EDUCATION, LAWLESSNESS AND POLITICAL CORRUPTION IN AMERICA

EDUCATION, LAWLESSNESS AND POLITICAL CORRUPTION IN AMERICA

By

HAROLD H. PUNKE

THE CHRISTOPHER PUBLISHING HOUSE
NORTH QUINCY, MASSACHUSETTS

PRINTED IN

THE UNITED STATES OF AMERICA

To My Brothers
Edward and William

GENERAL INTRODUCTION

Complexity in social structure can be defined in terms of the number and types of relationships in which the people engage, along with the geographical distribution and demographic composition of the population involved. As a society becomes more complex in the sense noted, more regulations to guide the people become necessary; and an increase in number of contacts among individuals means an increase in number of points at which transgressions and corruptions may appear. Regulatory expansion and growth in potential for transgression or corruption increase the demands made on the time and energy of society as a whole. One result is growth in effort to focus regulatory responsibility in particular agencies.

It seems natural for people to relax the sense of individual responsibility concerning areas for which special-agency responsibility has been proclaimed. And perhaps the major reason for establishing any special agency is that the problems of the particular area concerned have become too numerous and too involved for them to be handled on the basis of general diffusion among persons who have no special qualifications for dealing with them. However, with agency-orientation often goes overrelaxation or a popular assumption of greater transfer of responsibility to an agency than is actually possible.

The tendency to feel relieved upon transfer of thorny problems needs to be examined regarding the extent to which transfer is possible. The examination should clarify the point that no social agency can perform the functions which its theoretical framework describes without the continuing support of the general population for whom the agency is intended to act. While the foregoing applies substantially in any type of society, it is especially important in a democratic society where the people in general are expected to participate extensively in the design and control of government.

Failure in the support mentioned constitutes the point of origin respecting many of America's problems in the areas of lawlessness, corruption, and a related sense of immorality. Mild awareness of the situation is reflected in comments that the people do not well support their courts, police, educational institutions, or broad social expectations of moral behavior. Part of the difficulty lies in an inadequate popular conception of support, a conception which focuses too largely on taxation and the financial aspects of agency support. This conception gives insufficient attention to the need for some of the individual citizen's time and energy in supplying essential informa-

3

tion, evaluating agency performance, promoting measures for improvement, or otherwise contributing directly to agency operation and integrity.

A major theme of the present study is that lawlessness and related social problems will not greatly diminish until the people in general understand why they must support the agencies in the three areas emphasized (courts, police, education), understand how to perform the support functions, and accept commitment to provide the support and surveillance required. The study recognizes the extensive interdependence among institutions in any society. It nevertheless directs particular attention to the functions which our society expects agency personnel to perform as well as to the personal, moral, and jurisdictional qualifications they are expected to possess.

Emphasis is placed on the need for a broad understanding of the American social order, for a means of keeping that understanding continuously updated in relation to social change concerning both current activity and expectations, and for commitment to the ideals of that social order. While a considerable degree of social understanding and commitment has been reflected in the past by personnel in the areas of operation mentioned, the urge is for a different level and scope of comprehensiveness, understanding, and moral integrity— including new tools and new administrative relationships concerning some aspects of the process.

A further theme of the study is that Americans have greatly oversimplified the nation's problems regarding law and order, especially with respect to piecemeal efforts in seemingly isolated areas of social action. While the extent to which there is lawlessness and corruption in a society depends partly on how such terms as crime, morality, and respect for law are defined, it is possible to observe trends, within particular definitions which remain fairly constant. But the increase in reported crime in America during recent decades is not due in any major sense to shifts in definitions. Basic reasons must be sought elsewhere. Moreover, it is logical to assume that if the reasons and implications were simple, then simple remedies would have been applied and the difficulties overcome.

In dealing with lawlessness, or any other difficult area of social relationship, there is usually a substantial counsel of gloom and despair. The chief value which such counsel has for creative work in the field lies in its demonstrating one of the problems to be overcome. Individuals who support that counsel will vary in their responses to different types of information, as well as to reasoning that weaves the different types into alternative patterns of meaningful relationships and recommendations for action. Problems thus arise concerning situations in which the recommendations do not reach anything very fundamental and situations in which conditions have become desperate and approval of action embodies a gasp of hope or a willingness "to try anything." Creative social reform ought to become effective before desperation is reached. Faith in the experimental approach, which the natural sciences have found especially helpful, could be of great importance in the social fields.

A table of contents presents an overall view of the study as a whole. The main body of material is organized into five divisions. The basic themes of these divisions may be stated thus: (1) preliminary considerations on cultural development and the regulatory system; (2) the role of the courts with respect to educating the public on lawlessness; (3) the police and other law-enforcement and correctional agencies; (4) the schools and other basis agencies of popular education; and (5) general implications of the study. The divisions vary according to chapter and other internal organization. At the beginning of each division there are certain introductory remarks concerning the division. An outline of the division, as suggested by the table of contents, is carried through the text of the division. Each of the first four divisions is concluded with a section on the highlights and implications of the division's content. Footnotes appear at the end of each division.

An epilogue sets forth certain rather specific action implications, and also certain more inclusive considerations. There are three appendixes. The first two are essentially extensions or amplifications of Division IV, as indicated at the respective points in the text which specifically refer to these appendixes and as indicated by captions to the two appendixes. Appendix No. 3 is devoted to quotations from the literature, which bear on the themes of the five respective divisions. The justification for using quoted material appears at the beginning of the appendix presentation.

An index, along with a table of contents, facilitates easy reference to specific items and areas of discussion.

CONTENTS

Division III — The Police, Law Enforcement and Correctional Agencies

Epilogue

DIVISION I

CULTURAL DEVELOPMENT AND
THE REGULATORY SYSTEM

INTRODUCTION

This division deals with the evolution of human society in general and of American society in particular. Certain points are noted in which social evolution may be regarded as a projection of biological evolution. To some extent this idea runs through early conceptions of personal freedom in America and through related efforts to develop governmental regulations in harmony with those conceptions of freedom. Efforts to achieve harmony require an understanding of the nature of rights and duties, and achieving it in America requires an understanding of the doctrine of separation of powers in government.

Since any organized society must have a material base of support for the people, the way in which the society develops and uses that base will greatly influence other aspects of social organization. As a society becomes more complex, specific vocational and occupational fields become defined. With continuous development, these fields change and new fields appear. Through experience, some of the older or more popular vocational fields develop techniques for making their roles and prospects understandable to the general population, as well as techniques for enlisting the public support that is necessary for their specialized vocational efforts to be successful.

Certain aspects of these techniques often become applicable to other fields; that is, fields which may be more recent in systematic development, or which may deal with substantially different areas of the culture. Some aspects of procedure in developing broadscale appreciation and popular support in such fields as agriculture and homemaking, health, sports, and industry may thus embody clues for developing popular appreciation and support for the field of law and order. Although the latter field is not new in a chronological sense, since problems concerning orderly human relationships seem to have been reported throughout literate societies, the field of law and order in America is undergoing extensive change from the standpoint of new elements to be brought into the regulatory framework.

This division thus affords a backdrop for considering the developmental roles of our courts, our police and law-enforcement structure, our correctional agencies, and our educational institutions, within an evolving legal framework for a peaceful and creative democracy. The division is presented as two chapters: social regulations and evolutionary development; vocational and career experience, as guides in regulatory development.

Chapter 1

SOCIAL REGULATION AND EVOLUTIONARY DEVELOPMENT

Much is said in America about lawlessness and disrespect for our legal framework. Less is said about relationships between lawlessness and popular understanding of the culture's regulatory structure, or about the responsibility for developing and maintaining such understanding within the general population.

Broad contentions about preparing children to become good citizens constituted the basic argument used in legislatures 100 to 150 years ago in establishing public, tuition-free schools across the Northern states. But the practical civic education on how government actually works, and on the problems with which it deals, was gained outside the school—mainly through informal association in the community. Since that time, the inadequacy of our various educational activities in the area of civic understanding and civic responsibility has increased, along with an increase in social complexity and in problems which public agencies are asked to solve.

However, it should be noted that the public schools actually never have been considered to have full responsibility for civic education. They do not have full responsibility today. Moreover, it is doubtful if schools and the system of public education could be sufficiently broadened in conception and in support to do the job *alone,* even if some legislative or judicial fiat should declare such to be a school obligation.

Lawlessness, in a broad sense, embodies the aspects of civic education with which this study is mainly concerned. The approach stresses the development of regulatory structure in human society, the purpose and operation of major institutions in connection with that structure in America, and the need for the general population to understand and to support the institutions and regulations set up to achieve the ideals to which the people aspire. The purposes and needs are not new phenomena. They reflect a long evolutionary or developmental process, which apparently began before social groups were formally organized.

1. Human Society and Its Biological Antecedents

With respect to changing institutions and practices in an industrial society, the term "evolution" is often used. Thus we speak about the evolution of an educational or a legal system, evolution of the family or of the church as an institution, evolution in farming or in medical practice, etc.

In sociology, as in biology, evolution means the development of more complex organizations from simpler ones. While the biological process was apparently under way for numerous millenniums before man's governmental agencies became prominent, the social and the biological processes have much in common.

A basic consideration in each field concerns relationships between the individual and the group. In biology the species is perpetuated only through action by the individual; in sociology the same is true concerning language or institutions. In both spheres, evolution is possible only through variations or alternatives which arise among individuals. In biology, the pertinent alternatives appear mainly through sports or mutations; in sociology the alternatives appear mainly through ideas or imagination.

The crucial element in mutations lies in the chromosomes involved in mating;[1] the element in imagination lies in deposits of experience impressed upon the cerebrum. But chromosomes are produced by individuals, not by committees.[2] Likewise, ideas arise in the heads of individuals, although committees may provide certain experiences for particular individuals.

What happens to the mutants, or to the heads in which unusual ideas arise, depends on the general climate or environment in which the variant or the idea appears. Thus, when either the mutant or the idea varies too widely from the usual stream, the variant element does not survive. The crucial point, in biology and in sociology, is how broad a shift or change the group or general stream can accept *at one time*. When the changes are distributed in some tandem fashion, with a cumulative effect that points in a particular direction, evolution is present.

Without individual variation, none of the ideas or biological specimens would be any better able than others to survive in a particular setting. So, the individual is the source of both improvement and deterioration, both in the biology of the species and in the content of thought. Nobody knows what the ratio is in either field between frequency in appearance of positive or developmental variants and frequency of those which are negative—or perhaps neutral. However, estimates are common that the positive variants in either field constitute a small percentage of all variants. The concept of "positive" here implies not only that a variant appeared, but that it also survived and became a part of the subsequent ongoing stream.

Thus it appears that it is only out of a rather narrow band of the probable range in variation that either biological or ideational improvement or evolution must come. But as life in an area such as the United States becomes richer and more diverse, both as to numbers and types of people or other forms of biological life and as to ideas and related forms of cultural life, the gene or chromatin pool, as well as the pool of ideas and practices out of which variant new elements might arise, similarly becomes richer and more diverse. The cumulative effect is now easy to see in the changing cultural sphere, but anthropology suggests that such was not the case during the 30,000 or more years which preceded written language.

Somewhat by contrast, two reasons may be noted as to why some people think that biological evolution no longer operates with respect to humans. (1) Such people do not appreciate the slow cumulative process and the hundreds of millenniums involved in past biological evolution through which man emerged. (2) They overlook the probability that past evolutionary change within any one generation was likely minute, and probably for many generations nonexistent; that it was the long accumulation which makes the total result now look impressive; and that there may now be important inner changes taking place within man which our casual observations from generation to generation do not detect.[3]

In biology or in sociology, the primary concern at any particular time is with group survival and continuity—that is, survival of the species or the society, although the status or even the existence of individuals may be sacrificed. Thus, among biological species, the rate of reproduction is closely associated with the prospects that individual offspring will survive to reproductive age. And within organized society, when the interests of an individual conflict with the well-being of the group or state, the interests of the individual must give way. Courts have frequently stated this point and have indicated that, without adherence to it, there could be no organized society. Paying taxes and rendering military service as a draftee may be noted, illustratively.

In view of the foregoing, no great strain on the imagination is required to conceive of organized government among people as an extension of the individual-group (or species) relationship mentioned concerning the biological world.

While the various patterns of government that the world has known have all necessarily been concerned with relationships between the individual and the group, governments have varied greatly in the extent and mode of recognizing that human progress from the days of the cave dwellers has depended largely on great individual minds.

2. Cultural Predecessors to America, and Insights Into Individual Well-Being.

Before the present American cultural system arose, with its extensive encouragement and protection of the individual, rulers who were autocrats in varying degrees recognized the value and need for imaginative counsel and for responsible assistants who could be entrusted with social responsibility. Although the procedure involved may seem a crude method of recognizing individual differences and of making selections, the fact remains that it was such operations which created the base for more elaborate systems; i.e., systems which include reflection on the status and role of the individual and which include concern about that role which developed it into a socially accorded status of "dignity and worth."

Whether one considers the status concept involved to have had religious or political origins is essentially immaterial. However, the gradual implementation of the concept into operating systems of government has been of great importance. It is important for the present status of the individual, the accelerated growth in knowledge, and the rate of social change in contemporary America.

Monasteries and royal courts, which selected persons who differed from other individuals with respect to interest and competence in particular fields and which provided such persons a place to work and to associate with others who similary differed from the mass of individuals, were major bearers and developers of the culture. This is especially apparent in relation to periods which are now sometimes referred to as pre-scientific or pre-technical. Emphasis is sometimes placed on such developments of the period as related essentially to the arts, philosophy, early science, and entertainment. But the developments also included theories on reform in government. Rousseau may exemplify the latter area, and the lives of Leonardo da Vinci, Beethoven, or Dryden (poet laureate) are also illustrative.

3. *Personal Freedom in America's Early Value Structure*

Those Founding Fathers who came to prevail in America saw, more clearly than their European contemporaries, the importance of cultivating a wide swath of the population from which to recruit individuals with creative imagination and with motivation to follow its leads. Several influences contributed to organizing a governmental structure to promote the ends implied. One influence was the essential absence of some aspects of European culture. Earlier comment suggested concentrations of wealth and prestige at different levels of royalty, which enabled courts and kings to vie with one another as "patrons of the arts." This social structure did not exist significantly in frontier America.

Although the majority of the immigrants who came to early America were illiterate, they were motivated to achieve a better life through the disciplines of physical labor and deprivation. Hence, there was no leisure-class structure through which to identify and support individuals in the types of creative achievements that were recognized by contemporary European "patrons of the arts." Rather, it was necessary in America to exercise creativeness for survival in a rather harsh physical environment, for adjusting to the strange ethnic composition and cultural background of the Indians, and for teaching British rulers that a bunch of liberty-loving migrants could not be regulated according to autocratic notions of government emanating from a royal focus 3,000 miles away.

The idea that developments in the latter sphere were not creative contributions to the arts essentially reflects provincialism in conception of "the arts." The designation of "practical arts" as separate from "fine arts," particularly with advancement of the industrial revolution and boost to agriculture and engineering through the Land Grant College after 1862, has substantially expanded the concept of creativeness. It has accordingly expanded the status of "dignity and worth" in relation to persons who make contributions in the practical fields concerned.

While it is customary in America to attach great significance to the insight of the nation's founders in providing for extensive personal liberty and freedom of the individual, a practical observation should be noted. With freedom-seeking individuals of varied religious and ethnic backgrounds scattered over extensive territory or perhaps accumulated in scattered villages, and with each individual largely bent on achieving success in the way he saw fit—or in "doing his own thing," a high degree of central control was no more possible under American direction than under direction from England.

However, credit is due to at least some of the founders for recognizing that it is politically wise not to try to regulate by government the areas of human endeavor which government cannot regulate—or at least not without an expenditure of resources that is exhaustive relative to the benefits in view. The struggles over the Articles of Confederation, and over protection of individual freedom through the first ten amendments to the Constitution, is common knowledge in America. Thus, in the search for enough centralization of authority through the latter document to insure national survival, there is considerable historical testimony to problems concerning relationships between the individual and the group.

The millennial quest for differentiation between what can be regulated by government and what cannot be, through America's three-branch system or otherwise, is apparent today in the numerous disputes that reach the nation's higher courts. The same appears likely to extend throughout the foreseeable future.

4. Optimum Regulation by Government in America

Foregoing comments suggest that government in America, perhaps increasingly since the founding days, has faced in a somewhat unique way the difficulty of establishing optimum relationships between two basic facts. One is that creative minds develop and function only within individuals. The other fact is that those individuals have to live within organized society. Moreover, that society probably consists mainly of persons who are less creative than the individuals noted, but who must carry on the day-to-day work of the group. This work includes providing the various kinds of resources needed for so-called creative minds to function.

Earlier comment noted the extensive influence of social conditions and of legal provisions, with respect to comprehensive personal freedoms for the average American. Reference might be made to expansions of and supplements to the early provisions. Prominent among expansions has been extending the franchise—by race, sex, and age—and protecting its effectiveness through such measures as legislative reapportionment and supervision of elections. Also prominent has been concern with equality of opportunity for individuals with various types of backgrounds. The initial emphasis of a century ago on equality through a widespread system of free public schools, without regard to tuition or the economic status of the family, has been amplified through equalizing opportunity in different communities by such measures as grants from state and federal funds, rural school consolidation and pupil transportation, and some aspects of racial integration. Developments in public housing and restrictions in the rental or sale of private housing stress equality as the main objective.

However, a kind of dilemma may arise regarding the achievement of group or state objectives in the individual's exercise of his legally stipulated "rights." Compulsory school-attendance laws have thus been looked upon as reflections of the state's interest in an educated electorate. With growing vocational emphasis on educationally competent workers, the state's interest in educacation for developing an economically productive citizenry becomes more apparent.

Similar observations could be made concerning the state-assured "right" to serve on a jury, regardless of race, sex, religion, etc., and the "duty" to serve on a jury when called upon to do so. The same applies to certain rights promulgated by the state with respect to health, and compulsions as to the exercise of those rights—i.e., compulsory immunizations against specific communicable diseases, or compulsions regarding garbage disposal or other sanitary measures.

5. The Nature of Rights

Preceding observations on the state's interests and compulsions concerning the exercise of individual rights raise questions about the nature of rights. It should be noted that rights are conceptions of relationships among people. Nobody in Montana or in Florida has a right to sunshine, rain, or frost. Rights are most effective when stated in terms which are rather easy to understand and which gain fairly wide acceptance. But, in order to have wide application, they must be stated in general terms—as are the provisions of the federal Constitution. This means that the application of a concept to a particular situation requires interpretation—by a court, or by some other agency with adjudicative power and responsibility.

In a broad sense the state is officially interested only in such individual rights as concern the group. But in that broad sense a large portion of the things which the individual does are of state interest. As the state becomes more populous, with persons engaging in more types of activities, the areas of state interest in individual activity expand.

Thus, the reason that the individual has rights in an organized society is that the group or state has defined the kind of behavior that will be approved in particular areas of human relationships, and is in a position to enforce what has been defined. The action by legislative bodies, courts, and other regulatory agencies shows how rights may be defined—or how they may be changed or erased.

References that are sometimes made to "God-given" rights should be thought of as efforts by the speaker to make certain rights seem as important as possible. In recent decades, similarly loose reference has sometimes been made to rights "based on scientific experimentation," or on "statistical evidence." It should be clear that references of neither type have much to do with the way in which rights become established or disappear, although the associated propaganda may be significant.

While rights are typically thought of as protecting individual freedoms in particular areas, according to accepted recognition of the particular rights, the state must have a source of power in order to define and to enforce anything. In any society the people constitute the only source of such power that there is, although societies differ greatly concerning the avenues by which representatives or officials come into positions of authority for defining and enforcing. The way in which the masses demonstrate this source status may be through popular vote in some instances and through violent revolution in others.

Another way in which the people in general reflect source status is in the continuing, although perhaps undramatic, support which they give to state action. Some of this is verbal, some may be through acts of respect for the flag and comparable symbols of government, through paying taxes, and through rendering military or other important service, etc. Respect for law and order or for the nation's legislative and judicial system has frequently been mentioned in this connection. So has respect for family life, schools and universities, systems of employment and economic production, and other institutions in the basic social structure of the culture.

6. Duties Associated With Rights

Areas of respect and associated responsibility such as indicated are sometimes referred to collectively as duty.[5] To a considerable extent, lawlessness and meagerness in support for fundamental institutions can be stated as weakness in the sense of duty—among the people generally. The weakness becomes more conspicuous as a culture becomes more complex, with regulation of individuals in the public interest continually in need of revision and extension and of reinterpretation for popular understanding. It is possible for this sense of duty to decline to the point where there is a disintegration of the cement that is required to hold conflicting elements of society in some kind of tolerable working relationship. Broadscale corruption and lawlessness are neither the initial nor the final stage in this process, but a stage that should generate alertness to the need for remedial attention.[6]

It is part of the theme of the present discussion that responsibility for developing a greater understanding and related sense of duty must be extensively diffused throughout the social structure. However, that theme urges that responsibility for leadership should focus on four types of agencies or institutions: the schools, the police, the corrective agencies, and the courts, all of which are educational and formative in certain ways.

7. Coordination and Separation in Regulatory Operations

A special area of coordinating responsibility grows in significance as a technological society becomes increasingly divided into vocational and technical specialties. The implications for the division of labor, and for productivity in goods and services, is often characterized as progress. Thus, specialists in education, law, medicine, architecture, transportation, etc., tend to lose sight of comparable specialists in other fields. They may even lose sight of the need for an overreaching coordination. With emphasis on specialization, it is easy to overlook the natural continuity or interwoven relationship among factors in any ongoing culture. The artificial dichotomies involved in separating out particular areas for emphasis may thus have values but also limitations.

Accordingly, there are values in providing schools and universities as focal points of education, but limitations in assuming that they can carry the entire responsibility for educating Americans—regardless of home background, street influence, parks and playgrounds, vocational participation, forum situations, etc.

Reference is often made to overlappings among the three designated branches of American government, such as criticisms of the courts for "usurping" legislative functions. Most Americans know in general about the struggles of Jefferson, Jackson, Franklin D. Roosevelt, and others regarding the courts. And most Americans should recognize that the typical lawsuit involves some degree of judicial extension in legislative regulation, simply because the legislative pronouncement did not go far enough to make clear what should be done under the conditions at bar. If the whole matter was clear to both sides, there would likely be no lawsuit.[7]

One of the clearest illustrations of overlapping governmental function, in the general area of education and social relationships considered in the present treatise, concerns school boards. Such boards exercise a legislative function in making rules and regulations to govern school operations. They perform an executive function in hiring teachers, in contracting for the construction of buildings and in regulating other facilities. They exercise judicial functions in evaluating testimony on charges which may lead to employee discipline or dismissal. In several school cases which have come to court, the judge has said that the issue should have been settled by the school board and the superintendent. Boards in several nonschool areas have governing status comparable to that of school boards.

From the standpoint of the values and limitations of specialization in a complex society, the major conclusion emerges that the separateness of specialization has its clearest values in regard to general and theoretical considerations. These features emerge with growth in size of the operation.

However, when specific situations are adjudicated, overlappings among the separate specialties are necessary. They are necessary not only for justice, but for the forward movement of administrative operations. Some basic problems in education and social regulation are concerned with developing understanding among the American people respecting the situation described. Those problems seem most conspicuous with regard to practices which relate to court and other situations in a way that exemplifies, as far as possible, the equal status of the three branches in the American system of government.

Chapter 2

VOCATIONAL AND CAREER EXPERIENCE, AS GUIDES IN REGULATORY DEVELOPMENT

Where a complex society has numerous functions which are performed by public agencies, considerable similarity and interdependence tend to develop concerning the operations of those agencies. Hence, there are substantial opportunities for them to learn from one another. This may be especially true regarding such matters as developing and evaluating social expectations, the extent and types of popular cooperation needed, variation among members of a community as to ability or willingness to cooperate in particular areas, or the time and personnel needs involved in developing a service. Also, in some instances there may be anxiety about competition from an expanding area.

The idea of borrowing or seeking guidance may be especially important with respect to educational activities. This is partly because education and learning in a broad sense are involved in perhaps most of man's activities, which makes it conceivable that clues regarding a particular situation might come from a wide range of sources. The scope inferred is quite pertinent, especially when it is suggested that the American judiciary or law-enforcement agencies might render a broader service respecting the education of the general public on the nature of a society in which people live under rule by law and, also, on the status and function of our various educational and regulatory agencies among such a people.

It is hoped that the materials presented in this chapter, from different vocational and career areas, will be helpful in offering clues for possible use in developing a more functional and better respected system of law and social regulation in American society.

1. Agricultural and Home-Economics Extension Service

In the United States, efforts to reach a scattered and rather heterogeneous population concerning rural life and agricultural production has long been carried on by the agricultural extension service. Important among early objectives of that service was bringing to the farm population the knowledge and practices which had been developed by experiment stations and colleges of agriculture. The process involved translating pertinent materials into such form that farmers with limited formal schooling and technical background could understand and helping farmers to develop skills and attitudes favorable to applying the knowledge. Effective organization of the efforts concerned slowly grew out of the informal gatherings and demonstrations among small groups—which then gained public support from government at federal, state, and local levels.

Many Americans have vague recollections, from their own lives or the lives of their parents, concerning grange meetings, farmers' institutes, agricultural fairs, farm demonstrations, and visits by county agents. Extension activities, through such avenues as home-demonstration agents, greatly expanded the areas of adult education, the methods used in carrying on the educational work involved, and the general impact of developments on improving the standard of living in the rural areas of the nation. Development of 4-H Clubs and some other youth groups amplified the scope of operations and enlisted interest at preadult ages. The areas of agriculture and home demonstration involved, now typically referred to as The Cooperative Extension Service, provide a very instructive example of broad adult and community education in America. Much of what has been developed has been adapted to use abroad. It includes possibilities for use in other areas of adult and community education in America, particularly in regard to social needs of national scope which the schools and universities *alone* cannot adequately provide. "Extension" services of this type, and in the broad areas implied, also stimulate the thinking and horizons of youth concerning vocational possibilities.[8]

2. Health Problems and Mass Educational Efforts

Many agencies are concerned about educating the American people with respect to the field of health. Several of these agencies presently focus attention on drug usage. The United States Department of Health, Education, and Welfare has several publications in the drug field.[9] The National Clearinghouse for Drug Abuse Information distributes a Federal Source Book entitled: "Answers to the Most Frequently Asked Questions About Drug Abuse."[10] Some state departments of education have special materials on drug education.[11] Kiwanis International[12] has a program, including materials, called "Operation Drug Alert." The National Association of Retail Druggists[13] has a kit of materials entitled: "Drug Abuse Education Goes to School." In one Alabama county[14] the sheriff's office, along with a substantial group of merchants and professional people, distributed to every school child in the county a 20-page color-and-explanation brochure entitled "Facts About Dangerous Drugs: Their Use and Abuse."

The foregoing items are merely illustrative. During the past few years a great deal of material on drugs has been presented by the mass media, especially newspapers, popular magazines, and television. Numerous informal meetings, seminars, workshops, etc., have been held under the auspices of agencies such as those mentioned. The total effort constitutes an extensive enterprise in popular and adult education.

3. Popularizing and Regulating Sports and Entertainment

Spectator and participator sports constitute a major source of interest and entertainment for Americans and for many other peoples of the world. In America, there are many organizations which stimulate interest in sports. Several organizations formulate rules to regulate games and participants, try to clarify and police differences between amateur and professional status, provide playing facilities, and through various avenues educate and influence the public in ways which promote different areas of sport.

Menke[15] referred to the Amateur Athletic Union of the United States as "the most potent factor in the advancement of sports throughout the world." He added that the union "helped spread the gospel of amateurism into every city, town and village in this country" and that "it has carried its preachments into every civilized country on earth." He referred to the standards set up by the union as furnishing the pattern for the Olympic Games as revived (1896) in Athens, Greece. He commented that the union is not an organization of individual clubs, but of some forty-eight associations (1963) each of which represents clubs, colleges or other athletic groups. He further noted several allied members in the United States and other countries over which the union does not claim jurisdiction.

Also important in the general sports and athletics picture are collegiate conferences. Menke[16] noted that the National Collegiate Athletic Association is composed of 473 individual institutions which hold active membership in the association, twenty-five conferences which hold allied memberships, and varying numbers of other institutions and associations which hold associate or affiliate memberships. The National Federation of State High Schools Athletic Associations, with a membership of over 20,000 schools which enroll about 5,500,000 pupils in forty-nine states and four Canadian provinces, is concerned with interscholastic sports at the high school level.[17]

A type of sports-promoting education through television, other than a broadcast of games, may be illustrated by a Sunday television program.[18] The first in a two-part presentation concerned a negro lawyer in New York City, who on a part-time basis developed a sports and athletic club for negro girls in one of the economically less favorable residential areas of the city. At the time of the presentation, the club consisted of forty-five members, eight to twenty-seven years old, who trained for and engaged in various types of competitive track events. A major objective of the club was to develop in members a feeling of self-confidence through achievement. The lawyer-organizer commented that those who do well in sports also do well in school, substantially because of confidence in themselves. The second section of the presentation featured a woman who was a news commentator on sports, particularly football. She referred to developing more understanding and appreciation of football among women, especially among the wives of professional players and ardent fans. She also referred to the important intellectual aspects of the game, as revealed through a study of plays shown by the game book and otherwise, and to the need for understanding in order to share appreciation with a spouse who is a fan. She called attention to a high school course on football appreciation—taught by a woman—for adult women, enrolling about eighty persons.

Anybody who has been alert to international sports and athletic events during an Olympiad year, as well as many other persons, will of course recognize that the foregoing comments include only a few illustrative references to the educational and social impact which sports thinking and events have in America and elsewhere. Two avenues of impact seem obvious: one concerns the selection and discipline of participants; the other concerns the peak excitement at competitive events. Upon reflection, a third avenue emerges. It involves a comparison of methods and precedures concerned in the sports buildup and carry-through with methods and procedures which *might be* employed in other fields of national well-being that require broad education and enthusiastic commitment of a large segment of the population. The status of law and order in the nation's culture might be among such other fields.

Reference to the Olympic Games, and to their place as entertainment and as symbols of disciplined achievement in the culture of Ancient Greece, indicates that sports events are not new in the different roles mentioned. One might note that the Apostle Paul,[19] in trying to promote self-discipline among the Corinthians in accordance with the teachings of Jesus, reasoned and illustrated his point by reference to the dedication and self-discipline of athletes who took part in the regular Corinthian games—with which his audience was familiar. And one might observe that before Columbus reached the Western Hemisphere, the different nations of the Iroquois Indians had developed Lacrosse into a sport of considerable entertainment—as well as discipline for war and other activities.[20]

4. Focus and Continuity in Adult Education

The concept "adult education" has often been rather hazy and shifting in American life, much as have such concepts as "civic education," "patriotism," or "respect for our courts and judicial system." This situation may be substantially a reflection of two major factors. One is a greater sensitivity to social change, which could imply that shifting fields are looked upon as less fundamental or core in nature than other areas, and hence are first to feel the pressures of expansion, contraction, or modification of direction. The other factor may in part be a corollary, that shifting areas have not been thought through fully enough to establish stable anchorage. Does the situation then imply a paradox that a field may shift because it has not been clarified to the point of stable anchorage, but that if it continuously shifts it cannot establish bench marks for determining clarity or standardization? To some extent the condition described exists in any area of service which applies to persons who are on the outer fringes of social change. With respect to general considerations of education, the fringe characteristics of adult education are usually more apparent than those of the public schools and colleges.

After an extensive consideration of the origin and development or genesis of adult education, Knowles[21] commented on the situation indicated. He stated:

The institutions for the education of children and youth—elementary schools, high schools, junior colleges, technical institutions, and colleges and universities—had their genesis in a broad conception of general education that predicated a continuing process of learning with unity, sequence, integration, comprehensiveness, and articulation. The institutions for the education of adults came into being without reference to any such grand design. Rather, the developmental process of the adult education movement in this country has been one largely of *need-meeting.* When the new nation needed the former colonial subjects to be quickly converted into citizen-rulers, adult educational activities came into being for this specific purpose. When the agrarian population needed quickly to be taught the skills required by the industrial revolution, mechanics' institutes, apprenticeship programs, private vocational schools, and other institutional forms were invented to serve this need. When a flood of immigrants needed to be "Americanized," special programs were devised to meet this need. And so on through history, adult education's role has been one of responding to the needs of individuals and of society as they arose.

This characteristic has caused adult educational institutions as a whole to be more sensitive than most educational institutions to the changing pressures of society for service. If adult education has missed its cue at times, as it did in failing to provide for the intellectual emancipation of the slaves after the Civil War and in failing to prepare our citizenry for the role of world leadership forced on this country by World War I, its record on the whole reflects a high degree of sensitivity to social needs.

One implication of Knowles' comment is that "need-meeting" becomes urgent in different areas of a culture at different times, with the duration of urgency and concern about remedy varying considerably.[22] With the increase in crime during the last two decades, and our limited imagination and perhaps limited courage with respect to remedies, need for general public understanding of our regulatory structure and need for respect as to the courts and the law-enforcement system may be nearing urgency status.

5. Changing Needs and Industrial Education

There is considerable similarity between adult education and comprehensive industrial education. The similarity seems to be growing. It is related in part to a decline in such earlier needs as the Americanization of immigrants and the skill-teaching related to the initial large-scale urbanward migration of rural persons, such as observed by Knowles. It is also related to the development of technological unemployment and associated problems of jobs and productivity in present industrial areas.

One similarity concerns a close relationship between an immediate need and the educational effort that developed. One difference concerns the emphasis of current industrial education on the job, with the job looked upon as the avenue through which most individuals secure the money by which to participate in the economy. The emphasis includes attention to an updating of industrial understandings and skills, as related to a continuing speedup of technological developments and of economic expansion through national and global considerations.

While it is important in the present connection to note the national and global implications of economic relationships, it is also important to note that economic relationships do not constitute the culture's total social and regulatory structure. But procedures developed in the areas of industrial and economic education may embody clues for possibilities in broader regulatory areas.

In commenting on sporadic developments regarding industrial education, before a period of rather systematic development from 1870 to 1906, Barlow observed:

> Social need for industrial education developed in relationship to the economy of the nation. As industrial developments proceeded to become the dominant factor in the economic life of America, its educational implications commanded attention. For a half-century a variety of forces— schools, lyceums, mechanics institutes and associations of craftsmen— placed an emphasis upon the need for industrial education. They were more a convenience to society than an integral part of general social development.[23]

Barlow's comment on the importance of continuity in the growth of industrial education has implications beyond that field. As essential in the growth, he emphasized continuity in self-examination relative to changes in technology and industrial processes, and continuity of interest in the successful adjustment and well-being of the individual trainee throughout the program.[24] This interest in the trainee has probably been a significant factor in the support and encouragement which organized labor has given to industrial education, through legislative and other avenues. On the importance of this relationship, especially for goal achievement, Barlow stated:

> The mutual dependency of labor and industrial education must never end; otherwise the goals of each group will be far ahead of actual performance. One of the great problems of labor and industrial education continues to be the acceptance of industrial education on a par with other educational endeavors; this must be accomplished without predatory destruction of other educational areas. Labor has maintained this goal firmly since the beginning of the modern public vocational education movement.[25]

Barlow also commented on the importance of our learning from other countries in the early development of industrial education in America and on the significance of the International Vocational Training and Research Center at Geneva (Switzerland), established in 1961 by the International Labor Organization.[26] He implied a growing interdependence between the United States and other countries in the further development of industrial education and the significance of a center for the documentary appraisal of research and other contributions to the field.

It is easy to imagine similar international implications of cooperative development in promulgating and enforcing social regulations and the growing dependence of personal safety and security in any country on international cooperation. Recent attention to drug traffic, plane hijacking, terrorism against diplomats or other individuals, monetary valuations and swindles, etc., are significant aspects of the worldwide picture.

In the development of any kind of service, especially in an expanding culture, it is essential that both theory and practice grow in comprehensiveness—and that the growth reflects continuous harmony between the two. Theory is essential to coordinate fragmented efforts and achievements, to formulate long-range goals, to outline feasible procedures for approaching goals, and to forecast the probable results of pursuing different alternatives. On the other hand, practice is the only avenue through which theory has much influence on human behavior or through which theory actually becomes meaningful to the popular masses. Thus, without practice, theory is largely fantasy; and without theory, practice is likely to be a treadmill operation.

With respect to inadequacy concerning theory in industrial education, Barlow noted: "The hard work of keeping the program in operation has not been conducive to the production of philosophers, sociologists, historians, economists, or psychologists in industrial education, but this need too must be satisfied."[27] He subsequently expanded:

> The "educational mind" of America does not really understand industrial education and its potential. Few industrial educators have been able to demonstrate the real values of industrial education. They do not lack ability to do so; it just hasn't been done. Central in the future is *exploration in depth of the potential of industrial education.* (Emphasis by Barlow.)
>
> The stakes are high; therefore, if industrial education does not become involved in depth and in a much wider range of endeavor it is most certain that *some other agency will.* Already in the 1960's we have seen private industry and other branches of government take on a responsibility for education for which they have no previous tradition or history. A major part of this responsibility should have fallen to industrial education. (Emphasis supplied.)[28]

6. Engineering Extension and Experimentation in Popular Education

For several decades there has been considerable work in popularizing engineering technology through extension service similar to that noted for agriculture and home economics. Also, one should recall that engineering has been included along with agriculture among major functions of land-grant colleges which stem essentially from the Morrill Act of 1862.

However, instead of reviewing the field of engineering extension as an area of broad popular education respecting certain areas of nationwide import, as foregoing pages do with respect to agriculture and some other areas of the culture, attention here is directed to certain experimental and related developments in engineering education. The experiments noted are aimed at overcoming the isolating effect of educational and technical specialization and at integrating technical achievements with understanding and general acceptance or support by the common people.

Man-Made World and the National Science Foundation

One experiment concerned a secondary school course on "The Man-Made World," developed over a five-year period through a program called the Engineering Concepts Curriculum Project and supported by a grant from the National Science Foundation.[29] The ten major participants in developing the program included four from Bell Telephone Laboratories, four from engineering education in two technical schools, a high school principal who was an ex-teacher of science, and a director of high school science in the school system of a large city.

The authors referred to "the traditional divisions of education into physical sciences, life sciences, social sciences, humanities, arts, and their usual subdivisions," as being "leftovers from the time of education for the few who were to fill a narrow and select spectrum of society." They continued:

> Universal education must prepare students for a much broader variety of roles, and must do so while maintaining a mutually shared culture. Over the years, there have been attempts at "comprehensive" and "interdisciplinary" education for such purposes, but these have generally fallen by the wayside because their values proved transient or superficial. Perhaps the central question in education today is how and what to teach in a society where universal education to college and beyond is becoming a reality.

In a broad sense the course aims "to teach certain concepts useful to the thoughtful citizen living in a technological world," concepts which are not taught in any widely available course. These concepts are to be taught through a problem-solving approach, with the idea that when this approach is used on "wisely chosen" problems it is possible to move inductively from the specific situation of the particular problem to the broader implications of the concepts which make up the program.

With respect to their basic philosophy, the population swath to be reached, and anxiety about the future status of our expanding technology depending on a broad understanding and acceptance of it by the American people, the authors stated:

> From the beginning, the primary objective of the project has been a contribution to the technological literacy of young people. The target population consists of those high school students planning some education beyond secondary school, and those students who are not necessarily contemplating careers in science or engineering. It is this group which displays aversion to mathematics and science courses and among which is found the antitechnology sentiment so evident today.
>
> Thus the goal of the course is to provide this group of students with a basic understanding of the characteristics, capabilities, and limitations of modern technology. Political, economic and social decisions today are increasingly dependent on technology, whether that technology offers constructive results or whether it is a basic contributor to societal problems. As Congressman Daddario has emphasized, in his call for technology assessment, well over a thousand bills each year in the House of

Representatives involve strong technological considerations.

Two recent developments emphasize the problem. The first is the growing focus on technology as the culpable source of social problems—an attitude particularly strong among liberal arts students, but also familiar in the public press and in the halls of Congress. Technology is blamed for the more than 50,000 cars abandoned last year on the streets of New York City, and there is a frequent tendency to overlook the social, behavioral and economic factors which are equal elements of the problem.

The second factor is the common fear and distrust of technology, with the consequent thwarting of the benefits that technology is designed to deliver. For instance, automated health examination centers are being developed rapidly in an attempt to bring health and medical services to that portion of the population which has been totally separated from the health care system. The fear of technology on the part of central-city residents threatens to lead to utilization of such centers by only the sub-urban population—the group which already receives adequate care. In countless other examples, technology developed without adequate public education will result in accentuation of social schisms.

The authors noted two cautions regarding the course. One relates to its nonconventional nature and to resulting difficulty in fitting it into a school's departmental structure. The other relates to the lack of suitable teachers. The authors added: "This is indeed the handicap that any true reform of secondary education must face." A practical thread that ran through their presentation is concern about what they called a "cost-benefit tradeoff," in the sense that social costs and social benefits must be evaluated relative to each other, rather than on any basis of absolutes. The authors concluded:

. . . Resolution of many . . . problems depends upon the idea of costs and benefits based upon measures and valuations. With cost-benefit tradeoffs firmly in mind, public discussions could become more nearly rational and certainly more productive.

This is a worthy objective for engineering education generally. *But engineering education must widen its horizon to include nonengineers and the public* if it is to approach such goals. If it did so, engineering education itself and the profession would be the principal beneficiaries. (Emphasis supplied.)

In Appendix I of their report, the authors presented an outline of the course and of the textbook developed.

Dartmouth Supervised Projects

Another experimental development[30] is somewhat related to the first, in the sense that it involved teaching by engineering students from Dartmouth College (Hanover, New Hampshire), in two widely separate communities, of courses based on the *Man-Made World* book and on procedures developed by the Engineering Concepts Curriculum. One Dartmouth group was in a central-city ghetto high school in Jersey City (New Jersey), the other was in Tuskegee Institute (Alabama).[31]

With particular reference to Jersey City, Manasse commented as follows on the general aim, procedure, and difficulties involved:

The intent of the course . . . is to train citizens to understand and appreciate the role which technology plays in their lives; indeed to make them aware of their role in our "Man-Made World." It seems particularly appropriate that this kind of course should be taught in the inner-city high school, because these are the young citizens who will be most directly concerned with many of the kinds of problems which man is creating by his increasingly technological organization. However, it also seems apparent that the training which these inner-city youngsters have been getting in their school systems leaves much to be desired. This kind of course would not work very well under most circumstances, because of the poor quality of their teachers, inadequate finances for equipment, and also the basically poor quality of the students, especially as relates to their ability to read and to calculate.

The course has been taught at well over 100 high schools in the last couple of years. Most of these were primarily in well-to-do residential areas, parochial, or private schools. Whenever it has been attempted in an inner-city school it appeared not to go over very well, in part due to a combination of all the peculiarities found in those environments. Most significant, however, was the feeling that the poor teacher quality, lack of equipment, and poor preparation of the students in mathematics and English were the most important reasons for its failure. We felt at Dartmouth, then, that the role of our undergraduate students would be to try to eliminate these inadequacies. First, they must function as assistant teachers, and thereby retain the respect of the students; second, they must also function as tutors or coaches, and thus would need to acquire the confidence and friendship of the Jersey City students. In both of these roles our students acquitted themselves most commendably, due in no small part to their dedication.

At another point, Manasse observed: "Currently, the engineering program is represented in Jersey City by the presence of six (Dartmouth) students each year (two students per term) who help to teach an engineering-oriented course at two of the high schools in the city. The course is based on the Engineering Concepts Curriculum, 'Man-Made World', and is taught to seniors as a science elective."

With respect to the Dartmouth-Tuskegee involvement, Manasse noted: "This was the first time 'Man-Made World' was being offered at Tuskegee; indeed, one of the few times it had been taught on the university level." He indicated the Tuskegee goals as: (1) developing thought patterns essential for engineering study, (2) arousing general interest in engineering, and (3) reteaching poorly learned high school material. He mentioned considerable modification of the Tuskegee program in the second year—with an expanded teaching team composed of Dartmouth undergraduates, Tuskegee undergraduate and graduate students, and two members of the Tuskegee faculty. Program content was also extended and otherwise modified.

Manasse's final comment read:

In conclusion, then, these programs appear to offer a partial answer to meeting the needs of our society and expanding the horizons of our engineering students. The program works because the students give as much as they get, learn as much as they can teach, and act as much as they are acted upon. It is an excellent example of practical engineering and demonstrates cogently the opportunities which exist for engineers to remake our society, the so called "Man-Made World," into an environment which is more nearly satisfactory to all of us.

National Aeronautics and Space Administration

Most Americans have a general, although vague acquaintance, with the work of the National Aeronautics and Space Administration (NASA) and, to some extent, with its major experimental and research center at Huntsville, Alabama. Less is typically known about the several branch and associated stations and enterprises in various areas of the nation, or the "tracking stations" and other facilities located in other parts of the world.

Important in the present connection are the educational efforts by NASA to keep the general public informed as to its projects and achievements. For many people, in America and elsewhere, these efforts may have seemed most prominent in connection with the televised Apollo Missions (space shots)— and the more recent Skylab undertakings. However, the numerous booklets, brochures, and other materials which NASA distributes, set forth in detail many achievements that are of great benefit to the general population of the country, the national economy, and international well-being. Several achievements relate to the development and use of foods, clothing, industrial materials, and recreational possibilities.

Certain implications of NASA's extensive program in adult education and public relations should be noted. One implication could be looked upon as a current illustration of the Jeffersonian doctrine that when the common people have the facts presented to them in understandable terms, as for example regarding efforts and achievements in complex undertakings, the people arrive at sound judgments. To urge that the American court and legal system is technically or otherwise more complex and difficult to explain than the aerospace undertakings, may indicate a robust judicial ego or widespread professional indifference—but it does not indicate much insight into the learning processes of people.

Another implication concerns favorable popular image, to which considerable reference is made relative to the courts and law-enforcement agencies. NASA seems to recognize that its operations depend for moral and financial support on the attitudes and evaluation of the general run of Americans, concerning its requirements and its achievements. It would be a national asset if there was a clearer awareness of this relationship on the part of some other governmental agencies—as the operations of those agencies extend further into the lives of the common people and demand more in financial and other types of support, and as the people become more sophisticated in their capacity for critical analysis and evaluation. Much of the foregoing applies to several aspects of conventional education and of judicial procedures.

Chapter 3

HIGHLIGHTS AND IMPLICATIONS OF DIVISION I

The division introduction notes two major parts to the division: one on social regulations and evolutionary developments; the other on vocational and career experience as guides in regulatory developments. Concluding statements at this point follow the same pattern, with a short note added.

Social Regulation and Evolutionary Developments

Considerable perspective can be gained by looking upon the evolution of social institutions as a continuation or projection of biological evolution. Projection of an open-ended developmental process thus encourages the continuous reaching out of creative imagination into an indefinite and probably endless extension of man's conscious efforts. At the same time it recognizes an ongoing biological evolution through genetic mutation. Viewing the social and the biological as thus coordinated helps man to feel secure as to his anchorage and status in the universe.

(1) The text of the study emphasizes the aspect of evolutionary method which points to the discipline and perhaps sacrifice of the individual, so that the group or species may survive. Some reflection on this point should be useful, regarding areas in which a culture may tend to fly apart through exaggerated individualism or weakened social cohesion.

(2) Present-day Americans should expand upon the insights of their early compatriots, regarding the cultural vigor and prospects for growth that lie in the potentialities of the common people when given broad social opportunity for development. The political and educational systems of this nation have contributed greatly to this development. But as the general developmental framework moves forward through time, it needs more emphasis on responsibility to accompany opportunity; that is, greater recognition that opportunity and responsibility are interdependent social concepts.

(3) When material affluence is extensive and installment debt is at a high but continuously rising tide, it is well to remember that growth in any culture depends on saving. For saving to be significant in a culture, material productivity must be able to turn out more goods and services than are required for maintaining the population at its current standard of living. Growth or advancement of the culture then depends on using the surplus for research

and other creative undertakings. One difficulty as to maintaining clarity and dedication regarding this point arises from man's biological makeup, which emphasizes immediate pleasant sensory experience as the avenue to satisfaction. Attention to deferred satisfactions requires planning and other elements of cultural maturity.

(4) Considerations regarding law and order necessarily give substantial attention to human rights. Variations among nations concerning the rights which the people have, underscore the social nature of rights. Thus rights do not rain down or drift into a culture like springtime zephyrs; they grow out of contacts, struggle, and conflict in a complex of human associations.

Three pertinent items concerning rights should accordingly be noted: (a) rights are always relative to some social arrangement that has developed, and they tend to change with changes in that arrangement; (b) they reflect a significant element of *earning*, at least in the sense that the enjoyment of unusual rights or status is typically associated with making an outstanding contribution; (c) the culture must balance rights with duties. In some respects the duties might be considered avenues through which particular rights are earned.

(5) Every culture, regardless of its form of government or social structure, must continuously struggle with the concept of minimum regulation of the individual to insure maximum social well-being. One of the most difficult aspects of this struggle lies in the fact that creative ideas and developmental suggestions always arise in the heads of individuals, and they do not tend to arise under circumstances of external coercion. If a society is to be creative, every law-making and every law-enforcement agency must be guided by the philosophy indicated.

Vocational and Career Experience as Guides in Regulatory Developments

The text of the chapter refers to several areas of vocational and adult education and to career experiences of various kinds, which embody suggestions that might be useful in developing a broader nationwide understanding of the role of law and order in organized society and of associated responsibilities of the individual citizen. Comments and suggestions of the kind indicated are now extended.

(1) Benjamin Franklin seems to have been outstanding among Founding Fathers in recognizing the importance of vocational and "practical" education, partly as reflected through his academy in Philadelphia—chartered in 1753. And private normal schools for preparing teachers were becoming rather prominent in the 1820's, before they rather generally became organized as parts of state school systems. However, it was the Morrill Act of 1862, providing for state colleges of agriculture and engineering, that gave vocational education its first major boost. The Smith-Hughes Act and other acts during the first quarter of the present century extended vocational training in agriculture into the high schools. Various legislative enactments have since expanded the areas of vocational training and made it available to a large number of common people. Two points stand out. One is the increasing extent to which our expanding technology now brings a wide range of

vocational training into the academic sphere. The other point concerns the extent to which the development necessitates understanding, acceptance, and participation by a large part of the population.

(2) Increase in total population, geographical and social mobility, job categories and employment opportunities, concepts of equality as to rights under the Constitution, etc., increase the need of Americans for a broad understanding of regulatory structure in organized society and for expansion of that structure as the entire society becomes more complex. Popular understanding, acceptance, and participation thus become growing necessities. Question then concerns the degree to which rather extensive lawlessness and a low order of respect for the courts and other aspects of the regulatory machinery indicate neglect of law and lawful behavior relative to technological production. To what extent do the experiments on engineering education offer clues at this point?

(3) Knowles' considerations in adult education emphasize the idea that successful work with adults stresses teaching people *how* to learn, not *what* to think. This approach seems especially important with respect to the functions of government and one's personal responsibility concerning government.

(4) While the cost-benefit theory in evaluating alternatives in relation to possible change may seem easier to apply in technology than in government, it *must* eventually apply in both areas. In government some costs and some benefits may be more delayed or more intangible than in technology, but any ongoing enterprise *must* operate within its resources—in order to continue "ongoing."

(5) Technology typically places considerable emphasis on its role in developing a "Man-Made World." This role has indeed been impressive during the past century. But law and social regulations also have much to do with shaping that "Man-Made World," including the support and freedom for development which technology enjoys.

(6) At several points the vocational materials stressed the importance of harmony between theory and practice, partly with the idea that it is only through interaction between the two that either becomes meaningful. As to law and social regulation, perhaps theory in the sense of social and political philosophy supplies the goals, whereas operating regulations indicate the procedures by which goals may be attained. Moreover, operating procedures supply feedback on needed modification of goals, if attainment is to be feasible.

(7) There may be a significant difference between vocational outlook and political philosophy in regard to what a system of human regulation should attempt to achieve. It may seem fairly easy to determine success in one's own vocational efforts, since the framework of vocational evaluation lies within the larger social system. And one of the hearty perennials in the larger system, regarding governments of all types, is how far can the individual be relied on to determine what is best for him in a general setting among other people.

Cultures universally maintain that children cannot thus be relied on to make the determination, but every culture has problems concerning the age when a child becomes an adult. Accordingly, we have various "coming-out" parties, age of consent regulations, rights to exercise the franchise, etc. Dictatorships are typically thought to accord child status to physically mature individuals, on more issues than is true of democratic societies. In the United States, the federal Constitution is one of the instruments that is sometimes referred to as dangling before the people extensive rights to decide, but removing from the majority a right to decide certain important issues, and of often making the route to decision in other cases so long and tedious that efforts are likely to be abandoned enroute.

In fact, the whole idea of government under law implies that in most relationships in a complex society the individual cannot be relied on to determine what is best for him, except as a participant with others in reaching a group decision on general regulations. While much can be said about regulating *certain individuals* for the welfare of the others, the idea that the individual is often "his own worst enemy" includes more reality than it is possible to explore in the present connection.

(8) Much is said about the values for Americans to study the development of vocational education in other countries and about the usefulness of the vocational training information research center in Geneva (Switzerland) in connection with such study.

A parallel consideration regarding law and social regulation might ask about the extent to which a comparable study of the regulatory systems which different cultures have developed could help Americans, who have either lay or professional responsibility concerning the law, to gain new insights into both goals and procedures.

(9) One engineering study commented on the importance of the engineers' assuming responsibility for revising their conception of the people's role in the engineering field, so that there would be greater social understanding of what engineering and technology *attempt to do*, and perhaps greater feedback from the people on some things that the engineers *ought to do*. One implication was the need for a continuous reorientation and upgrading in the area of relationships indicated, and one the effect that if engineering societies do not assume leadership in the area indicated, other agencies will do so.

(10) Some of the literature on vocational education reflects scars of long struggle in a dichotomy between so-called "liberal" and "practical" education, with the stratification of social class which the dichotomy symbolizes. Two differences between the United States and most technologically undeveloped countries in the respects noted are that social stratification in the latter countries is typically more pronounced than in the United States and that vocational education is much less developed. While several of those countries may reflect democratic formulas in the official documents of government, they lack one basic element of a democratic society—insofar as such a society assumes broad equality of opportunity among its members. The lack concerns the low level of vocational or economic productivity on the part of the popular masses, and hence their meager participation in control of the economic base, on which many other aspects of democratic life depend.

Since most of these undeveloped countries are fundamentally agricultural and are engaged in a type of primitive low-production agriculture, the most feasible area of vocational education for many of them to start on is that of agriculture. Through this avenue, societies which are characterized by a primitive agriculture might develop an economic base on which to extend vocational and technical developments into other areas. But, as this base and related areas of economic participation expand, so do the possible avenues of conflict with the law and of general lawlessness. Noneconomic bases of positive lawfulness also expand.

(11) Countries which are primarily dependent on the economy of a primitive agriculture can learn much from vocational education in agriculture as developed in the United States. Many teachers at different levels have gone from the United States to such countries to help them explore their conceptions and procedures in the field of agriculture. Moreover, the ongoing nature of expansion and improvement in this nation's conceptions concerning possibilities in agricultural education and daily practices in farm operation outlines an open-ended philosophy for continuous development.

The open-endedness should apply to government and law, as well as to areas of more direct economic productivity. It is substantially through the avenues implied that vocational education increasingly challenges and erodes the older patterns of classical or liberal education, at the same time that the vocational absorbs growing portions of the so-called liberal content. One limitation of much education for the legal profession has been its classical emphasis, with too little attention to the general implications of its principles to present-day community life.

(12) With the land-grant college and subsequent developments in this nation's vocational agriculture, the field of American agricultural development offers one of the world's best illustrations of an improved standard of living for a large number of people through the avenue of vocational education. And no ag-college graduate in American need feel chagrined at his alma mater being referred to as a "cow college"—as long as beefsteak is tops in American gustatory aspirations and demands the continuing attention of price regulators in the nation's economy. Other areas of cultural development might well survey this field for possible clues to adapt for their own.

Agency coordination

A theme that is reiterated at various points in the study is that the educational needs regarding lawlessness in American society are too extensive for any one agency to undertake *alone*.

FOOTNOTES AND REFERENCES

1. Cf. David J. Merrell, *Evolution and Genetics* (New York: Holt, Rinehart and Winston, 1962), pp. 185-194.

2. Cf. Alexander Allard, Jr., *Evolution and Human Behavior* (Garden City, N.Y.: The Natural History Press, 1967), pp. 227.

3. Cf. Frederick S. Hulse, in *The Process of Ongoing Evolution*, ed. Gabriel W. Lasker (Detroit: Wayne State University Press, 1960), pp. 66-67.

4. Cf. D.H.J. Hermann III, "Justice and Order: A Preliminary Examina-

tion of the Limits of Law," *Washington Law Review* 45 (Apr. 1970): 335; Roscoe Pound, "The Future of Law," *Yale Law Journal* 47 (Nov. 1937): 7; Sidney Hook, "Law and Anarchy," *University of Richmond Law Review* 5 (Fall 1970): 47.

5. Cf. R. Bambrough, "Proof of the Objectivity of Morals," *American Journal of Jurisprudence* 14 (1969): 37.

6. Cf. T.W. Davis, "Law and Disorder—Our Scrambled Legal Heritage," *University of Missouri Kansas City Law Review* 39 (Spring 1971): 364.

7. Cf. R.B. McKay, "Supreme Court as an Instrument of Law Reform," *St. Louis University Law Journal* 13 (Spring 1969): 387.

8. For a comprehensive treatment of the agricultural and home ecomonics extension service, see H.C. Sanders, ed., *The Cooperative Extension Service* (Englewood Cliffs, N.J.: Prentice-Hall, Inc., 1966), 1-6, pp. XII + 436.

Also: Lincoln D. Kelsey and Cannon C. Hearne, *Cooperative Extension Work* (Ithaca, N.Y.: Cornell University Press, 1963), pp. VIII + 490.

9. Illustrative are:

    a. "How to Plan a Drug Abuse Education Workshop for Teachers," Public Health Service Publication No. 1162 (1969).

    b. "Curious Alice" (Cartoon and quiz item for children—an Alice-in-Wonderland approach), Publication No. (HSM) 72-9026 (1972).

    c. "The Social Seminar: Inservice Teacher Training Program," Publication No. (HSM) 72-9079 (1971).

10. The Clearinghouse (5600 Fishers Lane, Rockville, Maryland, 20852) is operated by the National Institute of Mental Health. The item cited was produced jointly by the departments of Defense; Health, Education and Welfare; Justice; Labor; and the Office of Economic Opportunity.

11. Two items available from the Alabama State Department of Education (Montgomery) are:

    a. "Drug Education Films" (1971), which lists films available to schools from the department.

    b. "The Classroom Teacher and Drug Education" (1972).

12. 101 East Erie Street, Chicago, 60611.

13. One East Wacker Drive, Chicago, 60601.

14. Office of James C. Pearson, Sheriff of Lee County, Opelika, Alabama, 36801.

15. Frank G. Menke, *The Cyclopedia of Sports*, 3rd ed. (New York: A.S. Barnes & Co., 1963), pp. 29-30.

16. *Ibid.*, pp. 298-309.

17. *Ibid.*, p. 639.

18. "The Christophers," 9:30 A.M. (C.S.T.) (9/24/1972).

19. I Corinthians 9:24-27. For amplification, see *The Interpreter's Bible* (Nashville, Tenn.: Abingdon-Cokesbury Press, 1953), vol. 10, pp. 105-106.

20. See *Encyclopedia Britannica* (1969), vol. 13, pp. 584-586.

21. Malcolm S. Knowles, *The Adult Education Movement in the United States* (New York: Holt, Rinehart and Winston, Inc., 1962), pp. XIII + 335, at p. 257.

22. For a comprehensive annotated bibliography on adult education covering 696 research and other studies, relating to the 1953-1963 period—

appropriately grouped into chapters—see George F. Aker, *Adult Education Procedures, Methods and Techniques* (Syracuse, New York: University College, Syracuse University, 1965), pp. ix + 163.

23. Melvin L. Barlow, *History of Industrial Education in the United States* (Peoria, Illinois: Chas. S. Bennett Co., Inc., 1967), pp. 48-49.

24. *Ibid.*, p. 290.

25. *Ibid.*, p. 406.

26. *Ibid.*, pp. 479-80.

27. *Ibid.*, p. 500.

28. *Ibid.*, p. 503.

29. Edward E. David and John G. Truxal, "The Man-Made World: A Trend in Education," *Proceedings of the Institute of Electrical and Electronics Engineering, Inc.* 59 (June 1971): 924-932.

30. Fred K. Manasse, "Engineering Students and the Education of the Disadvantaged—The Dartmouth Experience," *Proceedings of the Institute of Electrical and Electronics Engineering, Inc.* 59 (June 1971): 935-940.

31. See also Fred K. Manasse, "Getting Engineering Students Involved: The Dartmouth-Tuskegee Program," *Institute of Electrical and Electronics Engineering Spectrum* 7 (Dec. 1970): 59-64.

DIVISION II

THE COURTS AND GENERAL
EDUCATION ON LAWLESSNESS

INTRODUCTION

Any system of government must have regulations which direct the people. This implies arrangements for evaluating allegations of offenses committed and for assigning penalties. Concern about growing lawlessness, in America and elsewhere, is related to increases in population and to increases in contacts which persons have with one another—both within and among nations. Attention to international treaties, the world court, peaceful coexistence, etc., suggest that war is our most outstanding manifestation of lawlessness—although formulations exist which are referred to as the rules of war.

Originally the idea of a court denoted an enclosed place, and in architecture the term continues to be used in that sense. This early enclosed place housed the king, from whom all power of government was presumed to emanate. As different places were designated to be points at which adjudications might occur, and as special forms of courts appeared for dealing with particular types of disputes, the king's presence was assumed to prevail in each such instance. Each special setting was thus considered to be a part of the king's court (or curia regis). Moreover, during much of the period concerned, including the late Middle Ages, the judicial function was not separated from the legislative and administrative functions of government. And in the United States today we frequently hear references to the importance for a democratic society of a separate and independent judiciary, implying that some uncertainty lingers, especially at the philosophical level. Such references may be most likely in connection with selecting members of the judiciary or with calling persons who have become members to testify before legislative committees.

In America, one major function of courts is related to the enforcement of contracts. This fact highlights the role of the contract as a major avenue through which the individual manifests his freedom to enter into agreements, with other persons or with the state. Assessment of damages for breach is part of the picture, whether the assessment is made according to statutes, contract provisions, or equity considerations. Allowance of court costs and attorney fees, in some cases, further reflects court power.

Most Americans know in general about the federal system and the state systems of courts within the nation, as well as the steady expansion of the types of situations over which the federal system exercises jurisdiction. Most Americans have heard about variations among state systems and about overlapping jurisdictions and delays in the administration of justice. Part of the criticism made of the courts relates to such delays and includes recommendations for centralizing the control of certain operations and for greater overall efficiency. Moreover, a substantial part of the criticism comes from the judiciary itself.

With Americans living increasingly in a goldfish bowl, from the standpoint of international observation of the way our institutions function, the status and performance of the courts in respect to our heralded philosophy of justice in a democratic society becomes of growing importance. The growth is pertinent for the people of the United States and for other people.

Major considerations of this division deal with the status and role of judicial imagery in America, the judiciary and social change, and the courts relative to effective communication. In each of these areas, some attention is given to the responsibility of the courts for developing popular understanding of how our legal system works and of how its effective working depends on intelligent cooperation and support by the general public.

Chapter 1

IMAGERY AND JUDICIAL ETHICS

There is considerable lay and professional comment in America about an increasingly unfavorable image of our court and judicial system. The comment includes forecasts of dire consequences for the American conceptions of justice and democratic government if the trend continues. The nationwide political scandals, growing out of our system for electing high-ranking public officials and broadly designated as Watergate, fuel the anxiety and the comment. Particularly disturbing to average citizens is the basic immorality shown by numerous persons who are professionally trained in the law and in the American conception of justice, and who are sworn to obey and protect the law of the land, but who have knowingly violated that law for personal gain.

The situation described places a heavy emergency burden on members of the nation's higher judiciary and on the committees in Congress which are concerned with judicial matters. The burden is not confined to matters regarding an ethical code for disciplining members of the legal profession. It includes a less clearly recognized, but perhaps fundamentally more important, problem of reevaluating the American conception of three separate but equal branches of government and the somewhat rickety system of checks and balances which has allowed considerable drift. The presence of drift in the sense implied typically permits escape from responsibility for action by government in the case of some public officials and "empire building" in the case of others.

It is unrealistic to infer that the judiciary should assume full responsibility for improving the quality of government in this country, including the integrity of public officials. But the focus of popular criticism on the courts and on the flow of justice from them makes it realistic to assume that a considerable burden rests on the judiciary. This situation also makes it appear feasible to anticipate that current stress on the courts and on judicial imagery will stimulate scrutiny regarding the other branches of government.

The following exploration provides a brief sketch of the nature and basis of imagery, of relationships of imagery to judicial performance, and of imagery as related to retirement or selection of judges. Certain remedial suggestions are included.

1. Nature and Basis of Imagery

Reference to the imagery of a particular ethnic or other social group, as well as to an institution or practice within a culture, relates to general acceptability and popular support for the entity considered. Thus imagery regarding the judiciary, law enforcement, or other institutions and services is always anchored to a social setting. Imagery is cumulative. Thus it is a buildup of impressions connected with individual events which have been scattered over time and to some extent scattered over diverse circumstances, but which in a substantial measure have been witnessed by a common audience that carries impressions from one situation to another and that distills them into a kind of attitude stance or evaluation readiness.

Imagery regarding an institution or a professional body is thus comparable to imagery regarding the character of an individual. In fact, the image of an institution depends primarily on the performance of individuals who are or have been officially connected with the institution and who are or were presumed to act for it. Image is thus the basis of forecasting what to expect in particular situations of the future.

Moreover, imagery regarding an institution or a profession is always an evaluation in terms of what is considered to be best for the public well-being. Hence the growing fringe or the withering trail of imagery is inseparable from social change in the community or from changes in the kinds of problems which the people think their institutions and associated professional personnel ought to solve. Social changes which demand adjustments in institutional imagery might, for example, relate to science and technology, military exploits, epidemics of disease, or such natural disasters as floods.

As knowledge expands and man's ability to control such phenomena grows, acceptable institutional imagery changes from willingness to be satisfied with salvage operations following misfortune to demands for preventive measures. Controversy regarding such matters as air pollution, budgetary allocations, and ethnic status illustrate the types of conflicting interests that accompany social change and the kinds of problems that must be settled if there is to be a stable social order.

Another factor should be mentioned, as affecting relationships among people and the imagery of institutions. That factor is basic human selfishness. Our biological ancestry, for some hundreds of generations before the regulatory problems of government became prominent, seems to have been such that individuals who looked out for themselves first and for others later were the ones who survived. Individuals who lacked this trait did not participate extensively in the stream of biological continuity. However, perhaps a few new representatives of this kind appeared with each generation, and during the past few centuries there has been an increasingly concerted group effort to revamp personal selfishness in terms of collective well-being.[1]

Moreover, a primary job of the courts might be characterized as that of compromising opposed patterns of individual self-interest in the light of collective need for social stability and directional guidance. The point has been noted that courts say that where basic interests of the state conflict with those of the individual, the individual interests must give way.

Operating problems are not lessened when one notes that judges are initially equipped with about the same repertoire of personal selfishness as other persons are and that there is wide variation concerning their subsequent conditioning for submerging that selfishness in the public interest. The manner in which a judge conducts a court over which he has jurisdiction, or his willingness to step aside during a trial in which he might reasonably be said to have a personal interest, may illustrate the types of problems involved.

2. Judicial Performance and Imagery Status

With respect to the social basis of imagery, three factors are probably more important than others concerning what the general image of the courts is. These factors are: (1) what the people in general think the performance of the court is and ought to be; (2) what the courts themselves and the legal structure in general consider the function of the courts to be, and how well those functions are performed; and (3) the role of certain tyrannical judges.

Public Imagery of the Judicial Role

Judge Landis[2] recently mentioned the extensive comment on establishing a judicial code of ethics and the disappearance of myths about judges as "men of mystery garbed in black robes." He added: "It is no secret that the public no longer glorifies the bench or thinks of them (the judges) as members of an exclusive ethical cult. Rather, there seems to be a growing belief that judicial office is a political sinecure." He attributed much of the attitude described to a popular misconception of what judges and courts do. He noted a common popular belief that judges come to work between 10:00 and 11:00 a.m., take a long lunch period, and adjourn court early in the afternoon—after some four to four and one-half hours, close court during the summer, and take a vacation of two or three months each year. Landis commented: "Debunking these misconceptions is the responsibility of the judiciary. Unless the facts are made known, the reputation of judges must continue to be downgraded in the public eye." Concerning the role of judges in popular education with respect to judicial imagery, he elaborated:

> Judges know the facts; they can effectively evoke understanding of the judicial tasks, notwithstanding that they may not be experts in the field of public relations. Consequently, I urge each judge to assume a secondary role in the judicial stage, namely, to make himself available to address Chambers of Commerce, Rotarians and other social groups and service clubs to explain and define the work of the judge "the way it really is." I am confident that the contribution in effort and time would result in the enhancement of the judicial image.

Presenting a Worthy Judicial Picture to the Public

In a vein similar to that of Judge Landis, Judge Stafford[3] commented on judicial responsibility for popular education on imagery, for indicating in lay terminology the problems which judges face in making decisions, and for convincing the public of judicial integrity and impartiality. He inferred a continuing myth about dignity associated with black judicial robes and referred to judges who find it easy to "stick their heads in the sand with the forlorn hope that deteriorating public respect may rectify itself if left alone long enough." He added: "Many . . . judges avoid the issue by contending that it is beneath their dignity to discuss the judicial image, much less do anything about it."

Stafford implied that for the judiciary and the courts to benefit from a favorable popular image, they must deserve it. He said:

> True *understanding* and *respect* for the judiciary can be achieved only as a public response to our integrity, impartiality, fair play, conscientious attention to duty and simple courtesy. Public esteem will not be regained until each judge is willing to accept his personal accountability as an integral part of the responsible group. If we fail or refuse to do our part, no one else can or will rebuild the judicial image for us. As Edmund Burke stated: "Evil grows because good men do nothing about it." (Emphasis by Stafford.)

Judge Stafford referred to several aspects of judicial behavior which run counter to a favorable public image of the judiciary. These include: (1) unnecessary continuance of trial dates; (2) judicial wisecracks in the courtroom; (3) conscious effort by a magistrate to attract personal attention by peculiarities of dress or by habit idiosyncrasies; (4) reflecting partiality or dislike for certain attorneys; (5) discourtesy or oversolicitousness to particular witnesses; (6) "pre-trial discussions"—such as with an arresting officer, prosecuting attorney, or possibly a witness; (7) private interviews or communications regarding a trial; (8) activity which either labels one as a "prosecutor's judge" or a "defense judge"; (9) yielding to "get tough" editorialists or police officers, and thereby forgetting that a judge is "*not* a part of the law enforcement team"; (10) not insisting that conviction be based on proof, rather than on current popular acceptability; (11) failing to withdraw and summon another judge if a case involves personal interests; (12) transferring a hearing from the official courtroom to a place such as a high school auditorium because of wide public interest in the hearing; (13) failing to control the audience in a courtroom, and thereby transforming operations into entertainment rather than procedure to determine justice; (14) failing to render an opinion which indicates serious consideration of the rights of the parties, rather than only a stark ruling as to "guilty" or "not guilty"; and (15) allowing popularity or publicity to play a role in determining the nature or severity of the punishment.

In his reference to "all trial judges," Stafford mentioned a unique position in the judicial system held by courts of limited jurisdiction—that is, justice courts, police courts, municipal courts, and others that are not courts of record. Toward his conclusions on imagery, he stated:

> We cannot achieve public esteem by the simple process of wearing a black robe. The public has respect for and dependence upon the law, and *since we represent the law, the average man demands of us something*

much higher than he expects of himself. Although this may seem unrealistic, it is our burden, and we cannot avoid it. Because of their demand for higher principles, we have both our greatest challenge and our greatest opportunity.

In order to meet our obligation we must do more than attempt to justify our peculiar conduct in areas that are difficult even for the legal mind to grasp. We must do more than try cases with dispatch, carry a heavy caseload efficiently and fulfill the mere routine of legal research. *We must reach the highest ideals that are the foundation of our legal system, and we must continue to strive for them—lest we lose them through disinterest.* (Emphasis added.)

* * * * * *

Integrity, impartiality, fairness, dignity, understanding, courtesy, service and an honest search for the truth cannot be captured in books, documents and rules for convenient exhibition to the public as proof of our right to high public esteem. These things exist only as abstract ideals. We shall merit public confidence and a good reputation, or fail to do so, by the manner in which each of us copes with those ideals. In short, a high moral principle is our most compelling answer to the critics.

Dean Acheson,[4] former Secretary of State, commented on different aspects of judicial integrity and status. He referred primarily to the Supreme Court and to controversy which had often embroiled that court since the days of John Marshall. He focused on propriety of the nonjudicial conduct of justices, which he thought might affect their judicial work and which he thought also affected judges in lower federal courts. He emphasized the idea that for high-level members of the judiciary to perform their judicial function, it is necessary for them to be isolated and insulated from activities which may have appeal for other persons.

Five areas of impropriety were categorized. First, *supplementing judicial salaries by outside earnings* should be flatly forbidden, according to Acheson. This related largely to stipends for lectureships and earnings from writing books and articles. These activities and associated compensation, he observed, "may be saved for the often-boring period following retirement from active work." He thought that speeches, lectures, and eulogies of deceased jurists should be restricted to legal subjects discussed before legal audiences. "The judiciary will only invite trouble if it intrudes into other fields," observed Acheson. He added: "A judicial robe is poor insulation from folly. As the Arab proverb wisely pointed out: 'The ass that went to Mecca remained an ass.' " However, Mr. Acheson opposed the practice of judges and justices making a public listing of their investments, "as a needless invasion of a judge's privacy and an opening for much harassment from solicitors of all sorts."

Second, *judicial officers participating in nonjudicial work or organizations* should be prohibited, Acheson stated, because such participation distracts them from judicial tasks and involves them in controversies which interfere with needed judicial impartiality and aloofness. As illustrative, he referred to President Johnson's appointments of Chief Justice Warren on the commission to investigate the assassination of President Kennedy and to President Franklin Roosevelt's appointment of Justice Robert Jackson as chief American prosecutor at the Nuremberg war-guilt trials. He further noted that membership on civic, educational, and church boards or committees could likewise embroil judges in controversies which detract from a reputation of impartiality.

Third, *appointment of holders of judicial office to nonjudicial office within a number of years after leaving the former* should be discouraged. Acheson reasoned: "When a man shuttles back and forth between judicial and executive office, he does not give the assurance of impartiality and aloofness from current issues that the judge's special position requires." Illustrative reference on this point was made to Fred Vinson who left the Court of Appeals for the District of Columbia in 1943 to become Director of the Office of Economic Stabilization and who, after holding this and other nonjudicial positions, was appointed Chief Justice of the United States in 1946. Reference was also made to Mr. Justice Byrnes who left the court to become Director of the Office of Economic Stabilization and to Mr. Justice Goldberg who left the court to become United States Representative to the United Nations. Acheson observed that if a justice wants to leave the Supreme Court, the Thirteenth Amendment provides a route. He continued: "But when coaxed or pressured by the President to leave the bench for political office, the judge's reputation for independence, a highly important element in maintaining respect for the judicial office, will suffer."

Fourth, *the nomination of a sitting Justice to be Chief Justice* is an undesirable practice, thought Mr. Acheson. He commented that when a justice comes to the Supreme Court, the justice should have no further ambition. He added:

> To aspire to the central seat on the bench reflects a vanity that shows the sufferer from it unworthy of the presiding place. Even more, it opens the temptation to shade views and votes to enhance the chances of elevation. We can all be certain of one proposition: At any time there will be more potentially good Chief Justices off the Court than on it. The two occasions when the Chief Justice was chosen from the Court do not sustain the desirability or success of the practice.

Fifth, *a Justice counseling any person holding political office or any aspirant thereto* is bad for the court, reasoned Acheson. He recognized that much of this had been done in American history, but looked upon it as contrary to the separation of powers among branches of government. He again emphasized the independence and "special position" of judges, especially those on the Supreme Court, "who have powers unknown among judges anywhere else on this earth." Acheson noted the importance of this power in relation to a loss of public confidence in the competence of the court to exercise it and the public's association of any special loyalty or friendliness by members of the court to the President with an unjustifiable bending of the Constitution according to presidential desires. Among various instances of this kind, Mr. Acheson emphasized the relationship between Justice Frankfurter and President F. D. Roosevelt, which Acheson said "did harm to the public reputation of both the Court and the Justice."

Barry Goldwater's[5] evaluation of judicial competence, relative to judicial image, approached the matter through examining the criteria used by the Senate in approving nominees by the President for seats on the Supreme Court. His point of departure involved the criteria advocated by certain "liberal members of the Senate Judiciary Committee" in confirming Powell and Rehnquist for the Court. The senators involved "made no bones about" their standards, said Goldwater: "They were concerned with knowing whether the nominees' judicial and political philosophies fitted the same mold as their own views on the social issues of the day." He thought this point was especially apparent in the hearings on Mr. Rehnquist.

Goldwater reviewed a study made by two legal scholars, involving "a panel of sixty-five academic experts," who evaluated ninety-six of the ninety-eight justices who had sat on the Supreme Court before Powell and Rehnquist. The panel omitted Burger and Blackmun because of the recency of their appointments. With respect to panel evaluation of the ninety-six, Goldwater stated: "Only twelve were rated as 'great' by the panel. Of the rest, fifteen were considered 'near great,' fifty-five were rated 'average,' six 'below average' and eight 'failures.'"

The author then examined individually the backgrounds of the twelve "great" before they were appointed to the bench and compared the backgrounds with the contributions of these justices after their appointments. Backgrounds were studied in terms of the positions held and services rendered before coming to the bench, and contributions were studied in terms of decisions in which these justices subsequently played significant roles. The precourt backgrounds were also compared with the criteria insisted upon by the senators noted regarding the appraisal of Powell and Rehnquist.

The study caused doubt in Goldwater's mind as to whether several of the "great" justices would have been confirmed for appointment, if the criteria of the "liberal" senators indicated had prevailed at the time of those appointments. Nine of the twelve "great" were identified as Joseph Story, Louis D. Brandeis, Harlan Fiske Stone, Earl Warren, Hugo L. Black, Benjamin N. Cardozo, Oliver Wendell Holmes, Jr., Charles Evans Hughes, and Felix Frankfurter. The precourt backgrounds of several of these men seems quite conservative, as compared with their performance on the bench.

Mr. Goldwater evaluated thus:

> In truth, those who would use the judicial philosophy test are engaged in an utterly fallacious practice. I believe it is safe to say that, if the criteria suggested by the liberal element of the Senate had been applied to the twelve Justices selected as great, only one of them would have been assured his seat on the Court. There was something tangible and significant in the background of each of the other nominees that could have disqualified him from acceptance by the judicial philosophy advocates.
>
> There is a real spark of independence that ignites men once they become immune from all political pressures. As Justices, they sit as neither conservative nor liberal, but as intelligent human beings doing their utmost within their God-given capacities to search for and uphold the truth.

The author thought that the will of the people would come nearest to finding expression through the Supreme Court if the President had broad leeway in choosing nominees. He concluded: "So long as a nominee is a man of high ability, scholarship, integrity and diligence, without any significant conflict of interest in his past record, he should be confirmed by the Senate."

Tyrannical Judges and Court Imagery

One does not need exhaustive acquaintance with judicial functioning in order to recognize that not all judges function according to the ideals suggested by such writers as Stafford, Acheson, and Goldwater. Tyranny and authoritarianism exercised by men in positions of power have long been a part of human history. The doctrine of judicial restraint is a theoretical recognition of this tendency among judges.

Schwartz[6] studied this situation through considering the position of the trial judge, with particular reference to the performance of Judge Julius Hoffman in the Chicago case styled *United States* v. *David Dellinger*.[7] Schwartz commented on the "near-absolute power" of the trial judge in criminal cases and observed that "most of what trial judges do, particularly in petty criminal trials and generally in most trials, is quite unreviewable" by higher court authority. He indicated that court reporters, who work daily with particular judges, deliberately omit certain kinds of remarks made by the judge during the trial—and of course do not include gestures, inflections of the voice, etc. Schwartz referred to a general sympathy of trial judges in criminal cases with the prosecutors' and to the judges themselves as frequently having been prosecutors. He noted "the almost religious reverence which many lawyers have for the judiciary and the courts as institutions," thus enabling judges to expect and to get "almost fawning deference" from the bar, since most attorneys prefer to try their cases before a judge who at least is not hostile to them personally. The author suggested that the College of Trial Lawyers essentially approved the attorney-court relationship described.[8]

Schwartz referred especially to trials involving political and social deviants, and to the severe contempt penalties assessed for courtroom disturbances in some of such cases. At one point he stated:

> . . . In the last twenty years, the Bar has defaulted miserably on its obligation to defend the political heretic or other unpopular client. In 1770, John Adams and Josiah Quincy, Jr., defended the British soldiers who participated in the Boston Massacre. But, as Morris Ernst observed in 1962, "it is practically impossible to get leaders of the Bar in New York City at least, to represent whatever may be unpopular at the moment—a nudist, a communist, a Fifth Amendment pleader, a homosexual, an alleged obscene book, etc." . . . Given the acceleration of violent dissent and repression, the Chicago contempt rulings may render American justice even more suspect, by discouraging an active defense of dissidents involved.

The author subsequently stated: "The real cause of courtroom disruption is injustice, both inside and outside the courtroom, and not defendants who, in

Judge Hoffman's words, seek to 'cause . . . such disorder and confusion as would prevent a verdict by a jury.'" Schwartz added: "The manner of conducting both the trial and the sentencing, as well as the denial of appeal bonds, made it very clear that Judge Hoffman considered these men not merely as criminals, but as enemies of the State and prisoners of war to be dispatched for as long and as quickly as legally possible." Continuing, he stated that the Chicago trial confirmed "the views of those who see law and the legal systems primarily as an institution for 'legitimate' repression of dissenters."

With regard to judicial imagery or respect for the court and the need for objective studies on court performance as well as wider participation by members of the legal profession, Schwartz concluded:

> . . . One cannot demand respect for the office when the way it is filled deserves none. At the very least, we need a detailed study of the behavior of American trial judges to document and publicize the frequency of the abuses described here, and ways to curtail them, as well as recognition of the need for flexibility, latitude and understanding in trying defendants whose crime is based primarily on dissent from governmental policies. Some greater control by appellate judges may ultimately be in order, or by bar groups whose membership remains secret. If no controls are imposed, as is likely, judicial tyranny and courtroom disruption will probably escalate and the legal order will become even more discredited.

3. Court Imagery and Compulsory Retirement of Judges

As the idea of compulsory retirement upon reaching a specified age, accompanied by something that resembles decent compensation, becomes more generally accepted throughout American culture, increasing comment appears on the desirability of a stipulated retirement age for the judges in our courts.

Judge Calvert,[9] Chief Justice of the Supreme Court of Texas, recently indicated enthusiasm for compulsory retirement. He referred to from twenty-two to forty states as requiring the retirement of judges at ages of from seventy to seventy-five years, with the number of states depending on which survey report is accepted. He saw no guarantee that a judge who was quite eminent when selected would remain competent, rather than become tired and grow out-of-touch with social problems as he gets older. He commented that the foregoing applied to both federal and state judges and suggested that "a totally unselfish approach to improvement of our judicial system should impel those of us who are judges to lead the movement for mandatory retirement in both branches of the system." Calvert further noted: "The federal judiciary is one of the last bastions for employment of the aged. There seems to be some sort of pervading fear which makes it more or less untouchable and deters those who would speak out forthrightly." The author noted that business and educational institutions had "long since adopted mandatory retirement and limited service programs" and saw "no sound reason for believing that judges are a master race of people."

Judge Calvert reviewed the operation of retirement considerations in Texas and commented on a 1966 article by Major[10] on compulsory retirement of federal judges. Calvert agreed with Major that "advocacy of compulsory retirement is not the high road to popularity," and approved Major's comment that he had "never heard a valid reason why a judge should not voluntarily retire when eligible," but had heard many self-interest excuses. Calvert then identified four main excuses, which he rated in the following order of increasing importance. The judge (1) has developed no subsidiary interests to occupy his time upon retirement; (2) has a secret feeling that he is indispensable and essentially irreplaceable; (3) wants to hold on to the social standing and honors for himself and his wife which the job entails; (4) is not wanted around home because his wife over the years has developed other interests and routines which she does not want to have interrupted.

In conclusion, the author reiterated his appeal for judges to take the lead in promoting compulsory retirement, and thought that if a constitutional amendment was considered necessary to apply the idea to the Supreme Court of the United States, there would be no problem about getting congressional and legislative approval.[11]

4. Imagery and Mode of Selecting Judges

Goldwater's comparisons of performance by individual justices on the Supreme Court with the political-philosophy test as applicable to appointments led him to reject that test as a means of selecting well-qualified appointees. Comments by Stafford and others, as noted in this study, also have implications as to appointments.

Cutts[12] used a quite different approach to evaluating judicial competence in terms of judicial responsibility and as related to the appointive process. He analyzed several recent decisions by the Supreme Court in establishing his thesis that the court can and does exercise legislative functions. His main approach concerned judicial use of procedural due process under the Fourteenth Amendment. Cutts accepted the idea that the lawmakers should be representative of the people and saw nothing particularly wrong with judge-made law, provided the judges actually represent the people. He commented: "There are several ways to accomplish this," referring to the Supreme Court. Cutts elaborated:

> The most apparent method of selection would be choice by circuit—one judge selected from each circuit. Whether selected by popular vote, by vote of state legislatures, or even the recommendation of a majority of governors in that circuit, the purpose of responsibility would be accomplished. More important, *a term of office less than life should be established.* The idea of appointment and later vote by the people, such as is the California practice, is appealing. No particular scheme is essential so long as the objective of representation is met. Any of these alternatives will, of course, require a constitutional amendment.
>
> Another alternative, appealing but less guaranteed of permanence, is the formulation of due process standards by Congress under its Section V authority.[13] . . . Unless there is a definite provision in the Constitution, Congress is best suited to evaluate what is an "unreasonable" search and seizure, for example. Regardless of the alternatives selected,

the fact of judicial lawmaking requires a change in responsibility. (Emphasis added.)

Watson[14] was also concerned about the selection of judges, as related to their responsibilities and their status or acceptability to the people. He emphasized the possible role of a nominating commission composed of members of the state bar, such as had been developed in Missouri, which operated in accordance with a nonpartisan plan based on representation by four groups. The groups are: (1) the general public—whom Watson characterized as showing least interest; (2) attorneys—who think in terms of the kinds of clients and cases they have, and how favorable a prospective judge would likely be to their situations; (3) persons moving into judgeships—who were cronies of "good personality" when they were practicing lawyers; (4) judges who are already on the bench—and who reflect a type of colleague orientation.

Watson noted problems which societies have faced at least since the days of Plato in selecting public officials with both competence and integrity—that is, persons who were both wise and unselfish. Watson observed: "The most effective control which those 'outside the government' exercise over those 'inside the government' in a democracy comes through popular elections." He mentioned politically partisan and nonpartisan elections, with school and mayorality elections in the second category. "Put in simplest terms, there is no Republican or Democratic way to develop a curriculum or pave a street," he noted. Appointive offices and non-policy-making civil service positions were also mentioned as suggested avenues for selecting individuals to operate government.

"The plan has not entirely removed political considerations from the selection process," commented the author, but he thought that it was quite an asset to the governor in reducing the narrower aspects of partisan politics in judicial selection. He referred to public participation as the weakest part of the plan and suggested the need for improvement in that sector. He also noted that many attorneys who participated in a survey of operations emphasized the need for a procedure to remove incompetent and incapacitated judges from the bench. "Until such a procedure is developed, the Nonpartisan Court Plan will fail to live up to its full promise as a means of meeting the age old problem of 'judging the judges,'" concluded Mr. Watson.

In his documented and comparative report on voluntary plans for selecting judges on the basis of merit, Lowe stated:[15] "Twenty-five United States jurisdictions now use merit selection and tenure plans or parts of them, covering all or a part of the appellate and trial courts. . . . Merit plans have traditionally been instituted by means of legislative action, but in the last decade a new phenomenon, voluntary merit selection, introduced by executive decision, has become increasingly widespread."

Tabular comparisons were made of some thirty-one plans being used in twenty-four states and Puerto Rico. Details were presented of plans adopted through executive action in a few states. Lowe commented that no executive action had been taken to institute voluntary merit selection of judges for federal courts, but implied favorable prospects for the future.[16] He looked upon voluntary merit selection plans as a temporary expedient, until appropriate constitutional amendments are approved.

Chapter 2

THE JUDICIARY AND SOCIAL CHANGE

Much of what is said about an unfavorable judicial image in America, or about an unfavorable conception of law and lawful behavior in the nation, relates to updating the court and legal system so that its operations are more in keeping with the needs of a complex and socially mobile industrial democracy.

One aspect of complexity and upkeep involves the speed of change in human relationships, relative to the slowness with which adjudicated disputes come from the courts. And we hear about wisdom in the observation: "Justice delayed, is justice denied." Furthermore, many aspects of technology are more important in American life than they were fifty years ago. This implies the need for different machinery and evaluative competence to assemble and appraise relevant information on the wide range of conflicts which now arise for adjudication. This may imply greater judicial specialization than has yet occurred. Other types of problems relate to the growing role of jobs and employment in the nation's economy, together with the organizational status of vocational groups, and mobility of individual members of the labor force. Still other problems relate to the multiplicity of small and overlapping units of government, which linger although several of their earlier functions have declined. Many critics of the courts, including several members of the judiciary, fail to recognize the implications of changes such as those noted.

There is a considerable repertoire of rather specific criticisms that have been made of the courts concerning matters which help to undermine favorable imagery. A few of these relate to such matters as delays and docket backlogs; management of court procedure in the sense of differentiating between administrative and adjudicative functions, with a possible reallocation of the former; the need for incorporating certain aspects of scientific procedure, such as relate to experimentation or to statistical evaluation of judicial operations; and education of the public on what the functions of the courts are, as well as on the responsibilities of the people generally for the status of lawlessness in America.

1. Judicial Adjustment to Social Change

Probably, in a broad sense, most of the comment on loss of favorable imagery implies failure of the legal system, particularly the adjudicative aspects, to make the adjustments demanded by broad social changes in American life. To emphasize judicial modification as demanded by social change, one need not ignore the vagueness and the mythology embodied in assumptions that the system was ideal for conditions which prevailed in the days of the Founding Fathers, or assume that no significant changes with respect to justice have been made since that time. Consideration should be given both to needs and to remedial efforts.

Scope of Need

In commenting on needs, Senator Tydings[17] recognized that criticisms of the way in which justice is administered have long been a part of man's history, and stated: "Hundreds of years of criticism and yet our courts today are administered in essentially the same way as they were two centuries ago." With respect to waste, delay and excessive reverence for the past, he said: "The mills of justice are not only grinding slowly, they are grinding to a halt." He referred to the nation's 200 million people, and commented that in twenty years (1990) a population of 300 million was "not inconceivable."[18] Tydings suggested that each person in the population is a potential litigant. And one might add that in a complex society each person tends to have more contacts with other people than in a simple society.

"For the past fifty years," court reformers have advocated the creation of unified state courts, observed the senator, in place of a proliferation of semi-autonomous and in part overlapping courts—such as criminal courts, equity courts, probate courts, and domestic-relations courts. He mentioned the need for management consultants to handle court administration, such as introducing the use of computers and other business machines, as well as methods for dealing with such matters as dockets, court calendars, and the flow of cases through the system. This would conserve the judge's time for adjudicative functions, he reasoned. He thought that part of the reluctance of courts to use management consultants and systems analysis was "the notion that only judges and lawyers understand the real needs of the courts."

More directly than most critics, the senator observed: "The problems of the courts in general are magnified ten fold at the lowest level and it is at this level unfortunately, that the average American, the one with the traffic ticket and the small claim, forms his opinion of our judicial system." He added: "We must recognize the great capacity these courts have for affecting the lives of our people and either destroying or invigorating their reliance on the law as an instrument of justice."

The general competence and technical knowledge to produce effective court reform exist in our culture, stated Tydings, but the question remains of whether the will to accomplish it resides in the legislatures, executives, courts, lawyers, police, and general public. He quoted a federal circuit judge to the effect that for democracy to live, it must be efficient; for free government to be preserved in America, it must be good government; and that at no point does government touch the lives of the people more intimately than in the administration of justice.[19]

When Judge Tamm asked:[20] "Are Courts Going the Way of the Dinosaur?" he had in mind several of the delays, inefficiencies, and other shortcomings noted by Tydings. In focusing on delay and backlog, Tamm commented: "A court system that is on the verge of collapsing under the weight of its workload denies justice to litigants and to society." He added that if the foregoing seemed an exaggerated statement as of the present, "it may soon prove to be a distressingly accurate one." He noted a "massive outpouring of apathy" from "bored and indifferent brethren" some twenty years earlier when he advocated changes in the court system. "The pattern of the bland leading the bland has proved its own inefficiency," observed Tamm, as he urged judges to assume the obligations of leadership in reform.[21]

In his emphasis on need for objective and empirical information on which to base court reform, Tamm referred illustratively to the "scant consensus" on professional qualities which nominees to the Supreme Court should have; the absence of feedback on whether damages awarded in breach-of-contract suits were having the desired effects; the outcomes of remands to trial courts or administrative agencies for further proceedings, especially to the extent to which remands lead to repetitive exercises because the remanding authority failed to point out the particular defects of the original proceeding; and injunctions which are so vague or so harsh that litigants must return to court for clarification or for modification. Tamm thought that it should be possible to acquire meaningful statistics as a basis for sound generalizations on problem areas such as those indicated.[22] Clues such as those noted, along with computerizations and courtroom management suggested by him and other writers, could increase productivity and improve court efficiency, reasoned Tamm. He concluded:

> If we do not advance into the twenty-first century geared to meet the accelerated and demanding times that face us, then our judicial system will fail in its basic responsibility of promoting that security of life, liberty and property, which is the great end of society and government.

In part, Dean Laub[23] commented in a similar manner on the courts and social change. In connection with emergence from what he thought of as an ego-based arrogance reflected in a theory of judge-directed social structuring, Laub reasoned in part as follows regarding "aspirations for law."

> I am convinced that the principal role of the judge in this country, at least for some time to come, must now be to adjust the law to mankind's aspirations. Reduced to basics, these aspirations, in the order of their importance are: (1) survival, and (2) the good life.

Laub further categorized certain areas of special importance for law reform. First, under "law for survival" he observed that "abstract rights must give way to concrete perils," and stated: "The judge of the future must be more astute in protecting man against himself than in solving a constitutional rebus." As to problems which technology creates for law, he generalized: "Both science and the law must turn full-face to urban problems, for it is in the city where we face one of our gravest dangers. Science has already laid the groundwork for fantastic legal problems in the future." Second, with respect to "law for waste and pollution," Laub mentioned oil depletion, landfill programs, and electric highways, and noted that redevelopments cannot be on a piece-by-piece basis but must involve coordination regarding substantial areas—

perhaps comparable to the idea of macroeconomics versus microeconomics.

Third, in considering "law for model cities," he stated: "Judges must find a way to get social facts into the mainstream of litigation." Laub emphasized the need for judges to become "interdisciplinarians" who coordinate the research of social and physical science. He continued: "The time must come when every piece of litigation having an important impact upon society must first be researched and analyzed in a social laboratory before it will be converted into a law."[24]

Fourth, concerning "lay involvement in law," Dean Laub initially commented:

> Intelligent laymen are more and more going to make their voices heard with respect to the direction of law, and the bar, and the bench must keep in touch with public thought, not to discover the public's attitude on a particular case, but with respect to public aims and the administration of justice generally. Humanity's unquenchable thirst for survival, justice, peace and the good life, will impress itself more and more upon the judiciary and society will not tolerate disobedience for too long a time.

More specifically, the Dean referred to alteration of the Fifth Amendment, scuttling the so-called "enlightened bail practices" relative to "preventive detention," and he noted recent attacks on the entire Bill of Rights "by speakers who point to Australia as an enlightened jurisdiction which deliberately eliminated a Bill of Rights from its constitution." In conclusion, Laub observed: "In essence, the motto on the (judge's) chamber wall will continue to echo the question of Micah, 'And what doth the Lord require of thee, but to do justly, and to love mercy, and to walk humbly with thy God?'"

Reform Efforts

Some criticisms of court operations have been accompanied by detailed statements regarding types of reform and have described reforms which have been undertaken experimentally or otherwise. Senator Gurney[25] used this approach as he reasoned that present operations both victimize the accused and ignore the concern of citizens for their safety. He noted four reasons for docket backlogs: (1) actual increase in crime rate; (2) greater emphasis on due process, whereby more attention is given to hearings and appeals with greater burdens placed on the courts—without corresponding increase in personnel and facilities; (3) increase in administrative detail, such as transcripts and records which take up a considerable amount of a judge's time with paper work; and (4) the fact that most judges handle both criminal and civil cases, which Gurney considered to be "inextricably related" and looked upon as contributing substantially to the breakdown of criminal justice. But such factors, said Gurney, cannot be accepted as excuses for delays in bringing criminal cases to trial. He commented: "Under our system, our citizens have every right to expect that records will be properly kept and trial transcripts quickly made available." As extremes, he mentioned a twenty-year-old boy "who remained locked up for nearly eight months after all charges against him were dropped," and a man who was "kept in jail from April to September because a clerical error resulted in loss of his record of dismissal." He further noted: "Our legal system urgently needs more judges, prosecutors and public defenders. There is a critical need for more courtrooms and newer jails."

Senator Gurney offered various specific suggestions and comparisons for improving the situation, particularly with regard to personnel and jury procedure. He stated: "The principal (sic) function of a judge is presiding over a trial," but he saw little help in adding more judges so long as they were bogged down in paper work. He suggested: "One possible solution to this difficulty is the use of para-judges to arrange calendars, to hear motions and to follow up on procedural and administrative details," and he thought that the Federal Magistrate Act of 1968 should be helpful with respect to the federal district courts. He also looked upon the para-judge approach as "providing a useful and badly needed training ground for young men and women interested in a judicial career."

Other suggested improvements might include the training of court administrators for service comparable to that of hospital administrators, more extensive utilization of law clerks, and the use of computers and microfilm for data storage and retrieval. The senator noted: "It makes no sense, in this age of technology, to continue using such anachronisms as handwritten dockets, ledgers, and court journals." He saw encouragement in the training program of "the new Institute of Court Management at the University of Denver" and in the National Center for State Courts, which is intended to help improve the operation of state and local courts. He mentions a bill for a Judicial Assistance Administration which he introduced into Congress.

Particular attention as an expediter of operations should be given to Florida's six-man jury approach, upheld by the Supreme Court[26] and subsequently adopted by twenty-four federal districts. Senator Gurney observed that such juries result in considerable saving: of money; of the time of judges, lawyers, and jurors; and especially of the time of the accused. He also mentioned co-sponsorship of a senate bill which in criminal cases would require trial within sixty days of indictment.[27]

2. Functional Law and Order

One aspect of an administrative approach to considerations regarding the judiciary and social change appears in former Mayor Lindsay's comment[28] on the difference between problems of lawlessness as they are presented in survey reports and as they appear to one who is responsible for improving the situation. In an initial comment, he stated: " . . . If the machinery of law fails to work swiftly and justly, Americans will abandon faith in the Rule of Law." In his analysis, he stated:

> The issues are:
> whether people feel free to walk to the newsstand after dark,
> whether police arrest criminals
> whether courts convict the guilty
> whether correctional systems really rehabilitate.

The mayor referred to the sweeping recommendations of the 1931 Wickersham Commission for police, judicial, and correctional reform, but added that since the recommendations were largely ignored, the National Crime Commission repeated a statement of them in 1967. "And in 1968, the Kerner Report on Civil Disorders echoed the Crime Commission," noted Lindsay. He added that the Violence Commission's 1970 Report borrowed extensively from the Kerner Report. The latter commission estimated that implementing the needed reform program would cost six billion dollars. "Six billion dollars for more police and better courts, more rehabilitation and better corrections, more safety and less crime," reiterated the mayor. He observed that "Washington talks" about conditions and needs, but offers little financial support. Like the mayors of most other large cities, Lindsay apparently thought that the federal government should pay most or all of the additional cost involved.

"But all the work of reform and all reshaped structures will still fail unless we alter the correctional system," noted the mayor. "Rehabilitation deserves more than verbal tribute and a paltry 3% of our criminal justice funds." He emphasized the need for making correctional structures responsive and open —"responsive to the need for training and educational opportunities; open to paraprofessionals, who can communicate with released offenders and who cannot be fooled or conned by their clients; open to every person, every government agency, and every private institution that can aid down and out individuals." He continued: "Then we can turn more first-time criminals into productive citizens rather than repeat offenders."[29]

Lindsay stated that some of the needed reform in the system of criminal justice involved extensive social reform, but as illustrative of small changes that might be helpful he mentioned a revival of street life through such avenues as pedestrian malls and street bands for "recreating the streets as people places." He added: "And there *is* safety in numbers."

3. Specialists and Paraprofessionals

Several earlier references to court administration or management, and to systems analysis, infer a type of specialist or paraprofessional. Mayor Lindsay referred more directly to paraprofessionals, and Senator Gurney referred to para-judges. In a recent statement, Miller[30] referred to consultants for the court. He particularly mentioned academic or law-school consultants, management consultants, and technical consultants, and indicated several considerations to be taken into account with respect to employing consultants.

Pasquesi[31] mentioned "part-time lawyers" and "paralegals," or lay assistants for lawyers. He sought to define a paralegal as one who can function regarding a particular isolated task *almost* as a lawyer, but whose function would fall between the "legal" function of a lawyer and the "sublegal" function of a secretary. He commented on an increasing lawyer interest in paralegals as part of a "divide and conquer" approach to their increasing range and volume of legal work.

The author recognized problems in recruiting and training paralegals and in determining the work for them to do. He noted the following basic steps in putting the paralegal to work:

Determine the need to delegate a paralegal function to a nonlegal person;

Identify that function;

Isolate it from the remainder of the transaction of which it is a part;

Establish a formal, written office procedure to train your nonlegal personnel to perform the function in question; and

Constantly annotate and revise your written procedures to keep them up to date.

A community junior college in the St. Louis area, Lupo stated,[32] has developed the nation's first formal program for training legal assistants. He traced the development of the program from its initial conception in 1966, through the autumn of 1969 enrollment of fifty-eight students in the Legal Technology Program, to the first students who in June 1971 completed the one-year Legal Technology Certificate Program as they graduated from the community junior college. Regarding these graduates, Lupo said: "This means that they had completed 18 credit hours in general courses, such as American Government, English Composition, Accounting, Typing, etc. They had also completed at least 16 credit hours of legal technology courses." A 1968 questionnaire canvass of the 2,000 members of the Bar Association of Metropolitan St. Louis indicated that within the ensuing five years the law firms represented could absorb 400 full-time legal assistants. Up to the date of Lupo's writing, all students in the program were evening students.

Lupo commented on the wide publicizing of the program since the opening of classes in 1969 and noted the development of similar programs in Cleveland, Minneapolis, and San Francisco. He emphasized the importance of attorney supervision of training details and bar control of general program design and operation. At one point he stated:

Most essential, and something that cannot be over-emphasized, is the fact that the legal assistant must be trained to perform his duties *under the supervision of a lawyer.* A lawyer cannot delegate his responsibilities to a lay assistant. At all times the legal assistant must be under his supervision and the lawyer must be responsible at all times for the work, functions and tasks performed by the legal assistant. (Emphasis by Lupo.)

The author indicated the need for bar control to coordinate and evaluate operations by individual lawyers, as well as to evaluate possible new lawyer-client relationships and to check on unauthorized practice of the law. He referred to proposals for submitting the legal Assistant Program to the Supreme Court of Missouri, for a consideration of rules governing professional ethics and of standards concerning the role of Legal Assistants in American society. Lupo thought that such programs should not be encouraged without the active participation of the Local Bar Association, but that local, state and national bar associations should become actively involved in developing programs. He apparently looked upon such programs as one way to reduce load factors and delays in the American legal system.

Larson described the program at the University of Minnesota for training paraprofessional workers in legal fields.[33] He stated: "The curriculum is multilevel, offering a one-year sequence for legal secretaries, a two-year associate of arts degree program for legal assistants, and a four-year baccalaureate degree program for legal administrators. The program is open-ended so that a student may progress to the level appropriate to his individual interests and abilities." Among the advantages of the location was access to the professional guidance and support offered by the university law school, a substantial body of practicing attorneys in the Minneapolis-St. Paul area, and a good working relationship between the university and the legal profession.

Four components of the program were noted: general education, related business courses, specific technical legal courses, and internship experience. The technical legal courses are taught by practicing attorneys, who are available largely because of the twin-city situation.[34] A three-credit course meets for a two-and-one-half hour session in the late afternoon on one day per week over a ten-week period. Larson mentioned certain problems in internship placement because of the temporary nature of the service rendered.

The wide interest in the program indicated by the large number of potential enrollees was attributed in part to the small number of such programs available in the nation, but encouragement by twin-city law firms for their employees to enroll seemed also to be involved. With the program in operation for only two years, Larson referred to its potential evaluation by the job market: "Until we finally place our graduates, we have no way of knowing whether suitable career opportunities will actually be available. It is one thing for the legal community to voice support of our program and to acknowledge that the widespread use of paraprofessionals is a valuable innovation. It may be quite another for the profession to provide immediate employment for graduates in the kinds of jobs they anticipate and are prepared for." Larson mentioned a grant of $30,000 for a two-year period to help support a program for training law students to work with paraprofessional students.

In concern about uncoordinated specialties in the field of legal training and practice, Dean Pedrick[35] showed considerable anxiety about the lack of broad-visioned generalists to whom the legal profession and the broader culture must look for social leadership. He commented on specialists as contributing to technological and related success, but as weak in being able to use it for developing a better life. At one point, he observed:

> In some ways, it seems that as we get better and better at more restricted assignments, we are valued less and less on matters of general importance. Scientists, engineers, economists, sociologists, city planners, even accountants, sit with the mighty in seats occupied in former times by counsel. As Lord Radcliffe put it some years back, it is as though we lawyers, to a considerable extent, have become spectators while others are "where the action is." How often is the tax lawyer the general adviser to the corporation president? Not often, it is believed, if he is solely a tax lawyer.

The Dean noted great ferment in legal education, but parallel dalliance by the American Bar Association for fiteen years "over the wisdom of setting up a system for certifying specialists in the law." He thought that the situation was approaching dilemma proportions. By way of elaboration, he further mentioned the tax lawyer—particularly as connected with the Internal Revenue Service. He stated:

> A steady diet of the Internal Revenue Code can do things to a man—not very pleasant things either. IRC has at least something in common with LSD. Both tend to be habit-forming. They offer an escape from reality and produce in the addict illusions of pleasure and power followed by fits of depression and disorientation. Addicts get so they can't distinguish illusion from reality.

Pedrick recognized values in specialization, and looked upon the modern law firm as a counterpart of the medical clinic, "offering a wide range of legal services to be administered by specialists." However, he thought that specialist training should probably be given by practitioners, not by law schools—at least not in undergraduate programs. He mentioned the need for specialists in any area of the law to work part of the time outside their specialty—"just to maintain their peripheral vision." He mentioned public service work, legal aid, criminal defense work, and the juvenile courts as offering helpful opportunities regarding such vision. Dean Pedrick continued:

> Public service work must be seen not only as serving the interest of a clientele desperately in need of legal services and a public interest in need of champions, but as *absolutely indispensable to the equilibrium of the specialist himself.* The idealism with which most students come to the law is deeply ingrained. If the practitioner cannot reconcile what he is now doing with the idealism of his youth, he will, indeed, become cynical, bored and depressed. (Emphasis added.)
>
> The conventional work of the profession is not being dismissed as of no consequence. That conventional work is important and essential. Perhaps we ought to relate our work to the public interest more effectively in our own minds. . . . we hold to the view of a legal profession offering all the really demanding service society needs in relation to law. To maintain our place in a profession of such nobility and dedication, we must swim a bit outside the confines of a specialty.

Perhaps it would be appropriate to characterize Pedrick's view of a peripheral-visioned leader as a "noncollapsible specialist" with a broad core of general education and experience, plus one or possibly more nodules of specialization on the periphery. This characterization suggests the type of undertaking, as to civic responsibility of lawful behavior in American society, which it is necessary for the various agencies concerned with educational and social leadership to develop in the general population. Rapid social change intensifies the need and places it on a continuing basis.[36]

Chapter 3

THE COURTS AND COMMUNICATION

We say that the good teacher is knowledgeable and can communicate his knowledge to learners whose backgrounds differ widely from his own. However, learners vary not only in how much they already know that is useful as a foundation, but in how much they are interested in learning the particular material at hand or in the current situation. In school terminology, the latter is called motivation. Thus the teacher and school program have the task of determining what knowledge, attitudes, habits, etc., to teach—that is, the curriculum. But there is also the task of providing the facilities, situations, and procedures which are most likely to achieve the desired learning results.

Teaching problems and responsibilities regarding children in school resemble those involved in getting the general population to understand more about the role of law and order in a complex society, and about the rights and responsibilities of the individual concering that role under different types of social or governmental organization. In addition, the teaching problem regarding our legal framework includes the development and continuous functioning of constructive attitudes and habits.

When it is urged that the courts and law enforcement agencies assume greater responsibility for popular education about our legal structure, it is not assumed that schools and universities, including their programs for adult education and for training professional workers, will play no role. It is rather assumed that coordination among all agencies involved will become more important.

1. Communication Between the Courts and the Legal Profession

Several articles and reports previously noted show extensive two-way communication between the judiciary and other parts of the legal profession. Judges, law professors, practicing attorneys, political scientists, office-holding politicians, and law-enforcement officers have contributed extensively to the literature on the subject. Members of these groups have often been critical of their own systems and operations, although sometimes they see the shortcomings of others more clearly than their own.

While some writers urge judges and other members of the legal profession to address civic clubs and other nonlegal groups, there is considerable support for the idea that judges should keep their noncourt work within narrow limits. The latter approach would have judges restrict their addresses and writings to strictly legal topics, and presented only to members of the legal profession. The emphasis on this point by Dean Acheson, aimed particularly at the Supreme Court, is clear.

The Legal Profession's Closed-Circuit Operation

This study supports the view that members of the legal profession, especially the judiciary, have been talking too much to one another—and too little to the general public. The reasoning herein is that the seat of lawlessness and of disrespect for the courts, as well as the unfavorable imagery concerning government under law and concerning law enforcement in general, lies with a public which is meagerly informed and substantially disappointed and disillusioned. The competence of the profession and the public-spirited aspects of its orientation need broader impact on the public. Some of the items reviewed, which point to the need of attorneys and law schools for greater recognition of the public-service responsibility of the profession, support the reasoning indicated. However, the Acheson doctrine of aloofness and restricted contact with ongoing social changes, insofar as that doctrine can be judged by the one item on the subject included herein, does not support that reasoning.

The Law Schools and the Legal Profession

Substantially in line with the logic which urges a wider civic or public-service responsibility is a recent article by Swords on clinical programs for law schools.[37] He stated: "The primary educational objectives for law school clinical programs is to promote an awareness by students of the legal profession as a service profession with major obligations to broad segments of society that go largely unserved." He also pointed out that "a classroom component is an essential part of any clinical program."

Swords noted an important question that arose in developing such a program; that is, whether the program is primarily to extend legal service or to teach law students. He emphasized the latter. In the clinical aspects of the program, students "are expected to work one afternoon a week for at least three hours in a neighborhood law office managed by the law school and situated in a nearby ghetto." Swords added: "The office provides legal services to indigents of the community in the civil field. . . .Three attorneys comprise the full time staff of the office." He stated that the attorneys handle the more complicated cases. Theoretically, they also supervise the students, noted Swords, which in reality amounts to conferences that the student seeks with one or another of the attorneys. He noted that the attorneys are on university staff as instructors and attend faculty meetings, but do not hold regular faculty appointments.

The author rather lamented the heavy orientation of law-school courses toward preparing students for commercial practice which is geared to the attorney's making a living by practicing law.[38] He commented that when welfare or other government agencies deal with the rights of the poor, they operate in terms of what the agency thinks is the client's best interest rather than on what are the client's procedural and substantive rights. This is a part of Swords' rationale which emphasized the public-service aspects of law practice. To develop an understanding of indigent problems, he noted, "students should have extensive contact with poverty clients, assuming full responsibility for them as a lawyer." A subsequent comment logically followed: "The neighborhood law office is probably a better setting for a program than a clinic located in a law school. A neighborhood office is likely to have a wider range of clients. Moreover, it takes the students regularly into the community."

Justice Denecke,[39] Supreme Court of Oregon, made a creative plea for cooperation between the judiciary and law-school professors. His suggestions stemmed partly from the growing case load of judges, but more from the range of subjects which lawsuits involve and the limited range over which a particular judge can develop expertise. He noted a kind of antagonism between the professors and the judges: with some professors holding the judges in low esteem, not worth helping or capable of being helped; and with some judges looking upon the professors as "impractical," with neither the capacity nor courage to "make it" in the rough and tumble world of practice. Such judges, noted Denecke, do not think that the law teachers can render worthwhile assistance to the bench.

The author noted a classroom teaching load of six to seven hours per week in law schools, and goals of reducing it to four to five hours, with emphasis on substantial amounts of time devoted to preparation for classroom teaching, research and writing, and helping to solve community problems of local or wider scope.

Denecke urged the use of part of this "other time" in helping the judges on the bench with the range of difficult problems which they face. He implied waves of interest in law-reviews articles. He commented: "For example, articles on the various facets of *Miranda*[40] are filling the law reviews," whereas several problems of other types are bypassed or barely touched upon. He mentioned that such reviews were helpful, then added: "But if I could only have your thought-out views on my particular problem it would be of even more assistance." Some judges resent law-review articles which make specific attacks on their decisions, observed the author, as he referred to a comment by one judge at a joint dinner for the judiciary and law-school faculty. The comment was: "Teacher *B* is informed by one of the judges that the law review criticism of one of the opinions had about the same quality of judgment as that enjoyed by the fellow who created '*near beer*' (he was no judge of *distance*)." (Emphasis added.)

Justice Denecke emphasized a combination of practice and theory, which might be characterized as a combination of "How To Do It" plus "Thinking Through It." He thus noted that several types of problems on conflict, as well as other areas of adjudication, had come into prominence since the days when the justices on the bench were students in law schools. He also noted that a majority of appellate judges thought their work loads would not permit them to return to universities for general continuing legal education, even should governing regulations permit leave for doing so.

To circumvent educational difficulties and to develop coordinations of the types inferred, Denecke stated his hypothesis and outlined his suggestions. He said:

My thesis is that law teachers can render a great aid to the law and to the appellate courts by participating in some fashion in the presentation of materials to the courts in the cases that are being briefed, argued and decided today, rather than by attempting to educate judges by writing or teaching in a general subject area or by writing comments about decisions already written. I am suggesting (that) you directly enter into the battle when it is occurring and fire salvos which may bring about the winning or the losing of a case then in issue.

The author observed that his proposal would require that the teacher be admitted to the bar in the state in which he teaches, which it was suggested might be handled with or without a state bar examination. As members of the bar, continued Denecke, the teachers could aid the judges through preparing briefs, and perhaps presenting oral arguments in the role of *Amicus Curiae*. He nevertheless observed that some courts oppose the *Amicus Curiae* approach because of the additional material to be read and because most such briefs come from persons who are not really friends of the court but friends of one of the parties. However, the justice thought that the values justified his proposal. He referred illustratively to a case under the Uniform Commercial Code which was assigned to him and for which he had no formal education or practical experience. He commented: "A lot of judicial man hours and one judge's fear of being a fool would have been saved if we could have called upon one of you (teachers) who knows this area and ask you to submit an *Amicus* brief."

Justice Denecke further suggested:

I am concerned that in some cases we (judges) never see the problem until we read a law review critique a year after the opinion is handed down. One method of assisting us to locate the problem and assisting us in its solution would be to have the clerk of the court send copies of the briefs to the law schools reasonably soon after they are received by the court. Which is some months before oral arguments in our court and I'm afraid in most others.

He thought that some member of the faculty could then at least scan the briefs and offer his evaluation to the court. He added parenthetically: "Scanning the briefs also might cause you (teachers) to work a little harder upon your students' research and writing so that they will not repeat the errors of their predecessors."

As a further suggestion, Denecke noted:

Another means of creating and strengthening this bond between law center and the judiciary is by the court appointing you to represent indigent accuseds in criminal cases. I realize that not too many of you (teachers) claim knowledge in this field, but I am also of the opinion that in many law schools teaching in this area is becoming a sought-after chore.

And there is a need for expertise in this kind of representation.

The author also suggested that teachers sit as trial judges *pro tempore*, in certain types of cases which do not involve a resolving of fact questions. On this point he reasoned:

> What is more natural than having a law teacher, whose specialty is trusts, acting as pro tem judge in a case involving complicated trust problems? The regular trial judge is happy to have you come in and hear the matter. He has more cases to dispose of than he can handle and any case that is going to require a lot of study is an obstacle to his keeping up with his docket. The attorneys on the first go-around will probably have a "let's look and see" attitude. If you conduct yourself in a reasonable fashion, remembering that being a judge pro tem, like being a regular judge, does not make you any smarter or wittier, the lawyers will probably be glad to have you the next time and may ask to have you appointed.

The justice concluded his suggestions and his appeal thus:

> Well, there you are. We need help and you are in a uniquely capable position of providing that help. To secure your assistance will need affirmative action by the judiciary but the impetus to cause the affirmative action must come from you.

Continuing Legal Education for Lawyers

Writing as President of the American Bar Association in 1969, Gossett reflected enthusiasm for the bar's interest in continuing legal education for lawyers and put forth six criteria for constructive future growth.[41] Part of these criteria urge the broadened public service aspect of law practice emphasized by Swords, and the closer coordination of law school and law office stressed by Denecke. Gossett's first criterion emphasized the development of purposeful values and aspirations concerning public and professional needs and a sequence of programs to achieve the objectives proclaimed. Second, he urged a shift from the large-audience convention-type of approach to a more in-depth seminar-type course, with probably small numbers of immediate participants. He then suggested the further development of required programs, such as those currently illustrated by the operation of large law firms, government agencies, the judiciary, and corporate law staffs. He thought that requirements plus recognition for achievement would "tempt reluctant members of the Bar to utilize fully the opportunities that are provided." As his fourth item, Gossett mentioned self-discipline by persons who administer programs of continuing legal education. He observed: "Professional education cannot be a willy-nilly endeavor."

Gossett's fifth criterion emphasized continuing legal education as a *connected and cooperative aspect of a comprehensive educational effort*. On this point he elaborated:

> The linkage between prelaw education and law school on the one hand and between law school and continuing legal education on the other must be strengthened. Ways must be found to heighten the interest of

law teachers in greater involvement. Town and gown traditionally have been set apart from each other, each blaming a communication barrier, which, on examination, may be more mirror than glass. Each group should confess that it has been and is troubled by its own limitations, but those limitations should not inhibit dialogue now or coordinated efforts later.

The sixth criterion stressed the need for persistent creativity, if continuing legal education is to have a significant future. In this connection, Gossett said:

Our efforts in this realm of professional endeavor are just beginning: training for specialization; programs for the judiciary and other governmental personnel; *a meaningful educational program on public and professional responsibility*, meeting the educational needs of newly graduated lawyers; *integrating legal research and law reform into continuing legal education*; developing and fully utilizing radio, television and audio tapes. These are a few random but familiar illustrations that bear testimony to how far we still must go. (Emphasis added.)

After brief comment on the financial problems entailed in efforts by a "learned profession" to "continue the learning process," the author concluded on a combined appeal and eulogy. He recognized that ideals by nature can only be approached, not reached, as he stated:

. . . If we recognize the value of evolutionary progress, if we understand the need for constructive change, and if we are willing to join together in working toward our common goals, we can plan and develop a system of continuing legal education that will heighten the competence and enhance the social awareness of the members of a great profession.

Judge Ketcham[42] reviewed what Gossett called an in-depth seminar-type program. With the aid of "a generous financial grant" the program was conducted as a four-week summer session at the University of Colorado (Boulder), for thirty-four juvenile court judges. Two of the thirty-four were women, both lay magistrates from Great Britain. Ketcham mentioned representation by twenty-four states, mainly from large cities. He commented on a melting-pot ethnic composition as reflected by the genealogy of their names: Scandinavian, Jewish, Irish, Anglo-Saxon, Italian, Spanish, Chinese, Polish and French. He noted: "The Irish-Americans were clearly the most vocal."

The program was described as covering five days of each week, with lectures, discussions and field trips. The schedule was from 8:30 to 11:00 a.m. and from 2:00 to 5:00 p.m. It included discussions and films, and there was testing on two evenings per week. Prominent persons in various areas concerned lectured and led discussions. The first two weeks were devoted to a study of the behavioral sciences and their application to the system of juvenile justice. This background is quite important, thought Ketcham, in view of the status in American culture of most judges involved. He stated:

With broad statutory authority, a juvenile court judge can not only intervene in the life of a child to determine what changes in conduct or environment are necessary; he can also bring to bear forces to insure that his decisions are implemented. Few other individuals or agencies in our democracy can emulate such power. Hence, its use requires knowledge, caution and restraint lest it do harm as well as good.

As a part of the first two weeks, the seminar made a field trip to the Lookout Mountain School for Boys at Golden (Colorado), followed by a reciprocal visit by thirty-two boys from that training school to the Boulder setting. During the one-day reciprocal visit, each judge was paired off with a delinquent youth for interviews and conferences.

The third week concentrated on "The Delinquent Child and the Law," with lectures and discussions supplemented by field visits to the Denver Juvenile Hall and the Fort Logan Mental Health Center. Members of the seminar went in groups of six "to observe other juvenile court judges conducting delinquency hearings in Denver and Arvada," noted Ketcham, as he added: "Law enforcement was observed at the asphalt level when the judges toured the city of Boulder in police patrol cars during weekends." The author commented: "The right to counsel as set forth in *In the Matter of Gault*[43] was the most frequently discussed legal subject both in class and at the many bull sessions."

The last week dealt with "the proper use of detention, probation, institutional programs, and alternatives to commitment," plus a group visit to the Molly Brown Halfway House in Denver (the first such facility for girls in the country), stated Judge Ketcham. He further noted "three long, 'open end' sessions which explored judge-probation officer relations, the judge's responsibility in community affairs, and available state and federal resources for juveniles."

With respect to general interest in the type of program described herewith, the author referred to an earlier program based on a grant by the National Council of Juvenile Court Judges.[44] He recognized that the success of a program such as that conducted at Boulder "can only be measured by the subtle improvement in juvenile justice in the courts of the judges who attend— a very difficult result to note and one that needs time to assess." But he concluded: "It is good news that the Summer College for Juvenile Court Judges will be repeated next year."

The Judiciary and the Legislative Bodies

A substantially different type of communication between the judiciary and the legal profession concerns relationships between the judiciary and legislative bodies. While such bodies are not made up entirely of lawyers, members of the legal profession constitute a substantial part of the membership of such bodies, and most legislators devote a considerable portion of their time to the legal aspects of legislative sessions. Focus in the connection indicated may relate to Congress, as the nation's top legislative body. However some aspects of the foregoing considerations apply to public boards, which have authority to make regulations in minor areas of jurisdiction.

Prettyman,[45] a practicing attorney in Washington, D.C., discussed one type of responsibility of the Supreme Court to Congress. He set the stage for his discussion by a substantial quotation from a 1953 address, at the Fourth Circuit Judicial Conference, by William P. Rogers, who was then Deputy Attorney General of the United States. Prettyman quoted Rogers thus:

> . . . It seems to me it might be well for us to consider here tonight and in the days ahead a method of re-emphasizing to the people of the nation the great importance of the judicial process in a free nation. The work of the federal courts in this country has been outstanding. . . . But I doubt that the Congress and the people of the country fully appreciate the work of the federal judiciary. This might be a good time to consider a new and better way to see that this is done.
>
> With that in mind, I should like to suggest that Congress might well consider extending an invitation to the Chief Justice of the United States to appear each year before a joint session of Congress to report on the state of the judiciary. In this way both Congress and the public would be fully informed, from year to year, about the work and the progress of the federal courts of our nation. Such a plan, I think, might materially contribute to a better understanding among the three great branches of our government. For that reason, I believe that the initiation of it should deserve serious consideration.

Prettyman thought that the work of the judiciary was in even greater need of being explained to the country now than in 1953, referring in part to increasing judicial workloads, in spite of the 1968 authorization of nine additional federal appellate judgeships. He commented: "An annual address to Congress by the Chief Justice would give the country its first realistic look at the state of its judiciary, pinpoint current and long-range problems, suggest solutions, as well as areas for study, and motivate the Congress to effective action."

The author traced long and tedious hurdles of judicial committees and conferences, which must pass suggestions for reform and improvement offered by the federal courts, before they can be communicated by letter to the Vice President of the United States and the Speaker of the House of Representatives for presenting to the two respective houses of Congress. Committee and other procedures from that point on are more widely known to Americans.

Problem areas especially noted by Prettyman include a relationship between state and federal courts whereby a congestion in state courts stimulates attorneys to seek entry of their cases into federal courts; judges substantiating their personnel requests on the basis of last year's workloads, whereas even when legislative action is favorable it may be two years before any of the relief sought actually becomes available; and a point noted by Senator Tydings that the judiciary should approach the Congress on the basis of what the courts require in order to do their job, rather than on the basis of what they think the appropriations committee will allow. As to Tydings' criticism of the judiciary for timidity and reliance on hindsight, Prettyman observed:

> . . . The answer to both (limitations) would be a well-constructed, well-supported, forceful and public presentation to the Congress that the country as well as congressmen could evaluate. Nor should the Chief

Justice be restricted to the needs and problems of the immediate future; he could forecast the years ahead, the decades beyond, and offer suggestions for basic changes that would help meet the needs and obviate the problems.

The author mentioned several types of problems with which the Chief Justice might deal in an address to Congress, and reviewed a few specific instances of severe judicial difficulties. He emphasized the importance of a personal presentation to the Congress and the people, rather than the submission of reports. On this point he stated:

A report does not become "influential" simply by being designated as such. It becomes influential by the nature and quality of the people who present it, the people who receive it, and the forum in which the presentation is made. If influence is what is needed—and I think it is—surely an address by the Chief Justice is the more direct and natural way to achieve it.

In conclusion, Prettyman observed that an address each year, "or at the commencement of each new Congress every two years, would be proper and meaningful from a number of standpoints." He continued:

It would be a dignified approach from the head of one coordinate branch of government to the branch responsible for both legislation and appropriation. It would inform the public of problems in an area now largely hidden from public view, and so it would furnish impetus for appropriate remedies. It would force the judges to face the failings of their system and to evolve new ideas for dealing with them, and then provide them with an appropriate forum for the expression of those ideas. And, as Mr. Rogers pointed out sixteen years ago, it would provide an opportunity to demonstrate the extraordinary vigor and strength of our federal courts, the absolute necessity for an independent judiciary and the all-important role of the judicial branch in protecting society and human rights.

2. Communication Between the Courts and the Public

While it is impossible to draw a sharp line of separation between any professional group and the general lay population with which that group is intermingled and carries on its activities, there are differences in emphasis between professional and lay needs and interests. This statement holds true whether the profession relates to law, education, medicine, engineering, industrial management, or something else. Subsequent comment on judicial responsibility to communicate with the people generally points up the idea noted.

On the need for informing the public about the operations of the court and about the procedure for doing so, Marvin Berger[46] cited Wilson thus:

In an address to the National College of State Trial Judges last year, Thomas C. Wilson of Reno, Nevada, expressed the opinion that the major responsibility for communication between the people and their courts should devolve on the courts, but that presently, it seemed to lie in the hands of the press. "Many people," he said "are baffled by court decisions and procedures." And, often press coverage does little to clear up the misunderstandings. Press coverage of highly technical decisions, he noted, result in news stories that "defy comprehension by even educated laymen."

Berger also referred to statements by Mr. Justice Abe Fortas, regarding the Supreme Court, to the effect that some means should be found for communicating more information to the public about what the court does, so that the public can be both more open and more effective in criticizing it.

News Media and a Public-Relations Officer

In his plea for reduced aloofness and expanded communication between the court and the people, Berger urged the establishment of a public relations officer attached to the court. Much of the work of such an officer would be with the press, reasoned Berger. He would explain court procedures, the technical aspects of complicated cases, and other judicial matters to news reporters, in the hope that wider coverage and more intelligible stories would reach the public.

But in addition, Berger conceived of a more direct impact of such an officer on public education through the schools. On this point he said:

A public relations officer can also fulfill an important educational function directed not only to the media but to the school population at all levels and the citizenry at large. Such educational efforts are either ignored or left to the bar associations or to interested citizens' groups. Significant as such efforts can be, they cannot equal the effectiveness of a permanent and ongoing program explaining the operation of the courts and the judiciary by way of films, radio and television, publications, tours of the courts, demonstrations of their operations, lectures and the like. Justice Bernard Botein, when he was presiding Justice of the Appellate Division, First Department of the New York Supreme Court, pioneered brilliantly in this area by focusing public attention on bail bond reform in cooperation with the Vera Foundation, in setting up a 24-hour arraignment part for the huge Criminal Court of New York, and in educating prospective jurors in their responsibilities by means of an imaginative film for which he obtained a foundation grant.

In regard to feedback operations from the people to the courts, through criticisms or otherwise, Berger commented on the role of the public relations officer "as a conduit of information from sources outside the courts to the people on the inside." He added:

All of us, and perhaps judges more than others, tend to become isolated in the busy performance of our jobs and fail to see how the outside world views us. Here, a perceptive, inquiring, trained information officer can perform the essential task of feeling the public pulse and funneling available news and information to the proper people within the court system.

He suggested that courts on restricted budgets might start with a part-time information officer and perhaps expand his operations as experience and funds seemed to warrant. His closing statements referred to the law as a specialized area of social concern, comparable to science, and to the need for specialized preparation if one is to work effectively in that area. He commented further:

> Unless the courts appoint persons who can deal with such specialists, they will be at a disadvantage in explaining their needs and activities. We have long passed the stage in which any branch of government can afford to take itself for granted. Courts can be replaced, as witness the growth of administrative tribunals and arbitration. *If the courts do not update themselves to the point of making themselves understood by the persons who support them,* they will fail in their function as important instruments of our political and social system, and pave the way for a search for substitutes. (Emphasis added.)

In a subsequent article, Judge Berger[47] included the results of a questionnaire survey which he made of the court administrators or the chief justices of all fifty states in regard to amplifying the meagerness of objective data on the extent to which courts bring about public understanding of court functions, as well as the limits and obstacles involved in court operations. Among other things, he referred to indifferent news media, involving media ignorance of court operations and a lack of mutual confidence between court personnel and the media. He noted the frequent difficulty or impossibility of getting a judge to explain or amplify an opinion which he has written, and added: "Frequently, a judge's home telephone number is unlisted, and no one at the courthouse will even relay a message to the judge." With further regard to judge performance, Berger noted:

> A long or complicated decision, sometimes running to several pages, is not accompanied by a summary or emphasis of the significant portions of the opinion. Why, asks one reporter, is an opinion printed in the advance sheets with a head note explaining it to lawyers, whose training should enable them to dispense with a summary, and none provided for reporters who must interpret the decision, often under time pressure?

Among his other comments the author suggested that the court administrator or chief judge issue a periodic bulletin indicating the news on court operations, noting any new or changed rules and procedures, stating who would speak for the court in case of criticism, etc. He mentioned three states in which such bulletins were regularly published. Berger described what he called "a model system" for the public information program and noted the need for continuing effort to move in the direction of the model. With specific regard to "Reaching Laymen," he concluded:

> Judge Eugene A. Wright of Washington some time ago urged that every judge in America should give three major speeches each year to lay bodies. Such speaking engagements can be arranged through the public relations or speakers committees of local bar associations. Some years ago, the California Bar Association printed a speakers guide for

California judges which included eight suggested speech outlines. Such a guide would be of great value to state judges.

One aspect of the problem of communications basic to the entire concept of a healthy relationship between the courts and the public must be noted—the need for periodic reports on the administration of justice in the state. The Chief Justice of the United States, under the stimulus of Bernard Segal of Philadelphia, former president of the American Bar Association, innovated such reports with his speech on the state of justice to the 1970 annual meeting of the American Bar Association in St. Louis.

I suggest that each state's chief judge should emulate Chief Justice Burger in submitting to the legislature very early in its annual session a report on the administration of justice in his state.

This survey is by no means comprehensive but it touches on the major aspect of a problem which is not easy to define and is difficult to keep in focus. . . . But if the objective—that of maintaining the independence and stature of our courts is desirable, we must seek to achieve it by every means at our command, including the potent instrument of communications.

Making and Publicizing Judicial Decisions

A few years ago, Professor Grey briefly described the operational setting of the Supreme Court, its decision-making procedure, and its communications with the public. He commented on the essential "veto power" which the court may exercise over Congress and the President in determining the "law of the land," and on the place of judicial review in the exercise of that power. Important in the review is the determination as to which appeals from lower courts the Supreme Court will hear and the flexibility of the power residing in its position as interpreter of the Constitution.

However, Professor Grey noted a "complex mixture of fact and illusion" as to that power status because of its extensive dependence on the court's having the respect of the people. The dependence, he commented, is largely reflected in the role of the people through legislative avenues regarding control of financial support and regarding constitutional amendment. Thus the Court's image, what the people *think* that it is and does, assumes great importance. He mentioned the high occupational rating which the American people assign to members of the Court as one type of evidence concerning respect. But he also saw the mystique thus associated with the Court as a possible obstacle to communication with the people, since the popular image depends largely on what the people absorb through the mass media.

The author considered the Court's secrecy regarding its deliberations and its aloofness in communicating its procedures or justifications to the public. He noted recent modifications of the aloofness through the numerous appearances, voluminous writings, and counseling activities of such justices as Warren, Clark, Frankfurter, Douglas, Goldberg and Fortas, with recognizable differences in regard to "avoidance of controversy" through the kinds of topics dealt with.

A kind of mystic conception of the relationship between traditional aloofness and good judicial imagery was reflected in a 1938 observation by then Chief Justice Charles Evans Hughes. Grey quoted Hughes thus:

The courts have no advertiser, they have no one to publicize the extent of their industry; they work quietly, their work cannot be understood by many, and the reasons for decisions in many cases are beyond public comprehension. It is of vital importance that every step should be taken to keep the work of the courts so far as possible in the good opinion of the country. It is of greatest importance that everything should be done to conserve the confidence of the people in the administration of justice.

Grey saw both a pro and a con implication in aloofness. He mentioned the relative absence of machinery to anticipate possible controversial cases or associated lines of authority for public relations activities. One point concerned possible leaks of the Court opinion, before the litigants had been fully informed. A more dubious point was to the effect that the Court should be above image-making, or of broadly appearing to force its opinions on others. But Grey noted that estimates regarding governmental agencies may be greatly influenced by control in the flow of information about them, colloquially referred to as censorship. He observed: "By trying not to manipulate public opinion, the Court paradoxically, is manipulating public opinion." He continued:

The Court controls the flow of news by releasing only what it wants to say and by often leaving vague what it does not want to say. There is no direct answer from the public. The Court can say what it wants to; no press conference nor defenses are needed. The Court simply speaks and the country and parts of the world listen. Thus, while it can be argued that the Court shows great self-restraint and wisdom by being silent, it also can be observed that this silence may best serve the Court's self-interest. Not only may the Court feel it *does not need* or should not have public relations, it may also *simply not want* public relations. (Emphasis added.)

Professor Grey struggled with the difficult task of analyzing how a court arrives at a decision. He did not particularly deal with the illusive question of whether anybody is clearly aware of how he actually makes a decision, in view of the numerous aspects of one's value-attitude structure that have settled into his subconscious, and thus create a kind of unconscious judgmental-readiness that comes into play when particular types of stiuations appear. The aspects of personality suggested are not readily fathomed by efforts at self-analysis through reasoning.

However, Grey noted the analysis by Judge Jerome Frank that the process of judging does not ordinarily follow the traditionally heralded procedure of starting with a premise and working out a conclusion, but that it starts with a hunch or conclusion, and then seeks premises to substantiate it. However, when Judge Frank added that if one could not muster appropriate arguments to support a conclusion he would reject that conclusion "unless he is arbitrary or mad,'' the judge's comment might have been more forceful if he had suggested percentage estimates on frequency of occurrence of persons who are "arbitrary or mad." Frank's conclusion, that judicial judgments no doubt follow the pattern of other judgments—from conclusion to premise —seems naturally to follow. Grey added: "One result of this system is that formal logic can be used almost any way needed by a judge," thus building up precedent to support the judge's philosophy. He further noted that the whole decision-making process "can also be complicated when such factors as the individual Justice's personality, ideology, and background are added," and Grey accepted Frank's reasoning to the effect that "efforts to eliminate the personality of the judge are doomed to failure." In this setting, Grey thought: "The best course seems to be to recognize the necessary personal element and to act accordingly," although specifics for action were not illustrated in detail.

Since the court's opinion ordinarily presents the rationale associated with the decision, the opinion may have greater influence on subsequent litigation than the decision in the particular case has. A question then concerns the extent to which opinions are written to inform and influence the general public, in contrast with some small portion of the public. On this point Grey commented:

> For whom are the Justices writing opinions? A common notion is that judges usually write for posterity and other lawyers. One survey of state and federal appellate judges indicates there is at least some basis for this belief. The question: For whom do you write your opinions?— brought the following response: first, for posterity; second, for the bar; and third, for future judges.

Grey observed differences in foregoing respects, depending on whether the particular justice was writing a "generalized" opinion acceptable to the court's majority, or writing his own "individualized" opinion in a dissent or in a separate concurring statement. He commented that a dissent was more than "a creative outlet for judicial self-expression"; that it might seek to influence a vote on the bench, narrow the scope of the majority opinion, appeal to Congress or the President, or reduce in the minds of the profession and the public the status of the group who made up the majority in the particular instance. However, the professor stated: "Judges seem to have no illusions that they are widely read by laymen and doubt if the public is interested in much of what they write."

The author thought that particular difficulty in legal writing attached to "weasel words," such as "due process," and to "holy words," such as appear in rules, formulas, and standards which become "reduced to well-polished phrases." He also thought that the isolation and aloofness of the justice, both in public and in private contacts, insulated him from criticism of his literary style—criticism which he may seriously need, at least so far as broadening his audience of readers is concerned. In this connection, the author summarized:

> From a communication standpoint, one by-product of this whole decision making and decision writing process is that the task of under-

standing Supreme Court decisions is made difficult for both expert and lay consumer long before the Court's decision is ever announced.

In a general concluding statement, Professor Grey raises several pertinent notes on court action and on public information regarding it. He said:

Indeed, much of the communication problem exists because the Court is reluctant to do much about it. There are good reasons to resist some changes, but it would seem that the Court should be encouraging more informed dialogue about its activities. In fact, it would seem somewhat inconsistent for the Court to talk about such first amendment rights and freedom of the press as essential parts of democratic dialogue and yet to discourage efforts at improved public insights into the Court itself and the workings of law. The court so often talks about need for change in society and yet resists change in many of its traditions and practices.

Perhaps the Court itself has been as guilty as any bar group of wanting to "leave law to the lawyers." The call here is not for any impropriety of disclosure or to violate the seemingly correct view that written Court opinions should "speak for themselves." There is no need to go beyond the words of the opinions; this view simply says that the Court should pay much more attention to the problems of legal meaning for those not in the inner circle of awareness and sophistication.

Perhaps the public image of justice is distorted because we judges have turned our backs to the news media.[49] Only partial understandings of the courts and the law have been allowed to sift through the cloaks of secrecy and judicial language. All this has been true despite the belief that the citizen is entitled to know what the judges are doing.

Again, such an assessment does not argue for public disclosure of sensitive deliberations in the conference room or elsewhere; it does simply acknowledge that—like it or not—a Supreme Court decision is not just something that goes into a bound volume for lawyers and other judges. It is a declaration of governmental policy that (partly by definition of the press' role in a democratic society) also becomes a public "news" event. As an important institution, it would seem that the Court should not only show more empathy with the real problems of press and public understanding but also should consider seriously the full range of positive steps that could be taken.

Focus and Evaluation of the Criticisms

Perhaps a few observations regarding the form and substance of Grey's concluding remarks are in order. It might be pertinent to ask whether his initial reference to the Court's eagerness about first-amendment rights concerning freedom of the press, "as applied to others," manifests a deep-seated trait among ethical reformers that used to be associated with some religious promoters: "Don't Do as I Do, but Do as I Tell You to Do." A related question could be raised: do ideals tend to foster striving, partly because they exceed achievements? "If the reach does not extend beyond the grasp, what is heaven for?" we have heard. Among many other things, Aristotle seems to have suggested: If you can't be a god; act as nearly like a god as possible, as much of the time as possible. There seems also to be much of this sentiment in the teachings of Jesus, sometimes referred to as Christlike behavior. The point of the foregoing comment is that there could be a large element of unawareness in the Court's inconsistency about freedom of the press—a manifestation of a rather natural tendency to call attention to the speck in your neighbor's eye, before recognizing the mote in your own. But if so, Professor Grey renders an important service by helping to cudgel the court toward awareness.

Grey seems to imply that it would be possible to explain for lay understanding what a court sets forth in its opinions, without going "beyond the words of the opinions." This raises the fundamental question of whether it is possible to *explain* anything to anybody without going beyond the terminology, concepts, or general setting of the original appearance. If a teacher explains anything to a learner, the teacher does it through words, illustrations, and perhaps gestures that were not parts of the original appearance or presentation. The teacher thus goes *beyond* the original in order to find something with which the learner is sufficiently acquainted so that old and new can be integrated. Learning theory sometimes refers to the process as absorbing the new into the learner's existing apperceptive mass. The same process occurs whenever an adult learns anything—regarding court decisions and associated rationale, or anything else.

The basic theme of Grey's cogent analysis is in harmony with that of several other writers whose statements have been sampled in earlier pages of the present study. A general statement of that theme, shaped as the theme of the present study, is that the courts in general have the technical knowledge and the social status to contribute more than they do to an understanding by the people concerning the role of law and lawful behavior in organized society, and concerning a sense of popular responsibility for the kind of regulatory system in America that fosters maximal individual freedom within a framework of social development and growth. The theme also implies that for the courts to render the educational service inferred, there will have to be a greater two-way communication between the courts and the people. This applies to all courts, but in some respects it applies most comprehensively to the courts of record, and most especially to the appellate tribunals.

Some of the authors previously reviewed have referred to the vocabulary and style of writing which appear in many court opinions as constituting distinct obstacles to communication with the people, whether through the press or otherwise. These authors have implied that the courts should adjust their conceptions of dignity and aloofness, so as to reach the common people with the necessary food for civic understanding regarding law and our regulatory structure, and for commitment to that understanding. This should be apparent when the status and the power of the courts themselves depend on the respect which the people have for the judicial system. The idea might be stated in rural terms: "if you are going to handle your feeding chores from the loft through a chute, you have to put the hay down where the goats can reach it." And this is important when you depend on the goats for milk. In the thought and statement of many would-be intellectuals, the term "common herd" has not been restricted to goats.

Chapter 4

HIGHLIGHTS AND IMPLICATIONS OF DIVISION II

Much of the criticism leveled at the courts for failure to inform the people on what courts consider their function to be, how they go about performing that function, and the financial or other problems which they face in performing it, could be explained in terms of inadequate communication.

This author has suggested that a great deal of the judiciary's voluminous writing and speechmaking, especially that by members of appellate tribunals, is on somewhat of a closed-circuit basis, intended for other members of the legal profession. But the basic problem concerning judicial imagery and respect, as well as concerning the more general areas of lawlessness, resides with the mass of people outside that profession. However, some reference has been made by members of the legal profession to reforming court procedure, through the use of public relations officers and in other ways.

Nature and Operation of Imagery

In any area of social consideration, imagery should ordinarily be looked upon as the appraisal of an individual or a group by the community as a whole, although there may be an appraisal of one society by another, as in the case of international relations. The appraisals are based on achievements, with a gradual development of social expectations emerging from accumulated results. A close relation between expectations and achievements makes it possible to describe functions and to attach them to institutions. In a complex society the allocation of particular functions to specific agencies contributes to the image which the people hold concerning the agency or institution involved. A two-way situation is thus apparent: expectation can strengthen or weaken the image, and achievement can do the same. However, achievement or performance is the long-run base on which evaluations rest and in terms of which institutions are actually defined.

Variation Among Judges and Judicial Image

In an intricate technological social structure, members of many professional groups will likely be numerous. This means considerable variation among members in regard to the prestige of the position which they hold and to their performance in those positions. Materials reviewed in this division have variously referred to tyrannical, incompetent, and unimaginative performance by judges. Imagery is accordingly portrayed. For professions or for persons who are prominent within a profession to enjoy public respect and favorable imagery, they must deserve that status and imagery. In a democracy, and to quite an extent in any other type of society, the people find a way to exercise final judgment concerning imagery and status. Thus one might say that favorable imagery must be *earned* and that it is earned through performance before the public.

The process of earning favorable imagery is thus a process of developing favorable social expectation; for example, what is likely to constitute justice or procedural due process in the court of a particular judge. The materials reviewed illustrate both positive and negative imagery.

Public-Relation Contacts

While propaganda, censorship, and other ways of distorting the picture of actual performance acquired by the public can develop an unrealistic image, the "vigilant upkeep" required by distortion can become burdensome. The idea might be stated by saying that consistent distortion in a particular direction results in an accumulating load that becomes overwielding, and failure in consistency causes the structure to collapse.

Professor Grey's note on a court not wanting a public relations officer, because of uncomplimentary impressions which such an officer might give, points to the censorship factor. Perhaps the areas of American culture in which the people are most continuously propagandized to accept inflated images are those most extensively touched by commercial advertising. Political campaigns may be close competitors in presidential years. One might here recall Professor Grey's note on an observation by former Chief Justice Hughes: "The courts have no advertiser." Comments by Goldwater and others show the role of imagery in selecting justices for the Supreme Court.

This division emphasizes the terminology, and to some extent the illustrative treatment of content, in judicial efforts to communicate. In the kind of learning involved in this situation, as well as that involved in the kindergarten and in the graduate school, desirable content and the method of dealing with it effectively are inseparable. Both depend considerably on the audience to be reached. Three general audience categories are noted, with respect to communication by the courts: the legal profession, lay adults, children and youth. Each of these categories may need further subdivision when methods are thought of as including court reports, lectures, films, tours, conferences, and other procedures.

With respect to the competence and appropriateness of the judiciary in the field of adult education, it should be stated that previous comments on imagery are not intended to belittle the extensive respect and prestige which members of the judiciary in general have in the eyes of the American people. This means that in the general public there is considerable "listening readiness" for what members of the appellate tribunals have to say. Audience receptivity is important in any learning situation.

Suggestions on the potential of judges to inform the public about court functions and operations do not imply that every judge will suddenly become an expert in adult education. But they do imply that several judges might develop substantial competence in that direction, and they recognize that some judges have, through various avenues, already made significant contributions in this area. Perhaps a lightened case load could be given to judges who devote substantial amounts of time to inaugurating systematic programs for reform along the lines suggested, supplementing them with pro-tem judicial service. Such an arrangement would, of course, seem more feasible in some courts than in others. But it is conceivable that after such an educational program has been under way for a while, the judicial load respecting certain types of criminal and other cases would decrease.

This implies more emphasis on preventive measures, with the prospect of lessened demand for remedial and penal measures. Some aspects of the problem might thus be resolved by asking whether it is a matter of more judges, or of a different orientation concerning both judges and the public in ways that reduce the number of disputes which come to court. To some extent the question is analogous to asking if the answer to crime in the streets lies primarily in more policemen or in a different orientation of both the police and the public to responsibility for law and order in an industrial democracy.

Activist Courts

Much of the extensive reference to activist courts tends to identify activism with liberalism, and thereby to contrast it with conservatism. In rejecting this view, Kurland[50] stated: "An activist court is one that assumes capacities to govern in broader and broader areas. An activist court is one that interferes with legislative and executive judgments on the basis of its own contrary personal predilections." Thus he observes that an activist court may be either liberal or conservative, depending on the biases which prevail among its members. His analysis is essentially in terms of the Supreme Court during recent decades, and he suggests that the Burger court will probably be less liberal than the Warren court but not less activist.

There are several ways in which such terms as "conservative" and "conservation" may be interpreted. If there had not been extensive conservation from one generation to the next among our ancestors, civilization or progress would have been inconceivable. We currently hear a great deal about conserving certain species of wildlife and other features of an earlier physical environment. With regard to conservation in both the physical and cultural environment, it must be asked: conservation of what, by whom, and for what purposes?

Social regulation and government is one of man's earliest specializations, and the study of law is one of his oldest professions. Hence there is a much longer historical accumulation of material in law than in some new field, such as radiology. In any area of cultural development, there tends to be more of such accumulation in the hands of some persons than in the hands of others. The accumulation represents power in the areas concerned, and individuals who possess this power usually want to conserve if not to expand it. Persons with considerable power thus tend to champion the virtues of the system which produced the situation described, and reformers usually see virtue in other arrangements which would likely give them more power. Basic selfishness is thus preserved without showing preference.

It is sometimes commented that an extensive body of material and cultural accumulation is typically required for a person to acquire training in law and to become successfully established in the profession. More of both elements is likely to be required for attaining a judgeship. Such requirements, the argument runs, tend in general to make judges and other members of the legal profession conservative—although messianic and lesser crusaders appear from time to time in any vocation.

Scrutiny of this philosophy demonstrates an inadequate recognition of shifts in the value system of a dynamic society. With greater material affluence in the total culture, relatively less private accumulation is necessary for a comfortable social status or image, and new avenues for attaining favorable imagery arise more often than they formerly did. This nonmaterial orientation tends to affect the legal and judicial profession, although perhaps less than it affects some newer areas of cultural development.

Among the numerous ramifications of the foregoing considerations, those most pertinent for the present study emphasize the need for a continuing scrutiny of the values and practices which the past has brought to us and a reorganization of the retained elements in order to maximize the well-being of the people. Here, as in several other connections, final evaluation rests with the common people, and greater insight by them would contribute to a more favorable image of persons who have official power and responsibility. Favorable imagery through newer avenues thus comes to replace that associated with avenues which are at present more conservative. The groundwork for tomorrow's conservatism is thus laid down.

With respect to the liberal approach, some of the material reviewed in the present study referred to a "growing ferment" within the legal profession, to law-school programs as including more emphasis on the behavioral sciences, and to clinical experiences with public-welfare clients as increasingly reflected in training for the profession. The comments indicated suggest dissatisfaction with customary judicial orientation and conclusions and suggest a need for more judicial attention to current social developments, as well as to the status and aspirations of a broader swath of the population. Among the areas of concern are jobs, education, housing, health services, and voting, particularly as related to sex, race, and economic status. To some extent the concern reflects a more general expansion of consideration for individual rights and opportunities, which has in a growing sense characterized American life during the last few decades. It has also become more usual to look upon the courts as helping to deal with social problems, while operating within the existing regulatory framework. Expansions of the type noted are typically referred to as liberalizations.[51]

Some of the materials reviewed herein criticize censorship by the courts of information given out about their operations. In a society which encourages the people to inquire and become informed about how its institutions function, one should expect ferment when the people are denied access to the information concerned. Where there is free dialogue, unanswered questions do not accumulate to the point of generating ferment. And freer dialogue might well produce suggestions which some judges would welcome as means of improvement. Thus censorship might create rather than avoid problems for the court.

Personal Security and the Moral Integrity of Judges

The personal security felt by individual judges may bear on their moral integrity and independence of judgment. Dean Acheson indirectly referred to this point, respecting justices of the Supreme Court. It has been suggested that Plato considered well-to-do persons likely to be more honest than other persons in serving the state through public office, since they would be less likely than others to steal from the state so as to improve their personal status. However, conceptions of status, integrity, social change, and motivation are presently too involved and too much in flux for one to push this idea too far in the present connection.

Popular Stake in Government and in How It Operates

The American conception of democracy assumes that the people in general who are governed have a greater stake than anybody else in how government functions. To protect and advance this stake, it is further assumed that the people need to understand how the institutions of society operate and what the outcomes of operation are. This applies especially to the institutions charged with administering justice. The assumptions are reflected in recent controversy before the nation's higher courts dealing with the confidential nature of sources from which news reporters get information for their stories.

Court reports are public documents in the sense of being open to public inspection, in the same way that the recorded deed to a farm or corporation site is open to inspection. But court decisions are also a part of our governmental structure; they determine personal rights and obligations, much as legislation does. The right and need of the governed to be informed presumes ready access to official statements which are pertinent and also understandable. The present study emphasizes concern for more extensive and direct communication between the courts and the general public. Specific suggestions appear at various points in the text.

But a tenacious problem lingers with respect to practical implementation. Abundance of material implies some pattern of selection, by news media or otherwise, and individuals vary greatly as to the amount of explaining and illustrating that is required for their understanding. Developing and maintaining appropriate bases for selecting and for explaining are major ongoing problems in American society. The judiciary should assume more responsibility in this area than has traditionally been the case, with respect to court operations.

The Institution Versus Its Present Incumbents

At a particular time, most people think about a public institution in terms of the persons who currently hold office. This is partly because an institution cannot live apart from the individuals who carry on its functions. It is also partly because it is easier for most people to think in terms of human personalities than in terms of generalized or abstract institutional principles and goals.

But an institution develops its status out of a cumulative deposit from acts performed by individual incumbents. This applies to objectives which the society seeks to promote, such as education, and to objectives which it seeks to restrict, such as prostitution.

Imagery of the courts as bodies, and of members of the judiciary or of the entire legal profession as individuals, are such cumulative deposits. In addition, the image status is continuously being strengthened by the acts of some incumbents and weakened by the acts of others.

It is the strength of the image embodied in judicial reasoning on previous occasions that lends status to judicial precedent. Precedent thus carries authority because of this institutional relationship, and the degree of authority varies according to the hierarchical level of the particular court in the system and according to the status of the particular judge who wrote the lead opinion.

When it is understood that the vigor of a society depends greatly on the imagery of its institutions, the importance of collective effort for a continuous strengthening of that imagery is apparent. This is especially relevant when the institution is concerned with an aspect of the culture that is as important as justice is considered to be in America.

FOOTNOTES AND REFERENCES

1. Cf. Gerald S. Levin, "Law—Bridge to Justice," *American Bar Association Journal* 56 (May 1970): 458; R. Forrester and Commentators, "The Future of America and the Rule of Law," *Vanderbilt Law Review* 23 (Nov. 1970): 1297.

2. Benjamin Landis (Superior Court of California in Los Angeles), "Public Imagery and the Judicial Image," *Judicature* 53 (Feb. 1970): 282.

3. Charles F. Stafford (Superior Court of Washington), "The Public's View of the Judicial Role," *Judicature* 52 (Aug.-Sept. 1968): 73.

4. Dean Acheson, "Removing the Shadow Case on the Courts," *American Bar Association Journal* 55 (Oct. 1969): 919.

5. Barry Goldwater, "Political Philosophy and Supreme Court Justices," *American Bar Association Journal* 58 (Feb. 1972): 135.

6. Herman Schwartz, "Judges as Tyrants," *Criminal Law Bulletin* 7 (Mar. 1971): 129.

7. United States v. David Dellinger, reversed and remanded 472 F. 2d. 340 (11/21/1972); cert. den., 93 S. Ct. 1443 (3/5/1973).

8. Cf. W. F. Winter, "Judging the Judges—Techniques of Judicial Discipline," *Mississippi Law Journal* 41 (Winter 1969): 1; G. Edwards, "Commentary on Judicial Ethics," *Fordham Law Review* 38 (Dec. 1969): 259; "Judicial

Ethics—A Symposium," *Law and Contemporary Problems* 35 (Winter 1970): 1.

9. Robert W. Colvert, "Mandatory Retirement of Judges," *Judicature* 54 (May 1971): 424.

10. J. Earl Major, "Why Not Mandatory Retirement for Federal Judges," *American Bar Association Journal* 52 (Jan. 1966): 29.

11. Cf. P.B. Kurland, "The Constitution and the Tenure of Federal Judges: some noted from history," *University of Chicago Law Review* 36 (Summer 1969): 665.

12. John A. Cutts III, "Procedural Due Process: A Haven for Judges," *American Bar Association Journal* 54 (Dec. 1968): 1199.

13. Section V of the Fourteenth Amendment (article 14) states: "The Congress shall have power of enforce, by appropriate legislation, the provisions of this article."

14. Richard A. Watson, "Judging the Judges," *Judicature* 53 (Feb. 1970): 283.

15. R. Stanely Lowe, "Voluntary Merit Selection Plans," *Judicature* 55 (Nov. 1971): 161-168.

16. In this connection he cited: Hugh Scott, "Legislative Proposals for Reform of the Federal Judiciary," *Judicature* 50 (Aug.-Sept. 1966): 50.

17. Joseph D. Tydings, "Court of the Future," *St. Louis University Law Journal* 13 (Summer 1969): 601.

18. Census reports give the following population figures, in thousands, for the dates shown: 1790—3,929; 1830—12,866; 1870—39,818; 1910—91,972; 1950—151,326; 1970—203,185. (See U.S. Dept. of Commerce, Bureau of the Census, "Statistical Abstract of the United States" [1971], Table 1, p. 5.)

19. One suggestion for reducing the case load on the Supreme Court has been made by the Freund Committee study group. The group suggested the creation of a National Court of Appeals to screen cases to be heard by the Supreme Court. The pros and cons of the suggestion are argued in a group of three articles in the August 1973 (Vol. 59) issue of the *American Bar Association Journal*. These articles are:

    a. William J. Brennan (Sup. Ct.), "Justice Brennan Calls National Court of Appeals Proposal 'Fundamentally Unnecessary and Ill Advised,' " p. 835.

    b. Clement F. Haynsworth, Jr. (C.A. 4), "A New Court to Improve the Administration of Justice," p. 841.

    c. N.O. Stockmeyer, Jr. (Mich. App.), "Rx for the Certiorari Crisis: A More Professional Staff," p. 846.

20. Edward Allen Tamm (U.S. App., D. of Col.), "Are Courts Going the Way of the Dinosaurs?" *American Bar Association Journal* 57 (Mar. 1971): 228.

21. Cf. R.J. Traynor, "Judges and Law Reform," *Trial* 5 (Apr.-May 1969): 37; R. M. Byrn, "Urban Law Enforcement: a plea from the ghetto," *Criminal Law Bulletin* 5 (Apr. 1969): 125; R. E. Keeton, "Law Reform and Legal Education," *Vanderbilt Law Review* 24 (Dec. 1970): 53; H. J. Stiner, "Legal Education and Socio-economic Change: Brazilian Perspective," *American Journal of Comparative Law* 19 (Winter 1971): 39.

22. For recent considerations on the use of computers and computerization in judicial procedure, see:

    a. Malcolm MacDonald, "Computer Support for the Courts—A Case for Cautious Optimism," *Judicature* 57 (Aug.-Sept. 1973): 52-55.

    b. Robert B. James, "Computers Trim Backlog in San Diego County Courts," *Judicature* 57 (Aug.-Sept. 1973): 56-59.

    c. Laura Tatham, "Computerized Information Retrieval in Italy," *Judicature* 57 (Aug.-Sept. 1973):60-63.

Suggestions on electronic recording of trial hearings, rather than the usual court reporting, are made by Winfrey D. Houston, Fount Holland, and Wesley W. Beck, Jr., in "Instant Replay for Appellate Courts," *American Bar Association Journal* 59 (Feb. 1973): 153.

Caution against a misleading use of statistics in blaming a "liberal" judiciary for apparent increase in crime, is suggested by Hans Zeisel, "F.B.I. Statistics—A Detective Story," *American Bar Association Journal* 59 (May 1973): 510.

23. Burton R. Laub (Dean, Dickenson School of Law), "The Judges' Role in a Changing Society," *Judicature* 53 (Nov. 1969): 140-145.

24. James W. Curlin has similarly emphasized an interdisciplinary approach to the social and legal problems created by technology: "Fostering Understanding Between Science and Law," *American Bar Association Journal* 59 (Feb. 1973): 157.

25. Edward J. Gurney, "Crisis in the Courts; The Need for Reform," *The Florida Bar Journal* 46 (Apr. 1972): 196.

26. Williams v. Florida, 399 U.S. 78 (1970).

27. For a recent appraisal of the six-man jury and its relationship to other jury problems, see:

    a. William R. Pabst, Jr., "What Do Six-Member Juries Really Save?" *Judicature* 57 (June-July 1973): 6-11.

    b. David J. Saari, "The Criminal Jury Forces Future Shock," *Judicature* 57 (June-July 1973): 12-17.

28. John Lindsay (Mayor, N.Y. City), "Making Law and Order Work," *Trial* 6 (Aug.-Sept. 1970): 20, 28.

29. See Herbert C. Quay, "What Corrections Can Correct and How," *Federal Probation* 37 (June 1973): 3-5.

30. Richard I. Miller, "Choosing a Consultant: A Guide for the Courts," *Judicature* 57 (Aug.-Sept. 1973): 64-68.

31. Theodore A. Pasquesi, "Putting the Paralegals to Work," *The Practical Lawyer* 17 (Oct. 1971): 29.

32. David G. Lupo, "Paraprofessionals, Legal Technology, Legal Assistants—What's in a Name," *Journal of the Missouri Bar* 28 (Mar. 1972): 120.

33. Roger A. Larson, "Legal Paraprofessionals: Cultivation of a New Field," *American Bar Association Journal* 59 (June 1973): 631.

34. A procedure for improving the competence of trial lawyers, sponsored by the National Institute of Trial Advocacy and pioneered through summer school at Boulder, Colorado, was described by Edward A. Tamm (C.A., D. of Col.), "Advocacy Can Be Taught—the N.I.T.A. Way," *American Bar Association Journal* 59 (June 1973): 625.

35. Willard H. Pedrick (Dean, Col. of Law, Ariz. St. Univ.), "Collapsible Specialists," *DePaul Law Review* 19 (Summer 1970): 699.

36. Among other considerations regarding general practice and specialization in law work, two are noted:

a. The range in services which a corporation lawyer is expected to render could make him in effect a general practitioner, reasons Brian D. Forrow in "The Last of the General Practitioners," *American Bar Association Journal* 59 (Jan. 1973): 57.

b. A voluntary test-taking arrangement, whereby attorneys can check on how well they are keeping up with the flow of new problems and possibilities within their areas of specialty, is recommended by Curtis J. Berger and Michael H. Barnett in "Rx for Continuing Education: Lawyer, Examine Thyself," *American Bar Association Journal* 59 (Aug. 1973): 877.

37. Peter Swords, "The Public Service Responsibilities of the Bar: The Goal for Clinical Legal Education," *University of Miami Law Review* 25 (Winter 1970): 267.

Cf. Also, Chief Justice Burger, "The Special Skills of Advocacy," Sonnett Memorial Lecture, Fordham University Law School, Nov. 26, 1973.

38. M. Abram, "Educating the Lawyer as a Policy-Maker," *Trial* 6 (Apr.-May 1970): 11.

39. Arno H. Denecke, "The Judiciary Needs Your Help, Teachers," *Journal of Legal Education* 22 (1970): 197.

40. Miranda v. Arizona, 384 U.S. 436 (6/13/1966).

41. William T. Gossett, "The Future of Continuing Legal Education," *American Bar Association Journal* 55 (Feb. 1969): 132.

42. Orman W. Ketcham (Juv. Ct., D. of Col.), "Summer College for Juvenile Court Judges," *Judicature* 51 (Apr. 1968): 330.

43. In re Gault, 387 U.S. 1 (5/15/1967).

44. See *Judicature* 48 (1965): 225.

45. E. Barrett Prettyman, Jr., "The Chief Justice Should Address Congress," *American Bar Association Journal* 56 (May, 1970): 441.

46. M. Marvin Berger, "Public Relations and the Courts," *Judicature* 52 (Apr. 1969): 378.

47. M. Marvin Berger (N.Y. City Crim. Ct.), "Do the Courts Communicate?" *Judicature* 55 (Apr. 1972): 318.

48. David L. Grey, "The Supreme Court as a Communicator," *Houston Law Review* 5 (Jan. 1968): 405.

49. Quoting J. Skelly Wright, "A Judge's View: The News Media and Criminal Justice," *American Bar Association Journal* 50 (Dec. 1964):1125, 1129.

50. Philip B. Kurland, "The New Supreme Court," *The University of Chicago Magazine* 66 (July/Aug. 1973): 3.

51. George S. Swan reported a recent study indicating that regardless of activism, idealism, etc., most law-school seniors want lucrative establishment-oriented jobs: "Today's Law Seniors—Messiah or Moneychanger," *American Bar Association Journal* 59 (Mar. 1973): 277.

DIVISION III

THE POLICE, LAW-ENFORCEMENT
AND CORRECTIONAL AGENCIES

INTRODUCTION

In the development of civilization, a police force for maintaining public order and protecting lives and property from public offenders appears earlier than most institutions which are now considered to be essential for an industrial democracy. And much the same applies to non-democratic systems of government.

In some respects the earlier inclusiveness of the term *police* is now reflected by courts in America under the concept of police power, as extending to the "health, safety, morals, and welfare" of the people, and thus as essentially indicating the power of the state to exercise jurisdiction over all important public needs and activities.

The role of the police in respect to sanitation or during an epidemic, in respect to food inspection, race relations, the enforcement of building codes, to flood control and dam inspection, as well as early and continuing relationships between public education and the police power, reflect the relationship of early public education in America to the inclusiveness of the concept. Moreover, at the present time, traffic officers and other law-enforcement personnel in a populous and mobile society have a considerable educational responsibility concerning the general population. From another standpoint, the existence of police courts and the procedure by which an arrest typically precedes a court trial in criminal justice support the idea of early recognition of police action.

In the United States there is no nationwide police system under a minister of the interior, such as exists in several countries of Western Europe. By contrast, we have several thousand separate jurisdictions represented by federal and state governments, the sheriffs in our 3,000 counties, as well as police with city, town, highway or other jurisdictions.

Reform efforts to reduce jurisdictional overlapping and to develop the professional competence of the police force, as well as the growing importance of the Federal Bureau of Investigation from the national standpoint, have attracted considerable recent attention. So have the number of policemen killed in line of duty, bases for protecting their well-being and that of their families, and provision of the death penalty for certain types of crimes.

The corrective or rehabilitative aspect of our penal system should perhaps be looked upon as a recent development, when compared with an earlier philosophy of incarceration to protect the community and to provide revenge for offenses committed. Correctional and rehabilitation efforts may be considered remedial or repair work in education, needed largely because of inadequacy in earlier educational achievement through direct school and kindred approaches. It should be noted that during the past several decades there has been marked expansion in public education for the total population, as a major avenue for increasing the socio-economic and other values of human resources; as resources are viewed with respect both to the personal satisfactions of the individual, and the collective vigor of the group. As an aspect of the general movement concerning education and the development of human resources, it is reasonable to expect that considerable attention would be given to education through correctional and rehabilitation avenues regarding public offenders, who constitute one group in respect to which the nation's "total effect" through previous education has been ineffective or otherwise inadequate.

This division focuses attention on education as a branch of the police power; the duties and working relationships of the police force; competence and professionalization of police officers; recruiting for police service; relationships of officer qualification to the community served; delinquency prevention and correction; newer developments in corrections and rehabilitation; professionalization of corrections personnel; and priorities concerning corrections and other public needs and services.

Chapter 1

POLICE DUTIES AND OFFICER QUALIFICATIONS

When a society is simple in organization and in the relationships among its people, informal contacts afford the major avenue by which the people learn what is acceptable practice. It is also the avenue by which police officers learn what their duties are and what constitutes adequate performance of those duties. Hence the role of education in the procedure concerned does not attract much attention.

However, as a society becomes more complex, both the citizens and the officers need to know more about social relationships and about the role of personal discipline, as well as the role of group or state regulation in the well-being of the people. Moreover, as a society becomes more complex, there is a need for more types of regulations, and there are usually more people in the society to be governed. Thus, society can no longer consider the education secured through informal association in the community to be adequate for either the citizen or the officer.

In some respects American society has recognized this problem of adequacy, though more fully in regard to the citizen than in regard to the police officer. The need for the citizen in America to be literate and informed has been emphasized since the days when the Founding Fathers recognized that for government by the people to be successful, those people must be informed and educated in order to be able to evaluate the information available. The founders were thus emphasizing civic education, or the need for education in order to be good citizens in a democratic society.

When the founders referred to the police power of the state, they were thinking in more comprehensive terms than the power usually exercised by members of the police force in maintaining order and peace in the community. An earlier note mentioned health, safety, and the general welfare of the people as considerations within the police power. The continuing expansion in demands by the people in recent decades for more services to be rendered by government complicates the problems of law and order and, hence, of civic responsibility and associated education.

1. Education as a Branch of the Police Power

When America was developing its official base of free public education, the educational function was typically justified in legislative halls and elsewhere as a branch of the police power. One aspect of the reasoning involved was to the effect that if children in school develop certain areas of knowledge, attitudes, and habits, less police effort in the sense of physical force is later required to get them to conform to the general value and behavioral patterns respected by the culture. Reference to the process as "school keeping," and noting that the hickory stick was one of the main "aids to instruction," have sometimes been looked upon as reflections of education's police ancestry in America. The fact that both school and police alternatives in developing conformers have greatly expanded during the past half-century does not mean that formal schooling has ceased to be a branch of the police power or that physical force has ceased to be an instrument in the development of acceptable personality—in spite of a luxuriant growth of permissiveness throughout the American culture since World War II.[1]

Reference to education as a *branch* of the police power does not mean that all authority or responsibility of the state for education has been or could be transferred to the designated educational branch. The fact that the original granting or mother-police agency did not transfer all such authority and responsibility is reflected in numerous lawsuits involving such school matters as attendance, the curriculum, religious practices in the school, racial integration, teacher status, and supporting systems of taxation.

Realities concerning granting and retaining educational authority and responsibility are increasingly reflected through voluntary cooperation between school and law-enforcement agencies, as members of each profession increasingly recognize the vital importance of the other for its own specialized operations. This interdependence relates to both the deficiency-repair and maintenance education of adults in the area of lawlessness, and to the foundational and preventive education of children in the same regulative area. The fact that in any type of human relations violation of the code is a matter of degree, does not mean that the voluntary features within the granting-receiving framework may not be developed further than they have been, or that they do not need continuous attention in a changing society.[2]

2. Police Duties and Working Relationships

While many Americans find it easy to think of a "peaceful community" or of "street crime" in terms of the policeman on the beat, there is great misunderstanding about the responsibility which such policemen are expected to carry and about their qualifications for doing so.

For many persons, the policeman on the beat is the initial and most direct contact which they have "with the law." He mingles with the people on the street and elsewhere, and thus sees and is expected to evaluate many types of behavior. In specific situations he must decide whether to arrest a person or to explain something and perhaps reprimand or warn the person. He must initially decide whether the location or maintenance of certain property constitutes a nuisance or a health or safety hazard. He is often expected to investigate the facts regarding situations in which offenses occur and to appear at police or other tials of accused persons. On occasion, he is expected to direct traffic and render first aid. And policemen are increasingly being asked to speak to or work with public-school and other groups concerning law enforcement and its role in American democracy. The list could be extended.

While most policemen are not asked to perform all of the functions implied, a wide range of information and substantial maturity in on-the-spot judgment are required if a policeman is to perform effectively and justly.

During the last several years there have been numerous articles in legal and related journals on the status of crime and law enforcement in America and on the responsibility of the police in relation to education and to the legal profession in the situations concerned.

Christopher[3] emphasized action by the federal government through the Omnibus Crime Control and Safe Streets Act of 1968[4] as an initial step in "massive financial aid to improve and strengthen all aspects of state and local law enforcement." He commented on the role of the National Crime Commission in developing the idea of federal money to assist in state and local law enforcement, and on major areas of improvement for which grant money might be secured. His treatment emphasized planning grants; action grants; riot control grants, particularly for California; academic assistance grants, for tuition and loans to law-enforcement personnel or students who plan careers in the field; and grants for expanded training programs of the Federal Bureau of Investigation. After commenting extensively on the great promise of the federal grants for a new approach in the struggle of state and local governments against crime, the author concluded:

> It must always be remembered, however, that law enforcement is essentially a local responsibility. Each State and local government must plan with care to use the Federal funds which the new statute will make available and to dig into its own resources to help finance the improvements that are necessary.
>
> Only through dedicated cooperation and coordinated efforts at all levels of Government—Federal, State, and local—can we make the most of this historic opportunity to mount an effective attack on crime.

Murphy,[5] as Director of Public Order and Safety Studies at the Urban Institute in Washington, spoke in 1969 of being impressed by the meager lay understanding of dramatic changes in our system of criminal justice. He emphasized change from a few years earlier when mass demonstrations, civil disobedience, and group violence were rare occurrences, to present-day situations in which police administrators must give priority to preventive measures through police-community relations, disorder-prevention training, and crowd-control planning. He said that the new problems "do not signify a return to some romanticized 'law and order' approach." He looked upon that approach as a kind of nostalgia for the days of simpler problems and simpler solutions. He noted the importance for community relations of the action by the officer on the beat, in contrast with that of a staff unit on community relations, and the importance for all officers of progressive training in community and race relations.

On the effectiveness of the system of criminal justice, Murphy stated: "We are not arresting enough offenders, convicting enough of those charged, or rehabilitating enough of those convicted." He added that we go far in assuring a fair trial, then put convicted persons in a correctional system that does not correct. He estimated that 50 percent of offenders are repeaters and commented that for many offenders the "correctional institutions are revolving doors." The responsibility of mayors and chiefs of police was considered, implying a need for cooperation between the police department and other departments of city government. As to cooperation, Murphy elaborated:

> The parts of the criminal justice process—the police, prosecutors, courts, correction agencies—which attempt to deal with crime in a large city will have to work more closely together. With the present fragmentation of authority—city police departments, county prosecutors, county or state courts, county or state corrections agencies—cooperation will not come easily or with rushing speed. Fragmentation of the criminal justice system by governmental units poses severe hurdles for a program of fruitful coordination to control crime.

Murphy interestingly commented on the responsibility of leadership, in dealing with the complex problems involved, for being able to ask the right questions so that pertinent information might be developed through research.

In a subsequent statement, speaking then as New York City's Commissioner of Police and referring more directly to urban crime problems, Murphy stated:[6]

> There are three components to the criminal justice system; the cops, the courts and the corrections; and it is my belief that the police come closer to fulfilling their responsibilities under this so-called system than any of the other agencies.

The commissioner noted a 165 percent increase in felony arrests in New York City during the decade ending in 1971, and that of the 94,042 such arrests made in 1971, there were 552 brought to trial. He recognized the heavily loaded court dockets, shortage of prosecutors and other needed court personnel, and haste versus justice in some efforts to reduce docket backlog. Commissioner Murphy added:

> Knowing these things makes (it) difficult to explain the decision of all the Supreme Court judges in this city (New York) to close down the courts for several weeks of informal Christmas vacation—difficult to explain to police officers out there arresting felons at great risk, to prisoners awaiting trial, to citizens being raped and robbed during the Christmas holidays.

Murphy advocated a "selective enforcement program," focusing on serious offenses and paying less attention to others. He commented:

> . . . Perhaps we in the police service should emphasize, almost exclusively, quality rather than quantity in our arrest activity. Despite strong public pressure to clear the streets of junkies, prostitutes, numbers runners, loiterers and other offensive types who make up a major part of the arrest workload, perhaps we should leave them there.
>
> Fewer arrests might just provide better police protection. The key would be making those fewer arrests count for as much as possible, thus instill-

ing fear in the criminal communities. Our approach to this goal would be to define whole categories which deserve less police attention—or none at all—and to saturate the other categories and areas of crime with increased effort.

On court function, Murphy further observed: "The courts are not merely an operating agency. They are expected to be of vital educational and symbolic significance too. But are they? Let's not delude ourselves."

Attorney Williams,[7] in a 1971 address to the National Conference on the Judiciary, included several items comparable to those set forth by Murphy. Williams further stated: "Let's face up to the fact that we lawyers are the bastions of the status quo. . . . We view proposals for reform with suspicion and their advocates with derision. We stand 100 percent for progress and 100 percent against change." He proposed ten specific changes in the urban criminal justice system to reduce the slow-motion aspect of big-city justice. The proposals included reference to "outmoded, archaic" grand jury proceedings, the bail system, written motions, technological updating in such areas as the steno-computerized transcript, and reduction in the time often wasted in selecting a jury.

Regarding the nation's approach to certain types of crimes, Williams referred thus to the narcotics area:

> It is folly to think that we can solve the addiction problem by controlling the flow of heroin into this country. Last year 105,000 vessels entered our seaports, 345,000 airplanes crossed our borders and 65,000,000 automobiles entered the United States—225,000,000 people came in. There are only 1,400 men in the Bureau of Customs patrolling the ports and places of entry for narcotics. Thousands of dollars worth of heroin can be brought in a tobacco pouch. All the heroin used for a year in the United States can be brought in uncut in two trucks.

3. Officer Competence and Professionalization

The reference by Christopher to the availability of federal funds under the Safe Streets Act of 1968 noted personnel training programs as one aspect of the plan to improve law-enforcement services. There has been extensive comment and considerable action regarding upgrading the qualifications of policemen.[8]

In his 1971 address, previously noted, Williams remarked that as a nation we have grown fat and flabby, morally and otherwise. He stated: "Our preoccupation with self-centered concerns and personal pleasures has deflected us from public obligations and necessary collective endeavors. We have lost the spirit that changed a people into a citizenry and a territory into a nation." As one avenue of remedy, Williams suggested dedication to vocational excellence, a high level of performance or craftsmanship, regardless of what one's vocation is. With specific respect to police service on a professionalized basis, he said:

> . . . we must make law enforcement an attractive profession to our bright young college students. We must introduce the concept of of-

ficers' candidate schools for college graduates so that after a prescribed period of training, say 180 days, they can be commissioned.

We must create a West Point for law enforcement officers, an institution which qualifies interested young men and women for immediate commissions in our urban police department.

In short we must introduce and promote the concept of lateral entry into the commissioned ranks of our big city police forces for those who are qualified by education and training.

The abstract of an article by Craig,[9] who was director of Public Safety for Pittsburgh when writing, reads thus:

The key to real support of the police is to be found in the development of enhanced competence among the police officers. The truly competent policeman performs effectively despite the difficulties which stem from recent constitutional interpretations issued by the courts. Competency is more important than philosophy in police-community relations. The development and implementation of competency in police work depends upon scientific recruit-selection methods, broad support of higher education of police, freeing police from irrelevant duties, and the wise use of more sophisticated equipment.

Craig commented, as other writers on law enforcement have commented, on the *Miranda* decision[10] as offering problems concerning enforcement. Conversely, he referred to an observation by Chief Justice Warren in *Terry* v. *Ohio*,[11] which noted 335 policemen killed on duty during the seven years 1960-1966, and which, said Warren, pointed to "the need for law enforcement officers to protect themselves in situations where they may lack probable cause for arrest."[12]

Community Relations and Police Image

Craig particularly stressed the ramifications of officer competence with respect to community relations. On this point he reasoned and illustrated:

It is important to make clear that police-community relations is not a staff function to be confined to a specialized unit of the police; community relations depends, 99 percent, on the competence with which every man on the street performs his job. In community-relations training (euphemism for race-relations training) we're not concerned so much with changing police attitudes as we are with developing external actions of competent quality to reverse the spiral of worsening relationships.

Craig then added:

This brings into mind a certain policeman who was at the top of the civil service list for promotion to a supervisory rank. When we were considering whether to promote him, we noted his reputation for being a tough guy, for being a bit quick with the use of force. We debated this thoroughly and finally concluded that, since no actual disciplinary action had appeared against him on his record, we couldn't disqualify him. After he was promoted, we watched him closely. Oddly enough, this policeman, who could hardly qualify as a liberal articulator of the brotherhood of man, is so interested in police work that he does his job energetically. He responds to the needs of the ghetto community in which he has been stationed so well that he has become its favorite son. He has become the kind of police officer that is pointed to as the one who gives black citizens assurance of protection. Philosophical allegiance to particular attitudes is not expected because attitudes are notoriously unreliable. If the policeman is willing to spend sweat on the concerns of the ghetto community, that is really all the residents there want, just like the residents anywhere.

Craig was also interested in police image. In this connection he noted that currently the military is not at the peak among American ambitions and suggested that the police move away from military models and imagery. He apparently was thinking about titles, uniforms, shirts, ties, etc., as well as buttons, belts, shoulder straps and other forms of symbolism. Craig noted: "I think that image counts and can break down some barriers now separating the policeman from other men."

A California professor of criminology[13] presented an analytical study on needs and progress toward professionalization of law-enforcement personnel. He referred to the American policeman as a barometer of community values and noted a shift in values from property rights to human rights. He also noted a shift in pattern from the policeman working to a large extent independent of and perhaps suspicious of other governmental agencies toward a more co-operative approach on a teamwork basis. The shift toward cooperation involves the obligation of the professional policeman to "instruct the total community in terms of responsible citizenship." Professor Germann emphasized that respect for rule by law was crucial in police training and placed particular emphasis on the development of sound judgment and on officer attitude. In this connection he said in part:

> . . . It is easier and cheaper to teach a policeman the mechanical techniques of work—operating the radio, applying the police strangle, double locking the cuffs, writing the ticket—than it is to teach an officer the psychological, sociological, anthropological, legal, ethnical and human relations aspects of his work. It is easier and cheaper to teach an officer a few sections of the penal and vehicle code than it is to teach him how poor police work in the areas of arrest, search and seizure, will be rejected by the courts which assume their responsibility in enforcing the Constitution and Bill of Rights. It is easier and cheaper to teach an officer to "follow the book" than it is to teach him how to use his discretion wisely in performing his function. . . .

Professionalization Through College and Educational Preparation

Germann further commented: "When we talk about professionalization, we must talk about the educational qualifications for the work." He later added: "The modern police task, in my judgment, imposes as great a logic in requiring a college degree for the local law enforcement service as for the federal law enforcement service." He subsequently noted:

College men entering the service should be broadly educated, and equipped with the perspective and understanding obtained by courses in psychology, sociology, political science, English, history and philosophy. Our educational system must not overemphasize techniques and neglect conceptual understanding if it is to provide professional preparation. We have only to open our ears to the statements of uneducated police leadership to realize that narrow specialization over a number of years has resulted in a lack of ability to see the police operation in a balanced perspective. The American police service is in dire need of supervisors and administrators who are broadly educated generalists.

With respect to advancement toward professionalization, Germann observed: "Police training, *in-service* oriented, has progressed to the point where many departments operate police academies, provide for refresher (advanced officer) training, specialist training, supervisory training and executive development." As to expansion in college-level training, Germann said:

College programs at the junior college, community college, city college, and university level are expanding rapidly. At the beginning of 1966 there were some 160 such degree granting programs—and now (writing in 1967) there are 271—with 40 added in the past nine months! These programs enroll both full-time students and substantial numbers of working officers. In California we have seven programs which offer Baccalaureate and Graduate degrees, and 60 programs offering the two-year AA degree . . . . in the Spring of 1966 a survey was completed in Los Angeles County relative to working police officers and their educational attainment. Some 650 have the AA degree, over 475 have bachelors degrees, some 65 have masters degrees or above—and currently, in that one county, over 4,500 officers are enrolled in college programs.

Professor Germann did not comment on possible relationships between Watts-type incidents and programs for upgrading the qualifications of Los Angeles policemen. However with respect to program content in the improvement effort, he observed: "The studies are carefully balanced between the tool and vocational type course and the conceptual and research course," and noted that "students are expected to prepare for supervisory and management roles, even though their entrance is at the operational level."

At several points Germann noted the rule of law as the heart of American police action and the need for a high level of background training in order to combat what he thought of as an authoritarianism and anti-intellectualism that may become involved when promotion is based primarily on experience in the ranks. He commented: "The professional American policeman is very cognizant of the fact that in order to gain *respect*, he must be *respectable*." In conclusion, Germann stated:

Every policeman, representing the government, is in a position to be a force for good, for by his example he teaches the community and molds its attitudes. We cannot induce a spirit of respect for man if we tolerate evil means to accomplish good ends, or if we ignore human dignity in enforcing the law. We cannot induce a spirit of respect for law if we treat people who constitute our crime problem as if they were beyond the protection of the Constitution, or if we violate the law in enforcing the law.

Newberger[14] described special offerings in police science at the John Jay College, a part of the City University of New York (sic). The three phases of the course emphasized student involvement: first, within groups of students formed on a sociometric basis; second, in laboratory experiences related to the various aspects of dealing with arrested persons; third, in feedback situations in which students examined the difficulties which they had encountered. Newberger found the "human responses of students themselves, to live situations," to be an effective way to achieve student learning.

Burrow[15] indicated the development of a core program for preparing law-enforcement workers in Texas. A committee composed of representatives from the various junior colleges and universities of the state and from the law-enforcement profession recommended a core of eight courses carrying twenty-four semester hours of college credit. The coordinating board adopted seven of the eight courses as a statewide program. Private institutions which grant baccalaureate degrees in law enforcement were permitted to participate in the core program on a voluntary basis. On the significance of the program, Burrow stated:

> The core curriculum has become state policy by its having been adopted by the Coordinating Board, Texas College and University System. This means that every state-supported senior institution having a degree in police science law enforcement must accept the credits from junior colleges. This means that for the first time in Texas, the technical vocational programs offering the core are recognized as being academically oriented, thus lending more dignity to technical education. This means that the pure training courses which in the past have been taught in junior college programs will be relegated to the police academies where they belong. But most of all, this means that the student who is preparing for a career in law enforcement can begin his education at one of the 36 junior colleges, obtain his associate degree and transfer into one of the 17 baccalaureate programs with the assurance that his credits will not only be transferable but applicable toward his baccalaureate degree.

Jagiello[16] made certain comparisons of the relative adequacy of training for law enforcement as provided by the police academy and by the college program. His point of departure was essentially that of taking issue with a 1969 book which maintained that academic training for patrolmen was largely irrelevant. It was irrelevant, the book maintained, because it was unnecessary for patrol service; police academies provide adequate technical training; the authoritarian aspects of police work overwhelm any liberal impulse resulting from college experience; and a hapless law-training officer would appear as a symbol of educational failure.

In his refutation of the book's fundamental contention, Jagiello emphasized what he considered to be the expanding discretionary responsibilities of policemen—much as set forth by some writers previously reviewed. Moreover, he called attention to the short period of training that characterized academy programs and to the fact that police officers frequently do not enter the academy "until after they have been on the force for a period of time."

Newman and Hunter[17] reported data from a survey of institutions of higher education offering programs in law enforcement. Their data related to 99 institutions which responded, out of 128 contacted. One concern associated with interpreting the data was the small number of persons in these programs compared with the needs in the field, as those needs were set forth in the February 1967 report of the President's Commission on Law Enforcement and Administration of Justice. The authors noted that a majority of the educational programs were serving people who were already in law-enforcement work, but thought that as more and better programs were established, there would be an increase in new recruits. Among conclusions, the authors stated:

> One of the major problems which must be resolved if these programs are going to remedy the severe shortage of man-power mentioned . . . is that of attracting well-qualified and able young people into such programs and subsequently into the field. Many other of the less romantic and less well-paid professions (e.g., education, nursing, social welfare, etc.) are similarly faced with this dilemma, and competition in obtaining able and interested young men and women is becoming more difficult each year.

A somewhat unique suggestion, regarding the qualification of persons employed in the American system of criminal justice, relates to the use of Transcendental Meditation (T.M.) as a corrective technique.[18] In his preliminary comments on penal institutions, the killings in San Quentin and Attica, and a survey reporting that one-fifth of our jails are housed in buildings over 100 years old, Cox summarized: "Overall, the conditions found were suited only to maximize the primitive aspects of incarceration, with little attention directed to the rehabilitative goals of a correctional system." While he thought that newer structures and more "progressive" staff arrangements including psychologists and psychiatrists would probably be helpful, he noted that the recidivism rate was not greatly different under the more "progressive" programs. He referred to a root problem of criminal behavior which was not reached by the programs noted and suggested a growing readiness of prison administrators to try new possibilities. Hence the pertinence of T.M. in the preparation of law-enforcement personnel.

Cox described the technique of Yogi or T.M., with its crucial manifestation of deep physical and mental relaxation, and noted experimental evidence regarding changes in physiological processes related to oxygen consumption, carbon-dioxide and lactate levels, galvanic skin resistence, electrocardiograph and electroencephalograph readings, and general metabolic rate, during periods of deep relaxation. He referred to the use of T.M. in alleviating some forms of drug abuse and hypertension and to over 300 universities in the United States offering instruction in T.M. He commented on a social acceptability of meditation, since it was used by persons in various walks of life and did not stigmatize a practicer of meditation as being a criminal or a social outcast.

Cox thought that under the circumstances described, T.M. deserved "serious consideration" as a supplement to our system of criminal justice.

The need for interstate effort in personnel training was emphasized by Vanagunas.[19] His orientation was based essentially on that part of the 1968 Omnibus Crime Control and Safe Streets Act which deals with Law Enforcement Education Programs (LEEP). He emphasized the idea that people rather than hardware hold the answer to improved law enforcement, as he urged interstate cooperation in training programs. In thus urging state rather than federal initiative, he stated:

> A fine opportunity for the states to take the initiative in nation-wide criminal justice improvement lies in manpower development. Most training and education programs for law-enforcement, court and correction personnel are offered in state-supported colleges and universities or other agencies connected to state government. These programs should be made available not only to the individual state's criminal justice community but also to interested residents in other states. The most logical vehicle for achieving this goal is an interstate compact.

Vanagunas set forth his Model Interstate Compact in terms of nine formal articles, three of which have four or more subdivisions. With specific regard to the model, he stated: "Its purpose is to allow the states, by means of bilateral and multilateral contracts, to share existing training and education programs and to develop new programs mutually for police, prosecutors, public defenders, judges, correctional administrators, probation and parole agents, and other criminal personnel."

Two apparent limitations of the Vanagunas proposal might be noted. (1) Along with the personnel indicated in the foregoing paragraph, he should include teachers, guidance counselors, social workers, health-services personnel, employment and vocational placement personnel, and perhaps others who are concerned with crime prevention as well as with the rehabilitiation of offenders. Among others are those agencies which are involved in the educational aspects of the general field of crime and lawlessness in American society. (2) As to funding, he comments: "Perhaps it is natural that the intiative to improve criminal justice comes from Washington—that, after all, is where the money is. However, the states can and should take vigorous steps of their own to match federal efforts." The quote may embody conflicting implications. (a) The first sentence suggests a refrain that is popular in state capitals—for the federal government to supply the funds, to be used by the states as they see fit. Suggestions of this kind can make little claim to realism. (b) If the "vigorous" steps by states "to match federal efforts" include the use of state funds, arguments to justify the program sound more realistic.

Evaluation of Professionalization Efforts

The basis of organization in any type of society is some kind of value structure. It is often suggested that the basic elements in such a structure are human and material. But there is often a failure to recognize that in fundamental respects the two are inseparable. Material items have value because they enable people to survive and to achieve other goals. Conversely, neither survival nor any other human goal is achieved without material goods. Moreover, an increase in material goods typically causes man's world of goals to expand, while an expansion in goals causes man to seek and to create more and newer material goods. Hence, to suggest that human values are superior to material values, apart from biases in every culture as to whose values will prevail, is about on a par with suggesting that one leg is more important in walking than the other leg.

It follows that every type of activity in which people engage undergoes some degree of conscious or subconscious evaluation. With respect to professional services which constitute special and probably intricate areas of human relationships, and which depend on human and material support in a broad collective sense, the devices required for effective evaluation are likely to be complicated and difficult to create. Limits in competence, and natural drift toward easier activities, thus often contribute to postponement in developing effective procedures for evaluation. Most newly expanding fields reflect the shortcoming noted.

With respect to evaluating the efforts being made toward professionalization of the police force, attention is focused on two contributions.

The dependence of police professionalization on structural support within the police occupation was stressed by Maniha.[20] In reviewing professional literature on the subject, he referred to conflicts on the desirability of professionalization and on the goals to be sought in the process. He thought that there had been more professionalization in the administrative work of police departments than in patrol work and focused his attention on administrative matters. He looked upon the conceptualization of a profession as a matter of degree, and in his model he set forth as follows his conception of the crucial elements for evaluation: (a) development of specific theory or intellectual technique, (b) relevance to basic social values, (c) a training period, (d) motivation toward an ideal of service, (e) autonomy, (f) sense of commitment, (g) sense of colleagueship or community, and (h) code of ethics. He presented considerable biographical data on police chiefs in St. Louis, in substantiating his comments on professionalization work in police administration.[21]

A significant effort to appraise the arguments and programs suggested for professionalizing the police and law enforcement service has been set forth by White.[22] Her analysis focused on two main points: (a) the absence of "criteria for what counts as better performance of police tasks"; (b) meagerness of information "about the behavior that professionalization has produced or will produce." Her analysis was presented in three categories: she (a) presented a critique of the professionalization model of reform, (b) formulated certain types of police roles, to illustrate the various dimensions which professionalization might include, and (c) suggested applications of the type idea to policy-related research concerning police service.

White looked upon professionalization as "basically an argument for a certain kind of control on police behavior." The effort is to get individual policemen to internalize certain standards of behavior that are set forth by professional bodies which are external to them. The fundamental point thus becomes who determines the criteria by which the standards of professionalization are developed. White saw a conflict between commitment to certain principles of conduct which professionalization emphasizes and the necessity for police officers to exercise discretionary judgment on numerous occasions. She commented: "The prevailing mode of professionalized control in police departments today is deliberately centralized and nondiscretionary. . . , reflecting the dilemma in its most pragmatic form." She noted supporting research studies, although her conclusions differed substantially from those of some other authors on professionalization.

The effect of professionalization in causing the policeman to perceive himself "as a professional rather than as a necessary evil," makes the content of the perception a crucial element in professionalization. Whether there is a substantial gap between this perception and what the policemen meets on his job, depends on the realism that is incorporated into the professionalization.

The analysis hypothesized four types of police roles: tough cop, rule applier, problem solver, and crime fighter. White explained and illustrated these in considerable detail. She observed: "The typology of police roles, while not constructed from personality measurable data, is obviously related to basic personality differences among police officers. This relationship ought to be examined for both theoretical and policy reasons." She accordingly set forth twelve "testable hypotheses" to use in making the examination. She added: "There can be no solid empirical conclusions concerning the nature and effects of police professionalization until these and other related hypotheses have been tested. And without the sort of knowledge that such a procedure can yield the professionalist program remains an empty set of Slogans." However, she urged study of police role typology, with attention to the consequences that might follow from each model developed and with the aim of role content determining what constitutes professionalization. She concluded:

> . . . The different consequences which follow, rather than the appropriation of the label "professional," should be the focus of future concern. The rhetoric of professionalization and its accompanying politics only obscure the deeper problem, which is a basic confusion over the nature of the policing function itself.

Gyrations Enroute to Professional Status

With respect to practically any major social goal, the route between initial conception and basic achievement is not straight. It is characterized by wanderings, dynamic thrusts, setbacks, recuperation, circuitous movements, bickering, confusion, etc. It is only after the goal has been substantially reached that one can look back and draw a "fairly straight" line connecting the points of significant contribution.

The present study at various points, as in commenting on the Vanagunas Model Interstate Compact for professional training, suggests that one cause of the confusion concerning professionalization in the police force is that the policing function is too narrowly conceived, and this seems especially true with respect to involving the personnel of education, guidance, and industrial employment.

However, one should expect that efforts at professionalization in a new field, such as that of the police and law-enforcement agencies, will give attention to the goals, content, and results of professionalization in older areas. But major attention should probably be placed on the newer criteria that are being pressed upon certain of the older areas. Some of the newer criteria relate to a closer scrutiny and more precise statement of objectives. Some relate to more identifiable and measurable outcomes of training programs, such as are sometimes set forth in terms of performance-based qualifications.

One evidence of need for a broadened conception of professionalization is the growth in semiprofessional or paraprofessional designations. Growth and gradual upgrading in paraprofessionalization tends to dim somewhat the social halo that has often been attached to the idea of professional status. However, this development should be expected in a complex but expanding social structure, in which the level of preparation for employment is rising both consistently and rapidly. One might note by comparison that during the early decades of this century rather substantial prestige attached to graduation from high school and that during several following decades the same applied to graduation from college. But college diplomas are now looked upon as commonplace needs for many types of employment and for participation in several other aspects of the culture. The "commonplace need" may not alter the importance of the social service rendered as much as it alters the relative social status of the persons who render it.

4. Recruitment for Police Service

Newman and Hunter, previously noted, also commented on the need for more active recruiting effort, the need to gear programs toward improving the public image of the law-enforcement and correction professions as well as toward upgrading personnel and techniques, and the need for more systematic bases in determining salaries.

Hamilton and Bimstein[23] spoke about salary as an important recruiting tool. They observed that many police departments are requiring their men to acquire some college training and that some departments are requiring a college degree for new entrants. However, they stated that little research had been done among college students to determine what background and motivational factors lead students to choose police work as a career.

Accordingly, they studied the backgrounds and expectations of persons graduating in 1971 from a two-year Police Science program at Northern Virginia Community College, located some twelve miles southwest of Washington, D.C. The school enrolled approximately 4,000 daytime and 3,200 evening students, of whom 180 full-time and 120 evening students were enrolled in the Police Science program. Of the 80 daytime students entering the program in 1969, 29 graduated in 1971. Among reasons why the other 51 failed to finish the program on the two-year schedule were military service, financial problems, and family relocation in other communities.

The authors noted that the students of the college come mainly from local middle-class families, that most students have part-time jobs to help defray expense, and that the 29 graduates in Police Science were a representative cross section of the total 245 graduates in the 1971 class. About half of the 29 indicated a preference for uniformed police work and half for work in non-uniformed positions. Analyses indicated types of agencies with which work was preferred, and preferences as to municipal, county, or state service. Three of the 29 graduates were women. None of the evening students, many of whom were already in law-enforcement work, had sufficient credits to be among the 1971 graduates.[24]

An interesting and somewhat unusual approach to recruiting appeared in efforts to reach Americans in West Germany who were finishing their military service. In connection with Job Information Fairs and otherwise, Price and Bostik[25] held information and recruiting sessions of a few days each at different points in West Germany where large numbers of Americans were stationed. Representatives of American industry were also present, giving information and seeking recruits. From March 27 to April 7, 1972, some 5,925 servicemen participated in the program, which the authors thought constituted "a strong indication that there is a real need for the type of information and counseling provided by the visiting civilians." Regarding the police-recruiting aspects of the activity, the authors at various points stated:

> Much has been said recently about how young people are no longer interested in law enforcement as a profession. Our experience in Germany proves that this is a myth. We found many highly qualified young men who are very interested in law enforcement careers. They have some reservations. They need sound, up-to-date information to help them make career decisions. They certainly represent a highly qualified manpower pool for the nation's police departments (p. 53).

> More than 150 Job Fairs have been sponsored by the Jobs for Veterans Committee at military bases inside the United States, but these are primarily local affairs designed to match servicemen with employers who operate local businesses. The European Job Information Fair was international in the scope of businesses represented, and the program was aimed at the serviceman who had been away from home and was out of touch with the job market that would await him after discharge (p. 54).

> . . . Black servicemen expressed a high degree of interest in law enforcement careers. Blacks comprise an estimated 20 percent of the total audience that requested information. . . . Like misconceptions about young people not being interested in law enforcement, it had also been stated that blacks were not interested in law enforcement. The experience in Germany ran counter to that theory.

As the black serviceman prepares to return to civilian life, one of the things he considers is the possibility of serving the black community in some way. Since the policeman on the beat can provide one of the few role models available to black youth, the law enforcement profession may offer the black serviceman just that opportunity for service (p. 54).

There was also a great deal of interest in police work expressed by specialists who wanted to know if they could practice their specialty in police work. . . .

Two themes emerged as powerful recruiting devices from the Germany experience. One theme emphasized the vast variety of police duties. Another stressed the *service aspects* of police work in contrast to *purely enforcement duties*. It was repeatedly *emphasized that police work involved a far greater percentage of community service duties than those involving crime and violence* (p. 55). (Emphasis added.)

5. Relationship of Police Qualifications to Community Served

One general point, inferred by Jagiello and some other writers, deserves more attention than it ordinarily receives. It concerns the large and increasing percentage of the American people who have college degrees and the imagery status as well as the practical adequacy of noncollege officers dealing with such people in discretionary and judgmental situations. Through this channel, much could be said about the possible relationship between college training and police image in a community.[26]

Relative to this, one might note Manella's observation[27] that since youth under twenty-five years of age come in contact with the general population more extensively than members of any other age group, the police need a particular understanding of this age group—with respect to attitudes, actions, and reactions.

The theme suggested by Manella was substantially expanded by Younger.[28] He noted several developments and associated limitations in recent American society which make the problems of youth considerably different now from what they were a generation or more ago. He initially commented on the extensive permissiveness of our society, which, he suggested, is based on an assumption that "the best way to preserve our ideals and institutions is to constantly attack them." He thought that this situation generates undue tolerance toward individuals who perpetrate illegal and often violent acts.

Younger observed that some professors teach that violence is justified if the ends sought are noble, that some schools in our educational system are poor, and that there has been an erosion of the authority of the teacher to deal with violence—even in situations in which he or she would otherwise be capable of doing so. Younger reasoned that by the same token we have not trained many principals or college presidents in mob psychology, guerilla tactics, and other things which they need to know in order to operate effectively in the face of violence. He further noted that school and college administrators often hesitate to call the police during the early stages of threatening or developing violence and do so only "after learning the hard way"—perhaps through repeated lessons.

In extensive comments, Younger referred to differences between present teen-agers and those of a generation or more ago. He commented that with the expansion in knowledge, and in the leisure and permissiveness available to teenagers for learning and reflection, they are less ready to accept the values and pronouncements of their elders than was true of youth of former generations. He recognized a small percentage of professional troublemakers, perhaps 5 percent, but thought of the others as involved in traumatic experience without adequate guidance through school situations or the general regulatory frame-work of society. Teachers too, he noted, are different from those which teen-agers of previous generations had, making more effort to seek relief from their financial and other frustrations through teacher organizations.

Younger emphasized the interdependence of various agencies concerned with the development of youth and the dependence of social progress on peace and tranquility within a framework of law. Concerning the role of law en-forcement within the structure, he said:

> We cannot hire enough policemen to provide security unless we take steps to eliminate the basic causes of much of the dissatisfaction felt by the young people and other citizens today. While admitting our short-comings, and acknowledging the necessity for improvement, we are going to get rid of our inferiority complex and stop apologizing to students and and everyone else when we call for an application of police power to main-tain law and order.

He pointed to the responsibility of the police to protect lives and property, and stated: "Lives and property on campus are just as precious as off-campus." Subsequently he reasoned: "No one ever improved an educational institution by burning down the buildings on campus. No youngster ever got an educa-tion carrying a sign on the sidewalk in front of his school."

Chapter 2

DELINQUENCY PREVENTION, CORRECTION
AND REHABILITATION

From the long-range standpoint, the most important aspect of dealing with crime and lawlessness in America relates to prevention, and the second most important relates to corrrection or rehabilitation. Both prevention and correction are intended to reduce the social loss and disruption associated with lawlessness and to secure optimum social contributions from potential and actual offenders. Since the development of antisocial tendencies in an individual often extends over considerable time and is of sociological and psychological importance before it is generally looked upon as having legal significance, preventive measures deserve extensive attention. But the correction of a first offender, or even of a repeater, is intended to prevent further delinquency on his part. For this and other reasons, one should approach a separate treatment of prevention and of correction with a recognition of the limitations involved. Perhaps one should think in terms of areas of emphasis, rather than of separate or distinct categories.

1. Emphasis on Delinquency Prevention

The development of socially constructive knowledge, skills, and attitudes during childhood and youth, as related to holding jobs and to other approved ways of participating in the culture, is emphasized at several points in the present study, especially in the attention which Division IV gives to education. The need for close cooperation between the schools and other youth-service agencies is similarly emphasized. One such agency is the juvenile court, in its relation to other parts of the legal system and to other youth-serving agencies.

Interpreting Court Decisions

With respect to America's high rate of crime and delinquency, much has been written about a gap between principles set forth by the Supreme Court of the United States and the operating policy which actually governs criminal justice. Several studies which bear on the effectiveness of the Court as a policy maker regarding justice were reviewed by Duffee and Siegel.[29] They observed that agencies concerned with criminal justice must take sociological as well as legal considerations into account, and that legal explanations often fail to reach sociological implications. In summarizing certain studies of the type indicated, they stated:

There appears to be agreement that the Court's lack of influence over frontline agencies (e.g., police, trial courts and correctional agencies) is more accurately described in terms of misunderstanding rather than open conflict, misapprehension rather than insubordination. When judicial directives are not reflected in the daily operation in the system, it is often the case that the Court's message has been distorted to fit individual organizational needs. It is less the case that organizational officials have received, understood, and then knowingly ignored Supreme Court decisions. For example, if the policeman's version of the Miranda decision[30] differed from the original, the transformation lies in the values and goals that constrain individuals to work in the police organization. The Court obviously perceived the police role in such a way (as) to require that suspects be informed of their rights. The policeman, however, is rewarded for apprehending the guilty party and not for aligning his perceptions to harmonize with those held by the Court. Because the values important to the Supreme Court are not the primary criteria used by administrators to evaluate police performance, it is unlikely that judicial mandates concerning police behavior will have the intended effect.

The Supreme Court apparently thought that the juvenile court system was not working as originally intended for the protection of youth through rehabilitation service, reasoned Duffee and Siegel, and the Court in *Gault*[32] provided that juveniles were entitled to equal counsel to insure constitutional safeguards to fair treatment. This provision, observed Duffee and Siegel, meant that juvenile courts in their deliberations must subsequently deal with the contributions of counsel. However, these authors noted from available data that juveniles with counsel were more likely to be incarcerated than juveniles without counsel. They thought it likely "that the juvenile court is more willing to retain the juvenile as a participant in the justice system when the presence of a lawyer has insured the appearance of due process."[33] They further noted that the Court could set up minimal requirements as to counsel or other matters, but that in administrative operations the minimal soon became the norm. In regard to members of the juvenile court or of any other organization, these authors concluded:

If their work is to be more than minimally acceptable, their commitment to goals must be gained. Commitment, participation, and satisfaction cannot be legislated; they must be developed through innovative management. Organizational structures and interaction patterns must be developed in which officials will be positively rather than negatively sanctioned when their behavior is congruent with Supreme Court intent.

New Careers Involvement and Delinquency Prevention

The new-careers concept of preventing delinquency through involving youth in social change and its challenge of demands implies far-reaching integration of prevention and rehabilitation as well as extensive and ongoing changes in the general structure of American society. Among important elements in the conception are: (a) linkage of education from about the third year of high school through the graduate school of the university, with an internship of paid work experience in various types of social agencies; (b) direct integration of youth, through this linkage, into the process of social change; (c) the assumption that social change is an inevitable outgrowth of expansion in knowledge and that the rate at which knowledge expands is increasing; (d) no current adult generation can adequately equip its children by preparing them for the kind of life which the adults have been living; (e) crime and delinquency constitute a framework of games to which youth turn when they are shut out from participation in the approved social structure; (f) the social and educational system must find ways of screening into the system the actual and potential dropouts, instead of screening them out; (g) job-integrated educational programs constitute a major avenue of screening in, particularly with respect to new areas of employment; and (h) reformed or new-career delinquents will be important agents in tutoring peers and in other instructional service of the broad new-career development.

Grant[34] considered much of the foregoing and certain other implications in connection with a model new-careers program relative to institutions which are involved in the administration of justice (probation, parole, corrections, law enforcement, and legal assistance). He noted changes in the vocational world, with an increasing shift from blue-collar to white-collar jobs, and stated: "Health, education, housing, recreation, administration of justice, research, development, and planning are the jobs of the future." He observed that such "outgroups" as minorities, welfare clients, public offenders, and consumers will develop more organization and exert more political power, much as labor unions have done. He thus saw civil rights and civil liberties as being at the heart of the change process, with particular implications for the administration of criminal justice. Youth organizations and movements will expand, he suggested, and will demand roles in formulating social policy. He added: "We are going to see more examples such as that of the Mission Rebels in San Francisco (a youth organization) who have a contract with the school system to provide counseling service for potential dropout students." The extension of voting rights to eighteen-year-olds, with the large percentage of initial delinquents being in the age span of roughly seventeen to twenty-three years, may press for the restoration of voting rights to convicted offenders and for screening them back into cultural participation. Broader university service in providing technical assistance to clients in developing and operating their own programs was envisioned. Two comments by Grant deserve especial consideration. In regard to one, he stated:

> The emergence of parallel systems is becoming inevitable as we struggle with the change process. . . . We can look for more contracting with local groups for services presently provided by our large bureaucratic institutions. This trend will be one of the advocated ways to deal with the demand for local community control.

The comment may lead some school people to think about feeding, testing, or transportation service; about certain health, guidance, or vocational-placement services; and perhaps about in-service programs for upgrading staff personnel. If this indicates the pattern of Grant's thinking, perhaps a term such as "delegated responsibility" would be more feasible than "parallel systems."

The other comment for especial consideration relates to delinquency as a form of social deviation and places it in a broad perspective concerning different kinds of social and ideological variation, plus the note that social progress depends on tolerance for wide variation. The latter item notes that constructive ideas emerge from rich variety. In some respects delinquency could be looked upon as an experimental way of pointing out shortcomings in the social order and of initiating related urge for reform. The effect of prison riots during recent years, and perhaps some drug problems, may be illustrative.

How Much Centralization in Prevention and Correction?

Associated with his review of several prevention and therapy programs, Polk[35] emphasized the importance of community-based effort in contrast with programs based on correctional institutions. He observed that the relative success of the community-based programs has led to a considerable exploration of one community-type development—the Youth Service Bureau. He noted that juveniles might be referred to the bureau "by the police, the courts, parents, schools, and social agencies for counseling, education, work, or recreation programs and job placement."

Polk looked upon the function of the agency as being largely that of advocacy in working with other agencies to provide service, rather than acting as an agency which directly rendered the service concerned. He stressed the importance of getting qualified local residents to work in the program, to counteract the tendency of many local residents to resent the presence in their midst of delinquents who had brought disrespect on the community.

Probably the most important activities of the bureau are associated with securing the integration of youth into the mainstream of activities and decision-making in the community. Polk attached great significance to the way in which the American educational system has developed and implied the significance of future modifications of the system. He noted that with rapid technical development and urbanization, two important changes in the education of youth had taken place. One is a segregation of youth from participation in the life of the community in order to be educated, and the other is that as youth go through the current educational process they must play a passive role which denies them roles of responsibility and authority. The problem youth or public offender is particularly isolated and vulnerable, stated Polk, creating a kind of vicious circle. Within the circle, the youth has a low stake in conformity to community expectations, and the low-stake behavior aggravates segregation and lack of belongingness.

Concerning the role of the school, Polk commented that a major part of the delinquency of youth was associated with failure to do well in school and that school success was largely related to academic performance. He further commented that the point at which one enters the vocational world depends substantially on his school record. He added that school achievement depends on a narrow conception of ability, noting that in several instances of employment there is little correlation between school achievement and vocational success. He thought that a child got into a groove or track status rather early in his school career, as being a success or a dullard, and usually continued in that status. He commented: "Thus, it is no wonder that recent research studies have shown that delinquency is much more likely to occur among the academically unsuccessful without regard to their class background.[36]

Polk thought the Youth Services Bureau could serve as a *systems change agent*, which would create new kinds of educational relationships—or workflow concepts. He reasoned that the flow must provide an opportunity for the youth to "be somebody"; that is, to move into economically and otherwise rewarding positions, to be and feel competent, to participate in roles that produce a sense of worthwhile contribution, to feel a sense of belonging, and to receive counseling which overcomes the psychological residue of past failures.

The importance of a cogent theory concerning how the different agencies working through the bureau would function was stressed in conclusion, with "system-level theories rather than the individually-centered counseling approach that pervades correctional practice today, and which unfortunately has already infected the budding new Youth Service Bureau programs in process of establishment around the country."

A kindred type of development grew out of a 1970 meeting called by the Youth Development Delinquency Prevention Administration (YDDPA), of the federal Department of Health, Education and Welfare.[37] Persons attending the meeting were law-enforcement officers, educators, sociologists and practitioners, and researchers in juvenile delinquency and youth development. The strategy developed by the meeting and subsequently refined was implemented by federal and state governments through pilot projects in twenty-three communities throughout the nation. Other projects were planned. On strategy, the author stated:

> The strategy calls for the establishment, nationwide, of youth service systems which will divert youth, insofar as possible, from the juvenile justice system by providing comprehensive, integrated, community-based programs designed to meet the needs of all youth, regardless of who they are or what their individual problems may be.

Along with prevention as noted, emphasis was laid on "community-based rehabilitation programs as alternatives to placement of delinquent youths in traditional correctional facilities." Reference was made to reprogramming our social institutions so as to offer to youth roles which are responsible, socially acceptable, and personally satisfying. Emphasis was placed on youth involvement in all phases of the programs that affect them, with individuals working out personnel programs in conjunction with social workers.

It was recognized that evaluation of the project depended on measurable objectives, and the following objectives were differentiated: to provide socially acceptable and meaningful roles for youth; to divert youth away from juvenile justice systems into alternate programs; to reduce negative labeling which tends to stigmatize and further alienate problem youth; and to reduce youth-adult alienation. The latter item might concern youth-parent relations.[38]

In emphasizing delinquency prevention in an area of Chicago,[39] Treger pointed to several possibilities for cooperation between the police and social workers. He noted the skill that police develop in identifying people with problems which require professional service and the substantial body of knowledge regarding families which social workers typically acquire. He added: "Furthermore, the police officer can use his authority to stimulate a desire for services when internal motivation is not present." Also, the social worker can offer an alternative to police options of dropping a case or referring it to court and thus avoid a gap in services, with the indicated alternative supplying feedback to aid the officer in his disposition of the case. Through avenues such as mentioned, some people with problems could at an early time "be diverted from further entry into the criminal justice system" and be directed into appropriate services.

However, Treger thought social agencies could review their services in order to make them more available to law-enforcement personnel and to people who come to the attention of such personnel. He saw a university role in developing innovations, training personnel, and conducting research.

An article reporting on a Chicago regional planning development respecting crime control placed substantial emphasis on prevention through planning and through the coordination of agencies which were involved in criminal justice within the city.[40] Several aspects of the program also coordinated pertinent agencies in suburban Cook County. In his article, Matthews referred to the general project as the only one on such a large scale by a city government in America at the time, and noted some "seventy-six major projects to prevent crime and juvenile delinquency" in the region. Among major projects within the general program, he mentioned:

> . . . improved services for offenders such as training, education, half-way house placement; a comprehensive program to improve the security of children and teachers in the schools, including security patrols, better lighting and communications equipment and truancy prevention; provision of detoxification services to divert the chronic alcoholic from the criminal justice system; a comprehensive drug treatment program to be operated by the City's 18 community mental health centers; studies and demonstration programs to provide increased security to encourage industrial and commercial employers to remain in the City; programs for elevator security and vertical patrol to improve security in the City's high-rise, public housing units; and expanded training and education programs for criminal justice personnel.

One particularly innovative feature was a million-dollar program by the Chicago Civil Service Commission to place 100 parolees in civil service positions in major city agencies. Matthews noted the creation of "a working partnership representing all elements of the local criminal justice system." On this point he further stated:

> The necessity for leaders in the different phases of the system to meet and

discuss problems has created a new awareness of mutual needs and inter-relationships. This awareness, in turn, has led to the development of plans and programs which emphasize not only the needs of individual components within the criminal justice system but also the needs which transcend the responsibility of any one agency.

In conclusion, Matthews emphasized the capacity of local regional groups to plan as indicated in Chicago, provided the federal government supplies the funds and permits the local groups to use the funds as they see fit.

Revising the Criminal Code to Reduce Crime

It should in theory be obvious that one way to reduce crime would be to reduce the number of situations which are regulated by the criminal code. Thus, where regulations do not make drunkenness a crime, getting drunk is not a criminal offense. The practical implication is that with courts overloaded, penal institutions crowded and doing, in general, a poor job of rehabilitation, and with other aspects of the system of criminal justice rather ineffective, there should be a critical and continuing effort to scrutinize the criminal code. The scrutiny should include attention to possibilities of simplifying the code by eliminating provisions intended to regulate conduct that is not actually criminal. Thus a matter of definition arises, to differentiate crimes from misdemeanors, or from lesser offenses against socially approved behavior. But it should be observed that new enactments or repeals, and new court rulings in criminal cases, continuously revise the definition to some extent.

There has been substantial recent criticism of the criminal code and argument for simplifying it in the general sense described. Smith and Pollack[41] set forth this view with considerable illustrative detail:

An effective criminal justice system must be confined to dealing only with conduct which is *dangerous* to persons or property. It should not be concerned with either culturally determined behavior preferences which do not adversely affect others, or offenses so petty that they can be safely handled informally. This first step toward reform should be elimination of morals offenses, such as drunkenness, gambling, obscenity, Sabbath breaking, and unorthodox sexual conduct between consenting adults. Prohibition should have taught us that virtue cannot be legislated. The 18th amendment did not end drunkenness; it only increased organized crime. The thought of homosexual activity may be repulsive to heterosexuals, but such activity is not *dangerous.* The same can be said of gambling, prostitution, and to some extent of drug use. There is less scientific evidence of the harmfulness of using tobacco or alcohol. (While drug use is connected to at least half and possibly two-thirds of the crimes charges to defendants in our metropolitan criminal courts, such crime is related to the effort to obtain either the drugs or the money for the drugs rather than to the effect of using drugs *per se.*) If we cannot prevent smoking or drinking by law, we cannot prevent drug use (and many other morals offenses) by law. To the extent that such conduct can be modified at all, education and socialization are far

more effective than coercion. In any case we cannot *afford* coercion because the numbers of defendants created are causing the breakdown of
our criminal justice system and not permitting us to handle truly dangerous criminals. (Authors' emphasis.)

The authors urged treating drug addiction as a medical problem rather than
as a police problem, with authorized physicians able to dispense necessary drugs
on a free or economical basis, and with such personal psychotherapy and
such community therapy as seems appropriate. Criminal law would then
focus on illegal drug importation and peddling. They considered it dis-
astrous to try to limit the supply of heroine without providing a legal source,
and added: "Therapeutic rather than primitive handling for individual users
will take the pressure off the addict in the street to the end that the public will
be spared crimes of violence and the criminal justice system will be relieved of
part of its present unmanageable burden." They suggested that many forms
of behavior which continue on the criminal list might be handled through
informal administrative channels by personnel who operate essentially on a
civil-service basis. Such behavior includes "violations of the housing law,
factory and sanitary codes, as well as disorderly conduct, moving traffic
violations, loitering, minor shoplifting, and petty larceny."

There is a fundamental note of experimentation in the authors' suggestions.
They recognized that problems will arise but that the status quo will result
in further deterioration, perhaps with the kind of functioning union between
extremes of moralism and of gangsterism which characterized prohibition
days.

At his conclusion of a research study based on a fellowship grant by the
American Judicature Society, Boruchowitz[42] arrived at conclusions similar
to those of Smith and Pollack. He stated:

Half of the people in American prisons and half of the cases in American courts are there as a result of behavior in which no one was injured.
Delay in providing justice in other cases could be significantly reduced
and more just treatment could be given to the perpetrators of victimless
"crimes" if these kinds of behavior were decriminalized and removed
from the criminal courts to other public and private agencies whose underlying purpose would be to help, not to punish.[43]

2. Emphasis on Correction and Rehabilitation

During the past several decades there has been a growing trend to work with
delinquents on the basis of correcting their shortcomings and rehabilitating
them into full citizenship status, rather than on the basis of punishment and
isolation from the standpoint of revenge and of preventing their infecting
other members of the community. The growth has been slow, and as judged
by attitudes and practices that carry over from the past, such growth could not
presently be described as completed.

Both economic and humanitarian considerations have been involved in the
change, and some aspects of economic development have probably supplied

the foundation on which the humanitarianism has rested. In the latter respect, the rehabilitation of delinquents resembles the rehabilitation of physically or mentally handicapped persons.

Perhaps four avenues of economic consideration concerning rehabilitation might be recognized: (a) the cost of carrying on programs of correction and of general rehabilitation; (b) the extended custodial and associated cost outlays that would be involved if no rehabilitation were attempted; (c) the earning, taxpaying, and other social-contribution potential which rehabilitation makes possible; (d) the general influence and material standard of living which tends to accompany economic prosperity, with resources to support many rehabilitation or other undertakings which a century ago were beyond the reach of the American culture. Item four has been a major factor in the growth of compassion and of humanitarian idealism during the past century. Without material resources for implementation, lofty humanitarian ideals are rather empty.

Local Jurisdiction and Criminal Justice

Probably the average American does not realize the extent to which the county jail functions in our system of criminal justice, or the small extent to which jails have changed over successive decades relative to changes in other aspects of the culture. It should be observed that the rural nature and scatter of the culture in which the Founding Fathers worked and thought, and the mistrust which they had for centralized authority, made it easy to look upon the county as the responsible unit for handling most types of public offenders. The part of that responsibility which is of major concern in the present connection relates to the county jails.

Bates[44] reviewed historic and recent information on the nature of these institutions and their relationship to criminal justice. He noted the report of two French observers[45] who came to the United States in 1832 to study our prisons. They commented on new prisons for convicts with one- or two-year sentences, and on there being nothing comparable for persons of shorter terms or for persons who had only been indicted but not convicted. Bates quoted thus from their report:

> In respect to the latter (jail) nothing has been changed: disorder, confusion, mixture of different ages and moral characters, all vices of the old system still exist for them. . . . It is easy in fact to conceive, that he who has not yet been pronounced guilty, and he who has committed but a crime or misdemeanor comparatively slight, ought to be surrounded by much greater protection than such as are more advanced in crime, and whose guilt has been acknowledged.
>
> Arrested persons are sometimes innocent and always supposed to be so. How is it that we should suffer them to find in the prison (jail) the corruption which they did not bring with them. . . . There is evidently a deficiency in a prison system which offers anomalies of this kind.

Bates next commented on observations made about a century later by a Commission of Prisons for the British Isles[46] and reported in 1935. Part of Bates' quote, from commission statements on county jails, follows:

> Young and old, virtuous and depraved, innocent and double-dyed, are thrown into the closest association by night and day. For the most part, they spend the whole day in idleness, reading tattered newspapers or playing cards, herded in cages, devoid of proper sanitation, with little change of exercise or occupation. . . . There they sit and lounge and lie this day, rotting in the fetid air, and though all agree that these things are unspeakably evil, yet *they continue from year to year*, and the public conscience is not sufficiently aroused to demand a cleaning of the stable. (Emphasis added.)

The 1971 report by a senior probation officer from England, who was visiting prisons in the United States,[47] referred to the same conditions in some county jails that has been reported by the earlier French and English observers, although he noted a contrast "to this barbarism" in some of the institutions which he visited.

Police and county sheriffs who are in charge of local jails over the county, said Bates, usually excuse the deplorable conditions on grounds of lack of funds and lack of time and reform developments during short-term sentences. One need not deny the truth in these responses in order to recognize that great harm can be done in a short time, or in order to recognize two major unlisted shortcomings: lack of imagination on the part of responsible personnel, and lack of their commitment to the idea of rehabilitation in contrast with punishment.

Bates also quoted from recent statements by Americans with extensive experience in prison work. One federal prison inspector referred to the jail as "unbelievably filthy." He added that for the men and women who are confined there, not under sentence but simply awaiting trial, it "generally affords ample time and opportunity to assure inmates a complete course in every kind of viciousness and crime." It is, the inspector concluded, "a melting pot in which the worst elements of the raw material of the criminal world are brought forth, blended and turned out in absolute perfection." Bates also noted the observation of a former Commissioner of Corrections in a major city, who characterized the local county jail as "the prime gateway to our penitentiaries and reformatories."

There will not be much improvement in jail conditions, reasoned Bates, unless the state assumes complete responsibility for short-term prisoners. This seemed to be much like the state assuming such responsibility for mental hospitals, major highways, as well as important aspects of public education and public health services. He noted a nationwide jail census, made as of March 15, 1970, that showed a population of 160,863 in the 4,037 locally administered adult jails which had authority to hold persons for forty-eight hours or longer. Of this number, 52 percent had not yet been convicted.

The general situation described by Bates makes it easy to recall frequent reference in the literature to recidivism; the "revolving door" syndrome; programs and institutions for the correction of offenders, but which do not correct; etc. However, one should also note the extensive recommendation for prison facilities in small units and for general community participation in the rehabilitation of offenders—as subsequently reviewed in this study.[48]

Civil Disabilities Faced By Offenders

A difficulty often encountered in rehabilitating public offenders relates to civil disabilities—that is, the loss of rights because of being an offender. Some of the disabilities linger after the offender has met the penalties levied by the existing system regarding the offense committed.

Cohen and Rivkin[49] have commented thus:

> These "civil disabilities," imposed by every state and the Federal Government upon many convicted offenders, may deprive these persons of such privileges as voting, holding public office, obtaining many jobs and occupational licenses, entering judicially enforceable instruments, serving as juror or judiciary, maintaining family relationships, obtaining insurance and pension benefits, and many others.

Such disabilities, commented the authors, prevent the ex-offender from returning to the role of a responsible citizen with a stake in community well-being. They referred to the prospects of a person with a "criminal record" qualifying for public office and to the possibility of more limited restrictions which would adequately protect the public interest. They added: "It is also arguable that the United States should adopt the Swedish system of permitting informed voters to elect the candidate of their choice, irrespective of his criminal record."[50]

Many Americans are familiar with job application blanks, for both public and private employment, which ask if the applicant has ever been arrested or incarcerated because of some public offense. The authors commented on the particular role of this type of inquiry with respect to licensed occupations, with the increasing number of occupations which require license (i.e., barbers, chauffeurs, some food handlers, pharmacists, teachers, physicians).

After specific illustration of other disabilities, noted in the initial quote, the authors made certain recommendations for reducing the disabilities at the same time as providing adequate public protection. They recommended: (1) uniformity among state and federal jurisdictions as to what the disabilities shall be; (2) examination of the whole system of disabilities, and elimination of those which are not necessary for public protection; (3) scrutiny of the list of prohibitions, so that the offender loses only those rights and privileges which are related to his particular criminal offense; and (4) assurance that the disabilities will be removed as soon as the convict's rehabilitation process indicates that such action is warranted.[51]

A basic point of conflict in the disabilities situation should be mentioned. When the state proclaims its interest in rehabilitating public offenders, and invests substantial amounts of money and professional manhours in the process, it should not unnecessarily maintain other operations which inhibit the rehabilitative process. However, it seems reasonable to say that the state has even greater responsibility to protect its general citizenry from further criminality than it has to rehabilitate past offenders. But such general civic responsibility does not rule out the possibility of closer scrutiny regarding particular disabilities and the relationship between disabilities which apply to a particular case and the offense committed in that case.[52]

It is worthwhile to note similarities between the problems described concerning the relationship of disabilities to offenses and the appropriateness of disciplinary measures sometimes taken in educational institutions. These measures relate to the period from the primary grades through the college. While the remedial efforts in such institutions may not be called rehabilitation, the process of modifying future behavior so as more acceptably to fit the mores is much the same. Educational institutions often proclaim objectives concerning the moral growth and general development of competence in students, but maintain regulations and procedures which conflict with those objectives. Most educational institutions do not assume much functional responsibility for the student who drops out or is pushed out because of violations, but the state in general cannot assume comparable nonchalance regarding violators of the criminal code. And less nonchalance on the part of educational institutions might well reduce the subsequent offender case load on the state.

The Job as a Tool in Rehabilitation

The role of jobs in delinquency prevention and in rehabilitation has received attention from several standpoints, although many Americans seem to think in terms of handling delinquency largely through prison arrangements.

Writing in 1971, Rosow[53] commented: "Prisons, as bad as they are, get almost all of the corrections dollar." He supplemented: "It is estimated that of $1¼ billion spent on prisons, perhaps $30 to $40 million goes for rehabilitation." He noted that state employment services were typically asked "to shoulder the difficult task of job development services and placement, with little assistance and less advance notice," which he considered to be unfortunate.

Rosow elaborated on three aspects of rehabilitation which deserve more attention than they receive. One aspect concerns pretrial intervention by rehabilitation effort, which he thought was particularly important in the case of young first offenders. He reported on an experiment with selected defendants sixteen to twenty-six years old, charged primarily with economic offenses, and recruited from enrollment in a ninety-day period of voluntary participation before judicial review of their cases was made. Each defendant was given "job or placement assistance, group and individual counseling, remedial education, and other assistance as required." In evaluating three years of experience on the project, Rosow stated: "Of 753 young offenders accused of such things as petit larceny, attempted auto theft, forgery and simple assault, charges against 468 have been dropped, while 285 were returned to normal court processing, primarily because of unsatisfactory performance. Charges were dismissed at a rate of 76 percent for adult enrollees and 40 percent for juveniles." He added: "Favorably terminated participants committed further criminal acts at a rate less than one-half that of a control group which did not receive project services. Over 1,000 job and training placements were made, with the employment rate among former adult enrollees a year after leaving more than double that at the time of enrollment. At a program cost of a little over $500 per enrollee, the project exhibited a benefit-cost ratio of at least 2 to 1."[54]

On the basis of results with the first project, Rosow referred to extending the pretrial intervention work to seven other major American cities, thus expanding initial enrollment to over 4,000 new participants. He urged a massively expanded probation system which could utilize community educational, employment, and training resources. He noted: "Potentially much more effective than institutionalization and obviously cheaper, probation remains virtually an unexplored frontier for rehabilitation."

The second aspect of rehabilitation service which deserves increased attention concerned fidelity bonds, to insure employers of satisfactory work performance by ex-offenders whom they hire. On this point, Rosow stated that the Labor Department bought fidelity bonds for over 2,300 ex-offenders, "including inmates released after completing the skilled training programs. Only 30 defaulted." As to bonding, he further stated:

> Our studies show former prisoners able to hold jobs otherwise unobtainable without bonding assistance. Further, employers are often motivated to review their regular requirements for subsequent hires. As a result, we are now providing bonding assistance at all institutions where we provide skill training.
>
> We are going even further. We have so much confidence we are extending the program nationwide to make bonding assistance available through more than 2,200 local employment service offices for all ex-offenders who apply—and who can demonstrate that they are barred from accepting a specific job offer solely because of inability to secure a commercial bond. Significantly, the bonding company substantially reduced its rates to us and has now agreed to give standard coverage rates to any bondee for 18 months without a paid default (sic) if he is unable to get commercial bonding.

The third aspect of rehabilitation service, deserving more attention, relates to volunteer service by private agencies. Rosow especially noted volunteer work in corrections by the Junior Chamber of Commerce, and stated: "There are now all-inmate Jaycee Chapters in over 100 penal institutions." He thus mentioned specific chapter activities of inmates: "These men, who all-too-often have no other constructive activity available, are addressing thousands of envelopes for charity drives, and planning social service programs to mobilize assistance for the retarded, the blind, and the sick in the world outside." Rosow mentioned an Illinois development in which a statewide Employment Program for Ex-Offenders is sponsored by the Jaycees.[55] He also mentioned satisfaction expressed by Chrysler and by Caterpillar Tractor about their experience in employing ex-offenders, and he then continued: "When hundreds of employers have dispensed with bonding requirements after experience with ex-inmates, when thousands of men and women voluntarily devote hundreds of thousands of hours to working with offenders, we should be aware (that) something significant is taking place."

In concluding observations, Rosow emphasized greater coordination, both among different agencies of government and between private and governmental agencies.[56]

Centralized Institutions Versus Autonomous Communities

There has been extensive criticism of institutions as being unable to exert any lasting corrective influence on offenders, and praise for the great promise residing in community-based programs, which allegedly provide "normal" avenues for integrating the offender into community life.

Some of the comments along the lines indicated are reflected by materials listed in the accompanying footnote.[57]

A rather analytical comparison of institution-community status, dealing with when and how correctional efforts actually do correct, was made by Quay.[58] He reviewed certain theories on the causes of delinquency, such as one's being poor, lacking opportunity, having unfavorable family background, associating with criminals, etc. But he noted that most persons with such background influences do not become criminal offenders and that more specific analysis was necessary to determine why others do become offenders. He referred to the need for a conceptualization that recognizes behavior change as the core of correction and that such change demands individualized effort along social, emotional, educational, and vocational lines. Quay emphasized the need for better trained staffs, as well as better designed and less crowded facilities, to do the job. He also pointed to the need for follow-up or "aftercare," so that the "new behaviors and skills which the offender takes with him when he returns to society must somehow be maintained in that society." He observed that such aftercare as was being provided was seldom under the control of persons who were responsible for the institutional correction. Essential coordination was thus lacking.

Quay thought there was something resembling a fadlike shift from derogation of institutional effort to unanalytical recommendation of community programs. He commented that the shift in location where service is rendered "from the hospital to community has not proved to be the expected panacea for mental health. Neither will it prove to be a panacea for corrections." He continued:

> What is needed in corrections is some fundamental and basic changes (sic) in the nature of the service delivered. Inadequately trained personnel charged with carrying out poorly thought-out and minimally-supported programs cannot be expected to do any better in the community than in the institution. In fact, there is a good possibility that they will do worse particularly from the standpoint of the community itself. The community is, after all, entitled to some protection during the process of correction.
>
> We will be totally irresponsible if we continue to neglect the crying need for effective correctional programs in institutions using as the latest excuse the illusion that a loosely conceptualized and inadequately implemented "community corrections" will solve all of our problems.

He maintained that institutions could correct, when given proper facilities, adequately trained personnel, and feasible conceptualization of what corrections should try to do. He concluded:

. . . It is totally unrealistic to consider the mission of corrections as that of "holding" the offender for some period of time, perhaps years, until society is willing to tolerate him in the community—where he can then be treated. We must begin to bring about positive changes in the offender from the day he enters the correctional system by the specification of behaviors which need to be changed and the application of an effective technology for changing them. It is erroneous to say that corrections has failed. Corrections has not yet been tried.

A recent study of corrections in California referred to the "non-system" in that state.[59] Several lines of criticism were offered respecting particular aspects of the scattered operations observed, and several recommendations were made which pointed toward greater centralization. Sections of the report which reflect criticisms bore such captions as "no agreement as to goals," "inadequate programs and treatment," "poor intergovernmental relations," "outmoded organizational structure," "lack of training," and "inappropriate allocation of funds."

In their comment on need for statewide coordination and a new state-local partnership, the authors referred to concern for "3 R's" or correction: redirection, rejuvenation, and reordering." In order to convert the "non-system" into a system, they postulated a model with the following goal orientation:

The primary goal for all of corrections should be the protection of society, i.e., *minimizing the probability of new illegal conduct.* Secondary goals, compatible with that of protecting society, include deterrence (prevention), incapacitation, rehabilitation, and reintegration. (Authors' emphasis.)

With respect to community anchorage and involvement, they stated:

Corrections should be as local and as similar to real-life situations as possible. Service can, in the great majority of cases, be most effectively provided by community supervision, preferably in the offender's own home. Institutions should be utilized as a last resort and, even then, should be community based—i.e., adjacent to and involved in a high degree of interaction with the community served.

Their "model" emphasized greater statewide coordination, particularly with regard to cost-sharing, planning new institutions, administrative organization, and staff direction. With respect to staff training and work evaluation, they stated:

The state should establish a centralized training unit, to coordinate all training activities and resources relevant to corrections throughout the State. This program should include a network of local and State trainers, from corrections and other relevant disciplines, whose primary objectives would be to assist each other in maximizing the effectiveness of correctional training.

This centralized training unit, together with its agency network, should immediately develop and implement a certification program for all correctional personnel.

Each correctional agency needs to make a vastly increased commitment to the systematic evaluation of what it is accomplishing. The State Department of Correctional Services should assume the responsibility for overall coordination and support of such research and evaluative effort.[60]

The authors thought that their model might well apply to "progressive" correctional systems in other states. They observed:

There is little reason to believe that the situation among other states that are also national leaders in the field of corrections differs much from that of the Nation's most populous state. While the study was conducted in and for California, it is submitted that the findings, model, and recommendations have applicability for other progressive correctional systems today.

Along with the emphasis on coordination among correctional agencies, it may be worthwhile to inquire anew about the role of discipline in lawful behavior and to note that most informal as well as institutional efforts to shape human values and behavior through education are forms of discipline. The point then becomes one of when measures which are intended to be disciplinary actually help produce the anticipated results; that is, to ask what the positive as well as the negative or neutral elements in the regulations are, as related to specific situations. Observing parents, teachers, and law-enforcement officers know that regulatory or disciplinary measures achieve better results if variously applied, in the light of varying circumstances.

A note that grows out of the foregoing considerations asks when punishment is an important resource in rehabilitation, in contrast with being universally looked upon as a negative influence in the process of developing constructive human relationships. Hotis[61] criticized reform movements which reject the idea of punishment and thus look entirely to curative-rehabilitation treatment of offenders. He referred to interminable delays in trial and appellate procedures as being forces which reduce the deterrent effect of law and thus support the view among criminals that crime *does* pay. From the standpoint indicated, speedy trials and prompt resolution of appeals might have considerable value in the rehabilitation of public offenders.

Chapter 3

NEWER DEVELOPMENTS AND PROFESSIONALIZATION IN CORRECTIONS AND REHABILITATION

In considering educational proposals for dealing with public offenders, one should recognize the present as a period of marked transition from emphasis on punishing offenders and separating them from the general population for the latter's protection, toward a period of analyzing the causes of their antisocial behavior and of getting them back into the mainstream of society through education and rehabilitation. However, when shift in pattern of relationships among people is made on the basis of emotion and sentimentality, rather than on the basis of analyzing data from objective study, there may be considerable likelihood of the pendulum swinging from one extreme to the other. Recent comment to the effect that our practice now regarding conviction and rehabilitation shows more adjudicative and popular humanitarian concern for the criminals, than for their actual or probable victims, may illustrate the point. Out of this kind of background, reactions tend to develop.

As a part of the objective study mentioned, one should recognize that transition in any system of dealing with people must provide for considerable experimentation on alternatives. Moreover, if a fairly large number of professionally trained persons are concerned about possible improvement in the operations involved, as in regard to corrections and rehabilitation, one should expect substantial range in alternatives offered.

1. Recent Practices in Corrections and Rehabilitation

Several types of developments in corrections and rehabilitation deserve attention in the present connection.

Range in Suggestions Regarding Correctional Programs

In her review of program suggestions, McCollum[62] referred to a rather narrow conception of education and training which often prevails and which is formulated largely in terms of a high school diploma or something equivalent to a General Educational Development (G.E.D.) certificate, plus vocational skills developed to a job-entry level. She referred to need for a broader conception which also includes content and skills to "stimulate and facilitate involvement in social, economic, and cultural pursuits and the ability to seek entry into and to take advantage of available opportunity systems." She noted the substantial need of most prisoners for education and training, and stated: "Most of the 4,000 county and local jails in the United States offer no programs at all."

McCollum saw a basic weakness in programs which are offered by state and federal agencies because of their limitation to concepts of high school equivalency, skill training in four or five vocational areas, and a few college-level courses. She criticized this approach as ignoring the heterogeneity of the prison population, where the inmates have little in common other than a common address. She noted an age range of fifteen to fifty years or more, with a great range in interests, aptitudes, past educational experience, and achievements. She reasoned that the educational needs of such persons could not be met by conventional school curriculums, dealt with in conventional classroom settings, with instructors of the typical school pattern. She further observed that the manual skills included in the vocational programs were seldom related to the academic courses or to the kinds of jobs available outside the prison.

It was not to be expected, thought McCollum, that traditional procedures which had not been particularly successful in the nonprison world would be more successful with the prison population. She reviewed studies on the absence of relationship between prison vocational training and post-release jobs; studies indicating that post-release jobs were not lost because of deficiencies in specific skills but because of "poor attendance, hostile attitudes, overreaction to supervision, and other nonjob-content related issues"; and studies showing a "positive relationship between a person's involvement in education and training programs while in prison, post-release employment in some job, and 'success' in staying out of prison."

It is significant that inadequancy of education and training programs has increasingly been included among grievances for which prisoners' organizations seek redress.[63] This grievance item should be viewed in relation to the general development of broad participation by the large body of persons directly affected in the decisions and operations of social and vocational institutions—i.e., student participation in the decisions of high-school and college boards and administrators, labor participation in decisions on industrial policy and management, lay representation on medical boards and in decisions concerning the availability of health services.[64]

McCollum organized her suggestions around seven points:

(1) Concern about the need for "new delivery systems" has been noted with respect to individualization of educational programs. She mentioned the interest of various religious, civic, and professional groups in this development.

(2) She reviewed possibilities embodied in the vocational voucher system, whereby individual prisoners are given vouchers which guarantee them access to certain educational services in the community, upon their meeting specified standards of conduct and completing specified time periods.[65] The cost of vouchers was favorably compared with the cost of prison confinement, whereby McCollum noted: "In addition, we know that prison experience almost guarantees recidivism."

(3) The prison is a specialized learning center, she noted, suggesting small prisons to accommodate perhaps 200 persons which would be located near hospitals or other service facilities. She thought of different prisons specializing in different vocational programs, with the assignment of prisoners to particular institutions according to vocational interests and potentialities.

(4) Where the suggestions of item (3) do not seem possible, McCollum thought it feasible to develop the larger prisons into "all purpose" educational technology centers—with the broad individualization mentioned earlier. She emphasized "computer assisted instruction, dial access video-tape systems, and programmed materials packaged and delivered in a variety of ways," as offering both scope and individualization.

(5) She observed that Texas, Connecticut, and Illinois had created "statewide school districts which embrace correctional institutions in the state." The school-district approach was considered quite significant, with the program looked upon as providing one type of special education.

(6) Another possibility concerned "educational diagnostic and referral centers." This idea was related to the observation that many persons in prison do not actually belong there, but should be in "residential correctional facilities in which security is the last rather than the first priority." McCullom stated: "Basic literacy as well as industrial literacy programs might be offered on-site, but beyond that level the individual would be referred to an already existing education or training opportunity. The institution could be residential or nonresidential depending on circumstances."

(7) She also commented: "The nationwide chain of 1,100 community colleges offers another possible resource for relocating and redirecting correctional education effort." She thought that such schools could serve "as diagnostic and testing centers, developers of program plans for individual offenders, and effective referral agents to other community counseling, occupational, or educational institutions." She also referred to seeking out particular jurisdictions which might be willing to use the community and its college as "precommitment diversionary centers." She added: "These colleges could serve as facilitators in the delivery of any services necessary to divert the first offender from commitment to a correctional institution." McCullom was mindful of the extensive cooperation which such a program would require between professional workers in criminal justice, the general community and its college, as well as the parents and students personally involved.[66]

An item of basic social philosophy undergirds McCollum's suggestions on remedial measures. If a wide range of individualization is provided according to age, prior experience, aptitudes, interests, learning style, etc., for inmates whose chief common denominator is that of "serving time," when comparable individualization is *not* available to the nonprison or law-abiding population, is the culture actually "rewarding" the inmates for having become criminals? Should the development of individualized programs for inmates be accepted as a means of alerting the general civilian population to the mediocre job that the regular system of public education and vocational counseling does in the broad civic area of delinquency prevention?

To what extent are the individualized developments suggested, along with arrangements concerning educational vouchers, prisons as specialized learning centers, and other "treatment" possibilities such as McCollum reviews, to be regarded as comparable to "Head Start" programs for some negro and other culturally deprived children as aimed at developing readiness to learn in school situations, or comparable to minimum public welfare standards set up in other areas? Various philosophical gyrations about "compensatory education," or compensatory measures in some other direction, could relate to the prison or other programs noted.

Other gyrations might ask about the justice accorded by the system to individuals who live at standards lower than those provided for welfare or rehabilitation clients, but who must pay taxes to help provide the programs for those clients. If the reward for such taxpayers resides in some vague or mystic sense of independence and moral superiority, then what happens if these socially important characteristics are eroded by an easy forgiveness of shortcomings and an easy return of delinquents to full civic and moral status?

Creative value might lie in the usefulness which such "experimental" programs of corrections for public offenders have in alerting the general population to needed revisions and updatings in major aspects of our social structure; that is, provided the results of such programs actually become embodied in a broad approach to adult education. But if they are not looked upon as experimental in the sense described and are not embodied as suggested, they could become the basis of popular resentment and of reversion to an earlier emphasis on punishment of offenders and general disregard of "ne'er-do-wells."

Comparisons are often made in dollar costs of the special educational and rehabilitation programs for offenders, relative to estimated costs in future delinquency, court action, and custodial or welfare service which seem likely to result in case of failure to provide rehabilitation programs. The role of dollar considerations in these connections emphasizes two fundamental considerations in organized human relationships: (1) the role of interlocking between material factors and humanitarianism in determining ethics; (2) the tendency of persons who control the social structure to bask in the comforts of the status quo, until some explosion disrupts those comforts and demands a revision of practices. But such interlocking relationship between materialism and humanitarianism is not new, as applied to the rehabilitation of public offenders; it applies in general to tax-supported public education, public health services, police protection, etc., and perhaps to the opportunity of some individuals to conduct a business in the community at a profit.

Social Deviance and Presentence Rehabilitation

In his concern about the the role of the local community in rehabilitating public offenders, Gardner[67] stressed the idea of delinquency as a matter of social deviance; of such deviance as a problem that springs from the community, and must be treated as a community problem rather than merely as a correctional-agency problem; and of the greatest protection as resting on integrating the delinquent into a self-motivating and nondeviant role in the community. He emphasized the idea of partnership and coordinated relations between various community agencies, with particular reference to home-finding associations, educational institutions, goodwill services, community mental health centers, and the office of vocational rehabilitation. Passing reference was made to such other groups as Alcoholics Anonymous, Catholic Charities, Lutheran Social Services, the Salvation Army, and to various human relations commissions and educational opportunity programs.[68] He also referred to "state juvenile aftercare agents."

Gardner noted the important status of the district court, as "the institution that begins the whole process leading to any attempt at resocialization." He gave weight to a partnership relation among the different agencies indicated, and continued:

> The partnership can look beyond past criminal record, from a broader perspective than one of strict legal formality, to a time when programs can be discussed and feasible methods of control and rehabilitation can be formulated *before sentencing*. This would make the court the first community resource in any program of rehabilitation by enabling the adult parole and probation officer to enter the resocialization process at the earliest possible stage. Such a resource and partnership orientation would make the administration of justice a more fulfilling process for society and client alike. Criminal justice viewed thus becomes a process of rehabilitation and integration in a much fuller sense than just giving the offender "his day in court."[69] (Emphasis added.)

Scheon[70] described a Probationed Offenders Rehabilitation and Training program, which has served three counties in Southeastern Minnesota since 1969. It serves as a "live-in, community-based, community-directed, community-supported treatment program for adult and juvenile offenders." The program was conceived by two district court judges, who were dissatisfied with conventional probation or imprisonment. The program aims to control objectionable behavior by changing the lifestyle of offenders, in order to avoid prison and training-school experience.[71]

Juvenile Justice and Delinquency

With respect to juvenile justice relative to delinquency, Judge Young[72] traced the evolution over 250 years of the idea of justice for juvenile offenders. He commented that the basic ideas involved were developed long before legislation established juvenile courts, much as the basic principles embodied in the Magna Carta were developed before they were set forth in that document at Runnymede in 1215. Thus, in neither case was the resulting system an experiment, reasoned Young, in depending primarily on subsequent testing.

In determining whether the juvenile courts are a success, Young noted certain criteria. With respect to law, a principle is successful if it can be and is adopted for use beyond the area in which it arose. He observed that criminal courts and correctional systems are presently following the use of probation staffs, as inaugurated by juvenile courts. He further observed that the juvenile court doctrine of rehabilitation instead of punishment as the goal of justice was broadly accepted and "is now being loudly proclaimed by the Chief Justice of the United States as the solution for our problems of crime." Young continued: "The training programs for new judges which are now an accepted practice, even in federal courts, were first created by the juvenile courts. Imitation is not only the sincerest form of flattery. It is the hallmark of success."[73]

Judge Young made summary comments on individual juvenile delinquents whom he later knew as occupants of responsible positions in the community. He realistically commented that he did not "win them all," but stated that the juvenile court had been more successful in achieving its purpose than had, for example, the criminal courts. He reasoned that failure of the juvenile court system as yet to have reached its maximum potential afforded no justification for tearing down what had been accomplished. He inferred that community underachievers might use it as a guide.[74]

Drug Abuse

One area of newer concern in correctional programs relates to abuse in using nonnarcotic drugs. A recent report referred to a widespread and growing abuse of these drugs (barbiturates, amphetamines and other stimulants, sedatives, tranquilizers, antidepressants, and hallucinogens), available on the illicit market.[75] After reviewing certain empirical data, the authors estimated that "some 30 percent of the Nation's adult population are regular users of one or more of the tranquilizers, sedatives, and stimulants." They suggested that "a new substantial drug-abusing population is in the process of emerging and this fact has remained hidden from probation, parole, correctional and mental health personnel." From the standpoint of both abuse and treatment they gave especial consideration to three drug groups: barbiturates, amphetamines, and hallucinogens (mainly LSD).

In conclusion, these authors stated:

> The abuse of many nonnarcotic drugs is increasing in every segment of our population. Law enforcement, probation, and parole personnel can expect to encounter these abusers with increasing frequency. While such personnel would not be expected to administer indicated medical procedures, they must be familiar with symptomatic behavior and appropriate referral sources. In all probability, as trained interpreters of behavior with long-duration and high-frequency contact with their clients, these professionals will be the initial detectors of the abuse of drugs. They will be required to make the appropriate referrals for medical treatment, and will be the primary providers of long-term aftercare service.

From the standpoint of drug abuse in America as a medical problem rather than as a penal one, McNamara made a historical study regarding certain drugs.[76] He stated that for over 100 years drug abuse in America had been considered a medical problem, but that by 1925 our policy had changed so that drug addicts were made virtual outlaws. He further stated that the impetus for change came from the Protestant Missionary Societies and Temperance organizations. He added that these agencies were so thorough and successful in their efforts that the problem is still discussed in highly symbolic temperance rhetoric.[77]

Conjugal Visits and Home Furloughs

Perhaps it is as an aspect of a relaxed or nonrestrictive atmosphere in rehabilitation development that there is considerable attention to conjugal visits and home furloughs for prisoners. Hayner[78] studied attitudes toward conjugal visits in several countries of Latin America, and in the United States and Canada. He noted differences in the practice, as observed in the Latin and the Anglo-Saxon cultures. There were also some differences among Latin American countries.

While most of the Latin American countries permitted sex visits by wives, fiancees (novias), and sometimes friends or "companions of the home," there was substantial variation in whether prostitutes might make such visits. According to Hayner, Peru and Columbia permit no conjugal visits. He indicated that since there is no exact Spanish equivalent for the word "furlough," referring to sex visits by prisoners outside the prison walls, comparisons between the two cultures on this point were difficult. Apparently furloughs are prohibited in Columbia. With respect to Chile, Hayner observed: "Conjugal visits are not permitted but social visits are informal and 'petting' is permitted."

Apparently the situation in Anglo-America was more spotted and more restrictive. Hayner reported that in Canada by 1969, both furloughs and conjugal visits had been made legal, and that in Saskatchewan a correctional center was experimenting in this field. He reported an experimental development in Mississippi, including the observation that each woman who visits "must be legally married to the prisoner she visits." He stated: "One-half of 464 prisoners rated 'keeping marriages from breaking up' as the most helpful result of conjugal visits." Hayner also reported: "In California conjugal visiting seems to have reached its most acceptable form for Anglo-America." The program there apparently emphasizes preserving the family, with sexual intercourse as incidental to that objective. He cited a report from one prison which stated that many wives had expressed to the prison staff "that they were not at all sure they wanted to continue their marriage. However, after having family visiting they were able to strengthen the marriage and have abandoned separation plans." In a final statement, he observed:

> On the basis of impressions of Mexican penal institutions, conjugal visits seem to cut down but not eliminate homosexual behavior. They seem also to help create a more relaxed social climate. Some of these visits result in improvement of family life: in other cases problems develop. Little data are available, such as follow up studies, to test the actual results of variously administered conjugal visit or furlough programs. At least by the year 2000, and perhaps before that time, for inmates and their wives who meet certain standards, many prisons in Anglo-America will permit both furloughs to visit home and conjugal visits.[79]

Rights of Offenders to Rehabilitative Treatment

When it is proclaimed that the purpose of correctional agencies is to rehabilitate rather than to punish, it must be assumed that rehabilitation will demand some kind of treatment. The basic question then relates to what constitutes treatment; and also who has authority and responsibility for determining when particular kinds of treatment shall be provided, and what constitutes adequacy of treatment? Embedded in this question is the matter of what party of parties are intended to benefit from the treatment and can therefore be said to have enforceable rights concerning treatment.[80]

A substantial review of rights to treatment for prisoners was made by Snowden,[81] with particular emphasis on statutory provisions. After preliminary consideration of the long-standing failure of correctional institutions actually to achieve correction in offenders, the author traced the evolution of rights to treatment. He commented that such rights appeared with respect to the mentally ill because of the inadequacy of treatment afforded them. Whether failure to provide treatment is a violation of constitutional due process, on the assumption that the sole reason for placing an insane person in a mental institution rather than in some other place of detention is the expectation that he will receive treatment, has essentially been rendered moot because of specific provisions in statutory enactments—said Snowden.

He stressed *Rouse v. Cameron*[82] as the first American case to authorize a remedy based on a statutory right to treatment. As one point he stated: "Perhaps the most significant aspect of the *Rouse* decision is the remedial basis of the opinion. The court stated that continuing failure to provide suitable and adequate treatment could not be justified by lack of staff or facilities. The right to treatment was clearly a present right and not a matter of administrative grace."[83]

Sexual psychopaths constitute another specific category to which Snowden gave detailed attention. While significant differences exist between members of this group and mentally ill persons, Snowden observed that in the pertinent case reviewed the court followed *Rouse* in significant respects—particularly as to staff and facilities for treatment. He commented: "A violation of the individual's rights to treatment also violates society's right to self-defense."

A third category of persons involving rights to treatment consists of juveniles, which category Snowden reviewed in terms of *Creek* v. *Stone.*[84] In this case the court reasoned that failure to provide psychiatric care vitiated the justification for confining the youth in a receiving home, pending trial upon arrest for robbery. Another case[85] involved detention of a truant youth by the Department of Public Welfare, without affording him adequate treatment. The statute said that a child so detained shall be provided "custody, care, and discipline as nearly as possible equivalent to that which should have been given him by his parents." Failure to provide such care made the detention illegal.

Defective delinquents constituted a fourth category of persons in terms of which rights to treatment were considered. A Maryland act[86] provided for the "confinement and treatment" of a person who "evidences a propensity toward criminal activity, and who is found to have either such intellectual deficiency or emotional unbalance, or both, as to clearly demonstrate an actual danger to society." Confinement without treatment denied equal protection of the laws for the defendant, as compared with others who had committed the same crime but were not similarly confined.

Snowden emphasized two common factors, underlying the foregoing categories of persons, with regard to treatment. One was that the purpose of confinement is rehabilitation. The other was that the statutory language stipulated a duty to treat. He reviewed statutes from several states which embody the same factors. In this connection, he said: "The statutory language demonstrates that the enacting legislatures recognized the purpose of the prison system to be reformation of the individual and the protection of society." Considerable logic supports the view that the degree of protection afforded depends on the degree of reformation; also that the people in general have a right to expect that persons who are released from prison were benefited by their confinement and are hence less dangerous to the public.

After a review of the advantages of statutory provisions, Snowden devoted attention to machinery for enforcing statutory rights to treatment. He commented: "Almost every state has enacted some type of administrative procedure act," and noted that penal and correctional institutions are administrative agencies. Such acts are intended to require those agencies to provide the statutory treatment for offenders.

Another aspect of enforcement concerns standing to sue, either under administrative procedure acts or otherwise. Problems in this connection relate more to suit in the public interest, based on the statutory treatment as a protection for the public, than to the offender's right to personal benefits from treatment. While statutes often include vague statements about the rights of interested citizens, residents, and taxpayers to sue, problems of establishing a pecuniary interest in the case may be complex. In this connection Snowden said:

> Perhaps the most significant group of persons who appear to have standing (to sue) would be those organized especially to seek rehabilitation of prisoners. . . . Foremost among these groups would appear to be the groups which comprise the American Correctional Association. Certainly ex-offender groups across the country and groups of concerned citizens organized in good faith to promote prisoner rehabilitation would also be entitled to standing. All of these groups meet the test of being aggrieved in fact. They also meet the test of arguably being within the zone of interests protected by the statute. It would appear that if a right to treatment is to become effectual its enforcement would fall upon these groups.

Concerning the personal rights of individuals who are also in a position to assert public rights, Snowden noted from the Supreme Court: "That a court is called upon to enforce public rights, and not the interests of private property, does not diminish its power to protect such rights."[87]

One might note a trend for federal courts to intervene where state courts seem unable or unwilling to deal with problems of public interest; but Snowden mentioned a federal-court handicap in dealing with correctional matters, where the institutions involved depend on state legislatures for their ongoing status. He suggested that state statutes which provide enforceable rights to treatment avoid federal complications regarding constitutional mandates.

He concluded: "The right to treatment properly enforced, can insure that the field of corrections will not become insulated from the view of the public and that the opportunity to rehabilitate criminal offenders will not be lost."[88]

2. Nonprofessionals, and Professional Correction Service

A trio of writers[89] in the corrections field referred to a significant development in the form of "indigenous nonprofessionals." These persons are recruited from the same social class as the delinquent population served, and some of them may be former offenders. These authors emphasized two causal factors in the development: shortage of professional workers and "mounting disenchantment with some professional treatment models." The shortage was viewed in terms of the inefficient use of professional competence, through persons with professional qualifications being expected to do all of the different tasks involved in corrections; whereas a better use of said competence would result from differentiating among tasks and assigning many tasks to paraprofessionals, aides, and voluntary helpers, who were under the supervision and counsel of professionals. One reference compared the change to that in health fields, from the age of the country doctor to that of the clinic.

A major portion of the report by the trio dealt with a research study in Chicago, relating to Probation Officer Assistants (P.O.A.'s). The subjects were negro and white men, at least twenty-one years old, who resided in Chicago; who were probationers, parolees, or persons on mandatory release; and whose offenses fell within restricted limits. There was an experimental group of 161 offenders, and a control group of 141 offenders who received "normal" supervision from probation staff officers. Each subject in the experimental group was assigned a P.O.A., and the two professionals each supervised twenty P.O.A.'s. (Further comment on this study appears at a subsequent point.)

It should be noted that when reference is made to professionalization within a field of service, certain tasks or aspects of the field which are called professional are being differentiated from other aspects which are not so designated. This applies to professionalization of law-enforcement and correctional service, the same as it does to professionalization in other areas of society. Reference to change in the conception of health services, from the country doctor who is a broad generalist regarding various aspects of service to the clinic where there is a line of specialists, illustrates the point. However the general idea of differentiation should be amplified by reference to particular areas and by comparisons between corrections and other fields.

Gradation Among Service Tasks

Reference to professionalization implies that a large body of knowledge and responsibility concerning the professional field remains in a general category which is *not* selected out of the total for professional designation. Thus when knowledge in an area is sufficiently abundant for professionalization, it is assumed that much if not most of that knowledge lies in nonprofessional areas characterized by such terms as paraprofessional, aide functions, volunteer services, etc. In hospitals and related areas of health service, reference is made to laboratory or x-ray technicians, nurses' aides, orderlies, etc. In the educational field reference is increasingly made to teachers' aides, testing and statistical technicians, school nurses, guidance personnel, school accountants, etc. The legal field increasingly refers to legal aides and para-legals, dentistry to dental assistants, and somewhat the same appears in pharmacy, social work, and other fields.

With growth of knowledge in vocational areas and effort to differentiate categories of employees according to some type of competence and status arrangement, it is necessary for there to be a fairly sharp differentiation and gradation regarding the knowledge, tasks, responsibilities, etc., associated with the different employee categories. Moreover, in a dynamic society of substantial growth, the process of gradation and of redefining employee categories must be continuous. And in a service field in which profession-alization is rather new, it is easy for categories of persons who have recently become professional to continue doing chores which are carry-overs from preprofessional days. This is obviously a waste of professional competence, when under reasonable supervision those chores could be handled by persons with less extensive vocational training. Accordingly, professionalization demands an upgrading in job analysis, in testing and other evaluation of employee competence, in administrative insight and organization, and per-haps in legal or judicial conception of equal vocational opportunity.

Communication, Social Distance, and Rapport

The service vocations are characterized by providing things for people which the persons concerned desire or which the social group considers it desirable for designated categories of people to have. This means that the employees who provide the service need to know what the desires are or what the needs are considered to be. Substantial communication between those who receive and those who dispense is thus essential.

If dispensers and receivers belong to clearly different social, racial, reli-gious, political, or other categories, communication is inhibited. This is equivalent to saying that a comprehensive understanding by dispenser and receiver of each other depends on a substantial common background, not only of general knowledge but of lifestyle, trust, and commitment to improve existing conditions.

The communication, trust, rapport, capacity for personal identification, etc., is probably more important for some professional services than for others. Thus, the aspects of public welfare concerned with supplying food, clothing, or shelter may not place as heavy a draft on rapport as teacher-learner relationships in the classroom, physician-patient relationship some-times characterized as bedside manner, minister and denominational affiliate in religion, attorney and client in the legal field, or counselor and counselee in the various guidance areas. Charisma is one of the terms used regarding politicians and voters.

In the field of corrections and rehabilitation of public offenders, matters of communication and rapport may be especially important. This is because of the need which the disperser of benefits has for a substantial body of information in order to develop a constructive remedial program; the anxiety which the offender may have about possible further disciplinary action, if he reveals too much of a possibly rich background of delinquency experience; or the offender's surmise of possible futility in view of only a superficial interest of the case worker in the scope of the delinquent's problem and his need for rehabilitation.

Sensitivity to the communications and rapport situation concerning public offenders was noted in the report by Beless, Pilcher, and Ryan[90] in the selection of Probation Officer Assistants (P.O.A.'s) from the same social class, race, and cultural background as the offenders. Only negro P.O.A.'s were assigned to negro offenders, and only white P.O.A.'s to white offenders. Moreover, the P.O.A.'s selected were from the residential areas having high proportions of offenders included in the study, and some of the P.O.A.'s were former offenders. However, much the same point has sometimes been made concerning the rapport situation and teachers who are successful in ghetto schools, physicians who are successful in some types of isolated rural areas, ministers who do well in college towns or with other particularized types of congregations, etc.

The use of P.O.A.'s who have been offenders has implications beyond the corrections field. The point seems to be that one who has experienced social rejection and personal dissatisfaction because of the life he was leading sees a new life or feels a kind of rebirth of social opportunity when he is accepted back into full social participation. In addition to being able to establish a rapport with offenders who are in the process of rehabilitation, because of commonness of background with them, such a P.O.A. can look through his own dark background and perhaps see future opportunity more brightly than seemed possible before he had the dark experience. The use of previous alcoholics in the rehabilitation work of Alcoholics Anonymous and the use of former drug addicts in counseling young people or others who seem enroute to addiction are illustrative. Public school personnel have sometimes found that dropouts who have returned to school after a period of empty drift can be more effective than teachers in counseling potential dropouts to remain in school—unless the school program itself seems largely a matter of empty drift.

Perhaps with somewhat different orientation of the school to its community setting, more constructive guidance use than is typical could be made of delinquent youth who have been returned to the community from correctional institutions. The religious injunction "Ye must be born again" can thus have many broad and realistic implications.

There is another psychological dimension to the matter of rapport, in the sense of a person who is troubled by confusion, guilt, or anxiety being able to talk out his difficulties with an understanding and sympathetic listener—a kind of sounding-board therapy. The idea that sorrow or grief often relieves itself by words or other forms of expression, which are greeted with receptivity, has long been recognized by pastoral counselors and by other counselors in situations of emotional tension and conflict. In some religious settings much the same result may accompany prayer, especially if a feeling of response from the listening board can be thought of as the prayer being answered. Apparently some of our cultural ancestors experienced comparable relief and satisfaction through prayer and ritual carried out before statues, idols, sphinxes, stone lions, golden calves, bronze eagles, Wailing Walls, etc.

The key idea seems to be the release of emotional tension through some avenue that tends to be individualized by one's biological structure and habit patterns. Thus, some illiterate peasants have talked to their cows, some riding-club aristocrats have talked to their steeds, and some ten-year-old boys have talked to their dogs, all with varying degrees of certainty of understanding and rapport between the speaker and the addressee, and with indications of personal relief and satisfaction springing from presumed response by the addressee.

It would be unrealistic to assume that the emotional involvement of the typical public offender is less complicated or less amenable to a broadly based psychosocial therapy than the involvements mentioned in the preceding comments.

From Recipient to Dispenser

Preceding statements include several references to former recipients of corrective or rehabilitative service being reformed (reborn) and thus accepted into broad social participation, and through the whole experience becoming effective staff members for doing therapeutic work or dispensing rehabilitation service in recently identified cases of need. Certain further points should be noted.

(1) It seems to be a common observation in fields in which "religious zeal" is prominent that new converts to a cause are typically more enthusiastic about it than long-time adherents. While previous comment included a hint on this point, in referring to previous offenders when acting as counselors often being able to see future opportunity more brightly than they could before their delinquency and therapy, the point is noted further for emphasis.

(2) It has also been observed, by the trio reporting on the Chicago probation study and by other writers on correction and rehabilitation, that reformed clients who become counselors or dispensers of service are helped in their own further development through helping others who are walking in the former footsteps of these counselors. The universality and the extent of such further development probably depend greatly on the individuals selected.

(3) The quality of counseling provided by reformed offenders, as compared with professionally trained personnel with no comparable background or basis of rapport with current offenders, has been considered. The point nevertheless deserves emphasis since it may indicate certain myths and fantasies, in professional training and in popular attitudes, in regard to accepting into the community persons who are in the process of rehabilitation.

(4) Previous attention has been called to the possibility of reducing a functional shortage in manpower through the use of Patrol Officer Assistants or of aides and paraprofessionals in other fields. The possibility of utilizing

personnel with considerable vocational competence, but who do not have comprehensive professional training, has expanding ramifications in a culture which is continuously demanding higher levels of performance in services rendered to individuals.[91]

(5) Associated with supply of professional manpower is the dollar cost of rehabilitation and other service programs. While it may be easy to muster data to show net rehabilitation gains over probable costs for custody or similar purposes in the absence of rehabilitation programs, it is never fiscally sound to waste money through the haphazard allocation of personnel in a complex service organization.

Racial Separation and Integration

Notwithstanding the seeming position of some courts to the contrary, separation of ethnic groups in some considerations may contribute more to opportunity than integration contributes. Foregoing considerations on communication, rapport, and emotional involvement in correctional and rehabilitation work suggest the point.

In the Chicago study on Probation Officer Assistants, it was noted that only two ethnic groups were involved and that in the case of each offender the P.O.A. assigned belonged to the same ethnic group as the offender.

While rapport between authority and offender in a correctional situation may be of no greater importance than rapport between authority and learner in a public school situation, two differences are suggested. One is that although anybody who is learning is thereby modifying or reforming his personality and his stance regarding the general culture, the school child is accepted as being in a formative stage when great leeway for error is allowed.

Also, the school child is usually surrounded by favorable circumstances for making the adjustments which society approves. Much of this is reflected in methods of classroom procedure, in which teachers receive substantial preparation before they begin to teach. The importance of rapport, and of how to develop it, receive considerable attention in this preparation. In significant respects, emphasis on rapport in rehabilitating public offenders is calling attention to a need for their personality modification which is taken for granted with respect to the school child. And instead of being in a generally favorable setting, the offender is in one that is enshrouded in suspicion, if not in definite revenge. Hence, what may seem to amount to great attention to rapport in correctional work with offenders seems justified.

However, with perhaps more focal attention to race, in situations comparable to the P.O.A. arrangement, ethnic identity should become less important as broad cultural sensitivity to race declines. Concern for aiding or retarding this process may have considerable long-range bearing on correctional and rehabilitation work.

Orientation Procedure for Nonprofessionals

In any area of specialized service which is presumed to be available to people in a wide range of geographical as well as other physical and cultural circumstances, general preparation which is received in a university or comparable setting for rendering the special service must necessarily be rather general and deal with core matters. This means that there is a considerable residue of practical detail which is associated with any particular job or particular work situation.

Orientation of neophytes is thus necessary, and it is almost universally accepted in the vocational world. In fact, it is accepted beyond the vocational world. Thus, it appears when an individual transfers from one school to another, when a family moves into a new community, when starting expenses and other adjustments are associated with a new business, when newlyweds establish a household, etc. The significant point is that in each orientation circumstance, the orientation content deals as directly as possible with the situation concerned. While orientation in some of the situations noted is on a haphazard and "do-it-yourself" basis, in a professional service the orientation should be systematically planned and carried out. For the corrections worker, two focal points should be the individual personality of the offender and the job potential in the vocational world.

Nonprofessional Experience and the Recruiting of Professionals

It is fairly common for successful teacher aides to be sought as regular teachers, upon completion of their professional training. Aide status offers two-way screening. For some individuals, it can screen out teaching from further consideration as a possible vocation. For the teaching profession, it can screen out certain individuals as unpromising from the standpoint of prospective membership. There is no reason why the status of P.O.A.'s, or the status of paraprofessionals, aides, and perhaps volunteers in any field of specialized service might not have comparable value in recruiting professionals.

As the demand for public service in America becomes more extensive and more varied, competition among professions for competent recruits will increase, whereas competition from menial or from nontechnical skilled vocations will probably decline further.

With a rather long and apparently extending lead time in preparation required for several professions, the assets and limitations of fairly early nonprofessional orientation and try-out regarding particular fields should receive closer scrutiny. One type of scrutiny relates to prevocational participation as a way to help youth mature.[92]

Professional Preparation of Correction Workers

With respect to the professional training of correctional personnel, and their need and ability to harmonize their work with principles outlined by the courts, Statsky suggested the teaching of corrections law.[93] His initial emphasis emerged from the rapid changes that are taking place in corrections law and the growth in general visibility of corrections institutions during the past twenty-five years. He noted that courts are becoming less prone to follow a "hands off" policy, voiced on the ground that judges do not want to interfere with the discretion of the warden in administering an institution "unless unusual circumstances" exist. Statsky quoted Chief Justice Warren Burger's admonition to attorneys on this point:

> The system of criminal justice must be viewed as a process embracing every phase from crime prevention through the correctional system. We can no longer limit our responsibility to providing defense service for the judicial process, yet continue to be miserly with the needs of correctional institutions and probation and parole service.[94]

Statsky differentiated four training options: (1) Law Oriented-Ministerial, with training that is primarily informational, in that the instructor explains what must be done as a result of recent court decisions; (2) Law Oriented-Defensive, which regards "the law" an an enemy. "The training seeks to equip staff to provide a 'cover' to demonstrate to the courts that they are complying with the law." (3) Law Oriented-Preventive, to upgrade the staff, aiming to anticipate and avoid legal problems; and (4) Administration Oriented, in which the training emphasizes the common-sense power of the layman to address himself to common-law problems. An understanding of the law is built around the threshold concern. Statsky noted that there is too much law for a lay corrections official to pursue either of the first two options and then further explore the last two. Focus the approach on the problem of the learner rather than on the subject matter, he urged, as he set forth guidlines to help trainees to raise and answer the right questions about what they do on the job.

With respect to due process, he observed: "There can be *substantive restrictions* such as ordering an inmate to submit to a strip search or to transfer his job placement, and there can be *procedural restrictions* such as denying an inmate counsel or counsel-substitute at disciplinary proceedings or failing to give the inmate notice before he is transferred." In conclusion, Statsky commented that there did not need to be conflict between correction practice and judicial theory. His final statement was: "There is a distinct parallel between how and why courts solve problems the way they do and how correctional institutions solve their problems on their own *if corrections personnel will carefully analyze what it is that they are doing in the light of some basic guidelines*. (Emphasis by Statsky.)

Waldo[95] discussed research and training with respect to corrections personnel and service and with respect to the university's role. He saw need for a sharp dichotomy between research and training, with a further differentiation between research to develop and explore theory and research to improve the efficiency of daily correctional activities. The area of theory and the development of new information are for the university, thought Waldo, with the training of operating personnel and research on procedures to be handled by the correctional institution or a junior college. He would clearly differentiate between educating and training, and would not have universities carry on in-service training, but would have the university responsible for "educating the trainers." Recognizable "ivory tower" aloofness is essential for theoretical speculation, commented Waldo, and for setting up experiments which test theories but which can be rejected without operational trauma if outcomes are negative.

The general emphasis that Waldo placed on research at various levels and on the need for theoretical considerations in policy-making may be sounder than his rather firm insistence concerning allocation of personnel and institutions for carrying on the work. In regard to where his envisioned theoretical experiments will be tested out, or the role of close and continuous feedback in revising theory and experimental constructs, his discussion appears somewhat hazy. It is probably well for a university liberal-arts exposure to dispel existing myths about corrections, as Waldo infers, provided the exposure does not essentially substitute a different set of myths to replace the current ones.

Should one ask: are university professors and administrators, such as Waldo, likely to be overimbued with the university's ivory-tower and hierarchal status in the preparation and research supervision of both professional and operating personnel in corrections or other areas of the culture? At various points the present study has expressed the view that both competence and incompetence, with respect to both operations and policy-making, exist among both university and operating personnel. Recent emphasis by organized labor on opportunity to share in industry policy-making, and on prison inmates to share in decision-making concerning governing policy, are among developments which support the view suggested. One can note substantial value in Waldo's comments, without rejecting the possibility that operational leadership might have different ideas about the role of the university.[96]

3. Correctional Services and Cultural Priorities

It does not seem reasonable to suppose that a culture such as the United States will ever have enough material resources or trained personnel to pursue all of the social goals which imaginative persons might show to be desirable. Priorities are thus perennially involved.

From the standpoint of priorities, as related to prospective social contributions and public well-being, comparisons might here be made regarding efforts directed toward two groups: (a) public offenders and other groups who are broadly looked upon as handicapped and as being entitled to public rehabilitation provisions, in order to bring them up to some type of average status; (b) persons under thirty-five years of age who are not only free from handicaps in the foregoing sense, but who are outstanding in their past accomplishments and apparently in their future potential, and on whom the nation will primarily have to depend for its future developments and for "breakthroughs" in various aspects of achievement. One phase of the situation is reflected in statements to the effect that relative to potential, bright children and bright young adults are more handicapped and retarded than any other segment of the population.

But also from the standpoint of priorities one should note that so long as we can spend as much as we do on pet food; dog, horse, and automobile races; ball games and theatrical entertainment; resort luxuries; cosmetics, massage vibrators, and other merchantable "aids to shape and pulchritude"; television give-away shows; gourmet specials; etc.; we could provide much more richly than we do now for both the clearly handicapped and the great achievers.

Two major problems concerning professional leadership and lay support thus stand out. Probably of greatest importance is dwarfed imagination as to what could be done—what man might yet become. It is fairly easy for "leadership" to compare itself with the handicapped and conclude that the way to remove the handicaps is to do for the persons concerned somewhat more of what the leaders have seen done for themselves. This is largely, although not exclusively, a problem of method. But few "leaders" have yet envisioned the goals or conceived of the routes that would be most creative and developmental for the bright and the competent, or have yet thought of how to harmonize such goals and routes with doctrines on equality of opportunity.

In the presence of dwarfed imagination regarding goals, etc., there is little in the direction of the social aspirations noted to which broadscale social commitment can become anchored. Hence we as a people tend to wallow selfishly in a growing volume and diversity of material goods, seeking new forms of sensuous stimulation and immediate sensuous satisfaction.

Perhaps in every culture that has ever existed, there have been great differences among individuals in what they accomplished—or were capable of accomplishing. The fact that America has constitutional and other stipulations about equality may have caused numerous functioning or potential leaders to place an exaggerated emphasis on greater equality along with its unadvertised mediocrity, rather than to emphasize other types of social accomplishment.

For one to recognize broad individual differences, he does not have to place himself in the top group. However a primitive selfishness and yearning for power over other persons and over things might urge him to do so, much as a comparable selfishness stimulates many of those who are below the average to desire the power and status of persons who are above them in the hierarchy.

Probably greatest promise for a socially creative escape from the circular hazards inferred lies in developing individual satisfactions through personal identification with long-range social goals. This implies a substantial orientation away from the immediate sensuous satisfactions previously noted. Developments along the lines of social goals as noted could gradually erode the opposing force of the nation's elaborate advertising machinery, which largely beckons toward the immediate and the sensuous.

But the foregoing comments should not lead one to assume that American culture reflects no indications of long-range social interests and related commitments or precommitment speculations. Illustrative reference concerning such commitments and speculations might be made to space exploration and knowledge of solar behavior; weather forecasting, and perhaps control; knowledge of the human organism and its illnesses; developing and exercising the powers of peace rather than those of war; exploring the duration of sound and other vibrations in the atmosphere, and the other surroundings of the earth, as possibly revealing the content of past events; determining what happens in the central nervous system, in terms of electric potential or otherwise, during the formation of an idea—or ideas of different kinds; etc. Some information and gestures concerning these and other long-range and socially creative developments have appeared.

Potential for individual commitment, and the satisfactions of being identified with big undertakings and achievements, is currently inferred in comments to the effect that research is fast becoming a major area of employment. Research also demands rising levels of technical and perhaps genetic competence for effective participation. Would such a development also mean increased rehabilitation and custodial care for persons who fail to manifest the competence required for effective participation? Would it be important for population structure and growth? The ramifications of cultural priorities are thus extensive; they will continuously be with us, and perhaps continuously expand.

Chapter 4

HIGHLIGHTS AND IMPLICATIONS OF DIVISION III

Rather extensive public attention has recently been directed to the general area of service which the present study characterizes as relating to the police, law enforcement, and corrections. The attention has quite often appeared under a caption such as "safety in the streets." Certain of the considerations which the study gives to this area are emphasized through concluding observations.

1. General Ignorance

While theoretically "ignorance of the law excuses no one," in a practical sense much depends on how many people are ignorant and on the direction and scope of their ignorance. Efforts to teach the people about new laws or about changes in old ones obviously indicate that it is not possible to enforce a general law if only a small percentage of the people affected know what the law is—regardless of vague intent or abstract formulas by law-enforcement agencies to the contrary.

Brief attention is called to three aspects of ignorance. One concerns general popular ignorance of what the law is, in some particular area of regulation, as noted. A broader implication of this point involves general ignorance of the function of a regulatory structure and of how the particular law fits into that structure. The second aspect relates to popular ignorance about the role of the police and law-enforcement agencies and about general responsibility of the people for peaceful and orderly life in the community. The third aspect concerns ignorance on the part of law-enforcement agencies regarding the types of problems which they face and the availability of resources for dealing with problems of different kinds. Some authors emphasize the changing and more complicated problems which today face youth up to their mid-twenties, as compared with age counterparts of a generation ago, and the need for police officers to have an understanding of these problems.

2. Increasing Lawlessness

While much is said about growing lawlessness, much less is said about fundamental research on causes. Three points are mentioned in this connection. Since every person is a potential offender against some regulation, there is a statistical basis for assuming that increase in the number of people tends to increase the number of crimes. The tendency is pronounced where people are crowded together, as in urban areas. The second point is that when people move around extensively, each person ordinarily comes in contact with more other persons than when nobody moves very much. During recent decades, the mobility of the American people has increased rapidly. The third point concerns material affluence and contractual relationships. There are more types of goods and services now than at any previous time in our history, and a more extensive supply in several particular categories. Hence there are more types of goods to steal or misuse, and more types of relationships concerning which agreements may be made and broken. The areas of potential offense increase accordingly. The expanding participation of juveniles in the areas of the culture implied is of considerable importance.

When development of the regulatory philosophy and structure does not keep pace with increase in offense potential, increase in crime should be expected. Much of our concern about crime effervesces in superficial and thoughtless groans and lamentations about crime rates and increases in rates, whereas our lamentations should more largely focus on our lack of imagination and of sweat in analyzing and updating an obsolescent regulatory structure.[97]

3. Responsibilities and Qualification of Law-Enforcement Personnel

The materials reviewed indicate considerable effort to improve the qualifications and competence of police officers and other law-enforcement personnel. Part of the effort concerns training programs in universities as contrasted with training in police academies.[98]

The basic point involves upgrading qualifications somewhat in harmony with increased complexity of the service to be rendered. The problem could be stated in terms of alternatives that arise from the background of the service person concerned. The same problem arises with teachers when dealing with children in school situations. A police officer who has a broad background from university study in the behavioral sciences, along with other university experience and street experience on the beat, is likely to recognize more alternatives for dealing with particular situations that arise than an officer whose preparation has been narrow or routine.

While the officer must have authority to arrest an alleged offender and take him into custody, probably in most cases this procedure should be looked upon as the last resort rather than the first. It is noted that such matters as available time in the immediate situation, criminal record, social crisis in the community, etc., will affect priority among alternatives—such as, for example, whether the arrest alternative is near the top of the list. Social complexity seems to increase the proportion of offense situations in which officer discretion is essential, in order to achieve the civic goal of protecting the community and also enabling the offender to function constructively in it, and there can be little discretion when few alternatives occur.

In some respects the arrest alternative in law enforcement resembles the hickory-stick or expulsion alternatives in school practice. Hickory and expulsion should be last resorts, not first ones. But where they stand in the repertoire of a teacher depends on the scope of alternatives which he can muster.

The use of physical force as an educational and disciplinary instrument, in the home, school, street, etc., has long and firm anchorage in the human race. Hence substantial conditioning through personal education, as well as substantial development in community attitudes and service facilities, are required in order to render the approach through physical force less immediate or universal.

4. Recruitment

The effectiveness of training programs depends considerably on the avenue through which persons enter those programs. Thus, some importance should be attached to whether entry is by edict or order, affecting currently employed personnel; by less authoritative pressure from peers who are employed; by more voluntary procedures among young persons who are determining careers; etc.

Several authors emphasized the need for research in order to improve law-enforcement service. One author emphasized the importance of being able to ask the right questions at the right places, in order to secure useful information. A pair of writers studied the motivations of youth which led them to choose police work as a career. Another pair[99] studied interest in future police work shown by military personnel in West Germany, who were approaching discharge from military service.

With growing complexity in the nation's economy, and rising levels of education and general competence required for constructive vocational participation, competitive recruiting among potential employees, who may exercise considerable volition in career determination, is an ongoing reality of social or institutional life. Movement of the nation toward an all-volunteer military force and springtime recruiting campaigns by industry on university campuses illustrate the point. No ostrichlike policy of police or law-enforcement agencies, rationalizing assumptions that they can avoid the competitive struggle, should anticipate a bright future.

5. Correction and Rehabilitation

Belatedness in recognizing the importance of correction and rehabilitation in the treatment of incarcerated public offenders is probably associated with the revenge conception of dealing with persons who have gone "afoul of the law." Revenge is a well-anchored biological reaction, which education, humanitarianism, etc., are presumed to modify.[100] Considerable ingenuity regarding efforts to modify is required.

Humanitarianism and Economics in Correctional Philosophy

With the rise of criminology and associated behavioral services, humanitarianism and economics have gained in public attention. While any formative area of a culture involves some combination of ideals, myths, and emotions, the cluster of traits loosely referred to as humanitarianism has apparently undergone less systematic analysis and evaluation than those referred to as economics. Perhaps one of the more tangible humanitarian considerations could be stated by saying that a person in "normal" circumstances pictures how he would feel if he were in the position of his "unfortunate" brother—and moreover, that with increasing cultural mobility and shift, he may someday actually be in that position. Much of this kind of humanitarianism appears in social-security and related governmental programs.

The economic approach is more tangible. It does not require brilliant insight concerning humanitarianism or elaborate statistical manipulation to show that it is costly and wasteful to hold a man in prison for an extended period, when he might rather promptly be brought back into the economic world—to hold a job and pay income tax.[101]

If there is anything amazing about the situation described, it is that it has taken us so long to recognize the possibilities of rehabilitation and to devise ways to shape and maneuver it so that it can erode and replace the biological and tradition-based revenge approach. Some of the authors reviewed in the present study have lamented the inadequacy of our corrections system and the "revolving door" situation of "repeaters."[102]

Stability and Confusion in Correctional Development

In any kind of development there are usually several variants, probes, alternatives, sporadic activities, and other manifestations which may collectively be referred to as confusion. Development resides in the aspects of the total situation which describe a consistent movement in some direction, as the other aspects become recognized as surplusage and are discarded as fall-off. The process appears in biological and social evolution. When the process in a social setting becomes systematized and embodies planning effort to identify and reach specified goals, it tends to be called research or scientific experimentation. Creative imagination is involved in the systematization and perhaps sporadically in generating the preliminary confusion.

In a social development with as many facets as are involved in corrections and rehabilitation, it would be unrealistic to expect that all facets would at a particular time represent the same stage of advancement from confusion toward scientific foundation. Moreover, in any dynamic society it would also be unrealistic to assume that any facet has developed beyond the point of further growth in potential, except for certain personnel fossilizations and associated efforts to retain organizational power.

(1) The idea of vocational therapy, or rehabilitation through jobs, has been in American social thinking and practice for some time—although many efforts remain puny or clumsy. The place of the job in the rehabilitation of public offenders has firm anchorage in the broader American perspective that increasingly looks upon the job as a major avenue through which most individuals participate in the culture, and thereby develop

personal status, self-respect, peer associations, and other aspects of indi-
viduality. More emphasis on jobs, by professional workers, clients, and
the employing community, is accordingly justified from the rehabilitation
standpoint.

(2) Organizational patterns and lines of control, with respect to correctional and rehabilitation service, show extensive variation. This situation
reflects both a rather basic philosophy regarding the relative merits of home-
like and local-community settings for clients, in contrast with more specialized
services which a centralized institution might offer. Much remains to be
done concerning the particular kinds of service that are most effective in
rehabilitating different kinds of persons and probably concerning goals that
seem realistic in determining what constitutes rehabilitation.

(3) This division notes several types of practices which have been tried
and others which have been advocated. The procedure involved is essential
for broadening the objective base of operations, as related to both the competence and the self-confidence of professional workers in the field, and as
related to public attitudes regarding tax funds to support the service. However, it is of great importance that dependable procedures be developed for
evaluating the results of experimental efforts relative to costs involved.

(4) The study comments substantially on the use of paraprofessional personnel, with respect to correctional services as well as to educational and
judicial areas of service. Several influences contribute to the paraprofessional development. Among these are: (a) an expansion in recognized need
for the service; (b) a trend toward general upgrading in quality and differentiation in categories of service to be rendered; (c) substantial disappearance
of manual labor from the nation's economy, with growing stress on vocational
"relevance" of the more extensive educational opportunity available to
American youth; (d) a material affluence which enables the American people
collectively to extend humanitarianism more abundantly to fellowman, at
home and abroad; and (e) a recognition that on-the-spot paraprofessionals
may, through feedback-experience, gain insights which sometimes escape
professionals who may be further removed from active operations.

Provisions for "Aftercare"

There is growing recognition of the need which the offender has for help
after the penal term is over and after he may be located in a job. The aspects
of this help which are concerned with job economics or physical health may
be less difficult than those regarding psychology and community attitudes.
The division discusses part of the difficulty from the standpoint of civil disabilities. But much of the problem relates to personal contacts and informal
associations which would hardly be defined as among civil rights and obligations.

Preventive Rehabilitation

Much of the counseling in schools, in playground and recreational settings,
in 4-H and other youth clubs, in pretrial counsel efforts with youth and their

parents, etc., is aimed at preventing or reducing the trauma of delinquency experience. The idea that "an ounce of prevention is better than a pound of cure" deserves more realistic consideration in rehabilitation and corrections than it has received.

In regard to preventive rehabilitation in general, without particular reference to public offenders, the present author in another connection stated:[103]

> Several aspects of American culture have for some decades been shifting from the concept of service through recovery as from disease, accident, cultural deprivation, typhoons and other natural disasters, economic depression, "containing communism," etc., to service through preventing the misfortune or disaster from occurring as preventive medicine, safety education, highway design, pollution control, earthquake resistant construction, social and economic planning as to business and employment cycles, etc. In a broad cultural atmosphere of the kind implied, it is unrealistic to suggest that the rehabilitation field should circumscribe its future by orienting its outlook entirely on concepts of salvage, repair and restoration.

6. Coordination Among Agencies

In various connections, this study refers to divisions of governmental responsibility in a complex society and to the assignment of particular responsibilities or functions to specialized agencies. Agencies concerned primarily with law enforcement, education, or public health are illustrative. Reference has also been made to isolations, overlappings, etc., that tend to develop with respect to the functioning of such agencies. General interest in police image and community relations points in the direction suggested, as does more direct reference to coordination among agencies in the urban community,[104] or reference to a public relations officer and similar forms of communication between the courts and the public.

The further reference made here to coordination is to stress its importance. *Federal Probation* presented a synoptic statement by Charles L. Newman.[105] It read:

> Before we can hope to win our war against crime, each of us must believe in the principle that his share of responsibility complements the work of others in the correctional system. This means that the person at the reception center, the institutional counselor, the custodial officer, the school teacher, the classification officer, the tradesman, the field and institutional parole officer, the probation officer, the law enforcement agent, and social workers in public and private agencies must see themselves and each other as part of a total system, as members of a *well-organized team*. (Emphasis added.)

FOOTNOTES AND REFERENCES

1. Cf. J. L. J. Edwards, "Criminal Law and Its Enforcement in a Permissive Society," *The Criminal Law Quarterly* 12 (1969-70): 417.

2. Cf. L. Harris, "Changing Public Attitudes Toward Crime and Correction," *Federal Probation* 32 (Dec. 1968): 9.

3. Warren Christopher, "Toward Safer Streets," *Los Angeles Bar Bulletin* 43 (Oct. 1968): 493, 526.

4. P. L. 90-351, 82 Stat. 197.

5. Patrick V. Murphy, "Reflections on Changing Law Enforcement Problems," *Federal Probation* 33 (Sept. 1969): 10-13.

6. Patrick V. Murphy, "The Police, The Lawyer, and The Courts," *The Record* 27 (Jan. 1972): 23.

7. Edward Bennett Williams, "Crime, Punishment, Violence: The Crisis in Law Enforcement," *Judicature* 54 (May 1971): 418.

8. Cf. (a) A. F. Brandstatter, "Career Concept for Police," *Journal of Criminal Law, Criminology and Police Science* 61 (Sept. 1970): 438. (b) L. C. Laughrey and H. C. Friese, Jr., "Curriculum Development for a Police Science Program," *Journal of Criminal Law, Criminology and Police Science* 60 (June 1969): 265. (c) D. G. Williams, "Police and Law Enforcement," *Criminal Law Review* 1968 (July 1968): 351. (d) P. S. Ring, "Bar's Aid to Police: Too Little Too Late," *American Bar Association Journal* 55 (May 1969) 461. (e) D. Johnson and R. J. Gregory, "Police-Community Relations in the United States: A Review of Recent Literature and Projects," *Journal of Criminal Law, Criminology and Police Science* 62 (Mar. 1971): 94. (f) "Lawless Law Enforcement," *Loyola University Law Review (La.)* 4 (Feb. 1971): 161. (g) "Problems of Police Brutality," *Santa Clara Law* 10 (Fall 1969): 168. (h) R. B. Holmgren, "Law Enforcement Training for Today and Tomorrow," *Chicago-Kent Police Law Reporter* 2 (Oct. 1969): 3. (i) "Police Patrolman Selection," *Journal of Criminal Law* 63 (Dec. 1972): 564.

9. David W. Craig, "The Police in the Middle of the Conflict," *Crime and Delinquency* 15 (July 1969): 387.

10. Miranda v. Arizona, 384 U.S. 436 (436-545) (6/13/1966).

11. 88 S. Ct. 1868 (1968).

12. See also: E. A. Wenk, J. O. Robinson, and G. W. Smith, "Can Violence be Predicted?" *Crime and Delinquency* 18 (Oct. 1971): 393.

13. A. C. Gormann, "Education and Professional Law Enforcement," *Journal of Criminal Law, Criminology and Police Science* 58 (1967): 603.

14. Howard M. Newberger, "Action Level Methods in the Higher Education of Police Officers," *Police* 16 (Aug. 1972): 55.

15. Wordie W. Burrow, "Texas Core Curriculum in Law Enforcement," *The Police Chief* 39 (Sept. 1972): 48.

16. Robert J. Jagiello, "College Education for the Patrolman—Necessity or Irrelevance" *Journal of Criminal Law, Criminology and Police Science* 62 (Mar. 1971): 114.

17. Charles L. Newman and Dorothy Sue Hunter, "Education for Career in Law Enforcement, An Analysis of Student Output 1964-1967," *Journal of Criminal Law, Criminology and Police Science* 59 (Mar. 1968): 138.

18. "Transcendental Meditation and the Criminal Justice System," *Kentucky Law Journal* 60 (1972): 411.

19. Stanley Vanagunas, "A Role for the States: A Model Interstate Compact for the Training and Education of Criminal Justice Personnel," *Crime and Delinquency* 19 (Jan. 1973): 49.

20. John K. Maniha, "Structural Supports for the Development of Professionalism Among Police Administrators," *Pacific Sociological Review* 16 (July 1973): 315.

21. See also: Susan O. White, "A Perspective in Police Professionalization," *Law and Society Review* 7 (Fall 1972): 61.

22. *Ibid.*

23. Lander C. Hamilton and Donald Bimstein, "Attracting College Graduates to Police Departments," *The Police Chief* 39 (Aug. 1972): 40.

24. Cf. Daniel F. Ponstingle, "Wanted: Youth and Experience in Law Enforcement," *Police* 16 (Jan. 1972): 57. See also, J. T. Flynn and M. Peterson, "Use of Regression Analysis in Police Patrolman Selection," *Journal of Criminal Law* 63 (Dec. 1972): 564.

25. Clifford S. Price and Ronald J. Bostik, "I A C P Goes to Germany," *The Police Chief* 39 (Aug. 1972): 53.

26. P. S. Mitchell, "Optimal Selection of Police Patrol Beats, *Journal of Criminal Law* 63 (Dec. 1972): 577. See also: "Police-Community Relations: Police-Youth Ride-Along Proposal," *Denver Law Journal* 48 (1972): 559.

27. Frank L. Manella, "The Three Worlds of Youth," *The Police Chief* 39 (Sept. 1972): 53.

28. Evelle J. Younger, "Violence and Education," *Los Angeles Bar Bulletin* 44 (Sept. 1969): 513, 536.

29. David Duffee and Larry Siegel, "The Organization Man: Legal Counsel in the Juvenile Court," *Criminal Law Bulletin* 7 (July-Aug. 1971): 544.

30. Miranda v. Arizona, *op. cit.*, note 10.

31. Note the comments by members of the legal profession, as reported in this study—especially Division II, on including more study of sociology, economics, anthropology, etc., in the preparation of lawyers, and also comments in that division on communication by the courts to members of the profession and to the public. Also note the study's emphasis on coordination among agencies concerned with delinquency and lawfulness.

32. In re Gault, 387 U.S. 1 (1967).

33. Cf. M. H. Langley, "Juvenile Court, the Making of a Delinquent," *Law and Society Review* 7 (Winter 1972): 273.

34. J. Douglas Grant, "Delinquency Prevention Through Participation in Social Change," *Criminal Law Bulletin* 7 (July-Aug. 1971): 530.

35. Kenneth Polk, "Delinquency Prevention and the Youth Service Bureau," *Criminal Law Bulletin* 7 (July-Aug. 1971): 490.

36. See Also: Dean E. Frease, "The Schools, Self-Concept and Juvenile Delinquency," *The British Journal of Criminology* 12 (Apr. 1972): 133-146.

37. Robert J. Gemignani, "Youth Services Systems: Diverting Youth from the Juvenile Justice System," *Federal Probation* 36 (Dec. 1972): 48-53.

38. Cf. Mary Gray Riege, "Parental Affection and Juvenile Delinquency in Girls," *The British Journal of Criminology* 12 (Jan. 1972): 55-73. See also: W. Walker, "Games Families of Delinquents Play," *Federal Probation* 36 (Dec. 1972): 20.

39. Harvey Treger, "Breakthrough in Preventive Corrections: A Police-Social Work Team Model," *Federal Probation* 36 (Dec. 1972): 53-58.

40. Arthur R. Matthews, Jr., "Cities Can Control Crime—City Planning

for Criminal Justice: An Urban Offensive in the War on Crime," *Chicago Bar Record*, Nov. 1972, pp. 83-90.

41. Alexander B. Smith and Harriet Pollack, "Less, Not More: Police, Courts, Prisons," *Federal Probation* 36 (Sept. 1972): 12-18.

42. Robert C. Boruchowitz, "Victimless Crimes: A Proposal to Free the Courts," *Judicature* 57 (Aug.-Sept. 1973): 69-78.

43. See also: R. Bacon, F. Feeney, and W. Thornton, "Preventing Delinquency Through Diversion: The Sacramento County 601 Diversion Project," *Federal Probation* 37 (Mar. 1973): 13.

44. Sanford Bates, "How Many Years," *Crime and Delinquency* 19 (Jan. 1973): 15.

45. Gustave de Beaumont and Alexis de Tocqueville.

46. Sir Alexander Paterson.

47. T. D. Bamford, "A British Probation Officer Looks at Corrections in the United States," *Federal Probation* 35 (Dec. 1971): 23.

48. Cf. H. H. A. Cooper, "Toward a Rational Doctrine on Rehabilitation," *Crime and Delinquency* 19 (Apr. 1973): 228.

49. Neil P. Cohen and Dean Hill Rivkin, "Civil Disabilities: The Forgotten Punishment," *Federal Probation* 35 (June 1971): 19.

50. Cf. G. Marnell, "Comparative Correctional Systems: United States and Sweden," *Criminal Law Bulletin* 8 (Nov. 1972): 748. See also: M. C. Rossiouni, "Criminal Justice Systems of the Union of Soviet Socialist Republics and the Peoples Republic of China," *Revista de Derecho Puertociqueno* 11 (Oct.-Dec. 1971): 163.

51. Cf. J. P. Reed and D. Nance, "Society Perpetuates the Stigma of a Conviction," *Federal Probation* 36 (June 1972): 27. See also: S. Rubin, "Man with a Record: a Civil Rights Problem," *Federal Probation* 35 (Sept. 1971): 3.

52. In regard to removing unnecessary barriers to the rehabilitation of ex-felons, see Timothy W. Tweeton, "Rehabilitating the Ex-Felon: The Impact of Arizona's Pardons and Civil Rights Restoration Statues," *Law and The Social Order* 1971 (1971): 793. See also: "Restoration of Rights to Felons in California," *Pacific Law Journal* 2 (July 1971): 718.

53. Jerome M. Rosow (U.S. Dept. of Labor), "The Role of Jobs in a New National Strategy Against Crime," *Federal Probation* 35 (June 1971): 14.

54. Cf. M. S. Richmond, "Measuring the Cost of Correctional Service," *Crime and Delinquency* 18 (July 1972): 243. See also: L. Phillips and H. L. Votey, Jr., "Economic Analysis of the Deterrent Effect of Law Enforcement on Criminal Activity," *Journal of Criminal Law* 63 (Sept. 1972): 330.

55. See also: Wayne Hopkins, "The U.S. Chamber of Commerce: Its Concern About Crime," *Federal Probation* 35 (Dec. 1971):33. Among other things, Hopkins refers to a *Deskbook on Organized Crime* and a 133-page booklet: *Marshalling Citizen Power Against Crime*.

56. Certain related studies are cited, with brief annotation. There is little correspondence between current vocational training programs in prisons and current or projected future job demands, said Michael J. Miller, "Vocational Training in Prisons: Some Social Policy Implications," *Federal Probation* 36 (Sept. 1972): 19. He commented that most training programs are

related to meeting institutional maintenance needs. He also commented on recidivism statistics which indicate that only persons who had specific training which they were able to use outside the institution had good prospects of successful reintegration into society.

A California study of work-furlough programs covered 2360 minimum-security jail inmates (Alvin Rudoff and T. C. Esselstyn, "Evaluating Work Furloughs: A Followup," *Federal Probation* 37:48—June, 1973). Among findings were: (1) the inmates did not think of themselves as criminals, although the staff did; (2) specialized vocational rehabilitation service for the jail inmate was a high-cost low-yield venture; (3) work furlough inmates made a better adjustment in the post-release period than nonfurlough inmates. One aim of the study was to develop a model work-furlough program. The authors suggested that such a program would have to be on a par with local law enforcement and perhaps independent of enforcement. They foresaw this arrangement as making many community services available to the inmates "as a matter of right rather than as an act of grace." They commented: "This includes adult education, welfare counseling, employment services, motor vehicle training, tax-supported health care, financial counseling from private loan companies, legal advice, advice on union and veterans benefits, and much else."

57. See: (a) D. P. MacPherson, "Corrections and the Community," *Federal Probation* 36 (June 1972): 3; (b) H. Treger, J. H. Collier, and C. F. J. Henniger, "Deferred Prosecution: A Community Treatment Alternative for the Non-Violent Adult Misdemeanant," *Illinois Bar Journal* 60 (Aug. 1972): 922; (c) B. S. Griggs and G. R. McCune, "Community-Based Correction Programs: A Survey and Analysis," *Federal Probation* 36 (June 1972): 7; (d) T. C. Clark, "Courts, the Police, and the Community," *Southern California Law Review* 46 (Dec. 1972): 1; (e) J. W. Sterling and R. W. Harty, "Alternative Model of Community Services for Ex-Offenders and Their Families," *Federal Probation* 36 (Sept. 1972):31; (f) M. Burdman, "Community Re-Entry of Offenders," *Journal of the Beverly Hills Bar Association* 6 (Sept. 1972): 62; (g) W. Mandell, "Making Correction a Community Agency," *Crime and Delinquency* 17 (July 1971): 281; (h) C. W. Thomas, "Correctional Institution as an Enemy of Correction," *Federal Probation* 37 (Mar. 1973): 8; (i) D. H. Kelly and W. T. Pink, "School Commitment, Youth Rebellion, and Delinquency," *Criminology* 10 (Feb. 1973):473; (j) C. M. Mathias, "Everything Begins at Home: The Problem of Juvenile Crime," *Judicature* 56 (Dec. 1972): 189; (k) "Nondelinquent Children in New York: the Need for Alternatives to Institutional Treatment," *Columbia Journal of Law and Social Problems* 8 (Sept. 1972): 251; (l) "Neighborhood Patrols and the Law: Citizens Response to Urban Crime," *Fordham Law Review* 41 (May 1973): 973; (m) John W. Oliver, "To Whom Should the Prison Chaplin Minister?" *Federal Probation* 36 (Mar. 1972): 19.

58. Herbert C. Quay, "What Corrections Can Correct and How," *Federal Probation* 37 (June 1973): 3.

59. Robert E. Keldgord and Robert O. Norris, "New Directions for Corrections," *Federal Probation* 36 (Mar. 1972): 3.

60. Cf. L. X. Pusateri and R. K. Scott, "Illinois New Unified Code of Corrections," *Illinois Bar Journal* 61 (Oct. 1972): 62.

61. John B. Hotis, "A Law Enforcement Officer Looks at Sentencing," *Federal Probation* 36 (Mar. 1972): 23.

62. Sylvia G. McCollum, "New Designs for Correctional Education and Training Programs," *Federal Probation* 37 (June 1973): 6.

63. Note in general: Linda R. Singer and J. Michael Keating, Jr., "The Courts and the Prisons: A Crisis of Confrontation," *Criminal Law Bulletin* 9 (May 1973): 337. These authors consider nonjudicial methods as the best hope of bringing the rule of law into the administration of the corrective system. They suggested grievance procedure for both inmates and correctional personnel as a possible model to use.

64. Cf. J. J. Enomoto, "Participation in Correctional Management by Offended Self-Help Groups," *Federal Probation* 36 (June 1972): 36; M. L. Erickson, "Changing Relationships Between Official and Self-Respect Measures of Delinquency: an Exploratory-Predictive Study," *Journal of Criminal Law* 63 (Sept. 1972): 388; D. P. Farrington, "Self-Report of Deviant Behavior: Predictive and Stable?" *Journal of Criminal Law* 64 (Mar. 1973): 99.

65. See also: D. F. Greenberg, "Voucher System for Correction," *Crime and Delinquency* 19 (Apr. 1973): 212.

66. See also: M. A. Frey and C. P. Bubany, "Pre-Adjudication Review of Social Record in Juvenile Court," *Journal of Family Law* 12 (1972-73): 391.

67. Eugene J. Gardner, "Community Resources: Tools for the Correctional Agent," *Crime and Delinquency* 19 (Jan. 1973): 54.

68. Note also: B. C. Gibbour, J. F. Jones, and P. G. Garabedian, "Gauging Public Opinion About the Crime Problem," *Crime and Delinquency* 18 (Apr. 1972): 139.

69. Concern about prison aftercare and halfway-house possibilities in Ireland were indicated by Mary C. O'Flynn, "Prison After-Care in the Irish Republic," *The Irish Jurist* 6 (Summer 1971): 1-17. She thought that during the whole period of the sentence, attention should be given to resocialization and the return of the individual to society. She referred to the functioning of an interdenominational religious body, called Prisoners Aid Through Community Effort, and the establishment of halfway houses. She also thought that day release or temporary release to some outside training center might be better for inmates than training within the context of a prison.

See also: R. L. Rachin, "So You Want to Open a Halfway House," *Federal Probation* 36 (Mar. 1972): 30; D. J. Helms and R. Russell, "Odyssey House Model and Civil Commitment," *Federal Probation* 37 (Mar. 1973): 31; L. L. Riskin, "Removing Impediments to Employment of Work-Release Prisoners, *Criminal Law Bulletin* 8 (Nov. 1972): 761; Lawrence S. Root, "Work Release Legislation," *Federal Probation* 36 (Mar. 1972): 38 (This comparative survey reveals similarities in objectives and in bounds set for implementation.); N. Holt, "Temporary Prison Release," *Crime and Delinquency* 17 (Oct. 1971): 414.

70. Kenneth F. Scheon, "P O R T: A New Concept of Community-Based Correction," *Federal Probation* 36 (Sept. 1972): 35.

71. Note also: "Symposium: the purposes of corrections—directions for

improvement," *University of San Francisco Law Review* 6 (Oct. 1971): 1.

72. Don J. Young, "Is the Juvenile Court Successful?" *Federal Reporter* 35 (June 1971): 12.

73. Cf. P. J. Brantingham, "Model Curriculum for Interdisciplinary Education in Criminology," *Criminology* 10 (Nov. 1972): 324.

74. See also: C. J. Flammang, "Reflections on the Police Juvenile Enterprise," *Juvenile Justice* 24 (May 1973): 22.

75. Carl D. Chambers, Leon Brill, and James A. Inciardi, "Toward Understanding and Managing Nonnarcotic Drug Abusers," *Federal Probation* 36 (Mar. 1972): 50.

76. Joseph D. McNamara, "The History of United States Anti-Opium Policy," *Federal Probation* 37 (June 1973): 15.

77. See also: Robert L. DuPont, "How Correction Can Beat the High Cost of Heroin Addiction," *Federal Probation* 35 (June 1971): 43; "Addict Diversion: An Alternative Approach for the Criminal Justice System," *Georgetown Law Journal* 60 (Feb. 1972): 667.

78. Norman S. Hayner, "Attitudes Toward Conjugal Visits for Prisoners," *Federal Probation* 36 (Mar. 1972): 43.

79. See also: R. R. Smith and G. A. Milan, "Survey of the Home-Furlough Policies of American Correctional Agents," *Criminology* 11 (May 1973): 95.

80. On rights to treatment, with emphasis on juveniles, see: (a) "Person in Need of Supervision: is there a Constitutional Right to Treatment," *Brooklyn Law Review* 39 (Winter 1973): 624; (b) L. Kapner, "Juvenile Right to Treatment—the next step," *Florida Bar Journal* 47 (Apr. 1973): 228; (c) J. F. Pyfer, "Juveniles' Right to Receive Treatment," *Family Law Quarterly* 6 (Fall 1972): 279; (d) "Right to Bail for Juveniles," *Chicago-Kent Law Review* 48 (Spring 1971): 99; (e) J. A. Weiss, "Emerging Rights of Minors," *University of Toledo Law Review* 4 (Fall 1972): 25; (f) "Juvenile Legislation: Time for Change," *Houston Law Review* 10 (Mar. 1973): 720; (g) "Right to Treatment for Juveniles," *Washington University Law Quarterly* 1973 (Winter 1973): 157; (h) C. P. Malmquist, "Juvenile Detention: Right and Adequacy of Treatment Issues," *Law and Social Review* 7 (Winter 1972): 159; (j) W. M. McCarty, "Juvenile Justice: the Economies of Ineptitude," *San Diego Law Review* 10 (Feb. 1973): 250.

81. James A. Snowden, "A Statutory Right to Treatment for Prisoners: Society's Right to Self-Defense," *Nebraska Law Review* 50 (1971): 543.

82. 373 F. 2d 451 (D.C. Cir., 1966); 387 F. 2d 241 (D.C. Cir., 1967).

83. See also: B. J. Kubetz, "The Legal Rights of the Mentally Retarded—Symposium," *Syracuse Law Review* 23 (1972): 991. Dyslexia is one type of illness or handicap associated with poor intellectual achievement and problem behavior, which has probational implications. See: William Mulligan, "Dyslexia, Specific Learning Disability and Delinquency," *Juvenile Justice* 23 (Nov. 1972): 20. On chromosome abnormality as associated with criminal behavior, see: Nicholas N. Kittrie, "Will the ZYY Syndrome Abolish Guilt," *Federal Probation* 35 (June 1971): 26. See also: (a) P. E. Lohman, "Medical Model of Treatment," *Crime and Delinquency* 18 (Apr. 1972): 204; (b) E. I. Megargee and R. E. Golden, "Parental Attitudes of Psychopathic and Subcultural Delinquents," *Criminology* 10 (Feb. 1973): 427; (c.) B. Paludan-

Muller, "Modern Methods of Treatment of Offenders," *Federal Probation* 36 (Dec. 1972): 36.

84. 379 F. 2d 106 (D.C. Cir., 1967).

85. In re Elmore, 382 F. 2d 125 (D.C. Cir., 1967).

86. Sas v. Maryland, 334 F. 2d 506 (4th Cir., 1964).

87. Scripps-Howard Radio v. Federal Communications Commission, 316 U.S. 4, 14 (1942).

88. See also: (a) R. Plotkin, "Enforcing Prisoner's Rights to Medical Treatment," *Criminal Law Bulletin* 9 (Mar. 1973): 159; (b) J. A. Robertson, "Pre-Trial Diversion of Drug Offenders: a Statutory Approach," *Boston University Law Review* 52 (Spring 1972): 335; (c) "Federal Government's Role in the Treatment of Youth Offenders: Two Approaches," *St. Louis University Law Journal* 16 (Spring 1972): 459.

89. Donald W. Beless, William S. Pilcher, and Ellen Jo Ryan, "Use of Indigenous Nonprofessionals in Probation and Parole," *Federal Probation* 36 (Mar. 1972): 10.

90. *Ibid.*

91. Cf. M. K. Hos, "Application of Helper Principles in Working with Delinquents," *Federal Probation* 36 (Sept. 1972): 26; F. Ragulsky, "Innovative Peer Group Program that Works," *Juvenile Court Judges Journal* 22 (Summer 1971): 36.

92. See also: I. M. Schwartz, "Volunteers and Professionals: a Team in the Correctional Process," *Federal Probation* 35 (Sept. 1971): 46.

93. William P. Statsky, "Teaching Corrections Law to Corrections Personnel," *Federal Probation* 37 (June 1973): 42.

94. Quoted by *In re Tucker*, 486 P. 2d 657, 682 (1971).

95. Gordon P. Waldo, "Research and Training in Corrections: The Role of the University," *Federal Probation* 35 (June 1971): 57.

96. Cf. (a) C. H. Logan, "Evaluation of Research in Crime and Delinquency," *Journal of Criminal Law* 63 (Sept. 1972): 378; (b) J. L. Schrink, "Structuring a Student Correctional Research Program," *Federal Probation* 36 (Dec. 1972): 42; (c) R. S. Pront, "Analysis of Associate Degree Programs in Law Enforcement," *Journal of Criminal Law* 63 (Dec. 1972): 585.

97. Cf. Richard L. Thornburgh, "Are We Really Serious About the Crime Problem?" *University of Pittsburgh Law Review* 31 (Summer 1970): 587.

98. Cf. Jagiello, note 16; Germann, note 13; Burrow, note 15.

99. See Price and Bostik, note 25.

100. Cf. S. Reiben, "Revenge or Rehabilitation," *Trial Law Quarterly* 8 (Fall-Winter 1971): 56. See also: Robert Coulson, "Justice Behind Bars: Time to Arbitrate," *American Bar Association Journal* 59 (June 1973): 612.

101. Cf. (a) V. L. Williams and M. Fish, "Rehabilitation and Economic Self-Interest," *Crime and Delinquency* 17 (July 1971): 281; (b) J. M. Rosow, "Role of Jobs in a New National Strategy Against Crime," *Federal Probation* 35 (June 1971): 14.

102. See Murphy, notes 5 and 6.

103. Harold H. Punke, "Preventive Vocational Rehabilitation," *Journal of Rehabilitation* 87 (May-June 1971): 50.

104. See Murphy, note 5.

105. *Federal Probation* 36 (Dec. 1972): 58.

DIVISION IV

EDUCATIONAL INSTITUTIONS AND ACTIVITIES

INTRODUCTION

During the middle two-thirds of the past century, when public schools were being established generally over the nation, education was coming to be thought of as synonymous with schooling. Before separate institutions were thus established in America or elsewhere, education was essentially a casual part of informal association by children with other members of the community; although there were concerted religious efforts, vocational apprenticeships, and conscious attention by parents to teach the children certain things.

There are several reasons why the institutionalization of education in public schools led to greater expectations than the schools were able to meet, and why school operations as well as unrealistic expectations regarding them have increased as our culture has become more complex. Perhaps an initial reason is that when a special institution is set up to function in a particular area of social interest, there is considerable variation in the community regarding what the institution ought to accomplish. Some vagueness of officially stated purposes and expectations may be essential in order to secure acceptance of the idea that the institution should exist. Analysis respecting the content of the Constitution of the United States, and a review of our history in getting the original Constitution accepted, substantiate the idea regarding political value in generality and vagueness—with, perhaps, considerable exaggerated optimism.

Moreover, when public schools were being generally established, teachers were in many instances among the best informed people of the community, especially with regard to academic learning by children. To a considerable extent the same situation exists today, as continuous upgrading in teacher qualification supports justification for the view stated. Also, increase in complexity of the culture and in the learnings and adjustments which children have to undergo make parents less adequate as guides and mentors. Coupled with this is the fact that a substantial number of parents want to shuffle off the mortal coil of child rearing insofar as possible, through indifference and neglect or through transferring the responsibility elsewhere, and the school seems to be a logical recipient.

One consequence of preceding developments is the precipitation at school of many types of responsibilities. These relate to such matters as academic learning, social and emotional guidance, health and feeding services, moral discipline, vocational orientation and preparation, recreational opportunities,

housing needs, etc. The presence of empire builders among school administrators and some other professional personnel, characterized by an ambitious
reach, increases the precipitate.

School operations thus tend to encompass responsibilities which they are
not qualified to handle, at least not alone. Among several possible illustrations of this statement, focus in this study is on the aspect of civic education that is concerned with lawlessness in American society. Among the
reasons for the school's inadequacies in this area are the inadequacy in
teacher understanding of the American social structure and its relationship
to a democratic philosophy of life and government; inadequate board and
administrative concern about the need of teachers for freedom to instruct
and to discipline students; and inadequate conception in the school and in
the community in regard to the kind of facilities needed to develop in students the social insight and civic responsibility that law-abiding and creative
citizenship demands.

Undergirding the above comment in a fundamental way is the fact that
no *one* specialized institution in a complex society *can alone* provide the
type of civic education needed. With regard to the civic area, more than
with regard to some other areas in which schools are expected to provide
training for students, the undertaking is one in which the entire community
must participate; that is, participate in ways that reach the individual student
more directly than matters of financial support of the school do.

In dealing with the school and related educational areas of developing
civic responsibility, the body of the material in this division is organized
into four chapters. Chapter 1 considers the general background and competence of teachers, as related to the function of American public education
in developing civic understanding and responsibility. It is concerned mainly
with the philosophy and general outlook of teachers, their university preparation, their general orientation concerning research and new discovery,
the role of academic freedom, relationships between tenure and competence,
and the cooperation of schools with other agencies.

Chapter 2 assumes that teachers can profit by strengthening in the general
area of social philosophy and civil analysis. The approach used in this
chapter is to analyze several areas of social relationships to illustrate ways
in which teachers, through working with students, might analyze comparable
areas. The analysis includes the underlying social philosophies. It is
assumed that when teachers have a high level of competence to analyze and
evaluate, the direction and the scope of analytical and evaluative procedure
that is actually developed with students can be largely determined by student
competence rather than by teacher competence.

The chapter is treated in two parts. The first part deals with some fifteen
concepts of broad and general implication from the teacher-learner standpoint. The second part considers twenty items which are of more direct
controversial nature in present American society. The concepts dealt with
in part 1 are stated, with suggestions under each one of how it might be
explored. The items included in part 2 are examined in substantially greater
detail. It is thought that the procedure described indicates one method
which teachers could use in working with learner groups of different matu-

rity levels. A further note on procedure appears in section 2, chapter 2.

In chapter 3, a list of topics is suggested in outline form, which classroom or similar groups might use in developing an understanding of the cultural background in terms of which lawlessness in the nation must be considered. It is assumed that the outline suggestions will be expanded, contracted, or otherwise modified, as group considerations develop. It is also assumed that other topics will be used in the developmental process, and hence that the items suggested are intended only to be illustrative. The topics suggested are grouped into four categories, according to the major institutional or cultural areas involved.

Chapter 4 indicates a possible use of projects. It is assumed that students, working individually or in small groups, might broaden their understanding of community structure through pursuing selected project subjects, and thus get a clearer idea of why peace and prosperity in a complex society depends on intelligent cooperation among numerous individual citizens and agencies. Furthermore, projects can help students clarify what commitment means, why it is essential to an orderly and creative society, as well as why it is necessary to make and carry through on personal commitments.

There are two parts to chapter 4. One part presents a short list of philanthropic foundations, as an avenue toward recognizing the important role which foundations have played in the study of many educational problems. The other part lists individuals for possible biographical study, grouped according to areas of interest and of contributions made. These lists are intended to be illustrative, as noted regarding certain other materials in Division IV.

Where school facilities permit, or where communities offer broader library or bookmobile facilities, supervised project work can contribute a great deal to a learner's understanding of lawfulness and creative citizenship in America and of the range in types of contributions made by persons who have helped in the constructive development of the nation.

Certain further general comments appear at the beginning of each chapter. In some instances these comments include reference to materials presented in appendixes.

The chapter entitled "Highlights and Implications of Division IV" appears in an organization comparable to that of the three preceding divisions. Pertinent items regarding the present division are numbered for convenient reference.

Chapter 1

GENERAL TEACHER BACKGROUND AND COMPETENCE

Discussion in previous divisions of the study has made considerable reference to relationships between our schools and our courts, law-enforcement agencies, and correctional and rehabilitation institutions and services, as well as some reference to the role of the school in vocational and other relationships. Most of these references have concerned the schools from an institutional standpoint.

In the attention which the present chapter gives to the role of the school with respect to problems of lawlessness and associated remedial possibilities, the point of departure is more largely that of the individual teacher.

1. Teacher Philosophy and Commitment

The possibilities and limitations of the schools with respect to civic education are less directly related to skills and techniques of teaching, than to a basic philosophy regarding the ideals and structure of American society, or to a moral commitment to support and try to improve the ideology and structure concerned. Teachers are not professionally strong in their understanding of the competing forces in a complex society, of the function of government relative to those forces, of how the public interest or common well-being is continuously being redefined, or of the relative importance of different individuals within the power structure.

Remedy includes developing an understanding of the biopsychological nature and scope of human selfishness and prejudice, as well as an understanding of the reasoning and emotional conditioning involved in developing broadscale group cooperation in place of atomized individualism. Remedy also includes an understanding of why a substantial base of economic materialism is necessary for personal satisfaction and well-being, as a foundation from which cooperative effort may embark. Further included in a remedial approach should be a realistic analysis of both the strengths and the weaknesses of popular government, recognizing a major influence in a kind of biological drive for rights and power, accompanied by a shunning or lackadaisical attitude toward duty and responsibility.

Effective commitment involves understanding, but it also involves emotional reinforcement to support the choice which collective understanding has made, as the most feasible route to an improved existence. It recognizes limitations to the rational process of considering pros and cons and emphasizes need for physical action. This need appears in all types of administrative work, when one's reputation or even his existence might be at stake. The Founding Fathers pledged their lives, their property, and their sacred honor. To what extent can parents, teachers, school boards, textbook publishers, and others directly involved in public education today be expected to do the same?

2. The University and Teacher Preparation

An increasing responsibility of universities in America concerns the preparation of teachers for the public schools. Foregoing statements on philosophy and commitment ask not only how much our universities now contribute to developing the understandings and commitments noted, but also how much they should be expected to contribute. Answers to both queries should be made in the light of what other agencies our society has for making contributions, and also of the support and authority which society gives the universities for designing and carrying out the responsibility inferred.

Academic freedom has been prominent in the American university, partly because of our university's carry-over from its predecessor on the European continent. The continental university of the time concerned was strong on freedom to examine the pros and cons of theoretical considerations, but not on developing commitments to practical administrative situations. The general class structure of the society determined those commitments, and the university was a sort of class privilege on the fringes of the social structure.

In America during the past half-century, the university has moved substantially from fringe status toward the central stage. Among the factors involved are enrollments, both in regard to numbers concerned and to social composition of the student body. Broadening of the curriculum is also important, including many areas of vocational preparation for which high schools and other subuniversity institutions are no longer considered adequate. The university as a research center is of further importance, with respect to developing research competence in its own graduate students, and with respect to carrying on research projects sponsored by government, industrial corporations, foundations, and other agencies. Further implication relates to the university as a center of publication, especially for technical materials, with the large number of university presses and with the large number of books and articles written by faculty members. Football and other athletic events have central implications with regard to entertainment. Among numerous other considerations, passing reference might be made to what seems to be an increasing use of graduation exercises or other university settings as opportunities for public officials to air their political views.

With expansion in university activities, and with particular regard to the broad aspects of American life which are substantially affected by those activities, the pro-and-con argument-and-debate conception of academic freedom is an inadequate guide to university responsibility. More consideration is needed for commitment to a collectively accepted ideology and its activating institutional framework, on the part of individuals whose competence and potential influence have been greatly augmented because of their university experience. Maybe somewhere between propaganda and traditional conceptions of academic freedom, lies an area which universities should learn to develop creatively—especially with respect to the preparation of teachers, who are expected to exert considerable influence on the understandings and attitudes of young Americans. Patriotism and civic dedication, the role of discipline in life, the implications of common ideology embodied in the world's major religions, etc., might be suggestive of intermediate areas.

3. Teacher Competence and Academic Freedom

Since "academic freedom" is expanding to include every type of activity in which a teacher engages that may be looked upon as having some connection with school operations, considerable scrutiny of the concept of freedom is essential.

Comment elsewhere in the study develops the idea that a person cannot be free in any notable degree unless he becomes disciplined. Part of the discipline relates to the production of energy by his physical organism and to the use which he makes of that energy within a framework of time. Other disciplines include coming to understand the principles or laws according to which nature and organized society operate and accommodating one's personal actions to those principles.

A substantial background of discipline of the types suggested is necessary in order to judge what constitutes freedom in a particular teaching or other academic situation. The fact that many teachers have administrative supervisors who have immature or puny conceptions of discipline and freedom does not simplify the teacher's job. Neither does it excuse the teacher from the responsibility of working at the job with all the persistence and acumen that he can muster. Acumen may be especially important for teachers who work in the controversial area of social philosophy or in some of the more conventionally defined areas of social science.

In regard to freedom and competence with respect to developing an understanding and a mitigation of problems concerning lawlessness in American society, how far for example should a teacher explore with youth the relationships of energy shortage to long holiday weekends and the motor industry, relationships between American tourism abroad and balance-of-payment problems or dollar devaluation, equity and social class in taxing systems, lawlessness and revision of the legal structure, rehabilitation and employment of public offenders as a deterrent to future offenses, drug addiction and military or other international relations, etc.?

In situations of the kinds suggested, difficulty resides in the fact that freedom without competence is not likely to be constructive, but that competence cannot be developed except in a setting of extensive freedom. It is not realistic to expect teachers to contribute a great deal to the improvement of law and order in America until they have a better understanding of the social and regulatory structure than most of them have now, a firmer commitment to the responsibility for making such a contribution, and greater academic freedom than prevails in many communities. But it should be added that teachers in several communities, in subject matter areas such as noted, have more academic freedom than they want to use or know how to use effectively.

In a changing society, any person who would render constructive service to others on a continuing basis must grow with the culture. "Growing with" is not wholly a matter of following trends, but includes helping to shape the trends. Growth which is at a teacher's own initiative tends to occur earlier, reach farther, and be more satisfying than growth which is forced by school boards or similar outside pressures. But the key idea remains, that competence is basic to freedom and leadership, and that for initiative to remain viable, it must be exercised.

4. Research and Teacher Competence

Practically every culture has considered its future substantially in terms of begetting new life and of a developmental concern for its children. Emphasis relates to projecting the culture into the future and to expanding its base of physical vigor. Much of the current anxiety and propaganda about overpopulation in America could be more creatively stated in terms of a shortage of imagination than in terms of shortage of energy or of food, fresh air, etc.

Role of Imagination

No brilliant imagination is required to estimate the population of a nation at a particular future date, at a specified rate of natural growth. But considerable imagination is required to develop new sources of energy or new conceptions of energy needs; new conceptions of air and water purification or recycling; new ways to recycle human and industrial waste and update conceptions of overpopulation, including possible relationships among people as well as relationships between people and the physical environment.

Perhaps people who enjoyed buffalo hunts in the 1860's, or who made a business of such hunts as is said of William F. Cody (Buffalo Bill—1846-1917), would regard the plains area as presently overpopulated with farmers, industrial workers, towns, etc. Yet as judged by most criteria, the people who now live in that area enjoy a higher standard of living than the people did who lived there in 1860. The same applies to the remainder of the nation. Anybody with a nostalgic yearning to hunt buffalo has had to revise his conception of recreation.

Then should it be a cause of remorse if British extravaganzas known as "fox hunts" experience a similar change in the future? How about American deer or quail hunts, or sports fishing in "undefiled" lakes and streams? Is it feasible to mention the expansive areas devoted to golf courses, water skiing, wildlife preserves, etc., where one class of Americans can engage in and perpetuate the types of recreation which they like, without particular regard to the likes or needs of other present or future Americans?

To assume that the wheels of social change should be stopped at a particular turn, which individuals currently in power consider to be pleasant and therefore appropriate, probably reflects great ego or selfishness, but not great imagination or creativeness. Whether humanitarianism, compassion, etc., are reflected depends on who defines the terms, or on whose desires or whose well-being the focal point rests.

Biological and Intellectual "Begetting"

Foregoing comments could be interpreted as saying that during the last few centuries there has been a sharply increasing growth of new begetting and development of intellectual life reflected in cultural expansion, as well as new begetting and development of biological life reflected in population expansion. Whether one process is referred to as creative and the other as procreative is immaterial in the present connection. But relationships between the two are of considerable importance.

It should not be assumed that preliterate man who lived in caves had no exercise of imagination, but rather that it is on the basis of an accumulation of survival elements from his meager start that current potential for extensive imagining has grown. At least theoretically, it is feasible to conceive of current population concentrations over the earth as having had comparably limited beginnings. And it is easy to accept the statement that it is the products of imagination concerning ways to produce more food, to control disease, etc., that have made it possible for population to increase.

When Malthus (1766-1834) observed that population tended to increase geometrically and food supply arithmetically, he was essentially stating a relationship between imaginative or psychological creativeness and biological creativeness. One can recognize the usefulness of his observation without enslavement to the idea that it is mathematically precise, universal with respect to all regions and all times, or unalterable through activities of man himself. His observation reflects one element in the accumulation of imaginative output, as more tangible achievements in agriculture, bacteriology, engineering, government, etc., reflect other output. As voluminous and spotted as has been the world's growth in population during the past thousand years, that increase has been closely associated with the accumulation in imaginative output. Thus it is essentially meaningless to refer to overpopulation without consciously or subconsciously basing the reference on some status of the imagination as reflected in the arts of production and other aspects of the culture.

Research and Intellectual "Begetting"

In a complex society, it is largely through research and organized inquiry that the deposits of current imagination can add most to the accumulation from past generations. "Most" here refers to those elements which the persons who dominate the culture of the time consider desirable. Through organizing and orienting the creativeness or begetting of imagination as suggested, imagination increasingly assumed the role of major determiner of man's life, including the use of the physical environment and the cultivation, enslavement, or extinction of other species. One should go beyond the foregoing implication that "man is the master," and recognize that some men are more masterful than others and that the masterfulness of individual men depends largely on their ability to create and use new knowledge. This ability is more closely associated with research competence, broadly conceived, than with other aspects of contemporary life.

The logic set forth implies that knowledge about research inquiry and attitudes regarding it should be high among priorities in a child's learning. Ways to develop such knowledge and favorable attitudes in the sphere noted should therefore be major concerns in teacher preparation and outlook and in the organization of educational institutions.

Getting Children to Understand How Research
Stimulates Cultural Growth

Teacher preparation should emphasize ways of getting children to understand and to appreciate what research means in terms of the insights, commitment, and sacrifice of the persons who carry it on, as well as what it means in terms of influencing man's status in the universe. Children should also learn to understand and to appreciate what is meant by "the thrill of discovery" and by the feeling of identification with some one or more of the many undertakings what may change man's relationship to the rest of the universe. Along with this is an understanding of the probability that successive decades will see increasing proportions of gainfully employed Americans being engaged in some kind of research work and increasing proportions of our budgets and material resources being devoted to research undertakings.

Some grasp of the long history of hostility to new ideas should be included, with anchorage to illustrations of the persecution of religious and other leaders whose inspiration and inquiry led them to seek changes in the status quo. Also should be encouraged some grasp of ways in which most cultures have become more tolerant of deviant ideas, although noticeable differences among cultures presently exist as to the particular areas in which tolerance is marked. The learner should also understand that no culture could hold together and endure if it tolerated every kind of deviant that appeared. A moment's reflection on the nature of conflicts and the role of decision-making may amplify the latter point.

Along with the areas of knowledge and appreciations noted, children and youth should develop a sense of duty and commitment to make a contribution to the creation of new knowledge, with that sense becoming clearer and more focal as the individual moves toward mature participation in the vocational world. Perhaps the vocational implication can be thought of as having two features: some choice among areas which presently allow considerable room for creative inquiry on a personal basis; and prospects that most of the vocational world will move in the direction of creative inquiry as research becomes a more prominent feature of American culture.

Undergirding much of what has been said herewith about youth and creative inquiry is the idea of participation or personal identification with important and socially approved undertakings which can give the participant a feeling of significance and a stake in improving the social order. This can reduce the amount of "empty" milling around which characterizes many youth, in school or out of school, and thus reduce tendencies toward delinquency. Correctional agencies which emphasize the potence of local institutions from preventive or rehabilitative standpoints, might find it helpful to work with school personnel in the direction indicated.

Research Interest and Competence as Teacher Qualification

Many aspects of teacher qualification are inferred in preceding comments on pupil attainments. However, one point in qualification needs emphasis. There is considerable lingering mythology to the effect that if one is a good teacher he cannot be interested in research, and conversely if he is a creative research person he cannot be a good teacher.

Apart from the substantial embroidery of rationalized laziness and comforting linguistics that rises to defend the mythology noted, certain other points should be mentioned. One point is that, with respect to research in education, teaching is a useful source of feedback on the soundness of what look like findings of research effort. Also, teachers who are familiar with research procedures and who are alert to problem identification and hypothesis formulation can find many clues in the teacher's classroom, faculty, administrative, and community relationships.

Fairly active and continuous participation in research along these lines should help the teacher gain perspective regarding his own work, especially as related to developing research understanding and inspiration in students, and the participation might constructively modify the outlook of colleagues and administrative superiors. But if research competence and interest are generally to be looked upon as teacher qualifications, administrators need greater insight than many of them have as to what research is and greater competence in program development so as to provide teacher encouragement. It is quite conceivable that the learning opportunities of students could be substantially improved through a rather continuous participation by faculty members in some ongoing research activity. It might be added that the teaching profession of the future may offer less opportunity for persons who are devoid of research competence and inspiration, than some other professional areas might offer.

Illustrative Research Possibilities

Two research possibilities, of substantially different character and approach, are briefly sketched for illustrative purposes. The types of research thus illustrated are among numerous types which are particularly important for education.

(1) *Motivating youth toward good citizenship and away from delinquency.* It is not new for youth to appear restive under the general regulatory and institutional system established and controlled by their elders, but questions of "relevance" and defiance of the "establishment" have recently seemed more

pronounced than usual. Research in the area might seek experimental or other evidence on questions such as the following, with implications for changes in social practices.

(a) To what extent do youth feel critical or indifferent because our system of education and employment essentially denies them responsible participation in directing and controlling the system—in comparison with participation by the youth of other generations or of other cultures?

(b) Does our educational and social system fail to develop in youth an understanding of the role which personal discipline must play as to physical, social or moral, and perhaps other disciplines, if one is to have personal competence and resources for long-range achievements?

(c) Does American emphasis on personal freedom and independence exaggerate the idea that each person should be encouraged to do as he may desire, or do his own thing, without much sense of obligation to the group?

(d) Does the American system, during the individual's early childhood and adolescence, give adequate attention to how one comes to have values or to change them?

(e) What could teachers and school administrators learn about educational objectives and school regulation by having an elected council of high school students develop a body of school objectives and regulations, using whatever faculty or other adult suggestion or advice they see fit?

(f) How important is part-time paid employment for students in grades 7-12 in developing general moral and civic maturity and in motivation and know-how regarding good citizenship?

(g) How important for the development of responsible citizenship in children and youth are local or national models which might be admired and followed, either as public officials or as private citizens?

(h) In what respect might reform of our laws and general regulatory structure reduce delinquent tendencies and increase desires to support the existing system?

(i) Under what conditions might it be most fruitful to get youth to formulate social reforms that they think would contribute most to improving the status of American citizenship and their readiness to support it?

(2) *Brain structure and intelligence.* Educators are presumed to be at least as much concerned about intelligence and the ability of individuals to learn as members of any professional or other group in the population are. For two generations, there has been extensive concern about developing materials, methods, and social attitudes for achieving maximum learning on the part of mentally handicapped children. However, there has been no similar concern about achieving maximum learning on the part of bright or mentally superior children. Considerable attention has been directed to such matters as birth injuries, poor home or school settings, and general indifference toward development by mentally handicapped persons of whatever potential they may have.

In comparing different species with respect to learning potential, considerable attention has been given to the structure of the brain and central nervous system. However, little scientific attention has been devoted to said structure, from the standpoint of individual differences among human beings, as a possible basis for differences in general learning potential—or of potential for learning or adaptation to particular kinds of material or areas of learning achievement.

The development of substantial information regarding people along the lines indicated might greatly affect such matters as the grouping of children for learning in general or for learning particular kinds of material, the organization and presentation of learning materials, bases for judging maturity as to when certain methods and materials are most appropriate, feasible degrees of mastery for different learners, the evaluation of the vocational interests professed by students or their parents, span of years devoted to formal schooling, organization and location of school plants as well as learning equipment, etc.

From an essentially different standpoint, knowledge of differences in human brain structure as related to intelligence might lead to interest in and possibilities of modifying the existing structure, through surgery, physical supplements or appliances, diet, or perhaps disciplinary exercises. (If tensions and emotional controls can affect ulcers of the digestive tract and extensive aspects of our glandular structure, possibly they affect the structure-function relationship within the brain in ways that lay substantially outside the sphere of attitudes or paralytic "strokes.")

In regard to research procedure, such a project would demand a long-range approach. Perhaps much could initially be learned through a study of animals, with various learning exercises and dissections involving paired subjects and different species. Much might also be learned by postmortem study of humans, through comparison of discovered brain structure with known lifetime learning accomplishments. Strength or other characteristics of neurological impulses associated with different kinds of learning situations could afford useful clues. Possibly the affect on learning of certain drugs, in experimentally controlled and administered dosage, at least with respect to animal studies, might indicate relationships to brain structure. Genetic implications from the study of kinship groups might also have value, with respect to different species. So too might comparisons among different groups within species—as breeds of dogs by age and sex, or races of people by age and sex.

To some extent the vagueness and generality of foregoing comments on procedure reflect the magnitude of the challenge suggested. But space research, organ transplants, heart pacers, and other developments justify courage and experimental adventure. Reference to educational personnel in connection with a research study of the type suggested does not imply that the ordinary teacher of third-grade reading, junior high school algebra, or college philosophy would be able to design facilities or specific experiments, but such reference does imply that personnel might be recruited from pertinent university research areas, hospital staffs, industrial establishments, and other sources, who could embark on simpler aspects of such an undertaking and gradually develop competence and confidence regarding the more complex aspects.

Perhaps the most crucial point in research of the type suggested regarding brain structure and intelligence, or any other research undertaking, depends on probable values to be derived relative to cost outlays—including trauma costs in revising prejudices. The reference to space research seems adequately illustrative on this point. Hence, considerable emphasis on the possible value of outcomes from brain-structure research seems currently justified, although actual outcomes depend on research findings.

The Present Study and Research Interests of Learners

With regard to stimulating inquiry and research curiosity in school children and youth, and in some other learner groups, following chapters of this division indicate several topics for possible discussion with groups at varying levels of maturity. In addition, numerous individuals are indicated in chapter 4 of the division who have made significant contributions to the development of civilization. Most of the names are grouped, in appendix no. 2, according to areas of contribution; and the groupings carry some annotations on each person listed. With teacher and school resourcefulness, both topics and annotations can help awaken in many children a desire to know more about how contributions in different fields have been made in the past and arouse curiosity about what the future might hold—for society collectively and for themselves individually.

5. Teacher Competence and Tenure-Retirement Systems

In significant respects, the appearance in America of organized professional groups in the modern sense can be looked upon as beginning after the Great Depression of the early 1930's. To a considerable extent, the movement concerned has reflected earlier developments among workers in blue-collar fields. However, an important difference between the two areas has related to the interest which professional organizations have shown in ways to improve the service rendered to the people, with less exclusive emphasis on the financial and related status of the individual employee.

Also, teachers as a professional group in America have been employed mainly in publicly supported institutions and have accordingly been in a more direct focus of public attention. Service in such institutions has placed teachers rather directly under political pressures and jurisdiction, not experienced by employees of private agencies.

With the great emphasis on localisms that characterized the early American conception of handling public affairs, members of locally elected boards had essentially a free hand in hiring, supervising, and dismissing teachers. To a considerable extent, the hire-and-fire authority of local school boards early in the present century was in accord with an absolute right of the employer in the world of industry and general labor service. Hence, teacher employment probably reflected the continuing vigor of an even more extensive absolutism, the power of a master over his slave or servant.

Teacher Tenure and Pupil Well-Being

Anxiety among teachers about their jobs and livelihoods, under the circumstances described, came to be recognized as impairing their teaching effectiveness and, thus, affecting the opportunity of children to learn. Anxiety was often heightened by contracts or other employment arrangements which enabled the board to dismiss a teacher at will, and by one-year contracts which typically meant that during the latter part of a school term a major concern of the teacher was in seeking a job for the next year.

While in theory the teacher-employing agency had authority to establish tenure provisions as well as to hire teachers, in reality such provisions regarding many smaller communities depended on action by more central administrative authority. As a part of the general process involved, centralized authority became interested in variation among teachers regarding qualifications for teaching and in variation of teacher interest in rendering good service on a continuing basis. Qualifications for gaining tenure status thus became established.

Greater activity by centralized public authority also introduced a broader range of political implications regarding school and educational influence. One accompaniment of the broadened implication concerns the length of teaching service and its connection with retirement prospects. To a considerable extent, the argument on anxiety about future security status and quality of teaching also applied to the future prospects of a teacher as the end of his career in teaching drew near. To some extent, humanitarian considerations, formulated as rewards for long and dedicated service, became involved. Also, matters of fatigue or other developments became reflected in disability retirement.

Throughout the development of tenure-retirement provisions, public attention has been focused on the learning opportunity and general well-being of the schoolchild. However, since teacher organizations have become extensive and powerful throughout the nation and have tended toward resembling organized labor in philosophy and techniques, substantial intellectual ingenuity and perhaps some moral flexibility have at times been involved in showing how tenure and retirement demands aided learning by children.

Tenure Status and Teacher Growth

One problem in a continuously expanding culture relates to comparable growth or expansion in the qualifications or general competence of persons who carry extensive public responsibility. The avenue through which this problem affects teachers concerns the expansion in knowledge which society expects children to acquire and expansion in other responsibilities for child growth and development which rest on teachers.

In accordance with the problem indicated, most school boards have authority to establish teacher programs on in-service growth and development, although many boards lack the courage and the professional expertise to establish constructive programs. Moreover, universities which have responsibility for preparing teachers and for improving the general status of American education have often been limited in the suggested avenues of in-service teacher growth, other than through additional credit courses in subject matter and professional areas. However, field service by university faculties in schools of education are modifying this situation considerably.

Among teachers as among workers in other fields, there are many who tend to relax and coast after once having met minimum qualifying requirements. Such teachers operate on a philosophy "once qualified, always qualified," regardless of the changing educational needs of American citizens and of corresponding changes in teacher responsibility. At one time the "life certificate" was important in fostering the view indicated, and in some respects tenure extends that fostering atmosphere.

Hence, for tenure provisions to insure improvement in the learning opportunities available to children, the provisions must protect efficient teachers from dismissal and related security anxieties noted earlier and must also make certain that inefficient teachers either improve or seek employment elsewhere. The task implied is not easy, in view of such matters as legitimate differences as to what constitutes good teaching, budget and related problems in financing the upgrading of teachers, and nepotism or related aspects of political pressure which become involved in administrative operations. Nevertheless, in many communities the basic task concerns developing criteria for differentiating between acceptable and poor teaching, as judged by needs in upgrading or dismissal, as much as it concerns inadequate administrative courage and finesse in operating a program of differentiation so that it seems fair and acceptable to the general body of teachers. Various ways of influencing teacher morale, both positively and negatively, are thus implied.

Small Administrative Units

It has become customary among local politicians to extol the virtues of local units of government, in the face of obviously growing needs for and practices of centralized support and control of public services. Consolidations and centralizations have been spotty with respect to public services, but they have nevertheless been extensive throughout the culture.

With regard to school administration, consolidations and centralizations have varied in different aspects of school operations. At present, tenure and retirement provisions concerning teachers have fundamental statewide anchorage in minimum programs, although usually individual communities may exceed the minimums. Within the structure indicated, it becomes increasingly the responsibility of statewide authority to insure that adequate in-service growth provisions for teachers are offered—and enforced. While statewide provisions of the type noted allow for local imagination and effort, such provisions are essential for improving the quality of education available to children.

Statewide programs reduce the tyranny of local ignorance regarding the qualifications of teachers required to meet the expanding educational needs of children in American society. Such programs also provide a curb on local selfishness and nepotism in teacher employment, partly through providing a broader and often a professionally more alert audience concerning large-scale or statewide corruption.

Probably the most outstanding instance of local nepotism and corruption which has come to the attention of the author of the present study was before a Montana court in 1944[1] and is reported in considerable detail in another study.[2] Suffice it here to note that Nels Amundson, his wife, and his brother Sophus were the three trustees of the school district. The wife had been teacher of the school for six years, at the end of which time she claimed automatic contract renewal because she had not been notified to the contrary as required by an earlier court ruling. At about the same time, the trustees authorized removal of one district schoolhouse to Amundson's ranch, at district expense. Soon thereafter the brother moved out of the district. Not long after that, Nels, acting as sole trustee, sold this schoolhouse to his wife for $75.00, and as clerk of the board she claimed possession of the building upon tendering this sum to the county treasurer. Population decline had been such that the only children in the district were those of Nels and his wife. The county superintendent won his suit challenging legality of the employment and other procedures involved.

Professional Satisfactions and Teacher Growth

Every vocation is presumed to offer certain satisfactions, apart from monetary income and associated status. The satisfactions mentioned result from a kind of rapport or identification of the worker with the tasks and outcomes of his work efforts, and may thus embody a kind of emotional immediacy of satisfaction which is not associated with the pay route. The prominence of this element of satisfaction is broadly looked upon as a difference between professional and skilled-labor employment.

However, the extent to which this personal identification element of satisfaction is experienced by teachers, as by other professional workers, depends largely on two factors. One of these is the qualification of the employee to do well in carrying the responsibilities of his job at the particular time, plus an ongoing effort to improve his qualifications with successive years, and especially with the varied and changing backgrounds and needs of persons served—as broad social changes affect the total culture. The other factor is commitment or dedication, such as the teacher's wanting to bring about constructive developments in learners and putting forth considerable effort to achieve such developments.

It is the author's view that the problem with many teachers, who are no more than lukewarm to the enjoyments or satisfactions of teaching, is that they shut themselves off from greater exhilaration through limitations regarding a personal sense of adequacy concerning qualifications and through miserliness concerning dedication and related effort. Organization efforts regarding salary improvements, teaching loads, academic freedom, etc., are important as background conditions, but there is little reason to expect that they will generate the satisfactions heretofore noted relative to commitment or dedication. Furthermore, it is hardly realistic to assume that learners, at any school level, are unaware of the difference between a teacher with a substantially routine outlook on teacher-learner relations and a teacher who radiates the commitment noted.

However, foregoing comments on dedication versus pay, etc., should not blind one to either the pathology or the anarchism perhaps submerged in occasional teacher statements to the effect that they enjoy teaching so much that they would appreciate an opportunity to teach even without pay. Pathology may be reflected along either of two avenues. One is a psychologically undesirable interest in students, or in some particular students. The other is lighthearted or irresponsible twaddle. The latter becomes anarchistic when it is intended to curry temporary favor with *somebody* whom the speaker wants to impress and which tends to undermine the professional status of fellow teachers. For teachers in general, as well as for other employed workers, pay is the avenue that America recognizes by which to secure the material basis for a livelihood. If a few teachers have other income and do not need salary checks, they could turn those checks over to some philanthropic enterprise. But they should not seek special recognition through talk which belittles the status of other teachers.

Longevity and the Employment of Retired Teachers

The nation's social problems with respect to the employment and economic status of retired persons are growing. This is largely a consequence of three developments in American life. One is the increasing percentage of persons who are reaching the upper age brackets. This fact may be of especial importance for teachers, since in America women typically live longer than men do and since a considerably larger percentage of public school teachers are women than are men. Furthermore, retirement programs are becoming increasingly universal and increasingly placed on a compulsory basis attached to age, with some tendency to reduce the age level—at least for voluntary retirement. The third development concerns a tendency to expand the monetary involvement of public and other paying agencies, respecting individual retirees. Alternatives of increased taxes versus decreased benefit payments do not offer brilliant prospects for future retirees.[3]

Economic and related pressures may be important in forcing a reexamination of current practices regarding age and capacity to render constructive service to the community. This could be an area for greater individualization in evaluating competence, particularly with respect to teachers and existing educational needs. Developments embodying such individualization would probably entail administrative problems in developing suitable criteria for differentiation and in getting the application of the criteria accepted by teachers who think they are unfavorably treated.

Yet the complex of economic, professional, and humanitarian considerations involved might stimulate imagination and social effort to develop new prospects of professional and other possibilities for expanding the nation's system of paying jobs, so as to include additional areas of useful service. Such a development would be socially more constructive than paying individuals to retire vocationally before it is physically necessary, with such retirement tending to hasten mental and physical deterioration because of removal from basic aspects of the cultural stream.

6. The Teacher and Nonschool Agencies

When this study emphasizes the idea that developing a sense of lawfulness and civic responsibility in American youth is too big a job for any *one* or our social institutions to perform *alone*, it presumes that there will be coordination among institutions. While the study emphasizes the courts and law-enforcement agencies as prominent in the coordinations implied, operating practice will demand other coordinations, such as relate to social workers, health services, employment agencies, youth clubs and scouting groups, etc.

Although most transgressions by youth or adults might be characterized as variations in customs or perhaps as bad manners, the shift is gradual from such transgressions to those which are forbidden by law and have severe penalties attached. Teachers and other school personnel should recognize that along the gradient involved are various types of agencies which are especially concerned with the behavior and well-being of people. At a few or at several points along the line, the interests and activities of the nonschool agencies resemble those of the schools. Coordination of work at such points, rather than competition or indifference, indicates the avenue to greatest community achievement.

Since by law and by custom, the public school is the place at which more of a community's children and youth are brought together than anywhere else, the school is a natural center from which various services by coordinated agencies might well branch out—with respect to persons of the age and maturity concerned. Among some of the personnel involved, this situation may evoke the idea that teachers should assume major coordinating responsibility. While the assumption seems reasonable in regard to the use of facilities at the school plant, it probably will not be reasonable for immediate goals and procedures in many specific problem situations. Perhaps insofar as possible, visible leadership should rest at the point which the community is most likely to regard as normal.

Chapter 2

SOCIAL PHILOSOPHY AND CONTROVERSIAL ISSUES

When social philosophy or any other type of philosophy actually functions, it does so in connection with particular situations. Hence, attention to social philosophy in this and other areas of the present study emphasizes a pragmatic approach to the present and continuously evolving American social structure and to the place of that philosophy as both product and producer of the structure and the functioning concerned. The basic reason for this emphasis lies in the relationship of such a philosophy to the effectiveness of the teacher in developing constructive social values, insights, and commitments in students. The aspect of the development most immediately involved relates to civic education and most particularly to lawlessness in America.

Each of the two major parts of the chapter includes certain further preliminary comments.

1. General Concepts

The procedure in this part of chapter 2 is to state certain concepts or principles and then to list subsidiary statements for consideration as illustrative of how one might proceed in analyzing such concepts. There are fifteen concepts examined, listed from 1 to 15. For convenience, the concepts and subsidiary statements are set forth in outline form.

(1) Formulation and acceptance of social principles and ideals to be used as guides is an ongoing task which leaders in any society must perform.

(a) An ideal is a standard or model which indicates somebody's conception of how conditions might be improved or made more nearly excellent.

(b) People need ideals if they are to put forth much effort in any consistent direction of change or hoped-for betterment.

(c) Ideals can be realistic in the sense of being attainable with systematic and persistent effort, or they can be fantastic in the sense of being unattainable by any procedure that it currently seems possible to devise.

(d) Persons who can formulate realistic social ideals and get the people to move toward their attainment are among a society's most creative and valuable members.

(e) In the history of civilization, the general population has often persecuted or killed some of its greatest idealists—as, for example, Socrates, Jesus, and Ghandi.

(f) It is a constructive exercise for individual students at different levels of maturity to formulate ideals and then to discuss and evaluate them in conjunction with other students, teachers, etc.

(2) When does a history of past developments constitute a useful guide to the future, and when does it constitute an obstruction to future developments?

(a) The history of most countries reflects some glowing achievements for the betterment of mankind generally, and some outstanding corruptions and debaucheries of decent social ideals.

(b) Whether the accounts of the past which are presented in history have any lessons for the future depends on the use that is made of these accounts in trying to survey the future.

(c) In learning about the heroes of one's country, it is important to learn about their weaknesses as well as their strengths, but to recognize that the balance is in the direction of their strengths. (Most persons have made some mistakes.)

(d) For an individual to understand the role of history in developing the current status of life in the nation, it is necessary for him to understand both the socioeconomic attainments and the military operations.

(e) Studying the biographies of persons who have made significant contributions, to some aspect of a nation's culture, constitutes one of the best ways to study history.

(f) With an expansion in international relations, an understanding of the status and prospects of one's own country will depend increasingly on an understanding of other countries, as through world history.

(3) Regardless of the officially proclaimed system of government, the laws and regulatory framework of a nation must provide some avenue through which every substantial minority or other group can be heard with respect to making or enforcing the laws.

(a) Probably the free and independent vote of the people and open or forceful revolt by the people against operating authority represent the extremes along a continuum of the general populous being heard.

(b) For the voting route to be realistic and to seem preferable, persons who would act as leaders must formulate clear statements of the issues and must show commitment to the principles which they consider to be socially preferable.

(c) Political corruption is *always* a force which weakens popular faith in voting and moves the people in the direction of forceful revolution— or away from government by law, as that government is currently operating.

(d) For a democratic society to be socially progressive as well as politically stable, it is essential that a large percentage of the electorate be heard, either through the ballot or through some comparable avenue.

(e) Social evolution or change by vote, in contrast with change by forceful revolution, may or may not be more economical with respect to the utilization or the waste of cultural resources.

(f) Young Americans should recognize that democratic citizenship, which emphasizes voting based on an understanding of issues, demands more of the citizen than some other forms of government do.

(4) With the United States and other nations increasingly becoming involved in international relations, America's educational, financial, military, geographical, and other resources must increasingly be used for policing and other action to develop an enlightened system of lawful regulation on a worldwide basis.

(a) While international problems regarding lawful relationships may seem most conspicuous with respect to murder, drug traffic, plane hijacking, financial swindles, kidnapping and similar offenses, they are not confined to such areas.

(b) The United Nations affords a constructive although inadequate base from which to project desirable international regulations.

(c) Expansion as to international relations makes it more important that Americans understand the difference between this country and other countries, concerning the way in which law is conceived and enforced.

(d) For a system of law and social regulation to operate effectively, either within a country or among countries, there must be some basis for policing or enforcing the law and some basis for adjudicating violations.

(e) From the practical standpoint, responsibility for law enforcement and for lawful behavior in general within a country never has rested equally on all citizens. With regard to the enforcement of international relationships, one might expect a comparable situation as to the responsibility of different nations.

(f) There are some areas of law in which similarities among nations are more important than in other areas—such as maritime law, military law, offenders who are citizens of other countries, domestic-relations law, traffic regulations, negotiable instrument law, etc.

(5) Any country which desires to be broadly accepted by other countries in a setting of world leadership must demonstrate the presence of a desirable social status and opportunity available to its own people, on essentially an equal basis, and must demonstrate a competence and a willingness to extend the same opportunities and status to other peoples.

(a) Considerations such as race, sex, religion, age, physical and mental handicap, social class, etc., may be important with respect to equality.

(b) There are many countries, in Latin America and elsewhere, in which the constitutional and legislative framework makes elaborate provision for equality of status among the people, but which the society does not implement. Such countries are handicapped in offering leadership to peoples elsewhere who aspire to freedom and equality.

(c) With the great emphasis which the world now places on scientific and other knowledge, equality of educational opportunity may seem a basic avenue to other areas of equality.

(d) Where great emphasis is placed on knowledge, with the idea that knowledge is power, a nation which carries on extensive research and creates much new knowledge will ordinarily exert considerable leadership.

(e) There could be many areas of international cooperation in research and the creation of knowledge and in the use of that knowledge to improve the status of people in participating countries.

(f) Extensive programs of student and faculty exchange among nations could greatly help to improve international relations.

(6) One of America's greatest social problems during the next generation or so will concern the allocation of its resources to caring for and "rehabilitating" its handicapped and its nonproductive population, in contrast with carrying on research and experimentation to expand knowledge and man's power or control in the universe.

(a) To a great extent it is research and experimentation that has made the American food supply, housing, transportation, health service, etc., different now from what they were in the days of George Washington.

(b) To what extent do differences between research orientation and welfare orientation constitute differences in orientation between growth and productivity and a distribution of what has already been produced?

(c) Rehabilitation programs regarding various types of handicapped persons are usually aimed at improving the economic productivity of such persons and also at enabling them to get more personal satisfaction through broader participation in the culture.

(d) One criterion of the level of a civilization is the consideration and provision accorded its handicapped and biologically least fortunate members.

(e) A society which assumes considerable responsibility to provide for persons who are biologically handicapped or injured by accident should attempt to reduce from generation to generation the percentage of the population in those categories.

(f) Major responsibility in the relative allocation of resources to welfare and to research should rest in the hands of public agencies, which through the election process are presumed to represent all of the people.

(7) Social regulations regarding equality and differentiation among various groups in the population, such as relate to sex, race, age, physical or mental health or handicap, test-selection, etc., should rest on biological differences among individuals. In many respects, such an arrangement would demand research to develop more knowledge about biological and genetic differences than we have now.

(a) If people in general were better acquainted with what is scientifically known about human genetics, they would better understand why research in that field is more complicated than comparable research regarding many other species.

(b) People in general have a kind of fear or anxiety as to learning about their genetic backgrounds, lest the knowledge concerned bode ill for their futures.

(c) It is usually easier and more comfortable to think of family planning and population growth in terms of numbers than in terms of quality. This is only in part because we do not have very acceptable criteria as to what constitutes desirable quality, or very adequate knowledge as to why particular traits appear as they do.

(d) The percentage of its resources which a society uses for aid to physically or mentally handicapped persons will depend on its ideals or value structure, which must take many competing needs into account.

(e) With respect to physically handicapped persons, there is considerable statistical evidence to show that the taxes paid and other contributions made to public well-being after rehabilitation more than equal the cost of their rehabilitation.

(f) If a society may draft certain individuals for military or other service in which their lives are threatened, that society should also accept responsibility for influencing the competence of its future population by determining that certain kinds of persons should not beget children.

(8) Persons who are entrusted with official responsibility must have a more comprehensive and systematic orientation toward the future and the welfare of posterity than ordinary persons have. In some respects this civic orientation regarding unborn generations may be a tangible aspect of what some religious groups have referred to as a "hereafter."

(a) As the range and volume of knowledge in a culture expands, many concepts undergo new and more scrutinizing interpretations. Such an interpretation regarding a hereafter might include anything that happens after one's death—that is, after the "here and now" of his existence.

(b) In most cases, individual families as well as nations and cultures which plan for posterity are more likely to be represented on earth during future centuries than families or nations which do not do so.

(c) When it is said that individuals of a particular generation should live their lives as best they can and let posterity take care of itself, the phrase "as best they can" implies certain standards or criteria which actually take posterity into account.

(d) It is possible for public officials or others to be so concerned about posterity that they fail to take any action for fear of mistakes which will handicap posterity. Such persons are among a culture's worst enemies, with respect to its future.

(e) "Social planning" constitutes an effort to influence posterity, or the nearby hereafter, in accordance with certain ideals.

(f) As a society in general becomes more affluent, the individual does not need to direct as much of his effort toward providing for his own immediate personal necessities. Hence, he can devote more of his efforts to concerns which relate to posterity.

(9) For a technologically advanced culture to make further strides in development, it is important that the population include a relatively large number of persons in the older age brackets who have constructively used their earlier years for learning and development and whose health promises several additional years of life and productivity.

(a) We hear a great deal about individual differences regarding the learning capacity of school-age children and about the health services needed by handicapped and other persons. Possibilities of further services rendered by persons who are normally considered to be of retirement age should likewise be considered on an individual basis.

(b) When persons approach retirement age, they are more likely to be unemployed than they were twenty years earlier. It is therefore especially important for older employees that the economy operate on a "full employment" basis.

(c) With the rapid change in technology and in new kinds of jobs which appear, many of the skills and competencies of older workers may be essentially obsolete. This varies with type of job and should be evaluated from the standpoint of retraining.

(d) With a low birth rate and other changes in family pattern, older persons are not as important in the care and rearing of grandchildren as they were at one time in America.

(e) With more older persons in the population, a kind of "new industry" which appears is concerned with providing care and services needed by these older persons.

(f) The prophets and sages of earlier cultures were persons who had lived a large number of years, who had observed comprehensively during those years, and who reflected analytically on their observations. We now have books and libraries as storage places for accumulated knowledge and do not depend as greatly on older persons for storage and retrieval. In America, computers are of growing importance for storage and retrieval. However, there are some kinds of things which an individual cannot learn without having lived through several years of time and events, years which include experience concerning those things.

(10) When social change is rapid, it becomes essential to schedule specific intervals at which there will be a comprehensive examination and revision of the social structure, rather than essentially to leave revisions on the rather haphazard and fragmentary basis of annual or biennial efforts. Comprehensive revisions concern such matters as rewriting state constitutions or codes in particular areas such as motor vehicle codes, tax codes, drug and narcotics regulations, interstate commerce functions and powers, welfare provisions, etc.

(a) The scheduling of revisions for particular aspects of the social structure does not mean that revisions may not occur at other times, but it is likely to discourage off-schedule revisions.

(b) When major revisions are scheduled somewhat as indicated, the job is likely to be done by experts who know more about particular designated areas than members of a legislature ordinarily know. Hence, it is reasonable to expect that a more adequate job will be done on the revisions.

(c) Revisions which summarize and update the regulations in some particular area of the social structure make it easier for the people to know what the regulations are in that particular area.

(d) If legislators had more ready access to qualified legislative research service and had greater competence and willingness with respect to utilizing that service, the clarity and pertinence of successive crops of new laws might be such as to reduce the burdensomeness of consolidations and revisions.

(e) It might contribute substantially to lawfulness in America if more effort were made in both original enactments and subsequent revisions or consolidations to set forth the regulations in language which average laymen could understand, rather than in language which is largely that of the lawyers and the courts.

(f) The interests of law and order in America might be well served if the official agency which prepares a consolidation or a summary of the general laws of a state, or the laws concerning some particular area such as motor vehicles, worked with educators in preparing a briefer edition of the consolidation or summary for use in secondary schools. With the high delinquency rate among persons in their late teens and early twenties, such a cooperative approach might be useful in helping lawmakers to better understand the kinds of presentations which facilitate learning by adolescents, and it might help teachers better to understand the problems which lawmakers face in trying to provide a suitable regulatory framework for a democratic society.

(11) One avenue through which to help future generations to equal or exceed the accomplishments of their predecessors is to supply them with better tools than their predecessors have had. The idea of tools should not be confined to measures, gauges, or other mechanical devices, but should include such matters as language form, concepts, and other tools used in thought. Future generations of Americans could be greatly helped through simplifying the English language, thereby making the language easier to learn so that more time and energy could be devoted to learning other things.

(a) The English language has several irregular verbs such as the verbs "to be" or "to go." These verbs have several different forms, in contrast with such regular verbs as "to walk" or "to visit." If the irregular verbs could be regularized, that aspect of grammar would be easier to learn.

(b) The English language has numerous words with various meanings—such as man, thing, pick, stuff, nice. Would a reduction in the number of such instances and the creation of new words for some of the meanings involved make it easier to learn to use the language effectively?

(c) In the context set forth, what would be the situation regarding nonphonetic spellings?

(d) Would most adults, to whom our schools and broader cultural influences have taught the present language structure, oppose changes of the types suggested?

(e) With respect to possible language reform, as with respect to most other types of social reform in our culture, the schools cannot play a leadership role but must follow the patterns which are indicated by other aspects of the culture.

(f) If the reform job inferred seems to be a big one, does progress lie in postponing it while we work at smaller ones or in trying to break up the big job into smaller ones? If the latter, how should we proceed?

(12) Concern about living under a system of laws which one can participate in making through the action of his representatives, rather than living under

the personal rule of one official, must recognize the limitations of the law concerning what can be effectively regulated by law and what cannot be.

(a) Laws must be stated in general terms which can have broad application because there are too many specific situations to have a law which applies to each one separately.

(b) When laws are stated in general terms, there may be many specific situations in which courts are asked to indicate what the law means in each of those situations. This permits leeway for the courts to show variation or favoritism.

(c) Conflicts within the legal structure frequently appear because the extent to which the group can control individual behavior is always a matter of degree. Thus the concept "society" assumes some movement of individual within the group or some contact among individuals. But such contact means that it is possible for one person to kill another. Since murder cannot be prevented under circumstances of the type indicated, societies try to discourage it through the penalties attached.

(d) Reference has often been made to American prohibition regulations concerning the manufacture and sale of alcoholic beverages, which were established during a national emergency, as a kind of regulation which cannot be enforced because the people do "not believe in it." To what extent does this imply that no law can be enforced unless the people in general will support it?

(e) The extent to which the people generally understand the nature of law and social regulation greatly influences the extent to which behavior can be regulated by law.

(f) If lawmaking and law-enforcement agencies, as well as the courts, had a more comprehensive understanding of the ways in which habits, values, and aspirations (or social psychology) influence human behavior, they could more nearly provide a legal framework for the maximum amount of regulation by law that is compatible with democratic concepts of personal liberty and social development.

(13) A society which professes to operate in such a way as to help its members achieve the maximum in personal development and satisfaction must be so concerned about motivation as to get young people to *want* to learn all they can and to *orient* their learnings and other achievements toward the benefit of the group as a whole.

(a) In a society in which material productivity is high and necessities such as food, clothing, and shelter are fairly easy to obtain, motivation of accomplishment must be placed on more abstract bases. Greater abstraction, or remoteness from immediate needs for self-preservation, points toward orientation on group well-being.

(b) Learning achievement in a particular direction tends to make it easier to motivate further achievement in that same direction. Such motivation is part of man's natural curiosity to explore and to conquer ignorance as a part of the broad unknown to be challenged.

(c) The aspect of some religious faiths which urges young people to learn all they can may reinforce a natural curiosity with a form of mystic or supernatural urge.

(d) Most idealism which has motivated great individual and group achievements in the world has included certain elements of mysticism, in the sense of projecting some type of affiliation with external power which the demonstrable knowledge and analytical competence of the time have not been able to explain in provable terms.

(e) Apart from a biological urge to explore and to achieve or conquer, and apart from the more elementary aspects of material needs for survival, the directions in which one is motivated to put forth effort are determined largely by what the group approves and considers important.

(f) It should be a function of a creative society to develop and maintain leaders for the purpose of devising new social goals toward which to motivate individual effort and for the purpose of devising new ways to motivate effort toward achieving those goals.

(14) In emphasis on social philosophy, one should recognize that there are important areas of philosophy and related intellectual disciplines which are not social in implications; that is, which do not derive their orientation or significance from contracts among people or the values of human morality and ethics.

(a) When philosophy is referred to in the original sense of a love of knowledge or of wisdom, one might ask if all knowledge is in some way concerned with human involvement.

(b) If one looks upon philosophy as a body of theory or investigation concerning principles or laws which not only underlie knowledge and thought but which underlie all other aspects of reality, it might seem apparent that only a small part of the total is concerned with human relationships.

(c) Contact with the broader nonsocial aspects of philosophy should contribute perspective in viewing the aspects of the total which are characterized as social philosophy.

(d) One's sense of personal adjustment and stability in life makes it important for him to develop a social philosophy that is appropriate for his own circumstances, and to develop some acquaintance with the non-social aspects of general philosophy will aid him in the process.

(e) In the development of a social philosophy from either an individual or a group standpoint, it is helpful to look upon social philosophy as a kind of specialty that has grown out of the broad mother field of general philosophy, much as economic philosophy, religious philosophy, political philosophy, etc., are specialties.

(f) The degree of personal satisfaction which people feel in their culture, without particular regard to the level of the culture's technology or material attainment, may be an index of the extent to which a constructive social philosophy prevails.

(15) It is not possible to develop a scientific code of ethics or a scientific system of government under law.

(a) Scientific laws are general statements which are intended to fit a large number of kindred situations rather well, although these laws may not precisely fit any one of those situations. The same is true of laws passed by legislative bodies, which need interpretation by courts or similar agencies in order to fit particular situations.

(b) In regard to lawmaking, it would be possible to establish conditions for precise observations regarding the occurrence of murder, adultery, stealing, air pollution, etc., much as conditions may be set up for determining the occurrence of oil, iron, heat, vegetation, insect life, etc.

(c) Similarities in the basic tenets of the world's major religions suggest that people who live under widely varying conditions have found much in common in regard to relationships among individuals.

(d) Statistics on crime and delinquency constitute scientific reports on the success or failure of particular laws that are being tried out for regulating human behavior. Such reports may be the basis for revising particular regulations, much as a chemist might revise his experiment for a second trial.

(e) Several authors who are reported in the present study urge that the education and general background of law-enforcement personnel and members of the judiciary include more study of anthropology, technology, sociology, economics, etc. When or to what extent should study in such areas be considered scientific?

(f) It is sometimes maintained that religion and humanitarianism are the fields from which we get ideals concerning those human relationships and values that should constitute the basis of laws and other regulations, and that science can only try out the suggestions or pronouncements which come from these two sources. What are the strengths and weaknesses of this view?

2. Controversial Issues and Social Philosophy

The division introduction refers to the second part of chapter 2 as considering some twenty issues which are controversial in American society. These issues are examined in considerable detail. One reason for this is that controversial issues are the most difficult matters to deal with in any student or discussion group. A corollary to this reason is the assumption or hope that a teacher or other group leader can follow, with regard to other controversial issues, a procedure similar to that illustrated by the issues used herewith. In significant respects, the presentation used with any of the twenty items might be looked upon as a core around which to organize further exploration of that item. Major growth in learners and discussion participants will be associated with the extent to which they develop further situational concepts.

In consideration of general organizational format and balance among chapters, five of the twenty items are presented within the text of the chapter. The others, which follow the same type of analysis, are presented in appendix no. 1. (See pages 369-414.)

The titles of the items presented within the chapter are as follows:

Americanization and American Lawlessness

Leisure Time and Earned Freedom

Rights and Opportunities of American Indians
Romantic Environmentalism
Crime and Punishment

The titles of the items presented in appendix no. 1 are listed below. Subdivisions under some of the titles are not shown in this listing.

Hero Models in a Changing America
Drugs and the Moral Code
Motivation: Why Men Work
Boredom and Motivation
The Marketplace as the Cradle of Culture
The City as a Cultural Development
Urban Crisis
Minority Groups
Special Education for Handicapped Persons
Population Growth and Cultural Status
Church and State in America
Government and the Separation of Powers
Lawlessness and its Consequences
Scientific Method
Research and Welfare

The five items included within the chapter text are presented herewith.

Americanization and American Lawlessness

A major limitation of the nation's schools and their educational accomplishments, from the standpoint of respect for law and order, could be stated in terms of Americanization. Great emphasis on Americanization appeared during the decades between the Civil War and World War I, when large numbers of immigrants came from Europe—with their wide range in language, general literacy, and other cultural backgrounds. During the time indicated, Americanization emphasized development in the immigrant of enough acquaintance with the English language and with the general mode of life in this country so that he could get a job and become self-supporting. Major requirements for most jobs were a strong physical organism, ability to learn rather quickly from example, willingness to work, and readiness to endure hardship. A high degree of literacy was not essential to the abundant demand for physical labor in the agriculture, industry, and frontier explorations of the time. Furthermore, the activities of government were simple in design, and were carried out primarily in local settings wherein the results were rather immediate and rather obvious to casual observation.

Under the circumstances described, the Americanization which was considered to be necessary was conceived in terms of brief and limited effort that focused on a few easily achieved and easily recognized changes in the outward appearance and behavior of the recent immigrant. And much of the Americanization that was carried on took place through work crews and general association in the community, rather than through particular efforts by public schools and other educational institutions.

Americanization of a different kind seems to be a greater need at present, greater than the Americanization which was emphasized at the turn of the century was a need at that time. The current need is greater and more difficult to meet because of three main factors: (1) it affects most of the population, with what seems to be relatively less seed corn from previous decades to exemplify the process and its desirable outcomes; (2) it demands a more comprehensive understanding of the philosophy and implications embodied in the American theory of individual-group relationships with which government should be concerned, and demands greater commitment of individual duty and responsibility for a practice that carries the theory into operation; (3) there is no other populous, geographically expansive, and extensively industrialized society to which the nation can look for a model, but major pioneering is required.

It should be recognized that the formulations of government set forth in the official documents and other pronouncements, of those persons among the limited group of Founding Fathers who were strong enough to prevail, were a reflection of ideals and hopes rather than a description of current or easily attainable realities. Much the same applies to the Civil War Amendments, which seemed necessary because of failure to realize important aspects of the earlier hopes. With a much larger population now than during either of the earlier periods, and with greater mobility and affluence generated largely by higher levels of popular education and a greater range of vocational opportunity, many poorly understood and largely unrealized aspects of the proclaimed idealism leave the way open for extensive lawlessness and delinquency.

As a society becomes more complex along lines such as inferred, not only do more social regulations become necessary, but a higher level of voluntary cooperation by individuals with the regulatory agencies becomes necessary in order for the system to function as an organized society. One should recognize that present-day nations vary markedly concerning the extent to which social behavior depends on direct action by a police force. The extreme in this respect is sometimes referred to as a police state. But in any system of government, three chief considerations are involved in determining the extent to which proclaimed regulations actually govern what happens: an understanding of what the regulations purport to require, an understanding of the goals which the requirements are intended to achieve, and the cost in money and other sacrifice which enforcement involves. When the considerations describe a relationship that may be called balance, peaceful and orderly conditions prevail. When there is extensive disorder and violation of proclaimed regulations, some type of imbalance among those considerations exists.

When imbalance is extensive, cries of "crime in the streets" or of "general disrespect for law and order" become loud and frequent. Among possible remedial measures, two are noted in the present connection. One emphasizes an expansion of the police force and of jail facilities, with substantial reliance on fear as a deterrent. The other emphasizes education: to develop an understanding of the American theory and structure of government; to develop an understanding of how a peaceful and orderly society depends on the voluntary cooperation of citizens according to prevailing regulations, including accepted procedures for changing the regulations; and to develop a voluntary commitment by the citizens to assume responsibility for the cooperation needed to make the system work.

Emphasis in the present study is based on education to produce a broad range of understanding and commitment, in order to achieve maximum operation within the structure of organized society and with a minimum of cost through monetary and other areas of sacrifice. While the study recognizes that the schools and the formal system of education cannot do the job alone, and that extensive educational responsibility must be carried on by such elements as the courts and the law-enforcement agencies, this section of the presentation deals essentially with greater contributions by different aspects or levels of the educational system than they now make.

Two basic features of our culture which underlie all levels or aspects of formal education are first noted: (1) our emphasis on individual rights and our neglect of individual responsibilities, in the philosophy and framework of government; (2) failure to develop insights concerning needs and tools for analysis of our social structure as that structure has become more complex, and failure to bring about constructive changes in the structure.

Ability to govern is always related to what government is expected to accomplish with the tools available and with the dedication by officials to the social ideals which government is expected to implement. In America at present, moral integrity and commitment are areas of major weakness and neglect. And when the people in general take the position that public officials and politicians are all dishonest and that a considerable amount of graft and corruption in government is to be expected, the people fail in their responsibility as citizens of a democratic society and contribute to the disintegration of democratic institutions.

Effort at systematic analysis concerning the origin and scope of political corruption in America must include inquiry into whether the political idealism set forth in connection with one reform movement embodies the seeds of later corruptions. The question is not asked with sufficient frequency or penetration regarding certain basic documents of American government. For example, the Bill of Rights is appropriately referred to as a great power for individual liberty and justice in America, and much of the same is said about the Fourteenth Amendment. No comparable emphasis is placed on civic responsibility of the individual, if "government by the people" is to operate effectively; no clear emphasis on "procedural due process" in developing an adequate sense of civic responsibility.

Several factors may be involved in the emphasis on rights in contrast with responsibilities, in our basic framework of government. One is that the Founding Fathers were men of recognized competence, achievement, moral integrity, and personal honor—in their immediate communities and more broadly throughout the countryside. Hence, when they pledged their "sacred honor," it was *not* an empty pledge, unless spelled out in detail regarding specific types of situations. Also, the kind of central government in Europe, with which these men and other Americans had had experience, was government which placed many demands and duties on the common people but granted them few rights and privileges. It is easy to see how an arrangement which promised to reverse this situation would be popular in America.

Perhaps more important than either foregoing item is a fundamental biological selfishness in human beings, which quite generally presses for expression. As a simplified statement of the tendency, one might say that most persons enjoy life and feel happy when they can do what they want to do, without interference by other persons or obstruction by a hostile physical environment. This absence of restraint embodies one of the simpler definitions of freedom. It requires considerable sophistication to define freedom in terms of self-discipline, so that one uses his personal resources in cooperation with others, under group planning and for collective well-being. The collective approach is at the heart of government, and in a democracy it must depend in considerable degree on self-discipline rather than primarily on discipline from outside agencies.

Weakness of the development of self-discipline and moral integrity is important in America's problems concerning law and order. And as American life becomes more complex, more types of relationships appear in which new applications of integrity must be made. The absence of firm guidelines or commitment concerning such relationships means the presence of moral uncertainty or disintegration. Implications of the guidelines and commitments extend beyond the sphere of government, but encompass government as a part of their involvement. When theologians refer to the guidelines and commitments in terms of God, they are invoking the most forceful type of emphasis which they can muster. Whatever the vocabulary, the emphasis is essential for life in a democratic society.

Leisure Time and Earned Freedom

Americans who are somewhat beyond middle life have lived through a period of great increase in the amount of leisure time available in general to the nation's people. And with leisure, as with many types of material goods or other elements in a culture, when it becomes abundant its distribution among individuals is likely to be uneven and new uses for it tend to appear. Hence, one might expect older persons to be impressed with the amount of leisure that is broadly available and expect youth who are in the process of establishing life patterns to be confused by it. The relationship between the two situations needs to be better understood than it is, because in any culture it is the responsibility of the mature generation to guide the youth into patterns of life which will be personally satisfying and socially constructive, whereas youth should become aware of their responsibility for understanding the nature of constructive activity and for acquiring behavior patterns accordingly. Adult indifference, or attempts to operate on the theory that youth are always right, cannot support a stable culture.

Carrying the responsibilities noted, in the presence of a seeming abundance of leisure, raises questions regarding closer scrutiny of the definitions and values concerned. When man engaged for long hours in work activities which demanded large amounts of physical energy, leisure was largely freedom from such activity to allow for recuperation and physical renewal. However, it probably never was used entirely for such renewal, but included some imaginative speculation, daydreaming, and imitative play at his serious life activities—out of which variations and improvements in ways of carrying on those activities emerged. Evidence of such early "play-use" of leisure can be seen in the sculpture on the walls of some caves in France and Spain. Other evidence can be seen in the "free play" of some children, who try to imitate the serious activities of adults whom they observe.

The aspects of leisure emphasized through the two illustrations point to a function of leisure in "imagination stretching," as well as to the oft-mentioned function of physical recuperation. Man's natural tendency to engage in imaginative play, when he is not physically tired, has helped during recent generations to broaden the conception of recreation and has provided a basis for the idea that leisure rather than necessity is the mother of invention.

Important in redefining or reformulating the concept of leisure is concern for shift in emphasis from the physical role to the imaginative role. A part of the concern involves the role of freedom in man's endeavors and whether freedom *from* something should emphasize the idea of freedom *for* something else. There are both physiological and cultural implications of the relationship between the two. The human organism is physiologically so constructed that some types of activity are satisfying and also necessary for physical and mental health; yet there are many types which may be satisfying to the individual organism, but culturally destructive rather than constructive. The greater the range available for free imaginative activity, the more important this culturally positive-negative implication becomes; likewise, the greater the guidance responsibility of the mature generation becomes, especially that of parents and teachers, and especially in regard to the physical and moral discipline of the individual.

One of the most difficult but most important areas of discipline concerns the relationship between leisure and freedom. America's rapid emergence of leisure, as associated with technological development, and the political conception of freedom which has historically dominated the nation underlie the importance and the difficulty noted. Questions as to the social importance of relationships between the amount of leisure available and the way it is used, or as to when leisure is a curse, did not seriously arise when there was not much leisure. This point is sound, although our culture has long included observations to the effect that "idleness is the devil's workshop."

With emphasis on leisure's potential for developing imagination, scrutiny by parents and teachers about the nature of imagination assumes growing importance. One initial point is that imagination does not take place in a vacuum, but in a head that is well-stocked with knowledge and experience. An associated point is that personal discipline is necessary in order to acquire an extensive background of knowledge and experience and to have the energy required for rather endless imaginative play regarding possible associations and implications involving background materials. Habits respecting food, exercise, and other aspects of one's physical life are important in developing and maintaining an organism that can produce an abundance of physical energy—and can do so over a fairly long span of life. Other habits and disciplines are important regarding the ways in which one uses his energy, with a view to maximizing returns in proportion to imput. Youth should learn that effective operation in any type of cultural setting requires the development of habits and disciplines of the kind indicated, that the development is governed by principles which may be called laws of nature, and that he should both understand these laws and accept commitment to live according to them. For comparison, the youth might observe that for a farmer to produce a good crop of corn he needs to understand the properties or characteristics of seed, climate, soil, insects, moisture, cultivation, fertilizer, sunlight, etc.

Personal freedom thus becomes the capacity to exercise broad control over the development and use of imagination and energy along avenues which are satisfying, and to a considerable extent social or political freedom accrues when the personal satisfactions come from activities which contribute to group well-being. Freedom in the sense indicated must therefore be *earned*. It does not fall "as the gentle rain from heaven," nor is it possible to bestow it by legislative or judicial act.

Technology is growing in importance with respect to the leisure-freedom conception of discipline and habit. This is because technology is shifting the philosophy of employment from "a necessity to work" toward "an opportunity to work." This point is reflected in the shortening work week, anxiety about unemployment, "job therapy" in treating mental illness, job training and placement in the rehabilitation of public offenders in penal institutions, paid and voluntary part-time work for retired persons, etc. The leisure-discipline-freedom-job linkage implies that "empty leisure," including much that is associated with front-porch rocking-chair folklore, is burdensome and boring, and that it is eroding and emaciating with respect to physical and mental competence.

One problem relative to developing in youth the idea of leisure, as associated with freedom through discipline and through achieving commitment to some pattern such as that described, is that the general philosophy involved is not more than dimly understood by most teachers. It is never heard of by many parents. Much of this is due to an exaggerated individualism and associated permissiveness which has increasingly enveloped several aspects of American culture since World War II. The situation described is one among numerous causes of the so-called breakdown in respect for law and order, on which there has been extensive comment during the past several years. Considerable evidence regarding the scope of "breakdown" problems can be seen when one notes conviction for criminal activities, or involvement in political scandals, by high-ranking public officials in whom the people have placed confidence as being worthy of public trust and worthy as models for youth to emulate. The retinue has included mayors, governors, judges, members of both houses of Congress, and others; that is, before Watergate revealed grandiose operations.[4]

The road to a politically cleaner and more ethical system of governmental operations, to which self-respecting citizens can show interest and dedication, is a long and difficult road. But it is a road that must be traveled if a decent conception of the American system is to return and endure. And the travel must be by an extending sequence of next steps. It may be helpful to remember, with Chinese sages of former generations, "A journey of a thousand miles begins with a single step."

Rights and Opportunities of American Indians

The minority status of Indians in the United States seems less clear than that of other ethnic minorities. This may in part reflect polarization around two conflicting goals. One pole concerns historical rights and status as shown by treaties, designation of reservations, government wardship, and other stipulated relationships between tribal organizations and the regulatory agencies of the broader surrounding culture. The other pole relates to continuously expanding participation by members of a tribe in the broader culture, some of which conflicts with reservation and wardship status.

The point may be illustrated by reference to jobs and to contractual relationships. As the economy outside the reservation expands, there is an increase in the number and types of nonreservation jobs that become available. To hold such jobs and thus gain access to the goods and services which the associated wages bring within reach, it is necessary to compete with persons of nonreservation origin and training. To obtain the technical and social background required for successful employee status, young Indians must acquire extensive nontribal background. Interest in nontribal recreations and other associations become part of the picture—through such mass media as the press and television.

The same general idea applies to contracts. The broader culture looks upon the power to contract as a right to exercise freedom regarding one's commitments with others, which affect future relationships between the contracting parties. In varying degrees, children, mentally incompetent persons, and other wards of the state are not looked upon as competent to contract—and ordinarily are not held accountable under alleged contractual arrangements. The wardship conception of Indian status is significant in this connection.

The contract idea applies not only to those aspects of treaty relationships between tribal organizations and the federal government, which have been of concern in "Wounded Knee" and elsewhere, but also to contracts between individual Indians or tribal representatives and individuals or private corporations in the broader economy. Such contracts may relate to timber, oil, coal, grazing, or other development of reservation lands or of individually held properties.

The foregoing logic respecting contracts in no sense justifies the federal government in ignoring treaty obligations, nor excuses government from protecting one individual against "unconscionable" advantage taken by another in contracting procedure. Neither does it assume that the government has no responsibility concerning reforestation associated with timber cutting on tribal property or rehabilitation of lands subjected to strip mining. But it does infer that where the broader culture provides legal remedies for abuse of contractual relations, those remedies will be pursued by aggrieved parties.

Pursuit of such remedies in itself implies a type of maturity, relative to a complex culture. It means a removal of the struggle against alleged wrongs from the streets and the theaters of noisy demonstration, to the legislative halls and the courts. One might note by comparison a distinct maturity over the past two generations in the techniques of organized labor, or in the techniques used by some women's groups—relative to the bottle-smashing operations in certain early temperance struggles, or the activities of some early suffragettes. Techniques associated with the Whiskey Rebellion, or some early farm groups in the Middle West, may also be instructive.

However, some aspects of tribal emphasis and reservation polarity rest substantially on mythology. These aspects refer to the Indians as the "original Americans" and dream of "restoration" to some imagined pre-Colombian paradise of regional occupancy and control. Just how long particular tribes, which controlled specific territory at the time of signing treaties with the federal government, had previously been in control of that territory is seldom noted. But the tribal wars which apparently characterized at least the later part of the pre-Columbian period, and the early part of our national life, suggest considerable shifting in regional occupancy and considerable violence in gaining possession. The point is: how far should the rollback be carried in seeking "original Americans," with some kind of mystical entitlement to present possession? In some respects the situation resembles that of the present Jewish state of Israel, in the heart of the Arab World. However, several Indian tribes would need a rollback of scarcely two centuries to show substantial tribal organization and dominant regional occupancy, whereas the Jews seem to need a rollback of perhaps thirty centuries in order to support a similar regional claim.

Some presumed leadership of Indian well-being suggests that the federal government should make extensive sums available to tribal groups, for use by such groups as they see fit—"to make their own mistakes," with no federal supervision which reflects the benefits of experience gained elsewhere. The need for dollars to develop tribal resources appears to be sound. But suggestions of the kind indicated concerning supervision should not be expected to generate nationwide taxpayer enthusiasm for waste under some Indian label. A question of socioeconomic balance is involved: How much would the people of the country as a whole be expected to pay in order to repeat the development of elementary political insights and fiscal responsibility in local groups? The problem is continuously developing wider significance.

There is another implication of Indian separateness and of disservice rendered by some television and other programs which are pleading for a preservation and development of separate tribal cultures. Separation and special rights imply special isolations and discriminations. For an Indian child in America to come in contact with much of the world's culture, he must learn English rather than depend on a tribal language. To enjoy reasonably good health and comfortable housing, he must depend on the technology of the broader surrounding culture. His small tribal group, with its limited technical competence and functioning material resources, cannot carry on research to develop new knowledge and cannot even apply America's existing technology in the effective development of resources which lie within the tribal domain.

To restrict an Indian child to his tribal culture would be to condemn him to a life of emptiness and peripheral existence; that is, peripheral with respect to health, education, vocational prospects, home life, language and communication, etc. And it would deny the American people the potential of developed human competence, as well as defy heralded principles of American democracy.

In addition, the development of several scattered tribal cultures points to a cleavage rather than a unity factor in the broader culture of the nation. The cleavage factor was prominent in American life during the period of hyphenated Americanism (i.e., German-American, Italian-American) before World War I; it has often been noted with respect to private and parochial schools in American popular education; it is currently a problem in Brazil with some of its strong cultural minorities; and it demands ongoing attention in Canada with respect to some ethnic minorities.

Foregoing statements should not cause one to overlook a kind of tourist nostalgia that senses ground for remorse in a threatened disappearance of the opportunity to visit isolated communities of quaint costumes, housing, language, artifacts, etc.; nor overlook the economic interest of persons who hold jobs in agencies which promote tribal separateness, rather than promote continued expansion in the opportunity of young Indians to identify with the broader American culture. However, this is much the same idea as that embodied in trying to develop broader negro participation in the nation's total culture, rather than trying to develop a separate negro culture in politics, banking, finance, etc. Individuals who profess a humanitarianism or philanthropic interest in helping some culturally restricted minority should assume responsibility for a sufficient understanding of the social structure so as to know *how* to be helpful.

Romantic Environmentalism

A group of people styled environmentalists have attracted a great deal of attention recently, although it may be difficult to determine their objectives or to evaluate their achievements. If one assumes that they are interested in retaining the geographical environment as nearly as possible in its "natural state," problems arise as to what nature includes or what period in nature's evolution they dream about. If they mean the "good old days" of their youth, or the days when their parents or grandparents were young, on what justification would they halt the rollback at such chosen points? Why not go back to the days of Pocahontas in America, or to the days of King Alfred in England, or even back to the dinosaurs? Is it selfish vested interest, dwarfed imagination, or some other personal restriction that portrays some hazy rollback objective?

And how is one to manicure his conception of physical space or of biological life so as to make it idyllically acceptable? In the days of DeSoto or of Daniel Boone there were presumably many fish in the streams, much game in the woods, and an abundance of wild flowers. There were also a goodly number of unfriendly Indians, a large number of poisonous snakes, and an abundance of mosquitoes and malaria. And if one suffered from illness or a broken limb, he was essentially free from "encroachment" by any physician or medical service. Some accounts of DeSoto's trek across the Southeast indicate that he lost more men from snakebite than in combat with hostile people. Apparently rattlesnakes and water moccasins were important aspects of the natural life of the time, as were many species of insects—some of which might now be in danger of extinction, largely because of human predators. In other sections of the country, blizzards, dust storms, hail, tornadoes and floods have long been parts of nature. Earthquakes in San Francisco and in Guatemala extend the picture. Through prayer and through a few sporadic excursions of materialistic developments, man has long tried to ameliorate his suffering from such aspects of nature.

Much additional objective consideration could be set forth to show that many who rapsodize about "preserving" or "restoring" the natural environment are dreaming about some idyllic environment that never has really existed and probably could not exist along with any considerable portion of the present human race continuing to live and to enjoy things which they consider more important than fishing in creeks or looking at wild flowers in the woods.

A fundamental consideration which then emerges concerns the evaluation of different aspects of the natural environment and from what standpoint.

Competition among different forms of life is an important feature of the natural environment, as noted by Darwin and others in formulating the doctrine that the fittest will survive. "Fittest" means best able to survive under the environmental conditions that prevail in a specific place at a specific time. It does not mean that those conditions never change. If one inquires about causes of change, he notes that many causes are involved. On a large-scale basis he may note the effects of glaciation; of phenomena which raised much of the Mississippi Valley from sea bottom to its present level; of erosion which produced canyons along the Colorado River, badlands in North Dakota, and delta country along much of the Mississippi River south of Cairo; of volcanoes and earthquakes which have disturbed local areas of the earth's crust and the life sustained by it; etc.

References made by environmentalists and others to man *and* nature imply an artificial dichotomy which sets man *against* nature, whereas a more realistic consideration looks upon man as a part of nature. Man is thus conceived to be involved in the various competitions among species for survival and perhaps in competitions with nonorganic aspects of nature. In the sense noted, every species is in competition with every other species, and to some extent members within a species compete with one another. Presumably every individual utilized its physical mass, agility of movement, poisonous sting, or other special competence to better its competitive status. Cunning and intelligence are among the special competencies of humans, most of the higher primates, and some other mammals. Shifts in physical environment, or perhaps in competencies, result in changes in the relative status of different species. Hence, some species become extinct while others flourish. Thus man seems to be gaining on reptiles, especially alligators, whereas insects seem at present to be gaining on man.

If one assumes that fitness determines survival, then he is saying that the standards of evaluation noted earlier are based on fitness. Furthermore, if he speaks from the standpoint of a human rather than from the standpoint of a toad or a weasel, then he says that the competitive goals and techniques which promote man's status rather than the status of such other species are good or desirable goals and techniques. In short, he is saying that man is the measure or that man shall be the master. Man thus exemplifies a characteristic that is common to every living species, that is, each species bending every other species to its own needs or wants insofar as possible. The exploitative or utilitarian approach, in the sense noted, is thus universal.

When environmentalists or others speak about preserving wildlife, they are not ordinarily solicitous about rattlesnakes, mosquitoes, or poison ivy. The interest is thus in a selective preservation. So are the interests of most other persons. The farmer who is interested in raising corn or cotton, rather than weeds, has a selective interest in plant life. The same applies to housewives who are interested in vegetable or flower gardens, or to poultrymen who are interested in producing friers rather than foxes.

If there is a unique feature in the selectivity fostered by romantic environmentalists, it lies in the goal or purpose of their solicitude for particular species and not for others. It is in this direction that one must look to understand their anxiety about some tragic or irreparable loss if any of the "threatened" species on their list should become extinct. They would thus halt the natural process of competition to extinction, in order to preserve species which they think make a significant contribution to their own personal well-being. The doctrine that man is the master then takes the form of *which men* shall be the masters in the *particular situation* at hand. This of course is the way in which value judgments occur in all organized society. It would not require a great stretch of the imagination to see a comparable determination among other species, regarding which specific individuals dominate the group.

It is quite understandable, for example, that some environmentalists would consider it more important that they and others of similar persuasion should be able to fish in a neighboring brook, hunt game in a nearby woods, or stroll about a landscape enjoying wild flowers or autumn foliage, than to think that persons who hold different views should be entitled to benefits which other uses of the pertinent natural resources might yield. Effort by environmentalists of the type characterized to make their concern appear to be of great importance for the enrichment of posterity does not make that effort unique. And if competition is strong regarding their goals in contrast with opposing goals, a considerable embroidery of logic and rationalization may develop. The enlisting of recruits then becomes less selective, with an operating philosophy comparable to that of the proverbial captain of a sailing vessel— "any port in a storm." This process is sometimes called political jockeying.

Perhaps America's growing affluence should be noted relative to romantic environmentalism. Affluence in this connection means an abundance of leisure time and material resources. Both are inferred in earlier comments on strolling about the landscape or fishing in the brook and in providing the substantial areas of wildlife preserves at convenient locations which those activities seem to presume. Some people think of golf as similarly among expansive recreational possibilities, at least with regard to space and financial outlay relative to number of participants. Comparisons are sometimes made with so-called spectator sports and other recreations. However, in view of the gyrations in the bleachers at college football games, one might in passing speculate whether that game should be called a "spectator" sport.

A comprehensive view of man as a part of the natural environment, and of his being in competition with every other form of life, assumes that he, like the other species, will use whatever competencies he has in order to advance his status relative to the others. The fact that his mind, hands, and other parts of his organism enable him to fashion and use tools more extensively than any other species, should be looked upon as an aspect of his equipment for the competitive encounter. Man is not the only species that uses other species for food, but apparently he is the only one which specifically produces or raises certain species for food purposes. But at the hunting stage of man's cultural evolution, he was not a producer as the present-day farmer is. He was a collector, somewhat in the sense of a squirrel. And concerning some areas of using the environment, he is only at present emerging from the collecting or harvesting stage and moving into the producing stage. This can be noted in the reforestation of timberlands, rehabilitation of strip-mine areas, restoring the fertility of cropland, facilitating growth and restocking of fisheries, breeding of fur-bearing animals, etc.

Problems regarding environmentalism, and *which men* shall be masters in particular situations, are more difficult concerning nonreplaceable natural resources. Any system of priorities concerning resource allocation depends on which men determine the priorities. Should we use gold primarily for jewelry, to decorate members of particular social classes, or for money in a system of international trading and fiscal relationships? How should we channel the use of oil as a source of energy, relative to emphasis on developing nuclear, solar, and other areas of possible new sources? How concerned should we be about wildlife as related to offshore and other drilling to find new oil deposits, or what type of concern should we manifest relative to deep-well explosions to release additional pockets of natural gas? Is it more important to be solicitous that some caribou might slip on a soft spot in the permafrost along an Alaska pipeline, than to assure that people along the Great Lakes and in New England will have heating oil in the wintertime? Numerous other items could be noted, pointing up the significance of *which men* determine the priorities.

As to research concerning sources of energy and other natural resources, passing reference should be made to a concept in physics: that man can neither create nor destroy matter, but only change its form. Certain instances of atom-splitting have demonstrated one possibility associated with changing the form. Cyclotron and other research may discover other possibilities, and research on the recycling of waste might discover still others.

The theme of the preceding discussion is that man's environment has continuously changed since he first appeared on earth, that every form of life as well as inorganic forces have influenced the changes, but that man has steadily increased his capacity to influence the direction of the change. Growth in the capacity to influence change means expansion in man's use of other species to serve his purposes. However, it should not be supposed that there has typically been universal agreement as to the uses or other relationship between him and specific other species. One manifestation of the same situation today appears in the concern of some environmentalists. The policies and activities of environmentalists can be of great social value in generating scrutiny as to particular uses of the environment, so that the values of immediate uses are not gained at the cost of unnecessarily negating extensive future values. But romantic sentimentality about future values, without a public analysis of factual support, can be very deceptive regarding veiled forms of selfishness, and therefore highly negative respecting future social values.

Crime and Punishment

One of the things that made Dostoevski's *Crime and Punishment* rank among the world's great novels was his struggle with a continuing problem that faces every organized society. The struggle concerns the need of organized society for regulations to guide the behavior of individuals in their relationships with one another; to provide information and discipline for the transgressors so that the code will be respected and followed by the people in general; and to strike some balance between restricting or eliminating the offender for the protection of others and rehabilitating him so that he can return to a status of equality among those others.

Three features of the process are noted which make it perennial, both with respect to a particular ongoing society and with respect to comparing one society with another. One feature is that each generation is born without any background of habits or skills which equips it for approved behavior in the particular society into which it is born. Another feature is that the governing philosophy and guidelines concerning what constitutes approved behavior, or what constitutes appropriate balance between restriction and rehabilitation, changes from time to time. In part related to change in philosophy is a third feature concerning developments in technology which may expand or otherside modify the alternatives available for dealing with particular types of transgressors. Housing arrangements and supervised employment at some kind of work, or perhaps surgery or drug therapy, may be among technological developments.

Perhaps most of the attitudes and remedial procedures associated with crime are related to prevailing ideas of cause. The revenge approach, which would deal severely with the offender, is based on the philosophy that the fault or cause rests with the individual; that society, or the king, can do no wrong. Accordingly, the individual must pay, but the group determines the price; that is, the code of penalties for the list of offenses which occur. Under simple conceptions of justice, the code tends to be detailed and rigid. When the code shows flexibility so that a judge or council has leeway in assigning penalties and can take ameliorating circumstances into account, the idea is emerging that cause may be complex and that several causal factors may be involved—factors which vary in relative importance.

Somewhat farther down the line of possibility regarding multiple causes is the idea that in some situations there may be causal factors which are so diverse and interwoven that they embody a major portion of the community's social structure. Extremists down this avenue freely assign poverty, cultural deprivation, some kind of discrimination, or some other type of social cause for practically every type of individual transgression that occurs. This approach essentially absolves the individual of personal responsibility for developing the attitudes and competencies necessary for effective participation in the existing social structure. It emphasizes community responsibility for rehabilitation, with no more than secondary concern about the personal responsibility of the individual.

Perhaps the most important weakness of this approach is its neglect of the need for personal discipline, if the individual is to learn to develop and constructively utilize his physical and mental energies, time, and other resources so as to be able to participate effectively in any kind of organized activity—whether the procedure is called rehabilitation, or something else. The idea is sometimes expressed by saying that it is not possible to rehabilitate someone who has no interest in being rehabilitated and who is unwilling to cooperate in the process. Americans differ greatly in how far down the avenue described they consider our present-day social practice to be.

With respect to rehabilitation and otherwise, the problem of balance in relation to offense and remedy, needs and service, etc., is always present. One reference to balance appears in the statement: make the penalty fit the offense. Among the more vigorous current disputes on balance, before the courts and elsewhere, is one relating to capital punishment. In America and in other countries involved in such disputes, capital punishment is looked upon as the end point beyond which the state's exactions against the individual cannot go. While there may be discussion about different possible means of putting an individual to death, the discussion assumes that torture in the sense of persecution is not to be involved, as it has sometimes been involved in religious inquisitions and in other operations in different parts of the world.

Several considerations become involved in the balance approach to capital punishment. Some of these relate to religious and associated concern about the sanctity or inherent worth of human life, in evaluating relationships between the individual and the group. Promoters of the idea of abolishing capital punishment on the basis indicated are usually not bothered about consistency in social practice regarding the taking of human life on an individualized basis through such avenues as abortion or euthenasia, or on a wholesale basis through war. Operations on a quantitatively intermediate basis, as in the case of American industrial and highway fatalities, merely rate passing comment on weekend statistics.

A substantially different approach might emphasize socioeconomic considerations from the group standpoint and might recognize nature's pattern. This pattern is reflected when successive generations are replaced by new ones, or when other forms of struggle emphasize survival of the group or species, although individuals will be sacrificed in the process. Much of the rationalization justifying war rests on the latter basis. The approach which is here characterized as socioeconomic might also tend to ask how important is the convicted person for the well-being of others in the group, in contrast with the threat which his continued presence constitutes for tl n? This approach might further ask, in view of concerted efforts to reduce the birth rate and of broad indifference to premature death from such causes as illness and accident, what is the quantitative importance of an occasional person freed from capital punishment? The cost in time and effort for rehabilitating such a person, and the anxiety in a community which is asked to accept him back into an equalitarian status regarding civil rights and economic productivity, this logic might continue, would be greater than the value of any contribution that he might be expected to make.

In a society which provides for considerable individual participation in the direction of government, one intangible arises which bears rather heavily on the social or group approach. That intangible is that in the minds of numerous individuals the question arises: suppose I should be the convicted person? It is easier for most persons, whose value structures are rather narrowly or selfishly personal, to identify with a specific person who has been singled out by conviction than to identify with a broad social ideal which infers that "somebody" might be threatened by the convicted person's continuance. It is typically easier to focus on some identified person in regard to the general idea "don't do to another what you would not like to have done to yourself," than to focus on some potential but anonymous Mr. X. But the importance of this personal-identity view also has limits, as when conditioned on how many crimes of a heinous nature have been committed in the community within a comparatively recent time; that is, what is the prevailing level of fear and anxiety?

Several of the problems connected with identifying and punishing criminals, relative to some kind of balanced code, help justify great emphasis on crime prevention. In a vaguely general way, this concept of prevention has been in our culture for a long time—cf., "a stitch in time, saves nine." But indifference stifles inquiry into the application of the concept to new areas of human relationships, specifically with respect to what constitutes a stitch and where to apply it. However, growth of the preventive philosophy in medicine and public health, education and unemployment, industrial and highway design relative to accident frequency, etc., justifies hope regarding crime prevention and regarding prevention in other areas in which problems of rehabilitation tend to become extensive.

While foregoing comments focus on rather separate considerations of crime and punishment, operating programs necessarily include some combination of these and perhaps other considerations. Where the legal framework permits a judge or council substantial leeway in assigning penalties, one might expect substantial range of considerations to be taken into account. This situation emphasizes the importance of professional competence and moral integrity on the part of public officials, with respect to justice under the American system.

Chapter 3

TOPIC SUGGESTIONS FOR STUDYING
THE BACKGROUND OF LAWLESSNESS

For most study or discussion situations which emphasize the content aspects of learning development, it is desirable to have a topic outline. In high-school or more mature groups, each member with a copy of the outline can get an overview of what to expect and can offer modifications.

The accompanying outlines which suggest four topic areas are intended to illustrate types of areas which might be developed, with the specific items intended to reflect one approach that could be used regarding such topics.

The four suggested areas are: (1) popular education; (2) politics and government; (3) the courts, justice and the regulatory structure; (4) the police, correction, and rehabilitation. Several of the subtopics might be dealt with through one lecture or a short series of lectures, or in some comparable way. While the particular topics noted can have substantial educational or broader social value, it is presumed that the teacher or discussion leader will also use other topics. Some of such other topics may be better suited to certain groups or communities than those noted here.

1. Suggested Topics on Popular Education

Topics under this caption appear in two categories: general considerations and current issues in American education. For emphasis, it is reiterated that the topics listed are intended only to be illustrative.

General considerations
(1) Genetic inheritance and zero knowledge at birth
    (a) Values of reflexes and instincts as related to knowledge
    (b) Capacity of man and of other species to learn and adjust
    (c) Values if man could inherit (biologically) the knowledge of his ancestors
    (d) Freedom of the child from burdensome misinformation of his ancestors
    (e) Relationships and differences between biological and social inheritance
(2) Early avenues of learning and education
    (a) Early in the life of the individual, versus early in the life of the race

(b) Language and the mother tongue

(c) Parental supervision of learning in nonhuman mammals

(d) Parental "smothering" among humans and retarded development of maturity

(3) The human family as bridge between biological and social direction of learning

(a) What puppies, kittens, raccoons, etc., learn from their parents

(b) Incidental versus consciously directed learning in the human family

(c) Family-directed learning in the home and child contacts outside the home

(d) Community association and movement of people in early cultural development

(4) Contacts and competitions between home and community (or state)

(a) Compulsory education and civic training

(b) Public education as a branch of the police power
Education versus other avenues of social control
Compulsory taxation and compulsory school attendance

(c) State control, and child versus civic well-being

(5) Centralized versus local control of public education

(a) Control by a centralized state versus by a centralized church
Private schools and social cleavage
Anxieties about state monopoly and a "police state"

(b) Feasibility and mythology of central support and local control

(6) Adult education

(a) Incidental learning through casual association among people

(b) On-the-job training and vocational competence

(c) Formal classes and educational programs for adults

(d) Television as mass adult education

Current issues in American education

(1) Equality of educational opportunity

(a) Administrative and taxing arrangements

(b) Enrollment in more than one school system
Public and parochial schools
Curriculums of different public school systems
Vocational programs
Other differences in curriculums

(c) Educational opportunity and the development of human resources

(2) Racial integration

(a) Integration as a major educational objective
Racial understanding and socioeconomic strength of the culture
Reservation and tribal culture of American Indians
"Melting pot" concept as applied to race

(b) Gains and losses through forced and voluntary integration
Areas of greater learning achievement
Areas of learning sacrifice and loss

(c) Race and hero models for American youth

(d) Staff integration and employment rights

Racial quotas in employment
Objective tests, in staff employment and upgrading
(e) Busing to promote integration
(f) Problems concerning criteria of a unitary school system
(g) Integration and international relations
(3) State and church in American education
(a) Role of the church in early American life
Church as historic symbol and bearer of the culture in Western society
Control of the American school curriculum and staff
(b) Spread of popular education
As related to conflicting denominationalism
As related to financial support and administrative organization
(c) Social ethics versus sectarian doctrine
(4) Social ideals and lawlessness in America
(a) Understanding civic ideals versus commitment to support them
(b) Relationships between material and other values in a democratic society
(c) Technology and the origin of ideals
(d) Ethics and other theory in cultural development
(5) Vocational education and economic opportunity
(a) The job as avenue to cultural participation
(b) Complex technology and range of vocational opportunity
(c) Apprenticeships and intern experiences
(d) Collective bargaining and economic understanding
(e) Wage and price fixing in a complex economy
(f) Technological and other unemployment
(6) Methods and media in American education
(a) Role and limits of imitation as a method of learning
(b) Mass media in school and in nonschool education
Publicly sponsored educational television
Commercially sponsored television
(c) Experimental method and learning by doing
(d) Student responsibility for his own learning achievement
(e) Developing the capacity to formulate and interpret theory
(7) The group and the individual in a democratic society
(a) The individual organism as source of ideas, hypotheses, etc.
(b) Personal discipline as essential to creative imagination
(c) Social organization versus individual chaos
Status or respect as a social concept
Earned status versus inherent status
(d) Dependence of individual achievement on community resources

2. Suggested Topics on Politics and Government

Social structure and its operation as constituting the government
(1) Need of populous groups for internal organization and regulation

(2) Social change as cause and as result of regulation by government
(3) Cultural homogeneity and unity or centralization in government
    (a) Genetic and ethnic background as related to homogeneity
    (b) Communication and social mobility as related to homogeneity

Politics as the social consideration of public issues
(1) Formal and informal political discussion and debate versus group action
    (a) Governmental structure and delegation of power and of duty to act
    (b) When discussion and debate increase versus decrease the competence of the people to evaluate action taken under delegated powers
(2) Political science as not an accurate science
    (a) Role of variation among the people in competence and interests
    (b) Role of variation among officials in competence and integrity
    (c) Ways to make political science more objective, scientific, and predictable
(3) Basic importance of an economic or material foundation to provide resources for governmental or other action
    (a) Who shall pay taxes and how much
    (b) Who shall receive the benefits of governmental service, in what ways, and to what extent
        Machinery for administering benefits
        Duties owed by those who receive benefits
    (c) Budgets, deficit spending, and inflation
        Benefits as pauperizing the recipients
        Social philosophy and what the individual is entitled to receive

Functions of government in a populous and complex society
(1) Restrictive or compulsory functions
    (a) Restraining certain interferences with other persons and with their property, etc.
    (b) Compelling certain actions regarding other persons, etc.
(2) Positive service to promote the public well-being
    (a) Areas of overlap between restrictions and compulsions
    (b) Social philosophy and expanding areas of service in America
    (c) Service for public well-being as expense versus investment—i.e., public education, health services, police and fire protection, public highways and recreational facilities, public housing; also national defense and foreign relations, coining money and maintaining monetary stability, rendering postal service; etc.
(3) Providing for education, medicare, fire protection, highway travel, etc., at group or public expense as being community, communal, or communistic in social orientation

Ways of classifying political systems
(1) Number and homogeneity of the people governed
(2) Land or territory involved—as to amount, surface features, climate, geographical location, etc.
(3) Wealth, technology, and other bases of power which the culture reflects
(4) Mode and degree of popular participation in government operations

(5) Historic duration, adjustability, and ongoing vigor of the existing system

(6) Period or stage of cultural and economic development involved—Cf. tribal council, noted in anthropology; absolute monarchies and despotisms; oligarchies; constitutional monarchies; direct and representative democracies; totalitarian "democracies", etc.

Comparative study of political systems

(1) Determining what elements to study or compare

(2) Possible elements for comparison

    (a) Ways in which different systems insist that they govern for the welfare of the governed

    (b) General status of the common people

        Basis and importance of social class distinctions

        Role of inheritance

            As to title of nobility or some comparable distinction

            As to wealth, property, jobs, etc.

    (c) Nature and scope of the services which government is expected to render

    (d) Branches of the government and respective powers of the different branches

    (e) Mode of choosing and of controlling public officials

        Defining civil rights and duties

        Opportunity of the people to criticize their government

        Freedom to vote in showing disapproval as well as in showing approval

Information and propaganda in the operations of government

(1) The continuum-nature of relationships between information, propaganda, and censorship

(2) The right of the people to know (*know what*)—freedom of the news media and the philosophy of government

(3) Duty of the people to become informed and natural human laziness

(4) Duty of the people to act on the basis of information and reflection, and the courage and motivation to do so

(5) Education, propaganda, "news management," and public relations

    (a) Degree of realism in anticipating government wholly without propaganda

    (b) Differentiation between education and propaganda—by definition or otherwise

(6) Widespread concern by government about the content of education and of propaganda, as an indication that all governments regard what the people think to be important

(7) Research by government to expand information and knowledge

    (a) As to natural science and technology

    (b) As to ways in which government does or might operate

Statesmanship and corruption in politics and government

(1) Partisan politics as constituting opposing categories of selfishness and vested interest

(a) Patronage, as officially recognized and tolerated favoritisms and rewards for personal service as in campaigns, spoils politics

(b) Nepotism as pushing the characteristics of patronage too far, especially with regard to kinfolk—cf., "giving your grandmother a good job, for the welfare of the state."

(2) Innate selfishness versus group perspective and moral integrity as basic in all forms of corruption

(a) Personal selfishness as a trait having survival value in the relative isolation of precivilized life, but usually an obstacle to group cooperation on which civilized life depends

(b) Burden on education and psychological conditioning to overcome the inherent selfishness which is part of the equipment of each generation

(c) Will biological evolution eventually cause personal selfishness to fade through disuse as a human trait, comparable to disuse and the status of the vermiform appendix

(3) Lessons to be learned from Watergate

Models of government available for study by the Founding Fathers

(1) Problems of American government today which were nonexistent when the Founding Fathers attempted to work out a structure of government for the nation

(2) American and worldwide accumulation of information, since the nation was founded, on how governments actually function. Competence regarding our use of this information in attacking current problems of government

(3) Outlook for good government in America, now or in the future, without a motivation and a dedication comparable to that of the Founding Fathers

Democratic citizenship as a task to be worked at continuously

(1) The people as essentially deserving the kind of government that they have—totalitarian, repesentative democracy, or something else, depending on popular imagination and effort to develop good government

(2) Deservedness and collective responsibility for cooperative effort and surveillance, in contrast with personal indifference and associated selfishness

(3) A fundamental conflict in man's nature as residing in a tendency to shun responsibility and associated demands for sacrifice, but to desire power over others—with broad social approval. Effective operation, in government or in other areas of social relationships as demanding extensive harmony between these two characteristics

3. Suggested Topics on the Courts,
Justice, and the Regulatory System

Nature and origin of personal rights

(1) Religious and other conceptions of inherent rights

(2) Rights as formulated conceptions of justice in particular situations

(3) Rights as related to personal status and needs

(4) Enforcement as essential to the concept of rights

(5) Social change and shifts in rights

Social regulation and government in preliterate and pretechnical societies
(1) When and in regard to what is social regulation necessary
(2) Determining the scope and degree of authority accorded to regulatory agencies
(3) Perennial struggle as to competence and integrity in government
(4) Complexity of regulatory machinery and rate of crime and delinquency

Systems of government and social control
(1) Habits and customs as regulatory forces
(2) Emergence and scope of the common law
(3) When formal statutes supersede the common law

Government by laws versus government by men
(1) General implications
(2) Continuous evolution in systems of government by laws
(3) Varying degrees of personal rule in all regulatory systems

Constitutional law
(1) Basic government under a charter or constitution
(2) The British system
(3) The American system
   Federal constitution
   State constitutions
(4) The constitution and the courts in America
   Federal courts
   State courts
(5) The constitution as distrust of legislatures, and of shifting electorates, to govern
   Formal machinery for constitutional amendment
   Historical setting of amendments to the U.S. Constitution
   The United Nations Charter and constitutional government

Procedural and substantive law
(1) Importance of the procedure by which justice is determined
(2) What the legal rights are versus what they might be or should be
(3) Procedural law and individual status
(4) When procedural law actually becomes substantive law

Code systems versus the common law
(1) Major codes of the Western world
   Hammurabi (1955-1913 B.C.)
   Moses (13th century B.C.)
   Justinian (483-565 A.D.)
   Napoleon (1769-1821)
(2) Anglo-American common law
   Growth and flexibility of the common law
   Common law as law of the future (Holmes, Pound)
(3) Transfer of the common law into constitutional systems
(4) Oriental systems

Criminal and Civil law
(1) Seriousness of offense against public well-being
   As related to persons

As related to property
(2) Trial procedures
(3) Penalties
　　The history of capital punishment
　　Bases for evaluating other penalties
(4) Relation to correction and rehabilitation
(5) Shifts in social structure by legislation—from criminal to civil and vice versa

Trial of the accused before a jury of peers
(1) Theory of justice and fairness in judgment by equals
(2) Trial before a jury versus before a judge
　　Types of cases
　　Expediting procedure
　　Results as to justice meted out
(3) Venu and justice
(4) Constitutional protections and the tyranny of peers (public opinion)
　　When do mobs constitute peers
　　Criteria and procedure in jury selection

Evidence and proof
(1) Admissibility of evidence
(2) Validity of evidence
　　Expert testimony
　　Records and exhibits
　　When hearsay is all the evidence there is
(3) Adequacy of evidence
　　Amount and quality
　　Categories—documentary, testamentary, circumstantial, etc.
(4) Evidentiary hearings

Role and limitations of precedent—conservatism and activism
(1) As related to dependability in knowing what the law is
(2) As to flexibility and growth of the law in accordance with social change
(3) Split decisions by courts
(4) Reversal by an appellate tribunal of its own former decisions

Crime prevention
(1) Understanding the nature and role of law and of law enforcement
(2) Civic responsibility and participation
(3) Causes of crime
　　Economic considerations
　　Noneconomic competitions for power
　　Failure to repeal laws which are obsolete or not enforced
　　Perpetuation or extension of individual habits
(4) Law enforcement as a deterrent
(5) Respect for law versus fear of the law, and basic overlappings

Terrorism as a technique of human regulation
(1) Terrorism and law as natural alternatives
(2) Scope and application of terrorism
　　Among individuals—cf., some aspects of frontier life
　　Among ethnic groups—Arabs-Jews; negro-white; etc.

Among nations—North and South Korea; North and South Viet Nam; England and Ireland

Conservatism and reform in human progress
(1) The function of institutions in providing social stability and service
(2) Social progress as demanding both conservation and reform
(3) Respect for past creations as inspiration for new ones
(4) Social regulation and government as demanding continuously creative growth
(5) Respect for the legal structure as related to creative government
    Contempt of Court; Contempt of Congress
    Social image of the courts and of other governmental agencies

4. Suggested Topics on the Police, Corrections, and Rehabilitation

Defining and identifying crimes and public offenses
(1) Legal enactments as defining crime
(2) Relationship between increasing numbers of laws or regulations and increase in violations
(3) Existence of criminal acts which no law defines as such—Nuremberg Trials, Nazis (1945-46)

Police image in the community
(1) On what does image depend
(2) Ways in which image is important for community well-being
(3) Relative importance of perception (image) and of fact
(4) Perception which children have of policemen

Career concept for police service
(1) Interest and understanding of careers by youth
(2) Development of police science and the police career
(3) Decision-making by police in different kinds of cases
(4) College education for the patrolman
(5) Status of the police career among other careers in the public service

Community support of the police
(1) Responsibility of the individual citizen for a free and orderly society
(2) Problems of police-community relationships
(3) Police response to the domestic disturbance (family quarrels)
(4) Willful obstruction of peace officers by citizens
(5) Status of the policeman's right to free speech
(6) Support and coordination between bar and police

Riots and police action
(1) Why do people riot
(2) Bases for determining when a riot exists or threatens
(3) Special training for avoiding and for dealing with riots
(4) Riot and social reform

Police "brutality"
(1) When is behavior of one person toward another brutal
(2) The situation when one person has police authority over another
(3) Lawlessness in the enforcement of law

Paying the cost of damage caused by the police
    (1) Scope of damage and injury situations
    (2) Present burden on persons injured or suffering property damage
    (3) Tort liability of the state or municipality
    (4) Special insurance possibilities

Public attitudes and treatment of offenders
    (1) Revenge versus rehabilitation
    (2) Education as to procedures in criminal correction
    (3) Role of news media in treatment and correction
    (4) Justice and legal service offered after the trial

Correction and rehabilitation of public offenders
    (1) Correction as based on fundamental human dignity
    (2) Correction or rehabilitation as a community-wide enterprise
    (3) Changing habits, attitudes, competencies, so that the offender can be reintegrated into the total society
    (4) The halfway house concept in the rehabilitation process

Ignorance and the law
    (1) How far can the individual go in knowing the law
    (2) Individual and collective responsibility for the individual's knowing the law
    (3) Community-wide ignorance and the possibility of justice
    (4) Relationship between violence and education

Cultural bias and legal systems
    (1) Every legal system reflects the values of its culture
    (2) How goals and biases develop
    (3) Does fostering some goals rather than others mean bias
    (4) Majority versus minority biases

Parent versus state in the life of the child
    (1) Universal concern of organized societies for "citizenship" or civic education
        Rituals and disciplines in preliterate societies
        Literacy and law
    (2) The state and constitutional freedoms of the individual
    (3) School attendance, vaccination, and other state compulsions
    (4) Does expansion of state or civic authority and responsibility necessarily require contraction of home or parental authority and responsibility

Place of research in dealing with crime and correction
    (1) Research as a method of solving problems
    (2) Conditions under which particular types of crime arise
    (3) Results on effectiveness of different remedies used in dealing with crime
    (4) Relation of a "previous record" to present sentencing
    (5) Use and abuse of statistics in correctional research

Chapter 4

STUDY PROJECTS IN UNDERSTANDING LAWLESSNESS AND CIVIC RESPONSIBILITY

For some kinds of study, projects can offer a focus or thread of continuity which draws upon considerable time and a substantial range of material. A project can be adjusted to one or to several participants and may be fairly easy to accommodate to different rates of progress at different times. Moreover, projects often constitute a constructive way to acquaint learners with sources from which to secure pertinent material on a wide range of subjects and with how to organize such material effectively.

In regard to lawlessness and to individual civic responsibility concerning the regulatory structure of organized society, this chapter indicates two lines of project consideration. One line refers to philanthropic foundations. Its intent is to call the attention of learners to the nature of such agencies, and to afford learners an opportunity to study the kinds of activities in which foundations engage and the scope of influence which they have had on the development of education. The other line relates to a study of the careers of individual citizens who have been illustrious in the development of various areas of civilization. The biographical approach thus indicated sets forth a personal embodiment of the traits or qualities of good citizenship which are essential for the collective improvement of human existence.

1. Philanthropic Foundations

There are many philanthropic foundations in America, with widely different origins and bases of support and with widely different purposes. A recent listing noted 6803, which met the stipulated definition for that particular listing: namely, that the foundation either have assets of $200,000, or make grants of at least $10,000 in the year of reporting.[5] Only a few of the larger foundations are individually noted here.

The 1967 Foundations Directory[6] listed thirteen foundations with assets of over $200 million each. These foundations, with their respective assets and founding dates, were:

Foundation	Assets (millions)	Founding date
Ford Foundation	$3,050	1936
Rockefeller Foundation	854	1913
Duke Endowment	692	1924
Kellogg (W. K.) Foundation	492	1930
Mott (Charles Stewart) Foundation	424	1926
Hartford (John A.) Foundation	342	1929
Lilly Endowment	320	1937
Sloan (Alfred P.) Foundation	309	1934
Carnegie Corporation of New York	289	1911
Pew Memorial Trust	273	1957
Longwood Foundation	251	1937
Moody Foundation	244	1942
Rockefeller Brothers Fund	210	1940

2. Biographical Materials

The biographical materials are grouped according to areas of interest and contribution. Fourteen areas of the culture are differentiated. Obviously, other groupings might have been made of the particular materials included, or other areas of the culture might have been selected for illustrative groupings.

Each of the fourteen groups has two phases, which follow an introductory statement. The first phase sets forth "concepts for discussion," which relate to different implications of the area concerned. The second phase lists "individuals to consider" and presents certain information on each individual listed.

The individuals are persons who have contributed significantly to the areas noted. However, no particular effort is made to insure that these persons have made the most important contributions that have ever been made to the respective areas. One reason for this situation relates to problems of criteria as to what or who is most important, especially when a rather large number of persons is listed, as in the case of the fourteen areas. Another reason is that a rather wide range in types of contribution is indicated, in order to afford a range of avenues along which the imagination of learners might be stimulated. For this purpose, substantial contributions which may seem to a learner to be within his reach may be more stimulating than top-notch contributions which are easy for ordinary persons to look upon as representing achievement that is beyond their competence. In a few instances, one name may appear on more than one list. While most of the persons listed are Americans, some are from other countries. Insofar as the information is available, the life span is given for each person listed.

Most of the fourteen areas include several pages. Hence, with one exception, details on the materials are set forth in appendix form, rather than within the text of the chapter. The exception concerns agriculture, which appears in the text largely for illustrative purposes. The other thirteen areas are grouped under appendix no. 2. Each includes an introductory statement as an aid to perspective. (See pages 415-478.)

The thirteen areas under appendix no. 2 have been designated as shown herewith. Some designations are in terms of interests, and others are in terms of persons, whichever seems clearer.

While these materials are presented in appendix form, as an aid to chapter balance and organizational format, they should be read as an integral part of the chapter discussion at this point.

The thirteen area designations, apart from agriculture, are:

1. Banking and Finance
2. Business, Industry, and Labor
3. Clergymen and Religion
4. Inventors and Discoverers
5. Jurists and Legal Scholars
6. Literature
7. Manufacturing
8. Medicine and Health
9. Science
10. Teachers and Educators
11. Transportation and Communication
12. Women
13. Miscellaneous

Agriculture

Anthropology indicates that long before man developed literacy, he migrated, fought wars, starved, prospered culturally, and experienced other domination of his life because of the nature of his food supply. Less is said about clothing, either for protection or for personal ornamentation. The role of the United States as a producer of food for other parts of the world has been emphasized by two world wars and by drought and near-famine conditions at other times.

From the standpoint of land and climate, there are few large areas in the world which are as favorably situated with respect to the production of food as large areas of the United States. But technology has greatly influenced this country's productivity—through soil analysis and the development of fertilizers; through plant and animal breeding, with the development of more productive strains; through price and fiscal arrangements, which encourage the effective utilization of our land and technology within the nation's prevailing economic structure: and through a further technology of processing and distribution for transforming raw materials and making the results available at convenient points of utilization.

The foregoing indicates the complicated nature of today's system in America for providing food and other supplies which depend directly on agriculture. For well over a generation, most regular sessions of the United States Congress have been concerned with agricultural legislation and with designating subsidiary federal agencies to exercise regulatory powers and to carry associated responsibilities. Most states have taken similar action. Insofar as the future promises any substantial change in these respects, the change will apparently be in the direction of more extensive regulatory provisions. In the case of regulations concerning agriculture as concerning other fields, every regulation carries with it certain prospects of violation and problems of enforcement.

The list of persons suggested for feasible project consideration regarding the development and place of agriculture in the nation's regulatory system indicates many ramifications of the agricultural field and many stages in its development. Consideration of such persons and developments should help young Americans to understand the role of our regulatory system in the culture of the nation.

Concepts for Discussion

(1) Man can develop several arrangements for evening up the regional and the worldwide surplus-shortage fluctuation in food supply, which seem by nature to occur. Among possible arrangements, irrigation and storage of surpluses are only two. Others should also be considered.

(2) The cost of processing, packaging, refrigerating, and distributing foods through supermarkets or otherwise, constitutes a larger *percent* of the total cost of food for the American home now than it did before World War I.

(3) The land-grant college, and kindred programs in high schools and in extension service, direct too much attention to the narrow vocational aspects of agriculture and too little to other aspects of making the life of the student or learner personally enjoyable and socially constructive.

(4) Insofar as agriculture is an experimental science with respect to procedures in such matters as producing grain and meat, the regulatory structure concerning the role of agriculture in the total culture must also be experimental. Moreover, a similar experimental approach should be used concerning the laws and regulations governing most other aspects of American society.

(5) Farm organizations (i.e., National Grange, American Farm Bureau Federation, National Farmers Union, National Farmers Organization, stock breeder associations, etc.) have been concerned mainly with the nonvocational aspects of farm home and family life, rather than with increasing the production of food and fiber.

(6) The basic and final crop of any land or nation is its people, with food and fiber only as instruments for achieving population goals. Thus erosion, background fertility, international relationships of exchange and balance, permanent productivity and wastage associated with quality of management, etc., apply as much to the population crop as to the crop of corn, cotton, or beef.

Individuals to Consider

Adlum, John (pioneer in viticulture, Am. grapes; 1759-1836).

Aiken, David W. (agr. editor, militant agrarian ints. of S. C.; 1828-1887).

Allerten, Samuel W. (livestock, Chicago Stockyards, cornered pork market; 1828-1914).

Ames, Oakes (shovel mfg., pros. from agri. dev. of West and Civ. War; 1804-1873).

Armsby, Henry P. (agr. chem., metabolism in cattle; 1853-1921).

Atkinson, George F. (botanist, mycologist, *Studies of American Fungi*; 1854-1918).

Atwater, Wilbur O. (agr. chem., legumes and atmospheric nitrogen; 1844-1907).

Babcock, Stephen M. (agr. chem., Babcock milk-fat test; 1843-1931).

Bailey, Liberty Hyde (new conception of agr. lit., Bailey Hortorium; 1858-1954).

Baker, John W. (Eng., estab. exp. farm in Ireland, mfgd. farm equip.; ?-1775).

Bakewell, Robert (Eng., systematic inbreeding, dev. Liecester breed of sheep; 1725-1795).

Baussingault, Jean B. (Fr., org. chem., exper. sta. in Fr.; 1802-1887).

Beal, William J. (botanist, "new botany," corn hybridization; 1833-1924).

Beatty, Adam (agr. writer, *Essays on Practical Agriculture*; 1777-1858).

Bement, Caleb N. (agr. inventor, author, an influence to improve agr.; 1790-1868).

Brigham, Joseph H. (agr., Master in Nat. Grange, 4 terms; 1838-1904).

Buchanan, William I. (agr. dept. of 1893 World's Fair in Chicago; 1852-1909).

Burbank, Luther (plant breeder, dev. new varieties of fruits & vegetables; 1849-1926).

Burrill, Thomas J. (hort. microscopist, study of bacterial diseases in plants; 1839-1916).

Capron, Horace (scientific farmer, operated cotton factory; 1804-1885).

Carver, George Washington (botanist, chemist, peanuts; 1864?-1943).

Coburn, Foster D. (agr. ed., sect'y. Kan. State Bd. of Agr.; 1846-1924).

Colman, Norman J. (agr. journalist, lawyer; 1827-1911).

Coulter, John M. (botanist, morphologist, founded *Botanical Gazette*; 1851-1928).

Culley, George (Eng., improved breeds of cattle, pub. works on agr.; 1735-1813).

Davenport, Eugene (agr. dean, opposed fed. dom. of 1914 Agr. Ext. Act.; 1856-1941).

Davey, John ("father of tree surgery in Am."; 1846-1923).

Davy, Humphrey (Eng., chem., work on nitrogen and potassium, author; 1778-1829).

Delafield, John (banker, farmer, estab. model farm in N.Y. 1838; 1786-1853).

DeLaval, Carl Gustaf (milking machine; 1845-1913).

Dickson, David (farmer, agr. writer, introd. Peruvian guano as fert.; 1809-1885).

Downing, Andrew Jackson (landscape gardener, horticulturist, author; 1815-1952).

Dudley, William R. (botanist, univ. teacher, Dudley Herbarium; 1849-1911).

Dufour, John J. (pioneer in viticulture, vineyards in Ky. & Ind.; 1763-1827).

Dumas, Jean B. A. (Fr., chem., comp. of water & air, atomic weights; 1800-1884).

Eaton, Benjamin Harrison (pioneer in irrigation, Colorado; 1833-1904).

Fernow, Bernhard E. (Ger., trained forester, U.S. pioneer in sci. forestry; 1851-1923).

Fisher, Walter L. (leader in conservation of natural resources; 1862-1935).

Frederick the Great (Kg. of Prussia—1740-86, improved agr. & ind.; 1712-1786).

Fuller, Andrew (hort., small fruit, strawberry cross-breeding, editor; 1828-1896).

Gaylord, Willis (agr. writer, leader in N.Y. state agr.; 1792-1844).

Gilbert, Joseph H. (Eng., reorg. of Rothemstead experimental work; 1817-1901).

Goodale, Stephen L. (agr., Secty. Me. Bd. of Agr., stimulated sci. agr.; 1815-1897).

Gray, Asa (botanist, plant geog., hybridization, writer; 1810-1888).

Green, Seth (pioneer in fish breeding, selection, culture; 1817-1888).

Harshberger, John W. (botany and biology, naturalist, teacher, author; 1869-1929).

Heard, Dwight B. (Ariz. banker, farmer, U.S. Reclaim. Act of 1902; 1869-1929).

Hilgard, Eugene W. (geol., univ. prof., influenced soil study; 1833-1916).

Holmes, Ezekiel (botanist, estab. first farm jour. in Maine; 1801-1865).

Hopkins, Cyril G. (agr. chem., devised Ill. system of perm. soil fert.; 1866-1919).

Hough, Franklin B. (forest depletion, U.S. forestry, conservation; 1822-1885).

Husmann, George (teacher, pomology and viticulture in Mo. and Calif.; 1827-1902).

Jenkins, Edward H. (agr. chem., introd. shade-grown tobacco into North; 1850-1931).

Judd, Orange (agr. editor, relating chem. to agr., pub. agr. books; 1822-1892).

Kelley, Oliver H. (farmer, founder and secty. of the Grange in Pa.; 1826-1913).

King, Franklin H. (devised the round silo, wrote books on soils; 1848-1911).

Knapp, Seaman A. (dev. rice ind. in S.W., Farm Crop Demonstra. work; 1833-1911).

Lavoisier, Antoine L. (Fr., pioneer in chemist, plant physiologist; 1743-1794).

Lawes, John B. (Eng., 1842 patent on a superphosphate fertilizer; 1814-1900).

Le Duc, William G. (first miller of flour from Minn. sp. wheat; 1823-1917).

Liebig, Justus von (Ger., chemist, org. analysis, founded agr. chem.; 1803-1873).

Lindheimer, Ferdinand J. (botanist, Texas indep., collected Texas bot. specimens; 1801-1879).

Lyman, Joseph B. (agr. editor, emphasized crop diversification; 1829-1872).

Lyon, Theodatus T. (pomologist, orchard dev. in Mich.; 1813-1900).

McBryde, John N. (agr. prof., pres., promoted sci. agr. in So.; 1841-1923).

McCormick, Cyrus H. (invented and mfgd. a reaper; 1809-1884).

Manning, Robert (pomologist, introd. new varieties, correct nomenclature; 1784-1842).

Mapes, James J. (agr. chemist, first complete artificial fert. in U.S.; 1806-1866).

Mather, Fred (improved fish propagation at N.Y. hatchery, author; 1833-1900).

Meikle, Andrew (Scot., 1784 invented drum threshing machine; 1719-1811).

Michaux, Andre (silviculturist, studied forest trees from N.Y. to Fla., writer; 1746-1802).

Montogomery, William B. (introd. new grasses and cattle breeds into Miss.; 1829-1904).

Morrill, Justin S. (father of land-grant colleges, Morrill Act of 1862; 1810-1898).

Munson, Thomas V. (new-hort. varieties by hybridization, viticulture; 1843-1913).

Piper, Charles V. (agronomist, sudan grass as forage, author; 1867-1926).

Powell, George H. (hort., preserv. & trans. of perishable fruits; 1872-1922).

Priestly, Joseph (theologian, chemist, discovered oxygen; 1733-1804).

Pringle, Cyrus G. (plant breeder, herbarium at U. of Vt.; 1838-1911).

Pritchard, Frederick J. (plant breeder, sugar beets, disease resist. tomatoes; 1874-1931).

Randall, Henry S. (agr., educator, author—incl. *The Life of Thomas Jefferson*; 1811-1876).

Sanders, James H. (agr. journalist, first jour. on animal husbandry; 1832-1899).

Sargent, Charles S. (horticulturist, forester, conservationist; 1841-1927).

Sears, Paul B. (botanist, studies on pollen, hist. of climate ecology; 1891-   ).
Shaler, Nathaniel S. (geol., paleontology, conservation, writer; 1841-1906).
Shelton, Edward M. (prof. of agr., adviser on agr. to govt. of Australia; 1846-1928).
Simpson, John (farm leader, leg., guar. of cost plus for farmers; 1871-1934).
Spillman, William J. (agr. econ., sci. farm mgmt., prof., adviser to govt.; 1863-1931).
Stillman, Thomas B. (chemist, water and milk supply probs., author; 1852-1915).
Stockbridge, Horace E. (agr. chemist, editor, college pres.; 1857-1930).

Taylor, John (Rev. War soldier, statesman, contributor to sci. agr.; 1753-1824).
Thatcher, Roscoe W. (agr. chem., teacher, exp. station dir.; 1872-1933).
Thornburn, Grant (seedman, in 1812 issued first Am. seed catalogue; 1773-1863).
Thurber, George (bot., hort., expert on grasses; 1821-1890).
Titcomb, John W. (fish culturist, conservationist; 1860-1932).
Todd, Sereno E. (jour., wrote on systematic & econ. farm mgmt.; 1820-1898).
Tolley, Howard (agr. econ., relationships of production to price; 1889-1959).
Turner, Jonathan B. (educator, agr. leader, helped estab. U. of Ill.; 1805-1899).

Van Fleet, Walter (phys., hort., plant breeding, work on rose & chestnut; 1857-1922).
Vanderbilt, George Washington (founded nursery and forestry school; 1862-1914).
Van Slyke, Lucius L. (pioneer in dairy chemistry, casein, cheeses; 1859-1931).
Vick, James (imported & produced flower seeds, pub. annual catalog; 1818-1882).
Voorhees, Edward B. (agr. chemist, dev. agr. short courses for farmers; 1856-1911).

Wallace, Henry C. (agr. jour., conservationist, U.S. Secty. of Agr.; 1866-1924).
Warder, John A. (forester, pomologist, author, physician; 1812-1883).
Waring, George E. (agr. chem., san. engineer, exp. farms, urban drainage projects; 1833-1898).
Wickson, Edward J. (hort., prof., dean of agr., author; 1848-1923).
Wilder, Marshall P. (dev. fruit varieties and nomenclature, a founder of M.I.T.; 1798-1886).
Wilson, James (U.S. Secty. of Agr., estab. exp., sta. & coop. ext. work; 1836-1920).
Wohlschlay, Donald E. (ecology and energetics of fish population; 1918-   ).
Wood, Jethro (invented cast iron moldboard plow, 1819 patent; 1774-1834).

Chapter 5

HIGHLIGHTS AND IMPLICATIONS OF DIVISION IV

Throughout the study, attention has been directed to coordination and cooperation among agencies with major responsibility for the status of lawfulness and civic responsibility in America. Attention has also been given to an expansion in some types of service and a general upgrading in qualification of much of the personnel employed. This division focuses on the role of the schools and other educational institutions in the general connection indicated. Certain points are noted here for elaboration and emphasis.

Teacher Perspective

It is hardly possible to place too much emphasis on teacher perspective in understanding the role of the public school as an institution in American society. This relates to understanding by the teacher and also by the general public.

While it is important for teachers in their university study to learn how to teach children to read, add, spell, and use English grammar in a respectable way, it is at least equally important for teachers to be able to develop in children an understanding of why tool-subject and related learnings are more important for American citizenship now than they were a century ago and why these and other learnings will increase in importance during future decades. It is also important for children to understand why the "other learnings" are important for life in America.

Children and youth need to understand why American society, through compulsory school attendance and in other ways, emphasizes its interest in a broad popular knowledge of these subject areas, as contrasted with societies in some other parts of the world, and why our society continues the development of the school as the agency most directly obligated to achieve the learning indicated. As learners mature, teachers should help them to make constructive analyses of educational programs and to evaluate likely prospects under different alternatives.

Areas of Emphasis in Teacher Preparation

Even when teacher preparation includes sociology courses which deal with the school as an institution, along with the family or the church as institutions, there is typically some question of the adequacy of treatment of the school. It need not be derogatory of the church, and certainly not of religion as a field of human concern, to say that in the lives of most American children the public school is a more important institution than the church.

And with respect to the family, the school is increasingly being asked to take over functions that were formerly thought to belong in the home. Some of these functions relate particularly to moral conduct and lawful citizenship. There is considerable reason to expect a further extension of this trend, although there may not be any great urge to provide for it in programs for the preparation of teachers. To an important extent the preceding comment applies also to guidance efforts. While the vocational aspects of guidance effort are important, so are the broad moral and civic needs which tend to be associated with family disintegration. Although efforts concerning the moral-civic area noted relate partly to limitations of knowledge on techniques, they also relate in part to a false concern about invading the status of parents and the sanctity of the home.

Education and the Regulatory Structure

Many adult Americans seem hazy about the need that any organized society has for a basic system to regulate social behavior and why a dynamic society which attempts to operate on a democratic basis has a heavy responsibility for keeping that system up-to-date. The responsibility needs to be understood and to be accepted as being both individual and collective. Past contributions by many of our schools to developing the understanding needed have been too close to zero. Past neglect creates two present requirements: (a) to do a better job with present and future youth; (b) to do a repair job with adults because of neglect when they were youth.

Increases in crime and in problems of correction or rehabilitation concerning offenders mean a growth in burdensomeness of the repair job. When demands for repair expand substantially, the situation could be looked upon as the tail wagging the dog. But yet we seem quite slow to conceive and to implement adequate preventive measures.

Cooperation Among Service Agencies

With respect to cooperation between school personnel and members of the judiciary, law-enforcement personnel, and others in a community, it is hardly to be expected that the personnel of one agency need assume responsibility for leadership in all respects. Teachers might ordinarily be expected to know more than most others about how young people learn, in regard to both acquiring academic information and developing emotional conditioning, and also more about how to organize or present materials for effective learning. Yet much may depend on the content to be learned in particular instances or on community attitudes and types of behavior patterns sought to be established. Moreover, there may be considerable variation among communities as to how leadership in cooperative undertakings respecting the development of young people might be exercised, and variation as to the availability of present or potential leadership.

Active Participation by Youth

Some suggestions for getting the young people themselves to participate in the development noted are set forth in the outlines for discussion topics which appear in this division. Under astute teacher guidance in working with adequate materials, it does not take long for students to become serious about discussion content. Discipline of a few fickle ones by a substantial majority can be prompt and firm, but teacher supervision will probably be necessary to keep the discipline constructive.

The discussion and evaluation inferred offers an important opportunity to practice the idea of "learning by doing," which can be quite effective when well supervised.

Potentialities of Biography

Many schools overlook the potential of biography with respect to training in moral conduct and ideals. The biographical notes of chapter 4 suggest a wide range of constructive interests and social contributions which are probably more varied and challenging than those to which most students have access through ordinary textbooks, movies, or comic strips. And learning from examples or models has long been an important developmental technique, among humans and their mammalian ancestors.

Group discussion on the biographies of illustrious persons affords opportunity to show why those persons are illustrious and opportunity for individual youth to speculate constructively on what may lie ahead for them.

Developing New Learning Materials and Situations

Teachers in conjunction with law-enforcement personnel, members of the judiciary, or others, should not consider it beyond their competence or beyond their responsibility to develop biographical or other printed, graphic, or pictorial materials for areas which seem to be important, but for which little usable material is currently available. The experience of teachers in evaluating textbooks, brochures, manuals, films, and other curriculum materials, should give them useful insights into assembling and organizing biographical or other helpful materials. However, this experience should not cause teachers or other educators to overlook the insights of persons in the other categories noted, whose experiences have been substantially different from those of educators. Various kinds of materials, along with various kinds of firsthand experience, are essential for comprehensive learning and development.

Much of what is said about new materials applies to new techniques for using old materials.

Education and Future Delinquency Load

Participation by the courts in developing general civic responsibility and greater respect for lawful behavior could have substantial appeal for judges as a way to reduce future dockets. For comparable reasons, it might have appeal to personnel in law-enforcement and in probation work. Problems of school delinquency might also be reduced.

The approach suggested is of course that of extensive present investment in anticipation of extensive future dividends. This idea needs to be understood with respect to education and civic responsibility, as well as with respect to industrial finance and material productivity.

Paraprofessionals and Continuing Education

Comment in earlier parts of the study has referred to the interest of the legal profession in continuing education for its members, in paraprofessional personnel within the legal sphere, and in other developments which suggest reaching further into community life than the work of lawyers and judges ordinarily reaches. It is conceivable that such "continuing" effort in this field might be joined with efforts on continuing education for teachers and for law-enforcement personnel, as a kind of joint venture under university sponsorship.

Organization for such a venture, as a summer-school program conducted by law and education and perhaps other faculty participation, would suggest a more systematic and contentful effort than intermittent or improvised conferences usually imply. Furthermore, the systematic and coordinated features might be reflected in the off-campus type of course which meets one afternoon and evening per week for a university quarter or semester. University credit at the professional level, either in law, in education, or in training for police and probation service, should contribute to status and appeal. Some such recognition might be necessary for success of the project.

The Boulder (Colorado) program for members of the judiciary, noted in the present study, might embody clues. Interdisciplinary responsibility and service in the sense inferred in respect to different types of agencies might have considerable value. in acquainting the personnel of different service areas with one another and with their respective philosophies and techniques.

The University and Concern for Professional Study

But it would be unrealistic to let concern for paraprofessionalism and related developments cause one to overlook questions of need and eligibility for university study at the professional level. Such professional study must be recognized by the university and at times maximized by it.

Many American universities deserve extensive commendation for reaching out into communities of the nation with various types of service, and much can be said for the idea that a progressive state university should maintain a department with the function of *seeking out and identifying areas* in which *new services* would be distinct assets to the people. Some services of this kind might be rendered by the university on a joint basis with other institutions and appropriately set forth for regular budget and other recognition by each institution involved. The general idea is often reflected now in sporadic project appeals by universities to foundations or to federal agencies. Some universities now essentially maintain departments of the kind implied, although perhaps with less coordination of objectives than might be desirable.

Comments elsewhere in the study, especially in Division V, note that with substantial changes in the culture the existing institutions must change accordingly or new institutions come into existence—and move toward replacing currently existing institutions. Particular reference is sometimes made to post-high-school trade and vocational schools of roughly junior-college level and to the development of some of those institutions into technological colleges.

The implications of preceding statements for the type of coordinated professional course of university grade herewith suggested bear directly on three considerations: (a) how important is it for America to seek improvement in the competence of professional personnel who work in the areas of developing civic responsibility and lawfulness among the American people; (b) what should be the specific goals, content, and procedures which characterize efforts at improvements which are proposed; (c) does university auspices and university atmosphere offer a more appropriate setting for the effort implied than other institutions might offer?

Discussion at various points has stressed the need for improvement. Hence, nothing further on that point is included in this connection. With regard to the second item, one difficulty often faced by universities in meeting new service needs that develop is the strong academic orientation of university staff and policy, with a correspondingly dim view of how to make the university's program more functional in the lives of the people. "Functional program" here means one that makes a difference in the lives of the people, which the people themselves are able to recognize and which they accept as desirable. Experimental and operational activities in such fields as agriculture, engineering, health services, education, social work, vocational rehabilitation, journalism, and community planning, may be among the best illustrations of the idea inferred. However, these are not the only illustrations.

Essential in each operating area noted illustratively is emphasis on practical experiences in field or operating situations, where the people actually face the problems with which they need help. The health and educational fields have long emphasized internships as an aspect of qualifying for licensed service, and these fields increasingly refer to refresher programs and in-service efforts to extend and update the concern about practical experience. Perhaps the basic idea could be stated by saying that neither academic theory nor routine practice is very fruitful without the other.

The significance of preceding statements for the coordinated university course on professional status, which has been proposed, is that major emphasis on eligibility to participate should be the area and quality of relevant experience which an applicant has had and the prospect of his benefitting from university recognition of his work in the area. This means that pertinent theory and related academic involvements will be explained in terms which are understandable with respect to outcomes that can be recognized on the job. It also means that unrelated academic credentials which universities tend to emphasize will be minimized, both in respect to admission to the course program and in respect to degree recognition of accomplishment through the program.

The foregoing educational and training approach is not new. It has been involved for well over a century, in the nation's perennial but fruitful struggle over higher levels of recognition for the educational needs of persons in vocational and professional service. Preceding comments imply the need for a broadening in scope and a speed-up in rate at which the struggle moves forward. The coordinated program suggested offers promise for a step in the general direction indicated.

As to the third item noted earlier, regarding the university setting as an appropriate locale, one might recall statements from the literature reviewed in this study which relate to upgrading the qualifications of police officers and other law-enforcement personnel and which comment on the desirability of the university in contrast with educational institutions of lesser academic status as a desirable place in which to do it. One might also recall the note from members of the legal profession, urging that the training of lawyers include the faculty and student atmosphere of a sizeable and cosmopolitan university. The varied members of a coordinated class group of the type implied would learn a great deal about how different people look at the problems involved and how diverse suggestions might be organized into operating programs.

The Role of Scientific Method

It might be noted that the basic procedure involved in the course suggestion is essentially that of the scientific method; that is, a continuous interplay between pertinent theory and operating practice, with each strengthening the other and moving forward in joint improvement. A careful review of the biographical material presented in appendix form will indicate the extensive use of this procedure by many persons whose names are listed there.

In a broad sense the implication is for greater incorporation of the scientific method into preparing personnel for the various areas of service which this study has looked upon as involved in America's moving toward greater lawfulness and also for greater incorporation of that method into the daily operations of said personnel.

Learner Uses of Division Materials

Several specific suggestions regarding use of the materials of the division, with classroom or other groups, are made in connection with the presentation of those materials.

Experimentation with new materials and new techniques should be an important aspect of dealing with people in any changing society. Such experimentation is especially important with respect to an emerging area which is trying to coordinate scattered and perhaps at times contradictory fragments. Experimentation is a fundamental aspect of scientific method.

FOOTNOTES AND REFERENCES

1. State ex rel. Hoagland v. School District, 151 P. 2d. 168, 116 Mont. 294 (1944).

2. See Harold H. Punke, *The Teacher and The Courts* (Danville, Ill: The Interstate Printers and Publishers, Inc., 1971), pp. 212-213.

3. See "Special Report: Social Security; Promising Too Much to Too Many?" *U.S. News and World Report* 77 (July 15, 1974): 26-30.

4. Cf. "Corruption in Politics: How Widespread?" *U.S. News and World Report* 74 (June 4, 1973): 20-23.

5. *The Foundation Directory, Edition 3* (New York: Russell Sage Foundation, 1967), p. 16.

6. *Ibid.*, p. 9. The total number of foundations in the United States depends on how the term foundation is defined. The Directory notes 6803 which met its definition of either having assets of $200,000 or making grants of at least $10,000 in the year of record.

7. One type of implication for updating appears in a television comment on the arrest of nuns for shoplifting. It is hard to envision this kind of offense in the days of St. Thomas (Aquinas), 1225-1274.

8. Cf. Eric Hoffer, *First Things, Last Things* (New York: Harper & Row, 1967), pp. 21-24.

9. Various states have at different times enacted or considered legislation to provide for sterilization of mentally handicapped persons.

10. There has been some recent concern about the amount and content of television viewed by young children.

11. Pierce v. Society of the Sisters of the Holy Name of Jesus and Mary, 268 U.S. 510, 45 S. Ct. 751, 39 A.L.R. 468 (6/1/1925).

DIVISION V

GENERAL IMPLICATIONS OF THE STUDY

INTRODUCTION

The general principles which are reflected through the illustrative materials and discussions that appear in the foregoing divisions have extensive ramifications. Some of the ramifications reach quite deeply into the political philosophy of American democracy and into the faith and aspirations of the people with respect to their government and their general system of social relationships. Much of the nation's operating philosophy and value structure is thus reflected.

Division V attempts to focus on some of the more important principles involved in the situation described. The division is organized into eight chapters. With respect to several of the items considered, the attention given in this division extends substantially beyond the direct considerations which appear relative to kindred topics in the earlier discussions. However, a few items receive only brief attention in this division.

While each of the eight chapters could be viewed somewhat independently of the others, it is important to view them with attention to the relationships among them. Although the sequence used in presenting the different chapters need not be rigidly followed in reading them, following that sequence will probably make it easier to develop an overall evaluation of them.

Chapter 1

ORDER AND INTEGRITY IN PERSPECTIVE
AND IN GOVERNMENT

Order is one of the most broadly recognized needs in human relationships. However, attention may be called to the importance of order through apparently negative references, such as relate to international monetary or other relationships being in chaotic disarray or to the need for one to place his own house and personal affairs in order. In school and university settings, considerable effort is made to help students develop order or logic in their thinking and action. Any adult who has served as a member of a committee working on some difficult problem knows that some persons are more orderly or logical than others in their suggestions and procedures.

Compilations on "Rules of Order" for parliamentary procedure have developed out of experience, as guides for fruitful procedure in group situations which involve argument and debate. Such rules are intended to set standards. Moreover, particular groups may become dedicated to certain goals and hence set particular standards of conduct for members which their leadership considers important in relation to those goals. Thus, most Americans have heard of masonic and monastic orders, and many have heard of the Order of the Purple Heart in American military service, or the Order of the Garter in British knighthood.

Moral integrity in personal adherence to the rules or standards, and in trying to promote corresponding behavior among others, indicates the route by which integrity in government or other areas of public trust becomes essential for organized society. To a considerable extent, individuals in positions of public trust become models for others to admire and to emulate.

1. Law and Order in Cultural Perspective

At several points the present study uses the phrase "law and order." The use concerns relationships among people in organized society. However, this use is probably most meaningful when considered in a broader context of order and orderliness. The general concept in its human and even broader context has long been recognized by thoughtful persons in many cultures and in many types of situations. Some attention is given here to the recognition as perspective for examining the subject further in relation to government in America.

Literary Attention to Order and Orderliness

Numerous references to order and orderliness have been made in poetry and in other forms of literature. A few of these are noted, with some indication of the time and cultural settings in which each appeared.

The gods love those of ordered souls (Sophocles—495?-406? B.C.).

All things obey fixed laws (Lucretius—97?-54 B.C.).

Let all things be done decently and in order (Bible).

You must confine yourself within the modest limits of order (Shakespeare —1564-1616).

Set all things in their own peculiar place,
and know that order is the greatest grace (Dryden—1631-1700).

Order is heaven's first law (Pope—1688-1744).

Method is good in all things. Order governs the world. The Devil is the author of confusion (Swift—1667-1745).

Fretfulness of temper will generally characterize those who are negligent of order (Robert Blair—1699-1746).

Where law ends, there tyranny begins (William Pitt, 1st Earl of Chatham— 1708-1778).

Good order is the foundation of all good things (Burke—1729-1797).

The friend of order has made half his way to virtue (Lavater—1741-1801).

All are born to observe order, but few are born to establish it (Joubert— 1754-1824).

Order is the sanity of the mind, the health of the body, the peace of the city, the security of the state. As the beams of a house, as the bones of the microcosm of man, so is order to all things (Southey—1774-1843).

For the world was built in order
and the atoms march in time;

Rhyme the pipe, and Time the Warder,
the sun obeys them, and the moon (Emerson—1803-1882).

Order means light and peace, inward liberty and free command over one's self; order is power (Amiel—1821-1881).

Order is the primary regulation of the celestial regions (J. G. Saxe—1816-1887).

Order and system are nobler things than power (Ruskin—1819-1900).

Order is a lovely thing;

On disarray it lays its wing,

Teaching simplicity to sing (Anna H. Branch—1875-1937).

Order and simplification are the first steps toward the mastery of a subject —the actual enemy is the unknown (Thomas Mann—1875-1955).

America's Pioneering Job Regarding Law and Order

Critics on the status of law and order in America, whether they are of domestic or of foreign stock, should recognize the nation's pioneering status in developing a system of regulations appropriate for a large, technological, heterogeneous, and highly mobile industrial democracy. A few points may be briefly differentiated.

(1) No other nation with a fairly large population has as heterogeneous a body of people as the United States has—with respect to racial, ethnic, and cultural backgrounds. Moreover, the nation has historically been looked upon as a population and cultural melting pot, and the melting concept is broadening with respect to some racial considerations.

(2) Related to population heterogeneity, from the standpoint of maintaining a lawful and orderly society, is the great mobility of the American people, as compared with people in other parts of the world. Influences bearing on mobility are such matters as a nationwide highway system; allocations and transfers with respect to jobs and vocational opportunities; leisure and considerable affluence to support travel and touring over a substantial geographical area; and vehicle design in the sense of campers, plus various kinds of family trailers, with the presence of trailer-park accommodations. Rail travel has been important in the past. International travel and tourism, on the part of Americans, is an aspect of mobility.

(3) In several areas of scientific and technological development, America has gone farther than most countries have. This implies more rapid shifts in equipment and gadgetry, with corresponding influence on the lifestyle of the people. Changes in such areas affect the rate of obsolescence in the regulatory structure and in some aspects of its value base.

(4) A social policy which emphasizes trade and commerce regarding products of both foreign and domestic origin, implemented through a wage system that provides a high average level of per-capita income, maintains a broad flow of goods and services which are available through the channels of legitimate commerce. It also maintains a broad flow of smuggling and other peripheral trafficking which is outside of legally acceptable channels. Geographically broad frontiers with numerous points of entry, and often with little more than token surveillance of merchandise and often of persons entering, accentuate potential conflict with the regulatory structure.

(5) In the rather conglomerate setting indicated, there is also considerable social and political effort to expand the implications of democracy; particularly as related to such matters as personal freedom and equal opportunity—with opportunity rather abundantly available and with some freedoms pushing toward gross sensuous indulgence. Respect for the formal borders of permissibility is thus not high among individual priorities.

(6) Slowness in reorganizing the legal structure, as compared with rate of change in spheres of technology and personal affluence, retains on the law books numerous inappropriate regulations. They may imply that it is easier for man to understand the individual importance of change in transportation, housing, working conditions, or diet, than to understand the collective importance of updating the regulatory structure. In any culture, considerable lawlessness can result from obsolescence of regulations.

(7) The general conditions described embody numerous problems in respect to continuously redefining the kind and amount of personal freedom which contributes most to individual satisfaction and creativity, at the same

time that expanding needs for social orientation and control are adequately met.

The tasks elaborated in the enumerated items are collectively referred to as constituting a pioneering job because America is the first major country to be in the kind of situation described. Hence, this nation cannot look elsewhere for a model. Furthermore, the likelihood that world developments will move other countries along paths similar to those now being sketched by America makes the current and future world status of the nation depend greatly on success in the pioneering enterprise.

Eternal Vigilance as the Price of Freedom

In our emphasis on personal freedom as crucial in the nation's value structure and system of government, numerous safeguards are set up to protect individual freedom from encroachment by government. The historical background and psychological atmosphere of founding days made the initial framers of American government particularly sensitive on this point.

Hence it is not new to refer to eternal vigilance as the price of freedom, but it seems perennially desirable to do so. The present reference implies that freedom embodies pleasantness, whereas viligance demands effort. This study has variously referred to an inherent selfishness with which biological evolution has equipped us, but the study has also referred to the limited appropriateness of that equipment for life in a populous and widely variant industrial society. Modification of this trait is one of the most difficult, but most necessary and universal, functions of education and social regulation in modern society.

In a broad sense, the history of civilization reveals waves of rigid and narrow social controls, interspersed with periods of relaxation and drift toward personal licentiousness and a disintegration of social or moral structures. Some commentators point illustratively to the rise and fall of Rome or of some other political state, to the Reformation and Counter-Reformation period in Western religious history, to boom-and-bust cycles in modern economic affairs, to crime waves and "police crackdowns," etc. The pendulum-swing technique inferred usually leaves some residual contribution to the development of stability in human relationships, although accompanied by rather extensive anxiety and wastefulness of resources.

An important explanatory item regarding the pendulum technique lies in the fact that it is easier and quicker for man to react on the basis of emotion than on the basis of reason. The process of reasoning demands a tedious assembling of data, as well as new ventures in comparison and in formulating alternatives which may be tried out. While emotional response may be looked upon as a kind for which biological evolution has equipped us, reasoning is a process for which nature supplies varying potential but which requires cultural exposure and direction before it functions recognizably. It is in the setting of institutional and collectivised exposure and direction that problems of law and order in any society must be approached.

In various connections, the present study has referred to an expansion of individualism in America during recent decades, with varied reference to the psychology of individual difference, school programs, the courts, and other influence in the process of expansion. In the immediate setting concerning vigilance and freedom, a further note is added. The note is that the adults of recent generations have been too self-indulgent, lazy, and indifferent to develop the competence and put forth the effort needed for developing in children and youth an understanding of the social structure and the role of morality or collective values in civilized life, and for developing an analytical commitment to the existing value structure and to its potential for improvement. When it is said that the people of a country deserve the kind of government that they have, or that the level of relationships between a government and its people cannot rise higher than the level of moral integrity shown by its officialdom, it should be apparent that the integrity of teachers, parents, and other mentors of youth is in much the same category as that of the officials.

It follows that in a populous and broadly diversified culture, vigilance, like freedom, is a collective phenomenon. The idea has been reflected in observations to the effect: "United we stand, divided we fall." The idea has somewhat recently been substantiated by the personality disintegration of isolates in prisoner-of-war camps, in contrast with prisoners who could readily form small "buddy" groups with others who were in the same camps. The isolate's individualism included only a restricted base of elements in common with other prisoners on which to develop mutual understanding and respect, and the camp situation afforded little opportunity for the isolate to "do his own thing" as he might see fit.

An important problem that usually arises concerning the collective nature of freedom, and of vigilance regarding it, is that ideas concerning freedom or anything else arise in individuals and that any action which takes place concerning those ideas is action by individuals. But this does not mean that ideas and actions must be focused on a kind of separate or isolated well-being of the persons in whom the ideas or actions originate. Ideas and actions concerning group status also have individual origin; and as a society becomes more complex, the demand increases that more of the ideas and actions have group orientation.

However, one caution respecting group orientation should be noted. The individual must maintain a continuing identification with the group and with its responsibilities, and there are some things which the individual cannot turn over or delegate to the group collectively. One difficulty in developing morality and other socially desirable qualities in children and youth is that too many parents try to turn over the entire responsibility to the schools, welfare agencies, and police.

The situation described points up that aspect of the American philosophy of life and government which maintains that there are some powers and responsibilities of the individual which cannot be delegated to other individuals or to institutions. Among powers and responsibilities which the individual cannot entirely delegate is one which relates to participation in defining and in protecting freedom—and the associated role of vigilance.

To some extent in any type of society, and especially in one which attempts to operate along democratic lines, it is a major responsibility of leadership to develop understanding and commitment to the idea of nondelegability, as noted herewith. Foregoing statements constitute one way of saying that a democratic society demands more of its citizens than most other forms of social organization do. However, a democratic society offers its citizens more, particularly with respect to the satisfactions and growth potential associated with personal freedom. The American people need to recognize more clearly than many of them do that moral integrity and vigilance regarding the moral behavior of oneself and others are high among priorities in the area of democratic responsibilities.

Truth and Law

There are important respects in which law is one among several efforts of man to pursue his curiosity or adventure and thereby arrive at truth, with truth being vaguely conceived as some form of ultimate bliss. If a tinge of reality hints that this ultimate will never be reached because each increment of tangible growth enables man to extend his projections, many courageous and exploratory individuals will *find freedom* in an open-ended future which will accommodate their most fantastic dreams about what man may yet become. When one says that the most basic value in law and human regulation lies in its efforts to help man reach out as far as possible in the direction of what is here called truth, one should recognize that the same goal is substantially proclaimed through varied avenues of expression by philosophy, art, science, education, medicine, religion, business, and other lines of man's groping.

The situation described indicates the importance of cooperation among the various institutions of our culture in furthering lawful relationships among the people. The situation justifies some effort at examining the nature of truth, which has beckoned to man over many generations and in many different ways, perhaps along with some effort to appraise the results of the different ways. But appraisal is always a matter of relationships, in which particular items are compared with a standard.

In recent centuries the greatest conflict regarding standards has pointed to religion and science: with the conception of a pleasant and enduring hereafter based on celestial intervention, which religious leaders have imagined and formulated as an outgrowth of human achievements and disappointments; in contrast with conception from a different interpretation of human attainments and disappointments, which places the entire burden on man to depend on his own personal resources to improve his status in the universe.

Both approaches emphasize knowledge as essential to improvement, but recognize different sources of knowledge—divine revelation, empirical experimentation. Since man in the thinking process must depend on what knowledge he has, if knowledge along one line increases faster than along some other line, his thinking will be influenced by the differential. During the past two centuries, man's empirical knowledge has greatly increased, but what seems ordinarily referred to as revealed knowledge has not increased much.

If one accepts the view that there is no truth other than "empirical truth," then one questions the idea that truth can be established by logical reasoning —even though individual steps in the logical sequence may have substantially rested on empirical evidence. If one then assumes that "absolute truth" is that which takes into account all that is presently known on the particular subject involved, he circumscribes the term "absolute" and limits it to what is currently known to exist. Thus to deny the potential for growth in any area of knowledge is obviously parochial.

Accordingly, one finds himself on one of the routes to the conclusion that truth is always relative, that it is never complete, but continuously subject to revision upon the development of further information. Perhaps in more direct terms, one might say that the logician never knows when somebody will find holes or gaps in his sequence of steps, and the empiricist never knows when all possible alternatives have been taken into account. Our frequent reinterpretations of data and revisions of doctrine, in a culture of dynamic growth in knowledge, is testimony on the subject.

An additional note in the preceding connection relates to the "public" nature of empirical truth, which is open for anybody to challenge or verify, in contrast with phemomena of "private" experience which have been variously designated as divine revelations, visions, seances, hallucinations, etc., and which have sometimes been referred to as private pipelines to truth that are not accessible to the public.

Difficulty in the foregoing comparison lies in whether it is possible for an individual to have experience which is meaningful to him, but which may not be publicly verified or verifiable, and, if so, whether that private experience can be said to embody truth. An approach to this question which may be more fruitful than the approach concerning divine revelations, seances, etc., might concern the origin and nature of hunches, bright ideas, breakthroughs, etc., which occur in the thinking process. Most persons have experienced hunches, breakthroughs, etc., in thinking about difficult problems and probably have noted changes in the facial expressions of associates as those associates have had experiences which appear to be similar.

As long as our ignorance is as great as it is at present concerning what occurs in the human organism during the formation of an hypothesis or bright idea, it may be essentially irrelevant whether the occurrence is referred to as a divine revelation, phenomenon of chance, or in some other terms. The real point is that the occurrence takes place, that it takes place in the head of some individual, and that it is accordingly private before it is communicated to anybody else and thereby embarks upon a route toward public verification or rejection. To ask whether the content involved can be regarded as truth before it is publicly verified may overemphasize the process of social evaluation, at the expense of the content of the experience itself.

The upshot of preceding consideration implies a recognition of both private and public truth in the settings described, as well as a recognition of the relativity of truth under conditions such as indicated. Hence, reference to "absolute truth," whether in religion, science, law, or elsewhere, may tell one considerable about the circumscribed outlook of persons who use the term, while it contributes little to understanding the nature of truth.

Living in a world of relative truth generates anxieties, but it also fosters growth. The anxieties are largely among persons with routine minds who feel most comfortable in the presence of fixed guidelines which can be incorporated into habit. Growth possibilities are welcomed by adventuresome persons who want to explore and make things different from what they are. The growth potential may resemble that which is associated with the fact that a child does not inherit the knowledge of his ancestors, in the sense that he inherits the color of his eyes. The child thus escapes a great load of ancestoral superstition and false information, with related freedom for his own growth. However, the social heritage still conveys a great deal of falsity to a child, expecially when emphasis is placed on the kind of history that applauds "the good old days."

In law and in religion, the code idea embodies much of the *"absolute" orientation* and minimizes human potential for growth. But the common-law idea, which conceives of the regulatory structure as one of continuous adjustment through evaluating general principles in specific situations, more largely embodies the growth concept. In this connection, one should note the reasoning of our courts to the effect that constitutional and legislative provisions must be interpreted in the light of the particular circumstances in a case—i.e., that there are no absolute freedoms in such areas as religion, speech, assembly, etc., but only relative freedoms. While there is at present considerable overlapping in practice between code and common-law philosophies, one cause of lawlessness in America lies in the slow tempo at which reinterpretations are made and the tempo at which the machinery involved actually operates. In this as in other considerations of the nation's contemporary lawlessness, our courts, our law-enforcement agencies, and our educational programs need scrutiny, particularly from the standpoint of cooperation.

2. Moral Integrity in Government

Government, as group regulation of individual behavior, is one of man's oldest institutions. The operation of its principles in the family of parents and children, or in the large patriarchal group, need not be emphasized in the present connection. But it should be noted that government was important in the affairs of men before literacy appeared. Thoughtful members of various cultures have long sought to discern its basic principles.

Historical Reflections on Government and Related Morality

While critics of many kinds have reflected on the purposes and operations of government, those who regard it as a necessity and seek to improve its operations are usually the most constructive. But others too should be noted. A few observations, of varying and in part conflicting nature, should therefore aid perspective. The fruits of some of these efforts can be helpful in the present connection. A few of them are set forth.

Society cannot exist unless a controlling power upon will and appetite be placed somewhere; and the less of it there is within, the more there must be without (Burke—1729-1797).

Government is a contrivance of human wisdom to provide for human wants (Burke—*ibid.*).

No man undertakes a trade he has not learned, even the meanest; yet everyone thinks himself sufficiently qualified for the hardest of all trades —that of government (Socrates—469?-399 B.C.).

It is necessary for a Senator to be thoroughly acquainted with the constitution; and this is a knowledge of the most extensive nature; a matter of science, of diligence, of reflection, without which no Senator can possibly be fit for his office (Cicero—106-43 B.C.).

The very idea of power and the right of the people to establish government presupposes the duty of every individual to obey the established government (George Washington—1732-1799).

The depositary of power is always unpopular (Benjamin Disraeli—1804-1881).

All men would be masters of others, and no man is lord of himself (Goethe—1749-1832).

It is error alone which needs support of government. Truth can stand by itself (Jefferson—1743-1826).

The whole of government consists in the art of being honest (Jefferson—*ibid.*).

In all forms of government the people is (*sic*) the true legislator (Burke —*op. cit.*).

Nothing will ruin the country if the people themselves will undertake its safety; and nothing can save it if they leave that safety in any hands but their own (Daniel Webster—1782-1852).

The freedom of a government does not depend upon the quality of its laws, but upon the power that has the right to create them (Thaddeus Stevens—1792-1868).

Society is well governed when the people obey the magistrates, and the magistrates obey the laws (Solon—638-559 B.C.).

Virtue alone is not sufficient for the exercise of government; laws alone carry themselves into practice (Mencius—372?-289? B.C.).

In all government there must of necessity be both the law and the sword; laws without arms would give us not laws but licentiousness, and arms without laws would produce not subjection but slavery (Chas. C. Colton —1780-1832).

The principle foundation of all states is good laws and good arms (Machiavelli—1469-1527).

No government is safe unless buttressed by good will (Cornelius Nepos —99?-24? B.C.).

No one has long maintained a violent government; temperate rule endures (Seneca—c. 4 B.C.-65 A.D.).

No government can be long secure without a formidable opposition (Benjamin Disraeli—*op. cit.*).

I will govern according to the commonwealth, but not according to the common will (James I, Eng., to House of Commons, 1621).

An oppressive government is more to be feared than a tiger (Confucius —551-478 B.C.)

They that govern the most make the least noise (Selden—1584-1654).

If you would rule the world quietly, you must keep it amused (Emerson—1803-1882).

It is indeed astonishing with how little wisdom mankind can be governed, when that little wisdom is its own (Dean William R. Inge—1860-1954).

Nothing appears more suprising to those who consider human affairs with a philosophical eye, than the easiness with which the many are governed by the few (Hume—1711-1776).

In a change of government, the poor seldom change anything except the name of their master (Phaedrus—1st half of 1st century A.D.).

The foul, corruption-gendered swarm of state (Southey—1774-1843).

No government has ever been, or ever can be, wherein time-servers and blockheads will not be uppermost (Dryden—1621-1700).

Every actual State is corrupt (Emerson—*op. cit.*).

The deterioration of a government begins almost always with the decay of its principles (Montesquieu—1689-1775).

If I wished to punish a province, I would have it governed by philosophers (Frederick the Great—1712-1786).

There are no necessary evils in government. Its evils exist only in its abuses (Andrew Jackson, Bank Bill Veto, 7/10/1832).

Republics end with luxury; monarchies with poverty (Montesquieu—*op. cit.*).

A government that is big enough to give you all you want, is big enough to take it all away (Barry M. Goldwater—campaign speech, 10/21/64).

Of governments, that of the mob is most sanguinary, that of soldiers the most expensive, and that of civilians the most vexatious. (Colton—*op. cit.*).

Moral Integrity in American Government

In the aspects of Division IV relating to Watergate and in some other relationships, the present study has briefly commented on morality and the American political system. However, the role of moral integrity on the part of high-level public officials and their status as models for other citizens are so central to the American conception of social relationships and government that fuller treatment appears essential.

(1) *Material affluence and moral integrity.* It has become easy for present-day Americans, under the lengthening shadow of technology and its associated conception of the "good" as being dominated by that which increases material productivity per unit of time and human effort, to frown upon the emphasis by Puritan Fathers on moral commitment and related judgments. The fact that these forefathers and other socioreligious leaders stated their convictions and collective expectations in terms of a god and of divine influence should perhaps in a technological culture be looked upon as efforts to set forth those convictions and expectations in the most forceful language and symbolism that the promoters were able to muster. It should also be noted that the forcefulness of particular terminology or other forms of expression varies from time to time, in accordance with other changes in the culture. And during

the time since Puritanism was prominent in America, science and technology have become important in bringing about such other changes.

With regard to perspective it might be noted that the Hebrew prophets and the philosophers or seers of other cultures have essentially been moralists. That is, they have tried to summarize a wide range of experience and to indicate its importance for group life in the future. This was probably a relatively easy job in the somewhat primitive cultures implied, when the number of people in a tribe was small and when the level of material development was so meager that no great range in type of experience was possible. Under such conditions, a fairly alert and competent individual could encompass all of the kinds of knowledge and events that there were to think about and to evaluate. Although techniques for acquiring knowledge and observing events during the past two or three centuries have enabled competent persons to acquire and to observe more widely than at earlier times, capacity to evaluate and to project in terms of collective well-being (or moral status) has not received commensurate attention. The great emphasis in America on individualized material gain has been accompanied by a lag in group concern.

In the limited and materially primitive societies of the earlier centuries noted, as in any frontier and austere setting, persons who survive learn that they can do so only by following a narrowly charted path. There is little surplus by which those who deviate from that path can be helped to recuperate, and little tolerance for the threat which deviation constitutes for the group. Religious and other ideology and the various forms of police action must therefore cooperate to the end that the described path be followed. The existence of a state religion in some Western countries, with associated interlocking of church and state in regard to controls and well-being, substantially reflects the concepts indicated and, to some extent, reflects the associated operations.

By contrast with the early austerity noted, a materially rich and varied culture can afford a great deal of individualized and haphazard activity because of the surplus in resources which are available to recuperate from error. Certain manifestations of the situation described can be seen in the great emphasis in America during the past few decades on students' rights and on individualized freedoms and learning programs in educational institutions, or in the action of some courts in upholding the personal rights of adult offenders in suits against the group.

(2) *Vigilant attention to moral growth.* The present study has suggested that the rise in crime and violence in America is associated with a failure in our sense of moral obligation to grow, in proportion to growth in our socially disintegrative forces of individualism—that is, growth in the right of the individual to do as he sees fit in more of his widening range of circumstances. This point has been noted with respect to popular attitudes and imagery regarding the courts, public schools, police force, and other public agencies.

Public commentary on Watergate has referred to officials and their advisers as being considered above or beyond the law and, thus, of feeling free to violate the law when it appears to serve their individual purposes to do so. Efforts to rationalize the violations, in terms of unique insights as to public well-being, hardly seem convincing. Some of the defenses offered by alleged criminals who proclaim loyalty to a leader, or who plead the subordinate status of the offender when carrying out real or imagined orders from an official superior, are reminiscent of Nazi defendants on trail after World War II (at Nuremberg) for exterminating Jews. Should Americans remember the teachings of Hitler regarding a loyalty cult? The Watergate situation seems especially clear, in the sense that in several instances the accused knew when they engaged in the acts concerned that those acts were criminal—under the American legal framework. At least they should have known this, from their specialized training in the law and in related aspects of the nation's social structure, and from their position of trust and counsel within that system.

When the Watergate scandal is looked upon as symbolizing various forms and levels of current and past corruptions in American government, it lends support to the view that government in its relationships with the people can rise no higher than the moral integrity of its officialdom and associated advisers. Questions thus emerge as to responsibility for developing and maintaining the integrity required. This study has emphasized the idea that responsibility cannot rest *entirely* on any one area of society, such as the homes, schools, courts, law-enforcement agencies, etc., but is a responsibility in which several agencies must develop more extensive cooperation than they currently show.

One aspect of the cooperation indicated must harmonize moral integrity and commitment with technological development and material affluence. However, the emphasis should not be on "getting back to the good old morality," which unimaginative clergymen and teachers sometimes rave about, but on jointly working through the significance and applications of moral principles in present-day situations—i.e., what does moral integrity mean in teacher-pupil relationships, in coaching football, in superintendent-staff relationships, in merchant-customer dealings, in clergy-congregation service, in court procedure, in counseling high-ranking public officials, etc.?

Reference to one aspect of Roman history is sometimes made by stating that corn and circuses for the masses were not enough. Could the observation be made contemporary in reference to Americans by saying that bread, ball games, and automobiles are not enough? Montesquieu referred to deterioration in the principles of government and stated that "Republics end with luxury." Other quotes also bear on the subject.

Watergate and the American Political System

Any adult who has been living in the United States during the past five years and who has not heard of Watergate must have been extremely isolated. But the percentage of the people who sense the importance of Watergate for the American political system may not be great. Whether the system is naive or not, it places great faith in the dedication which elected officials are expected to have for the well-being of the community that they are presumed to represent, and hence it places great moral responsibility on those officials.

When the founders of our government embodied in the original framework an idealism that reached beyond typical practices as to public well-being and devoted service, they were acting in a manner characteristic of broadscale reform movements. The definition of social revolution typically embodies the idea of greater concern for the social group than that which has been accorded by the regime against which revolt is undertaken.

But is it naive for reform leaders to assume that the fringe members of their group, or their successors in future generations, will be likely or able to maintain an ongoing day-by-day commitment to the proclaimed idealism which the founders set forth and personally lived? Or is it more reasonable to expect that the appearance of new experiences and the retreat of memories concerning real and imagined old abuses will dull the spearhead of reform enthusiasm and cause the people to settle back into the petty selfishness that tends to characterize humans beings? Part of the concern about the tendency of a natural precipitate of narrow selfishness to prevail, whenever reform enthusiam lags, was expressed by some early leaders in statements to the effect that a country needs a revolution about every twenty years.

(1) *Moral integrity and temptation in high office.* In any organized society, the concept of high office implies a high level of power in the hands of officials and presumes a high level of understanding and moral commitment regarding the needs of the people in that society. But people are born without any particular moral qualification of the type required. The point then is whether the social system develops the need for an expanded conception of civic morality and for public dedication, faster than it develops in people the qualifications required to meet that need. Our widespread corruptions of sophisticated types and our increase in street crimes offer one answer. Perhaps we must either be content with that answer or develop the background for better answers.

When it has been implied from the days of Plato to the present that the people in any country deserve the kind of government which they have, it follows that possibilities for improvement in government depend on an understanding by the people as to what would constitute improvement and on devising ways to bring about the necessary changes. The contention throughout this study, that good government depends more on civic understanding of popular needs and on moral commitment to public well-being than on the particular framework or structure of government, recognizes that under some structural arrangements persons of mediocre understanding and moral integrity are more likely to do a tolerable job than under other structural arrangements. Part of the long-range significance of Watergate may lie in clarifying this point for the American people.

(2) *Congressional investigations.* An important clarifying instrument, in respect to national involvements, lies in bipartisan Congressional investigating committees. The bipartisan feature helps to curb those aspects of petty selfishness which thrive under patronage and other party devices, and when committee hearings are broadcast, the procedure constitutes one of the nation's most effective devices for adult education on civic matters.

Statements to the effect that such hearings thwart grand jury proceedings, as by prejudicing potential jurors, strike at the heart of the system. Such statements proclaim that popular and juror ignorance constitute the desired basis for justice and that the process of arriving at justice is vitiated if the veil of ignorance is raised by any agency that does not appear before the jury or fit into the judicial form of procedure and its conception of evidence. This arrogation of power and exclusiveness by one agency of government is not compatible with the right of the people to know without extreme surveillance over how they find out, and is not compatible with the doctrine that only an informed people is capable of self-government.

When the issue is stated as being *whether* the people should know *or* a few Watergate criminals should be convicted and sentenced, an artificial dichotomy is set up. Effort by a court-jury structure to prevent "poaching," as to sources of information, raises questions about structural fossilization rather than structural growth, particularly in relation to new technology for determining and disseminating truth. Although the dichotomy is defended on the paternalistic assumption that the immaturity and unsophistication of potential jurors require supervision as to the content and sources of information which they might consider in drawing conclusions, the inference may also be present that some members of the judiciary need comparable surveillance lest set procedural operations be challenged regarding flexibility. Both patterns of surveillance negate the prospects for growth in persons who function in our machinery of justice. A different approach might regard jurors as competent to evaluate varying types of conflicting evidence, no matter from what source the evidence comes. This approach would apply constitutional principles, concerning freedom of speech versus censorship, to jury and court procedure in determining justice, as well as apply them to other aspects of our culture.

Efforts to reduce the odium of Watergate by reference to corruptions of the Grant or Harding administrations, or by comparison with corruptions by individual senators, governors, mayors and other lesser officials, should be looked upon as aspects of a whitewash or cover-up technique. Presumably, by showing that corruption has been a part of the American system in various forms and over long periods of time, with the nation having survived and subsequently prospered, the ploy is that Watergate corruptions thus appear less serious. Aside from the weakness that two wrongs do not make a right, as inferred by Watergate being offset by some other corruption, there should be a basis for assuming that government under the American system is becoming less corrupt and more demonstrably in the interest of the people. Improvement is especially important for the nation's stance in relationships with other nations, particularly nations in the more populous areas of the world.

The real problem relates to honesty in government, as Jefferson observed, and to the crisis of the presidency, which is considered to be the top symbol of American democracy. Concern for the presidency, rather than for a particular incumbent, makes it imperative that the various ramifications of dishonesty and corruption be investigated, with the procedure and results presented before the American people. An important by-product of such investigative procedure is the better understanding which people in other nations get of the American system. Of great importance in the understandings concerned is the hazard involved when the chief law-enforcement officer of the nation, the United States Attorney General, becomes closely identified with party campaign managers in a nearby election—i.e., too close a relation between the judiciary and campaign politics.

(3) *Subfederal units of government and political corruption.* A further implication of Watergate involves the continuing concentration of governmental power in federal hands. To a considerable extent this concentration has focused attention and scrutiny on federal activities, with less scrutiny of governmental operations at state and local levels. While power-seeking governors and lesser public officials perennially refurbish their rationalizations for more federal grants with less federal supervision of the use made of the funds, they are not particularly informative as to subfederal levels of corruption. This situation lends some credence to the view that the sum total of the nation's "little corruptions" has greater dollar and morality implications than the smaller number of large federal corruptions. Apart from the sum-total note, it is probably from the small but familiar neighborhood operations that many Americans develop their skepticism as to the moral integrity and trustworthiness of politicians in general.

(4) *Educational responsibility of courts and schools.* Courts and schools, as agencies concerned with fostering honesty and moral trustworthiness in the American people, should find ways of addressing themselves to problems of integrity and corruption more effectively than they have and in several respects of working together in doing so. This should relate to both children and adults as learners, as well as to the development and presentation of various kinds of learning content and material.

International Implications

Typical Americans have not yet fully grasped the nature of responsibility concerning world leadership, which was thrust upon this nation with the outcome of World War I more than a half century ago and which has increased since that time. The nation has accumulating economic problems which now focus on general considerations of international trade and dollar status; the shortage crisis which currently focuses on fuel and food; and the narrowly economic aspects of drug abuse, including alcohol and nicotine. But there are also nationwide problems regarding "crime in the streets" and regarding broader implications of more sophisticated crimes, such as those associated with Watergate, which challenge the structure and integrity of the American system.

During the past 150 years, several developing countries have looked upon American technology and social institutions as worthy of extensive study and considerable emulation. Technological accomplishments in space, computerization, agricultural production, and other areas continue to challenge the imagination in most parts of the world, but the sociopolitical aspects of our culture seem now to have lost some of their international appeal.

Perhaps the sociopolitical loss implied is attributable to failure in our perspective and planning in these areas, compared with the perspective and planning reflected in technological areas such as those noted. To a considerable extent, the problem lies in heavy dependence on amateurism in the field of governmental structure and social regulation, whereas we use highly specialized expertise in technology and material production. Socrates noted this point roughly 2400 years ago. Comments in the text of this study on professionalization of law-enforcement personnel, greater attention to the behavioral sciences in the backgrounds of members of the judiciary, and understanding of the psychological as well as the economic aspects of job orientation among teachers and others who are directly concerned with the guidance of youth, point to the problem in a somewhat peripheral way.

For Americans to develop and maintain a sociopolitical system, which other peoples of the world on a continuing basis will look upon as deserving careful study and extensive emulation, Americans will have to work at the job with more perspective and planning. They should depend less on amateurism and nonchalance.

One implication of foregoing statements concerns the growing interdependence of different parts of the world, with the power of leadership resting in the hands of those who have the competence and the dedication to lead and with a widely acceptable system of social values which determines the uses that are made of technology occupying a high place on the list in judging competence. One could imply a need to move away from emphasis on highly personalized desires and toward the Puritan emphasis on social values, without emphasizing the particular code of values which characterized Puritanism. Differentiation among Puritan values is thus implied.

But from the international standpoint, there may be a creative fallout from investigating Watergate and kindred scandals, which many Americans overlook. There are many countries in which the existing government could not endure the process of washing its linen in public, day after day on television. Insofar as people in such countries have access to television presentations, or even to seepage through less open channels, many will probably raise questions about the contrast between American disclosures with emphasis on the right of the people to know and the situations in their own homelands. The ventilation of governmental corruptions, through Watergate and related investigations, may thus constitute an important American export.

Chapter 2

INDIVIDUALIZATION IN LAW AND LEARNING

For several decades there has been emphasis on certain individualizing influences on the official regulatory or formative aspects of American life. Two of these relate to our legal and our educational practices. For some time, the school use of intelligence tests and other evaluative devices, elective subjects available to students, and special provisions for handicapped students have produced substantial popular acquaintance with individualization in the school program. Current pressures for further individualization along foregoing and other lines seem strong.

1. Individualized Situations in Our Legal and Educational Structure

There is much reference to just laws, just penalties, and to other considerations of justice. Thus, we note that justice demands an evaluation of circumstances associated with a particular offense and an evaluation of the consequences which may be expected to follow the assessment of certain penalties. The foregoing is commonly referred to as a situational approach. Its cumulative outcome is the common law, which consists of an assembly of cases, each of which is presumed to reflect justice in a particular set of circumstances.

Out of the accumulated situational instances, certain principles are presumably distilled which constitute guides or precedents for future court rulings. Since the principles and precedents reflect past events, they embody strong elements of tradition. Among the various influences that determine how far a particular judge will follow precedent may be the following: his general inertia; familiarity with previous cases; respect for colleagues whose views are represented in the earlier cases; willingness and capacity to analyze a case at hand concerning its resemblance to precedent cases; and competence to see alternatives other than those embodied in precedent, along with courage to reject precedent in favor of a new alternative. Attention to new alternatives often appears in dissents to majority opinions.

Individualization may occur at more than one point in a functioning regulatory structure. (a) Legislation, custom, or other patterns of expectation may establish classes or categories with varying degrees of refinement, concerning offenses in particular areas of crime or other behavior. These classes are ordinarily established before the offenses which are to be adjudicated under them have been committed. The classes and refinements may be looked upon as legal individualizations, in contrast with provisions which are embodied in more general statements. (b) Individualization may also be noted in a judge's decisions, as previously suggested in comments on the situational approach to justice. A pertinent item often noted in judicial individualization concerns the kind or amount of supervision which is included in the statement of penalty. (c) There may also be individualization through the action of prison authorities or other personnel with responsibility for custody and rehabilitation. The activities of parole boards, halfway houses (between prison and freedom), and other operations also reflect types of administrative individualization. (d) A further type of individualization should be mentioned, although it may ordinarily receive less attention than the three already set forth. The further type relates to differences among police officers concerning their "readiness to arrest" or perhaps variation regarding a particular officer on different occasions. This police-test individualization may be more likely than the other three types to generate popular complaint about favoritism, but any of the four types may be subjected to political pressure or to other demands for favored treatment.

Individualization within the educational structure may be seen with respect to admitting particular students to particular schools, classroom assignments and promotion schedules, extracurricular activities, free lunches, student patrol service, academic overload, honors recognition and scholarship awards, etc. In the educational structure as in the legal structure, individualization is accompanied by opportunities for favoritism, and probably for favoritism in rather direct proportion to the number of points at which individualization may be attempted. This situation indicates the need for a high level of fairness and moral integrity on the part of persons who do the individualizing, if the situational or individualized approach is to be an asset in a democratic society.

2. Group Structure and the Concept of Fairness and Equality

Long experience with the favoritisms and corruptions of ruling heads, of both state and church, have been important in the development of rule by laws which have general application, rather than rule by men whose whims change with the social status of the accused. Rule by law as noted is often referred to as the foundation of a democratic society. Both England and the United States have had ongoing and widely publicized struggles about king or president being subject to the general laws of the land, the same as the average citizen is. This idea is crucial for the democratic conception of equality and justice.

It is not easy to harmonize the individualized or situational approach with the approach based on uniform law, but if government and such foundation services as education are to be provided with the consent of the people and for their general well-being, then a considerable degree of harmony must exist. Moreover the harmony cannot be looked upon as a fixed or static entity. There is no such thing as a governmental structure or an educational program on a once-and-for-all basis. Eternal vigilance and continuous development are among the necessary signs of life. And it is sham to say that certain things may be acceptable in theory but will not work in practice. Sound theory must be based on what works in practice, and vice versa.

With respect to harmony in the legal structure as growing out of the individualized situational approach of the common law, emphasis must be placed on the continuous search for general principles which constitute a thread and a common tie among the many individual case situations. This means that in addition to the common thread, each case will include other matters which cannot be ignored. As these "other matters" accumulate from different cases, new principles must be formulated and old ones revised or discarded. The process described is sometimes referred to as stating "the living law." Substantial writings on "the living constitution," as touching the lives of the people through court rulings, embody the fundamental idea. Looking upon the federal Constitution as a "Divine Instrument," as some Supreme Court justices have done—somewhat reminiscent of Moses and the "Ten Commandments"—does not alter the need for adjustment in order for the judicial pronouncements to live. This is one of several respects in which the two guiding documents reflect fundamental human experience.

With respect to harmony in the educational structure as conceived in America, attention must be directed to the purpose of education and to the appropriateness of educational agencies for achieving that purpose. While it may be realistic to think of the purpose category as pluratistic rather than as singular, it is also realistic to observe that in any system of values some purposes are more important than others. Furthermore, it is similarly realistic to characterize the apex of the resulting pyramid in terms of one purpose rather than in terms of several, if the one is appropriately stated.

In regard to purpose and related harmony, it is important in America to differentiate between public and parochial schools. The basic difference could be broadly stated by saying that the public school is oriented toward the status and well-being of the individual here on earth, whereas the parochial school is oriented toward status in a hereafter. In addition, since the public school is maintained and directed by the people generally, as a branch of the state, its role concerning the harmony mentioned necessarily emphasizes its connection with other functions which the state performs. The rights and responsibilities of the individual with respect to the various state functions define his status as a citizen.

Foregoing comments should make it easy to understand why the basic purpose of public education is to develop good citizenship. Otherwise stated, the only grounds for taxing a community to provide education for individual children is that the process will make these children better members of the community than they would otherwise be.

As our culture expands, with the state becoming involved in more activities and touching the lives of individuals in more ways, the concept of the good citizen must likewise become more involved and more inclusive. Accordingly, we find efforts to break up or individualize the general aim of good citizenship into various subsidiary goals or objectives. In this connection as in others, extensive splintering or individualizing increases the problems of maintaining harmony among the pieces. Also, as the society becomes more complex, with good citizenship making a wider range of demands on the individual, smooth civic operations require a higher level of harmony than might previously have seemed necessary.

It follows that for public education in America to achieve the harmony and smooth operations implied, it must continuously identify and emphasize the common thread of civic understanding and responsibility which constitutes the foundation of the various programs of individualized instruction, special education for the handicapped, adult education, etc.

Much of what is characterized as lawlessness and disregard for existing institutions implies that different areas of specialization have become alienated from one another; that is, the common civic thread has not been kept strong and functional. Specialists in all fields tend to develop a technological myopia, whereby prolonged focus on a narrow specialty renders them unable to see that their own specialty along with other specialties depends on a common base and that if the base crumbles then the specialty structure collapses. The foregoing illustrates why civic education must continuously be the most important goal of public education in America and why the concept of civic education must experience continuous growth and updating. The common need inherent in educational programs and in legal structures for continuous growth and updating seems to be more closely related to delinquency and lawlessness in American than several other aspects of our social structure are.

3. Scientific Method in Law and in Education

Some people in the social sciences reject the idea of applying scientific method to their fields, as that method may be thought of in chemistry or biology, and some people in law further reject the idea of their field being considered a social science. Two degrees of intellectual myopia are thus reflected.

When a judge analyzes the evidence in a particular case and compares it with that in other cases in seeking or formulating a principle to govern the situation at hand, he is engaged in the same procedure as a chemist who makes analyses and comparisons among samples in studying soil fertility or enzyme function. The same applies to analyses and comparisons regarding school programs, including the study of pictures by a football coach and team in attempting to improve their scores.

Greater uncertainty about how to apply scientific method in law or education than in chemistry or biology may be due in the main to recency of effort in the social fields, and to a tenacious but fading hope in these two social fields that they in some way gain or retain desired status by differentiating their content and ways of studying it from fields and methods that are acceptable in studying bugs or peanuts. Part of the hang-up is sometimes reflected by the use of such terms as "spiritual values" or "divine inspiration." And incidentally, part of the difficulty which the legal field has had concerning a favorable public image seems to rest with its efforts at separation and aloofness from the other social sciences. In earlier connections the present study noted efforts by some members of the legal profession to get more economics, anthropology, psychology, etc., included in the study of law. This author has commented on similar needs regarding the preparation of teachers.

Further emphasis should be placed on a characteristic which science, law, education, and several other fields have in common. That characteristic is an ongoing search for unity, at continuously higher or more inclusive levels. A science such as chemistry carries on the search through experimentation, in an effort to extend or to revise some accepted scientific principle or law. The extension or revision promotes unity through bringing a larger body of data within the scope of a general principle or explanation. The same goal of broader unity is sought when a court or a legislative body modifies a legal provision so as to include more types of circumstances under it; and school activities concerned with equality of educational opportunity are involved in expanding the common background of knowledge and competence among the people, which is the basis of greater unity.

The idea of a common goal and of movement toward unity through cooperative effort has frequently been mentioned in the present study, substantially in emphasizing the need for joint effort by various agencies with respect to problems of delinquency and lawlessness in America, and in pointing out that the job is too complex and too broadly inclusive for any one existing agency to handle alone. Understanding the implications of scientific method, and recognizing it as a common instrument, constitute important foundation material for the cooperation implied.

Preceding comment might lead some people to ask what scientific method, as here conceived, does to faith; does it erase the concept of faith? In response, it may be noted that few if any other aspects of American culture embody a conception of faith that is as inclusive or as tangible as that embodied in scientific method. This method implies great faith in man's essentially unlimited capacity to learn and to know, and justifies great faith in his power to control his own destiny through acquiring and applying knowledge. When a person with scientific orientation embarks upon an experiment, he has faith that either he or somebody else will live to complete it, that material and other resources for doing so will be available, and that the results will add to man's understanding of the universe. The lives of men of scrutiny and challenge, such as Jesus, Galileo, Einstein, and Pasternak, illustrate a common thread of faith. The democratic system of government in America embodies a great deal of faith comparable to that which science has in experimentation, including a great faith in the ability of the common people to govern themselves. But if faith is to be a positive force in a rapidly changing world, it too must continuously review its proposed sequence of tangible goals and its instruments for reaching them.

4. Values and Limitations of Individualization

In law and in education, as in many other aspects of individual-group relationships in America or elsewhere, there are always problems concerning optimum relative status of group and individual. Discussion elsewhere in this study has pointed out the dependence of the group on the individual for creative ideas in developing the group culture and the importance of extensive personal freedom in the appearance of such ideas. But it has also been noted that coordination and organization are necessary to establish meaningful relationships among diverse contributions to develop guidelines, principles, or laws reflecting them. Thus, extreme individualization without the social pressure of coordination is a certain road to chaos. This applies to the individualization of content and purpose in education, as it does to the individual-situation approach in law. Conversely, extreme emphasis on rigid adherence to a fixed code stymies the adventure which creativeness must have in order to grow.

Among the numerous facets of the recent drift in America toward greater individualization, three are emphasized. Considerable reference has already been made to two of these—our educational system and our legal structure. A third facet, which substantially produces a favorable psychology and the necessary resources for the other two, is the status of technology and the resulting availability of material goods. In present-day America, it is largely the existence of a material base which is abundant and varied that makes it possible for a wide range of personal desires and whims to be satisfied. The relative absence of such a base has led several technologically undeveloped countries to adopt the narrow patterns of communism.

But it is an important mistake to assume that maximum effort at further material production, and maximum individualization in the use made of the material output, indicate expanding democracy. They may be as likely to indicate expanding selfishness, indulgence and dissipation, or waste of social resources. Current energy problems in America are illustrative. If social well-being of the people as a whole over an extended period of time into the future is the collective goal, then the individual diversity of personal choices must be harmonized under general principles—much as a chemist harmonizes fragments from scattered experiments under a general law.

The foregoing indicates why under some conditions fairness or justice regarding law or education demands a rigid enforcement of regulations, whereas under other conditions the regulatory structure should be looked upon merely as affording guidelines. The situation described should help in understanding Justice Holmes' reference to the law as a prophesy on what the courts will do in the presence of particular facts. What is done by a court is thus likely to reflect some mixture of what the judge thinks the law is and what he thinks it ought to be. The relative proportion of the two elements largely determines the extent and direction of growth in the law through court interpretation.

With respect to individualization, in America or in any other industrial society that attempts to emphasize the personal freedom aspects of democracy, it is fundamental to differentiate between individualization of goals and individualization of methods. No organized society can permit individuals to pursue whatever goals they may desire, regardless of the effect on others, although a diverse culture such as the United States includes many possible goals which different individuals may be encouraged to pursue. But each of these goals must be considered subsidiary, with a major common theme to the effect that each person may pursue his subsidiary goal only insofar as it is compatible with public well-being. The extent of the pursuit will vary from one country to another, from time to time within a country, from one issue to another at a particular time, from one person to another at a particular time and place, and from other standpoints. Nevertheless, there is leeway for considerable individualization in procedure for achieving acceptable goals.

The variables noted imply numerous problems in determining what constitutes justice in a particular setting, including the need for consistency among similar cases, which in fact is the need for recognizing a general principle. The same problem is involved in the discipline and guidance of children by parents or teachers, or in the evaluation of teachers by a school personnel board, as the problem reflected by court rulings in lawsuits. Fairness and integrity are major qualification needs of persons in the adjudicative positions suggested. Televised Watergate hearings provided considerable adult education for Americans on fairness and integrity.

When there is extensive lawlessness and delinquency, as there is in America and in some other countries at the present time, it means that too many people are operating on an individualized basis with respect to too many activities. In America, more than in some countries, we have emphasized personal freedom to pursue individual desires at the expense of the substratum of social commitment that is necessary to hold a social structure together. At one time the idea of social commitment and concern for public well-being was substantially encompassed by such general concepts as patriotism, national loyalty, or common decency.

5. *The Contract as an Instrument of Democratic Individualism*

Expansion of personal freedom within a legal framework, which necessarily becomes more elaborate as social relationships become more complex, is generally accepted as a major goal of democratic government. One way to foster such freedom is for government to protect a wide range of opportunity for an individual to engage in various kinds of agreements with others, and to lend governmental support regarding contract enforcement and governmental insight regarding limited areas in which contracting is against public well-being. In a broad sense, contracts which would violate laws are in the forbidden category, such as contracts to promote child labor, prostitution, drug abuse, usurious interest rates, arson, etc.

The avenue by which contracting exerts a democratic influence is through its association with personality development in the individual. Scope and direction in one's development of personality depends on his status in the community, and that status depends on his relationships with other people there. Those relationships consist essentially of what one does or may be expected to do under certain conditions. Several of these relationships are governed by state regulations over which the individual has no direct jurisdiction, such as responsibilities of a man to his family or certain other kinfolk, responsibility for paying taxes, obeying traffic regulations on automobiles, etc. In such matters his options are limited to participation through representation in making the laws.

But in a society such as the United States there is a great range of agreements which one may enter into for the acquiring or exchange of real estate and merchandise or for the rendering of service. The number and kinds of such agreements which a person actually does enter into and the reputation which he establishes for living up to his agreements are a basic determiner of his status in the community. The key point concerns living up to one's agreements, which is necessarily associated with one's maturity in projecting what one is able to do, as embodied in the agreements when made. Responsible contracting thus assumes maturity of contracting parties, and government enforcement of the contracts which are made stimulates the development of that maturity. Status recognition in regard to maturity thus appears.

Furthermore, responsibility in the foregoing sense assumes equal competence on the part of opposing parties to a contract, so that each is able to project the implications for both parties of the contract provisions. Government has accordingly restricted the contracting power of children and of mentally incompetent persons, much as it formerly restricted the contracting power of women. Certain other kinds of protection also exist. Thus, in one's liability for a private debt, the debtor in most communities is entitled to retain a stipulated minimum of property which cannot be taken by a creditor through attachment. There is also the principle that one party may not take "unconscionable" advantage of the other. Additional protections may relate to particular contracting areas or legal jurisdictions. A point that arises out of situations of the kind indicated concerns how far such protections may go without exercising paternalism, coddling, or other influence which restricts the development of maturity and the exercise of freedom by the contracting parties. One among many types of paradox in social regulation thus appears, where different provisions intended for the general well-being of the people come into conflict.

In a complex economy such as the United States, many of the most important contracts are not among individuals as such, but among individuals acting for large corporations, either private corporations such as the Ford Motor Company or public corporations such as cities or public-school districts. Such contracts often involve considerable projection over time and great detail respecting what is to be done. Thus, in the construction of complicated plants or office buildings, detailed plans and specifications are drawn up and time provisions are included regarding progress reports. Another aspect of contracting with regard to such projects concerns financing and the issuance of bonds. Crucial points in bond issues are time projections concerning amortization and necessary sources of income, as well as interest accruals as payments for the use of borrowed money.

Preceding comments on corporate financing of large-scale projects indicate the extent to which contracting provisions enable individuals collectively to engage in undertakings of the scope which is now essential to further economic and social development in American society and to afford protection for the specific persons who become directly involved. One area of individual protection concerns the funds raised from a wide range of persons, through the sale of bonds or corporation stock. This protection is provided by way of various stipulations included in the bonds or in the stock certificates, and by way of general provisions such as appear in regulations of the Securities and Exchange Commission. Other protections relate to workers, through collective bargaining arrangements and union contracts, wage guarantees, accident insurance, etc.

Reference made to contracting, up to this point, should indicate something of the extent to which the American social structure depends on contracting and should indicate why "the sanctity of the contract" must be given legislative and judicial recognition. The alternative would be to invite a breakdown in trade and commerce, in any comprehensive domestic or international sense. The role of trade and exchange in the development of civilization, involving goods, ideas, and persons, is an area of major consideration.

There are two other facets, concerning the role of government in relation to contracting in a culture such as that of the United States, which require mention in the present connection. One concerns government responsibility for a high level of employment, so that the contracting system operates in such a way that practically the entire labor force is able to participate in the economy as consumers and through the consumption of items regarding which they have considerable choice.

The other facet of government responsibility relates to inflation and monetary stability. Most contracts involve the payment of money. This assumes that money at the time of payment should have about the same purchasing power as at the time of contracting, if the contracting is to have a stable base. Payment of debts in inflated dollars always cheats the creditors, unless they were able when contracting to include substantially ingenious guesses about future inflation. The opposite situation appeared in the depression of the mid-1930's, when inflated debts were to be paid in deflated dollars. The foregoing indicates why in America the debtor class has historically been interested in cheap money and the creditor class interested in hard money. The wreckage of economic panics with which the nation's economic history has been cyclically punctuated indicates the role of monetary stability and inflation control in the nation's social structure.

Freedom to contract cannot exercise a potent role, in expanding the individual's opportunity to participate broadly in the economic life of the nation, without a substantial degree of monetary stability so that one can know what the specific provisions of his contracts actually require. This will continue to be true, regardless of various forms of insurance to round off somewhat the sharpest corners and to offer salvage baskets for some of the worst economic casualties. Law and order in America have considerable anchorage to what the people look upon as democratic opportunity, and the contract is a major avenue through which opportunity becomes reality.

An earlier statement mentioned conflict among freedoms that contracting might involve and noted legal regulations governing such conflicts. Community attitudes, apart from laws, may also have considerable regulatory power in this connection.

But in some respects, contracting is based on an assumption of conflicting interests among the parties and is presumed to afford a peaceful method to resolve those conflicts. This idea may be most apparent relative to international treaties, which may be looked upon as contractual arrangements to settle international disputes. The main difference in this respect between nations and individual members of a particular nation is that the overarching power of the particular nation is able to coerce and exercise supervision over compliance by the individuals, whereas the historic absence of such an overarching power among strong nations has typically contributed to the causes of war. Gradual extension of the power vested in the United Nations Organization to exercise surveillance over different nations might thus become an important instrument of democracy, through extending the opportunity of individual citizens of one nation to enter more extensively and more freely into enforceable contracts with individuals in other nations.

The idea of personal freedom through opportunity to contract has another type of international implication. When the citizens within a major nation have an extensive repertoire of personal freedoms, the prestige of that nation is usually enhanced among the citizens of other nations. The citizen of the admired nation shares this prestige.

A commonplace instance of government agreement or contracting may help clarify the point noted. When a housewife enters a chain grocery, the appearance of merchandise on the shelves with prices shown constitutes an offer. Her placing successive items in a shopping cart and approaching the check-out cashier indicate her willingness to pay the stipulated prices or to accept the offer. Payment and departure with the groceries, then, consummates the contract. While the procedure is more complicated in buying a residence or a factory, the principle is the same. Also, the principle is the same in contracting for services—as wage contracts in industry, teacher contracts, or contracts for bus transportation, electric power, etc.

The point then regarding international status is that the freedom of the individual in a particular nation to engage in a wide range of agreements, such as implied, becomes a symbol of his nation's status on the world scene. Rationing of essential food or other items may erode this form of democratic status, unless it is made clear that limiting the freedom of some persons contributes to the general well-being of the community. When such contribution is shown, rationing belongs in the same category as limiting the speed of driving on public highways, limiting entitlement to public-welfare allotments, etc.

Chapter 3

INSTITUTIONAL CHANGE AND THE DEVELOPMENT OF SOCIAL VALUES

Probably one should recognize that social values are group or cultural projections of nature's drive for the species to perpetuate itself and to expand man's satisfactions and personal comforts if possible while doing so. Thus, any enduring value structure must be in harmony with the kind of biological organisms which people are.

Institutions may be looked upon as collective efforts to embody into practice within the group whatever net results the cumulative experience of the group has shown to contribute to the general purpose indicated. If the accumulation grows rapidly, there is a rapid emergence of new ways to achieve personal comfort and satisfaction. This generates a social or collective need to differentiate the new ways which contribute to the general social purpose from the new ways which result in dissipations and other antisocial behavior.

In any culture there is possible variation as to the direction and rate of institutional development, and some individuals are always more important in determining the direction and rate than other individuals. Hence, institutional structure tends to embody and to perpetuate the personal interests and biases of the powerful. Such biases often retard the appearance of institutional adjustments which would benefit the general run of the population. A power struggle thus results. The vigor of the struggle and the insights of opposing leadership then determine the direction and scope of institutional change.

In democratic societies, much of the struggle is carried on through legislative and other debate and through a judicial system to resolve controversies. Also, in at least a theoretical sense, educational programs are intended to perform the civic duty of acquainting the people with the general values and processes involved.

1. Social Development and Institutional Change

A study concerning law and social regulation must note that in dealing with human relationships, numerous variables become involved which are absent or less prominent when dealing with inorganic relationships. Part of the difference lies in the physical mobility of humans, but more lies directly in man's central nervous system.

Man's limited behavior patterns at birth, associated with his great learning capacity, are common knowledge. But the importance of these facts for relationships among people, or for necessary efforts to establish laws and regulatory systems to govern those relationships on a democratic basis, are not well understood.

Human Variables and the Mores

The existence of broad individual differences is widely known, as is the likelihood that in most families the differences among the children become greater as the children get older. The differences grow largely because there is no way to make sure that the experiences of any two children will be exactly the same. This applies also to so-called identical twins, whom parents may try to dress alike and to make act as nearly alike as possible. The differences influence the relationships in which persons can engage and the resulting satisfactions. Hence, in a society in which there is a wider range of potential experience than any person can undergo, the differences among persons will ordinarily be greater than in a society which has a narrowly restricted experience potential.

But while the sum total of biological and social background of one individual varies from that of another, the numerous backgrounds include many of the same elements. It is out of the core of common elements that the values and practices called "the mores" develop, and it is on this core that the regulatory structure must be built.

However, no great size of core is required, before it begins to act as a shaping factor concerning experiences which members of the group have. Language, rank order in the family and in the community, particular vocational practices, along with certain beliefs and superstitions, are among the influences in a child's early shaping. Later on, schools, religious organizations, general codes of law, etc., are set up in a conscious group effort to expand the core. Hence, the more complex and variant the experience potential of a society is, the more important it is to have an inclusive regulatory system. This is to insure a broad core area within which people can carry on their various relationships, in an atmosphere of considerable assurance and security.

Social Change and Social Obsolescence

Where social change results from some type of collective effort, the new relationship is better than the old; at least it is better from the standpoint of the persons who are powerful enough to produce the change. Replacement of an existing practice by a new one means that the old one has become obsolete. Speedup in change obviously means speedup in obsolescence. In a dynamic industrial democracy, this fact is often commented upon by older persons who compare the current rate of change with that of their young adulthoods.

It is out of those social structures and related idealisms which change slowly that concepts of eternal verities and fixed legal or regulatory systems arise. But any dynamic society is continuously involved in a process of crawling out of cocoons, from earlier spinnings, into an atmosphere of expansion in real or imagined freedom and comfort. With respect to the governing legal framework, most Western countries now place relatively little emphasis on codes—in the sense of the codes designated by Hammurabi, Moses, Justinian, or Napoleon—with more emphasis on current legislation and court rulings. In America today, perhaps constitutional provisions come nearest to symbolizing the code philosophy on durability.

Growth in the body of knowledge and dissemination of knowledge more widely and more rapidly among the people are probably the most revolutionary forces in present-day Western society. In America the mores include broad commitment both to developing new knowledge and to wide dissemination of knowledge through formal schooling and otherwise. This means that the development of techniques for continuous updating of our regulatory system and for the development of popular understanding and support as to the process involved become more urgent and more in need of systematic study.

Research on Governmental Function and Operation

Federal, state, and local governments in the United States carry on various types of research, as in agriculture, medicine and health services, education, highway construction, rehabilitation of handicapped persons, etc. But this activity does not include a great amount of research on the structure of government itself or on the scope and grouping of activities which government should perform. Occasionally state universities and public school systems engage in surveys or programs of institutional research, which result in moderate changes in structure or perhaps in function, but few of our major units of government maintain bureaus of research and experimentation which continuously review the structure and operation of those governmental units. Private industries often carry on much of this kind of research through their departments of research and development.

Perhaps the cultural lag regarding research on government results from a carry-over of philosophies and systems of fixed relationships, which developed before such forces as the industrial revolution came into Western society. And at present there are few countries in which these forces are as dynamic as they are in the United States.

In the present connection, two functions of government in America should be compared. One is the restrictive function, whereby government prevents certain individuals from encroaching on the socially defined rights of others. This is an early, continuous, and broadly recognized function, which does not need elaboration at this point. The other function looks upon government as an innovator or an agency for maximizing social accomplishment and the well-being of the people. The theory of police power as being intended to promote the common welfare, and as having jurisdiction wherever any substantial public interest is involved, reflects the idea. Building highways and dams, regulating public utilities, providing health or housing services, maintaining public schools, or granting subsidies and low-cost loans in certain instances, illustrate conceptions of governmental function which have recently become prominent but which were not in the thinking of the Founding Fathers. The emphasis in the present connection is that research and experimentation on governmental function and operation ought to be more extensively developed, that being so is within the innovative sphere, and that it should be geared to the welfare and benefit of the people who are governed and who pay for the services of government.

Natural History of Institutions

Sociological and other reference to the "natural history of institutions" implies that particular institutions come into existence to serve recognized needs and that if those institutions do not change as needs change, the institutions become ignored and insignificant. When Judge Tamm asked, "Are Courts Going the Way of the Dinosaurs?"[1] the foregoing is essentially what he had in mind.

Other writers have inferred that courts are not the only agencies that can judge and decide disputes and have pointed to the marked increase in administrative boards and agencies which exercise judicial along with other functions. School boards, commerce commissions, and boards of health are illustrative. In numerous instances the courts have apparently favored this development, as a means of reducing their own case loads. However, the problem always remains of how much can be given away, without giving away the right or need to exist.

During the past two decades of rise in delinquency among youth, with particular regard to lawlessness as focused on drug abuse and to complaints about lack of preparation for employment, much has been said about *relevance* of school programs to the needs of youth in facing present-day American life. Other skepticism regarding educational programs relates to whether programs for job and vocational training should be under the supervision of the Office of Education or the Department of Labor. Educators who remember the Depression of the early 1930's will recall the educational programs in camps of the Civilian Conservation Corps and the threat which they were thought to present to the orthodox high school of the time. Other crises have arisen in the evolution of America's extensive program of public education. The point with respect to the natural history of institutions is that in every such crisis lies a threat to the continued existence of some prevailing institution. If the institution makes the adjustments required by the new service demands, it enjoys renewed life. If not, it moves toward limbo.

A court item regarding lawlessness, which is pertinent concerning institutional history, relates to the independent judiciary. For perspective, the item should be viewed with regard to its growth from systems of government when the power of a ruling monarch was inclusive; that is, as to making, carrying out, and adjudicating violations of the law. Under the American system, the total authority and responsibility of government is distributed among three branches, which are presumably equal in stature and presumably independent of one another. However, since all three are concerned with regulating human behavior in an expanding culture, it is not difficult to understand how disputes arise as to jurisdictional gaps and overlappings, usurpations, laxity, unconcern about the public interest, etc.

However, in an increasingly complex and interdependent society, there is another standpoint from which the idea of an independent judiciary should be viewed. That standpoint relates to independence in the sense of judicial aloofness and of restricted communication between the courts and the people, with no substantial feedback from the people as to how well they think the courts are going about their job as a branch of government. Independence from responsibility to inform and serve the people may imply an extreme conception of judicial independence, but it points in the direction of some anxieties about an independent judiciary.

This study has reviewed extensive criticisms of aloofness, as well as numerous suggestions for remedying the situation. This author has consistently derogated the idea of judicial aloofness and has urged greater participation by the courts along with school and other agencies in working out programs for developing in youth and others a more constructive behavior regarding lawfulness and general responsibility for good government. The courts are in a position to render a unique service in the area suggested, and thereby to refurbish their image before the American people and to silence questions about the ways of the dinosaurs.

What is said about aloofness and obsolescence with respect to the judiciary and the courts has applied at various times and in various degrees to schools and universities. It has also applied to the areas of research and experimental inquiry called "pure research." It has sometimes applied to conceptions of vocational fields, as when agriculture used to be referred to as an "independent" vocation. However, with the disappearance of free land for homestead subsistence, the development of commercial agriculture, government loans and export concerns, etc., notions about agriculture as an independent vocation became myths.

Expansion of the foregoing idea on obsolescence indicates its application in varying degrees to every institution in a dynamic society. But the expansion also indicates that through social analysis and planning, institutions can greatly influence the future patterns of their "natural histories." The implications of this for lawlessness in America and for personal responsibility concerning good government are extensive.

2. Functional Development of Social Philosophy and Values

If one accepts a literal translation from the Athens of Socrates (c.470-399 B.C.) that philosophy means a love of wisdom and that wisdom consists essentially in understanding the meaning of things and events, one should not assume that the Athenians of that time were the first people who had ever been concerned about the meaning of human life or of the individualized experience of which man's life is largely composed. Among formal and partially recorded efforts, one might note those of Moses (13th century B.C.) or those of Micah and Hosea (8th century B.C.). One might also include some constructive surmises from anthropology about the lives of preliterate peoples who lived before or since the days of Moses or Socrates. Thus, the human tendency to seek meanings or to see relationships among situations and events preceded the appearance of what is now generally called civilization, but the tendency has depended more on written language for its growth and development than on other types of records concerning man's thought and action.

Throughout the effort to discover or create meaning runs the idea that meaning is a relationship phenomenon and that meaning consists of observing relationships between separate items and a central theme. The problem thus became that of determining the origin and nature of the central theme.[2]

Pre-Socratic Thought

The pre-Socratic Greeks looked for some rather simple and directly observable element of nature as embodying the central theme or touchstone of philosophy. When Thales (Ionian, 640?-546 B.C.) looked upon water as the central element, he probably had little if any modern knowledge about life having originated in warm sea water; most of the human organism consisting of water, and emphasis on plenty of pure drinking water as essential for health; a major portion of the earth's surface consisting of water; or of man's "farming and mining the sea" to secure food and minerals.

Much the same could be said about the background of Heraclitus (5th century B.C.) and his touchstone of ever-living fire, although it is not difficult to project his acquaintance with fire from volcanoes, lightning, or human efforts, and it is easy to recognize the ever flickering and leaping nature of flames. Acquaintance with geysers has apparently been a more recent human experience, as have technological concepts of piping heat from the earth's interior into communities for heating homes and generating electricity. Man's current dependence on heat for smelting ores and for many other industrial or commercial uses could be looked upon as projections from the earlier concept. Anaximines (4th century B.C.) looked upon air as the central theme or touchstone, whereas Empedocles (5th century B.C.) included earth and recognized the four elements: air, earth, fire, and water.

However certain other ideas appeared in pre-Socratic thought. Thus, in addition to the note in the foregoing paragraph, Empedocles had a bipolar concept of love and strife (or perhaps love and hate) and a concept regarding mixture and separation; whereas Pythagoras (So. Italy, 6th century B.C.) looked upon number (and the universality of quantity) as the touchstone.

Bipolarity raises questions concerning harmony and doctrines of unity. The idea of paradoxes was thus recognized at least as early as Heraclitus (5th century B.C.) and has attracted attention ever since. Paradoxes are currently recognized in the United States concerning such matters as individual freedom and group restriction, with repeated observations by the Supreme Court that no freedoms are absolute; creative drug use and criminal drug abuse; raising the wages or economic-take of one group at the expense of other groups, and the perennial oratory on catch-up or balance; what behavior in home, school, or court amounts to creative or rehabilitative discipline, and what behavior thwarts growth and the development of human resources. Out of the foregoing emerges a concept of degrees or gradation between the poles and of recognizing a feasible area of fruitful operation between the extremes. It is in situations of the kind implied that reasonableness acquires significance in respect to human relationships; i.e., such relationships as concern school regulations or court actions. The idea was probably in the thinking of Ben Franklin when he observed that there is reason in all things.

Search for Criteria of Moral Truth

Problems associated with efforts to find the touchstone of unity in simple and directly observable qualities of nature contributed to developing a line of philosophers who distrusted nature as observed by man through his sense organs and caused them to look elsewhere. Socrates apparently sought truth through critical reasoning, carried out in dialogue based on skillful questioning. He thus arrived at what he thought were objective truths and stable moral principles. This was contrary to the ideas of moral relativity, as urged by the Sophists in their rebellion against moral conservatism.

A crucial point in Socrates' doctrine was his agreement with the Sophists' premise that man must seek to satisfy his interests, but he claimed that man's real needs were not met by indiscriminate satisfactions of immediate appetites. Socrates emphasized a kind of long-range moral or spiritual health, in which justice and social living depended on the *way* in which one fulfils the needs of nature. Thus emphasis was placed on the form, order, or relationship of one's behavior to the structure of community life. This is the crucial idea in a modern system of law and order, in which individuals are regulated for the long-range well-being of the group.

Plato (c.427-347 B.C.) carried further certain ideas attributed to Socrates. Plato reasoned that particular instances of behavior in individual situations varied widely and were imperfect as guides and that full reality was to be attained only through universals or general ideas. He apparently observed that mathematicians deal with such abstractions as numbers and lines, but not with measurements of any particular house or body of water; and that biologists deal basically with types and species, more than with individual animals or other living things. Thus, there were the transient, imperfect, sensory impressions which one observes in particular situations of space and time, but from which one must escape in order to get at true reality which existed in general principles or laws. He thus relied on a kind of otherworld, which was characterized by such principles and laws. To some extent this process was similar to that of early Hebrew prophets and other sages, although their observations were probably less extensive and less systematically analyzed that those which characterized Plato, and perhaps the prophets were more direct in referring to the otherworld as focused on a god. In some instances reference is made to equally vague god-given orientation, in legislative and judicial behavior associated with modern government.

Aristotle (384-322 B.C.) gave greater recognition than Plato did to the idea that the only real existence which the general forms or principles have is in specific situations. He noted that every observable situation included both substance and form. Thus, a chair consisted of wood or metal, but arranged according to some design intended to serve a particular purpose. Human behavior always includes people, but they were doing particular things in accordance with certain purposes. Aristotle rejected Plato's flight from the real world, which he thought was based essentially on Plato's inadequate understanding of that world. This view resembles the view, which is sometimes more forcefully stated, that reliance on a god and otherworldliness symbolizes basic ignorance concerning the world of concrete experience in which we live.

However, if an Aristotle or anybody else tries to evaluate variation or change in situations, he must have some standard with which to make comparisons. This has been referred to as an immoveable force, which is called a "prime mover" regarding all other things. Aristotle used God for this purpose. He apparently reasoned that if one attributed purpose to God, one could recognize order or direction in the variation and change which Plato thought was chaotic and meaningless. Through this avenue, God's example of perfection could stimulate man toward lofty action.

To Aristotle man's highest achievement was in thought and contemplation. In his related view that labor was vulgar and fit only for slaves, Aristotle failed to carry through on his idea that real meaning has no concrete existence, except in specific earthly situations, and failed to show perspective regarding the slave-based society of Greece and of other parts of the world in which he lived and traveled. He thus did much to set the stage for the dichotomy between so-called liberal and practical education, which tended to blossom during the thousand years of intellectual enslavement of Western thought to Aristotle, and which has been carried into most parts of the present world that have been substantially influenced by European colonial and other relationships.

One difference between Aristotle and Plato should be further noted because of the importance and expansion of the Aristotelian idea in current American thought and practice. Aristotle was essentially an Ionian; and from that cultural background he got much of his early interest in nature study, including his interest in the details of biological differences among species. In addition, his father was court physician for Alexander the Great, which enabled Aristotle to accompany Alexander on many of the latter's military expeditions. In view of this background, it was probably easier for Aristotle to think in terms of growth and development, than for a philosopher who was strongly oriented toward mathematics. Thus, Aristotle's universe is sometimes characterized as dynamic, or as expanding and as becoming. Hence, each thing tends to move through a development, which is true and final, but also perfect—and natural. This appears in the numerous political insights that are noted in his *Ethics*: his idea about law as the true sovereign of states; about differences between a monarch who rules according to law and a tyrant who rules by personal whim; and about the right of the people, because of their capacity for collective judgment, to select their rulers and hold them to account. Several ideas thus bequeathed to posterity by Aristotle have subsequently been reflected in the thinking of Thomas Aquinas (1225?-

1274), John Locke (1632-1704), Thomas Jefferson (1743-1826), John Dewey (1859-1952), and recent Congressional investigations on Watergate.

Cleavages Following Aristotle

By the time of Aristotle's death, political stability and security among the Greek city-states had disintegrated to a substantial degree. Thus, old standards of judgment disappeared, and men sought new ones. The two major avenues of development that appeared reflected a dichotomy of that time—and of the present time.

The Stoic outlook was one of resignation, of living according to an established concept of universal law without complaint about one's fate, of suppressing the ups and downs of emotional life, and of following duty as indicated by reasoning based on established guides. It is not difficult to find conservatives in America today who reflect a comparable outlook.

The Epicureans emphasized reflective thought, but based it more largely on Aristotle's ideas about close observation of details in nature, including man. A sort of combination between science and ethics thus developed, although certain problems grew out of religious beliefs regarding an afterlife. Epicureans maintained that man's fears grew out of these beliefs, with the implied meddling of the gods in man's affairs. When man takes a scientific view of human life along with the rest of nature, discarding beliefs in divine providence and accepting the idea that death is the end, reasoned the Epicureans, he is freed from the anxieties and terrors inspired by religion. While Freud would probably not agree that the foregoing comment represents the entire repertoire of fear, the Epicurean view seems to be a rather clear forerunner of the current experimental and scientific approach to understanding the universe.

From Cleavage Toward Pragmatism

From the standpoint of current social values and educational thought in America, passing reference should be made to the influence of Thomas Aquinas on Catholic parochial schools; to the ideas of John Locke on education; to the contributions of Isaac Newton (1642-1727); to the role of science in a mechanistic conception of the universe; to the views of J. J. Rousseau (1712-1778) on the corrupt nature of civilization; to the critical analysis of knowledge and reasoning by Kant (1724-1804); to Fichte's (1762-1814) emphasis on the self or ego as the source of what others had considered to be objective; to Hegel's (1770-1831) idea that all types of human experience were manifestations of a universal or absolute spirit; to Kierkegaard's (1813-1855) concern about man's relationship with God as the only absolute, whereas other relationships are relative, and to certain implications of his doctrine for existentialism in education and elsewhere; to the stress by Karl Marx (1818-1883) on dialectic materialism and the rejection of religion, as supplying foundation stones in his philosophy of communism; to certain views on utilitarianism set forth by Bentham (1748-1832) and by John Stuart Mill

(1806-1873); and to the summary presentations and evolutionary implications noted by Herbert Spencer (1820-1903).

Achievements and Potentialities of Experimentalism

However, major attention from the standpoint of American developments should be placed on the evolutionary philosophy of Charles Darwin (1809-1882), as set forth in the *Origin of Species* (1859)) and as defended by T. H. Huxley (1825-1895) against widespread attack, and as exerting a marked influence on William James (1842-1910) and on John Dewey (1859-1952). Attention should also be given to the works of Charles Pierce (1839-1914), in the initial formulations of pragmatism to the effect that the basic truth of a doctrine is to be judged by the results that it produces; that is, what difference it makes to operate according to the particular doctrine, as contrasted with operating on some other basis. Pragmatism is now extensively thought of in connection with experimentalism, which assumes that experiments are specifically set up to test doctrines and to provide new information on the basis of which to revise doctrines. A continuous sequence of experiments and revisions has acquired great respect in America as a method of arriving at truth through the development of new knowledge.

With developments since World War I, it seems increasingly apparent that the operating philosophy of the American people is a combination or merger of pragmatism and experimentalism. The merger phenomenon is more apparent in some areas of the culture than in others. The areas in which its influence is greatest are those of the physical and biological sciences, where it has been easiest to set up experimental controls and make quantitative evaluations of results. But with experience, confidence, and the refinement of tools and concepts, the general philosophy of pragmatism is extending to government and to various other areas of social relationship. There has, of course, long been the practice in America of repealing laws which do not prove satisfactory—or do not achieve the anticipated results. However, there is marked slowness in developing techniques for evaluating achievements in this area and a continuing hesitance to making a broadscale application of such evaluation to human relations.

Slowness and hesitance here may be due partly to a continued religious influence concerning divine implications of man's existence, but probably they are due more largely to inertia and laziness with respect to attacking difficult problems. This is an area which well exhibits an important psychological fact; namely, that for most persons it is easier to extend rationalizations of why certain developments are impossible, or perhaps why *IT* was never intended that man should probe around in the area, than to devise and pursue varied modes of attack.

Broadening Experimentalism Into Social Areas

The crux of what has been said about applying experimentalism to human relationships in general can be illustrated by specific reference to education. The scientific study of education began with simple factual relationships, such as concern spelling or number combinations, and has gradually moved into areas concerned with defining and evaluating intelligence and rating personality development. But little has been done regarding scientific criteria in curriculum determination, objective appraisal of the more complex aspects of teacher competence, criteria other than the calendar to be used in establishing retirement, effectiveness of various disciplinary practices with respect to students or staff personnel, adequacy in school administration, implications of different procedures for levying taxes to support schools, appraisal of student competence upon graduation or at some point en route, etc. Reflection on items such as the foregoing supports statements to the effect that the scientific movement in education is in its infancy and may be in danger of being stifled through retreading old straw rather than being oriented toward great unexplored possibilities.

But education is only one of numerous areas of social relationships to which the term infancy thus applies, in considerable degree. Observations at various points in the present study indicate gestures along the lines of experimentalism with respect to some areas of law enforcement and of court functioning. Certain suggestions for other developments in these spheres are made. However, it seems that the "scientific movement" has done less in the field of law and order than in the field of education. Might one ask in this connection, perhaps with Aristotle, if a difference between the two fields should be expected, since education is primarily concerned with the growth and development of individuals, whereas law and order as presently conceived is concerned quite largely with restraining individuals and with conserving the group values and social structures of the past? It was suggested earlier in this study that the developmental functions of government, in promoting the general welfare, have been emphasized less than the restrictive functions of government, although considerable "promoting" has appeared in recent decades, especially at the federal level.

Philosophy has sometimes been referred to as the mother of sciences, since it is an old and vaguely inclusive field out of which newer and somewhat more sharply defined fields have emerged. With successive branchings, several generations of descendents have appeared. Among some of the nearer kinfolk, one might note such areas as the philosophy of education, philosophy of science, philosophy of religion, philosophy of government, philosohpy of communism; or one might more specifically note the philosophy of American or some other foreign policy, philosophy of public health services, philosophy of inflation and monetary control, etc. With further expansion in knowledge and human activities, and further scientific interest in differentiating detailed categories of observation, one should expect additional progeny to come from the general area of philosophy.

Perennial Problems of Social Philosophy

While forecasting is always hazardous, especially in a changing society, brief reference might be made to a few ongoing problems in social philosophy. (1) One problem concerns evaluation of the expanding body of knowledge; of devising better ways for determining what knowledge is of most worth and of worth to whom or under what circumstances. (2) Another problem involves continuous revision of relationships between the group and the individual, in efforts to harmonize greatest individual satisfaction with greatest social well-being. This implies continuous updating of the regulatory and judicial structure. (3) A more specific consideration may relate to man as a part of or a projection of other aspects of nature, probably with clearer recognition of certain biological traits as constituting great social handicaps. Such traits may include personal selfishness or the desire to dominate others Whether conscious effort will be made to breed a strain of humans in which such highly individualistic traits fade out is in the area of "far out" speculation; more social effort to modify such traits among currently living persons seems likely. (4) Reference, under $\#$ 3 above, to trait modification raises questions about revised or displaced religious conceptions about god and divine providence as factors in the social behavior of people. (5) Racial and ethnic considerations will likely continue to be prominent in the development of social philosophy during the immediate future, in America and abroad. (6) One aspect of the American regulatory structure which seems likely to undergo a review concerns permissiveness as it has developed in recent decades, especially with respect to some aspects of school practice and criminal justice. (7) Perhaps some examination should be made of our political philosophy on majority rule, with minority opportunity to be heard. The filibuster need not be the only focus of such examination. (8) Certain comments and references in the study have mentioned limitations of what can be accomplished through law. Similar considerations concerning limitations of what can be accomplished through experimental science or through education may deserve more attention than they receive. (9) Man has not found an adequate way to deal psychologically or philosophically with death as a human phenomenon. In view of probable further decline in respect for supernaturalism and an afterlife as avenues of reducing anxieties in the field, the prospects of a vacuum versus constructive replacements should be examined. There seem to be many Americans who are "tired of living and afraid of dying," but who sort of carry on in an ethical twilight zone. This is a zone which offers nothing particularly vigorous or creative, but embodies nothing that is overtly condemned. Broad erasure of an established pattern without developing a replacement could stimulate suicide, neurosis, and other behavior that is disruptive of the social structure. There are other bases for urging further thought and analysis in this area.

Chapter 4

CONSTRUCTIVE ACHIEVEMENT AND LAWLESSNESS
IN AMERICAN DEMOCRACY

The United States is often referred to as having one of the most creative and dynamic cultures in the world, yet one with a great deal of lawnessness. Probably several influences help support and also explain what superficially appears to be a contradiction in the two aspects of this observation.

One suggestion might be that the people are so busily engaged in creating new knowledge and new technological developments that they have energy and time only for the more serious forms of lawlessness and are not greatly concerned about many forms in which no victim is seriously injured, in person or in property. Also, it could be said that rapid change resulting from creativeness means that there is a considerable body of obsolescent regulations which does not really fit the needs of the time and that lawlessness occurs when such regulations are ignored. Some observers point to our extensive frontier history, with large regions of sparse population, with the population of the region consisting largely of rugged individualists who had strong motivation but little respect for legal restraint, and with a scatter which made legal surveillance and law enforcement difficult. Heterogeneity of biological and cultural background of the population has sometimes been noted, with respect to heavy representation from various parts of Europe, Africa, and native Indian country.

Perhaps two other items should be added to those already noted. One is a rather continuously growing emphasis on research and experimentation, which speeds up the rate at which new materials and procedures are introduced into the culture, with little planning on how best to make the necessary social adjustments. The other item is a substantial weakness concerning any comprehensive and systematic civic education, to explain to either youth or adults the nature of social regulation in a dynamic social structure and the responsibility which the individual citizen must assume in order for peace and lawfulness to exist under any kind of governmental arrangement. Several ramifications of aims, disciplines, achievements, lawlessness, and penal systems thus become involved.

1. Philosophy and Achievement in Education

To assume that learning or educational practice has always been on a conscious basis, or that the persons involved were always aware of goals to be achieved, may not seem realistic. This assumption could unduly minimize the extensive education which takes place as children grow up in a social environment and imitate what their elders do. But the imitation is accomplished through varying degrees of awareness, as a child observes closely in trying to follow in parental footsteps to gain many of the things he wants and as parents approve or disapprove the aims or methods of the children. Much education of this kind takes place in America today.

Aims and Outcomes

Whether one refers to nature as having purpose or aims need not arouse extensive quibble. One can refer to purpose or biological drive, or one can say that humans have evolved in such a way that for individuals to survive certain things must be done. One thing is to recognize that some items constitute food and that one must insure a supply of those items. Other considerations might similarly be noted. The upshot is that both purpose and achievement are essential to survival and that from the standpoint of practical results they are inseparable.

Yet as a society becomes more complex, one's purposes or aims become more numerous and varied. Hence, it becomes necessary to establish priorities among them and to resolve conflicts among aims as the general expansion occurs. The process described requires analysis of social relationships and the conscious establishment of regulations to foster a stipulated priority arrangement. When the regulations become numerous and are organized into a system, the result constitutes law and order.

Thus, the conception of what is good or desirable has expanded from a simple biological definition to a broadly inclusive definition which continues to expand with development of the imagination and of the productive arts. The expansion demands precision in stating aims and in measuring achievements.

Scope and Shift Among Aims

For achievement regarding any aim to be measured, the conception of that aim must be held fairly constant over sufficient time so that observation can produce data on the results. This depends on the units of measurement which are devised. It also depends on how adaptable those units are to aims which shift in a rapidly changing technology and on the rate at which new units and devices are created.

Developments in technology and in other aspects of American culture during the past several decades have generated great demand for instruments which can measure with increasing speed and precision. Further demand for instruments to manipulate and interpret the large bodies of resulting data are thus continuously generated.

The demand for precise measurement and for increasingly sophisticated interpretations of data has grown with mass-production techniques, with the emergence of large industrial corporations, and with the need for large numbers of employees who have widely varied qualifications. The needs of the individual, respecting measurement philosophy and procedures in order to participate effectively in the culture as either a producer or as a consumer, thus become apparent. To assume that pupil learning and educational programs can stand apart from demands for cogent statements of aim, or from associated measurement demands, is unrealistic.

Technological precision in stating aims and in measuring achievements does not eliminate falsification and propaganda intended to deceive the public so as to achieve private gain, but it demands a corresponding refinement in falsification and propaganda technique. Hitler showed the world how science in the fields of psychology and of broadcasting could propagandize large bodies of people and get them to become enthusiastic about aims and procedures which are contrary to much of their long-term cultural tradition. Considerable of the same is sponsored in present-day America through advertising by private enterprises regarding beauty aids and luxury equipment, television saturation with sports and theatrical personnel and events, and some aspects of corrupt politics with its monetary implications. By comparison, the techniques of Hitler, or of some American developments, make the procedures of the Church regarding the Turks during the Crusades or those of the Spaniards regarding the Indians in Mexico and Peru seem extremely crude and amateur. Considerable trickle-down of technique appears with respect to American political rallies, depending on persons and dollars involved.

There is another background item that affects the extent to which the propaganda of the present time is able to sway large bodies of people. This item might be called a "propaganda readiness" which is associated with an immediacy of goal demands. Immediacy is variously referred to as demands for "instant greatness," living in the "here and now," "live it up," "travel now, pay later," etc., with a general philosophy of letting posterity worry about the future.

Various influences in American life contribute to the outlook indicated. One is the abundance of material goods which have been easily available, with little preliminary sacrifice and saving required. Another is the broad coverage of welfare and insurance programs, intended largely to insulate from concern about the future, the substantial numbers of persons who are poor in money, imagination, personal discipline, and general competence. This tends to generate a large group which operates essentially on the philosophy "sufficient unto the day are the evils thereof," with planning as not being among the current day's evils. The idea of compassion, embodied in some religious practices as well as in considerable religious doctrine, may be part of the picture.

There can be important cultural values in helping the unfortunate or in using a broad range of material resources for enriching one's own personal life. But a society that aspires to a legitimate claim on the future must recognize that pursuing a virtue too far usually results in a vice, and that a viable social structure demands continuous scrutiny of both long-established ideals and freshly-conjured panaceas.

It is upon leadership that responsibility rests for a view of what lies beyond the here and now, and for the regulatory structure necessary to implement the social well-being embodied in such a view. It is not new to say that "where leadership fails the people perish," but it may be important to say it frequently and in various ways. Educators, courts, and law-enforcement agencies should be especially important in the statements and implementations inferred.

Developments Among Aims and Evaluations

An earlier comment referred to education through informal imitation and to movement from that situation toward a complexity of specializations concerning purposes and evidence of achievement. Further comment on certain steps en route and on certain consequences should be helpful.

Perhaps most Americans are familiar with the emphasis which early Puritan education in New England placed on religion and associated moral training, with emphasis on learning to read being associated with reading the Bible and thereby defeating the efforts of Satan. Arithmetic was a frill to the schools of the time.

But with the growth of handicraft and related expansion in the marketplace exchange of goods, the keeping of accounts became more important. And with westward expansion into "open country," which afforded opportunity for persons who were courageous and able to withstand hardship, surveying and some other practical arts gained in consideration. However, it was largely the tool subjects, along with ideas about thrift and associated moral precepts, that moved westward during the early nineteenth century —as the district school followed the prairie schooner across the continent's midsection.

The secondary school which timidly followed, pursued largely a classical curriculum well into the twentieth century. However, by that time trade competitions from industrial areas of Western Europe were an important force in gradually bringing the practical arts into America's public high schools, although frequently preceded by a period of developing private commercial and trade or mechanical schools.

Expansion of the high school curriculum as noted was part of an American socioeducational complex which included increased school enrollments; increased expenditures for education; rapid growth in mass-production industry; expansion of child-labor regulations; concerns of parents that the high school help their children develop salable skills; and preparation of selected students to participate in athletic events and certain other pageantry for the general entertainment of the community. These areas of development lent themselves to quantitative measurement and to reporting in such quantitative terms as impressed a population which was oriented toward material achievement and material wealth.

As Topsy grew, moral precepts stressed success in competitions—largely on an individualized basis, although gradually expanding into the power of industrial corporations. Attitudes regarding community responsibility, civic understanding, or the regulation of individual power in the public interest were reflected in expressions to the effect: "more business in government and less government in business," "tax-eating government boondoggling," "scurvy politicians," "patronage hounds," etc. Precepts were not comparably emphasized regarding such matters as personal growth through the collective development of others in community relationships. To some extent the shortcoming has been noted in expressions such as "united we stand, divided we fall," or in Franklin's Revolutionary War observation, "we will hang together, or we will hang separately." Several recent disclosures of flagrant corruption in high public office underscore our neglect regarding a high level of competence, honesty, and integrity on the part of individuals in positions of public trust.

The crux of much preceding discussion is that our cultural orientation toward quantitative evaluation has caused us to emphasize and develop those aspects of the culture which readily lend themselves to quantitative measurement, to the neglect of commensurate development in such areas as civic responsibility, moral integrity, public trust, or general honesty and respectability in dealing with fellow citizens, which are presently more intangible.

The importance of the neglect cannot be rationalized away by reference to our present inability to measure degrees of neglect or by saying that we have reached limits beyond which quantitative evaluation cannot go. An earlier comment in the present discussion inferred that statements of ideals concerning such matters as moral integrity and civic responsibility are essentially worthless, without some way of estimating progress toward achieving them. And the more precise the estimates, the greater are the prospects for revising techniques and evaluating progress. The inference suggests a need for more research and associated effort to develop instruments for measuring achievements in many areas of the culture which now seem intangible. Political corruption and betrayal of public trust, along with the creative achievements of education, the courts, and law-enforcement agencies in the fields concerned, constitute areas of high priority for the development of such instruments.

Furthermore, it is shortsighted to assume that America can be highly effective here at home in developing moral integrity, respect for individual creativeness, etc., when it shuns or neglects the opportunity to exert its national impact in these respects on the international scene. Thus, to rely solely on a quantitative dollar appraisal of food giveaway-sales to Russia, or on such an appraisal of their request for a most-favored-nation trade status, when Russia continues to restrict individual freedoms to migrate which are diametrically opposed to professed American ideals, will not contribute to strengthening those democratic ideals among the American people. If insistence on the personal freedoms mentioned is an interference in the internal affairs of Russia, so too is providing food to reduce hunger and associated political unrest there. With some variants, much the same applies to our immediate problems with Arabian oil, instead of our developing internal and other sources of energy through research and associated considerations. The procedures characterized reflect extensive adolescence and myopia in international relationships, rather than long-range humanitarianism. This may be one area in which America's operating government is more in line with the aspirations of grain and oil companies, than with the views and expectations of the general population.

In a complex industrial society in which the people have a relatively high level of general education and related sophistication, there is little ground for assuming that international *deals* which are contrary to widely heralded domestic *ideals* will help in achieving the ideals. Relationships between the confusion described, and the disrespect and confusion within this nation concerning "the establishment," may be more far-reaching than typical Americans realize.

The Modular Approach in Education

During recent decades much has been said in education about a modular approach, especially with respect to architecture and campus layouts. The idea appears in both public-school and university spheres. With respect to architecture, it assumes that a desirable pattern has been developed, which should be repeated in future construction. The repetitive element is apparent, somewhat as that element appears in automobile production or in other mass-production industry. Where flexibility appears, it may relate mainly to the intensity with which the pattern or model is used or to the length of time over which it is employed with minimal revision. In regard to school architecture, additional flexibility may relate to how much variation of equipment and school operation is possible within the module.

Considerable of what is said regarding building modules may also apply to the curriculum. Whether the segments into which the school program is divided are called school grades, semesters, modules, projects, contracts, or something else may make little difference with respect to creativity or other aspects of learning achievement which are sought.

If civic education in a quite broad sense is accepted as the chief single aim of public schools, then the modular approach must assume that some civic model or perhaps hero model will be replicated. One difficulty that arises in the modular approach, concerning any aspect of education, is associated with social change and the functions which the school is expected to perform. If modular patterns are set forth with substantial detail and firmness, then flexibility of program needs in response to changing conditions is cramped. Flexibility in learning programs thus tends to suffer until pressure accumulates for substantial remodeling or a new structure. If the modular pattern is widely flexible with great variation or individualization permitted within it, then the module becomes essentially a general guide that merely points in the direction of presumably desirable educational objectives.

The crux of the discourse on the modular approach in education is thus about as old as organized education itself: how much and what elements shall be rather firmly set in some required pattern; and how much and what elements shall be open to individualized goals and procedures, as developed through teacher-pupil relationships? Shuffling vocabulary in terms of grade promotions, modular progress, contract completions, etc., is not likely to have much long-range value. The basic considerations noted regarding the modular approach in education apply also with respect to juvenile delinquency or the broader scope of public offense and efforts at rehabilitation.

Recycling

Present attention to recycling seems to have grown from a merger of two industrial considerations: a prospective shortage of certain raw materials available at reasonable cost; and a burdensome accumulation of some types of waste. Containers for food, beverages, and certain other items are of concern with respect to both shortages and accumulations. Paper, glass, and some metals are important in the connections noted.

However, it does not require great imagination or involve any particular distortion of language to note the application of recycling concepts to other areas. For over a half-century, some of the nation's agricultural experiment stations have been emphasizing a permanently productive agriculture, based on a high level of soil fertility, apparently emanating from the early leadership of Dr. Hopkins at the University of Illinois. The program calls for crop rotations and the use of animal and commercial fertilizer for the restoration of critical soil elements that are removed in crop production. Through the restoration, or even an increase in effective fertility, the soil can be looked upon as undergoing continuous recycling with respect to its crop-producing capacity. When it is accordingly stated that a people who are ignorant of their history are condemned to repeat it, a recycling of mistakes is presumed.

Some students of social philosophy have referred to a restatement of certain ideals by prophets, seers, and advisers of successive generations or cultures as being essentially a recycling of those ideals. A few participants in the recycling are noted, in approximate chronological order—but recognizing variations as well as similarities: Hammurabi (1955-1913 B.C.), Moses, Isaiah, Pythagoras, Confucius, Buddha, Socrates, Plato, Aristotle, Mencius, Jesus, Mohamamed, Thomas Aquinas, Martin Luther, John Calvin, Benjamin Franklin, Thomas Jefferson, Simon Bolivar, Abraham Lincoln, Woodrow Wilson, John Dewey, Mohandas Gandhi.

When a scientist verifies or challenges the experimental work of a predecessor, he recycles the predecessor's concepts and conclusions through his own checking procedure. Should one perhaps infer that each time polio vaccine is administered, there is a recycling of evidence concerning immunology—until a new and more resistant strain is encountered? To what extent is the succession of people from one generation to another a recycling of genes or human traits? One of nature's greatest recycling processes relates to water—whereby oceans and lakes provide evaporation for clouds and precipitation, for plant and animal growth, as well as the many other uses to which water that falls on the land is put, as it progresses along its cycle back to the large bodies noted as major sources of evaporation. One might reach to the social science of economics and observe that most Americans beyond age thirty have had experience with economic cycles, along with the recycling of theories and twaddle concerning remedies. With more direct reference to educational practice, many school administrators have had experience in remodeling school buildings, in order to put the structure through a new cycle of usefulness, and in reassigning courses or regrouping course content, in order to recycle it through the thought and skill of another teacher. When should the hiring and firing of college instructors be looked upon as recycling chosen program content through new personalities?

Before high-school or college teachers have acquired much classroom experience, most of them have probably recycled some flunkers into repeating a course. To a considerable extent, reviewing for examinations, great and small, is a process of recycling material that is presumed to have been learned. In order to make the ideals and values which have been embodied in the lives of Biblical or national heroes into useful instruments for guiding the development of young Americans, it is increasingly necessary to recycle those ideals and values so as to show their relationship to present-day life. Inadequacy along this line is reflected in much of the delinquency of youth and adults and in the failure of rehabilitation programs actually to rehabilitate.

When educators convene to pool experiences and optimism about learning procedures, it is important to differentiate between a new body of words and a new body of concepts. Thus, urging that a body of learning material is a module, rather than a project, contract, or section of a school subject, can have limitations. Considerable has been said about "reinforcement" as involved in learning situations. Such terms as discipline or rewards and denials seem to be older synonyms. With due consideration of the abuses associated with corporal punishment, there have been times when the paddle was a useful device for reinforcing some types of learning.

A caution with respect to conferences among educators and others points to the ease with which persons who are allergic to rigorous inquiry assume that they have made a finding of breakthrough proportions, when they hit upon one of successive rediscoveries concerning basic concepts set forth by some of their predecessors—such as the men previously noted, beginning with Hammurabi. Perhaps one trouble with a knowledge of history is that it may deny such conference persons "the thrill of discovery." The same applies to discovery in law enforcement and in rehabilitation.

Career Education

A major difference between career education and vocational training lies in the greater breadth and time duration of the career concept, although there may currently be more overlapping than career theory would approve. Great potential for the career approach lies in systematically acquainting children in the elementary school with such matters as the general nature of the vocational world, the fact that most Americans make their contributions to the nation through some kind of job, that holding a job requires discipline on the part of both employer and worker, and that good citizenship during childhood includes looking forward to a productive adult life. Important in the setting described is the development of constructive attitudes and habits concerning job responsibility, with punctuality respecting job tasks, good workmanship, and ability to get along with co-workers as high among priorities in developing a constructive work ethic. But career outlook must be integrated with specific vocational preparation, so that the individual acquires the knowledge and skills which qualify him to hold some kind of job. General career background and favorable work attitudes during one's productive years, when taken alone, are not enough to turn out goods and services in exchange for paychecks.

A major consideration regarding the future of career and vocational education in America relates to a substantial change which the nation is going through with respect to the dignity and status of the job in our emerging conception of a democratic society. Some aspects of the change involve race and sex as related to vocational opportunity; collective bargaining with respect to professional and government service; provisions which govern such matters as paid leave, tenure, and retirement; employee representation in management's decision-making; minimum wages and cost-of-living escalations; protection against occupational hazards; work-load and overtime arrangements; etc.

Another development of substantial importance concerns the appearance of technical-vocational schools, which may first appear as post-secondary schools of about junior-college grade, but several of which tend to grow into technical colleges that respond to the nation's rising level of need for technological training and sophistication.

The appearance of these institutions retraces an interesting aspect of American educational history. Such institutions come into existence largely because the leadership of existing institutions is too orthodox and unimaginative to expand so as to provide for the growing technological needs. The situation is reminiscent of that roughly a century ago, when orthodoxy in the so-called liberal arts sphere could not provide collegiate study for agriculture and the mechanical arts—and the land-grant college appeared. One might also recall the separate normal schools for preparing teachers, since that vocational undertaking was likewise not a proper concern for the college of the time. Previous comment referred to corresponding orthodoxy in the high school at the turn of the century. At both secondary and college levels, private schools to teach auto and other mechanics, commercial subjects, and in some instances to prepare teachers, helped pave the way for public institutions to supply the needs.

It would indeed be a mistake to assume that American colleges and universities have a monopoly on institutional fossilization. In most other countries of the Westernized world, as for example Western Europe and Latin America, the universities in general reflect more classical orthodoxy and less concern about the general needs of the people than is true in the United States. Moreover, it was institutional fossilization and corruption in the church that precipitated the Lutheran Reformation. Comparable fossilization and corruption in the royalty of George III precipitated the American Revolution and led to the new nation. Similar developments brought the French Revolution and the subsequent Napoleonic bloodbath over Middle Europe. Developments leading to the revolt of the Spanish colonies in Latin America, to the Russian Revolution of the present century, and to the change of regime in China are fairly well known to most Americans.

The wreckage thus strewn along the path of recent history testified that institutions must grow and develop to meet changing needs, or perish. A previous reference to the "natural history of institutions" indicated the relationship of institutions to the rise, change, and disappearance of human needs.

Earlier comments have indicated the author's view on changes taking place in America regarding the technological, political, and ethical status of the job and of employment in the nation's culture. One educational manifestation of the change appears in the post-secondary trade and vocational schools and in the technical colleges previously mentioned. Apart from the area of trades and industries, two important areas that are in need of technical training, within an atmosphere which develops social perspective, are the health services and law enforcement. The materials reviewed in the body of the present study include several references to the need for a more comprehensive background of preparation on the part of police officers and other law-enforcement personnel, with substantial urging that the preparation be secured in a broad university program rather than in the typically more restrictive atmosphere of a police-academy type of institution. Rehabilitation needs of penal institutions can be looked upon as part of the above picture. The ongoing shortage of nurses and other health personnel needs to be pointed out in the present connection, although not particularly elaborated herewith.

Many living educators will recall the cumulating log-jam during the first third of the present century, creating pressure for expanding and democratizing American secondary education, and the burst of growth during several following decades. The growth came primarily from social strata in which youth had to look forward to working for a living and thus embodied youth who wanted an education that would help them in getting and holding a job. Some aspects of delinquency, which are associated with vocational incompetence, testify to the unfinished business of secondary education in the field described.

But with the rising level of American expectation regarding technical competence and its social implications, much of the bulge in demand and of the probable bulge in deficiency will rest at the door of the technological college; at least it will rest there unless universities, and especially land-grant institutions, get a clearer picture of current labor and vocational developments than several of them seem to have. National strength and solidarity lies in a broad common background of personal acquaintances and of social understandings among workers in the trades and the professions, not in a multiplicity of dichotomies and cleavages. And the common background suggested provides a relatively fertile background in terms of which to rehabilitate public offenders, as well as to rehabilitate physically and mentally handicapped persons.

Feasible Aims and Goals

For aims or goals to be feasible, they must be flexible so as to fit somewhat varying situations, and they must be measurable so as to determine what is being done toward attaining them. Feasible goals are best thought of as a sequence of rather short segments along a continuum which points in some direction. For a goal to be realistic, the direction of pointing must be consistent enough so that progress toward the goal can be recognized.

While measurement devices constitute tools for evaluating change, it is possible for the tools to become so complicated and involved that the user forgets the object of the measurement through busywork with the tools. This situation sometimes appears when there is a great deal of statistical processing on a few data. The opposite situation appears when there is a large body of data which the possessor does not know how to use. The problem of maintaining an optimum relationship between the volume and complexity of data and the most suitable processing instruments may not be easy. In any case, somebody must interpret and apply the results of the analysis made through using the instruments. Hence, the most difficult problems in the evaluation of learning achievement or of crime rate do not lie in statistical analysis, but in residual matters of applying the results of the analysis. However, this fact should not deter one from trying to press further in differentiating categories within the presently intangible areas of human values and relationships and from trying to measure the content of those categories.

It is hoped that foregoing comments will help dispel myths to the effect that constructive programs can be carried on in education, rehabilitation, personal discipline, civic and moral responsibility, or elsewhere, without concern for both goals and progress toward achieving them. What constitutes optimum relationship between philosophy and measurement must thus be a flexible entity.

2. Cultural Drift and the Decay of Imagery

When astute political and ethical observers comment that evil thrives because good men do nothing about it, they are in effect referring to the culturewide anchorage and implications of imagery or ideology. This means that members of the judicial, legal, or essentially any other profession must take the lead in building up and maintaining a favorable social image regarding their profession, or perhaps regarding a prominent area within it, but that wide support in the culture is necessary in order to make the imagery a constructive social force.

No comparable effort is required to produce deterioration from a respectable status of decency in one's relationships with others. Indifference and drift lead to deterioration. Thus, effort is required to maintain and improve anything which has required effort to build up. And when effort is required by the many, the burden for vigilance and insight is especially heavy on the leadership few.

Perhaps the situation indicated can be ascribed to a powerful leveling force that exists throughout both the physical and the social universe. In the physical universe, this force appears in the wind, rain, frost, waves, etc., that wear down mountains and erode seacoasts. It also appears in dwellings and other structures which are erected by man and which attract the attention of insurance statisticians and tax authorities. It continuously stimulates the curiosity and ambition of some men to find better ways to resist the erosion and leveling, so as to pursue a life style which is more to their liking.

The leveling factor in humans has often been referred to broadly as laziness, although in the sciences of mental and emotional concern more euphemistic synonyms appear—i.e., low motivation, dwarfed ambition, unawakened potential, thwarted self-expression, premature fatigue, etc. The basic fact resides in the wide range of circumstances in which relaxation is the natural state, with discomfort when relaxation is disturbed until new relaxation is achieved. The fact that the human organism is capable of education and conditioning, with respect to a wide range of present or imagined experience which can excite or quiet the individual, expands the scope of situations with which arousal or relaxation might be associated but does not alter the basic consideration on leveling.

The upshot of preceding statements on leveling and on imagery decay is that imagery which envisions behavior or achievement that can be attained only through more than average effort and sacrifice, will not be maintained when the effort and sacrifice level off to the average. The tendency then is for the average to sink toward the level of bare survival, and anthropology as well as history reports past cultures which have not survived into the present. Many living Americans who have had fairly broad experience, that has been spread over a considerable period of time, can personally recall former social movements and "good causes" which are now in limbo.

Further down the road thus projected, there apparently lurks a problem which troubled some of the Founding Fathers: how to keep *a large enough percentage* of the population imbued with democratic ideals and imagery *during enough of the time*, so that existing and future institutions are able to carry forward and to expand such principles of democracy as those which appear, for example, in the first ten amendments to the federal Constitution. Few Americans need to be reminded of the challenge to those ideals in the Civil War or of the continuing challenge since that time which appears in political campaigns, legislative debates, and court disputes. And there should be no need to dwell on the repertoire of medals, awards, scholarships, and other forms of recognition and bait used to amplify low motivation into the effort required for difficult and socially praiseworthy achievement. Individuals who are highly personal in their thinking might reflect on the need to dangle sugar plums which scent of good health and longevity, in order to get middle-aged Americans to limit their relaxation and take physical exercise.

The point is that in a dynamic society, ideals and social images are not museum pieces or deep-freeze specimens. They must be continuously involved where the action is or drift into limbo. In this connection, leveling and drift are essentially synonymous. One could say that the tendency to drift bears an inverse relationship to the favorableness of the social image. This applies to law and the judiciary, schools and the teachers, hospitals and the physicians, or to any other institution and its associated personnel.

Moreover, broad social judgments are never mathematically precise in allocating praise or blame, respecting the construction or destruction of favorable imagery in areas which relate to important social concern. Present anxiety about crime and lawlessness in America and about the inadequacy of those institutions which at least on the surface appear broadly responsible for the situation, seems particularly significant for the legal and the educational professions. And the legal implications are not confined to the judiciary, any more than the educational implications are confined to the teachers.

In commenting on implications of the Watergate scandals and associated lack of decency, for the entire legal profession, Meserve[3] recently spoke as President of the American Bar Association and said to the association, at various points:

Many Americans and most lawyers have been brought by the Watergate affair to remember once again the importance of fundamental constitutional principles and of morality in public life—of the meaning of the protections assured to each citizen by our Bill of Rights.

Many lawyers and members of the public are conscious of the responsibility of the bar to do something about the matter, particularly about the professional standing of lawyers who are proved to have broken the criminal law or ethical proscriptions or who admit that they have done so.

Ours has been a liberal and free society. Perhaps this sort of society can no longer exist in the brave new world we already have. It may be that those truths our fathers once held to be "self-evident" now must yield to a more compelling reality. If it happens, I hope it is not by reason of any default of ours as lawyers and citizens. Let it not be said that we closed our eyes to dangers or, seeing them, did not act because we did not care. In our public and private lives, until we are proved to be wrong, let us reaffirm the belief that the governance of our society ought to be carried on with decency, honor, and regard for law.

It is, perhaps, the belief in individual dignity and the deliberate promotion of mutual respect and tolerance that has been damaged most clearly by the pervasive totality of the events we have come to feel are comprised in Watergate.

We must act in the present era of anxiety to sustain and serve the moral and tolerant tradition that has taken generations of patient effort to create. . . .

President Meserve's statements are of mixed import. Few conscientious Americans would question support for the Bill of Rights, or decency and regard for law in government. But many Americans will recall statements to the effect that one mark of a profession is the ability to discipline its own members. And regarding closed eyes, etc.; the present study has emphasized the idea that open-eyed alertness on the part of the judiciary and other members of the legal profession and broad communication with the public as to what leadership in the profession sees and does, are basic to favorable imagery concerning the law and the nation's legal institutions. For leaders in the profession to wash their hands of past responsibility and rely on vague hopes for a brighter future, hardly provides a sufficiently tangible base for average Americans to improve national imagery regarding our legal structure and its professional personnel.

However, shortcomings in the area indicated do not all lie before the door of the legal profession. Many are at the door of our schools and members of the education profession, for inaction during the years before the Americans involved became oriented toward studying law—that is, the schools as institutions in which it has been considered more important to teach students to spell, add, type, sing, or throw a football, than to teach why a democratic society depends on each person's respect for other people and why honesty and moral integrity must be high among priorities in qualifying for any kind of public service.

And even more broadly, it is difficult to overemphasize the idea that, under *any kind* of social organization, matters of lawful behavior and respect for law and order have to be the concern of a substantial majority of the common people, and that this broad responsibility is particularly significant in a democratic society in which the people are assumed to participate directly in the more formal aspects of government. Professional leadership is essential; but unless professed leadership is in touch with the interests and understanding of the people so that they can follow, little constructive leading occurs.

Favorable imagery, on which vigorous institutions and associated service personnel must be founded, cannot be a matter of cultural drift.

3. Lawlessness in Democracy and the Development of Human Resources

There is considerable political philosophy to the effect that governments exist for the welfare of the governed, and that a key aspect of democratic government resides in the opportunity of those who are governed to participate in making the rules of government. A further point concerns the mobility of man's opportunity along a kind of status continuum from the most relative to the most absolute. The continuum might be appraised in terms of the opportunity of each person relative to that of others, as differentiated from a kind of average opportunity which the people of one generation may have as compared with the people of some former generation. A second kind of relative feature which is embodied in the "average" designation is of course apparent, as it would be in viewing one's prospects for health or longevity as associated with some particular vocation. Furthermore, in a democratic society, freedom is often stated in terms of equality of opportunity, but in numerous instances there is only a superficial examination of what constitutes freedom, equality, or opportunity.

The Disciplines of Freedom

The freedom of an individual is exercised in some kind of setting, which includes other people and various things. The number and the relationships among these people and things determines what one *may* do and also what he *must* do. His freedom is thus associated with learning what these relationships are and disciplining himself accordingly.

Part of the discipline involved concerns the use that one makes of his time and energy, with respect both to activities which are primarily physical and which are primarily mental. Physical fatigue thus becomes important, pointing up the idea that nobody's personal energy is inexhaustible and that if one uses personal energy unwisely for certain purposes, he has less to use for other purposes. High school and college students often note this situation concerning social affairs versus studying academic subjects.

A related aspect of the discipline involves a health regimen, whereby an individual develops and maintains an organism that is capable of producing a substantial flow of energy over a sustained period of years. Available time is essentially a fixed resource, allowing due recognition of longevity, but with discipline playing a considerable role in the uses made of time.

Other aspects of the discipline of freedom could be set forth, contributing to a summary observation that creative discipline is essentially the discipline which helps one to achieve desired objectives. The idea of earned freedom, earned respect from others, and the foundation of self-respect are parts of the general picture.

Discipline From Within Versus From Without

With respect to disciplines involved in one's relationships with other people, it is often stated that where there is little discipline from within there must be extensive discipline from without. Education, law enforcement, and various other informative and behavior conditioning influences thus become involved. The within-versus-without relationship could be described by saying that unless or until various educational and conditioning influences from without have left a deposit in the individual's behavioral structure which can guide him from within, there must be further informing and conditioning influence exerted from without.

Two points should be noted concerning the relationship stated. The relationship between the forces within and those without is not a sharp bipolar dichotomy, but a more-or-less continuum, with most adults falling somewhere along a broad midsection of the continuum. The second point is that since the individual is born without an established language or other set of behavior patterns which fit any particular culture, he *must* be conditioned from without *before* he is able to exert control from within. The control exerted from within reflects a value-habit-reflex structure that has been built up through physical and intellectual trial and error, in response to outside stimuli.

Hospital experiences, along with parental and home experiences, provide the earliest informative and conditioning influences on the child. Later comes the school with a more organized system of experiences, along with various kinds of general community and specialized vocational experiences. The law is a part of the general community framework, and for some persons the penal and corrective institutions seem to be necessary supplements to the other informing and conditioning influences.

Hence, it is totally incorrect to talk about self-discipline or discipline from within as if it had a supernatural or some other mystic origin, when its origin stems from experience with outside influences.

Penalty and Correction as Social Repair

From preceding comments it follows that the penal and correctional systems, which organized societies typically maintain, constitute a recognition that the various informative and conditioning agencies of society did not do an adequate job of developing acceptable behavior in the individual during his more formative years and that repair work must accordingly be undertaken. Where the system invokes the death penalty or permanent incarceration, the conclusion is indicated that the former neglect has been so extensive that it is not possible or not worthwhile to try the repair approach—in view of prevailing attitudes and the status of the remedial arts.

The present study reviews considerable evidence and exhortation to the effect that correctional or rehabilitative possibilities are expanding substantially and that social attitudes concerning public offenders should be characterized by remedial efforts instead of by revenge. Some attention has also been given to the legal rights of convicted offenders to receive treatment.

The corrective or remedial approach emphasizes the salvage and development of human resources, and points to economic and other social gains from doing so. The correctional and rehabilitation procedures noted are in keeping with the philosophy that government exists for the welfare of the governed and that a significant aspect of that welfare relates to developing the potential of the individual—both for his personal satisfaction and for social usefulness. But persons who are threatened by public offenders are also entitled to such welfare considerations.

Human Worth and Social Delinquency

Humanitarian considerations of human worth are important in the attitude background previously noted. The humanitarian approach stresses the idea that there is a common denominator of value and potential in all human beings and that the well-being of all members of society depends greatly on recognizing this foundation element and building upon it.

The philosophy involved reflects considerable faith. An obvious aspect of the faith concerns probable reform of the delinquent, along lines previously mentioned. Less obvious but perhaps more important is a kind of subconscious or intuitive sense that the line separating delinquent from approved behavior is often hazy and mobile, and that persons in the approved category might on some occasion become delinquent. The value of a prearranged tolerance framework may thus seem broadly apparent.

Difficulties in reducing the density of the haze and lessening the role of other problems may be associated with failure to take certain practical considerations into account. One such consideration may relate to appraisal regarding how to focus the central thrust or determine what the common-denominator factor is. The author has elsewhere suggested that exploration of this consideration might involve questions regarding whose worth; worth for what or in what circumstances; or what criteria are most appropriate for estimating worth. If one uses the phrase "inherent worth," should one be expected to show in what the worth inheres, how it comes to inhere there, whether the inherent quality expands or contracts in accordance with one's delinquency status, etc?

Ideological Projections and Human Worth Development

Ideological projections ordinarily involve considerable faith. Earlier statements referred to common elements of faith and inspiration in religion, science, politics, education, and other areas. How blind or enlightened the faith is ordinarily depends on the size and firmness of the evidentiary base from which the projections are made. The projections, then, are creations of the imagination, systematized in some degree concerning direction.

It is the view of the author that man's greatest handicap in his struggle up from the cave has always been a shortage of creative imagination in projecting from a reasonably firm base, with a continuous experimental exploration or projections for data to revise and extend the projections. Some of the greatest shortages relate to man's projections on exploring his own potentialities, in contrast for example with exploring interplanetary space, radiation and mechanical energy, photosynthesis or other synthesis of food materials, etc.

Study of brain and neurological structure, physiological functioning, dietary elements, etc., might throw light on such matters as why some persons become delinquent under particular conditions whereas others do not under essentially the same conditions; why some persons formulate speculative hypotheses more readily than others; why some persons learn more readily or learn certain kinds of material more readily than others, or show comparable differences respecting accuracy and comprehensiveness in remembering; etc. Further exploration of ongoing human evolution[4] might bear on several of the preceding and other considerations.

Much of the foregoing might be summarized in an ideology of what man may yet become if he is not too modest in his projections or too lazy and indifferent in his implementations. The hazards and the rewards of pioneering have long afforded man's greatest challenges. If imaginative teachers and other mentors can lead youth into paths of the kind suggested, fewer youths will find challenge in delinquent behavior.

Chapter 5

TRANSGRESSIONS RELATIVE TO CORRECTIONS
AND REHABILITATION

When an organized society shows concern about making regulations to govern the behavior of its members, that society must also be concerned about procedures for dealing with transgressors. The arrangements which are set up could be looked upon as extensions of the general idea of rewards and punishments, which is emphasized in the training of dogs or horses, as well as in many aspects of learning by children and adults.

As either transgressions or learning needs become numerous and widely variant concerning types of situations involved, problems emerge in regard to extending the scope of rewards and punishments and to allocating particular items according to the importance or the difficulty of the situation at hand. In the field of transgressions, the idea is broadly reflected by comments on making the penalty fit the crime. In high school and college education, the idea is reflected in making the credit and scholastic grade correspond to difficulty and significance of the learning accomplishment.

Effort to correct the behavior tendencies of public offenders and to rehabilitate them into socially constructive members of the community has received increasing emphasis in America for some decades. This approach emphasizes a basic worth in the individual, and it typically recognizes that weaknesses in the social structure have contributed to the offender's development of antisocial behavior. The approach is thus quite different from the older revenge or reciprocity emphasis, sometimes characterized as "an eye for an eye, and a tooth for a tooth."

Attention to corrections and rehabilitation has several implications as to thought and action regarding crime and delinquency in this country.

1. Errors and Corrections

The presence in any society of institutions for behavioral correction rests on three basic points: (1) the presence of some persons who deviate so far from approved behavior that it is a threat to the community for these persons to be allowed free circulation; (2) it is possible to correct or modify the behavior of such persons and make them sufficiently like the great majority so that they can circulate freely; (3) it is socially desirable to bring about the correction indicated.

Human Behavior as Less Than Perfect

When certain behavior is described as criminal or delinquent, it is implied that said behavior is in some way below the standard set for the group. Question then arises as to who set the standard and why it was set at the specific point involved. In a practical sense, the question may be resolved by saying that organized society must have regulations to describe and enforce behavior which the group considers acceptable and that the only way for regulations to exist is for them to be anchored at specific points or to govern particular kinds of behavior. Furthermore, the standard must be set at a level which is fairly easy for most of the people to reach, but which nevertheless rules out some behavior that tends to occur and that is generally considered to be destructive or antisocial.

Foregoing statements imply the competence of leaders to formulate ideals regarding types of behavior which will improve group well-being and to obtain general approval of the ideals. A governing code thus emerges. But with respect to practical operations it must be recognized that some persons will not follow the code. It is one function of jails and prisons to separate these persons from the general community. Capital punishment assumes that under particular circumstances a trial may prescribe that persons convicted shall be permanently separated. Possibilities of parole and corrective action, to justify a restoration of freedom, are associated with other penalties.

Local Jurisdictions and Social Mobility

As scattered settlements become organized into nations or other political units, a wide range of regulatory jurisdictions is usually involved, with substantial variation among jurisdictions of regulatory structure. Greater nation-wide uniformity has been recommended as a way to reduce lawlessness which had this origin. Varying degrees in recommendation and implementation relate to such matters as automobile travel, interstate commerce, illicit drug traffic, some types of personal assault, and some matters involving extradition of offenders from one jurisdiction to another.

Local jurisdictions have also been important with respect to correctional provisions made regarding public offenders. The present study reveals substantial conflict among recommendations for greater centralization in content and administration. Part of the conflict relates to such matters as the training and competence of correctional personnel, specialization in correctional facilities to which particular types of offenders might be assigned, and protection of communities into which rehabilitating offenders are being integrated. Some conflict also seems to persist regarding the purpose and general philosophy governing corrections.

Hazy Ideals Regarding Correctional Operations

It should be helpful to differentiate two categories of ideals which seem apparent in the attention given to corrections and to examine the content of each category. The two can be designated as ethical and economic, although overlappings should be recognized.

(1) *Ethical considerations.* Judgments regarding human behavior and the treatment of transgressors have throughout recorded history been important areas of conflict. Significant aspects of the conflict were reflected in religious considerations, before the rise of the modern civil state as an important separate agency in regulating human affairs. Thus, the Ten Commandments set forth by Moses are largely a body of Judeo-Christian doctrine for regulating human relationships. Similar pronouncements appear in other religions.

The American Founding Fathers noted the religious origin of certain ideals which they wished to emphasize in the civil state that they were establishing. Stress was placed on the importance of value attached to the individual human being in the political system under development, with the associated philosophy and usage employing such expressions as the "inherent worth" of the individual or the "sanctity" of his existence. Statements about "inherent rights" with which individuals are "endowed by their creator" and which are "inalienable" accept the status of the individual person as the fountainhead from which ethical reasoning emanates. Judgments may vary as to the practical importance of accepting this status as being of religious or of civic origin, but in any case the elaboration of ideological systems in Christianity and in democracy make extensive use of the worth status of the individual as a base.

However, both religious and civic expansions of the personal-worth ideology have had problems in harmonizing the ideology with the fact that in any society that has ever existed or that exists today, some persons are more important or worth more than others. The point is illustrated by the status, protection, rights, powers, etc., attached to heads of states, or heads of churches, universities, and several other types of institutions, in contrast with the status, etc., accorded the run-of-mill members of the organizations concerned. Much the same applies to persons who have made outstanding contributions to science, invention and the practical arts, business organization, literature, entertainment, etc., in contrast with run-of-mill consumers of the results which flow from such contributions.

Problems of the type noted have resulted in a rich embroidery of rationalizing gyrations and mythical doctrines to the effect that observed status and contributions of the type noted are mere peripheral items, of no particular consequence; that the real values of "inherent worth," "inalienable rights," all men being "created equal," etc., lie above and beyond the mundane considerations of status and achievement and may be quite difficult or perhaps impossible for some persons to grasp. Critics of the doctrine are presumably tops among persons having the difficulty. A practical response might be that difficulty for an enquirer should be anticipated, when there is nothing "out there" to grasp or examine.

Another problem faced by inherent-worth doctrine concerns *when* or under what circumstances the worth becomes inherent or the existence sanctified. In America and in several other so-called Christian lands, we have widespread advocation and expanding legalization of abortion. If the doctrine accepts this practice into a framework which pretends consistency, then it must develop peripheral cadenzas indicating that worth and sanctity have not yet been deposited in the life that is being destroyed. Perhaps one should recognize with early seafarers the idea of "any port in a storm" and hope that ethical logic in the future may become less haphazard—as sea travel has become.

Problems of the kind noted in foregoing paragraphs do not help to clarify the ethical basis of correctional programs for public offenders. If one is convicted of a crime, does he lose his inherent worth and sanctity? If not lost, at least this worth, "inalienable rights," etc., must undergo shrinkage—at least temporarily. Does this imply elasticity in worth, etc., or only a microscopic presence to start with? Longevity of the revenge complex, with respect to rehabilitating public offenders, is fostered by ethical confusion of the type described.

(2) *Economic considerations.* For some people it may seem rather easy to present economic justification for correctional programs regarding public offenders, especially when the dollar cost of the correctional programs is compared with the cost of prolonged incarceration and custodial service.

Several ramifications of the cost-accounting approach appear when one notes wide individual differences among offenders according to age, educational and vocational background, type of offense, prospects of extended employment following rehabilitation, etc. Different philosophies on how best to proceed with rehabilitation, the legal rights of offenders to rehabilitative treatment, role of legal and other "civil" disabilities which attach to the individual because of his offense, and other involvements that overlap with ethical considerations, also become pertinent.

One question about the economic-ethical overlaps, which some persons might reject as too materialistic but which every culture as an organized group eventually asks, is: who pays the monetary cost of the corrective operation, and can the payers expect to get as much or more from this use of the money as they might get from other uses? The fact of state action, as a collective agency working through taxation, does not alter the underlying economic consideration.

When effort is made to focus attention on *what other uses*, a wide range of value patterns arise for consideration. Probably those which are most appropriate to examine in the present connection relate in some way to the development and use of human resources. In various connections the present author has referred to the extensive neglect of our most competent and motivated young people, from the standpoint of what they *do* accomplish relative to what they probably *could* accomplish. Only a small percentage of these persons are among the public offenders. Growing attention is being given to "preventive rehabilitation," in the sense of various kinds of educational, guidance, social reform, and other developments which promise to reduce the incidence of crime and other delinquency. This study has emphasized job possibilities as an important avenue of prevention, especially with respect to teen-agers. However, much the same applies to adults. This study has also emphasized a broad scope of research, as a sphere of somewhat unique challenge as well as one affording extensive job potential.

One of the less frequently explored and perhaps more controversial areas of potential human resource development, with broad ethical involvement, concerns the lives destroyed through abortion. From the strictly economic standpoint, the question might be formulated: does it cost more to rehabilitate a convicted offender, relative to the economic contributions it seems reasonable that he will make thereafter, than to rear and educate a new model from the beginning? While somewhat greater statistical projection might be involved in the case of the new model than in the case of the corrected edition, the mathematics would hardly seem formidable. Strictly relating to the present consideration of human resource development, most other birth-control techniques belong in a different category from abortion.

Obviously under present conditions, economic considerations in the sense noted are of practically no importance as to what happens. Determination rests mainly on individual adult convenience and on other aspects of personal selfishness which are embedded in the ethical code. However, in comparisons such as that mentioned, economics is an aspect of ethics. The importance of economics as an influence in ethical determinations, relative to other influences, varies with circumstances.

"Underdog" as a Status Category

In America, much is said about sympathy for the underdog. Private charitable developments and public health and welfare programs rest substantially on that sympathy in their conception and operation. Idealistically, it has been suggested that the average person has a "natural" feeling of sympathy for fellowman, whose suffering appears to be pronounced or whose denials are conspicuously greater than one's own. The feeling might result from a kind of subconscious projection by this average person that he might some day himself be in an underdog position, in some of the numerous kinds of situations to which that status may apply.

Practically, it seems that the ideal is not likely to be activated into helping persons in underdog status until there is a substantial margin of personal satisfaction and of security through the presence of an "underdog" category, with the margin serving as a buffer for persons who would extend benevolence to the underdog. And in spite of sympathies and fantasies regarding fellowman or idealistic pleas to the effect that "it is not what you give, but what you share," the underdog recipient is usually more interested in the amount of giving than in the amount of sharing. While this may seem most apparent in regard to material goods, it applies also to personal counsel and to other intangibles.

One of the most difficult problems with which democratic citizenship must deal involves harmony between an idealistic goal of equality in opportunity and status, and individual differences in candidacy for transient or enduring underdog status. When the ancient Hebrews commented, "The poor you will always have with you," or when Lincoln allegedly observed, "The Lord must have liked poor people, since he made so many of them," the implications of poverty may have focused on material status. With growth in material affluence and in actualization of equal opportunity, concepts of poverty are expanding somewhat to include poverty of imagination, hope, motivation, initiative, self-confidence, sense of personal responsibility, etc. America may be at a point where a "hang-up" about material poverty as the root of all ills is an obstacle to progress through broader inquiry, rather than a remedial panacea which it has become routine to prescribe for underdog ailments.

In the area of social consideration noted, we not only have a substantial background of prejudice on both sides of the issue, but a large background of ignorance. Such ignorance is usually involved in supporting prejudice. One pertinent area of ignorance concerns the relative importance of genetic and social factors in producing the types of poverty that were previously mentioned, plus broad ignorance regarding the general idea that systematic and experimental inquiry in this area might yield results comparable to those yielded by research in many other areas.

2. Rehabilitation Prospects and Problems

Apparently organized society has always had problems with persons who varied markedly from the middle stream of the culture, either in biological traits or in social developments. While individual differences among people, as among rats or cows, have existed for many generations, the differences among people seem to become more conspicuous with successive generations.

Individual Differences and Rehabilitation or Education

Among possible reasons for the appearance mentioned, five are noted. (1) As a society becomes more tolerant of variants, there is more inducement for the variants to reproduce and to increase from one generation to another. While the genetic and the social processes involved are not the same, in some respects the net results are comparable. (2) With an increase in population, more gene combinations in offspring become possible. Hence, more genes which are trait carriers seem likely to join other carrier genes, which may enable more defective recessives to show up in outward appearance. (3) As a society becomes more complex in a sociological sense, more numerous and more varied types of social relationships appear. This typically means that there are more types of relationships which are beyond the effective competence-potential of many persons. These persons tend to become delinquent or dependent because of their limited competence. (4) And as a society becomes more complex socially and technologically, there are more ways in which persons become injured—through industrial accidents and otherwise. Whether the frequency and scope of accident involvement grows faster than remedial techniques and remedial attitudes depends on several factors (which are not explored here). (5) When a society becomes more affluent, it tends to expand its knowledge about causes of individual differences and to expand its concern about discovering and applying modifications.

Rehabilitation literally means a *restoring* of health, property, rank, privilege, or something else of value, which one previously had but which he has lost through accident, social deprivation, or otherwise. In a literal sense this means that when a program fosters the development of competencies which the individual never had before, the procedure is not restoration but new growth; that is, growth in about the sense that American public schools exist primarily to foster new or developmental growth in the health and competencies of America's children.

The developmental-growth approach may constitute a major reason for the close relationship between rehabilitation and general education. This includes an expanding consideration of rehabilitation as an extension of individualized instruction, with increased attention to individualized equipment and procedures, which the handicapped individual's particular difficulties make necessary for his achieving desired ends.

Material Affluence and Rehabilitation Concern

Each of the five designated items on individual differences has borne on the development and continuous expansion of rehabilitation concepts and provisions in America. However, the implications of affluence, including research and growth in knowledge, may be more important in defining terms and providing remedies than the implications of some of the other items are.

In rehabilitation, as in general education, public housing, unemployment insurance, medicare, and other areas to which substantial public funds are allocated so as to foster public well-being, there must be a frequent public reevaluation of the allocations in terms of the results gained as well as in terms of results which might reasonably have been expected from other uses of the funds involved. The evaluation rests on two major points; one is sentimental, the other is economic. Each of the two is independently important, but the extensive interdependence between them has biological anchorage.

Sentiment might be looked upon as a projection; that is, how would I feel under similar conditions of handicap and of collective possibility of effort to remedy the situation? But as the population increases, and as the culture becomes more expansive in geography and in terms of potential kinds of involvement, how far can a person realistically extend his projection and brotherly feeling to other persons? Thus, the projection increasingly becomes one of statistics rather than one of personal envisionment. Statistical accounts, without interpretations and associated prejudices, have seldom been strong arousers of sentiment.

Economic evaluations may not be precise, but they tend to have greater concreteness than sentiment. With regard to vocational rehabilitation of physically handicapped persons, considerable bodies of data support the statement that the amount which rehabilitated persons return to the state through taxes on earnings exceeds the rehabilitation cost paid by the state. The social gains expand when one adds estimates on custodial and other costs that would have been involved if rehabilitation had not been undertaken. Much of course depends on the level of custodial service on which the speculation rests, which in turn depends on economic affluence and on strength of sentiment.

Combining Sentiment and Economics

The aid or provision which any person makes available for another depends on some combination of sentiment and economics. Reference to "voluntary" aid means that the pressures of the mores are less precise and less crystallized than when stated in tax law, not that the pressures are absent. The evaluative feature continuously asks, in low or high key, what the contributor gets in return for his contribution.

Persons who seek to expand rehabilitation service, because of general sentiment, because of general socioeconomic well-being, or because of personal gain through receiving the service or through holding a job in providing it for others, should note an ongoing demand for accountability of how present funds are used and what is proposed to justify additional requests. This is one of many occasions when it is well in a complex society to recognize that honesty is not merely the *best* policy but that it is the *only* policy. In addition, where an intricate type of professional service is involved, a high level of insight and commitment are required in order that one may be both honest and effective.

Expanding Scope of Rehabilitation Philosophy

Foregoing comments relate mainly to physically handicapped persons and somewhat to persons who are mentally handicapped. But we hear increasingly about programs for the rehabilitation of public offenders in prisons, about concentrated efforts to train and otherwise develop useful qualifications in the "hard core" unemployed, about school-job arrangements for high school youth, about developing part-time and perhaps home-located jobs for mothers of young children, and about extending the useful and paid employment of competent older and retired persons. We also hear growing criticism of rehabilitation programs that do not rehabilitate, and note some inquiry about recently broadening programs of special education which might be in line for detailed scrutiny should the nation experience an economic squeeze.

Efforts to forecast the direction of scrutiny always seem hazardous, especially if the scrutiny is in a "maybe" status. However certain candidates for attention may be noted.

Preventive Rehabilitation

One of the suggested candidates is preventive rehabilitation, which currently receives some attention. The idea is that several delinquency problems might be avoided by taking appropriate measures before the delinquency becomes socially conspicuous. How long beforehand depends on the nature of the difficulty and the measures considered. The public school is thus basic from several standpoints. Entering school provides the first opportunity for a comprehensive review of the childhood population, with respect to early identification of handicaps and institution of remedial procedures.

Also, many such procedures are related to other aspects of individualized programs of school instruction.

Preventive orientation of the school program may deserve especial consideration with respect to rehabilitating delinquents and public offenders, since a large percentage of the first-time offenders are in their late teens and early twenties, and thus are or recently have been of school age. The situation described implies that the job of developmental education has not been adequately handled.

When the present study has repeatedly stated that the schools as presently conceived and constituted cannot do the job alone, it is not inferred that the schools could not have done better than many of them have done. This applies both to use of facilities at their immediate disposal and to work in conjunction with other agencies.

Two shortcomings in achievement seem obvious. One is the development of school-job programs, with significant nonschool jobs on a pay basis, for *all* youth during a substantial part of their high-school years. The other shortcoming involves developing a sense of moral or social responsibility and duty on the part of *every* student, in regard to his present and future relationship with the vocational world and with other aspects of the social structure. Statements elsewhere in the present study have mentioned the limited competence of many teachers for developing in students the responsibility noted and the broad absence of helpful orientation through university programs for preparing teachers.

With respect to public offenders and their rehabilitation, societies vary considerably regarding the extent to which blame is placed on the group in contrast with placing it on the individual. While sociology during the present century has shown rather objectively that social conditions may greatly affect an individual's orientation and development, it has not been shown that an individual is helpless in the face of a social determinism, or that the social influences may not include emphasis on the individual's personal responsibility. While the foregoing would seem to apply most fully to the individual with broad freedom of circulation, it can apply recognizably within prison situations. The survival rate and status of war prisoners help to illustrate the point.

Although Dostoevski in his considerations on crime and punishment may have thought that one could judge the level of a civilization by the condition of its prisons, this view must be recognized as parochial, as are other views which would use one narrowly-stated criterion for judging a broad civilization. For example, there would seem to be no close relationship between the conditions of a nation's prisons and the productivity of its agriculture, the status of its air transportation, factory output, incidence of automobile accidents or of malaria, involvement in sports events, etc. While Russian society in Dostoevski's time was simpler than American society is today, simplistic labeling of complex relationships is usually misleading. This general idea is especially pertinent in the present connection because it characterizes many statements currently made about lawlessness in America and about one-shot remedies.

Special Education for the Competent

With respect to individual difference and special education, there should be hope that America will someday become at least as concerned about identifying and making special provision for its bright and most competent children as it seems currently to be with respect to those who are most handicapped. There may be several reasons why such a development seems tardy.

(1) Perhaps one of the most subtle and pervading influences concerns philosophical variations, according to which the democratic ideal of equality is interpreted. The problem may have been launched through observations by the Founding Fathers to the effect that all men are created equal, but its subsequent involvements were not envisioned by those observations. Many successors of the founders have assumed that genetic or biological equality could not have been intended, since the genetic sphere was not then considered to be an aspect of politics.

Efforts to settle for "equality before the law" has involved a kind of peekaboo game between a rather hazy ideal and a tenacious reality, played in a general atmosphere of vague hope that things will turn out well. Attempts to objectify the ideal and speak of "equal opportunity" involve problems concerning such matters as whether the same provision made for each child constitutes equal opportunity, particularly in view of great individual variations among children as to needs and potentialities. Thus, the whole present conception of "special education"—plus earlier provisions for school-bus transportation, free textbooks, school feeding and health services, personal guidance attention, etc.—testify to rejection of the initial American conception of equality which was embodied in the idea of the one-teacher school with a set curriculum that was available to any child of the district who came to the school building and who had minimal qualifications for attendance.

Problems of the type inferred regarding opportunity have supported drift toward the ideal that equality means equal freedom or opportunity to achieve any goal which a child may profess. But the doubtful kinship between this ideal and reality seems clear if one asks about equal opportunity of *all* American children to become President of the United States, governor of a state, head of a large bank or industrial corporation, president of a major state or private university, or to sit on the bench of one of our higher state or federal courts.

A distillate that gradually drips from the preceding confusion is that every child should have roughly equal opportunity to become about like the "average" adult, with perhaps some general improvement from one generation to the next. The net result has generally been an extended consideration or special education for handicapped children, and drift for the most competent who are assumed to be able to take care of themselves in any future competitive struggle. Consideration of what particular individuals in the different groups seem likely to contribute to the nation's future is thus rejected, in the respects noted.

(2) A second line of influence, in the relative neglect of the brighter and more competent children, relates to technical matters of identification. Before

the development of intelligence tests and kindred instruments of evaluation, it seemed easier for the people in general to recognize and publicly identify physically or mentally handicapped persons than to identify and publicly admit that other individuals were probably superior to those average persons who were making the judgments. The foregoing may relate especially to judgments concerning children. At present, techniques for evaluating extreme superiority seem less well developed than techniques for evaluating extreme inferiority.

(3) A third type of influence concerns the development and use of appropriate learning materials. A common procedure has been to use, for both competency extremes, the materials which were developed for the average or general school program, with slowdown in rate of progress through the material being more usual than speedup in rate. As to grade promotions, the small number of accelerations relative to the number of retardations affords clues.

However, the situation described may be improved considerably for both fast and slow learners through the use of a growing variety of supplementary and enriching materials by imaginative teachers.

(4) Insofar as religion emphasizes "equality of soul" in all of humanity, there must be some carry-over of the idea of equality to daily relationships among living persons, or the "soul doctrine" must be looked upon as irrelevant so far as those relationships are concerned. Perhaps the soul doctrine as inferred is not as strong in America now as it was a century ago. This seems to be true of considerable other religious doctrine, but a subtle influence from the religious source may linger with respect to the conception of equality noted in learning opportunity.

(5) An additional influence relates to taxes and other costs in providing special programs for exceptional children. Since it is easier for the public to recognize the achievement limitations of handicapped children than to recognize the potential stunting of the most competent children, when both are subjected to school conditions that have developed for average children, it is easier to think in terms of special provisions for the handicapped. Also, parents often feel unburdened when their handicapped children are institutionalized. The broad absence of any comparable feeling regarding bright and competent children, may account substantially for the essential absence of comparable institutionalization for such children.

While teachers are distinctly above average adults with respect to guiding and supervising the learning of children in school situations, the question lingers as to whether average teachers can perceive the development boundaries and achieve the optimum regarding the most competent children, as well as they can regarding the least competent. The basic point deserves more elaboration than it usually gets—i.e., how well can the average university professor devise programs and activities for the brightest students? A fraction of recent student comment on "relevance" *may* bear on the situation noted.

Probably a realistic view of human characteristics and evaluations justifies the statement that throughout the foreseeable future American society will continue to include physically and mentally handicapped persons, delinquents and public offenders, "hard core" unemployed, old persons, and others who are *not* within the broad central stream of cultural vigor and productivity—or who are not looked upon as children, preparing through normal channels to enter that stream. Because of limited imagination, including obsolete and somewhat amateur conceptions about the allocation of resources, custodial provisions have afforded the major line of consideration for such atypical groups, although this situation is modified somewhat by rehabilitation and some other efforts. But neglect of the bright need not continue.

Sheltered-Workshop Possibilities

A prospect that deserves consideration relates to a continuing residual group, which remains after *reasonable* rehabilitation and associated efforts have been made. The prospect has sometimes been referred to in connection with the sheltered-workshop idea that often appears in the vocational rehabilitation of physically or mentally handicapped persons. The idea recognizes varying degrees of possibility for rehabilitation and recognizes a category in which the possibility will not make it feasible to anticipate future employment in the general vocational structure of American society. But the idea also recognizes that several persons in the category mentioned could make a continuing economic contribution through working on selected projects under the personal supervision which a sheltered workshop might provide. In some workshops of this kind which are maintained in state institutions, the productive output is distributed to other state institutions, or perhaps the work is performed on a contract basis for private agencies.

Two aspects of the foregoing statement should be amplified. One concerns economic implications. The idea of economically useful production under special or "sheltered" conditions could be extended to each of the other groups mentioned, although the characteristics of shelteredness would vary. Thus, the kind of shelteredness required for a person with a severe physical handicap would not be the same as that required for a prison inmate who has committed a heinous crime and who is not looked upon as developing possibilities for parole. Other variations of shelteredness might relate to the "hard core" unemployed. Still other variations might relate to older persons, who perhaps have retired from a career job or who otherwise find age to be a handicap to employment. Among variations of shelteredness might well be leeway regarding place of residence and personal life, apart from the work situation. But with regard to public offenders, extensive leeway in residence and personal life might not often be feasible.

Preceding comments on shelteredness have an economic orientation. There is also an important psychological consideration. Most people have a sense of belonging and of feeling significant if they are contributing something to the general stream of cultural life. Probably for most Americans a job constitues the usual avenue of doing so. The feeling of identification mentioned can reduce the rate of senile decline or other personality disintegration, and thereby reduce the amount of strictly custodial care that is required. For older persons, who constitute an increasing percentage of the nation's population, workshop potential might offer such identification, in contrast with strictly custodial "homes," sometimes called "death houses," in which the residents are essentially waiting to die.

Nothing in foregoing statements is intended to imply that the strictly custodial element in any category can be entirely eliminated or that any individual can live out a natural life without including some essentially custodial time.

Social Values and Economic Priorities

Preceding considerations on the general area of special education have made considerable reference to the cost or expense involved and some reference to the philosophy of priorities in allocating social resources. Comparisons have been suggested as to provisions for the most handicapped, relative to provisions for the most competent. However, broader comparisons should be made respecting priorities.

Americans seem to have a great deal to spend on deodorants and related cosmetic items, dog food and other pet requirements, a broad repertoire of sports, a substantial range of television giveaway shows, luxury automobiles with continuous addition of new pushbutton items, etc. The allocations or goals toward which the imagination, personal energies, and material resources of a culture are directed are basic determiners of whether the culture is a developing or a decadent one. Perhaps theoretically there may be a neutral stage between development and decay. Practically, it is doubtful if theorizing about neutrality is a useful exercise, although most any culture at a particular time includes some developmental and some decadent elements.

It is the author's view that under the circumstances described, "special education" should rate higher than it does among developmental priorities, especially as it comes to reflect greater concern for persons with broad or exceptional competence.

Chapter 6

THE JOB AND DELINQUENCY IN AMERICA

Concern about lawlessness and delinquency in this country and about job qualifications and placement have both been on the rise for at least two decades, but effort to explore relationships between the two has been limited. The limitation seems most pronounced in regard to whether our society should *invest* more extensively in vocational orientation and placement, along with some decrease in output per employee because of part-time or other limited competence to achieve; or should *invest* more in custodial, rehabilitation, or other costs of delinquency which are associated with one's inability to get and hold a job. In either case, the costs have to be paid out of the total productivity of the American people. Besides, either approach has long-range implications regarding quality of citizenship and personal usefulness in the community.

1. The Job Concept

In the sense inferred, a job should be thought of as including any type of employment which makes a positive contribution to the community, whether paid for in monetary terms or not. One of the most extensive forms of positive service, which is not on a wage or salary basis, is that rendered by mothers in the home through rearing children. While the importance of this service is widely recognized, although there is great variation from home to home in its amount and value, there has been no particularly commendable effort to evaluate it in terms of money. Also, in most communities there is considerable unpaid or volunteer philanthropic service that has important social value, and there is a great deal of intermediate service which might be partly paid and partly volunteer.

The complications suggested respecting gainful or volunteer classifications of service may not seem formidable from the income-tax standpoint, but they do raise questions about participation by high-school youth in services which are both satisfying to the participant and useful to the community. Kindred problems may relate to: (1) child-labor laws; (2) attitudes and expectations of organized labor; (3) employer attitudes regarding the cost of output with inexperienced or perhaps otherwise inefficient labor; (4) school and educational supervision of a total and coordinated work-study program; and (5)

community outlook toward subsidizing industry to compensate for sub-
standard labor efficiency, versus maintaining custodial and rehabilitative
services for delinquent persons. The last of these problems substantially
pervades the other four. It seems most firmly anchored in the philosophy
of dealing with delinquency on a penal or retaliatory basis, rather than on a
prevention or developmental basis. Constructive modification of the prevailing approach, as characterized here, involves several considerations which
require the attention of persons who are seriously concerned about the job
approach to reducing delinquency.

2. What the Worker Gets from the Job

Four kinds of rewards or outcomes are noted, which accrue directly to the
worker from a job with which he is contented.

Pay

Pay as an avenue for economic participation in the culture, through purchasing power, is a major value to the individual. The importance of this
value depends on take-home pay, after taxes and other required deductions
are made. An aspect of this value which is of growing significance concerns
the amount remaining for optional expenditures, after further deductions for
personal or family necessities are made. Expansion of the optional area in
recent decades has greatly expanded the sense of economic independence, if
not affluence, enjoyed by many Americans.

Personal Satisfaction

There is considerable immediate personal satisfaction for a healthy person
that accompanies physical or mental activity which involves a free expenditure of energy, at least to the point at which fatigue is approached. One
should not assume that this kind of energy-release satisfaction is confined
to the kicking and gurgling of infants, such as may carry on for a considerable period, until adequate relaxation for sleep occurs. Most adult recreations include some of the experience indicated, and some people find more
of the recreational or immediate-satisfaction element in their jobs than other
people find.

Sense of Power

There is a related form of personal satisfaction that comes through a sense
of power which a job ordinarily entails. This is a power to make conditions
different from what they were, which ordinarily translates into changing
things so as better to suit one's liking. The sense has sometimes been characterized as a will to power. The power may be sensed, for example, by
a craftsman who transforms a tree into furniture, or by a farmer who transforms hay and corn into beef. It is felt by a two-year-old who gets what he
wants around home by outwitting his mother; also by the political leader

who gets considerable of what he wants through promising and arm-twisting his followers.

Social Approval

The individual has need for social approval that is more inclusive than that implied by foregoing comment on power. The approval concerns respect of the group for the work in which the individual is engaged, which means that the goods or services that flow from his job have value for the group. In a complex society, several jobs may be grouped so as jointly to contribute to a desired outcome, and the outcome may be remote in time or locale.

3. What Society Gets From the Job

From several standpoints, society has a stake in the job and in a high level of general employment.

Goods and Services

A populous and complex society needs a large volume of widely varied goods and services, in order to maintain what is typically referred to as a high standard of civilization. In fact, the social fabric consists essentially of relationships among persons who are engaged in the production and distribution concerned.

Group Economic Implications

There are various direct economic implications for the group which are tied to the job situation.

E1) It is through income that people get money for paying taxes. Persons who do not depend directly on wages or salaries for income depend on interest paid or on profits earned. Receipts of interest or profits depend on somebody using available equipment, etc., in producing goods and services for the market.

E2) In an economically interdependent world, the trade and exchange implications of the job become international as well as nationwide. Thus, the international status of a country depends largely on the productivity of its people.

Employment and Social Stability

A country in which most of the people are happily employed, and thus has only a small percentage of unemployment, is likely to be rather stable. That is, it will have less anxiety, lawlessness, and social disruption than a country in which such employment conditions do not exist.

The seeming current paradox in America between a high level of employment and a high level of lawlessness suggests pertinent intangibles which are not covered by the foregoing statement. One such intangible concerns the nature of the prevailing crime and lawlessness and the extent to which it is associated with a high level of wage or other income. Another intangible relates to the complicated bases of personal satisfaction, which are enmeshed in a network of peripheral desires and competitions. In most cultures, human imagination begins to create such a network when basic necessities seem fairly well met. Thus, America's current affluence nurtures several forms of personal indulgence which our economic status of two generations ago did not encourage. A rather typical accompaniment of such affluence is stress on individualism, one aspect of which is general indifference to what other people do, so long as they do not infringe too directly on what one oneself wants to do.

Social Planning

A populous and socially complex society must be concerned about planning for its future; that is, with respect to energy resources, population growth, educational and health services, employment, international relations, etc. Planning depends on current and projected productivity, including the attitudes and skill-competencies of the people, as constituting a nation's most important resource.

Incidentally, the dependence of realistic planning on precise measurements and supportable estimates implies great emphasis on training programs to develop competencies and on attitude scales and test scores to evaluate individual developments relative to group needs. In a society with expanding emphasis on computerization of quantitative values, it is fantastic to assume that job competencies will not be included in the expansion. Alleged discriminations in the use of test scores in evaluating job applications may have considerable impact on job satisfaction.

4. Technology, Job Demands, and Leisure

It is commonplace to refer to technology as changing the nature of employment or the content of particular jobs, although less common to refer to jobs and employment as influencing the development of technology. The two-way nature of this relationship deserves more consideration than it gets. However, primary attention here concerns two major outcomes of the general relationship noted.

Research

One such outcome concerns research and other service vocations. For several decades the census data of employment have shown a decline in percentage of employed persons who work in the extractive fields, such as mining and agriculture, or who work in manufacturing areas, and an increase in the percentage who work in service vocations, such as education, health services, recreation and entertainment, or welfare programs. The pattern of change is sometimes described in economic terms by saying that the shift has been toward areas in which man's capacity for consumption is elastic and in which it can expand greatly when facilities for providing the services are available. Expansion in education during the past generation well illustrates the idea of elasticity, as elasticity could be illustrated by future contraction in education.

Further comment regarding service expansion is here limited to one area which has implications for many other areas and which may constitute a major area of future employment. That area is research and invention.

Research and invention can be looked upon as a service which produces knowledge and devices for use in various connections. With growing confidence in man's competence to solve his problems through knowledge and equipment gained by research as here characterized, the material and attitudinal base to support research expands. The two-way nature of the process should be apparent: as research produces an increasing supply of useful knowledge and devices it gets more support, and with more support the people demand greater achievements. Also, as knowledge inches outward through research, insightful leaders become more aware of the abyss of ignorance and of potential exploration that lies on all sides.

Popular demands for research will probably continue to be sporadic in emphasis and fortuitous in direction, until our culture develops sufficient maturity in the general area so as to manifest rather comprehensive perspective. Currently in the health fields we emphasize research on cancer and heart diseases, we carry on space exploration in astrophysics, we emphasize various areas of military ballistics and weaponry, and we call attention to certain aspects of energy usage and environmental outlook. In various connections this author has urged research on individual differences in brain structure, as related to intelligence and to various forms of academic and other conscious learning. He has also urged the study of dioxyrhibonucleic acid and other phenomena in human genetics. One does not need to be a genius to recognize the need for research on economic cycles and inflation, including the role of popular psychology, or to recognize the need for research on international trade and monetary relations. Much of the present study is oriented toward the aim of finding ways to reduce lawlessness and to develop and maintain ongoing institutions which can win and hold the respect of the people. Preceding comments point to a few areas in the abyss of ignorance, to which future generations might well devote research.

It should be obvious that research in any area, of the type suggested in the foregoing paragraph, implies work at different levels of complexity and with different degrees of comprehensiveness. It should also be obvious that research along lines such as inferred presumes employees who show different levels of competence. These levels could be thought of as existing in hierarchal form, much as the levels currently reflected by a large industrial corporation or a large governmental operation. In regard to comprehensive research operations, as in regard to comprehensive operations in other spheres, the chief bottleneck is usually at the top; that is, it relates to the imagination and organizational ability of leadership. Organizational imagination concerns material resources and facilities, personnel, and schedule of anticipated results.

The preceding observations mean extensive future *possibility* for jobs of various kinds, and they imply a future *necessity* for such jobs. As for youth who drift toward delinquency as they mouth slogans about the "relevance" of our present institutional and regulatory framework, participation in research under imaginative supervision can offer substantial challenge.

Leisure Time

The second major outcome of relationships between technology and jobs concerns the "boon or curse" implications of leisure in present-day America.

When men worked at heavy physical labor during most of their waking hours, leisure from work with its opportunity to recuperate from fatigue was usually an individual and a group asset. But when work hours are short, when machines do the heavy work, and when other developments contribute to the accrual of leisure before fatigue occurs, the net outcome is likely to be different. Such accrual of leisure in this country at present is very extensive. It stimulates much invention by private initiative, legitimate and otherwise, to absorb the time and cash involved. Several aspects of the personal indulgence, which thus slushes around within the gaudy affluence that accompanies such leisure, spills over the borders of respectability into various forms of delinquency and lawlessness. Under the circumstances described, leisure is a curse, not a boon—although the shift may seemingly occur by imperceptible degrees.

The curse features indicate a need for group supervision, but our timid and clumsy efforts at supervision imply broad ignorance of the social psychology involved. This psychology includes undue idealization of the virtues of private enterprise and perhaps an exaggerated judicial notion of personal freedom. Timidity and clumsiness also reflect a puny conception of the relationship between mental health and socially respectable employment. Work therapy in the rehabilitation of public offenders and in other settings has significant implications in the present connection. This study has frequently mentioned the role of jobs in delinquency prevention.

5. Formulating and Administering Job Programs

There has been previous comment on the need for coordination among agencies which seem most directly concerned with delinquency and lawlessness in America, especially our educational institutions, the judiciary and law-enforcement agencies. Several references to employment agencies have also been made. Hence, in the present connection, only sketchy reference is made to general areas of involvement.

Among such areas, attention should be directed to child labor and the national interest in the development and protection of children. A related area concerns organized labor, with perhaps a broader and more insightful conception of its own educational responsibility. Laboring people have more children in the public schools than any other social group has, not excepting welfare clients. A further area relates to the educational emphasis of rehabilitation programs, including the need for research to develop know-how so as to reduce complaints about rehabilitation programs that do not rehabilitate. More experimentation is justified on the involvement of churches and civic organizations, particularly with respect to the attitudes of employing agencies about jobs as instruments of education and citizenship development, as well as being instruments of direct economic production.

Previous comment has also dealt with the responsibility of universities in preparing personnel to serve as teachers, social workers, custodial and rehabilitation personnel for delinquent persons, personnel for service in the areas of physical and mental health, and other areas which bear significantly on the individual's civic and vocational responsibilities. Such comment has also emphasized a university responsibility for developing in the professional personnel of such areas the knowledge and attitudes necessary for coordination in providing some paid but nonschool work-experience for *all* American youth. This includes youth whose parents think that their children are or ought to be college bound. If college graduates are expected to hold positions of more than average power and responsibility, it is of more than average importance that they understand the sociovocational structure of American society.

6. National Consequences of Job Programs

Relationships which develop between jobs and the status of leisure, or of other factors bearing on delinquency, can greatly influence the pattern of American life. A few types of influence are briefly mentioned.

Shifts in Vocational Structure

Continuing modification of the relative status of different kinds of jobs in the vocational structure has been noted, particularly with respect to expansion in the service vocations and to expansion in the research component of the service field. Implied in the preceding statement is an increase in the relative number of persons engaged in some types of professional service. This carries new significance in view of a tendency for our more numerous professional workers to organize and to use strike or related tactics to attain collective goals. Recent activities by teachers, hospital workers, and firemen illustrate this point.

Broadened Vocational Understanding

Development of job considerations, along the lines suggested in foregoing pages, could have substantial influence on a broad understanding among Americans of the complexity of the vocational world. A joint relationship with other social developments bears on the situation indicated. One such other development appears in the probability that there will be a further increase in percentage of the American people who hold pay jobs. This is largely because of a likely further increase in percentage of women who are gainfully employed; that is, apart from further transforming into gainful jobs of considerable work which women have traditionally done around the home on a nongainful basis. However, it may also include more extensive participation by youth in the labor market through work-study programs and through other arrangements. Moonlighting and part-time employment may also become more important, as may a reconsideration of employment for retired persons. In addition, with growing interest in trade and international economic relations, the social implications of jobs in America increasingly have both domestic and international significance.

Broadened Sense of Responsibility

Implied in preceding statements on jobs and social understanding is a broadened sense of social responsibility for maintaining a high level of employment at reasonable wages. Part of this responsibility involves attention to the cost of unemployment, as reflected through such avenues as lost production and reduced volume of goods and services in the market, public outlays for relief or associated custodial demands, and sociopsychological impairment of confidence and respect concerning the social system as a whole.

The Job and Personal Life Style

Job orientation as an anchor point in personal life style would modify present conceptions of education, and of cooperation among institutions which have responsibility for different areas of education. Modifications would include general philosophy; staffing and servicing as related to facilities and to personnel qualifications; administrative organization, such as general adoption of the quarter system which is used in the business world; and the general values of academic, relative to other types of experience, in the backgrounds of persons on high school and university staffs.

Government Relationships to Job Structure

Another important national consequence of job programs would probably relate to direct government participation. Among the more obvious aspects of such participation is the availability of federal funds to support certain aspects of coordination among the different types of social and educational agencies mentioned. But along with federal funds is the need for concepts and guidelines which embody perspective, to reduce fortuitous gyrations among local communities. Moreover, significant economic developments and job status in America often depend considerably on federal action. One ramification of the dependence concerns the timing, scope, and location of public-works projects, viewed in terms of both immediate employment and of the long-range usefulness of completed projects.

A type of government participation in the vocational lives of the people, which operates differently in parts of Western Europe and Latin America from the way it operates in this country, involves the holding of political elections on Sunday rather than on some normal working day. Whether paid for by the employer or by the employee, time off the job for voting constitutes a vocational cost. Countries which seem to be as firmly dedicated to the vocal and ritualistic aspects of Christianity as the United States is, apparently see no desecration of the Sabbath by the political involvement of Sunday elections. Regardless of how our practice got started in an early god-fearing America, the present rationale seems to be that desecration would be manifested in voting but is not manifested in spectator sports or other pleasure-seeking activities. Experimental venture might yield worthwhile data on the percentage of the electorate that votes under the two patterns.

Increased Public Subsidy of Education

A major consequence of job programs, such as foregoing considerations have implied, might relate to a broadened conception of subsidized education. Typical reference to free public education in America neglects the fact that families pay a significant part of the cost of sending their children to school. Providing food, housing, health services, clothing, and often books, reflect significant family contributions, although public schools and relief agencies have increasingly expanded into these areas during recent decades. But the continuing responsibility of parents helps clarify the use of the term subsidy for the public contribution.

Relative to work-study situations for high school youth and to other comparable situations, the present study has suggested the subsidizing of industrial and other employers for the increase in unit cost of output which results from the low level of productivity which *may* be associated with inexperienced or as yet inadequately trained employees. Whether that allocation of public funds would increase or decrease the public outlay relative to total learning accomplishment could be determined only by information gained through experience. However, such experience should further demonstrate two things: that schools alone as presently conceived are unable adequately to do the necessary educational job; and that closer coordination among agencies, which presently have educational responsibility in the area concerned, would probably improve learner attitude and other aspects of employability.

Two other avenues to funding could be suggested. One would be for legislation to make it a duty of employers to participate in educational developments about as preceding considerations have described, with the expense involved being considered a part of the cost of doing business or the cost of being permitted to carry on productive activities in the community. This would mean that the cost would be passed on to consumers. That is, it would come out of the general resources of the people; although in the case of any one producing establishment, the individuals who make up the public of consumers are not identical with the individuals who make up the public of taxpayers. Another approach to funding might be through astute business management, whereby employee achievement more than offsets educational cost. This might come through such avenues as increased hourly output per employee, reduced absenteeism, reduced wastage or breakage of materials and equipment, employee suggestions for improvement in operations, reduced loss through work stoppages or slowdowns, etc.

7. Nostalgia for Normalcy

When a person refers to seeking normalcy in job or educational relationships, he is likely to have had recent experience with a type of change which he did not like. Normalcy thus comes to infer some past experience that was pleasant or similar conditions that one has heard about, including a halo of mythology typically associated with the "good old days."

Dynamic Normalcy

However, in a dynamic society, normalcy cannot be defined in static terms. It must be thought of as a shifting entity. Furthermore, it cannot be thought of as a moving dot which leaves only a thin line in its wake. It must be thought of as a broad band, permitting substantial variation in behavior that is acceptable. Operating on the basis of a static or narrowly defined conception of normalcy is one of the more common ways to stymie personal freedom and social growth, with considerable unrest and lawlessness typically involved.

A static and rather narrow conception may appear in government when a group in power wants to perpetuate its status and is not able to look far or realistically enough into the future to discover a way to do so. But even a group that may nominally be in power cannot expand or insure its power status without thinking in terms of a changing normalcy.

One reason why it is easy for many individuals to think in terms of a static normalcy rests in their development of a system of habits and expectations which involve their usual contacts with persons and things. Normalcy then resides in the body of circumstances which allows the most extensive or satisfying operation of the accumulated habits.

Needed Thread of Continuity

Regardless of any characterization of nostalgia, organized society requires a thread of continuity from one generation to the next. Although the course of the thread may be far from straight, its past course must be fairly easy to discern, and there must be some reasonable basis for forward projection. Areas of disharmony along the route are variously referred to as the generation gap, social unrest, delinquency and lawlessness, etc. While it is necessary for some conception of normalcy to be embodied in the goals of an ongoing society, struggle and adjustment in a dynamic society will be less violent if normalcy is conceived as a fairly broad band rather than a narrow line. In a society in which the technical and vocational world is as vigorous and dynamic as it is in the United States, job content and job status in relation to lawful behavior may offer a fruitful area in terms of which to think about normalcy.

Normalcy and a Vocational Core in American Education

In considering the judiciary, the police, and certain other agencies connected with law enforcement and correctional service, frequent reference has been made to the public image of the agencies involved. The image is the general picture which the people have in mind when they refer to the particular agency. The image might be thought of as the "normal" picture, with corresponding relationships between imagery and normalcy.

The general image or normal view of education in the nation's schools is not one which places a comprehensive vocational understanding and orientation in a central or core position. Hence, when it is suggested that one's anticipated vocation or job be made such a core, extensive modification of the traditional image is implied. Image in the foregoing sense is essentially a body of habits concerning the mode of viewing or appraising particular situations. While each person involved acquires the habits concerned, the habits as a cultural influence may reflect an accumulation over several generations. Such an accumulation has been important in a historic dichotomy between vocation and education, which to some extent still lingers in America.

The dichotomy seems to have got started when slaves or serfs did the work, which was viewed as primarily menial, whereas a free upper class learned to read and engage in arguments on politics and speculative philosophy. Throughout the apprenticeship of the handicraft period, and well into the present era of mass-production industry, educational needs associated with jobs have been considered inferior to the so-called liberal-education experiences of the nonlaboring upper class. Categorization of vocational and liberal courses became usual in American high schools and often in colleges.

The dualism implied still prevails in much of the nation's educational imagery. However, the imagery has been substantially modified by the rising demands for both general and technical education, in order for one to hold a job. With America's rapid development in technology, the rate at which the dichotomy is eroded speeds up. Accordingly, there is considerable pressure now from both parents and youth that high schools teach salable skills; and the large university is essentially a collection of vocational or professional schools, in the sense that most students who attend expect to get better jobs than if they did not attend.

However, the change in imagery reflected by the trend described is a considerable distance from accepting the idea that for students below the college level, the vocational world should be made the *core* around which other aspects of education are organized and through which the other aspects get their basic significance. But when one notes that the job is the major avenue through which the average American gets money for participating in the culture through the marketplace; marked governmental anxiety if unemployment exceeds five percent of the labor force; concern about wage rates, collective bargaining, hours and conditions of work, as well as leave and retirement benefits; the role of wages and productivity in international trade; and the personal and family friendships which develop through co-workers on the job; then the importance of the job as a core factor in one's life style should be apparent.

From the core status in life style as indicated, tradition and imagery will perhaps gradually yield further toward a comprehensive understanding of the vocational as becoming the core of education for *all* American youth—i.e., it will be looked upon as constituting normalcy.

8. *Normalcy and Creative Guidance for Youth*

For at least a generation there has been extensive talk about and substantial action as to providing guidance for youth, particularly through the efforts of school programs. The efforts have reflected both personal desires and satisfactions of individual youth and social implications for the community. Attention has also been given to the prevention of delinquency and the development of human resources.

But when one observes that more public offenders are in their late teens than in any other comparable age span, and that teenagers are ordinarily presumed to be or recently to have been extensively involved in school programs, it looks as if the schools have not done a good job in the guidance sphere. Among the numerous factors involved in this situation, a few are mentioned for emphasis.

The Generation Gap

The historic generation gap, sometimes characterized as a disease whereby youth rather automatically look upon their elders as senile, can easily grow in importance as the rate of technical and social change speeds up. In any rapidly changing society, the pattern of life which the parents lived when they were young cannot be an adequate guide for their own children who are currently in the youthful age span. While it may seem rather easy for most parents to recognize this point in a reflective or rational sense, it seems difficult for many of them to internalize its importance in their attitudes and general behavior.

The foregoing means that each generation must gain considerable of what it needs to know through the avenue of "learning by doing." But it also means that the scope of what must be learned on this basis expands as the culture grows, and that expansion occurs in the possible areas of doing—and of wrongdoing. However, the situation indicated does not mean that there is nothing which youth can learn from their parents or from other lay elders about the nature of change, the bases of projection regarding areas of change, the penalties which society is likely to assess for ignoring or defying the aspects of the mores which are highly revered, or the problems that are involved in recuperation from major error or defeat. Certain threads of this thought were apparently observed by our religious-oriented predecessors when they referred to the dire "wages of sin."

While learning by doing or learning through the "school of hard knocks" may be the only way to learn some important things, and perhaps the best way to learn some others, progress of the human race depends largely on the mentors of youth devising more certain and more economical ways for the youth of successive generations to learn much of the new material which technical and other developments bring forth. Preceding comments on teenage delinquency and hints about neglect in the development of human resources suggest that the mentors have not been particularly astute in devising the learning procedures inferred—and perhaps not firmly committed regarding an obligation to do so.

Conversely, the youth should learn, through hard knocks if not through less abrasive procedures, that as a practical matter these elders whom they might tend to regard collectively as fools are actually quite numerous, and that as the youth pass through subsequent years they will inevitably have rather extensive contacts with members of the elder group, while the youth themselves are moving along with Father Time and becoming full-fledged members of said elder group.

Providing Jobs

A suggestion which this study has emphasized, of providing a part-time job for *every* high school student on a continuing basis during his school years, would involve considerable reorientation in the nation's vocational practice. It would also involve broad changes in socioeconomic thinking, with respect to likely public subsidy of employment and related productivity as contrasted with public expenditures typically associated with delinquency or unemployment. Significant administrative problems, such as getting a considerable number of youth who attend consolidated or other schools in small communities where there is little employment opportunity into other communities with more such opportunity, would probably be involved. However, a tendency of many industries to disperse into rather sparsely populated areas or of new industries to become established in such areas could be important in the preceding connection. Possibilities concerning expansion in research work as a major area of employment should be considered in this relationship.

In connection with youth development through the job as here proposed, as in proposals regarding any other large undertaking, computing costs and returns is a complex responsibility. It is especially complex in the setting concerned because of the numerous respects in which it is contrary to traditional American thinking and expectations.

Project Exploration

Division IV includes numerous project suggestions whereby youth can be guided into the exploration of challenging vocational possibilities. These suggestions, including the appendix listings and annotations, point to many individuals who have made significant contributions to various aspects of civilization. They should thus offer challenge to young people, through a wide range of present or potential interests.

During youth it is normal for the physical and intellectual life of a healthy person to expand rapidly. This means that the youth seeks challenges to overcome, "worlds to conquer." If the adults who have responsibility for guiding the social order do not have enough imagination and concern to offer challenges which are within the framework of social acceptability, they should not be surprised if youth become involved in challenging various aspects of the social framework. Complaints by youth about "relevance" are peripheral challenges; various types of delinquency are more central, but often grow out of the peripheral.

The present study emphasizes two avenues of challenge: (1) jobs for youth, with associated educational and economic ramifications; (2) biographical considerations of the lives and contributions of outstanding persons. Learning by example and involvement is often noted as an easy and direct way to learn. Jobs and biographies afford examples, as well as varying degrees of direct and vicarious involvement.

9. The Job as Basic Avenue to Democracy

It has been suggested that many teachers, parents, and others who have responsibility for the education and personality development of youth, fail to recognize the importance of a paying job in the maturity of an adolescent.

Assuming that the adolescent has control of his earnings and that he may decide how to use them, after consultation with persons who have guidance competence and status, a paying job offers an important type of independence and of sharing in the adult community. The independence is important for the adolescent, who typically wants to be considered an adult and to leave childhood things behind him. Recent legal developments at federal and state levels, to extend the franchise as well as other rights and duties of full citizenship to persons eighteen years of age, increase the importance of job-holding by persons of that or immediately preceding years as a factor in the individual's maturity.

For a person over fifteen years of age, earned income through job responsibility is in a quite different category from direct allowance grants made simply because the young person exists. The same point has been stated regarding direct monetary or similar grants to relief clients, in contrast with employment on constructive public-works projects, through which employees can sense their making a significant contribution to the broad cultural stream. For most adult Americans, income through a paying job is the basic avenue of identifying with the economy and of securing money with which to exercise power in the market place.

A major portion of American social philosophy concerning work and employment is in a groove that was furrowed out when most men did not have much leisure and when any increment of leisure that could be gained through a shortened workweek was highly prized. But when leisure is abundant, additional leisure may become burdensome, and persons who hold full-time paying jobs may come to be regarded as fortunate. The situation described places a substantial burden on the nation's leadership to maintain a high level of employment and of general economic activity.

A significant aspect of the job from economic and mental-health standpoints seems to be emerging with arguments about a thirty-hour workweek, where the thirty hours may be distributed over three days rather than over five or perhaps six days. For commuters, the three-day arrangement would reduce travel problems. For the community, it might decrease the number of jobs growing out of commuter service. For employees generally, the three-day arrangement would increase the feasibility of a second job. Two sets of three-day employees might increase plant output and thus reduce overhead costs. Several revolutionary possibilities for nationwide employment might grow out of a widespread three-day arrangement. And not all of the possibilities are directly economic.

In Division II, considerations on "Motivation: Why Men Work," and on related areas, bear on the idea of the job as democracy.

Chapter 7

VICTIMS OF CRIME IN AMERICA

Two major components in the growth or expansion of a culture are increase in population and expansion in the number and types of activities in
which the people engage. An increasing number of social regulations accompanies the expansion inferred, and every regulation constitutes a possible
source of violation. Thus, every individual is a potential transgressor against
the person or property of others; also, every individual is a potential victim
of transgression by others. Every transgression involves both an aggressor
and a victim, and one function of the state is to insure justice in the kinds
of situations implied.

The concept of justice is a social concept, which can exist only in organized
society. It does not exist in the biological world. The concept reflects a
social recognition that some individuals will violate the group code and that
penalties will minimize the violations and thus enhance group status. A
schedule of penalties is accordingly worked out, with serious offenses carrying serious penalties. The schedule thus reflects the idea of balance and
constitutes the scale of justice.

1. Foundations of Balance

The social conception of balance or justice must be harmonized with a
biological drive for personal survival. But the individual learns that in a
group setting his own prospects for survival depend on cooperation with
c hers, and hence on the modification of highly individualistic tendencies.
Much of a society's educational effort is directed toward the modification
indicated.

However, the educational and other socializing efforts have a further biological anchorage. It is that when one's most elementary biological needs
for survival are met, one's perspective broadens to include other considerations. Some of these considerations relate to observation of the experiences
which other persons have, and recollection or projection as to what one's own
feelings would be under similar conditions. It is out of the common biological background plus the common body of experience that conceptions
of justice, or of what relationships ought to exist, are actually formulated.

Although the biological background of survival may be about the same for persons in different environments, it follows that differences in the experiential element will result in differences in codes of justice. Thus, to some extent the specific content of codes is relative to the society concerned, yet to some extent those specifics are constant from one society to another. Social values which are reflected in codes of behavior are combinations of biological and social elements and should be expected to change as changes in the elements occur.

The concept of balance and justice, from both individual and group standpoints, might be characterized as describing a continuum along a line which reflects different degrees of materialism. Thus, some things and events have greater material value to the individual than others have, and some individuals make greater material contributions to the culture than others make. The injury or damage which public offenders cause to victims, together with the economic problems of apprehending them and keeping them in custody, constitute negative material contributions. Compassion and a feeling of empathy for fellowman is in the present connection looked upon as a non-material value. The emotional load associated with compassion sometimes leads to contrasting it with the exercise of intelligence. While there has been great variation in the relative emphasis placed on economics and on compassion in the systems of justice which the world has known, every system has apparently included some of both elements.

2. America's Greater Concern for Offenders Than for Victims

The framers of early government in America may have been overly impressed with their status as rebels and as liberators from oppression when they emphasized the protection of the individual against encroachment by centralized government. Personal freedoms set forth in the Bill of Rights and elsewhere are essentially freedoms and protections which the state assures for the accused, not protections which the state guarantees for the potential victims of offenders. In addition to concern about the accused, there has also been concern about the status of government and about state authority and power to make and enforce regulations. Concern by new governmental organization about its power status has by no means been confined to the history of the United States. It seems broadly characteristic of new forces which take control of government through some coup or similar action.

Perhaps the American patterns of justice might thus be characterized as guaranteeing a broad swath of rights for the accused, and intending to assure respect and power for government, but substantially limiting to "regrets" its concern for the personal well-being of victims and their families—who suffer death, personal injury, or loss of property.

In the present connection, one situation is examined to show the state's concern for the accused and one to show its lack of concern for the victim.

Initial Assumption of Innocence

In American law, the "assumption of innocence until guilt is proven" has an interesting status. One element of status reflects transition from a highly individualized to a highly collective relationship between the individual and the group. A long and widespread influence of frontier life in America has done much to extend and perhaps exaggerate individualism in the nation's culture. An earlier comment suggested an "oppression psychology" among some of the Founding Fathers and their protection of individual rights against government encroachment. Perhaps it is in part a manifestation of the revered status of the individual in the system to assume that, when accused of some code violation, he is innocent until proven guilty. But there is also an important practical consideration from the standpoint of public administration. When it is much easier to accuse than to prove or convict, a large portion of the members of a community might be thwarted as to civic participation through mere accusations; that is, if there were no need to prove in order to establish civic unworthiness.

However, other aspects of the American legal system tend to protect the accused and essentially ignore the victim. One influence in the "innocence framework" relates to what constitutes proof of guilt. With worldwide news gathering and presentation, it is easy to sense present differences among countries in procedures for obtaining convictions. This country has extensive legislative and judicial law on procedural due process. One feature of said process relates to guilt "beyond a reasonable doubt," and another concerns the procedure by which a verdict of guilty may be reached. Additional features include problems on what constitutes evidence and on how the evidence is secured. Recent enlightenment of the nation in this sphere with respect to wiretapping and other Watergate operations, is rather extensive. But the extent of doubt that is reasonable, and other aspects of the "reasonable man" doctrine, present problems. Should one think of reasonableness as a matter of degree, reflecting distribution along some continuum from zero to one hundred? If so, then is a 10 percent doubt to be considered reasonable or may it extend to 40 percent? Or is reasonable doubt intended to reflect something implying a 50 percent phenomenon—as in voting shares of corporation stock?

The requirement of a unanimous jury, recently modified by the Supreme Court, has been part of the picture. Might one ask: in what other area of human controversy must action await a unanimous decision? This nation has gone to war on much less widespread agreement and has used various procedures to intimidate minorities—cf., Woodrow Wilson's reference to "a little band of wilful men" in Congress. And to what extent are members of a jury reasonable persons, rather than tenacious embodiments of prejudice and emotion?

Equal Protection of the Laws

American legal theory emphasizes equal protection of the laws. While American society never included the various grades of nobility and related social stratifications which characterized the European society that was vivid in the minds of the Founding Fathers, it would be unrealistic to infer that monetary affluence plays no role in the ability of American litigants to employ qualified counsel, who can ferret out "loopholes" which are advantageous for their clients or who can engage in delaying action through appeals and otherwise. Yet renowned jurists have observed, "Justice delayed is justice denied," and this nation's basic legal framework provides that the accused shall have a fair and speedy trial. It is probably easier for legal and other thought to focus the interest which an individual criminal has in escaping punishment, than to focus the scattered interests of the general public in safeguarding potential victims, regarding whom personal identification is at the time impossible. But when does yielding to what is easy constitute the feasible administration of justice?

3. Capital Punishment

The simple balance of retribution which is reflected in some early conceptions of justice, and which is epitomized in expansions of the idea of "an eye for an eye and a tooth for a tooth," did not envision any complex group machinery for either defining or enforcing justice. The matter seemed to be largely in the hands of the victim or his immediate family and associates, with the remedies being physically direct in content and prompt in time. Feud justice is sometimes referred to in the connection indicated.

The collective procedures which have become prominent in the social and legal complexities of the past century have deemphasized physical types of punishment and have broadened the use of other types. It may be noted that as a society becomes more complex, there are more ways in which the interests of an individual can be reached—in the sense of either reward or punishment. But it has also been noted that the complexity mentioned increases the number of points at which violations of regulations may occur. To some extent America's growing lawlessness should be viewed in this perspective.

Among the general accompaniments of growth in lawlessness is loss of respect for the police and other law-enforcement personnel; anxiety and fear of many people for their personal safety; and growth in the feeling of resignation and apathy, suggesting that it does not help to try to work with the police and that nothing can be done to improve the situation. If growing lawlessness includes a substantial increase in conspicuous crimes against persons, such as assault and murder, a further accompaniment is likely to be a popular request for restoration of capital punishment in connection with certain crimes, in spite of some judicial notes that it constitutes cruel and unusual punishment, which in America is constitutionally frowned upon. Thus disgust and mistrust, regarding sophisticated collective procedures and guarantees, leads to a desire for more direct and vigorous action which is simple and easily understood. During the past several years, America has experienced considerable revival of sentiment in favor of capital punishment. Several types of consideration are thus raised, apart from the judicial one mentioned.

Some of the most difficult civic and moral problems in America are brought to the surface when attention is given to capital punishment. One reason for this situation seems to lie in the finality of such punishment, so far as the individual criminal is concerned. Perhaps another lies in a rather narrow understanding of social or individual-group relationships in organized society. There are several ways in which American society, as well as other societies, sacrifices individuals for the welfare of the group. Drafting young men to fight wars may be one of the more ready illustrations. The sacrifice seems necessary, largely because the elders of these men were too selfish or too unimaginative to prevent the war crisis from developing.

Religious and other emphasis on the value and sanctity of human life, that often gets whipped up in connection with discussions on capital punishment, is typically ignored or rationalized away by clergical and associated logic with respect to war casualties. The same essentially applies to the large number of preventable deaths by accident in this country—on highways, in industry, etc. In addition, we have more knowledge than we use on how to prevent or delay deaths from hunger (malnutrition), disease, etc. And the nation provides tax-supported clinics to facilitate the deliberate destruction of thousands of lives each year through abortions.

Thus promoting doctrines about the sanctity of human life in relation to the capital punishment of criminals suggests a circus tightrope job, in which each step must be carefully taken and must be governed by a very narrow focus of vision. The situation might be characterized as reflecting highly selective vision and insight within a broad field of general blindness and with the selectivity focused on individuals who have committed heinous crimes against other persons. To what extent should one discard the "reasonable man" doctrine, concerning situations of the kind described, and assume that humans will operate on the basis of individual selfishness and emotion—somewhat as other mammals do?

To assume that with capital punishment there would never be an error in arriving at convictions is unrealistic. In this kind of situation, as in every other kind of social judgment, the state is responsible for a balancing act with its scales of justice. Whether a life is more valuable if ended because of crime, than if ended because of war, preventable accident, or the basically personal or selfish considerations associated with abortion, is a judgment which must eventually rest with the social group. Foregoing comments do not argue for or against capital punishment, but for something resembling consistency and reason in outlook and in practice regarding the general areas of life values and human relationship concerned.[5]

Comments have been made at various points in this study on education, employment and other ways of preventing crime, much as reference is often made to preventive versus remedial medicine, preventing severe swings in economic cycles, etc. The only further note on crime prevention at this point relates to mental cases. The note could be stated by asking how much longer we will continue to ignore possibilities, and wait for the mentally deranged person actually to commit some serious crime and for his sophisticated counsel to plead "innocence because of insanity," before we develop procedures for detecting the probabilities of his doing so, for getting public acceptance of the procedures, and for working out necessary programs of prevention.

4. *Victims of Crime, and Tort Liability of Government*

The liability of a private citizen in court action for injury or damages to another person because of negligence or wilful acts by that private citizen, which are not a part of some contractual relationship, is quite well established in America. However, the nation is now engaged in a struggle to revise its long-standing policy of state immunity from comparable liability, in the absence of contractual obligations. With expansion in relationships between government and the citizen and expansion in the protections and related services which government is expected to provide for the well-being of the citizens, greater importance attaches to liability for injuries or damages that might occur through government operations. Some of the considerations involved are examined in further detail.

Background and Status of Government Immunity

Present-day government in America has many types of contractual relationships with citizens, in which government acts much as a private contracting party might act. Contracts for the purchase of materials, for services rendered by employees, and for interest on bonds probably indicate the most usual areas of government liability under contracts. However, government liability in tort concerns injury caused by government in ways which are not concerned with breach of contract. Injuries resulting from the negligent or other acts of government employees in connection with their jobs have resulted in many lawsuits over government liability for the injuries concerned. Laboratory and playground injuries to school children have often been involved in lawsuits alleging liability of the school district in tort for the injuries sustained. The same applies to pupil injuries through school-bus transportation. Private agencies carrying on profitable educational operations would in comparable circumstances be liable in tort for the injuries indicated, and the dispute concerns state immunity in circumstances of this kind.

The doctrine of immunity is part of our legal heritage from England, where the king was looked upon as the symbol or representative of the people as a whole, and where the idea developed that nothing which the king did in dealing with individuals who were his subjects could be considered a wrong. In the absence of a king, the doctrine in America took the form that the citizen could not sue the state for tortious injury unless the state had specifically consented to such a suit. The ordinary avenue of consent has been statutory enactment, which usually means that at common law the state has been immune from tort suits. Some states have enacted statutes which abrogate this immunity. During recent decades the highest courts of several states have, through court decisions, abrogated immunity in certain types of cases. In some instances through court action, immunity has long been denied.

At the present time tort immunity is a more important factor in the respect and imagery which the citizen has regarding the state, than it was during the early days of the republic. Among the reasons for this situation are the increase in population, with the greater number of citizens now to be considered. Also, government at different levels now touches the lives of individual citizens in more ways than it did in the earlier days. Compulsory school attendance, vaccinations and other public health services, providing and patrolling highways, city police and fire protection, inspection and surveillance in food and drug distribution, and the certifying or licensing of practitioners to render various kinds of personal service are illustrative of areas in which governmental involvement is now of great concern to the individual citizen. Perhaps a third consideration regarding the greater present importance of tort liability, in addition to growth in population and expansion in areas of governmental liability, is the *expectation* of a higher level of governmental performance with respect to the services which it does undertake to render than was the situation roughly two centuries ago.

In America, imagery, respect for professed democratic ideals, loyalty to governmental leadership, willingness to make personal sacrifices for the social well-being, and other behavior or manifestations of attitudes which are sometimes referred to collectively as good citizenship are important for the stability of government as reflected through the lawfulness of the people and their willingness to support the form of government that exists.

A few specific illustrations may be helpful. If compulsory attendance laws force parents to send their children to school, and school operations include laboratory or playground activities through which pupils are injured, or if violence among pupils results in injury, how is the imagery formed by parents regarding the state affected when the state washes its hands of fiscal liability concerning the injury? Should the state be in a position to compel, such parents may ask, when it assumes no responsibility for personal injuries resulting from its compulsion? The same applies to transportation injuries, when the school bus is essentially the only means by which many children can get to the school which they are required to attend. As to busing, some parents might further ask whether the courts should be as vigorous about providing district liability in tort for bus-related injuries as they are about across-town or other busing to achieve racial objectives. To what extent does such across-town busing result in increased bus-related injuries?

If a citizen is falsely arrested or is charged with various offenses regarding which he must spend considerable in time and funds for his defense, should he upon acquittal be reimbursed or should he be compensated for impairment of his status in the community? How about time and expense involved in court delays which are rather direct results of docket load or general low-gear court procedure? What should be the liability of the state in these types of situations?

If government is looked upon as a cooperative enterprise between the citizen and the state, an enterprise which recognizes that the state cannot function without the cooperation of the citizen, should the state be as ready to accept responsibility for tortious errors and accidents which occur at its behest, as it expects the citizen to be when suit is between private parties? One should expect that general tort liability on the part of the state would involve expenditure of state funds as a result of tort suits. He might also expect greater care on the part of the state to reduce the number of situations which generate tort claims.

Perhaps the crux of the matter could be stated in terms of political ideology. Should enlightened or progressive democratic ideology, which proclaims that government exists for the welfare of the governed, be concerned about responsibility for personal injury resulting from the way in which government renders those services which it has accepted a commitment to render? To what extent do other countries, which may be less vocal about democratic ideology than we are, accept such governmental responsibility?

There are, of course, arguments on both sides of the question, otherwise there would be no issue. But the arguments in favor of state liability gain relative weight through increase in the complexity of American society and increase in areas of governmental activity, as previously noted; and also through increasing concern on the part of government about general lawlessness in the nation, and the anchorage of lawlessness in general disrespect for government and for public officials.[6]

Further exploration of these and other pertinent questions occurs at various subsequent points.

The Legal Profession and State Immunity

For several years various leaders in the legal profession have attacked the doctrine of state immunity in tort as being unjust, obsolete, in conflict with democratic ideology, etc. A substantial body of literature on the subject has developed,[7] embodying both criticisms and suggestions for improvements. Partly as a result of the concern indicated, several states in this country and some other jurisdictions under the general umbrella of English common law have modified the immunity by statute or court ruling, or both.

In its general support for limiting or abolishing state immunity, the literature mentioned has noted practical considerations relating to costs, administrative procedure, extension versus abuse of justice, etc., as well as the general idea of completely abolishing immunity in a society in which government is as broad and vigorous an influence in the lives of the people as is the case in the United States. Subsequent sections of this study examine some of these considerations from an illustrative standpoint.

5. Social Worth of Offenders and of Victims

It is commonplace to say that the basic reason why people put forth effort to accomplish goals is that the satisfactions more than offset the efforts, although some of the satisfactions may lie in anticipation or in other respects may at the time of effort be nonmaterial. Present freedoms, or broad social concern about future freedoms, may be largely in the nonmaterial category. Also, the evaluative concepts relate to people as well as to things and are generally tied to situations which are described in terms of relationships. Thus, an employer evaluates prospective employees with respect to what he thinks they will be worth to him, and the worker evaluates prospective jobs from a comparable standpoint. A coach evaluates his bench of second-string players in terms of his estimate of needs at a particular time. And we often hear references to individuals as making good wives or good husbands.

The idea of social evaluation may similarly be oriented on public offenders and on their victims, as two categories of people. Scattered references have previously been made regarding positive contributions to society which might be expected from members of the two categories, relative to the outlays of social resources and effort required by such members. Consideration has been given to concern by law-abiding citizens for justice in dealing with the accused and for the latter's freedom and opportunity to defend himself against accusations, because of a feeling that the person who is now law-abiding may some day be among the accused. The potential which each of us has to become a criminal has thus been a basic factor in building up a strong case for the accused.

But the potential victim also has rights, such as a right *not* to be robbed, molested, beaten up, or murdered. In exploring this subject, Sidney Hook[8] observed that most of the rights guaranteed in the Bill of Rights are irrelevant if one is murdered or is maimed to the point where he cannot exercise those rights. Hook reasoned that any right of a victim to damages depends "upon the prior recognition of his moral right not to be victimized by the law-breaker." He noted certain conflicts among rights. He cited the "right of a person out on bail for a crime of violence, to receive bail when he is charged with committing the same type of violent offense, and to be granted bail even when he is charged with committing the offense a third time—a right which he legitimately claims since he has not yet been found guilty of the first offense." The second and third victims can thus claim denial of rights because of specific rights guaranteed to the offender.

Hook reasoned that with the marked increase in crime, there is greater likelihood of the citizen meeting disaster as a potential victim than as a potential defendant in a criminal case and that the rights of potential victims should have priority. He referred to the Supreme Court of the United States as actually extending into state jurisdictions of criminal law certain provisions of the Bill of Rights which were intended to relate to violations of political rights by the federal government. He thought part of the difficulty lies in an absolutistic judicial interpretation of certain constitutional freedoms and protections for the accused, whereas reality demanded interpretation in terms of circumstances. On this point specifically, he commented:

> When crimes of violence are rare and infrequent we may justifiably lean over backwards to protect those accused of serious crime from a possible miscarriage of justice. But it is not justice but only compassion that leads us to say that "it is better that nine or 99 guilty men escape punishment for their crime than that one innocent man be convicted. . . ."
> . . . Compassion, if it is a virtue, must itself be balanced and equitable. Where, we ask, is their compassion for the Myriads of victims of violent crime? At what point do the victims come into their ethical reckoning?

Hook emphasized the need for a reevaluation of some basic assumptions in American jurisprudence, with an updating relative to present conditions of interpretations given to the principles involved.

6. Emerging Concepts of State and Individual Responsibility

Apart from Hook's emphasis on rethinking basic jurisdictional assumptions, comments on speedup in court administration and jury operation to expedite trials, and calls for extended public responsibility through broadened school programs, other social developments bear on concepts of state-individual responsibility.

One pertinent area of social development concerns the whole field of public welfare, the social insurances, low-cost loans, and various other federal and state aids to personal well-being. Such developments generate an atmosphere of expectation and justification for government to reach ever farther in its provisions for the well-being of the citizen and in its implementation of the doctrine that government exists for the welfare of the governed—i.e., for rendering service to the people. Moving toward state liability in tort, or other provision for indemnifying the victims of crime, thus becomes enlightened social and governmental policy. If one wanted to emphasize the balance or social-contract theory of government, he might note that the victims of crime are not being given the protection which they paid taxes or rendered other service to secure. In principle the idea applies to a dweller in a small college town whose garden hose is stolen from the spigot on his dwelling, the same as it applies to urban purse-snatching, or bank embezzlement in communities of various sizes.

The other side of the story emphasizes growing apathy and indifference on the part of average citizens toward their responsibility for law enforcement and for a generally peaceful and law-abiding community. Senator Mansfield[9] looked upon apathy as perhaps the only nonpunishable recourse open to the average citizen who pays taxes, etc., for protection that he does not get, and who receives no indemnification by government when he is victimized through crime. At one point he stated:

> Reflecting this growing apathy has been the significant increase in the number of cases where victims refuse to become involved; not as witnesses, not to assist the prosecution, not in preventing the crime, not in assisting a police officer. It should be added that this reaction is not limited to the immediate victim but is extended to witnesses, to the victim's relatives, to his friends, and neighbors. This is not surprising, if you recognize the fact that less than 2 percent of the victim population ever received any type of restitution.

In his emphasis on the civic responsibility of *all* citizens, he commented: ". . . today, citizens must recognize that through their plain apathy, they commit crimes against society." He added: "The elected representatives need to become cognizant of the need for legislation that would encourage, in fact reward, acts that were socially responsible." In his earlier concern about compensating victims, the senator looked upon compensation in the collective justice and lawfulness of a complex society as replacing the revenge concept of justice as administered by individual and feud action. Collectivization places reliance on the police force, he observed, with compensation in case of police failure as being essential to respect for the collectivized police system. He subsequently stated:

As a matter of public policy, social compensation programs are not revolutionary notions. Indeed there is great similarity in rationale and origin between the notion of compensating workers, assuring them a reasonably safe place in which to work, and compensating victims of crime, assuring them a reasonably safe society in which to live. Just as rapid industrialization increased hazards for the worker, so did the rapid urbanization of the 20th century create social conditions which set the stage for the substantial increase in recent crime statistics. Furthermore, just as the worker was frustrated in his attempts to recover damages, so too, has the victim of crime today been frustrated. In many cases the offender is not apprehended. When he is, he is often destitute. Further complicating this latter difficulty is the fact that present penal methods deprive the offender of his ability to make restitution, as he is deprived of any means of obtaining a gainful livelihood.

An important note respecting the critical importance of apathy resides in the fact that the police rely largely on private citizens to initiate the action which police take, through citizens' reporting offenses to them. From the standpoint of reporting, and also of contributing to precipitate victimization, Hawkins[10] emphasized citizen responsibility in crime rates. He noted the importance of further reserach on certain aspects of crime, such as the settings in which victimizations occur, factors which bear on the extent to which citizens report instances of crime, and contributions which citizens make to victimization through exposing themselves to criminal attack.

Hawkins referred to "tolerance limits" regarding the violation of different norms and to change in the life pattern by some individuals who feel themselves threatened by crime. He offered three hypotheses about the extent of citizens' reporting on victimization. The hypotheses are: (a) where there is confidence in the police, the greater the feeling of threat, the greater the probability of reporting; (b) persons whose work includes the enforcement of norms are more likely to report victimizations than persons engaged in other occupations; (c) if one holds a deterministic rather than a free-will view of human behavior, one is less likely to report transgressions. The hypotheses were tested through a summertime survey of households in Seattle.

Three major reasons for nonreporting were thought by Hawkins to be indicated by the survey: (a) there was no payoff, it did no good to report to the police; (b) a fatalistic outlook that there was nothing which could be done about the situation; (c) individuals did not want to take the time and trouble to become involved. He thought that state compensation for the victims of crime might be one way to increase the proportion of crimes that are reported. He also referred to studies on victim-precipitated crimes of violence and thought that courts might have to play a more active role in evaluating degree of victim precipitation. The concept seems reminiscent of contributory negligence in accident cases.[11]

7. Compensation Procedures

Any system for insuring individuals, or for compensating because of damage or loss in similar connections, must have some basis for determining whom to compensate and how much. Blum[12] explored certain problems in this area, through the use of several hypothetical situations. Comparable injuring and resulting incapacities were presumed in different situations, although resulting from different causes. Some causes involved crime, others did not. Blum's approach concerned an attempt to determine which of the causes should be entitled to public compensation and which should not, in a society in which the mores and legal regulations provide insurance or other compensation to alleviate various kinds of personal accidents and other misfortunes.

Blum's hypothetical situations included a person injured when being robbed by a drug addict, another when he was pushed by a policeman who was chasing a suspect; one who was bumped by an unidentified cyclist, whereas in another case a cyclist was admittedly negligent but wholly impecunious and without liability insurance; one man's injury resulted from stepping into a hole in the street, another's when he reached out to grab a young child to prevent her from being struck by a car; still another lost his balance because of a sudden spasm of nonrecurring nature, and one's injury resulted from a stroke of lightning.

Among considerations were the lack of recognized public responsibility in regard to the drug addict, the police shove, and the hole in the street. But if the community had provided more playground facilities, the child would probably not have been running in the street; and if separate paths were provided for cyclists, they would not be involved in so many pedestrian accidents. Also, to what extent does society provide help for victims of stroke or other health hazards? The point is that personal injuries which are associated with crime and with other settings, and regarding which considerations are pertinent as to public sharing of the burdens involved, do not fall into sharply defined categories. They describe a continuum which includes practically every type of physical misfortune that human beings experience. Moreover, community resources are always limited, which means that some agency must have responsibility for assigning priorities.

Blum emphasized a piecemeal approach to compensation for community shortcomings, with legislative and other debate on accumulating experience constituting the way to develop "the best policy." This stance projects an intermediate or growth area, between immediate and perhaps overbroad coverage on one hand, and inordinate hesitance and delay in the hope of perfection before enacting legislation on the other hand.

Lamborn[13] reviewed various methods used by governments in the regions of the world which emphasize the common-law in compensating victims of crime. He recognized four categories of administrative procedure: (a) those associated with the criminal court which tries the offender; (b) those designating civil courts to assume the responsibility entailed; (c) those allocating the task to general administrative agencies which also have other duties; (d) those which establish special crime-victim compensation agencies.

He recognized advantages and limitations of each approach, but as a summary of observations he concluded:

The programs are of minimal utility unless applications by victims for the benefits are facilitated through publicity regarding the nature of the programs and through easy access to them. Programs that are otherwise beneficial are rendered less useful if they are unresponsive to victim's needs because of unnecessary formality, lack of expedition, or insensitivity to applicant's dignity. Even the program that is operated in a generally fair manner is deficient unless the availability of internal and judicial review ensures the appearance and the actuality of fairness at all times. On the other hand, lesiglative review of compensation decisions may endanger the adequacy of the program as a remedy for victims of crime. These problems, common as they may be, are not insoluble, and attention to the successes attained in some jurisdictions should prove useful in solving them in all.

"In 1963 and 1964, New Zealand and Great Britain adopted the first modern crime compensation programs," stated Brooks.[14] He added: "These programs compensate for injury and death caused by a criminal attack upon an innocent victim. Although the reception given to these programs has been quite favorable and there have been additional adoptions by other jurisdictions, the total number of program adoptions remains small." He noted "six general crime compensation programs" adopted in the United States "during the past six years." The states involved were California, New York, Maryland, Hawaii, Massachusetts, and New Jersey.

Brooks was interested in the political considerations regarding the cost to the state of such programs, and studied cost factors for each of the six states. He mentioned some modifications in the programs since their inauguration, but saw nothing formidable involved. He referred to efforts to put compensation on a nationwide basis, through bills introduced into Congress by Senator Mansfield and Senator McClellan. He noted provisions in these bills to encourage state adoptions of crime compensation programs, by the federal government paying 75 percent of total program costs.

With respect to considerations of cost through tort liability or other compensation, and apart from the contributions by Brooks, one might ask: if the state can afford large expenditures for conducting trials and for incarcerating and attempting to rehabilitate convicted persons, can it afford to recognize liability to victims—who are typically innocent and reasonably law-abiding? Furthermore, if substantial state outlays were required on a tort or other compensation basis, would citizens, who frequently look upon crimes as passing news items from remote situations, recognize a more immediate concern for their responsibility as citizens? That is, how significant is the purse in fueling civic interest and commitment? In addition, since the days when state immunity from tort was broadly established in this country, several changes in American society have come about. Among these changes is growth in state affluence through access to richer tax resources and a decreased basis to fear tort as a bankrupting drain on the public treasury. Also, extensive private corporations have developed as sound operating agencies, although the equivalent of tort allowances are often granted against them.

From the standpoint of compensation, as well as the police protection actually afforded, some comment in legal circles has related to discriminations against minority groups in the "inner city." The "program budget," with systematic allocation of police department resources to specific areas of activity, has been urged as a means of ensuring equal police protection. One commentary observed:[15]

Attractive features of the program budget include the following: allowing the public to observe and modify police practices, illustrating where allocated money goes and how it is spent, showing the emphasis that the police give to each major task, and publicly acknowledging the exercise of discretion. Implementation of these and similar programs by police departments across the country will improve police public relations and lead to a solution of the underprotection problem.

As to legal framework versus judicial responsibility, this commentary added:

The Constitutional and local statutory tools presently available adequately guarantee the rights of equal police protection and other municipal services. What is lacking is enforced judicial recognition of these rights. The alienated residents of the "inner city" need an improved image of the police and local government. Jurisdictions that recognize these facts may well have fewer racial disturbances and incidents of crime as a result.

A form of compensation which is somewhat unique for America has been urged by Cooley,[16] largely as a means of shoring up respect for the legal machinery by which criminal justice is administered. He proposed a Trial Delay Indemnity (TDI), payable to the defendant. Reference is made to the constitutional right of an arrested person to a reasonably speedy trial. However, Cooley suggested that adopting the European rule of compensating *every* legally arrested person who is subsequently acquitted might tempt the police to make haphazard arrests without constitutionally probable cause, on the presumption that "no harm" would result from the arrest. He recommended the retention of stringent guidelines for determining probable cause and of then attaching the rights of compensation to actual government delays in conducting an orderly prosecution of the case. Establishing a "reasonable time frame" would be involved.

The rationale is that the arrested person should not have to bear the costs which fall on him because of imperfections in the administration of justice. Cooley thought that the compensation for delay would speed up court action and that "it could serve as a check on court administrative efficiency, particularly in the near future when computer programming methods and trained court administrators become commonplace in our judicial system." He pointed out the need for an accounting differentiation between delays which were attributable to the defendant himself and those attributable to the government or to exceptional circumstances.

Cooley looked upon the TDI as an essential instrument in the general overhaul of our judicial system. He observed: "In the federal jurisdiction and in the state jurisdictions which have already implemented plans to compensate the erroneously convicted, such statutes could easily be expanded to encompass the notion of indemnity for the dilatory acquitted (on a finding of innocence)."

8. Evolution of the Idea of Compensating Victims of Crime

The line of evolution in compensating victims of crime has been irregular, punctuated by spurts and gaps. It would be unrealistic to assume that interest in such compensation is wholly a recent phenomenon. The Code of Hammurabi (Babylonian king, lived approximately 20th century B.C.), as quoted by Lamborn,[17] stipulated:

> If the robber is not caught, the man who has been robbed shall formally declare whatever he has lost before a god, and the city and the mayor in whose territory or district the robbery has been committed shall replace whatever he has lost for him.
>
> If (it is) the life (of the owner that is lost), the city or the mayor shall pay one maneh of silver to his kinfolk.

Lamborn also cited Jeremy Bentham (1748-1832) as having stated: "Has a crime been committed? Those who have suffered by it, either in their person or their fortune, are abandoned to their evil condition. The society which they have contributed to maintain, and which ought to protect them, owes them, however, an indemnity, when its protection has not been effectual."

Voltaire (1694-1778), as noted by Cooley,[18] attacked the criminal justice in the France of his time especially the Criminal Ordinance of 1670. Regarding that ordinance, he asked: "Should it (justice) not be as favorable to the innocent as it is terrible to the guilty?"

With more direct regard to reimbursement and to indemnity of an accused person who is subsequently acquitted, Cooley also cited the action taken by Frederick the Great of Prussia in 1766. Cooley set forth a Prussian law involved, as providing.

> If a person suspected of a crime has been detained for trial, and where . . . he has been released from custody, and in the course of time his complete innocence is established he shall not only have complete costs restored to him, but also a sum of money as just indemnity to all circumstances of the case payable from the funds of the trial court, so that the innocent person may be compensated for the injuries he has suffered.

Cooley further noted that as of 1932 some twelve European countries or municipalities had laws for compensating innocent detainees and that by 1969 two other countries were added to this list.

Developments in certain other countries respecting compensation of innocent defendants in criminal cases, along with procedural delays such as noted in 1970 by Chief Justice Burger,[19] point up an important area of needed consideration in America regarding concern for the victims of crime. In addition to various social developments which bring more cases before the courts, the Chief Justice observed with respect to procedural time:

Experienced district judges note that the actual trial of a criminal case now takes twice as long as it did ten years ago because of the closer scrutiny we now demand as to such things as confessions, indentification witnesses and evidence seized by the police before depriving any person of his freedom. These changes represent a deliberate commitment on our part—some by judicial decision and some by legislation—to values higher than pure efficiency when we are dealing with human liberty. The impact of all the new factors—and they are many and complex—has been felt in both state and federal courts.

9. The Mores and the Imagery of Crime

From earlier comments on judicial imagery or on the imagery of the law-enforcement agencies, it should be clear that a public image may be developed concerning any person or any institution with extensive public functions or public contacts. Imagery thus grows out of service or disservice actually involved, in comparison with what the people in general think should be provided. The imagery of crime thus becomes what the people consider the status of law enforcement and of violations to be, relative to what the status ought to be.

But the status or image changes as the people substantially learn to survive and live with existing uncertainties about security. This means that imagery respecting crime becomes more permissive, more to the effect that the "wolf, wolf" cries about crime have been exaggerated and that the individual on his own will have to exercise more ingenuity to avoid being victimized. If this approach is pushed very far, it erodes the idea of general safety through collective action on which organized society is based. In this connection Senator Mansfield warned of the dangers of apathy. Under eroding conditions such as described, regulatory practice retreats toward a kind of presocial or guerilla situation, in which there is security for the strong but only anxiety and sacrifice for others.

Substantial emphasis in the present study has concerned the role of image makers; that is, the culture's major agencies for popular education and for the shaping of public opinion. Television as a prime medium of mass communication has been emphasized from the technical standpoint, with the courts, the law-enforcement agencies, and the public schools as major imput sources. This is especially important regarding imput of content to be communicated, and hence to become enmeshed in the value structure and actions of the people. The study has also emphasized the idea that the job involved is too big for any one of the nation's social agencies to undertake, that coordination among three agencies is essential, plus marked responsibility on the individual citizen.

Consideration for the victims of crime is a neglected area in the broad undertaking necessary for developing a more constructive picture of crime in America and of the implications which crime has for the nation's future.

Chapter 8

IDEALS AND REGULATORY STRUCTURE
IN AMERICAN DEMOCRACY

It is important to recognize the interdependence of social ideals and the organizational structure of the society out of which those ideals arise. Since ideals embody hope, faith, aspirations, and goals, along with commitment regarding behavior which seems likely to help realize those hopes, etc., it follows that the action required will depend on the social structure. But people tend to act in accordance with their goals. Hence, the social structure that emerges in the society concerned is shaped by the ideals.

In the sense described, ideals and structure can be regarded as different ways of looking at the same phenomenon. The relationship could be stated by saying that without a structure to carry through on implementation, ideals would be only fantasies. Conversely, without ideals there would be no consistent direction or orientation in accordance with which structure could function. Disintegration or weakness in social ideals thus becomes associated with an uncertain or fluctuating situation in social structure.

Stability in social structure requires an understanding of why both goals and operating procedures have developed to be what they are and why close relationships between the two are essential. Furthermore, when a society gets started moving in a particular direction as to ideals and structure, the movement produces an atmosphere or setting which fosters additional movement in that direction.

However, "breakthroughs" or sharp changes in the direction which idealism takes within a particular society depend on individuals who are outstanding. They are typically outstanding in regard to their insights, but perhaps more so in regard to their courage and persistence in promoting those insights. Thus, imporance must be placed on the interdependence of ideals and structure, if anything socially constructive actually happens. But at the same time considerable flexibility in the structure is essential in order to allow freedom for encouraging creative persons to introduce hypotheses or alternatives to be tried out. The age-old problem of a most favorable balance between personal freedom and group discipline is not an easy one to solve.

1. Coordinated Effort Among Educative Agencies

At earlier points in the study, considerable has been said about coordination among agencies which have educational responsibility concerning lawlessness and corrections in American society. There are two grounds for additional reference at this point to such coordination. One ground concerns emphasis, which the author thinks is justified. The other ground concerns two further implications, which are noted as follows.

The International Setting

In significant respects, lawlessness in any particular country depends on international relationships and on the status of law and order in other countries. With expansion in international relationships, this point is of growing importance. Three illustrations are noted.

(1) Much crime and lawlessness in the United States is traceable to illicit drug traffic, with associated limitations on trying to control imports. The roles of Turkey, France, and parts of Latin America in the presence of marijuana and heroine on our streets, college campuses, and elsewhere in this country, have been extensively publicized. The publicity includes reference to the large number of points and means of entry into the country, which are associated with our expanding international relationships.

(2) With respect to embezzlement and certain other crimes, the refusal of foreign countries to extradite Americans who have escaped from the scene of crime in this country aggravates problems of lawlessness in America. To some extent, international monetary relationships, investments, and swindles become a part of this picture.

(3) Airplane hijacking and the kidnapping or murder of American diplomats and businessmen in some countries reflect a kind of rule by terror rather than by law, in such countries. The term "mafia" causes some Americans to think of international terrorism. The terrorism in some Western Hemisphere nations is complicated by a jealousy of the cultural achievements and economic power of the United States, with an eagerness by leadership in those countries to promote their own brand of selfishness and local exploitation through what they call an independence from the United States.

Each of the preceding areas indicates an international influence on lawlessness in the United States. An important aspect of the influence concerns prospective efforts by this country to rely on peaceful negotiations with other countries, or to let accumulating frustrations on both sides lead to more forceful or retaliatory procedures.

American Tradition

There is a deep-seated factor in American culture which supports the separateness of institutional effort and the general lack of coordination noted. This factor is partly a result of the scatter in early settlement of the people over a broad geographical area, particularly with the "opening up of the West." Under the conditions of scatter, local control and responsibility was probably about the only kind of government that could function. Habits and values from this experience linger in the mores.

Possibly more important than scatter was a deep fear of and antagonism toward central government, which dominated the political philosophy of the Founding Fathers. The fear and antagonism became embedded in several aspects of governmental structure, to limit the power of central government and to set up extensive protections for individual freedom and for other aspects of individualism. Various influences bore on the several states to establish the same framework regarding centralism and individualism that the federal government emphasized.

With growth in population, facilities for transportation and communication, scope of available employment, educational opportunity, material affluence, international contacts and responsibilities, and other developments in American life, many features of the early conception of personal freedom and comprehensive individualism have had to be modified. Social and economic mobility, along with other phases of interdependence in American life, require a continuance of the nation's trends toward coordination and centralization. This kind of centralization has substantially characterized the past century. During the last half of that period, the process has been consipicuous with regard to corporation development in business and industry, the consolidation of school districts and some other local units of government, certain areas of professional education and research, and some types of health and comparable public service. There has also been coordination and perhaps consolidation among agencies concerned with law and order, in the ways noted concerning agencies emphasized in the present study.

With respect to need for research in governmental structure and operation and to implementing the findings of such research, the idea may be illustrated by pointing to coordination among the agencies which are focal in this study. The research and implementation necessitate considerable scrutiny of long-accepted ideas concerning individual status, obsolescence and evolution of institutional functions, qualifications and interests of operating personnel, monetary and other costs which society is asked to pay, values to society of the services received by intended beneficiaries, etc.

Often one of the most thorny among necessities relates to leadership competence among personnel in the different areas involved. Two kinds of thorns are noted. One relates to creative imagination on how improvements in service might be achieved through more extensive coordinations. The other relates to a widespread human trait which is commonly referred to in terms of protecting vested interests or fostering aspirations of empire-building. Problems of research in government should include problems on the orientation and control of ambition, among persons in leadership positions.

2. Balance of Power in Government

Any society in which different agencies have power and responsibility to govern, must provide some basis of relative jurisdiction by those agencies. Since the 1972 campaign for the American presidency, and with the subsequent retinue of investigations and allegations respecting corruptions of persons in high public office, extensive nationwide attention has been focused on jurisdictions. The attention involves the authority of one agency to exercise surveillance over the personnel and acts of another agency.

For several decades the question has involved the authority of the Supreme Court to reject enactments by Congress or acts by the President. Rejection is presumably based on power of the court to interpret the Constitution. Whether that power was intended by the framers of the Constitution or was usurped by aggressive judges in the face of weak executives and legislative bodies may not at present be as important as the nation's having extensively acquiesced in the process.

For a smaller number of decades there has been an obvious gravitation of power from the Congress to the President, partly because of imaginative and aggressive presidents and partly because of emergency situations in which prompt and nationwide action has been considered necessary. Out of the situation indicated, question arises as to when the President needs to consult Congress on contemplated action. Dispute has related to conducting war on foreign soil, impounding funds which the Congress has appropriated for domestic purposes, etc. Critics of the President state the argument in terms of whether he is above and beyond the reach of the law of the land, or whether his rights and responsibilities should be governed by the law the same as those of ordinary people are governed. Such critics reason that the justification for law is that all persons may know before acting what the group procedure is to be under stipulated conditions, rather than for the procedure to be determined later by the personal views of a dictator or other head of state. The idea has often been stated as government by laws rather than by men.

In a dynamic society, smoothness in operation of the balance-of-power concept is continuously disrupted by new situations which do not fit into accepted grooves or by some new encumbent in office who senses discriminatory growth in power by one of the other branches at the expense of his own branch of government. Complaints by members of Congress about the President or the Supreme Court depend on whether, for party or other reasons, they like or dislike what is being done by the executive or the court.

There seems to be little basis for the American people to anticipate a time when their government will be free from interbranch complaint and sniping. There are several reasons for this view. One is that governmental activity tends to be continuous in time and in scope of coverage. As government is asked to carry on more activities, any natural links or joints in the continuum increasingly fade. Thus, division of governmental function into three branches, or some other number, becomes increasingly artificial. As a society becomes more complex, more arguments can arise about fitting new relationships into the procrustean branch framework. But some kind of framework is necessary for there to be peace and lawfulness rather than social chaos.

Probably another reason for perennial complaint and sniping lies in human nature. Two aspects of human nature are indicated. One concerns man's limited capacity to handle difficult situations, including the development of varied modes of attack. The other aspect concerns a tendency to blame other persons for our collective failures, but to claim personal credit for our successes. Political parties often provide fertile territory for the operation of these characteristics.

The constructive role of educational and other formative agencies does not lie in withdrawing from the situation described, but in accepting responsibility for more direct and more extensive participation. The crux of that participation rests in developing and maintaining a high level of honesty and moral integrity on the part of the general population and in imbuing that population with a sense of personal responsibility to share in conducting governmental activities. Comment elsewhere has emphasized the magnitude of these two jobs and the role of educational, legal, and other institutions in the process.

3. The Public's Right to Know, and Competence for Knowing

Personal rights consist of particular relationships among individuals within the group; and such rights exist because the group has defined them, has made general pronouncements that they do exist, and stands ready to enforce them. The definition or pronouncement of rights assumes that there is competence and readiness on the part of the intended beneficiary to exercise the rights.

Thus, when the legal framework of a century ago established the right of children to free public education, it was assumed that the child was capable of learning and of benefitting in general from the school experience and that the family was able and ready to feed and clothe the child and get him to school. While the competency expectation and associated rights have been modified by subsequent developments concerning pupil transportation; immunizations, test scores, and other admission requirements; school feeding; special provisions for physically and mentally handicapped children; and other developments regarding school programs; the idea of a competency requirement for exercising the rights has not been eliminated. This point is frequently illustrated by court disputes over whether a particular child is legally entitled to bus transportation, free meals, special consideration accorded handicapped children, or whether he resides at a point which entitles him to attend a certain school.

Changes in Competencies and the Status of Rights

Preceding statements, regarding competence for exercising the right of attending a public school, apply essentially to the exercise of other rights. Nevertheless, consideration of an opposite approach asks in effect if improving or otherwise modifying one's competence entitles him to rights which previously were not available to him. The answer should be obvious in the case of a person who suffers permanent physical handicap because of an automobile accident. But does the same logic apply to one who has improved his competence to understand domestic or international economic and other relationships? For example, does such a person have a more inclusive right to know why government takes certain actions in these areas than a person who possesses less competence in this respect; or should the former have a greater voice in government than the latter? When only one or a few cases are involved, it may seem that rights should be commensurate with competence, in these cases as in those mentioned concerning public education. But complications arise when broad application of the idea is considered. The American Founding Fathers emphasized the need for raising the political competence of average persons, if government was to be determined by popular vote. Yet voting restrictions based on age, sex, property, and race rested on criteria of competence. The social stratifications of Europe rested on certain conceptions of competence to share in government. The same now largely applies behind the Iron Curtain, and to some extent elsewhere.

However, one should observe that at present the general educational level of the American people is appreciably higher than it was two centuries ago: much of the additional education through school programs concerns government and social relationships; the people travel more and in this way learn about conditions in various parts of the country; and through television and other mass media the general population has greater access to news and commentary than in the earlier days. The foregoing could be summarized by stating that the average American today has greater competence for understanding government potential and involvement than his counterpart had two centuries ago. But it should also be noted that the involvement of government in America has become more complicated.

One accompaniment of more widespread knowledge and understanding among present-day Americans, and of more complications in arriving at understanding, is greater demand to know who among public officials is doing what, why they are doing it, and what the results are. The demand for knowing applies to the courts, although perhaps *not yet* to the same extent that it applies to the other branches of government. The extensive communication between the courts and the public that is thus implied makes judicial aloofness seem anachronistic. Watergate indicates that the popular demand to know applies to the chief executive. The public schools have never operated in aloofness to the extent that the courts have, which is perhaps one reason why it is emphasized that the schools are public from standpoints other than tax support.

Right to Know and Responsibility to Act

Along with growing demand concerning right to know, should go a growing sense of responsibility for informed action. Without insistence on responsible action, the right to know may be merely a vent for idle curiosity and gossip. At the gossip level, knowing about the activities of public officials contributes little more to good government than knowing the results of golf competitions or dog races.

Should the right to know then be evaluated in terms of "readiness" to act responsibly, with readiness including both competence to act and willingness to do so? The problem involved has apparently been troublesome since the rise of organized government; that is, how to ensure efficient operation in government, without promoting self-interest and exploitation by public officials. As government becomes more involved, this continuing problem becomes more difficult.

Which Public?

Reference is often made to "the public" or "the public interest," as if the people constituted a homogeneous unity. Such a unity has obviously not existed during the milleniums when there have been wars and other struggles among groups. Struggles within large groups are in fact struggles among smaller groups or subgroups. Debates before legislative bodies are struggles between groups, and essentially the same applies to parties involved in court disputes. It also applies within the judiciary, at least regarding ideology, when reference is made to activist courts and conservative courts. Within any sizable group of professional educators, comparable subgroupings and struggles appear.

If "the public" at a specific time consists of such combinations of small shifting subgroups as are able at that time to agree sufficiently on a particular issue so as to dominate the others with respect to that issue, then certainly "the public" consists of different individuals whenever different issues arise. This situation can be recognized without proclaiming that the idea of "a public," with considerable ongoing stability, is entirely a myth.

The situation described is perhaps typical of human relationships in which matters of degree are usually involved and in which officials who make or who interpret the regulatory system speak of reasonableness. The operation has sometimes been characterized as cruising around in a large field where the borders are always uncertain and where there may be only a hazy inkling as to where the central focus is.

Perhaps in more concrete terms one might refer to "the public" as always embodying some degree of fluidity and note that shifts from little to great fluidity or to volatility can take place suddenly. Peaceful and violent revolutions usually illustrate volatility.

A dynamic society implies substantial volatility. But in any society some aspects are more volatile than others. Thus the American Revolutionary War shifted some aspects of politics, religion, and social class, but Americans retained the English language, the Anglo-Saxon system of jurisprudence, private property, weights and measures, and many concepts of personal rights.

With respect to a peaceful and law-abiding society or to crime in the streets, the idea that the American people in reality embody several "publics" rather than only one, means that in the continuous struggle for status among small groups or "local publics," those which seek peacefulness and law-abiding relationships must maintain the power to prevail—or there is no peace. Maintenance is a continuing job. In a society which encourages as many local groups and clubs as America does, and which permits a person to hold membership in several of them at the same time as well as to make easy transfer from one to another, the maintenance of a substantial degree of stability and of orderly change constitutes a bigger job than in a society which permits less personal freedom in the foregoing respects.

Young Americans should understand the foregoing relationship between the one and the many insofar as "the public," "public well-being," etc., are concerned. They should also understand that problems associated with the relationships are substantially products of the American system of personal freedoms, but that to some extent those problems exist under any type of social organization.

4. Democracy as America's True Religion

Since man is an organism which cannot exist without considerable integration among activities and aspirations, efforts to classify his ideals and hopes into distinct categories are somewhat arbitrary and overlapping. Part of the problems involved have been reflected in the cultural growth of the past millennium respecting such categories as family, religion, politics, business, education, and health. However, for attempts to compare two such categories it is necessary to have in mind a fairly stable conception of each category, including attention both to their core of similarities and their peripheral differences. Concern here with political and religious categories requires developmental observations regarding both of them.

Religious Developments

An initial consideration of religion in America involves denominationalism. The Founding Fathers had favorable things to say about God and about religion in a general or rather abstract sense, but great skepticism about religion as denominationalism. Yet, denominationalism is the usual way in which religion in America is institutionalized and made tangible through personal involvement. Government is concerned with similar relationships between institutionalization and personal involvement. Question thus arises about the personal-social nature of religious experience and of political experience.

It is obvious that if religion is manifested in a particular social situation, it is manifested by some person or persons. But this is much the same as saying that if a law is violated, some person violates it; if taxes are paid, somebody pays them; or if children attend school, some teacher is in charge of them. The fact that individuals violate laws, pay taxes, or attend school does not negate or belittle the related fact that it is only in a social setting that individuals are able to act in the ways indicated.

A crucial point then is whether an individual can be religious by himself, alone and apart from group or cultural influence or participation. If one notes that moral considerations and laws are prominent in religious doctrines and proclamations, for example in the code of Moses or in statements and proverbs set forth by other prophets, the social implications are obvious. Moral codes exist to govern relationships among people, and proverbs tend to become succinct or epigrammatic statements through the process of being polished and handed on by successive persons. Insofar as ritual is involved, formulas recited, tales narrated, holy days kept, specific places visited or avoided, there is the assumption of a performer-observer situation, or perhaps of some broader group relationship, with varying degrees of participation by different members of the group. Religious evangelism and camp meetings offer current illustrations of varying participation. Reference to law, church law or civil law, is clearly a reference to group regulation and control of the individual.

Another side of the story relates to a feeling of personal weakness in the face of difficulty. And the difficulty need not be social, at least not directly so. In a primitive or an advanced society a person might fear destruction through lightning, flood, fire, pestilence, earthquake, etc., without his recognizing any direct social causes. This situation continues to exist, although a technological culture recognizes communicable diseases, floods resulting from unsupervised timber cutting, forest fires due to negligent campers, etc.

Recognition of personal weakness and inadequacy suggests a greater power beyond man, which he may not understand but to which in desperation he may appeal. In his natural desire to arrive at explanations, it is easy for man to personify this unseen power in terms of a superman or god, since human embodiment is the most intimate form in which man has become acquainted with power. The phrase "God, the Father" may remind some persons of a psychiatric observation—that in religion, god is a father image; that is, kind, generous, and loving in some instances; harsh, demanding, and jealous of power or authority in other instances. While the individual may not need social reinforcement in order to sense personal inadequacy and fear in situations of the kind noted, a superman projection implies previous experience with men who vary in degrees of potence. And the father image reflects social relationships within the family.

In some connections religion has been referred to as prescience, in reflecting man's exercise of a natural curiosity and desire to explain through the use of symbols and parables, when he does not have adequate information or analytical competence to offer explanations in more precise or consistent ways. This view further maintains that what we now call science developed gradually out of the clouded situation indicated, through a succession of experiences; that is, experiences which added further information, then revised the explanation, and then again sought further information to check the revisions, and thus reflected a sort of continuous recycling process. When such a checking-revising process becomes fairly well systematized, it is called scientific method.

One of the difficult problems concerned in movement from prescience toward science, along lines such as noted, relates to the creation myths of most religions. These are efforts to indicate how things got started and to embody hints on how they may end. Defense of creation stories is usually in terms of divinely revealed knowledge, which is referred to as "beyond" the reach of other human inquiry. But as understanding and respect for scientific research and technology in America grow, including Biblical research and anthropological studies on religion, explanations based on revealed knowledge decline in status. A major difficulty in the scientific explanations of beginnings and ends is that science itself has up to the present not offered explanations which are particularly understandable or convincing. Thus, the immediate future promises substantial leeway for arguments, pulpit thumps, and laboratory fumes.

Political Democracy

When statements such as the foregoing on religion are thought of in relation to a democratic political system, several possible alternatives should be differentiated in trying to recognize common elements. If one considers *representative* democracy, which seems fairly common in the world today, he must recognize that the Greek idea of direct democracy, with all people of the community participating directly in essentially every community decision, is not workable as to populations which are large or widely dispersed in geography. He must also recognize the emergence of *totalitarian* democracies, in which government is avowedly *of* and *for* the people—but not *by* the people. Other considerations on democracy may relate to particular areas of a culture, such as political democracy, eceonomic democracy, religious democracy, educational democracy, ethnic democracy, etc.

Perhaps the extent to which religious denominationalism may be looked upon as representative or as totalitarian depends on how firm and jealous of power the governing philosophy considers the gods to be, in contrast with stressing forgiveness and compassion. Should the democratic state look upon the law as the iron framework of power and upon the correctional institutions and rehabilitation efforts as manifestations or forgiveness and compassion? Whether wayward members and behavioral deviants are looked upon as sinners, lost sheep, or public offenders, the prevailing system must find ways to deal with them or else suffer breakdown of the entire structure.

One thread that runs through most considerations on democracy relates to equality in opportunity and treatment of all members of the community; that is, regardless of such matters as sex, race, economic background, family lineage, political views, age, etc. And it implies that opportunity and treatment concerning participation in every department of public life is equally open to all members of society. Rousseau maintained that no man could be morally responsible or really consider himself to be a man, unless he participates in the formation of concensus in relation to the whole community. This somewhat formalized statement points to the mores as a body of values and practices that emerges out of the common life of the community, in which members actually participate in varying degrees, but in which all are presumed to have equal opportunity to participate.

With the development of knowledge in such areas as genetics and psychology, and with a growing recognition that statements by the Founding Fathers to the effect that all men are created equal have been significant as political metaphors but cannot be used as scientific guides, the popular vocabulary has shifted so as to tolerate preliminary implications of individual differences and hence to refer to equal opportunity for each to develop his potentialities. But thorny problems remain concerning such matters as differentiating between equality and identity of opportunity; types and extent of innate individual differences; the influence of education and other environmental conditions on the potential of different individuals; and personal recognition as being related to the contributions which society may reasonably expect from different persons.

An important type of confusion that appears among several of America's numerous minorities can be illustrated by reference to employment. When there is insistence on racial, sex, or other quotas of persons employed in particular types of work, without much regard to the knowledge and skill qualifications of the individuals concerned, the insistence is for economic and vocational disintegration rather than for growth and development. With broader recognition of this point, concern about equality may be shifting somewhat toward emphasis on equality through education or other means to become vocationally qualified, as preliminary to emphasis on obtaining particular jobs. Probably most observers of American life would note that since World War II there has been considerable equalizing of opportunity to become vocationally qualified, along the lines suggested, although occasionally the insistence by some court on "instant equality" as related to employment quotas may cast a shadow on the developmental process.

Evaluating the Status of American Democracy

While America's culture and its political system are not perfect, as judged by most theoretical treatises on democratic ideology, several considerations are essential in evaluating that culture. These must be considered relative to its own past, relative to other present-day cultures, and relative to its own trends concerning the future. Certain preceding comments make comparisons regarding the past.

With respect to personal satisfactions associated with one's current participation in a culture, much depends on the diversity and richness of the culture and on the availability of different avenues of participation. America now exceeds most countries in offering a range in such matters as the following: types of existing jobs; geographical climate and associated living conditions; educational opportunity; participation in civic and political life; health services; recreational opportunities; and freedom to move about regionally and socially.

Pioneer life in America may have afforded greater freedom from taxation and from several other present-day restrictions. But it also afforded greater opportunity to starve or die of disease without help from public services, to freeze in winter and swelter in summer, to get stuck in mudholes during attempts at short journeys, to sit and look at bare walls in poorly lighted homes during long winter evenings, to be free from contact with or participation in the news and events of the world, to be spared the excitement of sharing in the thrills of scientific and other exploration by one's countrymen, etc. The foregoing enumeration presents a few samples from an extensive repertoire of sharings and participations which help make present-day life in America more satisfying and culturally richer than in many parts of the world.

With respect to future trends, there are several developments in the nation which point toward greater equality of opportunity. Some of these relate to civil rights in voting and in holding public office; others to employment, education, place of residence, recreation, social mobility, etc. They also relate to sex, ethnic background, physical and mental handicap, rehabilitation from penal status, etc.

By direct statement and by implication, foregoing paragraphs have emphasized equality of opportunity as a major aspect of American democracy. Those paragraphs have thus reflected great support and amplification of Jefferson's faith in the common people and in their capacity to exercise sound judgment, when they are informed and are free to communicate with one another.

By comparison, one might inquire about the extent to which present-day churches promulgate religious doctrine and ritual that the common people of the present time have helped to work out. The sermons and associated ritual in most churches seem intended to persuade congregations to accept doctrines and practices which were developed some centuries ago, and on the basis of some combination of revealed insights and eternal verities to manifest reverence but not inquiry, concerning the field involved. While clergymen vary considerably in the scope of their personal efforts to interpret religious ideals in terms of current life in America, and representatives of most denominations have expanded their activities in this direction during the last few decades, such activities do not typically characterize the main thrust of their operations. The fact that affinity for revealed insights and eternal verities has a low order of priority or expectancy in the dynamic experimentalism of American democracy seems as yet to have made only a superficial impact. But perhaps mature reflection should observe that in education, religion, economics, politics, and other fields, the total operating personnel includes numerous slow learners.

Separation of Church and State

Much has been said in America about separation of church and state, and there has been extensive legislative debate and court action on the subject. Question has sometimes been raised about whether our legal framework has thus decreed separation regarding social interests and activities which cannot actually be separated.

Part of the confusion may result from inadequate attention to what the legal framework actually provides. It should be noted that the provision is not for a separation of *religion* and state, but a separation of *church* and state. It would be unrealistic to assume that religion is the only interest of individual churches or of church hierarchies. Most church hierarchies are interested in exercising power, and probably in a substantial measure use religion as a secondary or ancillary means of getting at major economic, political, or military avenues to power. In significant respects it seems that the scope and duration of a hierarchy is related to its power status.

In reference to church versus religion in America, it seems feasible to equate "church" with "denominationalism" and in a substantial way to equate denominationalism with hierarchal status and power. The view suggested enables one to look upon the pronouncements of most Founding Fathers on such matters as God, the Christian Bible, Jesus, and the religious anchorage of the nation as being consistent with their attacks on the organized church. It might be noted that the struggle by Jefferson and Madison in Virginia, before the religious controversy arose regarding the federal Constitution, did not relate to the Roman Catholic Church—which became strong only with later immigration—but to conflict among Protestant denominations. The doctrine of separation was looked upon as a major instrument in protecting individual freedom against encroachment by a politico-ecclesiastical power complex, such as prevailed in most of Western Europe at that time.

Nevertheless, any organized state must be concerned about the moral codes and social regulations which govern its people. In this area there is great overlapping between the interests of the organized state and the interests of organized religion. Thus, in America there are both political and religious sanctions against murder and against lesser attacks by an individual upon his neighbor or on his neighbor's possessions. Positive behavior is also prescribed by both, such as obedience to the moral code, whether the prescription is set forth as a legislative enactment or extolled as a commandment of God. In comparable vein, other areas of dual interest relate to the wellbeing of other persons, whether embodied as public-welfare legislation or as admonition to do unto others as one would like for them to do unto him. Other areas which are essential to both the state and religion could be added. An earlier comment emphasized the essentiality of these areas to the organized state. One current basis of criticizing religious activities for emptiness or irrelevance is their meager concern for service in the areas inferred; that is, in areas which the people consider to be important. It involves minimal concern about good works or the social gospel as exemplified here, but maximal concern about doctrines focused on a hereafter.

From the practical standpoint, one should recognize that American pioneers were not as materially affluent as their present-day cultural descendants are. This situation was reflected in the limited ability of pioneers to provide separate material facilities to serve different types of community interests. Accordingly, one community meetinghouse often functioned as church, school, and town hall, to serve religious, educational, and civic needs—such as were judged by the community to be appropriate. This arrangement was more common in some regions than in others, but it seemed to exist to some extent throughout the country and seemed to move westward with popular settlement. During recent decades it has not been unusual for public schools and religious groups to use each other's facilities, on something resembling an emergency basis. But recent court disputes on new variants concerning the overlapping use of personnel on a continuing basis, or on tax concessions for tuition paid by parents to parochial school, illustrate the sensitive problems now involved in separating church and state.

Faith in Religion, Politics, and Other Aspects of the Culture

In religious literature and preaching, extensive emphasis is placed on faith. Earlier comment in the present discussion mentioned the faith of Jefferson and others in the common people to govern themselves and to build a civilization in the American wilderness. One might also refer to the faith of Horace Mann (1796-1859) in free public education, of Horace Greeley (1811-1872) in the possibilities of western development, of Abraham Lincoln (1809-1865) in the potentialities of free negroes, of Edward Henry Harriman (1848-1909) in American transcontinental railroading, of John D. Rockefeller (1839-1937) in an American petroleum industry, of Woodrow Wilson (1856-1924) in a League of Nations, of Franklin D. Roosevelt (1882-1945) in the economic future of a depression-ridden nation, of Albert Einstein (1879-1955) in the theory of relativity, of NASA personnel and astronauts in possible space travel beyond the moon, etc.

Should one ask in what ways the faith of these men concerning various aspects of American democracy and culture was different, in origin and nature, from the faith shown by Paul of Tarsus (?-67?) in his missionary travels for preaching Christianity in the eastern Mediterranean, from that shown by Francis of Assisi (1182-1226) in establishing the Franciscan monastic order, from that of Western leaders during the Crusades (11th-13th centuries A.D.) who butchered Turks for the grace of God and "recovery of the Holy Land," from that of the world's great evangelists, or from that of leaders currently attracting attention through the religious quarrel in Northern Ireland or in India?

Nature and Operation of Faith

Faith can be looked upon as a projection from a present base toward something which is conceived to be different and better or to be in some ways desirable to attain. This includes persistence and motivation toward attaining the goal implied. The psychology of projection is about the same in all of the instances previously noted, with differences in the goals and the associated strengths of motivation.

Methods of procedure in attempting to implement action toward achieving the faith-goal depend on the operating tools which the culture of the time makes available. When Paul was preaching Christianity to the Corinthians, Thessalonians, and others, he did not travel by airplane or speak in large stadiums over television, as Billy Graham does in America and abroad. When Pope Urban II in 1096 called for the First Crusade, with the admonition that God Wills It, he was probably using the most potent instrument of agitation and propaganda that the culture then afforded. During World War II this country pursued the Manhattan Project of developing the atom bomb, substantially with the idea that American survival demanded it. This project, as well as recent space explorations, shows how technology is now employed to design specific tools for promoting certain orientations of faith. Both Manhattan and space work indicate extensive retooling in the area of propaganda since the days of Urban II.

Progressive aspirations and projections of faith are always made from successive past achievements or frustrations, as useful new bases or points of departure. It is easy to see this in the case of railroading, surgery and organ transplants, or ambitions to probe space beyond the moon through using manned vehicles. Success in the area of religious faith has often been gauged in terms of converts and cathedral-building. Teachers and guidance workers often expatiate on minute achievements of slow learners and handicapped children, as instruments of motivation and hope. Some of the same technique is used in rehabilitating public offenders, to rekindle their faith in the social order of which they went afoul and to seek out fragments on which to base encouragement.

A related feature of the hope and faith, embodied in projections of the kind mentioned, concerns a practical orientation as to what else there is to do that is equally or more challenging. The extreme of this feature may be desperation, such as the effort of prisoners in war camps or elsewhere to attempt escape in the face of what seem to be impossible odds. Perhaps suicide lies further down any road which is empty of definable challenge.

Probably as most persons move into and through adult life, they can recall persons, institutions, and activities or movements as earlier focal points of great faith and promise regarding future strengths and developments, but regarding which the outcomes were disappointing. This has related to faith in gods, relationships between parents and children, the potential of scientific method, the future reign of international peace or of domestic law and order, the concept of progress, and many other types of interest to which projected development and faith have been attached. Watergate scandals, police briberies, and partisan politics in court appointments often produce disappointments respecting faith in the integrity of individuals who hold high public office, particularly in regard to their value as models to emulate. The disappointments radiate into skepticism of democratic institutions with which such officials are associated. The text of the present study makes specific references to this situation with respect to members of law-enforcement agencies and of the judiciary.

Blind and Enlightened Faith

A basic question, about the disappointments noted, relates to blind faith and to a general popular responsibility to keep faith enlightened and thus to recognize its possibilities and its limitations. Problems of continuously scrutinizing and updating faith to keep it viable thus follow the same developmental or evolutionary pattern noted in early sections of the present study. Among the problems is the anticipation of some error and disappointment, as a result of faith that is too blind, but a recognition that systematic analysis and other aspects of scientific method offer clues for reducing the frequency and the seriousness of error.

Important in the analysis is due consideration of probable obstacles. For example, in the area of social and political reform, Western culture shows that the lot of a reformer is often a hard lot. Most Americans know in general about the life and death of Socrates and of Jesus. Some know about John Huss (1369?-1415) who was burned at the stake in Bohemia by the church for efforts at religious reform, and about the struggles and escape problems of Martin Luther (1483-1546), associated with similar reform efforts. People in this country are quite generally familiar with the experience of Roger Williams (1603?-1683) and of Anne Hutchinson (1591-1643) in Colonial New

England, and indeed with the experiences of two Kennedy brothers and of Martin Luther King during the nation's recent history. And few Americans could have missed the answer which Russian tanks recently gave to reform efforts in Czechoslovakia, thus recycling the Soviet pattern noted in Poland, Hungary and East Germany. Although the foregoing illustrations may seem dramatic, lesser instances abound in man's continuous struggle to reform his system of social regulation.

While the difficulties involved are many and hard to predict, even in a society which shows considerable tolerance for change within a preestablished theoretical framework, the value of insight based on comprehensive knowledge and analysis seems apparent. So does the importance of a high level of dedication, which must rest on faith. The democratic ideal of a right to speak out and express one's views on social and political reform runs through all foregoing instances, from the hemlock poison of Socrates to the Russian tanks in Czechoslovakia.

Earning or Deserving Faith and Devotion

For some people the reference to Jesus in the preceding connection indicates overlap between Christian and democratic idealism. Earlier comment noted the basic requirement of a body of common ideals and practices for effectiveness in government and in religion. It might be added that whether human needs are met by religious or by political institutions—as concerning needs for food, shelter, mental health, employment, peace and security on the streets, etc.—will probably impress average persons as less important than that those needs are actually met and that they are met at reasonable cost in personal freedom, material demands, general regimentation, etc.

With the rapid expansion in recognized human needs which was initiated by the economic depression of the early 1930's, and with subsequent expansion in conception of what is needed in order to live decently, the needs have increasingly exceeded the imagination and the material resources which religious agencies had previously embodied regarding their affiliates. Also, large numbers of persons without church affiliation became needy. Recent disaster-aid and other allocations update and expand the picture. In some cultures such affected persons are likely to be forced into a denominational mold, with church grip tightened on other persons, by the state making its funds available for distribution through church machinery. Along with strong traditions opposing such procedure in America, there have been constitutional provisions and court rulings on separating church and state—with associated complaints about breaking down the "wall of separation."

One consequence of the situation described has been a transfer to the state of much of the faith which individuals previously had that religious organizations would come to their aid when they were really in need. Another aspect of the American mores which contributes satisfaction in the transfer noted has been the freedom which the people in general feel to attack the government and its operation and to indicate "how things ought to be run," without popular faltering or getting bogged down in any haze or pretense about divine inspiration or eternal damnation.

However, one area in which the state has been slow to deal effectively with need is mental health and the various related problems involving personal psychology. In many instances religious confessionals and pastoral visits have probably rendered important service in this connection. The extent to which previous religious conditioning and indoctrination contributed to developing the problems involved is less widely heralded.

Emphasis on democratic ideals of personal freedom and equality of opportunity, as formally stipulated by legislation and court rulings and as informally practiced by the people while personal affluence and social mobility expands their participation in a richly diversified culture, continuously generates greater faith and dedication in support of the democratic state.

Democracy and the Nation's True Religion

Through the immediately foregoing statements, and throughout most of the entire study, runs the idea that the faith, loyalty, and dedication manifested by the people in general toward particular individuals or institutions must be earned or deserved. This point was noted particularly with respect to court imagery in America and the behavior of certain members of the judiciary. The idea also applies to other social institutions, either as initially established or as subsequently maintained.

Christianity arose largely on the promise of new service and new hope for man and a lightening of his burdens. The same applies to many of the denominational splinters, within the broader Christian fold, that have appeared in America.

But institutions can become embalmed in ritual and doctrine, direct their energies primarily toward internal hierarchy, property, or material power, and forget about service to the people. When they do so, they forfeit any right to material or other support from the people. Under any kind of social or governmental structure, the people will be the final judges of where faith, support, and devotion shall reside.

Popular judgment is likely to be rendered most quickly, and perhaps most painlessly, in a democratic society which provides extensively for education, for academic freedom and for freedom of speech and association in other settings, and for equality of personal status. In America, judgment and dedication fostering democratic idealism and its implementation, rather than church denominationalism and its associated practice, does much to make democracy the real religion of the people.

FOOTNOTES AND REFERENCES

1. See Edward Allen Tamm, "Are Courts Going the Way of the Dinosaurs?" *American Bar Association Journal* 57 (Mar. 1971): 228.

2. In his analysis and evaluation of experience in a Nazi concentration camp, Frankl emphasized hope for a better future, which he constructed out of pre-camp experience, as the theme around which he organized his camp life and was thus able to survive through increasing intensity of deprivation and torture. He looked upon the establishment of meaningful rela-

tionships as essential to sanity. (Frankl, Viktor E., *Man's Search for Meaning.* N.Y.: Pocket Books, Simon & Schuster, Inc., 1973 printing, pp. xiii, 266).

3. Robert W. Meserve, "The Legal Profession and Watergate," *American Bar Association Journal* 59 (Sept. 1973): 985.

4. Cf. Gabriel W. Lasker, ed., *The Process of Ongoing Human Evolution* (Detroit: Wayne State University Press, 1960).

5. Hugo Adam Bedau, "The Death Penalty in America," *Federal Probation* 35 (June 1971): 32.

6. Cf. "What About the Victims? Compensation for the Victims of Crime," *North Dakota Law Review* 48 (Sept. 1972): 473; H. Edelpherz, G. Geis, and D. Chappell, "Public Compensation of the Victims of Crime: a Survey of the New York Experience," *Criminal Law Bulletin* 9 (Jan.-Feb., Mar. 1973): 5, 101.

7. One type of development has been indicated by LeRoy L. Lamborn, "The Methods of Governmental Compensation of Victims of Crime," *Law Forum* (U. of Ill.) 1971: 655. See also: James Brooks, "Compensating Victims of Crime: The Recommendations of Program Administrators," *Law and Society Review* 7 (Spring 1973): 445; Richard O. Hawkins, "Who Called the Cops: Decisions to Report Criminal Victimization," *Law and Society Review* 7 (Spring 1973): 427.

8. Sidney Hook, "The Emerging Rights of the Victims of Crime," *The Florida Bar Journal* 46 (Apr. 1972): 192.

9. Mike Mansfield, "Justice for the Victims of Crime," *Houston Law Review* 9 (Sept. 1971): 53.

10. Richard O. Hawkins, *op. cit.*

11. Cf. M. K. Block and G. L. Long, "Subjective Probability of Victimization and Crime Levels: an Economic Approach," *Criminology* 11 (May 1973): 87.

12. Walter J. Blum, "Victims of Crime and other Victims," *Chicago Bar Record*, June 1971, p. 463.

13. LeRoy L. Lamborn, *op. cit.*

14. James Brooks, *op. cit.*

15. Comment, "Crime Victims: Recovery for Police Inaction and Underprotection," *Law and the Social Order* 1970: 279.

16. John W. Cooley, "Trial Delay Indemnity—Insuring our Criminal Justice Machinery," *Notre Dame Lawyer* 48 (Apr. 1973): 936.

17. LeRoy L. Lamborn, *op. cit.*

18. John W. Cooley, *op. cit.*

19. Chief Justice Berger, "The State of the Judiciary—1970," *American Bar Association Journal* 56 (Oct. 1970): 930.

EPILOGUE

INTRODUCTION

To a considerable extent this study emphasizes the idea that the development and maintenance of a regulatory system, which seeks to maximize the amount of personal freedom that is possible in organized society, is the most important single function of government in a democratic society. The study recognizes that the goal stated has many ramifications, in regard to some of which the citizen must carry extensive personal responsibility, at the same time that major collective responsibility is placed on certain institutions.

While it may be easy to indicate the general importance of perspective and reasonableness in developing and operating a regulatory system, it is essential to point out conflict situations through which such concepts as perspective and reasonableness develop their significance. It is also essential to recognize that basic conflicts in goals and procedures arise in any type of social organization, and that resolving such conflicts necessarily results in modification of the governing structure.

The study attempts to present and review materials which reflect varying degrees of specificity, in the hope of contributing to the development of the perspective and reasonableness mentioned. This epilogue includes two categories of presentation, in the further attempt at this concluding point to contribute to that development. These categories are styled: (1) specific action implications; (2) broader and more inclusive considerations.

1. Specific Action Implications

Several areas of need as well as suggestions for remedial action, concerning lawlessness in America, are noted as follows.

Types of Crime and Causal Factors

In the United States, many forms and causes of crime are interdependent. Hence, remedial efforts must be comprehensive in design and implementation. Various educational, judicial, correctional, employment, religious, civic, and other areas of the culture should therefore participate in working out the design. They should also divide operational responsibility, according to material resources and specialized competencies.

Titular leadership for project undertakings should probably rest with the agency which has the most direct responsibility or the most resources. But variation among communities ordinarily means considerable variation in where designated leadership does actually rest. More important than titular leadership is real leadership competence. Where title and competence do not coincide, the burden for insightful operation rests on the competent. They are most able to look beyond immediate personal credit or recognition, to broader collective well-being.

Perhaps in numerous situations, coordination within particular states might be initiated by the state superintendent of schools, the state attorney general, and some outstanding labor leader. Civic and religious organizations might be able to offer constructive leadership. In most extensive undertakings, various echelons of leadership are required. Also, it is important for numerous persons to be engaged in operations at the end of the performance line, rather than only at some level of supervision.

Basic Role of Popular Education and of Teacher Competence

There should be no hesitance about recognizing education at the most fundamental approach, provided one's conception of educatin is sufficiently broad. The conception must include the entire population from the kindergarten throughout life, with needs and obligations tailored according to age, vocation, and civic status, and somewhat according to sex or minority status.

(1) *Areas of emphasis in popular education.* The American educational system justifiably places emphasis on English grammar and composition, and from the kindergarten through the college there are compulsory courses and study programs in this area.

In our growing social complexity with a continuously expanding system of regulations, is there comparable justification for compulsory effort at securing general understanding of rule by law and a general sense of duty to accept and to promote such rule?

With respect to both the status of the language and the status of the law, there is both personal usefulness and group necessity. Before the American people became vigorous about establishing public schools and developing universal literacy, roughly 150 years ago, illiterates who had never studied the language found ways to communicate. And lawlessness was probably no more universal and no more overt than it is now.

It has been noted that in America broad civic education was the ground initially emphasized for taxation to support public schools. Comparable service to the state through some avenue of civic service is also the present ground for tax exemptions accorded religious and eleemosynary agencies.

One deduction from preceding comment is that our educational concern for a general understanding of the law with a sense of duty to support it or to modify it through regularized channels has not kept pace with our concern about effective use of the English language, vocational competence, provision for handicapped persons, or several other aspects of cultural change.

(2) *Shared responsibility in achieving the needed popular education.* With respect to operating procedures, emphasis has been placed on the responsibility of universities in developing teacher understanding and teaching com-

petence, so that teachers can develop in gradually maturing learners a sense of the place of government by law in American life. Comparable reference was made to boards and administrators, as to opportunity and encouragement for teachers to exercise a broader competence in classroom and other learning situations.

Textbook publishers might ask themselves whether their long-run net profit and business status would be improved by accepting less net income from publishing school and college texts and readers in the area concerned, if they pay less in taxes to reduce crime or if they suffer less in direct loss through vandalism, arson, or other lawlessness.

Television networks might present "specials" on popular responsibility for understanding and promoting law and order in America's industrial democracy, perhaps as compared with practices in some other countries. The utilization of educators, criminologists, employment agencies, judicial and correctional personnel, etc., in connection with such presentations would seem to be expected. Such presentations might be more constructive than detailed factual reporting by networks on prison riots or breakouts, with little attention in such reporting to causes or to remedial possibilities.

Attention by civic clubs, women's organizations, and similar groups might focus on two avenues of approach: general concern about the need for the education indicated, and sponsorship of specific projects. Both approaches could be developed so as to direct attention to conditions in the local communities in which the club groups function. Aid from nationwide or perhaps international representation of such club groups might be helpful in several ways, especially with regard to perspective.

Perhaps many church groups could find organized effort, concerning lawlessness and pertinent understanding along with remedial suggestions, to constitute one of the more effective ways to make a difference in their respective communities. Several of the teachings by Jesus and other religious leaders, of both Christian and non-Christian orientation, could be quite helpful in this connection. One might note that during the past decade several religious leaders have been active in this direction, both Christian and non-Christian, in America and elsewhere.

Fantastic Individualism

There is a kind of exaggerated, irresponsible, arrogant, and perhaps wanton individualism abroad in America, which is rather basically opposed to regulation of the individual by the group and broadly opposed to the assumption that all such regulation should be for the well-being of the group as typically symbolized by the majority.

A fundamental assumption, which is largely a product of fantasy, is that the natural state of man is one of personal freedom and that any effort to modify that freedom has a burden of showing how the modification would benefit the majority in ways which are *commensurate* with the restrictions placed on the individual. The idea of "commensurate" is not the only slippery spot in the assumption. Man's natural state was one involving a relentless search for food, a continuous struggle against physical forces and competitive species for survival, extensive suffering from disease, and victimization by other manifestations of ignorance and isolation.

It was when individuals began to cooperate and to pool their intellectual and other resources that collective development appeared which benefitted individuals. This collective feature appears in group cooperation in the hunt for food, tribal war of defense or aggression, tribal dances and other recreation, and the development of language and other symbolic communications.

In present-day America, the collective feature appears in all of our institutionalized activities, as well as in many others. Thus, reference might be made to "public service" rendered to individuals concerning education, health, housing, transportation, jobs and vocations, food inspection and distribution, police protection and national defense, etc.

It is largely because of these collective developments that the individual is able to survive earliest infancy and to participate in what most youth and adults call enjoyments.

Perhaps two major notes should be mentioned concerning the American doctrine about primacy of the individual. One is a kind of biologically inherent selfishness, to the effect that most persons do not like to have their impulses interfered with, if they can avoid it without putting forth so much effort as to make opposition counterproductive. The other note concerns fantasies or myths which the more influential among the Founding Fathers incorporated into basic documents during the establishment of the republic; although at the time when they were propounding the doctrine of individualism, they spent several years in struggle to develop enough collectivism so that, to cite Benjamin Franklin: they would hang together rather than hang separately. Generations subsequent to the founders have been concerned primarily with mouthing the early proclamations, not with analyzing them.

While exaggerated individualism may be looked upon as somewhat primitive among cultural traits, it is basic in the general lawlessness of the American people and in the broad retinue of problems that we have concerning our regulatory structure.

Remodeling of the attitudes and value background demands a comprehensive approach to matters of innate selfishness and to its subsequent expansion through catering to it more largely than reshaping it by cultural developments. This is an important reason for emphasis on the process of general understanding and value development, from early childhood throughout life. However, one should probably anticipate some struggle in formulating criteria for designating persons and materials to be given priorities in the process.

Remodeling and Expanding Our System of Rewards for Service

One gesture on remodeling, variously mentioned within the study, relates to developing greater interest and status concerning nonmaterial rewards for outstanding service and achievement. More specific reference was made to medals and honors awards.

Complications arise when one asks what makes a reward material. Is it material only when it is in the form of money or of tangible property or assets which can readily be turned into money? But political influence or character reference may play a role in who gets desirable jobs or who gets "reconsideration" concerning undesirable penalties or social demands.

Does the foregoing mean that there actually is no reward, unless there is some tangible difference between givers or receivers of the reward as constituting one group of persons in terms of the particular situation at hand, with persons who are not givers or receivers, concerning this particular situation, constituting another group? The situation may relate to scores in a tennis game, votes in a political campaign, teacher approval in a second-grade class, subscription in a community-chest or other charitable "drive," evangelistic activity regarding religious converts, the status of affection between parents and their children, appropriate or appreciated gifts for friends, etc.

The preceding may be manifestations of an old problem: must anything that exists actually exist in some quantity, although people may not be able to measure the quantity and, in many cases, may not even be aware of the existence? When quantity is humanly recognizable, does value become attached to possessing it or to avoiding it? Then do particular things, manifestations of status, etc., which some people seek, constitute matters which others desire to avoid?

The situation described indicates that considerations concerning rewards, which are suitable to motivate effort toward socially desirable accomplishments, involve numerous complications. As a society becomes more rich and varied in possible motivations and achievements, the complications become greater. This implies the exercise of considerable imagination to devise new rewards for which men will work, in the new kinds of situations that arise. Thus, substantial individualization of rewards according to socially desirable accomplishments is inferred, yet they must not be so highly individualized that they cannot be understood or appreciated except by a very small number of people. So in the final analysis, any kind of reward actually lies in the response of people whom the recipient considers to be important.

A pertinent social question then becomes: with regard to moral integrity in government, constructive use of leisure time, dedication to vocational service, relationships among members of the family, physical and mental disciplines of one's personal organism relative to functionality and longevity, etc., should organized society consciously direct a substantial amount of creative imagination into developing rewards which stimulate men to reach farther and farther into the unknown? To what extent is natural curiosity an adequate stimulus for this purpose? What is the function of research and invention in the sphere characterized?

When boredom, a desire for thrills and "kicks," etc., are important as immediate causal factors in lawlessness, developments in the area inferred deserve considerable attention. Guidance activities of numerous youth organizations point in the directions suggested, provided the activities involved do not in themselves become routine and boring. The percentage of criminals, especially first-time offenders, who are between about sixteen and twenty-two years of age, implies that our schools, youth organizations, employment agencies, etc., have not been doing an adequate job concerning such persons. To paraphrase President Kennedy, concerning youth and their elders, it's time for America to get going again. To reduce boredom as a cause of lawlessness, a dynamic society must continuously provide more stimulating and more satisfying things to do. This demands continuous but graduated expansion in knowledge, vocational potentialities, availability of goods and services, money supply, recreational possibilities, involvement in world affairs, man's power regarding natural forces in the universe, etc.

The basic comment thus becomes: fight crime by reducing boredom, and reduce boredom by providing challenges to youth and others through interesting and socially fruitful activities. The pattern suggested has never been thoroughly understood by any society. The rate of social change in America and the role of adventure and related achievement in the nation's history and mores mean that America will have to assume pioneering responsibility in the area of inspiration indicated, or deteriorate through the lawlessness and waste of human potential that is associated with boredom.

Many teachers are aware of the role of boredom in classroom discipline and learning. Awareness needs to be extended to all age levels and to all aspects of the culture, and it needs to be activated into operating programs if significant progress is to be made in reducing lawlessness and associated waste in the nation. The status of respect for the nation's economic and political system is more a result than a cause of the delinquency situation noted.

The Courts and Popular Education

The study has variously referred to communication between the judiciary and the public. The comment has mentioned addresses by members of the judiciary to various civic and professional groups in nonlegal fields, and public-relations approaches through the press and other mass media have been noted. The possibility of a special public-relations person attached to the court was mentioned. Important among things to be communicated are such matters as what the functions of the courts are in the American social structure and how well the speaker as a member of the judiciary thinks the courts are performing those functions. Also important is an explanation in lay terms of the most significant portions of complicated decisions.

The underlying principle is that lay understanding is essential to favorable court imagery, and that favorable imagery is essential for optimum translation of court decisions into community behavior.

Science and the Criminal Code

Much can be said for a more scientific development of criminal codes. This implies greater sociological and economic consideration of causal factors in crime and sharpens differentiation between misbehavior which results in the injury or death of persons or in damages to property and misbehavior which results in none of these outcomes. Discussion in this book's text refers to drunkenness and certain other forms of misbehavior as illustrative of the point mentioned. Revising the code so as to decriminalize behavior of this kind could free the police and the courts from a burden of relatively unimportant matters so that they could focus on serious commitments against persons (assault, robbery, murder) or against property (arson, bombing, looting).

What is referred to as a scientific approach would also relate to penalties for offenses and to corrections, rehabilitation, parole, etc. Psychological considerations respecting deterrents and remedial possibilities are prominent in the foregoing connection, as are economic considerations regarding the cost in time and materials for personnel engaged in police, court, and prison service.

Furthermore, as social relationships among people change, some types of offenses which may have been important at one stage in cultural evolution essentially disappear at a later stage, and new offenses appear. Horse stealing and the general field of vehicular traffic may illustrate the point. Consolidations and revisions of the criminal code, more often than they ordinarily occur, might make it easier for both laymen and members of the legal profession to keep up with what the law actually is.

Economics and the Prison-Correction System

Another possibility regarding crime and prison experience relates more to the economic implications of prison life, than to the revenge features of penal treatment or the correctional and rehabilitation features associated with possible return to free civilian life in the community. It is concerned especially with persons under long-term or life sentences.

The economic consideration relates to the production of goods and services by offenders who are under sentence, for parallel and competitive sales' status in the marketplace with the output produced by the general nonprison population. Two major economic considerations are noted. One is aside from therapeutic or rehabilitative features of a prisoner having a job, at which he produces something which is useful in the outside world and which connects him with that world. It concerns various economic costs of prison riots and of maintaining relative peace and order within a concentration of substantially bored and maladjusted persons. It also takes economic cognizance of the fact that the vocational training often afforded inmates in prisons relates to jobs within the prison rather than to jobs in the outside world and to operations by technically obsolete methods. Offsetting the implications for updating this situation is the cost of changes in equipment associated with keeping abreast of current industrial procedures in the general employment world. Related to this problem is a suggestion reported in the study, of different prisons specializing in different kinds of service. The suggestion implies the transfer of inmates to particular institutions, according to their interests, competencies, and needs, as judged by staff personnel.

The other economic consideration relates to feared competition, emphasized probably by organized labor outside the prison, if there is a flow of production into the marketplace from prison sources where costs are subsidized by public funds. Perhaps the type of competition inferred can be illustrated by a contract between an outside corporation and the prison employment service for a specified number of identical items, produced essentially on a piecework basis.

Three points are noted. Perhaps least important among the three is the extent to which the goods now produced through prison facilities as suggested are redistributed for use by other prisons or similar public institutions. The second point concerns the percentage of the nation's productive capacity that is reflected by production through prison settings. The third point relates to a constriction in leadership imagination, insofar as it is unable to conceive of a nationwide expansion in goods and services so that the total market can absorb the small percentage increase in the total which might have prison origin. The latter comment is not unmindful of the fact that in a free-market economy, a small surplus or small shortage in some particular area may substantially affect prices in that area.

With direct reference to the mechanics and administration of feasible production within the prison framework, one should consider the "sheltered workshop" concept as a possible continuous productive operation for offenders who are under long-term sentences. For some time, the "sheltered workshop" idea has been employed in institutions for physically and mentally handicapped persons, with varying degrees of economic success and general public acceptance. To some extent problems concerning disposal of products through the free marketplace have been involved. One of the less advertised aspects of the operation is the reduction in taxes to maintain the institution, as a consequence of the value of goods which it sells. Political considerations are of course involved, concerning who pays taxes versus whose jobs are challenged. However, the general workshop idea might be examined with respect to long-term incarcerated persons who are under pronounced civilian handicaps.

Morality and Government

In a rather direct sense the concept of morality comes from the sociological term *mores*, and embodies a type of condensate or distillate from those customs and folk practices of the group which are looked upon as important for group survival and well-being. Hence, moral behavior is socially approved behavior; and as a society becomes more populous and engages in more varied types of behavior, a network of approved action develops and becomes a moral code. Ordinarily, persons who achieve leadership status in the group have been outstanding in exemplifying the disciplines and behavior which the code proclaims. They thus become models for others to emulate.

It is through considerations of the type indicated that concerns about moral integrity in government have their anchorage. The anchorage is especially important in a democratic society, in which the people in general are presumed to exercise substantial peaceful influence on their government. One point of especial importance in American democracy is the idea that the same law applies to everybody and that nobody is above that law. This is a major foundation for other ideals about equality.

It is essentially because of the situation described that publicized investigations on Watergate, as a top-level affront to the idealism embodied in the code, has major educational importance for the American people. It may also have kindred importance for people in some other parts of the world. An objective and detailed review of the Watergate phenomenon may thus do more to strengthen America's status in the world during the next few generations than loans and other material aid to large and small countries of opposing or dubious political orientation.

One related point in the American system requires further comment. It concerns the way in which we get our candidates for public office and then the way we choose among candidates. The system fails to differentiate between the competence required to run a successful campaign and the competence needed for rendering effective service as a public official. The idea has in part been reflected by noting that elected officials have legislative and administrative power to set up licensing and other requirements to be met by workers in numerous categories of service. So why not set up comparable requirements for candidates; that is, requirements other than general considerations of age, citizenship, place of residence—and vote-getting ability? Qualifications with respect to licensing teachers, physicians, barbers, lawyers, and persons in many other types of service, are quite different from the qualifications which were considered necessary at the time that our governmental framework was established. So too are the requirements for exercising intelligent legislative and administrative power, as previously noted. It would be an asset to the American people if Watergate inquiries led to an exploration of such related matters bearing on candidates.

Special Days for Emphasizing "Law and Order"

Special reference is sometimes made to "law day," presumably as a day when emphasis through public addresses and other avenues is given to the nature of America's legal structure and to ways to protect and improve that structure. Much can perhaps be accomplished through one-day program concentrations, provided they are designed so that their impact is on a continuing basis.

However, the memories of most persons are rather short, especially when there is a broad range of daily impressions which flows through consciousness. Additional programs or focal days of emphasis may thus seem desirable, with some rather effective distribution over the year. Considerable of what is inferred takes place on Independence Day (July 4). To some extent Thanksgiving Day might serve a similar purpose. Gradual focus of attention on two additional days which are strategically located with respect to the calendar, making four in all, would seem to be a reasonable initial suggestion. Perhaps one such day might be called "Supreme Court Day," or one might be called "Legislative Accountability Day." Additional days and designations could be useful.

Research Needs and Prospects

In any culture the people could probably make better use than they do of the information which they already have. But often the best way to do this is to secure new information and integrate it with information that already exists. From this and other standpoints, development in any area of a culture is associated with growth of knowledge in that area. A few areas concerned with lawlessness, in which research might seem quite fruitful, are therefore indicated.

(1) Through case studies and related avenues, there has been considerable research on types of crime according to such matters as age, sex, race, employment or economic status, and education.

Information in such areas might be supplemented by further study on the place or locale at which offenses tend to be committed, holiday relationships involved, time of day or season of the year most often involved, or relationships between crime and economic cycles.

(2) What results accompany guidance efforts; as, for example, regarding the extent and content of such efforts, the preventive versus remedial intent of the efforts, and when the efforts are made? With the high percentage of first-time offenders being sixteen to twenty-two years of age, preventive effort seems especially important for work in educational institutions.

(3) How can we best develop in the general public a greater acceptance of the idea of crime prevention instead of remedial treatment, with a willingness to invest money and time in various kinds of experimental efforts in the preventive area? America's broad acceptance of the experimental method in other areas of the culture should be an asset in this connection.

(4) With respect to jobs and employment, three notes are emphasized:

(a) How can we get schools and employers to work more closely in identifying and creating part-time work possibilities for students?

(b) How can we assure established employees in industry of personal safety and self-respect when recent offenders become their co-workers?

(c) How should employers budget production costs which may be related to needs for employee guidance and protection or to decreased efficiency in output, etc.? Consideration for tax allowances relative to "rehabilitation outlays" might here be taken into account.

(5) Modifications in child-labor laws and perhaps in some conceptions of compulsory school attendance seem desirable, so as to permit greater flexibility in utilizing employment as a means of helping adolescents progress toward social maturity.

(6) What kinds of qualifications reflected by police, correctional, or other personnel who are officially responsible for dealing with offenders actually make a difference in the results achieved? This includes such matters as personal traits, formal education, experience, philosophy of "law and order,"

etc. It also includes orientation on what may be expected in different kinds of offender situations and on how to deal with those situations.

(7) How can court procedures be speeded up and punishment for crime be made more certain and more speedy? This point emphasizes the idea that a peaceful and law-abiding society demands that justice be prompt and certain.

(8) Further study should be helpful as to *when* punishment is a deterrent to criminality. This implies attention to the type, promptness, and certainty of punishment as related to the type of crime. It also implies attention to the relationship between penalty assessed and rehabilitation provided.

(9) The area broadly referred to as chemotherapy deserves more attention than it gets. Evidence seems to be accumulating that shortages in certain vitamins or glandular secretions are related to some forms of mental illness. Experimental study of possible relationships between such illnesses or shortages and criminal tendencies might yield useful information. The role of drugs with respect to lawlessness and corrections should not be thought of too largely from the negative standpoint.

A report on artificial coloring in food and drinks as related to "problem children" appears in *U.S. News and World Report* 77 (July 29, 1974), page 43. Also, to some extent a "comment" in the *Kentucky Law Journal* 60 (1972), page 411, deals with Transcendental Meditation (Yoga) as related to internal body chemistry. The comment is entitled: "Transcendental Meditation and the Criminal Justice System."

(10) The schools and civic groups in many communities might seek ways to cooperate with representatives of local, state, and national bar associations in the development and use of educational materials on lawlessness and on the general status of respect for law in the nation. An important lead exists in the "Directory of Law-Related Educational Activities" (2d ed., Working Notes No. 6), by the American Bar Association Special Committee on Youth Education for Citizenship (Norman Gross, ed., Chicago, Illinois: The American Bar Center, 1155 East 60th Street, 1974, 81 pages).

(11) During the past half-century there has been extensive and constructive research on sociological factors which bear on crime and lawlessness. Achievements along these lines do not mean that no biologically inherited influences are involved. More effort at studying possibilities of biological heredity is justified.

(12) From the standpoint of a broad understanding of the role of law and order in organized society, it would be helpful if the American people in general, and if teachers and law-enforcement personnel in particular, knew more about the social and legal structures of societies other than our own. Anthropology presents considerable material of the kind implied relating to preliterate societies, and the field of comparative law presents material relating to modern industrial societies.

2. Broader and More Inclusive Considerations

An earlier note in this epilogue referred to a second category of presentation, involving considerations which are broader and more inclusive than those noted in the first category. Several areas in the broader connotation are presented herewith.

Interdependence of Biology and Ethics

While it is easy to recognize arguments of the past century regarding the roles of nature and nurture in the development of man, it is important to recognize a long period of biological evolution before nurture in the sense of cultural growth became a significant influence in man's development. The gradual appearance of culture can thus be looked upon as an outgrowth or by-product of biological evolution. Perhaps the point could be stated by saying that with the physiological evolution of the human cerebrum and central nervous system, substantially characterized by memory and imagination, the development of tools and other basic aspects of culture was inevitable. Man's erect posture, as well as his hands, his oral cavity and other parts of his anatomy which facilitated the development of language along with manual tools, stimulated the growth of culture. But the main difference between man and his biologically adjacent primate ancestors lies in the cerebrum and the central nervous system in general.

If culture is looked upon as a by-product or outgrowth of biological evolution, then must ethics as a code of human regulation within the cultural structure be regarded as occupying secondary status? It should be apparent that no code of ethics could prescribe behavior which is outside the physical possibilities of the human organism. However, practical implications of this idea are not likely to appear with respect to impossibility of performance, but with respect to undesirability or the amount of effort and discomfort that might be entailed.

Reference has often been made to enforcement difficulties associated with our Volstead prohibition legislation (1919-1933) and some other enactments, because they interfered too much with the satisfaction of large numbers of Americans. Two points thus stand out: (1) in any type of social structure, the general run of the population in the final analysis determines what laws can be enforced; (2) the determination is made largely on the basis of current or anticipated satisfactions, which substantially rest on a biological foundation.

But as cultural developments become more extensive and involved, they exert noticeable effects on man's biology. Some of the effects appear in infant mortality and in general longevity, in personal health and physical comforts, in the content of one's intellectual life and the scope of his inspirations, or in who may reproduce and thus contribute to the biological stream of the future. Moreover, reference is now made to a development in genetic surgery, whereby certain genes can be identified and eliminated from the biological stream, without broadscale elimination through the denial of reproduction to certain individuals.

If one projects from the cutural and ethical developments mentioned, does he arrive at the conclusion that ethics will eventually revise and reshape man's biological foundation, on which it has been inferred that ethics must necessarily be based? If significant revising is looked upon as at best a slow process, one might note that several hundred generations of evolution have been involved in bringing man to his present biological or generic status.

From the standpoint of law as that aspect of the culture which is concerned with regulating man's behavior, and especially with the phase of democratic government which accepts responsibility for initiative in promoting human well-being, a closer coordination between ethics and genetics might seem desirable. This implies systematic research for developing basic information and operating techniques.

Law and Continuity in Knowledge and Behavior

Since there is a continuity or a kind of fluidity with respect to all knowledge, rather than unbridgeable separation of distinct segments, the point at which to discontinue the consideration or ramifications in a particular treatment is somewhat arbitrary. Hence, some ramifications which are considered in the present treatment might have been either omitted or more fully extended, and other ramifications not herein considered might have been included. Much the same applies to most subjects of intellectual interest, whether or not they deal with human relationships.

Considerations of law and human regulation should thus be thought of as radiating outward from a central core of firm demands, to peripheral areas of variable customs and "good manners" in which little attention is paid to the way in which one may conduct himself. In the peripheral areas, anything that may be looked upon as a "pattern of behavior" is in continuous flux.

Out of this flux or general void, which the creation myths of religions typically accept as a starting point, some forms of behavior move by means of repetition and group evolution toward broad acceptance as laws or commandments. Other forms are forgotten and disappear, or they drift into a category which is antagonistic to the approved behavior and are outlawed. Much of man's earlier terminology referred to these social excretions as works of the Devil, to be exorcised from organized society through varying levels of discipline and penance.

Contemporary jurisprudence refers to the varying levels in terms of criminal and civil codes, which are crystallizations out of the general range of possible human behavior. Several aspects of the present study have noted a growing rate of expansion in that range, as a society becomes more populous and includes more kinds of things or situations with which persons may in some way be related. In America, concern regarding the direction of expansion, so as to avoid or minimize antisocial crystallizations, has not been vigorous.

Broadening of Behavioral Patterns

In a dynamic society the stream of behavioral patterns and potentialities, which emerges from the "void" and moves with a central push toward law and associated regulations, broadens and can be said to increase in rate of flow. Perhaps in some respects the phenomenon might be likened to "magnetic storms" which boil up from the sun's interior and send out waves of radiation which man as yet knows little about and has little conception as to constructive adaptations or possible controls.

It should not seem fantastic to infer a similar scope and present incomprehensibility respecting potential human behavior in future settings which reflect currently unforeseeable environmental relationships and probably unpredictable genetic modifications of human intellectual competence. Neither should it seem fantastic for man to envision a future in which his struggle to devise constructive laws and social regulations will be itensified, or in which he will simultaneously be harassed by continuous demands for adjustment in order to survive and be blessed with an open-ended opportunity for growth in doing so.

By contrast, it would indeed seem fantastic to envision a future in which all of the problems of law and social regulation, with associated violations and related disciplines or rehabilitations, had been worked out and set for continuous smooth future sailing. Any historic patterns which may be looked upon as regulatory absolutes, whether set forth as divine commandments or otherwise, will thus require expanding interpretations. The dynamics of life are not compatible with the stability of the tomb.

Relativity and Universality in Law

The relative status of the individual and the group has long been looked upon as a core idea in government. The Supreme Court of the United States is among agencies which in effect reason that the amount of consideration which shall be given to the desires and interests of the individual shall be determined by what is for the welfare of the group. When variations in size of "the group" are considered, one can note the same type of conflict respecting local versus central government as appears respecting the individual and the group. When widespread domestic or international trade and communication are considered, the same conflict appears between localism and broader regionalism or internationalism.

The conflict mentioned should not be looked upon as parochial, in the sense of being limited to human relationships of the type suggested. It is apparent in the various sciences when an experimenter attempts to determine whether the principle which he formulates is applicable only to the body of data at hand or has more extensive or universal application. The same applies to operating procedure which a particular business enterprise may develop, the method of securing learner rapport and cooperation in school or other learning situations, the attitudes and relationships between a physician and his patient, the efforts of a tax board to develop an assessment program which embodies acceptable conceptions of justice and which may be used for several successive years, etc.

With respect to universality as concerning law, one might note efforts of the United Nations to formulate governing principles which can be applied throughout the world. Broadening the scope of its operations and improving the worldwide reception accorded the efforts of the United Nations gradually expand one's orientation from local specifics to conceptions of broad application.

Each foregoing illustration infers movement from a circumscribed local application, where orientation is in a high degree relative to a particular locality, toward circumstances which are more general or universal in their demands.

Relativity and universality, in law or elsewhere, should be thought of as concerned with broadly separated points on a continuum, with many evaluations shifting back and forth between the two points, according to changing conditions. Perhaps in acceptable phraseology the situation concerning relativity and universality in law and human regulation could be stated by saying that with increasingly worldwide contacts, formal statements of the law will more and more appear universalistic and will entail growing responsibility on courts and administrative boards to make necessary local or relativistic applications. Thus, the idea of a clear dichotomy between relative and universal is too simple to be of much long-range help, and conscientious effort at applying democratic ideology complicates simplistic efforts.

Cleavages and Coordinations in Law and Understanding

It is easy to see the path of unity in a simple society, where essentially every member participates in every social activity that is carried on. But as a society becomes populous and grows in number of activities in which people engage, specializations develop which are characterized by growing loyalties to fellow specialists and by weakened loyalty to the overall group. Vocational specializations, or the economic divisions of labor, are prominent in spawning cleavages of the type suggested.

But it is observed that specializations typically supplement one another, thereby supporting a wider range of satisfactions and a higher general level of civilization than would otherwise be possible. Hence, it should be recognized that increased efforts at coordination are essential in order to insure that constructive supplementing actually occurs, rather than interspecialist rivalry and chaos. Such interspecialist rivalry, etc., points out one of the routes to lawlessness and delinquency.

Two considerations bearing on such rivalry and lawlessness are noted. Less information and perspective are required to sense one's immediate vocational interests, than to sense the general economic and cultural relationships of the nation or the wider setting into which one's own specialized vocation must fit. The second consideration relates to basic human selfishness and the responsibility of leadership to show the general population that long-range self-interest is best served through coordinating the multiplicity of specialized vocational interests with an inclusive social well-being. This well-being is a concern of civic education, focusing on our legal and educational structure but involving all of our social institutions. Need for coordination is thus apparent.

Adult Responsibility for Developing Behavioral Perspective in Youth

A society which aspires to a future that is both satisfying and enduring should accept its duty to develop in young people a view of the ongoing problems and opportunities in human regulation which are in keeping with views on biology and ethics, continuity in knowledge and behavior, broadening of behavioral patterns, etc., as indicated in this epilogue. It should be apparent that the extent to which the aspirations are fulfilled will depend substantially on the extent to which the duty is understood and performed.

It should be observed that a basic element in fulfillment concerns attitudes and broad reasonableness. While majorities need considerable tolerance for deviants, minorities should nevertheless recognize that any small group can make an intolerable nuisance of itself by continued insistence on peculiarities in which it professes to see essential although unique values. This is particularly significant when these claimed values cannot be supported by objective evidence and explanations which appeal to individuals with backgrounds and perspectives that differ from those of the particular minority. The hope that lies in Aristotle's golden mean, or in the broad reasonableness of men like Franklin and Jefferson, offers greatest promise for continuous development and satisfaction on a long-range basis.

It follows that the continuous expansion of objective and verifiable information regarding wide range of social and material content, plus help for young people in acquiring and evaluating the information, constitutes a major aspect of the duty mentioned. Specific implications of reasonableness appear concerning parents in the home, teachers in the school, patrolmen and alleged offenders on the streets, judges on the bench, legislators in their chambers, scientists in their laboratories, etc. The interrelatedness among the elements indicated suggests the interrelatedness of varied aspects of the general culture, to which the system of law and order must effectively relate.

Social Implications of Age Gaps

It is not new to refer to an age gap or to note the recently expanding comment on *the* age or generation gap in America. Much haphazard thinking results from failure to note imprecision at two points. If one says that a generation covers twenty-five years, then does the age period from five years to thirty years constitute a generation, or the age period from forty to sixty-five? Or may one use such other beginning and end points as he finds convenient? To infer that the nation's population consists of two generations, the younger generation consisting of persons five to thirty years of age and the older generation including everybody over thirty years of age, could hardly be called realistic. Apart from leaving out those under five, the two-generation concept implies much greater homogeneity within each of the two generation groups than actually exists.

It is of interest that for census purposes, school attendance, voting, marriage, several areas of employment and retirement, and for other purposes, more precise age categories are used. Census enumerations are used in many types of demographic considerations, particularly the census data which accept individual years as age categories.

Part of the difficulty lies in the scope of individual differences which exist within practically any class or category of persons that may thus be set forth. Sex is probably the most consistent exception to the foregoing statement. But even in regard to this category, much depends on the range of characteristics which are used in defining the sex category. Certainly there are great variations among males or among females of any particular age, when one refers to physical traits, cultural background and status, learning ability, or other qualities.

Classifying people according to some quality such as age or maturity resembles classifying them according to political issues—i.e., membership in different political categories shifts as the issues change. The situation is reminiscent of referring to the people *en masse* as the *public*, in contrast with recognizing that there are probably as many publics as there are social issues and that the persons who make up the "concerned public" on a particular issue will not consist entirely of the persons who make it up on some other issue.

The confusion typically associated with reference to "the generation gap" might thus be reduced by differentiating among issues to be dealt with in a social context and then recognizing that both supporters and opponents on most issues will be found among persons who vary in age more than any reasonable conception of a generation could imply. Moreover, insofar as there may be recognizable concentrations by age with respect to some issue, differentiation on the basis of issue-content is more in keeping with civic deliberations and with justice, than some vague categorization based on a loose concept of age. The foregoing statement becomes increasingly important as the rate of social change and the mobility among population categories speed up. The intellectual laziness embodied in vague references to "the generation gap" thus becomes an increasingly pronounced handicap to social analysis and social progress.

Lawmakers and the Making of Legislators

Students of government have long been interested in the origins of the law. Particular attention might in this connection be called to three excerpts set forth among historical reflections, in chapter 1, section 2, of Division V. These excerpts read:

> The freedom of a government does not depend upon the quality of its laws, but upon the power that has the right to create them. (Thaddeus Stevens)
> The whole of government consists in the art of being honest. (Jefferson)
> In all forms of government the people is (sic) the true legislator. (Burke)

The social analysis reflected by the excerpts means that in the final analysis the general population constitutes the lawgivers, as well as the judges concerning lawfulness. This basic fact underscores the importance of broad understanding by the people as to how organized society depends on law and why no legal system can function without broad support by the people. It also underscores the insight shown by American educational pioneers of 150 years ago, who urged that civic education in a broad sense was the prime reason for establishing a public school system. It further underscores the neglect of attention to collective well-being through civic education, which an exaggerated individualism and permissiveness in recent decades have helped to bring about.

The path of creative discipline and civic commitment, which it is necessary for successive generations to tread, is not easy to discern and follow—or to keep updated with respect to needs. But it should be clear that indifference, incompetence, or misconceptions of the personal liberty to be accorded to children and youth by their mentors, become reflected in lawlessness and in disrespect for existing institutions as well as for the personnel officially associated with those institutions.

Various aspects of this study have attempted to point out the consequences of this neglect, etc., and to suggest avenues along which remedial possibilities might lie. The comprehensive and coordinate nature of the responsibility involved needs continuing emphasis.

Limitations of the Law

When law is thought of as formal or institutionalized regulation of social behavior, then limitations of the law must be thought of in terms of what the law is expected to accomplish. If it is assumed that a body of law is intended to be an asset to members of the society concerned, then it could be stated that the broad purpose of the law is to assure the people a maximum of satisfaction and accomplishment through a minimum of sacrifice and frustration.

The concept "limitations of the law" might imply a continuum from a point A at which there is great satisfaction and little sacrifice, to a point B at which there is little satisfaction and great sacrifice. Obviously the greatest contribution made by law is in the areas near the A end of the continuum, with an increase in limitations as one moves toward the B end. Perhaps the smoothest movement along the line suggested is that embodied in the common law, which grows directly out of settling court disputes over specific situations that have arisen. By contrast, statutes substantially hypothesize about situations which may arise in the future, in contrast with suits over current situations.

The condition described has left statutes somewhat suspect, in some thinking on the philosophy of law. Perhaps evidence of suspect status lies in the declared intent of some statutes to limit the application of other statutes. An important type of restriction exists in the numerous areas to which "statutes of limitation" apply. Thus, one who may claim statutory damages because of personal injury or loss of property must file his claim within a limited time, and in a specified place and form, or he has no valid claim. Other specific illustrations of limits, among the great number similarly involved, are installment contracts; action against architects, engineers, and building contractors; suits on medical malpractice; and challenge to the provisions of a will. The underlying philosophy is that persons who think they are aggrieved should press their presumed statutory rights within a reasonable time, or discard and forget about them, so that stability prevails as the basis for progress in community affairs.

To some extent the setting up of administrative agencies with broad discretion to establish rules for governing their internal affairs, such as school boards or boards of health, reflects limitations concerning the feasibility of direct enactments by legislatures. And to some extent, conflicts in the laws point to another kind of limitation. Such conflicts often arise, for example, in respect to granting and recognizing divorces, extradition of public offenders, remedies available to creditors, victims of airplane crashes, life insurance litigation, legislation concerning usury or defamation of character, choice of venue regarding corporations with activities which extend over several jurisdictions, etc.

Two limitations should be noted which may seem nontechnical but which are nevertheless fundamental. One concerns a general popular understanding of the results which it is reasonable to expect from specific enactments or from the legal system as a whole. The other limitation concerns the insight and sense of public responsibility on the part of lawmakers in analyzing issues and in drafting legislation or judicial interpretations. Indifference and haphazard legislative drafting can contribute greatly to overloading the courts and to distorting justice. Such legislation does not help in developing a favorable popular image of politicians or of government in America.

The responsibilities of citizenship in the nation should include a considerable understanding of the limitations of the law; that is, what it is reasonable to expect laws to accomplish. Much has been said in the present study about the educational implications of situations of the type involved.

Paradox of Democracy in Personal Freedom and Group Control

There is a significant paradox in the democratic ideology and theory of government. The ideology places great stress on dignity and worth of the individual and on the doctrine that governments should be operated for the welfare of the governed. However, government is a collective enterprise, which proceeds on the assumption that when the welfare or desires of an individual conflict with those of the group, the welfare or desires of such individual must give way. Implications of arithmetic thus become involved, whereby individuals with similar views on some aspect of well-being are added up, until something called a majority is reached. In a rather loose sense, the majority then determines the collective framework within which the well-being of the minority is presumed to be fostered—or at least respected.

When it is urged that the dignity and worth of persons who make up the minority should be treated with respect and tolerance by the dominant majority, it is responded that each member of the majority has as much dignity and worth as a member of the minority has. Accordingly, the arithmetical sum of dignity and worth vested in the majority exceeds that vested in the minority. When there is conflict between the two pools of dignity and worth, assuming considerable homogeneity within the minority, then by court ruling, the laws of physics, or some other persuasive criterion, the mass or power of the strong must prevail.

Apart from finesse and circumlocution, the difference between this conclusion of ideology and the operating rule of the jungle that the strong shall prevail may be somewhat hazy. But humans often seem to prefer roundabout avenues to illusive conclusions. One reason may be that they can then entertain themselves with fantasies along the way.

But a fundamental thus emerges: to what extent should a system of law and order be geared to promote this pattern of satisfactions? What should be the respective roles of fantasies and of reason in the development of civilization?

Utilizing the Past in Shaping the Future

The concept of development in any cultural relationship implies building upon the past with respect to present operations or future projections. The idea of progress has its anchorage in the situation described. Criteria of what developments to seek emerge from what man likes or thinks he will like, which is fundamentally rooted in the nature of the biological organism. If one assumes that basic likes will not change over extensive future time, he essentially denies the continuance of biological evolution, so far as the human species is concerned. Biological evolution has always been influenced by the environmental setting, but man is rapidly increasing his capacity to modify the environment. And with respect to modification and fitness for survival, in a democracy as in other forms of social organization, some individuals are more important or play greater roles than others do.

As to utilizing the past, one should note that there is no way to escape utilization. But with development of capacity to think and analyze, it is possible to make conscious selections and to plan. Yet physical proximity in a geographical sense continues to be a factor in selectivity, although not with the rigid narrowness that governed our early human ancestors. The same applies to sensory equipment in putting man in contact with the world, although he has devised tools for supplementing sensory acuity. Current struggle with shortages of food or energy, or with certain virus infections, illustrate the tool relationship.

The fact that we can and must learn much from the past should alert us to recognizing how the past enables us to expand our curiosity and our exploration of the future. The quotations presented in appendix no. 3 and elsewhere necessarily emphasize those observations by our predecessors which seem to have substantial current validity. This does not mean that those predecessors made no observations which subsequent experience has shown to be invalid, or perhaps ridiculous. This raises questions about "eternal verities" or about "how enduring" the "verities" are which have been formulated by the leaders of one era and which have been echoed during subsequent eras by persons of restricted imagination.

Thus, a major problem in regard to interest in the past concerns understanding and analyzing it for what it can offer in shaping and controlling the future, rather than worshiping or becoming enslaved to the past and its great leaders—with the past serving as a kind of wailing wall or kindred stone god.

Hence, present-day Americans should use the quotes and other contributions of our predecessors less as finished products or final achievements from which we may be content to enjoy an ongoing flow of benefits, than as starting points and hypotheses from which we may carry further and in more diverse ways than the predecessors did. This applies to contributions respecting government as set forth by the Founding Fathers, religious doctrines set forth by founders of major religions, nuclear and other research contributions by physical scientists, money and credit systems devised by financiers to support worldwide trade, learning theories and procedures developed by psychologists and educators, etc.

It is unrealistic to assume that our predecessors such as those quoted in the present study, especially those who are distant in time, were more reflective than ourselves because they were less pressed by a multiplicity of current happenings. It is more realistic to assume that they had a smaller background of information and experience in terms of which to reflect and that they were accordingly forced to look upon human personality as shaped by a more limited range of forces and as functioning in a narrower context. The fact that many of them at times have used what now seems to imply expansive concepts or perspective should be viewed in terms of expansion and diversity in meaning which particular vocabulary takes on as a culture expands. Many words and phrases thus come to be used with additional connotations.

The basic point then is *how* we utilize the past which we inherited from our predecessors, as we try to expand and shape the future, and thus bequeath to our successors a richer and more comprehensive past than we ourselves inherited.

APPENDIX NO. 1

Controversial Issues and Social Philosophy

(Continued from second part of chapter 2, Division IV. The first five items appear in the text of the study; see pp. 185-200. Footnotes are with Division IV.)

Hero Models in a Changing America

Much of the reportedly increasing crime and delinquency in the United States is often referred to in terms of a decline in moral ideals and standards or a disintegration of the forces of moral discipline. The kinds of ideals which are emphasized in any society and the consequences associated with their disintegration depend on the type of society concerned, or on which of a substantial body of ideals seem most directly involved, and on what emerges in the areas where disintegration has occurred.

Heroes are embodiments or personifications of ideals, and the acclaim that attaches to a hero at a given time indicates how well his behavior is thought to reflect the ideals or values of that time. The status of a particular hero may change considerably from time to time, or he may be substantially replaced by some other model.

During most of our national life, the United States has been a culture of more rapid change than most cultures of the world. Among the factors which have contributed to this situation are the heterogeneity of ethnic and ideological backgrounds of the immigrants who came to this country; the historic westward-moving frontier along which population was sparse and law enforcement often nominal or uncertain; an intense motivation for individuals to improve their status through acquiring material wealth, as a major criterion of success; and the rapid rise in technology during recent decades which speeds up the rate of creating material wealth and which brings many changes in daily associations among the people. Housing, social and geographic mobility, vocational activity, and material affluence have especially affected those associations.

One consequence of the environmental and associational changes noted is that no one hero model or personification of ideals is likely to seem appropriate for any very long time. By contrast, when a group of people live in much the same geographical and cultural setting for several generations, a concise body of ideals and a code of behavior become more clearly established.

This has been the situation in Europe, and certainly in the Orient apart from Japan, during essentially the whole period covered by United States history. Thus, one might expect more lawlessness and disrespect for traditional values and authority in this country than in the other lands noted.

However, an effort to explain extensive lawlessness in America's revolutionary culture is not necessarily an effort to justify that lawlessness. Part of the difference between explaining and justifying lies in recognizing the need of a culture for heroes and in the problems of keeping the heroes up to date if they are to be useful agencies of social integration and cultural growth. One implication of updating, as for example concerning the hero role of the Founding Fathers, may relate less to the precise acts or statements involved than to the theme of early endeavors as related to present-day life in America.

A problem involved in teaching ideals in any field—such as religion, patriotism, family life, etc.—is to keep the ideals stated and illustrated in ways which the contemporary audience can readily understand and can see how to join regarding operations. This applies to the ideals of Jesus, St. Paul, Captain John Smith of early Virginia, Washington, Lincoln, etc. But it is necessary to recognize that there are now several fields of achievement and service in our culture, fields affording ideological orientation, which were either nonexistent or relatively unimportant even as late as Lincoln's time. A few of these are scientific research; business and finance; teaching and developing educational materials, at university and other levels; medical and health services; and international diplomacy. America needs hero personages in these and other current fields, to serve as models for young people. Moreover, model performance by a few outstanding persons in any field has a socially beneficial effect on other adult workers in the field concerned.

The problem of models to emulate and to use as guides has sometimes appeared especially difficult with respect to girls and negroes, as members of these two groups participate more widely in the vocational and other aspects of the culture. But with the spread of unisex mores and the fading of racial differentiations, the importance of a sex or race model with which to identify becomes less important. This does not mean that identification with a person is entirely replaced by identification with a pattern of achievement; it rather focuses more on those characteristics of the person which are most important for the field of achievement concerned. The biographical suggestions in chapter 4 of this division offer potential in the direction implied.

Perhaps the religious and military fields have emphasized the role of heroes longer and more extensively than other fields have. Testimony on this point appears in the various levels of saints, which flourish in organized religions of long standing, and in the monuments commemorating military leaders or military events, which are generously distributed over much of the Western world. While the use of heroes *can* offer an easy method of learning, with almost universal appeal to persons of wide range in age and cultural background, to do so the heroes must personify the contemporary values and hopes of those people. Implications of this point for hero updating have been suggested. To a considerable extent the seeming low status of religious and patriotic appeal in America today stems from ideological obsolescence—that is, a failure to update hero ideals.

In America, persons elected to high public office and others in broad public service have extensively been accepted by youth as models to emulate and have been expected by others to lead exemplary lives. Legal controversies about immorality and unprofessional conduct on the part of teachers and university professors indicate popular and administrative attitudes regarding teachers as models and the incidental learning that results from teacher-pupil association and pupil imitation. Earlier sections of the present treatise deal with the "public image" of the judiciary and law-enforcement agencies.

The hero role of persons in high public office and trust is placed in high relief by such events as the Watergate scandals. The scandals have two major implications from the standpoint of hero ideology. The first is shock at the hypocrisy and the shell of pretended respectability that are shown to pervade many aspects of high public office in America. This shock sweeps away large areas of faith in the American system of government. However, the educational and other leadership on which the nation must depend for updating and "teaching" constructive hero ideology should recognize the scandals as an indication that the teaching job has not been adequately done. The scandals reemphasize the idea that eternal vigilance and public effort are essential to political freedom and to moral decency among public officials, and that man's inherent selfishness and reach for power cannot be allowed to operate without continuous public surveillance.

The second major implication of the Watergate scandals may well prove the most important. It concerns the surveillance role of Congressional investigative committees in holding nonadversary hearings to determine what happened that constitute the scandals and in televising those hearings as a kind of adult education; that is, education regarding the types of persons whom our system has placed in high public office, the responsibility of the people in general for the results shown, and proposed legislative or other remedies for the situation that exists. One phase of this implication is that there are some aspects of American culture in which the people as a whole must rather directly act as agencies of education and surveillance, and not assume that the job can be handled by the schools along with formal legislative and judicial action.

As a part of television and other effort in adult education to develop understanding of the American system and commitment to it is the development of adults who are able and willing to act as hero models in the political sphere. This implies more meaningful recognition and rewards for persons who render significant public service of any kind—as in scientific research, teaching, business organization, invention, philanthropy, religious exploration, law enforcement, philosophy, art, etc. Recognition includes pay in a monetary sense. But beyond a certain pay level, nonmonetary recognitions are likely to be more important. The creation of more kinds of awards, medals, and celebrations is suggested—possibly more holidays, which are not particularly attached to weekends for the benefit of business or tourist interests.

Perhaps attention can be focused on the key idea of preceding comment about hero models by saying that any culture needs individuals to play the hero role through personifying the essential ideals of the culture, depending largely on the insight and the vigilance with which the ideology is continuously updated, and that the job of updating and of developing personnel for carrying forward the responsibility is a job for the entire population, rather than one which can be delegated wholly to public schools—either alone or with other branches of government.

Drugs and the Moral Code

Concern about drug addiction and illegal drug traffic among American young people is not unique because of conflict with the moral code. Every sudden development and shift in the field of human relationships conflicts with aspects of the code bearing on those relationships. Conflicts really ask why the code exists and how it came into existence.

While sociologists may agree that the mores consist of a body of accepted practice which has grown out of communal life, one should recognize degrees of approval and disapproval among practices that exist. Thus, morality is theoretically based on the best knowledge of the time as to what is for the well-being of the group as a whole. But when ideals appear in practices which are carried on under the direction of particular individuals who are in power, the ideals tend to become warped by the personal interests or selfish desires of those individuals. Whether code elements appear as the ten inspired commandments of Moses, the Constitution of the United States as the fundamental or organic law of the land, the guidelines of lesser prophets which different cultures typically produce, or in some less conspicuous form, they must be applied and judged by men who are subject to human frailties.

When foregoing observations are oriented on recent anxiety about drug use by Americans, it is the rapid increase in the use of *new* drugs such as marijuana that attracts attention, not the continued appearance, for example, of alcoholism on a nationwide basis—which seems to be firmly established in the mores. When reference is made to alcohol as America's number one drug problem, as with regard to highway casualties and other forms of human wreckage, the comment moves across the viewing screen as a passing statistic of no imperative concern. It may be followed by an advertisement promoting the use of some alcoholic beverage. Some persons may be impressed by comment on religious sanction for the use of wine or other alcoholic beverages, or by reference to the use of such beverages by our ancestors as being older than our national existence, or by the importance of jobs and dividends supplied by the liquor industry in the nation's economy.

We hear that actions speak louder than words. And we observe that the beverage mores of our cocktail culture are determined less by the disunited individuals and agency forces which emphasize social losses by way of health and associated impairment of function through alcohol, than by sponsors of personal gain for those who own or direct the industry. For some generations, schoolbooks have carried bland statements about "the evils of alcohol," and various public health studies have presented somewhat inert statistics on the subject.

One should probably exercise caution regarding conclusions that economic materialism determines the mores in particular areas of American society, but with regard to alcohol and some other drugs the extent of that determination seems great. Recent developments in some states to lower the age at which youth may legally purchase liquor adds to the picture. State liquor stores reflect one type of public or moral sanction of the wide-spread use of alcoholic beverages.

Much of what is said about alcohol applies to the drug element and to associated cancer-producing potential of cigarettes. Two conflicting embel-lishments of the picture in this case appear: federal subsidies for tobacco farmers; federal effort to regulate cigarette advertising through some of our mass media. It may be too early to judge whether the recency of effort to regulate advertising indicates growing attention in the mores to the health of the American people, although the gesture might suggest a technique for wider application. But the subsidy-regulation dichotomy reflects effort to appease conflicting elements in the mores, plus general moral confusion.

Recent concern about marijuana and associated drugs reflects some of the same type of conflict. Should one ask: to what extent is the sharp anxiety about these drugs due to recency in their appearance, including speedup in rate of financial profits and a retinue of problems regarding health and social disorganization, to which the culture has not yet had time to adjust? Should one further ask about the nature of cultures in those parts of the world which have had a nonprescription use of these drugs longer than we have, or ask how the use of these drugs in America is related psychologically and pharma-cologically to our widespread and somewhat promiscuous use of sleeping pills or drug stimulants?

If one suggests that problems and inquiries of the types inferred should be approached on the basis of reason, he should note that reason does not prosper in a vacuum. It requires data. Attitudes inherited from the past, including those favoring a wide range of potential for private profit, should be evaluated along with other data. Physiological data and sociological data, concerning the influence of a particular drug on human tissue and glan-dular functions as well as the retinue of social consequences, are important types of data. Hospitalization, public health services, law enforcement, rehabilitation projects, etc., indicate areas of public concern which are re-flected in part through tax requirements. To say that physiological or some other technical data indicate that marijuana or some other new drug *is no worse* than alcohol or some other older drug, should such be indicated, is no positive defense of the new item. To say that something new is *no worse* than something which is generally recognized as bad, although of long standing, does not justify adding to the culture additional elements which are known to be bad.

Comments on technological data and inherited prejudices as factors in determining the mores, plus earlier comments about morality as based on the best knowledge of the time, may lead one to ask if there can be a scientific basis for morality. Considerable depends on one's view as to what science includes, but also on recognizing that the mores determine what kind of scientific experimentation will be allowed. The allowability feature has recently been pointed up by publicity on drug companies operating through medical facilities in using human "guinea pigs" for testing new pharma-ceutical products and on the syphilis experiment associated with Tuskegee,

Alabama. Much seems to depend on the gradualness or incline of the gradient according to which the new elements are introduced and the skill in propaganda or public education associated with the introduction. In the respects noted, considerations regarding drugs are much the same as considerations regarding sky-labs and space research, curriculum changes in high schools and colleges, creeping versus galloping corruption in American politics, etc. The point may be illustrated by a note associated with the first railroads established in this country. The note stated: the people simply will not consent to being hurled through the air at the tremendous speed of fifteen miles an hour.

But when reason is associated with an interest in improving the general well-being of the people, and when science generates considerable new knowledge that is useful in the improvement, then it really becomes a part of the mores to base an ongoing and developing morality on the most pertinent knowledge available. But in addition to organic chemistry and physiology concerning the effect of particular drugs on human functioning, the data involved must include sociological contributions on the nature and power of prejudice, on how community values emerge and change, on how to channel and transform man's selfish drive for personal power into community well-being, etc. Thus, when science is conceived with sufficient scope as embodying scientific method, it includes the kinds of observations that made the early prophets historically noteworthy, and it describes a design for improving the process and projecting it into the future.

If the foregoing type of scientific approach to moral development is oriented on the cocktail, tranquilizer, and cigarette aspects of our culture, through educational and economic efforts relating to children and adults, substantial improvements seem likely. The orientation must consider the technical problems of developing instructional materials and of informing teachers and laymen; the curiosity and search for thrills or "trips" on the part of young people; the economic and other obstacles to be faced within the nation; international implications regarding trade and economic development, policing national borders, foreign travel by Americans, overseas military involvements, subsidies for developing nondrug crops in the agriculture of certain countries, etc.; and rehabilitation or salvaging the wreckage of persons, who become a part of the domestic retinue at some point along the line of consequences.

With respect to all preceding comments on drugs and the moral code, perhaps major emphasis should be placed on one point: the will of the people to *become informed* and to *accept commitment* to act for the general public well-being. This implies the courage to apply penalties which have been socially defined as appropriate. Developing the acceptance of effective commitment is probably the most difficult part of the process. But in the absence of commitment there will likely be further relaxation and settling into the quagmire of social disorganization, to the refrain and sentimental bemoaning of how bad conditions are getting to be, while commercialism and illegal profits further dominate the mores concerning the field.

Motivation: Why Men Work

Questions as to *why* people do what they do have always been involved in efforts to regulate conduct. During a period of learning or conditioning by forces outside of himself, the individual is usually aware of the conditioning force, although on some occasions imitation may be so easy that awareness is at low ebb. But awareness of the kind indicated should not cause one to overlook an inherent biological regulator, which urges us to do what is immediately pleasant and satisfying while we are doing it.

An important aspect of cultural development, then, consists of causing the individual to shift from biological to social motivations. Social emphasis means that various relationships with people and things influence what one wants to do, but the wants vary greatly as to the nature and extent of the influence. Moreover, as a culture becomes more complex, more types of contacts with people and things become possible, and important differences appear among the contacts as to urgency. With multiple possibilities and interlacing variations in urgency, the problem of developing consistency becomes greater. In a development of the type described of a rich and varied culture, conscious social effort to develop acceptable ethics and patterns of moral behavior is the only alternative to social chaos. When social disintegration approaches chaos, people increasingly fall back on biological selfishness as a prime motivator.

Chaos based on a dog-eat-dog selfishness cannot support as large a population at as high a standard of living as can be supported by a cooperative social structure in which individuals are disciplined according to a carefully developed group code. Movement toward chaos constitutes the type of situation in which a growing sense of desperation provides background for a "strong man," who has some kind of program that promises direction plus considerable mental stability, if not immediate physical improvement. Some scapegoat as an enemy focus is then sought or created, around which to unify the social fragments which chaos has scattered. A new core philosophy or body of motivation thus appears. The situation described is often associated with the rise of Hitler, and the history of Europe during his heyday testifies to the power which a strong-man operation may have in a populous and technologically advanced culture.

A subsidiary point needs moderate elaboration in this connection. As a culture expands, many new activities come to be looked upon as *work* in a vocational sense. Thus, most of what in America is now called the service vocations did not exist a century ago, and other activities in the general area concerned were carried on in an amateur and haphazard fashion. We also speak of a *workout* in the development of athletic skill or in maintaining personal health. We refer to some student activities as being *academic work*, and we devise credits to measure the amount that has been accomplished. News comments relate to the President doing his *homework*, in preparation for a high-level international conference. We say that the engine in an automobile does not *work* as it should, and the courts are interested when certain pharmaceutical products do not *work* as television advertising promises. The upshot is that when the concept of *work* expands in a dynamic culture, motivations which come to be associated with different *kinds of work* necessarily change.

The term corruption is usually associated with conscious intent to violate some aspect of the social code so as to secure personal gain. Corruption should thus be differentiated from accident due to ignorance, and perhaps from negligence due to indifference. A member of the Senate Watergate investigating committee expressed wonder at the motivation of some of the people who testified before the committee. He referred to these persons as young men with unusually favorable social and educational backgrounds and with bright promise for the future. Then why do they commit perjury and deliberately violate other aspects of the code of law and decency?

Answer to the inquiry is not easy, and implementation of what emerges as an answer will probably involve widespread modifications in our social structure. Four items are mentioned here, as candidates for consideration in developing an answer. One is to reduce the exaggerated emphasis on the whimsical aspects of individualism, that in recent decades has dominated much of our educational practice, judicial philosophy, and material affluence. A corollary to the reduction is greater emphasis on responsibility of the individual to the group and on need for discipline of the individual organism in the development and use of personal resources in order to achieve anything significant in any field.

A second and related point concerns a discriminating loyalty to current leadership, which enables one to evaluate objectives as well as to pursue them, rather than a blind loyalty that embodies a type of personality cult. The cult idea was strongly manifested in regard to Hitler and perhaps some Soviet leaders, and some of it has appeared in Watergate testimony with respect to President Nixon. Evaluation asks whether there may be some objectives or methods which are approved by a leader, but which a loyal follower might refuse to accept.

A third point relates to certainty and adequacy of group discipline for deliberate wrongdoers. Certainty includes promptness, with the thought that "justice delayed is justice denied." Certainty also includes the idea of a visible end to appeals, delays, and stallings in court action. Part of the remedy on delays, etc., may lie in legal reform of judicial procedure, but more of it probably lies in the hands of judges who currently hear cases. Adequacy of discipline may imply a more difficult problem. While the object of discipline should be reform rather than revenge, reform implies deterrence from future acts by the particular offender or by any other person who might be in comparable circumstances. While there has been substantial recent attack on punishment as a deterrent to future crime, especially in regard to capital punishment as the penalty for murder, the problem of devising disciplinary measures that actually deter is a continuing problem with which American society must deal.

The fourth point relates to growth in the regulatory structure, recognizing that as a culture expands and shifts in basic trends, new loopholes in the old structure appear and emerging types of relationships need surveillance. Part of the newer need concerns speedup in the judicial process, to accompany speedup in the rate of social change. Point three above also notes this item.

Foregoing comments are intended to show that in a complex culture the motivations which cause men to work are quite complex and that the further motives are influenced by the culture to turn away from immediate biological motivations, the more difficult the motivations become to forecast or to shape. The growing difficulty indicates a growing need for constructive social effort to develop ethical concepts and moral behavior, with a wide range of agencies necessarily engaged in the process.

Boredom and Motivation

When inquiries concerning motivation ask "why men work," it would not be wholly facetious to respond that many of them work because of habit and because they have nothing else to do that is more interesting. A supplementary comment might add that the person is fortunate who really enjoys performing all of the various specific tasks which make up his job.

There is increasing recognition among alert personnel workers in industry that boredom is closely related to worker output, absenteeism, and accident rate. Imaginative teachers and guidance workers in schools have noted comparable relationships between boredom and poor academic achievement, dropouts, and school disciplinary problems. Student comments on "relevance" of the establishment are parts of the same picture. Some law-enforcement personnel have mentioned a relationship between boredom and drug trips, thrill aspects of automobile thefts by youth, and some suicide or murder attempts.

Insofar as preceding statements are illustrative, they imply that boredom is increasingly becoming a major negative factor in the American way of life. Moreover, the increasing amount of leisure available to the American people in general, unaccompanied by effort to develop ways of utilizing leisure which produce long-range satisfactions, causes leisure to become a bore—and a hazard. The point has sometimes been set forth by comparing abundant leisure, as noted, with unemployment, where the absence of a job cuts off a major avenue to satisfaction through physical and economic participation in the culture.

Some of the inferred relationships between boredom and antisocial behavior on one hand and personality disintegration on the other have been recognized for several decades by astute observers regarding individual cases. Broader social implications have become more apparent in recent decades. Perhaps the development of technology, with emphasis on precision and routine regarding schedules, achievements, test-evaluated competencies, recreational participations, diet and health regimens, monetary contributions to "good causes," retirement emptiness, etc., has important boredom implications.

The aim of present comment is to note that boredom is becoming of sufficient individual and social importance in America that we should devote more extensive and more systematic study to causal and remedial possibilities.

The Marketplace as the Cradle of Culture

Reference is often made to America as a business-dominated culture, with the inference that there is something derogatory about a business and trade orientation—in contrast, for example, with a culture dominated by religion, military power, colonial development, or some other orientation. Part of the haze and confusion in the views suggested can be clarified by an examination of the basic concept of the marketplace and its role as substratum of the business community.

The role of the marketplace in the meeting of people and the exchange of wares, ideas, and genes at a rather elementary level can be seen in village "market days" among Indians in the plateau areas from the American Southwest to Northern Argentina. Many of the rural Indians who come to the village on these days to exchange pottery, blankets, news, acquaintances, and other items, seem to live substantially for the market days. In several respects these market villages resemble the "Saturday night towns," with from a few hundred to several thousand inhabitants, that still function as local "bright light" centers in much of the United States—where people meet, gossip, see what's new in the stores and in the movies, join in a square dance, learn who is trying something new in home or vocational life, hear about new babies, etc.

Most Americans have learned considerable about the fur trading of early settlers, the frontier trading posts, sometimes with forts as accompaniments, and the exchange of wares, ideas, and gunshots that substantially made up the culture of the time. Such terms as Hudson Bay Company, West India Company, and East India Company still ring through the pages of early American history. The Boston Tea Party, Stamp Act, "Madison's War," blockade runners, "Sea Hawks," Barbary Pirates, Whiskey Rebellion, etc., acquired political implications largely because of their significance in the flow of merchandise and the associated tolls levied. Many types of development and exchange found their way into the cultures of this and other countries through avenues of the types suggested.

Persons who are familiar with the history of Europe know about the role of fairs, particularly as related to the growth of cities during the late medieval period. The fair, as a major educational institution associated with a broad conception of the marketplace, continues to play an important role in Western countries, through the somewhat sporadic appearance of World's Fairs in different cities, and to play a more local role in the numerous state, regional, and county fairs of contemporary America. With the growth of industry in volume and diversity, exhibits of specialized types of merchandise somewhat replace the more general fair idea—i.e., automobile shows, furniture exhibits and marts, displays of electronic materials, farm implement shows, exhibits of construction and road-building equipment, etc.

The trucking industry with the associated highway system, including farm-to-market roads, is now fundamental in this nation's economy in the production and distribution of food, fuel, construction materials, household equipment, books and periodicals, etc. For many consumers, the marketplace concept seems to focus in the neighborhood shopping center, which typically includes one or more "supermarkets" for food or more general merchandise. The numerous curb markets for fresh fruits and vegetables constitute part of the picture, as certainly do the widely known markets for livestock, grain, industrial stocks and bonds, and commodities (i.e., copper, onions, wool, eggs, lumber, scrap iron, molasses).

Expansion of the marketplace concept, with its extensive demands for management, labor, plant and distribution centers, equipment, and funds, has essentially brought along the industrial corporation, organized labor, and a retinue of agencies to regulate pay rates, working conditions, quality of products, installment buying of consumer goods, etc. It has also brought vocational education to develop salable skills, etc. The emergence of the industrial corporation, with ownership distributed through shares of stock, makes it possible to accumulate resources for giant economic undertakings from a large number of small investors. In the United States today there are several business and industrial corporations with operating budgets larger than the budgets of many small nations. Great power over people and things is thus concentrated in a few managerial persons, with great economic and political importance both nationally and internationally.

In significant respects the contract has grown out of and been developed through business and through marketplace relationships concerning goods and services. Written contracts enable individuals and groups to project relationships concerning large numbers of persons and things and to project them over long periods of time. Construction contracts for large buildings or for highway and bridge development, with blueprints and specifications and perhaps with extensive subcontracting, are indicative of scope. Contracts are thus one of America's most important forms of disciplined freedom, in which a great majority of Americans become involved through labor agreements or in other ways.

By helping to define the scope of possible content that may be involved in contracting, the competence and status of individuals who may become contracting parties, what constitutes arrival at an agreement or a "Meeting of the Minds," and by enforcement of contract provisions, the state does much to make contracting one of the most important forms of relationships among the people. The "sanctity of the contract," as a framework of human relationships associated with the marketplace status of goods and services, symbolizes a quite pervading discipline of our culture. It affords one of the culture's best illustrations of how extensive freedom to act in complex human relationships must depend on commensurate responsibility, indicated through detailed provisions governing the rights and duties of the parties who contract.

The current interest of several prominent nations in increased peaceful trade and reduced saber rattling is another indication concerning the potential of the marketplace as an instrument of civilization and cultural development. Wheat and technology from the United States to Russia in exchange for natural gas and raw materials *may* illustrate the point in the future, if Americans become satiated with tours by ballet dancers. Recent trade developments between Russia and West Germany or between Japan and the United

States further demonstrate the role of the marketplace in worldwide cultural developments, as does the whole balance of payment consideration and the international status of the American dollar. The aspects of American foreign-aid programs which urge more trade and less aid have a marketplace orientation. So do those aspects of our relationships with underdeveloped nations which refer to helping them learn how to help themselves—that is, help themselves to enter more fully into the world economic community, through bringing forth something to exchange through trade.

It would be an asset to most Americans during childhood and mature life if they developed a concept of the marketplace comparable to that suggested in foregoing paragraphs. The business community is more open and frank about competition and material motivation in its operations than some other aspects of the culture are, but typically less hypocritical and perhaps less unethical. The missionary work of different organized religions is a competitive enterprise with the elements of respectability and ethics sometimes hardly recognizable. The same may be true of ball clubs and other athletic teams. Watergate and associated developments may make contemporary politics seem especially competitive and characterized by "corrupt-practice acts."

The attitude of organized labor about immigration, and about "exporting jobs" through importing goods produced in the foreign plants of multinational corporations with the home base in America, is competition and market oriented. Any practical view of romance and marriage should recognize competition regarding whom you might want in contrast with whom you can get, and with varying degrees of trickery ingeniously woven into the process. A basic justification for constitutional protection of free speech lies in access to free competition in the marketplace of ideas. This point was emphasized by the Founding Fathers and has been echoed in numerous court decisions since that time.

It would be constructive for Americans to look upon the marketplace, in the sense described, as among the most creative forces in American life. Through the wide range of people, ideas, and merchandise which it involves; its research to develop new knowledge; and its life sustenance in improved commodities and services to "outdo the competition"; marketplace orientation has been a major factor in improving the material and other standard of living of average Americans. However, the foregoing does not imply that the business community is free from corruption and unethical practice. Nor does it justify corruption in this field to suggest that there is as much or more corruption in some other fields. But objective analysis should be helpful in developing competence and a sense of duty among the people generally for constructive evaluation of the role played by the business community, and helpful in remedying shortcomings in ways which are in accord with the public interest.

From preceding considerations it follows that in a modern industrial democracy such as the United States, the schools and educators—including the media of adult education—have extensive civic responsibility to develop the competence and courage inferred, and not only regarding the business community, but regarding every other major phase of the culture. Much of America's operating weakness and social disintegration is due to inadequacy in its moral and philosophical core as illustrated by reference to the market-place concept and the business community.

The City as a Cultural Development

For some generations, before urban crime and decadence became items of almost daily news comment, sociologists and others often referred to the city as the ultimate habitat of man, in his broad cultural evolution. The reference was based on the importance of the exchange and intermingling of ideas, wares, and genes, which was commonly associated with urban proximity, in contrast with rural isolation and rural anchorage to seasonal rhythms. The stimulus which this exchange gave to the imagination and to material achievement helped to cause the urban community to be considered progressive and revolutionary, in contrast with a slow-moving rural conservatism. The ultimate-habitat concept was associated with the idea of man's increasingly freeing himself from an enslaving dominance by nature, through expanding his knowledge about how to control nature. The development of cultural life in the cities of Egypt, Mesopotamia, and Persia supported the view indicated, as did development of the Greek city-states and the growth of walled cities in Medieval Europe. The grouping aspect of colonial settlement, as in the colonizing activities of Phoenicia, Greece, Rome, England, and Spain, further supported the idea, and so did the heavy urbanward migration in America and elsewhere during the past century.

In consequence of developments such as noted, many people have come to look upon cities as centers of wide vocational opportunities, superior school and university facilities, theaters and entertainment, deposits of past achievements in libraries and museums, hospitals and superior medical services, experimentation and the development of new knowledge, and generally comfortable living conditions. In contrast with the evolving situation in America and other Western countries, reference has sometimes been made to the Indian villages of the upper Amazon Valley, or some of the villages of India, where life apparently has not changed much for some thousands of years.

It is possible to consider the development of cities in terms of stages,[8] much as a long historical development of anything else can be segmented into periods or eras. Thus, one might refer to early trading centers along rivers, caravan routes, the shores of inland seas, and other lanes of travel where goods from various lands were brought and exchanged. The development of handicrafts stimulated the process, with some mayors trying to prevent artisans from leaving their cities. Leagues of trading cities, such as the Hanseatic League, reflect the period. Probably transition to the manufacturing city was gradual, perhaps based initially on water power, but soon based on steam, with the rate of change speeding up. In America much of the speedup has been associated with growth in population and in economic affluence, to provide a market for an increasing flow of goods. Important, too, has been the growing emphasis by large manufacturing companies on research and development, to bring forth new products and new market appeal.

Two consequences of the second or industrial speedup stage are the emerging shortages of energy and other natural resources, and the growing burdens of waste and refuse heaps. Reference to Medieval cities should include a note on pestilence, dramatized by the Black Death which substantially reduced the population of Europe and parts of Asia during the fourteenth century and which resulted largely from failure of sanitation and waste disposal to develop to an extent commensurate with the population concentrations involved. Slowness in developing sanitation and medical knowledge regarding diseases has been noted as important in the slow growth of cities which prevailed until slightly over a century ago.

Several factors are involved in what might be called a third stage in city evolution, concerning which reference may be focused on the United States. Along with shortages of raw materials and problems of waste disposal, affecting urban concentrations of industry and population, is the suburban dispersal of population and a wider dispersal of industry. Transportation to work, school, and elsewhere generates traffic problems and aggravates fuel demands. Some types of crime remain in the city; other types migrate to the suburbs.

There is a type of urban problem with which cities in American and elsewhere have not learned to deal effectively. That is the problem of sanitation and waste disposal. Abundance of industrial waste aggravates the problem. During much of man's prehistoric existence, he apparently sought to move from one habitat to another, as the former became cluttered, polluted, and filthy. Some cave explorations reveal different layers of deposits indicating different periods of occupancy, with some intervening cover-up.

The amateur nature of present urban disposal efforts may perhaps be described as having three major characteristics. As to sewage, the procedure is to empty it into rivers and lakes, typically with a considerable area of pollution around emptying points. As to garbage, the procedure is to dump it into somebody else's back yard or community, with so-called "landfills" increasingly becoming large-scale examples. The third characteristic is to "move away from it," previously suggested as historically the oldest of the three. This characteristic is perhaps most apparent now in the flight to the suburbs—or beyond, to the "open" country.

A realistic approach to most problems of waste disposal, in a populous industrial society, will have to engage in the comprehensive artificial speedup of nature's recycling process. Natural processes transform human body waste into plant food as fertilizer, which plants through photosynthesis transform either into food for animals that become human food or into cereals and other plants used directly as human food. Research in connection with space explorations and other developments have included some recycling. Some may be accomplished through the use of algae, and perhaps some through omitting the chemistry of photosynthesis. Research on the chemistry of recycling, and on the psychology of using as food certain materials which were very recently expelled as human waste, might contribute substantially regarding supply and disposal problems. Considerable agricultural recycling of animal waste into food for animals of the same species seems now to be under way. As to recycling the solid waste of garbage—paper, metal, glass, plastic, etc.—the problems do not seem formidable.

Certain other developments increasingly affect the status of the city as the ultimate habitat of man, apart from housing, vocational opportunity, and waste disposal. One of these developments concerns television and other mass media of information and entertainment. Another concerns education, with the widespread development of rural consolidated schools, higher qualifications for teacher certification, establishment of junior colleges in many nonurban communities, and the growth of graduate and research programs at state universities or at experiment stations which have no particular city attachment. Furthermore, extensive facilities established by industrial corporations for research undertakings are being established away from cities. Thus cities, as they are now generally thought of, do not constitute the outstanding centers of intellectual and cultural development that they once did. Anxieties about urban crime and personal safety are also important.

But the cities, like other aspects of society, need not be conceived of as being in the future essentially as they are at present. Urban renewal could include more comprehensive developments than are usually mentioned regarding housing; vocational opportunities; food, sanitary, and health services; schools and education; play and recreation; creative work; crime control; etc. Enclosing large portions of a city under one or more extensive roofing arrangements, similar to those enclosing some athletic fields, might greatly influence the nature of city life. Should such a development occur, it would represent a fourth stage, beyond the stage previously characterized as a flight to the suburbs and the open country. There could be substantial migration back to cities of fourth-stage nature. Fourth-stage possibilities respecting megalopolis areas, such as that from Richmond to Boston or that from Milwaukee to South Bend, afford opportunity for considerable speculation. In an important sense the extent to which America's future will be determined by the cities depends on fourth-stage developments. While it is not possible for any culture wholly to neglect or ignore large segments of its total makeup, it is possible for segments to rise or decline in relative importance, as the agricultural segment in America has declined relatively during the past century. The significance of the world's present and prospective food problems relative to expansion in what the general concept of agriculture includes, as to food needs and sources, is presently speculative.

Urban Crisis

There is frequent television comment to the effect that the future of America depends on the cities. The substantial degree of realism in the comment is clouded by the exaggeration which it embodies. With the current level of food prices, worldwide demands, and adverse weather conditions in food-producing areas, there is at least equal justification for saying that the future of America depends on the farms. There are also many intermediate areas of functional importance, which are involved in production, communication, and finance as well as in politics, health and educational services, law enforcement, etc., and which may not be dominated by cities.

The point is that cities are part of a total social structure and are to be understood or improved in that type of conceptual setting. To some extent there often is value in breaking out certain fragments from a complex network and focusing some type of study on a particular fragment, so long as one continuously has the idea in mind that the real meaning of the fragment lies in its relationship to the whole. So it is with the cities and the farms of America, and so it has been throughout their growing interdependence. Some examination of the interdependence may help clarify the problems involved and may indicate some of their educational implications.

(1) *Development of "the urban crisis."* It would be unrealistic to assume that all city problems are economic. But it would be naive to act as if city relationships did not depend on an economic base of material productivity, the same as any other social organization does, in America or elsewhere. The central position of human skill and competence in productivity has been emphasized by economists who maintain that labor is the fundamental source of all wealth. In evaluating the line of reasoning suggested and orienting it on the urban setting, it is necessary to ask about the urban labor supply.

During several decades preceding 1900, immigrants from Europe contributed heavily to the urban labor force in America. These immigrants were predominantly men, in their twenties and early thirties in age, who in a large measure came without family dependents. Thus, the urban labor force was greatly expanded by the addition of large numbers of young mature workers, who had been reared and to some extent educated at the expense of Europe and who upon their arrival were ready to enter upon production without any preliminary American investment in their rearing and development. While the economic harvest reaped by cities of the time was not called a subsidy, its influence on the development of urban productivity was much as if it had been called that.

A second factor of more domestic origin but of similar economic implication developed significance near the turn of the century. It expanded greatly with the disruption of immigration from Europe during World War I and also with the marked restriction of that immigration after the war. This was the migration of Americans from rural areas to the cities. Those migrants, like the immigrants from Europe, were predominately male and were in their twenties and thirties in age. These migrants, similarly, were reared and basically educated at the expense of the rural areas; when they became productive, the harvest was an urban bonanza. Obligations associated with the farm mortgage did not accompany these migrants to the city; but upon the death of the parents and the settlement of estates, the migrants' share expanded the urban bonanza accrual.

However, during the last several decades various forces have contributed to eroding the productivity advantages noted regarding the urban labor supply. Among these factors has been a reduction in size of the rural family, although a considerable out-migration from rural areas has continued. Deterioration of housing and industrial plants in the central city with age and continued use, and the development of transportation systems as well as newer architecture and building design which enhanced suburban locations, have been involved. The "further out" developments, sometimes referred to as exurbia, stimulate abandonment of the central city. The deterioration and abandonment affect community spirit and civic responsibility. Crime and social disorganization are thus facilitated, along with considerable disintegration of individual personality. Public education and law enforcement are among the services affected by the situation indicated.

It would of course be unjustified to infer that every section of every major city has undergone material deterioration or social disorganization of the type suggested; that there are no areas of redevelopment along imaginative lines; or that there have been no ongoing centers of cultural interest such as museums, libraries, theaters, universities, etc. However, the expanding influence of deterioration and disorganization in many cities negates the cultural updraft of the centers noted, attracts nationwide attention, and generates considerable despair, especially among persons who are low on imagination, initiative, and income.

(2) *Renewal and rehabilitation.* If the idea of progress has validity, then the concepts of human relations that exist at a particular time, plus the regulations and physical structures which are intended to implement those concepts, become obsolete and need replacement or rehabilitation. New conceptions of human relationships and of social institutions are thus inferred.

It is of course easier to refer to a need for new concepts of city development than to outline the content of a feasible list of concepts, and much easier than to implement the list. Considerable has been said about new housing design and arrangement to improve pedestrian safety, local recreational facilities, and community spirit. Considerable has also been said about recycling waste, in contrast to hauling it "out of town" to so-called landfills, which contaminate some other community. Experimental undertakings in recycling seem quite timid. Mass transit and other transportation arrangements to reduce traffic congestion and air pollution have received extensive comment. Some attention has been given to the attitudes of workers and to developing their understanding of the stake which they and the community have in an industrial system that is highly productive. The role of foreign competition is sometimes emphasized in this connection, as are workers sharing in management decisions and in company ownership. Perhaps more than average attention has been given to urban political structure and functioning. Particular attention has related to such matters as boundaries between political units, as highlighted by court action on dissolving school-district or county boundaries in suits on racial integration of schools. There has also been attention to the internal organization of local government, regarding mayor-council versus other forms of city government, and vocal attention to corruption in government, as highlighted by Watergate and other developments.

A concern that is increasingly recognized in renewal undertakings is the breaking up of existing ethnic patterns and the establishment of new ones. More understanding of the psychology of socially positive and negative aspects of such patterns could add to the constructiveness of some urban renewals and some school integrations. The recent election of negroes as mayors of several important cities might involve considerable experimental interest with respect to governing insights and rapport, since negroes typically constitute a large portion of the slum dwellers and since the slums constitute problem areas. Ramifications and implications of Watergate-type corruptions are a perennial concern in urban politics. The wide range of associations and activities which characterize urban life require a large number of regulations, each of which affords opportunity for violation or for corruption in regard to enforcement. The American people have never extensively understood political implications, such as those mentioned, or considered it a part of their civic responsibility to understand and act constructively on them.

(3) *Urban life and national unity.* Geographical scatter in America and suspicion of authoritarian central government in Europe were important influences in the provisions by the Founding Fathers for a weak central government in America. The subsequent drift toward greater centralization has been continuous, although the tempo has varied from time to time. Several factors have been pronounced in this development. These include the extensive development of industry and a market economy, in place of an economy based largely on self-sufficient agriculture; nationwide systems of rail, highway, and air transportation; large-scale corporate and government financing; seasonal and other internal migration of people; increasing range of governmental services requested by the people and rendered by the federal government; growing importance of wars and other international relationships, in which the people act through the central government; expanding power of federal courts, in broadening the nationwide implications of their judgment on a large range of issues.

Developments such as the foregoing mean that it is unrealistic to assume that any part of our national life can effectively be considered apart from its relationships to the other parts. It is thus integration of the total, and not fragmentation, that needs emphasis. The necessary integration demands a broad assemblage of information and the application of sophisticated statistical techniques for analyzing data and forecasting probable outcomes of pursuing different alternatives. Many large-scale undertakings demand a scope of financing that only the federal government can undertake. Information and commentator evaluations of most large federal projects are heralded across the nation through mass media. The implications of federal subsidies for agriculture, housing, health services, urban renewal, highway and other transportation developments, and price regulation are among numerous instances of the influence exercised by central government on the nation's economy. Other influences relate to the cost of national defense, foreign aid, etc. Great perspective is required to interpret the findings and the recommendations.

(4) *The role of the universities.* A further important consideration, regarding the relation of urban status to national well-being, concerns the leadership role of universities in developing a broad analytical understanding of urban problems—and in solving those problems. A larger portion of this responsibility than at present could be incorporated in the preparation of students for service in industry, government, and the professions. This is part of the integrative and perspective emphasis previously noted. However, universities might also be more constructively engaged in research on specific urban problems than many universities usually are.

Minority Groups

At present, considerations regarding minority groups receive a great deal of attention in America. Efforts to foresee the future of minority problems emerge and disappear, as well as the limited conception which minorities usually have of community well-being. The relation of minority status to changes in the general value structure of society should also be noted.

In any populous society which has a broad geographical expanse and a considerable variety of economic or vocational enterprises, minorities of some kind are almost certain to emerge. While minorities in America tend to be thought of in such terms as religion, race, national origin, economic status, vocational interest, etc., minority status may not always be associated with number of persons in a particular group but with the power which the group wields. This can be seen in respect to political parties or in respect to promoters and opponents of specific developmental projects in a community. However, groupings on this basis tend to be fluid and transient. In some instances, persons who are not in minority status numerically tend to have a kind of minority psychology or seek to promote group objectives much as numerical minorities do. American women are sometimes referred to as using a minority approach in furthering some of their objectives. Two important considerations regarding minorities thus relate to their origin and disappearance and to their limited outlook regarding community well-being. A third consideration relates to cultural change and change in value outlook associated with minority status.

(1) *Mobility and minority status.* The origin of biological and cultural minorities may be thought of in terms of isolation. Inbreeding is a biological consequence of isolation, with genetic mutations which occur becoming fixed within a group, but not spreading outside that group. The cumulative effect of this process over several hundred generations can account for wide physical and perhaps mental differences among population groups which have been isolated from one another over long periods of time. Racial characteristics as well as lesser ethnic differences have often been explained on this basis. It is thus easy to see how such cultural traits as language, status accorded to members of the two sexes or to persons of different ages, conceptions of family life or community government, etc., might develop along quite different lines among different peoples.

The melting-pot phenomenon in America shows how mobility broke down many cultural and minor genetic differences, which varying degrees of isolation had developed among the Europeans who came to the nation's shores in great numbers during three generations preceding World War I. The public schools and compulsory school attendance played an important role in melting-pot operations; but so too did jobs and other aspects of economic opportunity, as well as rather easy access to formal citizenship and voting.

But melting-pot achievements regarding European immigrants were easy in a biological sense because the different national groups represented close branches of the white race, without many people from the Arab world or from the so-called "aryan" parts of India. However, with the near-elimination of immigration from Europe following World War I, a marked dispersal of negroes occurred on a nationwide basis, and large numbers of persons came into the country from Mexico and some other areas of Latin America, whose biological ancestry was partly that of local Indians. Dispersal from the West Coast during and following World War II of persons who reflected

Oriental ancestry added to the biological heterogeneity of the people in several parts of the nation. Before much biological "melting" occurs with respect to these groups, or absorption of them by the white majority, considerable further melting or absorption in the cultural sense may be necessary. The history of intermarriage among descendents of European immigrants support the view that in the present world cultural melting generally precedes biological melting. In some respects minority considerations regarding American Indians in the United States resemble considerations noted regarding other ethnic minorities; but complications relate to their special land and reservation status, as related to their life here before white control was established. "Wounded Knee" disruptions may be symptomatic of future minority rumblings involving Indian groups.

(2) *Minority psychology and social outlook.* One characteristic which helps to identify minority groups is their typical concern for promoting rather narrowly conceived developments for the benefit of their minority, without much regard to the well-being of the rest of society, except as a by-product of helping their group. Few minorities use the reverse approach, with emphasis on general well-being and with their minority group benefiting through general participation along with others. The orientation described does not stimulate warmheartedness on the part of the majority toward the minority. The characterizations indicated may relate to minority behavior associated with religion, race, sex, or any other basis of minority grouping.

As long as the foregoing situation prevails, minorities are likely to look upon themselves as being persecuted and the majority is likely to hope the minorities will stop making nuisances of themselves. Reference is sometimes made to modern Israel in the connection indicated, as complaints of persecution arise because of local objections to carving a Jewish state out of an area of the Arab world. A major point concerns *who* should assume initiative for ameliorating minority-majority antagonisms. Minorities usually are more limited than majorities in human and material resources, and perhaps in imagination, but majorities have to spread their resources and attention over a wider range of society's problems. Also, the immediate interest which individual members of minority groups have in the measures which their groups sponsor, might justify their assuming the initiative for showing how those measures contribute to general community well-being—as well as to improved minority status.

Some members of the white majority in America see considerable hope for movement in the direction noted, lying in the recent election of negroes to high public offices. Thus, the election of Edward Brooke from Massachusetts to the United States Senate, the election of Thomas Bradley to be mayor of Los Angeles, or the election of negroes as mayors in several other American cities of considerable size could not have occurred without a large supporting white vote. Such a vote often means that a substantial portion of the white majority think that the member of the ethnic minority has the perspective and the commitment to handle the responsibility of the office from the total-community standpoint, rather than from the more limited minority standpoint. This represents a big step toward cultural absorption and a reciprocal step from minority restriction toward civic maturity. It thus represents effort to improve conditions through the political machinery of government, rather than through parades and other presently outdated civil-rights activities which have often been associated with Dr. Martin Luther King. Apparently the "Wounded Knee" technique concerning plains Indians remains more primitive, although the situation there is complicated by reservation status. However, some comparisons such as noted may be complicated by ethnic status in particular cities as contrasted with the nation as a whole.

(3) *Cultural growth and changing values.* Several changes have occurred in America since the beginning of World War II which bear on the implications of minority status within the nation. Some of these relate to the economic need for labor in industrial production and to federal regulations concerning racial discrimination and fair employment practices in industry. Federal legislation and court rulings on public transportation, housing, health services, use of recreation facilities, and public school attendance expand the picture in erasing minority-majority differences. America's international involvement, particularly with respect to the nonwhite majority of the world's population, has substantial implications for race relations within this country.

Moreover, significant nationwide interest has become focused on broad-scale economic and research undertakings, which make some of the older focal points of value orientation look puny and irrelevant, especially to persons under thirty, who have had little of the old-style indoctrination. Foreign aid to help technically and economically undeveloped countries of varied racial backgrounds illustrates the economic sphere; space exploration illustrates the research area.

Scientific, technical, and statistical developments in business, industry, government, and some aspects of education have generated considerable emphasis on objectivity in evaluating achievements and on the potential of different individuals for achieving. The objectivity seems particularly visible with regard to race and sex, although we still have hang-ups with respect to age, and some judicial thinking continues to paw around in a fog concerning racial quotas in job allocations.

Considerable future development seems probable concerning objectivity in evaluating people, with respect to such matters as school placement, job qualifications, public-service needs, etc. It is unrealistic to assume that no complaints or disgruntledness will accompany the process, as with respect to the evaluative instruments used, the procedure in administering or using them, or the interpretations placed on scores. But the *fact* that a person twenty years old cannot read or add above a fifth-grade level may be more important concerning a particular job than *reasons* offered as to why he cannot do so.

Objective evaluations might either support or negate conceptions of a superior-inferior scale of competencies, which is often associated with majority attitudes concerning some minorities. When scientific research pushes objectivity considerably farther than is possible at present, some aspects of such a scale will probably be established, although perhaps not along lines that either a majority or a minority will find wholly comfortable. Because extensive research in genetics is lacking, there is still much space for guessing about the nature of intelligence and its variation from one person to another. However, studies on educational opportunity have narrowed that space by showing that environment can substantially influence measurable intelligence. Research may reveal additional external or internal physical traits which affect a person's health or functional capacity and which have racial anchorage; as, for example, sickle-cell anemia is now considered to be essentially a negro disease, and hypertension a frequent negro problem. Perhaps every racial group has genetic traits which are obstacles to effective survival. Whether genetic or chromosome surgery can modify this situation now seems speculative, but research presently offers the best method of finding out.

In attempting to examine majority considerations from the standpoint of race, some attention might be given to research in anthropoloy. Such research might relate to so-called indigenous cultural developments in parts of the world which apparently were inhabited for several thousand years by persons of a particular racial background, without extensive migrations or mobility in other modern respects. Two culture areas stand out in this respect: the Congo area of Africa and the area of the Americas. Neither of these areas developed a culture status comparable to that of China, India, the Mediterranean Basin, or Western Europe, although the Aztecs and the Incas did reach noteworthy achievements.

Where race consciousness is strong, there may be a strong sense of personal responsibility on the part of outstanding negroes or Indians to demonstrate that their racial background does not embody any handicap for developments of the kind indicated. Outstanding achievement by individuals who pioneer in a kind of "breaking the ice" for group recognition has been felt by the first women in American politics, the rise of peasants to positions of high-level recognition in class-conscious Europe, and by members of other groups. Evaluating achievement on an individualized basis tends to reduce this group overhead, although individualizing may have an atomizing effect. For negroes, the white-based and the substantially individualized culture of the United States probably offers the world's best opportunity to reach outstanding individual achievement. There is considerable reason for thinking that the special burden to achieve that rests on the leaders of racial and other minorities will have to be borne until "outstanding" achievement becomes fairly common among members of the minority; that is, until the group thus comes to be looked upon as being "like the rest of the people." Broad cultural absorption, or disappearance of minority status, will then be well under way.

When public schools and other agencies minimize differences among minorities, they foster absorption and identification with the whole. Agencies which continue to emphasize minority differences and to promote special minority interests tend to perpetuate minority identification. The perpetuations foster majority resentments that are likely to be directed toward groups which are characterized by a narrow selfish interest that cannot be generally shared. Negro political leaders of the type previously noted do much to point the way from a narrow minority conception of life to broad cultural participation. But of course politics is not the only path leading in the direction suggested. Other paths may relate to business, scientific research, education, mechanical invention, the arts, etc.

Special Education for Handicapped Persons

For a half-century, causal and remedial designations concerning physically and mentally handicapped persons have continuously moved from superstition toward science. The ignorance that had earlier prevailed in this field, and had essentially looked upon the devil as causal and upon prayer as remedial, should be thought of as an extension into this particular field of the simple god-demon approach which primitive man's limited knowledge and imagination enabled him to formulate. The approach should be considered an advance over our primate ancestors who did not seem to recognize much causal relationship in connection with events which occur. But once the idea of cause becomes a part of a person's intellectual life, he begins to replace earlier conceptions of cause and response with newer conceptions which are associated with results that he likes better.

Apparently for some hundreds of generations there has been variation in the extent to which man has applied the idea of cause in his relationships to the physical world and in relationships among people. The variations involve the areas of relationship here concerned, and the particular individuals who consider the relationships. Both variables relate to the status of knowledge and action regarding physically and mentally handicapped persons, as they relate to every other area of human interest.

(1) *Major considerations in providing for the handicapped.* Among possible considerations concerning handicapped persons, three are considered.

(a) *Science and technology.* The superstitions noted in an earlier statement probably retarded the entry of research orientation and experimental procedure into areas concerning handicapped persons. But with the expansion of knowledge covering a broad range of interests, these areas also became involved.

One aspect of experimentation to develop knowledge involves trying out suggestions to alter the existing situation. Various prosthetic devices and remedial procedures relating to handicapped persons have thus come into use, with forward projection in additional possibilities. And man's usually tardy projections backward into preventive considerations is gradually being examined. As preventive hypotheses attract more experimental attention, fatalism as a cause becomes further eroded, both in relation to genetic and other factors which are loosely referred to as congenital and to a cluster of postnatal developments which our current ignorance and indifference finds comfort in allocating to chance and calling accidents. Imaginative workers in the field of special education and rehabilitation should look upon the "accident" category of explaining cause as being comparable to the term "devil," which was used by our ancestors as a kind of universal.

Critics of foregoing comments can muster substantial argument about the role of chance, in regard to both congenital and subsequent misfortune. Part of the argument is that chance or flukes affect chromosome and postnatal phenomena because people are less than perfect and accordingly defy efforts at errorless forecasting. The extent to which such argument seems reasonable depends on the extent to which "chance" is considered synonymous with "ignorance." Thus, as differentiations among causal factors and remedial efforts press further, chance as an explanation recedes. But at any stage in the expansion of knowledge it is worthwhile to recognize that at that particular stage knowledge helps to dispel old myths at the same time that it may help lay the foundation for new ones.

(b) *Humanitarianism.* One aspect of humanitarianism might be characterized as doing unto others what you would like for them to do unto you. While the theory indicated has been recognized for many centuries, the implementation has never been conspicuous. Reciprocity is apparent in the statement, as suggested by the idea: "he is a human being about as I am, and probably has likes and dislikes about like mine." Perhaps a more developed statement of the idea would be: "the same misfortunes might befall me as have befallen him, and if they did I would appreciate some help." When the idea has developed sufficiently to be projected on the group in a complex society, the margin of protection or security involved becomes a system of insurance.

Experience with initial operations of the system is likely to lend appeal for extension of the protection or insurance coverage, both for additional types of persons and additional degrees of need. A substantial margin has great importance for the emotional stability and mental health of the "normal" individual, since it enables him to feel that if great misfortune should befall him, there is a substantial difference between his present status and that position lower on the scale at which he would not be entitled to group help. The assurance and freedom from anxiety enables him to function more efficiently in his daily activities as a "normal" person. Most Western industrial countries now embody the idea in social insurance and to some extent embody it in tenure and retirement systems. Gradual extension of these systems to afford wider coverage is a familiar event. The development and expansion of special education and rehabilitation services concerning handicapped persons should be viewed in the perspective indicated.

However, an important note on further perspective should be added. Much of the benevolent "do unto others" sentiment floated about for several centuries before science and technology developed the skills and the material goods for implementation. It is largely through scientific and technological developments that benevolent sentiments have become more than sporadic gossamers.

But interrelationship between science and sentiment gives another significance to sentiment. Prevailing sentiments have much to do with the areas which science will be permitted to explore and with the uses made of knowledge gained through the exploration. Thus, will science be encouraged to develop new drugs or new prosthetic appliances for mentally or physically handicapped persons, or will it preferably develop new deodorants, sports prizes, dog foods, etc? The sentiments of a particular time may be crucial in regard to priorities in the allocation of resources, such as time, energy, and knowledge. The clue for science in this setting may be to devote more time to the psychology of sentiment manipulation. The rather new field of public relations in industry illustrates the point. Yoga and transcendental meditation may henceforth bear on the situation.

(c) *Economic materialism.* Foregoing comments embody suggestions concerning the fundamental nature of a material base, if sentiments or ethics concerning the "welfare of fellow man" are to be implemented. The long absence of substantial implementation has been due largely to the absence of material wherewithal for the implementation. Another way to state the absence would be to say that a person ordinarily seeks to provide for himself up to what he considers to be a fairly comfortable level, before he is concerned broadly about the needs of fellowman. There are, of course, variations in sensitivity about those needs, depending on such matters as propaganda, nearness of the fellowman who has the needs, etc.

Preceding statements infer that much of what is currently said about human values being superior to material values is essentially idle chatter. It is idle because human values do not really exist without dependence on material goods. Thus, if there is not enough food to go around, the ordinary man would prefer that it be somebody else's family which starves rather than his own. The dog-eat-dog implication is nature's survival of the fittest, when near to its lowest common denominator.

If earlier statements on margin of security are harmonized with immediately preceding statements on survival, it should be clear that the material status of handicapped or other minority groups depends, more fully than is true of the general population, on a high level of material productivity in the total economy. In a substantial degree the same applies to youth, older persons, the poorly trained, and others who are on the periphery of employability or of associated concepts of usefulness.

Workers in special education and rehabilitation thus have at least three significant professional interests in a highly productive economy. One concerns the resources that can thus be made available for research and service intended to help the mentally and physically handicapped or other rehabilitation clients. Another is that a highly productive economy implies an abundance of job opportunities and greater ease in placing individuals with peripheral employability. The employability may relate both to training programs and to post-training placement. A third interest notes that a highly productive economy can afford more jobs for professional personnel in providing for handicapped persons.

(2) *Demographic implications.* Some people call attention to eugenic implications of marriage and associated family responsibility on the part of mentally and physically handicapped persons. Much depends on the nature and degree of the handicap and probably on the attitudes of the persons most directly involved. Considerable also depends on the fact that marriage need not be followed by begetting and rearing children. Possibilities regarding sterilization and other birth-control procedures are frequently mentioned in this connection.

When it is said that in America the "right" to beget and rear children is one of the individual's most fundamental rights, some inquiry into the nature of rights is necessary. A preliminary inquiry asks if rights must be equated with competence and willingness in relation to commensurate responsibility. A more fundamental inquiry observes that individual rights are of social origin and that accordingly such rights vary substantially from one culture to another. For example, the reason that an American child is entitled to free public education is that the American people collectively have said so and are able to provide the facilities required. The situation regarding the Hottentot child in Central Africa is quite different, not because of the vegetation or wildlife of the region, but because of social structure. The same applies to entitlement concerning a job in one's preferred vocation, to health services, police protection, special education, etc.

Historic practices regarding infanticide or euthanasia, exacting the death penalty in relation to certain crimes, drafting individuals for hazardous military service, determining which applicants shall have priority for receiving organ transplants in modern surgery, or who may have lifeboat priority on a sinking passenger ship, are among many situation in which society ignores proclaimed individual rights. The point here is that rights are ordinarily stated in broad general terms, but applications in specific situations often involve curtailments. Thus, the Supreme Court has stated on numerous occasions that there are no absolute freedoms, that constitutional freedom of speech, religion, etc., is relative to the particular situation at hand.

When the preceding thought is applied to who may have children, various considerations concerning community responsibility for the children arise. Some of these relate to education, health services, vocational opportunity, and type of contribution to the group's biological stream. But here again, ignorance about genetic and many other causal factors in mental and physical handicap prevent any very creative development on individual rights and group controls in regard to begetting and rearing considerations. While one may accept the theory that a society has the right or duty to reduce the percentage of handicapped persons in future generations, implementing a theory requires knowledge and other resources as noted earlier. The required knowledge for comprehensive programs in the field concerned does not now exist.[9]

However, greater concreteness is possible on one aspect of eugenics. The point involves the logic in our social concern about the "rights" of persons with hereditary physical or mental defects to beget and rear children, when other aspects of our culture place great emphasis on birth control and on no-population-increase with respect to normal or superior persons who presumably could beget and rear normal or superior children. It is socially irresponsible for proclaimed leadership to suggest that logical consistency in situations of this kind is irrelevant or that such consistency should give way to contrary sentiment.

Population Growth and Cultural Status

In countries which have for several decades emphasized broad popular education at increasingly higher levels, it is not difficult to conclude that a sizeable and competent population is a nation's greatest resource, as compared with agricultural land, timber, coal, oil, iron or other metals, etc.

Question may thus arise as to the relative emphasis to be placed on "sizeable" and on "competent," or the relative emphasis on personal satisfaction and on national strength.

(1) *Population as material power.* Before the increased material productivity of the industrial revolution was well under way, there was broad acceptance of a political doctrine to the effect that the relative power of kings depended on the number of their subjects. Part of the support may have been based on a vague psychology which placed human subjects in the same category as broad acres and large herds of cattle, but part of it was based on the idea that more subjects meant more soldiers to fight neighboring countries. The emphasis on mere numerical superiority probably had some foundation when equipment and modes of fighting were simple. However, when progress in the industrial revolution showed that a smaller number of men with superior weapons and other equipment and with superior training constituted a more effective fighting force than the larger number who were poorly equipped and poorly trained, emphasis on sheer numbers declined.

Much of what is said about numbers versus equipment in the military sphere applies generally to industrial production for the consumer market. But when a small labor force that was well trained and well equipped could produce enough goods in the areas of material necessities to supply a population of a given size, two somewhat new situations arose. One concerned the availability of a rather large number of people at home and abroad to serve as consumers and thus to constitute a market. The other concerned the development of new products and new conceptions of human well-being, with advertising and propaganda to make the people think they needed the newer items.

Perhaps at the state of industrial and technical development inferred, the competitive search by industrial nations for markets resembles aggressiveness sometimes noted in militarily strong nations which appear to seek out weak neighbors on whom to exercise their military strength. Two world wars and subsequent military operations in different parts of the world may indicate considerable overlap between commercial and military aggression, but such wars also indicate that other causal factors are involved.

The former comment on new products and advertising implies that as the basically recognized necessities for material goods are met, to a degree which is currently regarded to be adequate, more leisure time is generated. Among the lines along which the leisure stimulates creative imagination are various forms of nonmaterial productivity. Out of this atmosphere arise such creations as literature, the arts, speculative philosophy, further mechanical invention, theories of government, and other developments which may loosely be referred to as luxuries; that is, developments which luxuriate when basic material needs have been met.

Then does it follow that a country with a large population, which enjoys extensive leisure and engages in extensive luxuriating, will reflect a higher level of cultural development than a country with a smaller population? Efforts of small industrial nations of Western Europe to draw together into a larger population and economic unit through common-market politics, as compared for example with the United States, may be instructive in this connection. On the other hand, comparisons between the United States and India in population mass and standard of living, might lend support to certain arguments about overpopulation.

(2) *Optimum population density.* A fundamental weakness of theories which refer to overpopulation strictly in terms of numerical density is that they overlook the most basic criterion of human well-being—namely, the standard of living. In the territory within the present forty-eight contiguous states of this nation, there are now several times as many people as there were in the days of Columbus, of Virginia's Captain John Smith, or of Daniel Boone. It would be fantastically unrealistic to suggest that the average person at any one of those earlier times enjoyed a standard of existence as high as the average American enjoys today, if standard is judged by adequacy of food, housing, health services, range of vocational opportunity, knowledge of world events, scope and freedom in personal association or travel, longevity, or any of numerous other elements which present-day Americans consider important to their lives. Few Americans would look upon these present values as having been offset by opportunities of our predecessors to watch squirrels jump from tree to tree, focus attention on a bear that emerged from a nearby woods to look over the new invaders, shoot a wild turkey now and then, or experience rhythmically alternating chills and fever which the widespread malaria afforded.

If one recognizes that the status of the arts and the sciences, along with the form of government and social regulations, constitute the basic determiners of the standard of living, then he recognizes that numerical density of the population has no more than secondary status. Optimum density implies number *relative to* the status of the arts, science, and government. Considerations of an optimum would relegate doctrines of absolute numerical overpopulation to the same museum as increasingly houses conceptions of absolutes regarding personal freedoms, political power, personal health, religion, property rights, etc.

When one reflects on foregoing views regarding optimum versus absolute considerations, some doctrines on "no population increase" in present-day United States seem especially curious. One way to characterize the underlying philosophy might be to say that the birth rate should be restricted in the United States—where children have as good an opportunity as anywhere in the world for adequate food, health services, education, vocational choice and satisfactions, freedom of expression and of personal association, participation in government, varied recreation, etc.—and that this should be done so that present adults in America have more time and resources to help feed, reduce mortality rates, and otherwise increase the population of India or some other have-not area of the world. With respect to anything resembling world population strategy, it seems to be a curious practice to operate on the assumption that future population increases should come from areas of the world which are least well qualified to rear and provide for children, rather than from the areas which are best qualified to do so. When the foregoing is coupled with a world tendency toward freer international migration of people, the implications of the philosophy described should be even more apparent.

(3) *Balance between growth in population and growth in the arts.* When

reference is made to *balance* among social phenomena, some conception of standards or ratios is assumed, although perhaps not stated. The basis of one's standards resides in what he likes or in the emotional satisfactions which he anticipates from particular activities which are being considered. However, the high degree of similarity among persons of biological potential for emotional satisfactions affords a substantial common base of preferred satisfactions. The preferences thus become community standards.

But the preferences or standards that prevail at a particular time depend largely on what the arts and other aspects of the social setting make possible at that time. It follows that standards change with changes in the setting noted. One problem of change now confronting America concerns research or further development of the arts with respect to new sources of energy. A corollary is the acceptance of life patterns which consume less energy or are less demanding on other natural resources. Fox hunts, deer hunts, golf, sports fishing, etc., have sometimes been considered forms of recreation that are wasteful in utilization of animals, land, and water relative to the number of persons accommodated.

There has been marked evolution in American recreation since the days of John Smith or Daniel Boone. To assume that the evolution should stop because a group of environmentalists or other persons imagine they would like things better if conditions were restored to a situation thought by the environmentalists to have existed a couple generations ago is no more realistic than to assume that the older conditions of job possibilities or household lighting should be comparably restored.

It might be essentially dealing with small potatoes and be otherwise unsound to suggest, as is sometimes done, that the movement for "no population growth in America" is promoted essentially by middle-class or upper-class women and others who have extensive leisure and who seek social recognition through "good cause" orientation rather than through rearing families. However, there can be little doubt about the potential of technology in medicine, agriculture, etc., to support a substantial or perhaps rapid increase in the nation's population. But such potential increase should be thought of in terms of some relative concept regarding optimum, rather than of some absolute which implies a numerical maximum. More emphasis on advancement in the arts, sciences, and social regulations, which largely determine the standard of living, might hold great promise in the connection noted. And it is basically in the setting described that lawlessness and delinquency have whatever relationships to population density and growth, if any, that they actually do have.

Church and State in America

American colonists who were instrumental in forming the American union and in writing the Constitution had had experience regarding state religions in the colonies, in England, or elsewhere in Europe. They were impressed with the way in which the military and taxing power of central government cooperated with clerical manipulation of religious faith and superstition, in exploiting the common people. State power embodied in the king was looked upon as exercising direct control over daily life and church power as exercising indirect control through alleged "pilot service" during a threatening hereafter. In return for economic and military support, the church provided psychological support and obedience—it was contended.

(1) *Degrees of separation.* Americans today are presumably familiar with the struggles by Jefferson and Madison in developing the provisions for freedom of religious worship and freedom from taxation to support a church, which they got into Virginia's legal framework and later into the Constitution of the United States. But there is always a question as to how far it is desirable or possible to separate the functioning of different institutions which are alive and active in any society at a particular time. One need not go so far as to urge that the activities or influence of any institution in a society reverberate from the point of origin throughout the remainder of the social structure, in order to recognize overlapping or conflicting reverberations between religion and government. The extensive powers of government which the church had historically exercised along several lines were being denied by the state in America. One line concerned the right to tax the people for the support of a particular church. Another concerned the right to force the people to attend a particular church or to forbid their worshipping publicly in any other church.

Halfway measures of separation in America have long been associated with some of the numerous activities in which churches engage, but in which sectarianism may not be the most conspicuous societal characteristic and in which there is a continuous problem of determining the correct path for the state in neither aiding nor inhibiting worship according to a particular religious faith. Maintenance of hospitals and orphanages illustrate the point. Exemption from taxes of the property devoted to use in such connections is thus part of the picture; so too in recent years is eligibility for certain public grants. The absence of either state aid or inhibition has generally been interpreted as justifying exemption from taxation of the church sanctuary or other property used directly in worship services. But in recent years the tax exemption has been under attack in several states, as different units of government are increasingly pressed to find new sources of revenue. However, under most immediate attack is the exemption from taxes of income-yielding property owned by churches, which competes with privately owned and taxable property. Church-owned office space, housing facilities, wineries, farmlands, etc., are examples.

(2) *Church and state in education.* At the time that our federal Constitution was adopted, in most parts of Europe the schoolroom aspects of education intended for children and youth reflected an extensive degree of church control. More state participation gradually appeared. Early America reflected much the same picture. While America's federal Constitution provided for separation of church and state in regard to religious worship and associated facilities, the Constitution did not provide for public education. The efforts of individual states to provide universal free public education within the constitutional framework of religious liberty have resulted in developments which show considerable variation.

Of major importance in the struggle between church and state for the control of education has been the idea that whoever controls the social and intellectual life of the child from the age of five or six years will essentially control the future pattern of society.[10] Concern has been less with classroom and textbook learning in English grammar, spelling, arithmetic, elementary science, personal hygiene, etc., than with such matters as orientation and humility respecting God, loyalty and respect for particular institutions, personalities to be used as hero models, or rights and entitlements regarding the distribution of tax revenues. The first group of items are looked upon as personal in nature and perhaps as involved in holding jobs; whereas the second group is considered to be policy determining, as to who will dominate and control the social order.

Persons who are familiar with the history of church-state controversies in America know that the early anxieties and disputes related to control by the various Protestant denominations. However, with the subsequent immigration of Catholics from Southern and Eastern Europe, and more recently from Latin America, the picture has substantially changed. In several of our states now, 80-90 percent of the children in parochial schools are in schools controlled by the Catholic Church, where activities follow a centralized pattern of denominational orientation.

Some leaders of the parochial-school development apparently think of the public schools as being in fact Protestant schools with anti-Catholic orientation. Protestants tend to react that whatever anti-Catholicism there·is in the public schools relates to school recognition of religious liberty under the Constitution. Some Protestants refer to a step-by-step "encroachment" of organized Catholic power on the tax base supporting the public schools. In this connection they point to state provided textbooks for children in parochial schools; to transportation at public expense for children attending parochial schools; to publicly provided feeding and heath services for parochial-school students; to dual enrollments whereby parochial-school students may take mathematics, laboratory, vocational and other "tool subject" courses in public schools, but take literature, social science, and other "policy-forming" courses in the parochial school; and to other *parochiaid* developments which courts accept under an expanding "child-benefit" theory as being constitutionally permissible.

Somewhat peripheral to the "child-benefit" theory but yet pertinent in the present connection, perhaps conceived of as a logical next step following dual enrollment, is effort to secure public funds to pay teachers in parochial schools who teach secular subjects. Teachers in parochial schools who are under personal religious vows of poverty might thus make a significant monetary contribution to the church, at the same time that there is an elimination of any religious hazard related to the association of the parochial-school students during part of the day spent with public school students in an educational atmosphere which is quite different from that of the parochial school.

Beyond peripheral consideration and indicating a quite new focus, it has been urged, is effort to get some kind of reimbursement for parents to cover the tuition or related payments which they make to parochial schools. This has been characterized as the "parent-benefit" theory and thus as going beyond the "child benefit" theory. A common form of effort in the "parent-benefit" category is to seek concessions on state and federal income taxes for the tuition payments. Perhaps efforts for concessions by lesser taxing bodies might trail along later, as might efforts to secure direct reimbursement of parents for tuition paid. However, it may seem premature to speculate on whether "parent-benefit" could serve as a way-station between "child benefit" and some type of "institutional benefit," possibly under some such caption as "benevolent charity."

(3) *Divisiveness and unity.* Any organized society has problems concerning divisiveness and unity, sometimes stated as the individual versus the group. The problems are especially difficult in a democratic society, in which the individual voter exerts considerable direct influence on government and in which government is supposed to be conducted for the benefit of the governed rather than of those who do the governing. Maximum freedom for the individual implies a high level of divisiveness in numerous aspects of social doctrine and social practice. The same applies to a great number of minority groups, which vary in size, orientation, and potential for power. Religious denominations in America are among such minorities.

There is a kind of political theory to the effect that *every* minority has a right to try to become a majority, but this right is circumscribed by formal rules and by public opinion as to how the "trying" may proceed. However, there is a parallel right of *every other* minority to try to prevent *a particular* minority from becoming a majority. A multiplicity of conflicting minorities thus constitutes a fertile seedbed for divisiveness.

Two important causes of divisiveness in America, since adoption of the federal Constitution, have been race and religion. Divisiveness concerning race mushroomed into the economic and political ramifications of the Civil War, with a retinue of reconstruction, separate-but-equal, school integration, and other forms of racial strife and divisiveness that linger today. While domestic and international pressures during recent decades have forced considerable racial unity, by restricting the individual freedom of some so as to increase that of others, shortcomings of both negroes and whites retard the development of creativeness within unity.

The situation concerning religion and social unity describes a quite different pattern. Early political reaction to religious diversity was to declare broad freedom for religious practice, through the Constitution and otherwise, and in effect to say that insofar as the state and participation in government are concerned, one's religious beliefs and practices are irrelevant. In practice, this theory has never been literally followed. This fact is shown with respect to religious practices on plural marriages; religious holidays of particular sects and public school attendance; religious objection to loyalty oaths and state employment; etc.

Foregoing comments on religious differences and social unity have related essentially to individualized and rather sporadic situations. Scattered events in the sense noted seldom threaten the kind of divisiveness that may be associated with a numerically large and highly organized minority that seems to follow a long-range plan of successive steps in eroding the unity and power of the majority or the state and in transferring that power to itself. Herein lies the basis for the anxiety which sponsors of American public education see in a highly organized system of parochial schools, which maintains a constant pressure for reaching further into the public treasury to support its programs. Divisiveness in this setting should be evaluated in terms of the creative and the destructive implications of individual and minority aggrandizements in their more general respects.

Part of the anxiety about divisiveness, relfected by present leaders in American public education, relates to private elementary and secondary schools which are not parochially oriented. The tendency of both parochial and nonparochial private schools, it is contended, is that they develop in their students the feeling that they represent a superior social and intellectual group who are receiving an education which is superior to that received by the public-school hoipolloi. According to this view, persons from nonpublic schools should be entitled to a higher social status and level of authority than persons of public school background. Such leaders in public education point to the class structure and social cleavages in some countries of Western Europe, where tax revenues for education are divided between public and parochial schools.

Those leaders further note that in racial or ethnic background, and in most aspects of historical development, the European countries indicated have been more homogeneous than the United States has been. The melting-pot function of the American public school may be noted in this connection, with its major contribution in developing cosmopolitan American citizens out of polyglot raw material of varied ethnic and cultural backgrounds. Exponents of racial integration, persons concerned about education for children who live in poor school districts, and people who are interested in educational and related opportunity for physically and mentally handicapped children are not the only ones who hope that the melting pot will not be replaced by a deep freeze.

(4) *Compulsory taxation and compulsory school attendance.* During the establishment of public school systems in America through the last two-thirds of the preceding century, there was great dispute about compulsory taxation to support public schools and about compulsory attendance when the schools were established. Controversy over state authority to require attendance at public schools has arisen intermittently since that time, although the Supreme Court in an Oregon case[11] established the right of parents to have their children educated in nonpublic schools, provided those schools met reasonable state requirements in regard to the education necessary for effective citizenship. In addition to the "necessary" education, the nonpublic schools might include religious or other materials. Since that decision was rendered in 1925, there have been various disputes about what constitutes equivalency in meeting the state program and about inspection of nonpublic schools by state agencies. Disputes over equivalency exist today, with varying degrees of vigor.

Amish in some states present a special equivalency problem, in their resistance to public education without providing a clear-cut institutional program to replace it. The point regarding compulsory taxation concerns justification for taxation to provide compulsory schooling if attendance is not in fact compulsory. This is a different form of attack on compulsory taxation from that advanced by Catholics respecting tax concessions for tuition which parents pay to private schools.

(5) *Justification for the constitutional prohibition.* It is not difficult to find Americans who respond by reflex to action which is considered to be "unconstitutional." This may have value regarding promptness or certainty of initial response in some types of situations. The point that certain provisions are in the Cconstitution is important, but much more important is an understanding of *why* they are there. To understand why, it is necessary to understand the divisiveness and strife associated with denominationalism in North America before adoption of the Constitution, the picture of that and subsequent times of divisiveness in Western Europe, and reemerging divisive influences in this country. These are important considerations as to why the provisions for freedom of personal worship, and against the use of state money or other state power either to promote or to inhibit the activities of particular religious denominations, became and remain parts of the Constitution.

Government and the Separation of Powers

In any organized group, certain regulatory functions must be performed. These functions are: (1) formulating regulations; (2) carrying out or administering the regulations; (3) identifying the violators; and (4) assigning disciplinary measures. The role of these functions can be seen in the home, school classroom, social club, church, business corporation, and the state. Interdependence among these functions can also be seen at all of the levels suggested. Thus, some conceptions of home or school regulation are easier to carry out than others are. The point is often made in regard to the drafting of state and federal legislation, as to the care given by the legislative body respecting content and form in drafting, versus "letting the executive and the courts worry about that." In somewhat more formative days of our nation's history, President Jackson is cited as having said: "Now that the court has made its decision, let them enforce it."

If taxing power rests essentially in the legislative branch, as in the American three-branch system, it is obvious that the other two branches depend on the legislative branch for operating funds. In 1973, dispute on this point attracted nationwide attention through the President's refusal to expend certain funds for the specific purposes indicated in Congressional appropriation and through refusal of Congress to appropriate funds for some of the war actions taken by the President as Commander in Chief of the Armed Forces. Similar conflict has appeared at lower governmental levels.

The philosophy of separation is associated with the idea of "checks and balances," which might be characterized as reflecting a basic distrust in the fitness of anybody to govern anybody else. The idea seems to be that fitness is limited more because of a biological drive to exert power over others to make them do one's bidding than because of ignorance of the needs or satisfactions for which others seek fulfillment. Implicit in the doctrine is the idea that when competing patterns of selfishness and drives for power must be acted out in a public forum, a kind of distillate or precipitate of public well-being results. Emphasis on broad freedom for news media is part of the picture, and Watergate points up hazy but nevertheless genuine conceptions of decency as to how the competitions shall be carried on. The matter of decency is sometimes noted in respect to business contracts, in which one party is not permitted to take *unconscionable* advantage of the other. However, cooperation among agencies which the system expects to compete is under suspicion as collusion or corruption. We also have a substantial body of regulations concerning mergers and monopoly activities of business corporations. A pint-sized edition of similar corruption sometimes appears in college athletics and in horse racing.

A crucial point regarding checks and balances concerns how far the system may be carried. The point has sometimes been stated by asking who will supervise the "checkers" or who will spy on the gestapo? In the simpler societies of our cultural ancestors 3,000 to 4,000 years ago, the situation may have seemed wieldy, in the sense that an absolute monarch held all of the important strings of control in his own hands. But attempts by dictators of the present century to employ this technique have not been particularly successful, especially in fairly literate and complex industrial societies. Then if relationships become so numerous and varied that no one person can exercise anything resembling direct supervision over all of them, some basis for trusting his associates with responsibility must be developed, including a system of delegating power and responsibility to others. A significant calamity appears in modern government when the leader of a state cannot trust the advisors in whom the system or the leader personally has placed confidence.

Problems of how to secure both honesty and competence in government are not new, nor are they likely to be concluded by investigations which may be concluded during the lives of youth who are presently in school. Plato wrote about "The Republic," and Aristotle was concerned about "Politics." Some other Athenians of the "Golden Age" were also concerned about government. So too was Confucius in another cultural setting. Sir Thomas Moore (1478-1535) and other writers on utopias have likewise been concerned about good government. Some of our cultural ancestors have suggested that wealthy men are more likely than others to be honest in government, since they do not need to steal directly or indirectly from the state in order to live in material comfort. This doctrine has a fairly obvious weakness, but also a strength. The weakness lies in failing to recognize adequately that material wealth is a major avenue to power over others and that the lust for power seems more insatiable than the sheer drive for material goods. As industrial nations achieve greater material affluence, the historic relationship between wealth and power could thus undergo revision.

The strength mentioned is less obvious. It assumes that in persons generally there is a kind of natural philanthropy or sensitiveness and respect for the needs and appreciations of fellowman; that is, a quality which remains submerged during a material struggle for survival, but which emerges when material security is attained. Many perceptive adults have noted this characteristic among their associates, including a great deal of individual variation concerning the breadth and depth of its manifestation.

Considerations regarding wealth as power and regarding fellowman philanthropy could have unique implications for America's future. One implication of power might relate to more emphasis on avenues other than wealth. Patriotism and personal service for the well-being of others have long been recognized avenues—even when wealth may have predominated. Private philanthropy, by wealthy individuals or perhaps by corporations, indicates attention to the uses made of wealth. The interest which substantial numbers of young Americans now show as to careers in scientific research and exploration or in some areas of teaching and health services, in contrast with careers in business and industry, may symbolize a degree of shift in power orientation. When the results of research are made public, in the sense of being available to everybody, the idea of substantial fellowman orientation does not seem particularly far-fetched.

Furthermore, the research approach with the accompanying development of new knowledge about space, disease, travel, natural resources, etc., has considerable appeal to intellect and to the satisfactions associated with manipulating ideas. This approach, however, should be evaluated in terms of the statement that comprehensive theory is the most valuable knowledge that man has. An economist might state the point in terms of the elasticity of intellectual wants in contrast with the inelasticity of physical wants, including related implications as to levels of satisfaction.

The favorable comments just made about research and service in contrast with material wealth, as avenues to power, should not be looked upon as effort to describe a panacea. Persons with substantial research experience know about competitions for credit as to successes attained and for responsibility as to failures in research. There is considerable substance to the idea that a great deal can be accomplished through cooperation, if there is not too much concern about who gets the credit. But most groups which embark with announced unselfish and cooperative objectives tend to produce or attract loafers and barnacles of intellectual inertness. To minimize the tendency, some focus of evaluative and administrative authority is necessary. The problem that remains continues to involve assurance that persons in the focal status will not show bias and favoritism in order to promote their own selfish ends. This is another version of the idea of who will check on the gestapo.

However, the circular relationship inferred does not rule out further identification or development of what was earlier called a natural fellowman sensitivity and philanthropy. Insofar as such a characteristic exists, it might be significantly developed, especially among children whom the older concepts of competition have not yet conditioned otherwise. Earlier suggestions on revising the avenues to power through social recognition become especially pertinent in this connection.

Provision for separation of the functions and powers of government in America should be examined in terms of a fundamental skepticism about the fitness of one man to govern another, which should further be considered along with the basic fact that some form of government and regulatory power is necessary in organized society. Americans of all age levels should therefore expect an ongoing competitive struggle among the three branches for the new power that inevitably lies in applying abstract constitutional or other statements of power to concrete situations. It is important to realize that in government, as in science or elsewhere, the life of a principle or theory lies substantially in the generality of form in which it is stated, so that subsequent developments can be woven into the earlier fabric through new interpretations.

In a democratic society, which assumes considerable participation in government by the general population, argument and debate are essential aspects of the process of interpretation. The role of a free press and forum is again emphasized. Perhaps more important is academic freedom in schools and universities. For people in a democratic society, with emphasis on government by the consent of the governed, freedom to examine the structure of their government and to review the action of incumbents whom they have entrusted with power is the most important freedom they have. It provides the basis and framework for the other freedoms.

Lawlessness and Its Consequences

Certain problems regarding lawlessness and peaceful association in a complex industrial society relate to knowing what the law is regarding a particular area of human relationships, which essentially means knowing the extent to which stated principles or regulations are enforced. With a large number of decentralized agencies enacting legislation, passing ordinances, and adopting regulations to govern small political units such as school districts, there is a great body of regulatory material which is intended to guide the behavior of the people. Considerable acquaintance with this body of material is essential for even the well-intentioned citizen to know when he is conducting himself appropriately.

(1) *Need for systematic study of the law in public schools.* American practice with respect to developing the acquaintance indicated has largely been that of leaving it to the incidental social contacts which the child has as he grows up in the community. That is, whatever acquaintance he comes to have is acquired primarily through sporadic comments by parents, teachers, other pupils at school, police, juvenile courts, and other uncoordinated sources. The primitive learn-by-doing technique inferred may have been adequate for the simple regulatory structures of preliterate societies, but it has shortcomings in fulfilling the needs of a complex industrial structure. Student participations in patrol service at street crossings, or participations in certain innocuous campus activities euphemistically called student government, have some value. But they are too restrictive in conception and in results. For creative citizenship in American society, systematic classroom and laboratory experience concerning the field of social regulation and the disciplines of enforcement would seem as important as systematic aspects of the school program relating to mathematics, language, the vocational field, etc.

The foregoing suggestion does not imply that school children could be expected to learn *all* of the law. No lawyer or judge does that. However, helpful results might well follow efforts to organize ten or so areas of the law which seem to be most important for typical Americans; to show *why* the legal provisions of these areas came to be what they are; to indicate the general principles of relationship between constitutional provisions, legislative enactments, and court ruling; etc. It has been suggested elsewhere in this study that development of learning materials and instructional procedures for the type of law study implied should be a joint responsibility of schools, the courts, and the law-enforcement agencies.

(2) *Violence in the antisocial heritage of Americans.* When any regulation is formally enacted, the enactment is usually intended to redirect some type of behavior from a course of undirected growth which is proving to be anti-social. Some aspects of the redirection are intended to modify the simple biological law that the strongest and most cunning are fittest to survive. One result of the procedure is that more sophisticated conceptions of strength tend to emerge, with emphasis on intellectual strength partially replacing physical strength.

Out of experience in human relationships, a kind of preliterate conception of justice emerges, as to what is right or what ought to be expected under certain conditions. An early Hebrew conception stipulated: "an eye for an eye, and a tooth for a tooth." The stipulation indicates a kind of reciprocity or a balance of violence. No "turning of the other cheek" is shown here. It is also implied that the family or clan is the enforcement agency. Feuding gangs in some metropolitan areas of the United States, and in some aspects of Israeli-Arab relationships, currently suggest this conception of justice. At a more respectable level of human association, as for example concerning relationships among nations, considerable vocabulary has developed about *just wars.* Perhaps this observation should be footnoted with the suggestion that the nation or combination of nations with the greatest strength determine what is just—especially when due attention is given to moral and pro-paganda strength.

Updated manifestations as to the *balance of violence* may be stated in terms of an East-West arms race or a balanced reduction of armed forces by Western and Iron-Curtain countries in Europe. Negotiations between the United States and Russia on stockpiles of nuclear weapons are sometimes referred to as efforts to reduce the *balance of terror,* so as to operate at somewhat lower levels. Reference is sometimes made to the overkill which the lowered balance would still authorize.

The fact that conceptions of god and associated religious doctrines at present seem less potent as motivators of terror than they were during the Crusades, or during the Reformation Wars and the Inquisitions, does not imply that recent motivations are less intense. But if one drifts into a surmise that religion is no longer a significant motivator, he might note the recent struggle between India and Pakistan, some aspects of the Arab-Israeli continuum, and the uncontrolled shootings in Northern Ireland.

As to present-day conceptions of justice and methods of achieving it, at several places around the world, one should also note the activities of terrorists against the diplomats, business leaders, and athletes of some countries. He should further note the hijacking of airplances for ransom, for the release of political prisoners, etc.

Reference to terrorism and balance of violence in the present world causes some people to reflect on Jewish experience under the Nazis. A key item in the terrorism of that period, along with the other periods noted, is the need of some *enemy focus* as symbolizing a goal to be accomplished. Adroitly conceived and skillfully developed propaganda may be needed to foster enemy hatred far enough so that it can serve the focal purpose. On a nationwide basis, Nazis, Communists, and at times Americans have directed great effort into this field. Some Americans like to refer to the phenomenon as propaganda when others carry it on and as patriotism when we do it.

The matter of enemy focus has various implications. The enemy characteristic which becomes the focus must be one that can rather easily be made to seem important, otherwise the results of propaganda efforts are mild. Then, should the *enemy scapegoat* modify the focal characteristic so that it can no longer be made conspicuous? The point could be referred to as removing bait or as a responsibility of the enemy scapegoat to remedy the characteristics which make him seem a *thorn* in the flesh to those who desire to persecute him. The idea applies to Jews in Nazi Germany or in Communist Russia, much as it applies to foreign diplomats and business leaders in some chaotic have-not countries of Latin America or elsewhere.

(3) *Role of forgiveness and rehabilitation.* At various points in this study it has been suggested that man has a trait of humanitarian consideration for fellowman, with a tendency to forgive the shortcomings of others, which has anchorage in the organism that is second only to traits which are geared to self-preservation. Like some other forms of idealism, forgiveness and associated rehabilitation or help for the fallen brother to rise again have long been stated theoretically in religious doctrine. But also like some other idealism, practical implementation in a large measure had to wait until material productivity supplied means other than words.

While both forgiveness and rehabilitation exist in degrees and have much in common, they are not synonymous. Forgiveness implies some form of transgression of an accepted code, with a considerable degree of acceptance back into a status of respectability. The acceptance usually comes after some kind of penance or other personal discipline which the group has defined as constituting justice. But the humanitarian implications of rehabilitation extend beyond the idea of transgression and reach persons who have committed no offense, but who have not shared in the endowments of nature and of the community to the extent that the prevailing sense of justice considers to be fair and decent.

In a complex society, such concepts as forgiveness and rehabilitation undergo considerable expansion, with growing dependence on reason and logic in determining what is fair and decent under particular circumstances. This situation indicates that in a complex society there are more things to reason about and more items which may be allocated in demonstrating fairness. The fairness appears along a continuum that recognizes increasingly more refined degrees of justice. In America at present, courts of equity have a substantial chore in the sphere indicated. But before technology stimulated the development of material affluence, idealism about rehabilitation extended to "the halt and the lame," even though causal factors might fall into categories now labeled as congenital or accidental.

Foregoing comments sketch a pattern which growth in technical knowledge and material productivity can greatly expand and complicate. With the increase in goods that may be distributed and the refinements in justice that may be administered, there are also more ways in which selfishness, favoritism, and corruption may enter. Martin Luther's concern about the process, referred to as the "sale of indulgences" by the church, ought not lead one to suppose that the church was the only agency then engaged in this form of merchandising. Princes, moneylenders, and others did much the same, insofar as their status through wealth and power allowed. Aspects of the process which later became generally accepted were sometimes referred to as "good business." Since churches in America do not presently have any great repertoire of special privileges and favoritisms to dispense, which the people consider important, the indulgences now are more likely to appear in secular form. Thus, we note ambassadorships or other appointive offices allegedly available in exchange for contributions to the campaigns of successful politicians. Alterations in the relative power status of different institutions thus result in greater shift in the distributing agent, than in the ethics of distribution.

Preceding statements suggest a route by which forgiveness can become a major avenue to corruption. No great insight is required to note how "a little humane generosity" for a few relief clients can lead to a substantial trek or even to permanent migration to urban or other areas which the grapevine evaluates as having an "enlightened" practice regarding the needy; to note how a few quarts of bourbon for precinct friends near the end of a close political campaign can flow into a considerable bootleg enterprise; how tips on the horses at the upcoming derby might become systematized through bookie shops that acquire "protected" status; how a "couple joints of grass" for a friend, as a projection beyond nonprescription tranquilizers from the corner drugstore, might grow into a drug matter of international fiscal and political importance; etc. Some conception of forgiveness may be reflected in each type of situation mentioned. The snowball effect implied emphasizes a point of the strict constructionist and the moral code—whether the code is set forth in the Constitution or otherwise.

Another type of consideration respecting forgiveness should be noted. There are practical limits to which it is feasible to push any ethical principle. The Supreme Court has often mentioned this point relative to the freedoms and other personal rights stipulated in the Constitution. How far a society will go in identifying and disciplining offenders will depend partly on how serious the offense is considered to be and partly on how difficult it is to identify and to discipline in the particular case. The fact that considerable history and legend attaches to the efforts of the Canadian Mounted Police in apprehending offenders is a testimony to a more relaxed approach by most law-enforcement agencies. There is no fixed point at which a decision *must* be made regarding further efforts to solve a specific problem. This applies whether the problem relates to law enforcement, dredging a river for a lost body, providing medical service for the ill, locating jobs for the unemployed, developing feasible programs for college students, or anything else.

The point then becomes: when do corrupt practices become involved in determining where that point is or in what constitutes corruption in the particular situation? The best that society seems able to do is to create some type of council or establishment and then expect that the establishment will be under continuous attack by persons who do not like the justice meted out. Recent attacks on the courts and the American judicial system illustrate this point.

Among the vested interests concerned about promoting or obstructing reform, inertia and lack of know-how are probably most important. The same applies to educational programs. If the fact as stated seems unpleasant, one should note that the traits concerned became deeply rooted in the organisms of our ancestors when those traits probably had survival value, although such traits now appear to be major handicaps and imperfections.

Scientific Method

During the past century the general population in America and elsewhere has developed great respect for scientific exploration as a means of finding solutions to problems. While astronomy and certain other areas engaged in limited amounts of such exporation during earlier centuries, the real burst of growth in scientific exploration has been recent. Although reference to experimentation or to setting up experiments is widespread, many people who use such terms are rather hazy about the nature of experimental procedure or why it has produced the results indicated.

The main difference between experimentalism or the scientific method and other procedures for arriving at conclusions on which to base operations lies in the emphasis placed on precise observation of phenomena being studied and on analysis of the data recorded. Hence much attention has been given by developers of the method to the creations of technical devices for making precise observations in many kinds of situations and for recording and analyzing what is observed. Much attention has also been given to close relationships between the data and the explanations offered as to why certain things have occurred or might be expected to occur in the future. Causal relationships between theory and data thus acquired new perspective, with preeminence attached to the observed fact.

Another important characteristic of scientific method is that the facts and interpretations are open to anyone who might desire to challenge or to verify them. That is, the findings and associated theories are public, in a democratic sense of being equally available to all who may be interested, with no status accorded to claims about mystic revelations or other private pipelines to truth. Partly as a consequence of free accessibility, there is extensive attack by researchers on the validity of data reported and on the interpretations or theorizing with respect to the data. Under the dynamic conditions indicated, there is continuous experimentation to test theoretical statements and continuous revisions and extensions of theory to take the new data into account. The process described, plus abundant funds in countries like the United States to support research, are of great importance in the rapid pace at which knowledge is presently expanding.

It should be noted that the greatest expansion in knowledge resulting from widening use of the scientific method is in the sciences and associated technology. Four items are mentioned as partial explanations and implications of this situation. (1) When scientific method arose, there was not much knowledge that could be called scientific in any modern sense of the term, whereas experience and theorizing in such fields as religion, philosophy, and government had been accumulating for several centuries. (2) Exploratory and follow-up work in the virgin territory now called science produced tangible results that could easily be seen and evaluated by persons without any extensive theoretical training. (3) The people liked many of the results because life was thereby made more comfortable for them. (4) The openness and availability of science gradually armed the common people for attack on some aspects of prevailing social systems which the people thought were exploiting them. In this connection reference has been reflected in controversies over separation of church and state.

Two important areas of "unfinished business" regarding scientific method should be noted. One is that precise observation of phenomena and scrupulous respect for facts should be extended more broadly than they have been to such areas as social science, philosophy, and theology. In each of these fields there are several theories, dogmas, claims, etc., that could be ventilated through objective study. The point here could perhaps be characterized as making wider use of the armor noted under item (4) above.

Possibly somewhat counter to suggestions in the foregoing paragraph is the idea of clearer recognition as to areas of the culture in which scientific method has little to offer. The point is sometimes illustrated by asking whether it is possible to devise a scientific code of ethics or whether this field must essentially be in the domain of philosophy and theology. The arguments could be extensive. Suffice it here to suggest that scientific method can itself become dogmatic, in failure to recognize the value of adjustments as it moves from one area to another, and to suggest that the prophets and sages of our earlier cultural background practiced much of what is now often characterized as scientific method. They practiced astute observation concerning human behavior and offered analytical evaluations of the observations made. Considerable present-day adjustment in scientific method seems feasible, without discarding basic respect for precise observation or for grounding conclusions on facts.

Research and Human Well-Being

There seems to be growing criticism in America of large expenditures for research and the expansion of knowledge, when we already have considerable knowledge which might enable us to live better in many respects than we do. It is natural to focus criticism on large expenditures for research in such areas as space, nuclear or solar energy, cancer and heart disease, or other areas which are so technical and complex that they are difficult for laymen to understand. It is equally natural to focus the associated recommendations on individual and social conditions which can readily be seen as improvable, and improvable through small units of expenditure that laymen comprehend.

Several developments contribute to the situation described. These must be viewed in perspective, if a constructive appraisal of expenditure trends and of criticisms is to be made. Exploration on small projects has been going on for some centuries, with the accumulation of numerous, somewhat related techniques and bits of information. Piecing these bits together generates courage and know-how for continuously more ambitious undertakings. Moreover, growth in technology and affluence of the American economy provides more funds and a greater array of materials to consider in planning.

But along with the foregoing there has been a lag in popular education, through television and otherwise, regarding the possibilities and the implications of further exploration which technology and affluence make possible. Hence popular education and commitment tend to focus on housing, food and other welfare problems of the poor and of associated have-nots; or on pet food, deodorants, clothing styles, liquor, etc., for the indulgent well-to-do. Add to the foregoing a growing cultural emphasis on individualism, substantially promoted through judicial attention to the constitutional freedoms and liberty of the individual as involved in different aspects of his relationships in the community, and further add the school's emphasis on individualized instruction and on teaching students how to organize and present their views regarding "the establishment" or other matters in which they reflect an interest.

An important social limitation of the development indicated lies in the way in which individualism functions; that is, in a rather inherent biological individual selfishness, as elaborated through judicial and other cultural emphasis on personal freedom, without commensurate emphasis on social obligation and the development of social perspective. The basic limitation is not new. It was involved in relationships between the individual and the group before man developed literary or formal government statements about freedom. But individual differences are such that for many generations some persons have seen that a major way to improve individual status is through group cooperation.

Group organization implies the emergence of leaders, who are authorized to discipline others. The exercise of discipline means that there are always individuals who get less than they want of some things and are forced into unpleasant sharing with respect to other things. The forgoing result is the same whether top leadership is thought of as a dictator, president, king, politburo, or governing council. The social values accepted by the leadership largely determine the pattern of cultural development and personal sacrifice.

The basic theme of the preceding logic, as related to science and technology for general development versus food and housing for the poor, is that collective imagination concerning ways for utilizing resources grows faster than available resources grow. Hence, the perennial involvement with priorities. Also, persons in leadership status often sense greater potential for expansion in their own prestige and power through expansion in knowledge and in the total content of the culture, than in a more even distribution or accessibility of the content that exists at a particular time. Sufficient attention to distribution so as to avoid open revolt which would upset the general structure, including research and expansion programs, is of course necessary on a continuing basis. How much attention is thus required depends on such matters as conceptions of what constitutes a decent standard of living, spread of ideas through social mobility and education, form of government and its sensitivity to popular demands, etc.

It was the power of the Pharaohs to allocate the use of time and other resources that enabled Egypt to build pyramids. It was comparable power of Greek leaders a few centuries before Christ that enabled them to develop art, philosophy, geometry, certain aspects of medicine, and concepts of democratic government. At a much later time it was the power of Ferdinand and Isabella to control a substantial portion of the wealth of Spain that enabled them to support the exploits of Columbus. The same can be said respecting the various governments of Western Europe that were active in exploration and colonization during the next four centuries, particularly in the Western Hemisphere. The idea of power exercised by leadership through government also appears in establishing nationwide systems of popular education and university study, health programs, or highway and other transportation systems. When the social system fosters the accumulation of large private fortunes, with substantial philanthropic orientation concerning the use of the funds involved, the basic theme of power to accumulate and to allocate remains the same, although the machinery of operation varies somewhat.

At this stage of the present discussion, two points need emphasis. One concerns the power of leadership to accumulate and allocate resources and the broad social perspective which much of that leadership has demonstrated in the allocations made. It is largely through this avenue that the cultural developments which we call civilization have appeared, with a continuous process of imaginative projection appealing to agencies that control resources for potential implementation and with a selective allocation of those resources. Current project formulation by universities, to tease resources out of government or foundations, does not reflect anything especially new so far as basic philosophy of cultural development is concerned.

The second point involves sacrifices and deprivations among the people generally, so that the mentioned accumulations and allocations can be made. To assume that nobody in Spain was hungry or poorly housed, during the time that Ferdinand and Isabella were financing Columbus and other explorers, is extremely naive. The same applies to the Egyptians and the Greeks during the periods noted and to the countries of Western Europe during their centuries of exploration and colonization. It applies to foreign aid, to many types of research, and to other areas of cultural development which are sponsored by public and private leadership in America at the present time.

A few of life's numerous paradoxes show up in the situation described. One paradox is that current sacrifice and deprivation is always involved in working for future growth and enrichment. "There is no gain without pain," it has been observed. Thus, for the people as a whole a particular standard of living and personal satisfaction must currently be accepted, in the hope of a fuller life in subsequent decades or for future generations. Furthermore, it usually means that the sacrifice is not spread equally or according to some equalitarian conception of justice in evaluating ability to bear sacrifice. The social perspective of those with enough imagination to formulate and carry out comprehensive projects of cultural development is quite often tempered by personal selfishness to the effect that other persons make most of the sacrifice involved. Whether this type of selfishness is presently inevitable among humans may be an open question, but general publicity and lay competence to analyze and evaluate can help to minimize it. Publicity can also help limit the waste, debauchery, lust for power, etc., to which leadership sometimes becomes addicted.

Another paradox concerns humanitarianism, in the general picture drawn here. Perhaps a brief definition of humanitarianism might be to characterize it as the amount of consideration that one human being owes to another, simply because both are human. From the organized or group standpoint, the idea becomes essentially: how much does the group owe the individual, simply because the individual exists? Such phrases as "inherent rights," "God-given rights," etc., reflect more euphemistic efforts to say the same thing. A major difficulty concerns when humanitarianism contributes to general community well-being and when it erodes that well-being.

If there is going to be cultural growth and improvement concerning man's status in the universe, effort on the part of *somebody* is required to bring about the changes implied. Individual differences among people are such, genetically and culturally, that some individuals will contribute more than others. Apparently in any culture there are some individuals who constitute a negative influence, from practically any point of judgment. The upshot of this paradox is that any culture which speculates on a bright future must maintain a substantial margin between the rewards which it offers to those who contribute significantly and to those who do not. The paradox is not eased by practical difficulties in setting up a scale of rewards geared to significance of contributions, with widely different conceptions of value relationships. Present dominance of television and some other media by individuals in the sports and entertainment world, in contrast for example with individuals who are important in producing the nation's food and fiber, or with individuals who are engaged in the drudgery aspects of research associated with seeking a "breakthrough" in some area of knowledge, illustrates the point concerning values and paradox. Intensity of the paradox is not reduced by noting that the television dominance indicated is mostly under the sponsorship of advertising aimed at private profits.

A low level of susceptibility to an objective scale-relationship between contributions and rewards, including a large number of rapidly changing variables in a dynamic society, implies that American society will continue to rock along on the basis of guesses and pressures. This relates especially to the reward margin between contributors and noncontributors. The fluidity inferred emphasizes the importance of a clear philosophy regarding the direction in which reward practice should be oriented. The philosophy noted is especially important with respect to youth, in whom curiosity and motivation are particularly amenable to formative influences, whether the influences relate to "drug trips" or to other trips.

An editorial in the *Atlanta Constitution* (5/26/73), appearing when the Skylab Mission was enveloped in uncertainty, sets forth a popular statement in line with part of what is indicated in foregoing paragraphs. The editorial, entitled "Saving Skylab," reads thus:

Even if it should prove impossible for the three astronauts now in orbit to salvage the Skylab space station, the very fact that they thought that they might, and were willing to chance it, is breathtakingly impressive.

It is an indication of not only what tremendous technological strides we have made, but also that the human spirit has not been daunted or dulled in the process.

Perhaps we are overly romantic about the space program, but it seems to us to represent some of the finest of human virtues: Optimism, perserverance, courage and selflessness—all in the pursuit of knowledge—and always in the face of a terrible and lonely death.

APPENDIX NO. 2

*Biographical Materials for Study Projects on Understanding
Lawlessness and Civic Responsibility*

Continued from the second part of chapter 4, Division IV.
(See pages 212-218)

Banking and Finance

Most people think of banking as being associated with money and credit and thus as being concerned with a fairly complex system of exchange regarding goods and services. The use of money increases the flexibility of exchange over and above direct barter, since a person who gives up an item can accept money in return—and need not have any use for a specific product which another person would give in a barter exchange. The value of the item given up is accordingly transferred to the money, where it may be stored for future use.

To state precisely when money came into existence would be arbitrary, depending greatly on how money, exchange, barter, and other terms are defined. Anthropology indicates that preliterate peoples have used various items as money—shells, jewels, certain metals, wampum, etc. Most Americans know about the use of gold and silver as money in the United States and about the present status of domestic and international considerations regarding the value of the dollar and its importance in economic relationships.

For such relationships to be adequate within and among modern industrial societies, banking and finance must go much further in respect to trade and exchange than preceding comments imply. The extension concerns credit, loans, and various other symbols of value, debt, etc. Thus, most persons who buy a refrigerator, automobile, or comparable item pay for it by issuing a check or a series of checks on some installment basis. Few persons pay through directly using such paper money as is generally accepted to be legal tender or through using gold, even in countries which permit the private ownership of gold as money.

The use of banks as depositories for money and the development of a complex system of credit and loans place great power in the hands of bankers, when they have extensive control over the deposits and over the conditions upon which loans may be made. American history reflects growth of public interest in the nation's system of money and finance, as indicated by such matters as President Jackson and the national bank, various money panics and boom-bust economic cycles, the Federal Reserve System, and the numerous other federal and state regulations for inspecting bank operations, protecting deposits, restricting loan charges, etc.

Many creative measures and many swindles have been involved in developing the present national and international system of money and credit. The numerous recent conferences on trade, inflation, and monetary systems indicate the growing importance and growing complications of the nation's and the world's monetary and credit relationships. The persons whose names appear in the accompanying list have been important in developing present relationships. Some of them will play major roles for some years to come. Considerable insight into the system can be gained through acquaintance with the lives and works of such persons.

1. Concepts for Discussion

(a) Banks in the modern sense seem to have arisen in Venice, as a Chamber of Loans, about eight hundred years ago. Why does this seem to be a feasible time and place for such an institution to arise? Have similar reasons applied later to Barcelona, Frankfurt, London, and New York as financial centers?

(b) For individuals to buy or build homes, attend college, or establish homes and families, etc., it is often necessary for them to establish credit and to borrow money. The same applies to corporations with respect to plant development, securing raw materials, employing labor, etc. In order that these operations may take place, it is necessary to have a stable system of money and credit.

(c) If banks are going to have any money to lend, somebody must save part of what he receives and deposit it in the bank for the purpose indicated. The interest which the depositor receives is his reward for saving. The interest which the borrower pays is a charge made for using somebody else's money, plus the cost of carrying on the lending operations.

(d) As the employed population of an industrial society increases, there is an increase in the number of persons who can save small amounts. There is also an increase in the need for corporations and individuals to borrow money. Hence, as the total economy becomes more complex, banks become more essential and also more in need of state or federal regulation so as to serve the general public interest.

(e) As trade and the movement of people increasingly extend beyond national boundaries, the well-being of the people within the United States or any other nation depends increasingly on a stable international system of money and credit.

(f) For the nation's and the world's banking and economic leaders to develop and maintain a system of money and credit relationships which contributes a maximum to the economic well-being of the people, the people in general will have to know enough about the system to be able to insist intelligently on persistent and conscientious effort by the leaders. The knowledge must include an understanding of the basic legal structure involved and the corresponding machinery for law enforcement.

2. *Individuals to Consider*

Abs, Herman J. (Ger., bkr., reconst. loan corp.; 1901-).

Aldrich, Nelson W. (fin., Aldrich-Vreeland Act on bkg., tariff; 1841-1915).

Armstrong, Samuel T. (bkr., whig politician; 1784-1850).

Astor, John J. (cap., high int. on gov't war loans 1812, Astor Lib. in N.Y.,; 1763-1848).

Bache, Harold L. (bkr., stk. exch., coffee & sugar exch.,; 1894-).

Barclay, Robert, J. P. (Eng., Barclays Bank Limited, bank mergers; 1843-1913).

Barker, Jacob (merch., fin., 1812-15 support for fed. govt.; 1779-1871).

Barnum, Zenus (cap., pioneer in tele. and rail industries, hotel keeper; 1810-1865).

Biddle, Nicholas (fin., author, struggle with Pres. Jackson over nat., bk.; 1786-1844).

Bingham, William (founded Bk. of No. Am., land specu., Pa. pol.; 1752-1804).

Bliss, George (bkr., dry goods merch. during Civil War; 1816-1896).

Brainerd, Lawrence (Vt. bkr., steamboat & ry. dev., pol.; 1794-1870).

Chaffee, Jerome B. (founded F. Nat. Bk. of Denver, first U.S. sen. from Colo.; 1825-1886).

Coe, George S. (bk. pres., helped estab. N.Y. Clearing House; 1817-1896).

Cook, James M. (cap., 1856-61 Supt. N.Y. St. Bkg. Dept.; 1807-1868).

Cooke, Jay (bkr., distributed large fed. loans—1862-63, panic 1873; 1821-1905).

Corcoran, William W. (bkr., dry-goods merch., Corcoran Gallery of Art; 1798-1888).

Creighton, Edward (bkr., telegraph builder, Creighton Univ. in Omaha; 1820-1874).

Davison, Henry P. (Bkrs. Trust Co., 1917-19 Red Cross War Council; 1867-1922).

Drexel, Anthony J. (bkr., brokerage house, founded Drexel Inst. in Phila.; 1826-1893).

Eckels, James H. (fin., comptroller of currency, bk. pres.; 1858-1907).

Ellis, John W. (merch. bkr., headed F. Nat. of Cincinnati; 1817-1910).

Fairchild, Charles S. (fin., prosec. "Canal Ring" frauds, Sect'y of Treas.; 1842-1924).

Fessenden, William Pitt (fin., lawyer,; 1806-1869).

Field, Cyrus W. (cap., merch., promoter of 1st Atlantic cable; 1819-1892).

Fisk, James (cap., spec., attempted 1869 corner on gold business disaster; 1834-1872).

Folger, Henry Clay (Std. Oil Co. of N.Y., Folger Shakespeare Library; 1857-1930).

Gage, Lyman J. (bkr., labor-capital relations, 1900 gold-std. act.; 1836-1927).

Grace, William R. (internat. bkr. & steamboat op., mayor of N.Y.C.; 1832-1904).

Guggenheim, Meyer (fin., imported Swiss embroidery, ore smelting; 1828-1905).

Hanna, Marcus A. (merch., cap., broker, organized M. A. Hanna & Co., pol.; 1837-1904).

Hatch, Rufus (fin., stk. broker, coined the phrase "lamb of Wall Street"; 1832-1893).

Heard, Dwight B. (inv. bkr., Ariz. farmer, 1902 Recla. Act; 1869-1929).

Hepburn, Alonzo B. (lawyer, author, bk. pres., fin., diplomat; 1846-1922).

Higginson, Henry L. (bkr., founded Boston Symph. Orch., bene. of colleges; 1834-1919).

Hunnewell, Horatio H. (Boston bkr., ry. fin., foreign exch. specialist; 1810-1902).

Hutchinson, Charles L. (bkr., pres. Chi. Bd. of Trade, treas. U. of Chi.; 1854-1924).

Knox, John J. (fin., comptroller of the currency; 1828-1892).

Lamar, Gazaway B. (bkr., ship owner, Confed. blockage runner; 1798-1874).

Littlefield, George Washington (cattleman, bkr., org. 1890 Am. Nat'l Bank; 1842-1920).

Lucas, James H. (St. Louis bkr. & cap.; 1800-1873).

Mellon, Andrew W. (indust., fin., Alum. Co. of Am., Nat'l. Gal. of Art; 1855-1937).

Mills, Darius O. (merch. bkr., invest. dir. in Calif. & N.W., "Mills Hotels," philan.; 1825-1910).

Mitchell, Alexander (bkr., ins., pres. Chi. Mil. & St. Paul Ry.; 1817-1887).

Moffat, David H. (Colo. bkr., inv. in land, mining, railroads; 1839-1911).

Morgan, John P. (domest. & internat. bkr., U.S. Steel Corp., philan.; 1837-1913).

Morris, Robert (shipping merch., fin. of Am. Rev., tobacco exporter; 1734-1806).

Newberry, Walter L. (bkr., land specu., railroader, Chi. Newberry Lib.; 1804-1868).

Nixon, John (merch., 1792-1808 pres. Bk. of No. Am.; 1733-1808).

Perkins, George C. (Calif. shipowner, bkr., pol.; 1839-1923).

Pollock, Oliver (planter, fin., personally financed munitions for Am. Rev.; 1737-1823).

Pratt, Enoch (iron merch., bkr., fire ins., E. Pratt Free Lib., Balt,; 1808-1896).

Price, Hiram (bkr., railroad builder, U.S. Com'r of Indian affairs; 1814-1901).

Rockefeller, William (fin., indust., oil, brother of J. D. Rockefeller; 1841-1922).

Rothchild, Meyer A. (Ger., bkr., founded bkg. house of Rothchild; 1743-1812).

Sage, Russel (fin., ry. dev., creat. Wall Street "puts and calls"; 1816-1906).

Salomon, Haym (merch., bought "Rev. paper"—1780-84—to aid govt. credit; c. 1740-1785).

Schneider, George (ed., pres. Nat. Bk. of Ill., org. Ger. vote for Lincoln; 1823-1905).

Seligman, Arthur (N. Mex. merch., bkr., pol.; 1871-1933).

Seligman, Joseph (founded bkg. house of J. & W. Seligman & Co.; 1819-1880).

Shaw, Leslie M. (bkr., chr. Internat. Monetary Conv. 1898, Sect'y. of Treas.; 1848-1932).

Smith, George (bkg. & ins., Chi. real estate, Wis. Marine & Fire Ins. Co,; 1806-1899).

Sprague, Charles E. (early C.P.A., wrote textbooks in accountancy and finance; 1842-1912).

Stevens, John A. (pres. Bk. of Commerce—N.Y. for 27 yrs.; 1795-1874).

Stillman, James (indust. bkr., pres. of Nat'l. City Bank for 18 yrs; 1850-1918).

Straus, Simon W. (fin., built skyscrapers financed by real estate bonds; 1866-1930).

Taggart, Thomas (bkr., hotel prop., Indiana pol.; 1856-1929).

Thatcher, Mahlon D. (bkr., stock-raiser, F. Nat. Bank of Pueblo, Colo.; 1839-1916).

Vanderbilt, Cornelius (fin., steamboat and ry. promoter, "Commodore"; 1794-1877).

Warburg, Paul M. (bkr., mem. 1st Fed. Res. Bd., warned of 1929 panic; 1868-1932).

Ward, Samuel (fin., lobbyist in Wash., D.C., "King of the Lobby"; 1814-1884).

Warfield, Solomon D. (Md. mfgr. and fin., pres. of Cont. Trust Co.; 1859-1927).

Whitney, Harry P. (fin., dev. railroad and mining concerns, sportsman; 1872-1930).

Winslow, Sidney W. (N. Eng. fin., mfgr., formed United Shoe Mach. Co., publisher; 1854-1917).

Yeatman, James E. (St. Louis bkr., civic leader, philan.; 1818-1901).

Business, Industry, and Labor

One present-day criterion of a retarded or undeveloped nation or region is the percentage of the population engaged in the primary task of producing food. Growing awareness of this situation increasingly causes underdeveloped countries to seek industry, and within the United States the more largely agricultural areas of the South and of the Plains typically seek to expand industrialization. The underlying philosophy is that industry which can turn out finished products that are in demand can ordinarily create jobs and income faster than agriculture can. What applies to products or goods in the foregoing sense increasingly applies to services.

A possible weakness in the logic set forth concerns a steady market for the output of industry, at a price which persons in other areas of the total economy can afford to pay. Unemployment, idle industrial plants, surplus agricultural commodities, curtailment of essential public services and other disruptions of a smooth-operating economy thus result. "Overindustrialization" of certain areas is also a problem, but more a problem of the location of industrial plants within such areas than a problem of industrial productivity in the total culture.

Business in a broad sense can be thought of basically as that aspect of our social structure which is concerned primarily with the exchange of goods and services, within the expanding system of production indicated. This relationship has been recognized for numerous decades in the marketing departments of industrial corporations and is recently attracting attention in the aspects of agricultural production designated as agribusiness.

Perhaps business may thus be thought of as a middleman type of relationship, but one which is essential to maintaining connections among the various areas of production and between producers and consumers, with a realization that individuals who are producers of some items must necessarily on balance be consumers of other items. "On balance" means that most producers are also consumers of some of the items which they produce, as farmers consume some of the food produced. But the excess of an item which is not consumed by those who produce it, and which results mainly from specialization throughout the world of production, is the basis of commerce and the associated business. In a complex economy there are various types of professional and other services which are rendered on a fee or price basis, but these merely represent extensions of the producer-exchange-consumer arrangement which has been characterized.

As the economy becomes more complex in the sense of more people engaged in producing more different kinds of goods and services, the exchange relationship described as business becomes more prominent in the total economic development. Various forms of advertising, credit, and organizations among employers and among employees become involved. Thus, government regulation of increasing portions of business and industrial developments becomes a natural part of the total picture.

The sample of names listed in part two of the present appendix gives some indication of the range in types of competencies, aspirations, methods, and practices; and also some indication of the militant aggressiveness, physical endurance, selfishness, ruthless disregard for the welfare of others, and additional elements which make up the repertoire of traits that characterize the dynamic groups of society. But many humanitarian and philanthropic elements are included, as well as much creativeness and personal sacrifice for the well-being of others. The fact that business in the sense noted may be associated with any type of productive, labor, professional, or other enterprise may mean that the personnel of the business community more nearly represents a cross-section of America's gainful employment than any other particular area of the economy.

1. Concepts for Discussion

(a) Since business is a kind of secondary or associated type of relationship among other aspects of the total economy which may be looked upon as more fundamental or primary, business cannot thrive or prosper unless the other aspects do.

(b) If business relationships become more extensive and more varied, as America comes to include more production workers who are engaged in a wider range of jobs, the demand for more complicated business machines may become greater than the demand for more complicated machines and comparable devices in other areas of the economy.

(c) Members of the business world, who are interested in the long-range development of communities in which they locate, emphasize service to both producers and consumers with a middleman or exchange cost which enables a particular business firm to grow or shrink at about the rate of the total economy. Such firms must oppose other firms which would insist on gains or profits that are considered exhorbitant by typical standards, or firms which hope to make a "quick killing" and then leave the community.

(d) Public schools, highways, fire departments, community health clinics or hospitals, and many other agencies or services which are maintained by government through taxes on the community are in effect community, communal, or communistic enterprises. As America becomes more populous and its economy more diverse and involved, the general growth will include an expansion in communal enterprises and also an expansion in private-enterprise operations.

(e) At the present time, American business and industry are engaged in international operations to a greater extent than most other aspects of American society. This means that the attitudes and impressions which people in other countries develop with respect to the United States will depend greatly on what the members of this business group do in these other countries. It may also mean that an increasing number of young Americans should anticipate employment which will involve service in some foreign country.

(f) If other countries engage in international commerce and travel to an extent comparable to that often noted with respect to the United States, there will be a growing emphasis on a common language for communication and perhaps more intermarriage and other biological mixing. Several types of social consequences might flow from the circumstances indicated.

2. *Individuals to Consider*

Arbuckle, John (coffee importer, ship owner, invented mach. to package food; 1839-1912).

Atkinson, Edward (ind. econ., Boston Mfgrs. Mut. Ins. Co., safe factory const.; 1827-1905).

Bissell, George H. (promoter oil ind., urged drilling, helped org. 1st U.S. oil co.; 1821-1884).

Blodget, Samuel (merch., arch., E. India trade, Ins. Co. of N. A., real est.; 1757-1814).

Carey, Henry C. (econ., author, favored Am. econ. expan. as opp. by Eng.; 1793-1879).

Crimmins, John D. (contr., cap., built much of N.Y.C. elev. & subway system; 1844-1917).

DeBardeleben, Henry F. (org. & magr. of B'ham steel and coal prop. in Ala.; 1840-1910).

Delmonico, Lorenzo (restauranteur, influenced dev. of restaurants in Am. cities; 1813-1881).

Drake, Edwin L. (Pa. oil ind., 1st well—1859, used pipe to keep drill hole open; 1819-1880).

Drew, Daniel (early cattle driver, ry. & real est. speculator, went bkpt.; 1797-1879).

Duncan, James (labor leader, A.F. of L. in formative days, V-Pres. 1900-28; 1857-1928).

Eckert, Thomas T. (Civil War mil. tele., adm. of Gould cos., pres. W. Union; 1825-1910).

Faesch, John J. (ironmaster, gov't. contr. in N.J., cast shot for Cont. Army; 1729-1799).

Field, Marshall (founded Marshall Field & Co., Chi., worldwide mdse.; 1834-1906).

Forten, James (negro sail maker, prom. Phila. business man, philan.; 1766-1842).

Gantt, Henry L. (ind. leader, labor rel. and ind. mgnt., "Gantt Chart"; 1861-1919).

Gates, John W. (promoter, specula., org. Am. Steel & Wire Co., stk. exch. manip.; 1855-1911).

George, Henry (journ., econ., reformer, Single Tax, *Progress and Property*; 1839-1897).

Grinnell, Frederick (ind., pat. automatic fire-exting. sprinkler and alarm; 1836-1905).

Guffey, James M. (large landowner and oil prod., also partnership; 1839-1930).

Gunton, George (ed., author, influenced Am. econ. thought on wages & hrs.; 1845-1919).

Hadley, Arthur T. (econ., Yale pres., author, gov't adviser on Interstate Com.; 1856-1930).

Haish, Jacob (contr., mfgr., invented "s" barbed wire—pat. 1875; 1826-1926).

Haywood, William D. (labor leader, co-founder I.W.W., sedition 1918, fled to Rus.; 1869-1928).

Heinz, Henry J. (prep. foods, founded H. J. Heinz Co., "57 Varieties"; 1844-1919).

Heinze, Frederick A. (copper miner, operator, speculator; 1869-1914).

Hering, Rudolph (eng., dev. sewage systems re: yellow fever in Am. cities; 1847-1923).

Herreshoff, John B. (yacht designer & builder, co-founder H. Mfg. Co., racing yachts; 1841-1915).

Hogg, George (glass mfgr., river & lake shipping, pioneer in chain stores; 1784-1849).

Holliday, Cyrus K. (bldr. & promoter of Topeka, got charter for A.T.S.F. Ry.; 1826-1900).

Jenks, Jeremiah W. (econ., served on gov't. bds., influenced trust leg.; 1856-1929).

Kress, Samuel H. (5-10¢ stores, estab. S. H. Kress & Co., philan.; 1863-1955).

Laramie, Jacques (pioneer trapper in unknown S.E. Wyo., Laramie River Area; ?-1821).

Law, George (contr., fin., co-founder U.S. Mail Steamship Co., N.Y.C. horse car lines; 1806-1881).

Le Barge, Joseph (Mo. R. navigator, fur-trader; 1815-1899).

Lucas, Anthony F. (oil eng., examined Texas coastal "domes," Spindletop; 1855-1921).

McClurg, Alexander C. (Chicago book dealer, publisher; 1832-1901).

McDougall, Alexander ("whaleback" vessel, built shipyd., founded Everett, Wash.; 1845-1923).

McNulty, Frank J. (pres. Internat. Bro. of Elec. Workers, negotiation of disputes; 1872-1926).

McVickar, John (Epis. clergy., taught pol econ. as moral philos., *Hints on Banking*; 1787-1868).

Niblo, William (hotel & theater mgr., fashionable Niblo's Garden in N.Y.C.; 1789-1878).

Nicholson, Samuel D. (Colo. mine op., prospector, mgr., bus. investor, pol.; 1859-1923).

Olyphant, David W. C. (merch., China trade, dir. Presby. Mission in China; 1789-1851).

Peavy, Frank H. (built Minn. grain-elev. empire, org. Peavy S. S. Co.; 1850-1901).

Phillips, Thomas W. (oil prod., relig. writer, pol.; 1835-1912).

Pinkerton, Allen (fed. counterespionage, wrote "real life" detective stories; 1819-1884).

Prince, William (Am. pioneer in selling budded or grafted nursery stk., new var.; 1725-1802).

Rae, John (econ., attacked Smith's doctrines, time-disc. theory of int.; 1796-1872).

Rezanov, Nikolia P. (Rus., civ. serv., founded Rus.-Am. Co. for dev. Alaska; 1764-1807).

Robert, Christopher R. (merch., founded Roberts Coll. in Constantinople; 1802-1878).

Rosenwald, Julius (Sears mail-order bus., estab. J. Rosenwald Fund; 1862-1932).

Sawyer, Philetus (Wis. lumberman & pol., bond int. probs., attacked by Lafollette; 1816-1900).

Schirmer, Gustav (music pub., G. Schirmer Inc. of N.Y., encour. Am comp.; 1829-1893).

Schoenhof, Jacob (lace merch., econ., author, forecast "Henry Ford" doctrine; 1839-1903).

Sears, Richard W. (founded S. Roebuck & Co. in Minn. before it moved to Chi.; 1863-1914).

Shedd, John G. (merch., philan., was partner & pres., of Marsh. Field & Co.; 1850-1926).

Sibley, Hiram (bus. promoter, co-founder W. U. Tel. Co., land & ry. specula.; 1807-1888).

Sibley, Joseph C. (oil refiner, stock breeder, Pa. pol.; 1850-1926).

Sigman, Morris (labor leaders, Internat. Ladies Garment Workers' Union; 1881-1931).

Stamp, Josiah (Eng., econ., tax expert, ry. and industry director, Nobel Industries; 1880-1941).

Statler, Ellsworth M. (hotel owner & op., "The guest is always right," Statler Hotels; 1863-1928).

Stettinius, Edward R. (Morgan & Co.'s superv. of 1915-17 war prod.; 1865-1925).

Stevens, Henry (bookman, coll. rare Americana, bibl. on hist. of Eng. Bible; 1819-1886).

Sully, Daniel J. (cotton speculator, dominant in N.Y. mkt., 1902-04; 1861-1930).

Sulzburger, Cyrus L. (textile merch., leader in Jewish affairs, philan.; 1858-1932).

Thompson, David (Hudson Bay Co., surveys in N.W. of U.S. and S.W. of Can.; 1770-1857).

Tiffany, Charles L. (estab. store in 1837 which preceded Tiffany & Co., jewelry; 1812-1902).

Tompkins, Daniel A. (pamphleteer on ind. in South, dev. cottonseed oil mills; 1851-1914).

Van Cortlandt, Oloff S. (merch., Dutch W. India Co., real est. specula., pol.; 1600-1684).

Van Dam, Rip (colonial merch. and pol. in N.Y.; 1660-1749).

Wanamaker, John (pioneer in dev. of dept. stores from novelty shops, pol.; 1838-1922).

Ward, A. Montgomery (mail-order, 1st catalog was 1 pg., Chi. lake front conserva.; 1843-1913).

Warner, Adoniram J. (dev. oil & coal lands, built 2 short-line rys., pol.; 1834-1910).

Wedgwood, Josiah (Eng., potter, dev. pottery trade & industry, philan.; 1730-1795).

Wellman, Samuel T. (eng., nearly 100 pats., adm. of steel & mfg. cos.; 1847-1919).

White, Horace (journ., econ., ed., Chi. Trib. rep., free trade & annexation probs.; 1834-1916).

Wolfskill, William (Calif. trapper, fruit rancher, 1st area ship. of oranges commercially; 1798-1866).

Woolworth, Frank W. (establ. chain of low priced stores, underselling others; 1852-1919).

Wormley, James (negro, estab. Wormley's hotel & catering serv. in Wash. D.C.; 1819-1884).

Clergymen and Religion

Through science and the development of knowledge along other lines, man's understanding of himself and of the external universe has expanded a great deal during the past few centuries. But man is aware that there are many areas in which his capacity to explain is very limited and that each increment of knowledge seems to unveil further areas of ignorance, concerning which he was previously unaware. When man's sum total of knowledge was small and his ignorance in most directions was more overwhelming than now, it was probably natural for him to think of events which he did not understand as being caused by big and powerful men—called gods, or consolidated as one god. Even today we often hear reference to man's ignorance set forth in expressions to the effect that answers to pertinent questions are "hidden in the bosom of God."

Much of man's early effort at improving his status in life was directed toward god appeasement, so that the "boss man" would be kindly disposed toward earthly man's weaknesses and his pleas. In some respects denominationalism may be looked upon as a differentiation or specialization in appeasement techniques, as people became more numerous and more affluent in the sense of being able to support more people to think up congenial doctrines and develop associated ritual.

During the early years of settlement in America, north of Florida, there was great turmoil and persecution in Europe concerning which religious doctrine and ritual should prevail. This meant that a large proportion of the early settlers came to America in the hope of securing religious freedom. Most of these early immigrants were illiterate, as were most of the people in the European communities from which they came. However, the immigrants included a rather large number of clergymen, who represented one of the best educated classes in Europe at the time.

In consequence of the situation described, the early clergymen performed several functions in the New World, which present-day Americans would not think of as being among clergy functions. For example, they were often prominent in civic affairs as public officials, and they were essentially in charge of education and of the early schools, as such institutions became established. By habit, expanding institutional interest, and a kind of hazy folk demand, much of this religious interest extended through the first half of the nineteenth century. Under dynamic evangelism, in a somewhat romantic and fiesta atmosphere associated with evangelical meetings, various ramifications of a similar interest appear today. The role of religious affiliation and strife and the role of clergymen as a vocational group has thus been important in the development of American culture.

1. Concepts for Discussion

(a) Reference has sometimes been made to ideological similarities, and differences, between the teachings of Jesus and the practice of American democracy. Does this mean that the American people are gradually incorporating their religious ideology into their political system.? Was there a similar incorporation in the European system against which Luther revolted? Does harmony between church and state demand such incorporation?

(b) Some countries in Europe and several in Latin America have an official or state church, which is supported by taxes levied on the community or state. In what ways may the relationships between this practice and religious freedom be restrictive, and in what ways may they be expansive?

(c) Apparently some American clergymen have recommended that members of their congregations should violate or disobey certain laws which the clergy looks upon as being in conflict with church doctrine. In what ways may such recommendations bear on civic imagery and respect for law and order in America?

(d) There are important forces for evolution in religion which are comparable to forces for evolution in law or in medical service, or which may be comparable to forces for extending the Darwinian concept of biological evolution. But there are also important obstacles for extending the concept of evolution to religion.

(e) As America has more contact with Japan, China, and other parts of the Orient, religious understanding and tolerance in America will broaden. More of the religious idealism which concerns relationships among people, in a fellowman sense, will thus become incorporated into the American political system.

(f) Much of the teaching procedure in American public schools, which is referred to as individualized or small-group instruction, follows several of the procedures which were used by Jesus as a teacher.

2. Individuals to Consider

Barrett, Benjamin F. (Swedenborgian writer, founded Swedenborg Pub. Assn.; 1808-1892).

Beecher, Lyman (pres. of Lane Theol. Sem., father of Harriet B. Stowe; 1775-1863).

Blanchard, Jonathan (Presb., pres. Knox College in Galesburg, Ill.; 1811-1892).

Breckinridge, John (Presb., public debate on Prot. vs. Cath.; 1797-1841).

Buchminster, Joseph S. (Unit., founded Boston Athenaeum; 1784-1812).

Cartwright, Peter (Meth., frontier preacher—Tenn., Ohio., Ind., Ill.,; 1785-1872).

Chadwick, John W. (Unit., wrote in favor of Darwinism; 1840-1904).

Chandler, Thomas B. (Angl., pamphleteer on church matters; 1726-1790).

Channing, William E. (Unit., liberal, estab. "Channing Unitarianism"; 1780-1842).

Cummings, Joseph (Meth., pres. Northwestern Univ.; 1817-1890).

Edwards, Jonathan (Cong., philos., writer; 1703-1758).

Einhorn, David (Rabbi, Am. leader in reform Judaism; 1809-1879).

Farley, John M. (Cath., became archbishop and cardinal; 1842-1918).

Finley, James B. (Meth., evang. pioneer, co-founder Wyandot Indian Mission; 1781-1856).

Fisk, Wilbur (Meth., pres. Wesleyan U., Conn.; 1792-1839).

Fosdick, Harry E, (Bapt., interdenom. Riverside Ch., prof., author, radio; 1878-1969).

Fox, Robert John (Cath. msgr., soc. worker; 1930-).

Funk, Isaac K. (Luth., editor, founded Funk & Wagnalls Co.—publishers; 1839-1912).

Graham, William F. (Billy) (Bapt. evang., internat. tours, T.V. programs; 1918-).

Gros, John D. (Ger. Reform, philos., chaplain, univ. prof.; 1738-1812).

Hartwig, Johann C. (Luth., ranged from Me. to Va., estab. a seminar; 1714-1796).

Hennepin, Louis (Cath. miss. with La Salle, captured by Sioux Ind.; 1640-post 1701).

Heschel, Abraham J. (Jew. theol., writer, prof. Jew. ethics & mysticism; 1907-1972).

Hirsch, Emil G. (Rabbi, univ. prof., editor of *Jewish Encyclopedia*; 1851-1923).

Hooker, Thomas (Cong., *Survey of the Summe of Church Discipline*; 1586-1647).

Hopkins, Mark (philos., theol., teacher, coll. pres.; 1802-1887).

Huntington, William E. (Meth., 1904-1911 pres. Boston Univ.; 1844-1930).

Kenrick, Peter R. (Cath. archb., opponent of papal infallibility doctrine; 1806-1896).

Kimball, Heber C. (Mormon leader, with the migration to Utah, counseled B. Young; 1801-1868).

King, Martin L. Jr. (Bapt., negro civil-rights leader; 1929-1968).

Kneeland, Abner (Univ., edit. *Boston Investigator*, 1st Am. rationalist journ.; 1774-1844).

Knox, Samuel (Presb., educator, sought national system of education; 1756-1832).

Larrabee, William C. (Meth., editor, 1st St. Supt. of Ind. public schools; 1802-1859).

Lindberg, Conrad E. (Luth. synod leader, seminary teacher; 1852-1930).

Mahan, Milo (Episc., seminary prof. and rector, wrote church histories; 1819-1870).

Mather, Cotton (Puritan, writer, helped excite people on witchcraft; 1663-1728).

Mayhew, Jonathan (West Church, Boston; relig. and pol. pamphleteer; 1720-1766).

Mombert, Jacob I. (Episc. pastor, wrote theol. works and biographies; 1829-1913).

Muhlenberg, William A. (Episc., educator, drafted liturgical reforms; 1796-1877).

O'Connor, Michael (Cath., seminary rector, bishop, became a Jesuit; 1810-1872).

Pemberton, John (Quaker, imprisoned for opposing armed resistance to Eng.; 1727-1795).

Perry, Rufus L. (negro Baptist clergyman and leader, journalist, editor; 1834-1895).

Potter, William J. (left Units. in 1867 to help found the Free Relig. Assn.; 1829-1893).

Rauschenbusch, Walter (Bapt., prof., author, dev. of "social gospel"; 1861-1918).

Rittenhouse, William (Mennon. preacher, pioneer paper manufacturer; 1644-1708).

Ryan, Patrick J. (Cath., leading preacher and orator, St. Louis, Mo.; 1831-1911).

Schroeder, John F. (Episc. preacher, prin. of girl's school, rector; 1800-1857).

Schultze, Augustus (Moravian, author, editor, coll. pres.; 1840-1918).

Silverman, Joseph (Rabbi, relig. lib., became strong Zionist; 1860-1930).

Smith, H. Preserved (Presb., seminary teacher, librarian, author; 1847-1927).

Smith, Joseph (Mormon prophet, published *Book of Mormon*, imprisoned and shot; 1805-1844).

Spencer, Anna G. (indep. clergyman, journalist, women's rights; 1851-1931).

Talmage, Thomas D. (Dutch Reform, lecturer, publisher; 1832-1902).

Van Rensselaer, Cortlandt (Presb., dev. parochial schools and academies; 1808-1860).

Wiggin, James H. (Unit., revised Mary Baker Eddy's *Science and Health*; 1836-1900).

Wigglesworth, Michael (Cong. preacher, practiced med., wrote poetry; 1631-1705).

Williams, Roger (clergyman, crit. Mass. Puritanism, founded Providence; c. 1603-1683).

Wise, Isaac M. (Rabbi, taught lib. Judaism, founded Heb. Union Coll., author; 1819-1900).

Witherspoon, John (Presb., statesman, educator, pres. Coll. of N.J.; 1723-1794).

Woodbridge, John (Puritan pastor, colonial magistrate, banker, publisher; 1613-1695).

Young, Brigham (2nd pres. of Mormon Ch., colonized Utah, 56 children; 1801-1877).

Zahm, John A. (Cath., author of theol. and sci. books, univ. teacher; 1851-1921).

Zollars, Ely V. (Disc. of Christ, author, coll. pres.; 1847-1916).

Inventors and Discoverers

The word "invent" is used in varying connotations, much as are such words as agriculture, education, science, etc. Thus reference is sometimes made to the invention of a theory, a system of practice, or an alibi. However, there is considerable feeling that the word invent typically refers to some product or device which directly changes man's physical relationships with the environment and hence expands his power in the universe. Thus, we say that Edison *invented* the phonograph. The more limited connotation is the usual guide in the listing on names which appears in section two of this appendix, although there are some exceptions.

Contact with biographical sketches of persons who have made significant inventions, at various times and in widely varying fields, should help enlighten present-day youth as to the limited background opportunity and strong motivation of many inventors.

While inventions vary in significance, the full potential of any invention may never be realized. But a large proportion of inventors make it possible for several later inventions to grow out of an initial achievement. This can easily be seen regarding such items as the camera, farm plow, microscope, or internal-combustion engine.

One result of the situation described is that a culture which is as richly supplied with devices of various kinds as America is at the present time has many more starting points from which further inventions may embark than a simple or undeveloped culture has. Adroit use of biography can stimulate the imagination of young Americans along the lines of possible future invention.

1. Concepts for Discussion

(a) A prominent American inventor is credited with saying that creativeness is 5 percent inspiration and 95 percent perspiration. What does this mean regarding the inventive potential of an ordinary American?

(b) It is often said that necessity is the mother of invention, but in reality leisure time in which to reflect and try things out is more important than necessity.

(c) Whether a particular invention is good or bad for the people depends more on the use that is made of it than on the specific content of the invention. This can readily be seen with respect to firearms, automobiles, airplanes, telephones, etc.

(d) The natural ability to invent is like most other abilities in being distributed throughout the population, rather than being concentrated in a few persons.

(e) Regardless of the material wealth or affluence of a family or a nation, motivation and encouragement are essential to stimulate fruitful inventiveness—and to overcome the disappointments of successive failures.

(f) The extent to which a nation can exercise world leadership depends largely on the scope and direction of the inventiveness of its people, including the support and encouragement which the group collectively gives to the individual who tries.

2. Individuals to consider

Arkwright, Richard (Eng., spin. and carding machinery, other textile machines; 1732-1792).

Babbage, Charles (Eng., math. calculus, speedometer, train cowcatcher, computer; 1792-1871).

Bell, Alexander G. (telephone, phonograph records, educ. of the deaf; 1847-1922).

Bessemer, Henry (Eng., Bessemer process in steel making; 1813-1898).

Bevan, Edward John (Eng., viscose-rayon; 1856-1921).

Bigelow, Erastus B. (power looms for carpets and coach lace; 1814-1879).

Billings, Charles E. (tool maker, drop forging, mach. prod. of pistol frames; 1835-1920).

Cartwright, Edmund (Eng., mechanical loom, rope-making machine; 1743-1823).

Celsius, Andres (Swed., earth's magnet. declin., invent. centigrade thermo.; 1701-1744).

Claude, Georges (Fr., chemist, expansion method of liquifying air; 1870-1960).

Cockerill, William (Eng., invented spinning and weaving machinery; 1759-1832).

Colt, Samuel (revolving-barrel, multi-shot pistols; 1814-1862).

Cooke, William F. (Eng., electric telegraph and railway signals; 1806-1879).

Crompton, Samuel (Eng., spinning mule, basis for muslin manufacture; 1753-1827).

Diesel, Rudolf (Ger., diesel engine; 1858-1913).

Dolland, John (achromatic lens, microscopes, telescopes, optics; 1706-1761).

Donkin, Bryan (Eng., paper-making and printing machines, food canning; 1768-1855).

Dunlop, John Boyd (Eng., invented pheumatic tire, Dunlop Rubber Co., Ltd.; 1840-1921).

DuPont, Alfred I. (mechanical procedure in gunpowder manufacture; 1864-1935).

Edison, Thomas A. (phonograph, quadruplex teleg., incandes. lamp, Gen. Elec. Co.; 1847-1931).

Fairbanks, Henry (scales for weighing grain, elec. generator, Congreg. preacher; 1830-1918).

Faraday, Michael (Eng., experimenter in elec. and mag. laws of electrolysis; 1791-1867).

Fitch, John (steamboat, predecessor to R. Fulton; 1743-1798).

Ford, Henry (motor vehicles, Ford Motor Co., introduced mass production; 1863-1947).

Gambey, Henri P. (Fr., scientific instruments, dipping needle; 1787-1847).

Gatling, Richard John (Gatling gun, farm tools, hemp-breaking machine; 1818-1903).

Goodyear, Charles (vulcanizing rubber, author; 1800-1860).

Gutenberg, Johann (printing from movable type, the 300 Gutenberg Bibles; 1398-1468).

Hanna, Clinton R. (microphones for sound movies, gryo, aircraft autopilots; 1899-   ).

Hargreaves, James (spinning jenny; 1720-1778).

Heath, Russell L. (equip. for nuclear spectorscopists, gamma-ray spectra; 1926-   ).

Henry, Joseph (electromagnetic motors, dir. of Smithsonian Institution; 1797-1878).

Heyrovsky, Jaroslav (polarography in chemistry and electricity; 1890-1967).

Hoe, Richard M. (rotary printing press, web press; 1812-1886).

Howe, Elias (invented and made sewing machines; 1819-1867).

Hyatt, John Wesley (celluloid, plastics, roller bearings, billiard & bowling balls; 1837-1920).

Kjeldahl, Johann Gustav (Dan., rapid estimation of nitrogen and protein; 1849-1900).

Krupp, Alfred (Ger., cruc. steel, rifles & superior cannon barrels, war material; 1812-1887).

Lawrence, Ernest O. (physicist, invented cyclotron, helped develop atom bomb; 1901-1958).

Leeuwenhoek, Antony (microscopist, structure of teeth, skin, capillaries; 1632-1723).

Lenoir, Jean Joseph (first effective gas engine, gov. for elec. motors; 1822-1900).

Liebniz, Gottfried W. (math., physics, calculus, work on calculating machine; 1646-1716).

McCormick, Cyrus H. (reaper, pioneered in business methods; 1809-1884).

Marconi, Guglielmo (It., wireless telegraphy, short-wave transmission; 1874-1937).

Marg, Elwin (tonometer to test eye pressure, prevent blindness from glaucoma; 1918-   ).

Maxim, Hiram S. (incandescent lamps, machine gun, smokeless powder; 1840-1916).

Macintosh, Charles (waterproof fabrics; 1766-1843).

McMillan, Edwin M. (co-discoverer of neptunium and plutonium, phase stability; 1907-   ).

Melnick, Matilda B. (methods to identify viruses re: cancer, infect. disease; 1926-   ).

Mergenthaler, Ottmar (linotype, organized Nat. Typographic Co.; 1854-1899).

Napier, John (logarithms, trigonometric functions; 1550-1617).

Nasmyth, James (steam hammer, reflecting telescope; 1808-1890).

Noyes, La Verne (farm machinery, windmills for farms; 1849-1919).

Otis, Elisha Graves (elevators, mechanical lifts, use of steam power; 1811-1861).

Otto, Nickolaus A. (four-stroke internal-combusion engine; 1832-1891).

Packard, James W. (electrical apparatus, motor cars, chassis construction; 1863-1928).

Planck, Max Karl (quantum theory, heat radiation and optics; 1858-1947).

Pullman, George M. (sleeping cars, organized Pullman Palace Car Co.; 1831-1897).

Ramsden, Jesse (instrument maker, improved sextant, micrometer, barometer; 1735-1800).

Rand, Addison C. (compressed air rock drills, organized Rand Drill Co.; 1841-1900).

Schmidt, Bernhard V. (Schmidt telescopic camera; 1879-1935).

Sequin, Marc (railway suspension bridges and tunnels, tubular boiler; 1786-1875).

Shrapnel, Henry (bursting charge in spherical projectiles, fuses; 1761-1842).
Singer, Isaac M. (sewing machine, successive patents to improve it; 1811-1875).
Sobrero, Ascanio (It., discovered explosive power of nitroglycerine; 1812-1888).
Sperry, Elmer A. (gyroscope, dynamos, mining mach., arc lamps; 1860-1930).
Sprengel, Hermann J. P. (vacuum pump, studies on specific gravity; 1834-1906).
Stanley, Francis Edgar (steam driven automobile; 1849-1918).
Sturgeon, William (electric motors and magnets, dynamos; 1783-1880).
Swan, Joseph Wilson (incandes. filament lamp, photography, bromide paper; 1828-1914).

Torricelli, Evangelista (mercury barometer, method of drawing tangents; 1608-1647).

Vogel, Hermann Wilhelm (photochemist, spectroscopist; 1834-1898).
Volta, Alessandro (electric battery, volt as unit of electromotive force; 1745-1827).

Walker, John (friction match, drug and chemical business; c. 1781-1859).
Watts, James (two-chamber steam engine, centrifugal governor; 1736-1819).
Wedgwood, Josiah (pottery, china, cameos, colored earthenware; 1730-1795).
Wedgwood, Thomas (photography, light-sensitive silver nitrate; 1771-1805).
Wesson, Daniel B. (winchester arms, rim fire percussion cartridge; 1825-1906).
Westinghouse, George (electrical devices, railroad frog, air brakes; 1846-1914).
Whitehead, Robert (mobile torpedo, compressed air motor; 1823-1905).
Whitney, Eli (cotton gin, interchangeable gun parts, milling machine; 1765-1825).
Wilkinson, John (boring machine, used in cannon-foundry, etc.; 1728-1808).
Wright, Orville (aeroplane, heavier than air machine; 1871-1948).
Wright, Wilbur (aeroplane, heavier than air machine; 1867-1912).

Zeppelin, Ferdinand (Zeppelin airships, dirigible balloons; 1838-1917).
Zsigmondy, Richard A. (ultramicroscope, ultrafiler; 1865-1929).

Jurists and Legal Scholars

Establishing and maintaining social regulations is one of the earliest and most pervasive responsibilities of organized society. At the present time there is great variation among the regulatory systems that prevail in different parts of the world, and the systems become more involved as the social relationships among the people become more numerous and complex.

America is among the Westernized industrial societies which in recent decades have been plagued by an increase in crime and violence. There seems to be considerable uncertainty about how to deal effectively with the problems involved.

Perhaps one should ask whether the uncertainty will continue and the associated difficulties mount until America, probably in conjunction with other countries, develops the courage and the insight to attack problems in the field with an analytical and evaluative objectivity which resembles the attacks now made on problems of insect control in agriculture or problems of human and material qualities in space exploration.

1. Concepts for Discussion

(a) For the people of any country to constitute an intelligently law-abiding citizenry, it is necessary for the individual citizen to understand and respect the law and to assume responsibility for helping to enforce it.

(b) The history of cultural development in any field is largely a history of the persons who have made significant contributions to that field. With respect to America's current legal and regulatory structure, such contributions have been accumulating longer than in some areas of our culture.

(c) For student government in school to be useful in helping students to understand the operation of government in American communities, student representatives must participate in making some of the important school decisions and must then abide by the consequences of those decisions.

(d) As America develops increasing contact with the Orient, it is probable that our law will include more concepts that have originated in that part of the world.

(e) When courts continuously refer back to earlier decisions to find principles or bases for settling current disputes, they overemphasize the continuance of traditional practices and restrict the opportunity for new growth and development.

(f) If teachers, factory workers, civil service employees, and most other persons who work for large employers have to retire at a specified age, there should also be an age at which judges have to retire.

2. Individuals to Consider

Ames, James Barr (legal writer, prof.; 1846-1910).
Ames, Samuel (jurist; 1806-1865).
Aquinas, Thomas (It., philos. of canon law; 1225-1274).
Aristotle (Gr., philos., pupil of Plato, *Ethics*, *Politics*; 384-322 B.C.).
Austin, John (Eng., jurist and author; 1790-1859).

Barbour, Philip P. (lawyer, jurist, statesman; 1783-1841).
Beasley, Mercer (jurist; 1815-1897).
Bentham, Jeremy (Eng., jurist and philos., rules of evidence; 1784-1832).
Black, Hugo L. (jurist, civil liberties; 1886-1971).
Bouvier, John (judge, author of law dictionary; 1787-1851).
Brackenridge, Hugh Henry (jurist, author; 1784-1816).
Bradley, Joseph P. (U.S. Sup. Ct., fed. gov't. has inherent powers; 1813-1892).
Brandeis, Louis D. (jurist, Sup. Ct., judicial liberalism; 1856-1941).
Breckinridge, William, C. P. (lawyer, Confed. soldier, editorial writer; 1837-1904).

Cardozo, Benjamin N. (jurist, writer, Sup. Ct.; 1870-1938).
Chase, Salmon P. (compiled stats., Free Soiler, C. J. of U.S. Sup. Ct.; 1808-1873).
Cicero, (Roman statesman, philos., writer; 106-43 B.C.).
Cobb, Andrew Jackson (jurist, law teacher; 1857-1925).
Coke, Edward (Eng., jurist, statesman, writer on law; 1552-1634).
Colbert, Jean B. (Fr., statesman, emergence of Fr. Civil Code out of feudalism; 1619-1683).

Comstock, George F. (jurist, equity lawyer; 1811-1892).
Cooley, Thomas M. (jurist, prof., edited *Michigan Reports*; 1824-1898).
Creighton, William (lawyer, Ohio's 1st Sect'y of State, U.S. Dist. Atty., whig; 1778-1851).
Cushing, William (jurist, U.S. Sup. Ct.; 1732-1810).

Depew, Chauncey M. (lawyer, ry. pres., 1st U.S. Minister to Japan; 1834-1928).
Dillon, John Forrest (jurist, author *Municipal Corporations*; 1831-1914).

Endicott, William C. (jurist, Sup. Judicial Ct. of Mass.; 1826-1890).
Erskine, John (jurist, fed. judge in Ga. who opposed secession; 1813-1895).

Forbes, John M. (lawyer, diplomat, charge' de' affairs at Buenos Aires; 1771-1831).
Frankfurter, Felix (jurist, Sup. Ct. of U.S., teacher; 1882-1965).

Gaius (Roman jurist, writer on civil law; c. 110-c. 180).
Goldthwaite, George (Ala. jurist; 1809-1879).
Gray, Horace (jurist; 1828-1902).
Gray, John Chipman (lawyer, prof., author, authority on real prop.; 1839-1915).
Greathouse, Clarence R. (lawyer, diplomat, legal adviser to Korean gov't.; 1845-1899).
Griswold, Matthew (Conn. jurist; 1714-1799).
Grotius, Hugo (Dutch jurist and statesman; 1583-1645).

Hamilton, Alexander (lawyer, statesman, soldier; 1757-1804).
Hamilton, James Alexander (lawyer, politician; 1788-1878).
Hammurabi (Babylonian king and lawgiver, 1955-1913 B.C.).
Hancock, John (Texas Unionist, lawyer, land laws; 1824-1893).
Harlan, John Marshall (jurist, univ. lecturer, "great dissenter" in 316 cases; 1833-1911).
Hemphill, John (jurist, "the John Marshall of Texas"; 1803-1862).
Hobbes, Thomas (Eng. philos., author—law of nature, *Liberty*, *Leviathan*; 1588-1679).
Holmes, Oliver Wendell (jurist, soldier, prof., author, U.S. Sup. Ct.; 1841-1935).
Hornblower, Joseph C. (lawyer, C.J. Sup. Ct. of N.J.; 1777-1864).
Hughes, Charles Evans (jurist, politician, C.J. U.S. Sup. Ct.; 1862-1948).

Jackson, Mortimer M. (jurist, diplomat, U.S. consul at Halifax; 1809-1889).
Jay, John (lawyer, statesman, diplomat; 1745-1829).
Jhering, Rudolph von (Ger. teacher, wrote on morals and law, *Spirit of Human Law*; 1818-1892).
Jones, Leonard A. (jurist, author, "Jones Legal Forms," securities; 1832-1909).
Justinian I (Roman lawgiver, "Justinian Code"; 483-565).

Kant, Immanuel (Ger. philos., reason and Divine Will as supreme law; 1724-1804).
Kent, James (jurist, *Commentaries on American Law*; 1763-1847).

Lamar, Joseph Rucker (jurist, U.S. Sup. Ct.; 1857-1916).

Langdell, Christopher C. (law school dean, teacher, author, case method; 1826-1906).

Lehmann, Frederick W. (lawyer, practised in Iowa & Mo., U.S. Solicitor Gen.; 1853-1931).

Leibnitz, Gottfried W. von (Ger. philos., writer on law and law reform; 1646-1716).

Livermore, Samuel (jurist; 1732-1803).

Livingston, Robert R. (jurist, stamp-act work; 1718-1775).

Lowell, John (jurist, U.S. Dist. Ct. in Mass.; 1743-1802).

McFarland, Thomas B. (lawyer, jurist, Sup. Ct. of Calif.; 1828-1908).

Manning, Thomas C. (lawyer, jurist, Confed. soldier; 1825-1887).

Marshall, John (C. J. of Sup. Ct., fed. powers, judicial review; 1755-1835).

Mason, Charles (jurist, patent law, Iowa Code; 1804-1882).

Mason, John Y. (U.S. Atty. Gen., usually supported Jacksonianism; 1799-1859).

Maxwell, Samuel (lawyer, politician, Sup. Ct., of Neb.; 1825-1901).

Mittermaier, Carl J. A. (Ger. crim. proc. law, mediator of Ger. and other leg. sci.; 1787-1867).

Moses (lawgiver, religious leader; 13th century B.C.).

Papinian (Roman jurist and writer; 146-212).

Peckham, Rufus W. (U.S. Sup. Ct., wrote noteworthy opinions; 1838-1909).

Pinkney, William (lawyer diplomat, Const. interpreter; 1764-1822).

Plato (Gr. philos. and moralist, *Meno, Republic, Laws*; 427-347 B.C.).

Plowden, Edmund (R.C. lawyer, used common-law reasoning against king and parl.; 1518-1585).

Pomeroy, John Norton (legal writer, teacher; 1828-1885).

Pothier, Robert J. (Fr. teacher, wrote extensively on law and its hist.; 1699-1772).

Pound, Roscoe (teacher, philos. of law; 1870-1964).

Pufendorf, Samuel von (natural law, confed. of Ger. states, more C.-Prot. harmony; 1632-1694).

Putnam, James Osborne (lawyer, educator; 1818-1903).

Quincy, Josiah (lawyer, writer; 1744-1775).

Rutledge, John (jurist, statesman; 1739-1800).

Sanford, Edward Terry (lawyer, jurist, "Pocket Veto"; 1865-1930).

Savigny, Fred C. (Ger., rights of possession, traced Rom. law thru Mid. Ages; 1779-1861).

Schofield, Henry (law teacher, author; 1866-1918).

Scott, William (Lord Stowell—Eng., laws on marriage, admiralty, internal. rela.; 1745-1836).

Selden, John (Eng., hist., wrote on legal subjs., emphasized freedom; 1584-1654).

Solon (Athenian lawgiver; c. 638-c. 559 B.C.).

Stone, Harlan Fiske (jurist, prof., C.J. of U.S. Sup. Ct.; 1872-1946).
Stone, Wilbur Fisk (jurist, Southwest Spanish land titles; 1833-1920).

Taney, Roger Brooke (jurist, statesman; 1777-1864).
Thayer, Amos Madden (Mo. jurist, soldier; 1841-1905).
Todd, Thomas (judge, important in Ky. land law, on Sup. Ct., supported J. Marshall; 1765-1826).
Tyler, John (Va. jurist, opposed fed. Constitution; 1747-1813).

Vattel, Emerich de (Swiss jurist and diplomat; 1714-1767).
Vico, Giovanni B. (It., philos. and jurist; 1668-1744).

Wait, William (lawyer, author; 1821-1880).
Warren, Earl (justice, politician, C.J. U.S. Sup. Ct.; 1891-   ).
Wayne, James M. (Ga. lawyer, Civil War Unionist, U.S. Sup. Ct., admiralty law; 1790-1867).
Wright, George Grover (jurist, C.J. Iowa Sup. Ct.; 1896-1920).

Zouche, Richard (Eng., internat. law, domicile, ambassadors, neutral., contrabd.; 1590-1661).

Literature

As cultures emerge, there is usually considerable development of song, dance, ritual, and folklore before literacy appears and makes it possible to write down the verbal aspects of the total phenomenon. Rhythm is one aspect of song and poetry which is early apparent as an element common to both fields. This point should be noted relative to the large number of persons who made early contributions to the field of literature through the avenue of poetry. While the meter in both poetry and song becomes more complex as a culture develops and as literacy becomes usual, considerable poetry nevertheless continues to be set to music.

But as a culture becomes more complex, there are many situations in which meanings must be as precise as possible. Poetry and song are important means of communications where emotion and sensuous response are involved, but those media are ineffective where response depends on science and technology. Thus, astronauts do not communicate with ground stations by song or poetry, but by the most technical prose that their programs have been able to develop for designating minute differences or changes. Sanitation, agricultural production, and sound monetary policy are not areas that respond well to communication through poetry or song. How, for example, would one sing statistics to a group of cattlemen or a group of bankers?

As anthropologists report on elementary cultures, it sometimes appears that every form of recorded inscription is looked upon as a part of the literature, whether recorded on stone, wood, bone, parchment, clay tablets, paper or some other material. Such a conception is probably adequate for a primitive culture in which there is not much to record. But as a culture develops, many new kinds of information appear and many new events occur.

A fairly advanced stage of the development indicated can be seen in the

United States, where there are many specialized areas of science, art, economics, government, religion, etc. Each specialized area develops a special body of recorded material, or literature, which relates mainly to the particular area. Thus, a person who is studying chemistry would not be likely to find literature on religion to be especially helpful. If a student attempts an experimental study on insect control, one of the first things that he does is to "review the literature" of the field, to find out what has already been done on his particular subject.

As various specializations develop in a culture and draw specialized materials out of the broad sum total of all that is recorded, the remainder still retains the status and largely the functions associated with literature under the prespecialized conditions. The situation is similar to that regarding philosophy, which has been referred to as the "mother of sciences," as various special areas split off from the parent body, but which still retains its identity and basic functions as philosophy. The same phenomenon appears in law and social regulation.

The literature considered in the present appendix designation is that which fits the undifferentiated residual category—with perhaps one significant exception. The exception relates to the various aspects of literary criticism, which can be looked upon as a specialized area within the field of general literature.

Persons who study literature in public schools and colleges should come to recognize the different connotations in which the term "literature" is used, and to recognize that as a culture becomes more complex one should expect additional connotations or specialties to appear. Through project and related study in the area of literature as described herein, considerable insight may be gained into why a complex and developing society needs more law and more areas of specialized regulation than a simple society needs—or could use. Follow-up comparisons of the type inferred affords great opportunity for a teacher. Throughout the exercise student orientation in poetry as in science, suggested Goethe, should be toward the future rather than toward a far-off or mystic past.

1. Concepts for Discussion

(a) An imaginative study of the numerous ramifications embodied in literature can help the student learn to integrate or hold together in a meaningful pattern the diverse experiences which he has as a student—and which he will later have as a responsible adult.

(b) During their formal schooling, young Americans should have some organized contact with the literature which people in other countries have developed and considered important, as one aid to constructive participation in the affairs to an interdependent world.

(c) In present-day America, a person who specializes in the study of literature at a fairly advanced level has fewer vocational opportunities associated with his specialty than a person who specializes in the study of agriculture or law.

(d) It should be a function of literature both to inform and to entertain, and the author who reaches the highest level of literacy achievement is the one who can both inform and entertain at a high level through the same pieces of writing.

(e) In view of the nation's extensive lawlessness and violence, more of our general literature should be aimed at informing readers about the nature and basis of law and social regulations and about the freedoms and other personal satisfactions associated with living in a stable and law-abiding society.

(f) A propaganda element is always present in literature, even when an effort is made to be strictly informative, because judgment and preference are always involved in designating the subjects on which information will be presented and in determining how much information to present.

2. *Persons to Consider*

Adams, Abigail (letters and correspondence reflecting life of the times; 1744-1818).

Aeschylus (Gr., poet and dramatist; 525-456 B.C.).

Aesop (Gr., writer of fables; c. 620-c. 560 B.C.).

Aldrich, Thomas B. (short-story writer, poet, novelist; 1836-1907).

Alger, Horatio (writer of boys' stories, novelist; 1832-1899).

Anderson, Hans Christian (Denmark, stories and tales; 1805-1875).

Aristophanes (Athenian, poet and writer of comedy; 448?-385? B.C.).

Arnold, Matthew (Eng., poet, essayist, critic; 1822-1888).

Attar (Pers. poet, moral maxims, lived 114 yrs.; 1119-1233).

Austen, Jane (Eng., novelist; 1775-1817).

Balzac, Honore de (Fr., novelist; 1799-1850).

Beard, Charles A. (social and economic hist. of U.S.; 1874-1948).

Blab, Phelair (Pers., author of astron., moral, pol. and lit. works; 1729-1825).

Boccaccio, Giovanni (It., writer and poet; 1313-1375).

Boethius, Anicius (Rom., philos., trans. into A/Sax. by Kg. Alfred, c. 890; 480?-524?).

Boswell, James (Scot., author, biographer of Samuel Johnson; 1740-1795).

Brewer, Fredrika (Swed., author extensively trans. into Engl; 1802-1865).

Bridges, Robert S. (Eng., poet, essayist, poet laureate 1913-30; 1884-1930).

Browning, Elizabeth B. (Eng., poet; 1806-1861).

Bryant, William C. (Am., poet, nature themes; 1794-1878).

Bunyan, John (Eng., preacher, wrote *Pilgrim's Progress*; 1628-1688).

Burns, Robert (Scot., poet; 1759-1796).

Byron, George G. (Eng., poet; 1788-1824).

Carlyle, Thomas (Scot., essayist and historian; 1795-1881).

Cather, Willa (novelist; 1876-1947).

Cervantes, Miguel de (Sp., novelist and short-story writer; 1547-1616).

Chang, Eileen (Chin., fiction writer, peasant life, revolutionary period; contemporary).

Chang, Tien-i (Chin., novelist, short-story writer; 1907-).

Chaucer, Geoffrey (Eng., poet, *Canterbury Tales*, wide range of sentiment; 1340?-1400).

Chekhov, Anton P. (Rus., short-story writer and dramatist; 1860-1904).

Ch'ien, Chung-shu (Chin., novelist, satire, *The Besieged City*; contemporary).
Chou, Tso-jen (Chin., essayist, translator, univ. lecturer; 1885-1958?).
Cicero, Marcus T. (Roman, statesman, orator, writer; 106-43 B.C.).
Comenius, John A. (Boh., refugee in Poland, wrote Boh. lit., bishop; 1592-1670).
Cooper, James F. (novelist, some mythology about frontier life; 1789-1851).

Dante, Alighiere (It., poet, *The Divine Comedy*; 1265-1321).
De Foe, Daniel (Eng., novelist and political journalist; 1659?-1731).
Dickens, Charles J. (Eng., novelist; 1812-1870).
Dickinson, Emily E. (poet; 1830-1886).
Diderot, Dennis (Fr., philos. critic, encyclopedist; 1713-1784).
Dostoevski, Feodor M. (Rus., novelist, ranked next to Tolstoy; 1821-1881).
Dreiser, Theodore (novelist; 1871-1945).
Dryden, John (important among founders of Eng. prose, poet, critic; 1631-1700).

Eliot, T. S. (Eng., poet and critic—born in U.S., Nobel Prize, 1948; 1888-1964).
Emerson, Ralph W. (essayist, poet; 1803-1882).
Erasmus, Desiderius (Dut., humanist, theologian, writer; 1466?-1536).
Erskine, John (novelist, poet, essayist; 1879-1951).
Euripides (Gr., dramatist; c. 480-406? B.C.).

Fichte, Johann G. (Ger., philosopher, orator; 1762-1814).
Field, Eugene (newspaper reporter, poet; 1850-1895).
France, Anatole (Fr., novelist, essayist, Nobel Prize, 1921; 1844-1924).
Frost, Robert L. (poet; 1874-1963).
Fuller, Henry B. (novelist; 1857-1929).
Futabatei, Shimei (Jap., pioneer of modern novel, analysis of Jap. life; 1864-1909).

Galsworthy, John (Eng., novels, short stories, drama, Nobel Prize, 1932; 1867-1933).
Garland, Hamlin (novels, poems, short stories, Wis. and Dak. settings; 1860-1940).
Ghazzali (Pers., Islamic theologian and mystic, prolific writer; 1059-1111).
Goethe, Johann W. (Ger., dramatic poet, novelist, philosopher; 1749-1832).
Gogol, Nicholas V. (Rus., novelist, Cossack background, *Dead Souls*; 1809-1852).
Goldsmith, Oliver (Irish, poet, playwright, essayist, novelist; 1730?-1774).
Gorki, Maxim (Rus., novelist, dramatist, short-story writer; 1868-1936).
Grey, Zane (novelist; 1872-1939).
Grimm, Jacob and Wilhelm (Ger., fairy-tales; Jacob, 1785-1863; Wilhelm, 1786-1859).

Hamit, Abdulhak Tarhan (Turk., poet and dramatist, prom. in mod. Turk. lit.; 1852-1937).
Harris, Joel Chandler (journalist, author, Uncle Remus stories; 1848-1908).
Hawthorne, Nathaniel (novelist, short-story writer; 1804-1864).
Hay, John M. (poet, fiction writer, journalist, statesman; 1838-1905).

Hazlitt, William (Eng., critic and essayist; 1778-1830).

Hearn, Lafacadio (Eng., author, newspaper reporter, novelist; 1850-1904).

Heine, Heinrich (Ger., poet, journalist, critic; 1797-1856).

Herder, Johann G. (Ger., philosopher and poet; 1744-1803).

Holberg, Ludwig H. (creator of mod. Danish lit., wrote on law, hist., satire; 1684-1754).

Holmes, Oliver Wendell (poet, novelist, essayist, physician; 1809-1894).

Homer (Greek, epic poet, *Iliad and Odyssey*; c. 8th cent. B.C.).

Horace (Rom., poet and satirist; 65-8 B.C.).

Howells, William D. (author, critic, editor; 1837-1920).

Hugo, Victor (Fr., poet, novelist, dramatist; 1802-1885).

Hu Shih (Chin., scholar, author, diplomat; 1891-1962).

Huss, John (Boh., author, orthog., relig. reformer, burned at the stake; 1369?-1415).

Ibsen, Henrik (Norw., dramatist and poet; 1828-1906).

Irving, Washington (popular Am. author, *Sketchbook, O. Goldsmith*; 1783-1859).

James, Henry (novelist; 1843-1916).

Johnson, Dr. Samuel (Eng., poet, critic, lexicographer; 1709-1784).

Kalidasa (poems, dramas, some trans. into Eng., "Hindu Shakespeare"; fl. 5th cent. A.D.).

Keats, John (Eng., poet; 1795-1821).

Kipling, J. Rudyard (Eng., author, Nobel Prize, 1907; 1865-1936).

Lang, Andrew (Scot., poet, prose writer; 1844-1912).

Lanier, Sidney (poetry and music, literary scholar; 1842-1881).

Lao-Tse (founded Taoism, nonresistance, influenced Chin. poetry; 6th cent. B.C.)

Lenin, Vladimir (Nikolai) (Rus., revol. leader, propagandist, Sov. premier; 1870-1924).

Lessing, Gotthold E. (dramatist and critic, Lutheran Reform of Ger. lit.; 1729-1781).

Lin Yutang (Chin., author and philosopher, in U.S.; 1895-).

Livy, Titus (Rom., history writer; 59 B.C.-17 A.D.).

Longfellow, Henry W. (poet; 1807-1882).

Lowell, James R. (poet, essayist, diplomat; 1819-1891).

Lucretius (Roman, poet and philosopher; 97-54 B.C.)

Macaulay, Thomas B. (Eng., historian, author, statesman; 1800-1859).

Machiavelli, Nicolo de B. (It., statesman, writer on history and government; 1469-1527).

Mansur, Abul Kasim (Fedusi) ("Homer of Persia," royal praise and satire; 940?-1020).

Mao Tun (Shen Yen-ping) (Chin., novelist, short-story writer; 1896-).

Mardhekar, Bal Sitaram (Marathi—India, poet and critic, newer trends; 1907-1956).

Marx, Karl H. (Ger., economist, philos., socialist, author *Das Kapital*; 1818-1883).

Maupassant, Guy de (Fr., short-story writer, novelist; 1850-1893).
Mencius (Chin., philosopher; c. 380-289 B.C.).
Mendele, Mocher S. (Jewish, novelist, traveling bookseller; 1835-1917).
Mill, John Stuart (Eng., philosopher and economist; 1806-1873).
Milton, John (Eng., poet; 1608-1674).
Mishima, Yukio (Jap., prolific writer of novels, drama, short stories; 1925-1970).
Moliere, Jean B.P. (Fr., actor and playwright; 1622-1673).
Montaigne, Michel (Fr., essayist; 1533-1592).
Moore, Thomas (Irish, poet, satirical use of comic rhyme; 1779-1852).
More, Thomas (Eng., humanist, author, statesman, canonized in 1935; 1478-1535).
Morley, John (Eng., journalist, biographer, critic, statesman; 1838-1923).
Murray, Gilbert (Eng., classical scholar, statesman; 1866-1957).
Mutanabbi (Arab., poet, most quoted Arab. poet, murdered near Baghdad; 916-965).

Niemcewicz, Julian (Pol. poet, wrote some fables and plays; 1757-1841).
Nietzsche, Frederick W. (Ger., philosopher, author; 1844-1900).

Omar Khayyam (Persian, poet and mathematician, *Rubiat*; d. 1123).
Ovid (Roman, poet; 43 B.C.-17? A.D.).

Parrington, Vernon L. (literary historian and critic; 1871-1929).
Pasternak, Boris (Rus., author, *Dr. Zhivago*, Nobel Prize, vilified in Russia; 1890-1960).
Pavlov, Ivan P. (Rus., physiologist, author, Nobel Prize for med. 1904; 1849-1936).
Petrarch (It., poet and scholar; 1304-1374).
Pien Chih-lin (Chin., poet, "new verse," trans. Eur. works into Chin.; 1910-).
Poe, Edgar Allen (Am., poetry and fiction, shady aspects of life, critic; 1809-1849).
Pushkin, Alexander S. (Rus., poet, short-story writer; 1799-1837).
Pu Sung-ling (Chin., collector of ghost and fairy stories, Liao-Chai tales; 1640-1715).

Ram Mohan, Roy (Bengali, synthesis of Hindu & Chr. ethics, Brahma/Sabba; 1774-1833).
Rey, Mikolaj (of Naglowice—Polish poet, religious literature; 1505-1569).
Riley, James W. (poet; 1849-1916).
Robelais, Francois (Fr., satirist and humorist; c. 1490-1553).
Ruskin, John (Eng., author, art critic, social reformer; 1819-1900).

Saadi (Pers., poet and moralist; 1184?-1291?).
Schiller, Johann C.F. (Ger., poet, dramatist, historian; 1759-1805).
Scott, Walter (Scot., narrative poetry, novelist; 1771-1832).
Shakespeare, William (Eng., poet and dramatist, Reform. period, humor; 1564-1616).
Shaw, George B. (Ir., dramatist, critic, novelist, Nobel Prize, 1925; 1856-1950).
Shelley, Percy B. (Eng., poet; 1792-1822).

Shen, Ts'ung-wen (Chin., novelist, short-story writer, critic; 1902-   ).
Shinran, Rennio (Jap., religious writer; ? c. 1500).
Sholokhov, Mikail A. (a great Rus. novelist, Nobel Prize, 1965; 1905-   ).
Sinclair, Upton (novelist, socialist, reformer; 1878-1969).
Sophocles (Gr., dramatist; 495?-406? B.C.).
Spengler, Oswald (Ger., philosopher, *Decline of the West*; 1880-1936).
Steinbeck, John E. (novelist, Nobel Prize, 1962; 1902-1969).
Stevenson, Robert L. (Scot., novelist, essayist, poet; 1850-1894).
Stowe, Harriet Beecher (novelist, abolitionist; 1811-1896).
Swift, Jonathan (Eng., satirist, clergyman, born in Ireland; 1667-1745).
Swinburne, Algernon (Eng., poet and critic; 1837-1909).

Tagore, Robindranath (Hindu, poet, Nobel Prize, 1913; 1861-1941).
Tennyson, Alfred (Eng., poet laureate, religion based moralist; 1809-1892).
Thackeray, William M. (Eng., novelist, born in India; 1811-1863).
Thahkin Ko-daw Hmaing (Burmese, poet, playwright, historian, pol. satirist; 1876-1964).
Thurber, James (writer, caricaturist, illustrator; 1894-1961).
Tolstoy, Leo N. (Rus., novelist and social reformer; 1828-1910).
Tu Fu (great Chinese poet; 712-770).
Turgenev, Ivan B. (Rus., historical novelist; 1818-1883).
Twain, Mark (Samuel L. Clemens) (humorist, novelist, *Tom Sawyer*; 1835-1910).

Untermeyer, Louis (poet, journalist, anthropologist, critic; 1885-   ).

Veblen, Thornstein (economist, socialist, author; 1857-1929).
Vergil (Rom., poet, author, *The Aeneid*; 70-19 B.C.).
Voltaire, Francis M. A. (satirist, Fr. dramatist, *Candide*; 1694-1778).

Wells, H. G. (Eng., rom. and sci. stories, novels, *Outline of History*; 1866-1946).
Westcott, Edward N. (novelist, *David Harum*, song writer; 1846-1898).
Wheatley, Phyllis (poet, born in Africa; 1753?-1784).
Whitman, Walt (poet, contempt for conventionalities; 1819-1892).
Whittier, John G. (poet, 1807-1892).
Wordsworth, William (Eng., poet, 1843-50 poet laureate; 1770-1850).

Xenophon (Gr., historian and essayist; 434?-355? B.C.).

Zola, Emil (Fr., novelist; 1840-1902).
Zoroaster (Persian, religious teacher; fl. 6th. cent. B.C.).

Manufacturing

In America a large percentage of the population makes a living through some form of manufacturing. The percentage seems especially large if one includes persons engaged in supplying raw materials to manufacturing plants and in distributing manufactured products. At the time of this nation's first census of population in 1790, most of the people were engaged in agriculture.

In an important respect the expansion of employment in manufacturing and other nonagricultural vocations has resulted from the increased capacity of the individual farmer to produce food, fiber, forest products, etc. The increase makes it possible for fewer farmers to produce the food needed by the nation. However, much of the increase has been due to improved farm implements, availability of fertilizer, and better marketing equipment. These items in turn are largely products of manufacturing.

If it is difficult for youth to get a clear picture of the American industrial and economic system, help in getting such a picture can be secured by reviewing the range in types of contributions made to the system through manufacturing, as shown by a list of persons such as that submitted herewith. Further help can be gained from reading the biographies of several persons who are listed.

1. Concepts for Discussion

(a) In a dynamic economy, a vigorous manufacturing sector depends on a continuous flow of new inventions and discoveries.

(b) Since a growing economy has a continuing need for new or expanded plants and facilities, part of what is earned through the economic system must be saved for investment in these facilities.

(c) A competent and ambitious young person can look forward to making as important a contribution to America through industry as through medicine, teaching, or other areas of professional service.

(d) Throughout the field of industrial work, the health and development of the employee should be regarded by management as its most important source material.

(e) If certain important items can be manufactured or otherwise produced with less effort in some parts of the world than in other parts, international trade and tariff arrangements should be such as to encourage their production where economy indicates.

(f) The educational background of every able-bodied American youth of either sex should include some work experience, in a nonschool pay-job, before he leaves high school.

2. Individuals to Consider

Appleton, Nathan (textiles, cotton, power machinery, cheap female labor; 1779-1861).

Babbitt, Benjamin T. (baking power, soap, held numerous patents; 1809-1889).
Billings, Charles E. (drop-forging of tools; 1835-1920).
Bridges, Robert (Saugus Iron Works, 1st in the Colonies; d. 1656).

Carnegie, Andrew (iron, steel, capacity for industrial organization; 1835-1919).
Chickering, Jonas (pianos, 1st one-piece cast-iron frame piano; 1798-1853).
Chisholm, Hugh J. (paper, a founder of International Paper Co.; 1847-1912).
Coates, George H. (flexible shafts for grinding machines, hair-clipper mfgr.; 1849-1921).
Colgate, William (soap, benefactor of Colgate University; 1783-1857).
Colt, Samuel (multishot pistols, revolvers; 1814-1862).
Converse, John H. (locomotives, pres. Baldwin Locomotive Works; 1840-1910).
Crittenden, Albert R. (marine hardware; 1843-1921).

Deere, John (plows, farm machinery; 1804-1886).

Dennison, Aaron L. (watches, factory produced items with interchangeable parts; 1812-1895).

Douglas, William T. (shoes, built a retail chain of 117 stores nationwide; 1845-1924).

DuPont, Eleuthere I. (gunpowder, worked under Lavoisier in Fr., came to Am.; 1771-1834).

Earle, Pliny (cotton machinery, patented a carding machine; 1762-1832).

Eastman, Atthur M. (firearms, promoted ocean cable between Europe and U.S.; 1810-1877).

Edison, Thomas A. (background for General Electric Co.; 1847-1931).

Emerson, Ralph (farm mach., knitting estabs., Emerson Inst., Mobile, Ala.; 1831-1914).

Estey, Jacob (organs, melodians; 1814-1890).

Faber, John E. (pencils, 1st to attach rubber erasers to pencils; 1822-1879).

Fairbanks, Henry (scales, electric generators, pulp-making machine; 1830-1918).

Flagler, John H. (pipe and tube mfgr.; 1836-1922).

Fleischmann, Charles L. (yeast; 1834-1897).

Ford, Henry (automobile inventor and manufacturer; 1863-1947).

Frick, Henry Clay (steel, coke, helped form U.S. Steel Corp.; 1849-1919).

Gary, James A. (cotton mfgr., banker; 1833-1920).

Greenleaf, Moses (map-maker, author; 1777-1834).

Gunther, Charles F. (candy mfgr., rare book collector; 1837-1920).

Hammond, James B. (typewriters; 1839-1913).

Hewitt, Abram S. (iron, 1st Am. open-hearth furnace; 1822-1903).

Hogg, George (glass mfgr., pioneer in chain stores; 1784-1849).

Howe, Frederick W. (machine tools, milling machine; 1822-1891).

Howe, John Ireland (rotary pin-making machine, physician; 1793-1876).

Ingersoll, Robert H. ("dollar Ingersoll" watches; 1859-1928).

Judson, Egbert P. (powder and explosives; 1812-1893).

Lindsay, William (textile mfg., author; 1858-1922).

Luckens, Rebecca W. P. (iron, Brandywine Iron Works; 1794-1854).

McCormick, Cyrus H. (farm mach., harvester, Internat. Harvester Co.; 1859-1936).

Mallinckrodt, Edward (chemical mfgr.; 1845-1928).

Mason, William (power looms, locomotives; 1808-1883).

Nelson, Nelson O. (bldg. and plumbing supplies, labor dispute arbitrator; 1844-1922).

Oliver, Henry W. (iron, Oliver Iron & Steel Co.; 1840-1904).

Oliver, James (foundry work, Oliver Chilled Plow Works; 1823-1908).

Osborn, Henry S. (map maker, metallurgist, Presb. preacher; 1823-1894).

Otis, Charles R. (elevator mfgr; 1835-1927).

Owens, Michael J. (glass, 1st automatic bottle-blowing machine; 1859-1923).

Packard, James W. (Packard automobile mfgr; 1863-1928).
Patterson, John H. (cash register, helped build Nat'l. Cash Reg. Co.; 1844-1922).
Patterson, Robert (Louisiana sugar, textiles; 1792-1881).
Pillsbury, Charles A. (flour, C. A. Pillsbury and Co.; 1842-1899).
Pinkham, Lydia Estes (patent medicines, "Vegetable Compound"; 1819-1883).
Pitcairn, John (Pittsburgh Plate Glass Co.; 1841-1916).
Post, Charles W. (prepared foods, Postum and Post cereals; 1854-1914).

Reese, Isaac (brick, "Reese Silica Brick"; 1821-1908).
Remington, Philo (arms, typewriters, farm equipment; 1816-1889).
Rittenhouse, William (paper, 1st paper mill in the Colonies; 1644-1708).
Rogers, Thomas (locomotives, built the "Sandusky," 1st west of Allegheny Mts.; 1792-1856).

Sage, Henry W. (lumber, philanthropist; 1814-1897).
Scranton, George W. (iron, ry. developer; 1811-1861).
Slater, John Fox (cotton and woolen mfgr.; 1815-1884).
Spalding, Albert G. (sporting goods, A. G. Spalding and Bros.; 1850-1915).
Sprague, William (textiles, lumber; 1773-1836).
Sprechels, Claus (sugar, especially in Calif. and Hawaii; 1828-1908).
Steinway, Henry E. (pianos, built Steinway Hall for musical life, N.Y.; 1797-1871).
Stetson, John B. (hats, John B. Stetson Univ., Fla.; 1830-1906).
Stiegel, Henry W. (iron, glass, Stiegel glassware; 1729-1785).
Studebaker, Clement (wagons, automobiles; 1831-1901).
Stutz, Harry C. (automobile manufacture, Stutz Motor Car Co.; 1876-1930).

Timken, Henry (wagon maker, roller bearings; 1831-1909).
Towne, Henry R. (locks, Yale Lock Mfg., Co.; 1844-1924).

Wagner, Webster (railway sleeping cars, drawing-room cars; 1817-1882).
Warner, Worcester R. (telescopes, turret lathes; 1846-1929).
Washburn, William D. (flour, W. D. Washburn and Co.; 1831-1912).
Weaver, Philip (textiles, cotton, early operation in Spartanburg, S.C.; 1791-1861).
Westinghouse, George (ry. airbreaks and signals, Westinghouse Electric Co.; 1846-1914).
Wharton, Joseph (refined nickel prods., Wharton School of Fin., U. of Pa.; 1826-1909).
Winchester, Oliver F. (firearms, shirts mfgr., author; 1810-1880).

Ziegler, William (Royal Baking Powder, partron of No. Pole sci. expeditions; 1843-1905).

Medicine and Health

The tribal organizations of most preliterate peoples include persons recognized as priests and medicine men, who usually have responsibility for the health and physical well-being of the tribe—and perhaps responsibility for producing illness and debilitation within enemy tribes. Various combinations of magic and herb concoctions are major items in their ritual.

Western civilization and its antecedents have had an organized concern for medicine and health for about 2500 years, or at least since the time of Hippocrates, who is often referred to as the Father of Medicine. However, it is only with the rise of experimental study and close observation, which characterize modern science, that rapid progress in medical knowledge and service has been made.

One implication of the situation noted is that early contributors were much less specialized than contributors are today. Hence, in the early period a person might have been recognized as a philosopher or a theologian as well as a physician. By contrast, many recent contributors have worked within rather narrow specialties.

However, narrowness tends to drift toward isolation, with a weakening of the social cement that is necessary to hold society together. Thus, extensive diversity and specialization actually increase the need for highly competent generalizers, who have perspective to organize a great many details into meaningful relationships with one another. The need for developing and maintaining perspective as suggested is no less essential in the field of medicine and health than it is in politics, economics, education, or any one of numerous other fields. Problems of perspective in the kind of setting inferred constitute one of the areas of greatest difficulty facing a complex society.

1. Concepts for Discussion

(a) The physical and mental health of the people is the greatest single asset that a nation can have. It is important for the individual to learn why and how to foster his own personal health and to learn the ways in which individual differences are important in doing so.

(b) In a richly varied culture such as the United States, an undisciplined indulgence in food, or other things that are immediately pleasing to the sense organs, tends in the long run to be contrary to good health.

(c) While there are important group responsibilities for community health and sanitation, the individual must from childhood onward assume a major responsibility not only for his own personal health but also for his relationships to community health needs.

(d) There are quacks and charlatans in every field of human relations, although in some fields they may be more numerous than in others and in some fields they may be called swindlers or something else other than quacks. The antisocial attitudes and consequences of such persons are about the same, regardless of what they are called.

(e) If quackery, swindling, hypocrisy, etc., exist in varying degrees, most individuals must have *some tendency* in the direction implied. If such a tendency is strong, there is a heavy demand for public regulations to assure the public well-being.

(f) There is no foreseeable limit regarding the extent to which man's life may henceforth be extended through medical research and practice. The extensions which occur will not eliminate man's problems, but will produce changes in their nature and relative intensity.

2. *Individuals to Consider*

Allen, Edgar (Am., anat., disc. estrogen, studied fem. reprod. cycle, endocrines; 1892-1943).

Aspinwall, William (Am., phys., mil. surg., 2nd Am. hosp. for smallpox; 1743-1823).

Barnard, Christiaan N. (So. Afr., surg., cardiology, heart transplants; 1922-).

Bartlett, Josiah (Am., phys., jurist, politician, signed Decl. of Indep.; 1729-1795).

Bell, Charles (Scot., anatomist, surg., studied nerve functions; 1774-1842).

Billings, Frank (Am., phys., concept of focal infections, helped dev. Chi. med. schools; 1854-1932).

Billings, John S. (Am., surg., lib. designed for J. Hopkins Hospital, co-founder Index Medicus; 1838-1913).

Blalock, Alfred (Am., surg., co-perfector of operations for blue babies; 1899-1964).

Bushnell, George E. (Am., surg., specialist on tuberculosis, author; 1853-1927).

Cameron, Thomas W. M. (Scot., parasitologist, diseases of animal relative to man; 1894-).

Carey, Eban James (Am., phys., studied origin of bone and muscle, med. exhibits; 1889-1947).

Carrel, Alexis (Fr., surg., suturing blood vessels in organ transplants; 1873-1955).

Celsus, Aulus C. (probably the chief medical author of antiquity, Roman Hippocrates; fl. 14-37).

Channing, Walter (Am., phys., ether in childbirth, pernicious anemia in pregnancy; 1786-1876).

Colombo, Matteo R. (It., anat., discovered pulmonary circulation of blood; 1516-1559).

Cournand, Andre F. (Fr., cardiac and pulmonary physiol., heart catheterization; 1895-).

Crawford, John (Am., phys., theory of contagion; 1746-1813).

Cushing, Harvey W. (Am., pituitary gland, brain and neurosurgery; 1869-1939).

DeBakey, Michael E. (Am., surg., invented surg. instrts., decron tubing for blood vessels; 1908-).

Delafield, Francis (Am., phys., pathol., nephritis, colon diseases, author; 1841-1915).

Dragstedt, Lester R. (Am., phys., gastric physiology and ulcers; 1893-).

Faget, Jean C. (Am., phys., diff. between yellow fever and malaria; 1818-1884).

Ferrier, David (Scot., cerebral anat., neurol. of cerebral localization; 1843-1928).

Forssmann, Werner T. O. (Ger., phys., disc. in 1929 a method of catheterizing the heart; 1904-   ).

Fracastoro, Girolamo (It., phys., attrib. disease to tiny particles, gave syphilis its name; 1483-1553).

Francis, Thomas Jr., (Am., phys., epidemiologist, isolated diff. influenza viruses; 1900-   ).

Fuchs, Leonhart (Ger., phys., botanist, critic of Galen and Arab med. dogma; 1501-1566).

Galen, Claudius (Hellenistic phys., experimental physiol.; c. 129-c. 199).

Goodpasture, Ernest W. (Am., pathologist, viruses, studied formation of fibrinogen; 1886-1960).

Gorgas, William C. (Am., surg., trop. med., yellow fever, Panama and Ecuador, sanitarian; 1854-1920).

Graham, Evarts A. (Am., surg., cancer of lungs and bronchi, pneumoectomy; 1883-1957).

Gray, John P. (Am., phys., alienist, revolutionized asylum practice; 1825-1886).

Hahnemann, C. F. Samuel (Ger., phys., founded homopathy, said tiny orgs. cause cholera; 1755-1843).

Harvey, William (Eng., phys., discoveries on circ. of blood, embryology; 1578-1657).

Hays, Isaac (Am., phys., ophthalmologist, studied astigmatism and color blindness, editor; 1796-1879).

Herophilus (Gr., phys., father of sci. anat., 1st syst. study of pulse, comp. anat.; fl. 300 B.C.).

Hippocrates (Gr., phys., father of med., rejected demoniac causes of disease; c. 460-c. 377 B.C.).

Holmes, Oliver W. (Am., phys., showed puerperal fever to be contagious, author; 1809-1894).

Jacobson, Leon O. (Am., phys., hematologist, neoplastic diseases of the blood, radiation injury; 1911-   ).

Jenner, Edward (Eng., phys., pioneer in smallpox vaccination, 1796 was his first; 1749-1823).

Jung, Carl Gustav (psychiat., 2 dimen. of uncon., phys. & psy. aspects of disease; 1875-1961).

Keeley, Leslie E. (Am., phys., treatment for liquor and drug habit; 1834-1900).

Kocher, Emil T. (Swiss, surg., 1909 Nobel Prize, worked on thyroid gland; 1841-1917).

Koller, Carl (Bohemia, introd. cocaine as local anesthetic, author; 1857-1944).

Laennec, Rene T. H. (Fr., phys., invented stethoscope, auscultation in diagnosis, prof.; 1781-1826).

Landstiner, Karl (immunology, antigen chain, blood groups and transfusions; 1868-1943).

Lang, Tzu-Wang (China-Taipei, cardiologist, heart and vascular research; 1929-   ).

Langerhan's, Paul (Ger., pathol., discovered Islets of Lang. in pancreas that prod. insulin; 1847-1888).

Leites, Samuel M. (Rus., pathol., fat metabolism, endocrinology, liver diseases; 1899-).

Lister, Joseph (Eng., biol., founded antiseptic surg., isolated pure-culture bacteria; 1827-1912).

Loeb, Robert (Am., phys., metabolism disorders, electrolyte physiol.; 1895-).

Loewi, Otto (pharmacologist, chem. of nerve impulse transmission; 1873-1961).

Long, Crawford W. (Am., anesthetist, procedure to use sulphuric ether; 1815-1878).

Mayo, William J. (Am., surg. at Mayo Clinic, stomach surgery; 1861-1939).

Medawar, Peter B. (immunology tolerance, res. on aging, tissue transplants; 1915-).

Mesmer, Franz A. (Ger., phys., laid foundation for modern hypnosis; 1734-1815).

Minot, George R. (Am., phys., liver treatment in pernicious anemia; 1885-1950).

Muller, Johannes P. (Ger., physiol., founder of modern physiol., res. in anat.; 1801-1858).

Nightingale, Florence (Eng., nurse, hosp. reform., sanita. in hosp. serv.; 1820-1910).

Osler, William (phys., res. on spleen, heart, blood platelets, angina pectoris; 1849-1919).

Palmer, Alonza B. (Am., phys., cholera edpidemic of 1854, author, editor; 1815-1887).

Paracelsus, Theophrastus B. (Swiss, phys., attacked ancient authority, med. chem.; 1493-1541).

Pare, Ambroise (Fr., surg., cauterized wounds, ligature in amputa., invent. instrts.; 1510-1590).

Pasteur, Louis (Fr., chem., microbiol., germ theory of disease, vaccines; 1822-1895).

Peck, Franklin B., Sr. (Am., phys., diabetes and new insulin modifications; 1898-).

Perutz, Maz F. (molecular biol., res. on proteins, hemoglobin crystallographer; 1914-).

Pickett, Morris J. (Am., microbiol., med. bacterio., immunity in undulant fever; 1915-).

Rammelkamp, Charles H., Jr. (Am., phys., epidemiologist, rheumatic fever; 1911-).

Redi, Francesco (It., phys. & poet, showed that flies come from eggs, not spon. gen.; 1626-1667).

Reed, Walter (Am., phys., studied typhoid and yellow fevers, mosquitos; 1851-1902).

Sabin, Albert B. (Am., phys. born in Rus., virolog., oral polio vaccine; 1906-
).
Sachs, Volkmar R. (Ger., phys., blood transfus., genetics of blood groups,
  Nu. Hematol.; 1922-   ).
Salk, Jonas E. (phys., epidemiologist, dev. anti-polio vaccine; 1914-   ).
Sanctorius, Santorio S. (It., phys., helped found study of metab. & quant. med.;
  1561-1636).
Serturner, Friedrich W. (Ger., chem., apothecary, discovered morphine in
  opium; 1783-1841).
Sherrington, Charles S. (Eng., neurophysiol., functions of neuron, synapse,
  etc.; 1856-1952).
Spalding, Lyman (Am., phys., vaccina., hydrophobia, founded U.S. Phara-
  macopia; 1775-1821).
Squibb, Edward (phys., pharmacologist, research, manufacturing chemist;
  1819-1900).
Sydeham, Thomas (Eng., phys., urged clin. observa., not theory; "Eng.
  Hippocrates"; 1624-1689).

Theiler, Max (phys., virol., dev. 170 vaccines against yellow fever in humans;
  1899-   ).
Tullis, James L. (Am., phys., isolate & preserve coagula. factor in blood for
  med. use; 1914-   ).

Underwood, Michael (Eng., phys., Underwood's disease—tight skin—in
  children; 1736-1820).

Wangensteen, Owen H. (Am., surg., res. on ulcers and bowel obstructions;
  1898-   ).
Ward, Arthur A. (neurosurgeon, epilepsy, function of cerebral cortex, brain
  research; 1916-   ).
Warren, J. Collins (Am., surg., healing of arteries after ligature, editor,
  author; 1842-1927).
Wasserman, August (Ger., bacteriol., immunologist, syphilis test; 1866-1925).
Wharton, Thomas (Eng., phys., discov. submaxillary saliva duct, "Wharton's
  Duct"; 1614-1673).
White, James W. (Am., surg., genito-urinary surgery, author, translator,
  editor; 1850-1916).
Whytt, Robert (Scot., phys., neurologist, studied reflex action; 1714-1766).
Willis, Thomas (Eng., phys., brain anat., cerebral arteries, disc. 11th cranial
  nerve; 1621-1675).
Windaus, Adolf O. R. (Ger., chem., 1928 Nobel Pr. in chem., res. on steroids,
  Vit. D; 1876-1959).
Withering, William (Eng., phys., botanist, mineralogist, med. uses of plants,
  digitalis; 1741-1799).
Wittman, Heinz G. (Ger., molecular biol., res. on viruses, helped decipher
  gene. code; 1927-   ).
Wojewski, Alfons (Polish phys., urologist, res. on carcinoma of the prostate;
  1912-   ).

Zakrzewski, Marie E. (phys., prof. of obstetrics, estab. N. Eng. Hosp. for W. & child.; 1829-1902).

Science

Probably the most important cultural development in the Westernized world during the past two centuries has been the rise of science. The influence of science has related not only to the physical or material aspects of daily life, but also to the mode of thought and general outlook on life and on man's confidence in his capacity to change the world according to his liking. Moreover, the influence not only concerns relationships among people within countries, but concerns the movement of people among countries and the general patterns of international relationships.

It should be added that the accumulated body of scientific knowledge and techniques implies a further acceleration of foregoing developments within the areas now reached by the so-called Westernizing influence and also implies that the influence will gradually extend to the rest of the world. It further implies that several areas of the culture which at present are not looked upon as having a scientific orientation or as being particularly influenced by science will gradually be influenced by the types of observations and evaluations that are typically referred to as scientific method. Questions about the use of scientific procedures in forecasting and controlling economic cycles, or in examining and modifying systems of ethical and religious values, are suggestive of the expanded influence concerned.

The developments indicated necessarily affect the rate of obsolescence in the existing regulatory structure and affect other problems related to the continuing effectiveness of that structure. It follows that for a citizen to function effectively in the life of a community, through vocational and other avenues, he needs considerable understanding of the nature and development of science and of what look like reasonable expectations regarding the future influence on the culture as a whole.

Acquaintance with the lives and contributions of individual scientists, particularly when gained under the coordinating guidance of a teacher or other leader, affords one avenue for developing the understanding required.

1. Concepts for Discussion

(a) The crux of scientific method lies in the objective recording of events, analytical interpretation of the data, freedom for others to attack or defend the data or conclusions of any researcher, and an open-ended recognition that all of the possible data on the expanding ramifications of any subject will not be available at any one point in time.

(b) A major concern about the future of science in American life relates to the extension of its method, perhaps with some modification, to additional areas of the culture; such as the adequacy and growth of the regulatory structure and the institutions with primary concern for law and order in the community.

(c) Much of the heralded conflict between science and religion results from an inadequate conception of either or both fields.

(d) Scientific research has not become so involved that there is nothing which the individual scientist can do, apart from extensive laboratory or comparable facilities which only the government or the large industrial corporation can make available.

(e) The development of a career interest in science frequently begins before adolescence.

(f) Progress in science depends on community values and attitudes, particularly in regard to what areas of possible interest science will be encouraged or permitted to study.

2. *Individuals to Consider*

Adler, Alfred (Austrian, psychol., psychoanal., emphasized emotional disturb.; 1870-1937).

Agassiz, Jean R. (zoologist, naturalist, contribs. to Nat. Hist. of U.S.; 1807-1873).

Albertus Magnus (Bavarian, scholastic philos., naturalist; 1193?-1280).

Ampere, Andre M. (Fr., physicist, electrodynamics; 1775-1836).

Amundsen, Ronald (Norw., polar explorer, dirigible flier, author; 1872-1928).

Anaxagoras (Gr., natural philos., explained moon phases and solar eclipse; c. 500-428 B.C.).

Archimedes (Gr., math., physics, invented hydrostatics; 287-212 B.C.).

Aristotle (Gr., philos. basis of science, nat. hist., dissected animals, medieval influ; 384-322 B.C.).

Asimov, Isaac (biochemist, extensive writing on science and science fiction; 1920-   ).

Audubon, John J. (artist, ornithologist, author, *Birds of America*; 1785-1851).

Avery, Oswald T. (phys., biol., pathol., res. on pneumococcus bacteria; 1877-1955).

Babcock, James F. (chemist, Mass. assayer of alcoholic beverages; 1844-1897).

Bacon, Francis (Eng., philos, based sci. laws on observa., universal lang. idea; 1561-1626).

Bacon, Roger (Fran. monk, scientist, experimenter, inaccuracy of Julian Calendar; 1214-1294).

Baeyer, Johann F. (chem., sleeping pills, dyes, molecular structure of indigo; 1835-1917).

Balfour, Francis M. (comparative embryologist, author; 1851-1882).

Barr, Murray L. (res. on sex chromosomes and mental retardation; 1908-   ).

Bartlett, Frederick C. (experimental psychol., devised mach. to test men in WW II; 1886-   ).

Bateson, William (geneticist, theory on origin of trait linkage; 1861-1926).

Belyavev, Pavel T. (Rus., astronaut, first orbital flight with walk in space; 1925-1970).

Black, Joseph (chem., spec. heat, inv. ice calorimeter, quant. analysis; 1728-1799).

Bohr, Niels H. D. (physics, spectroscopic data on structure of the atom; 1885-1962).

Bosch, Martin H. (indus. ammonia syn., synthetic gasoline in WW I; 1874-1940).

Boye, Martin H. (chem., geol., joint discov. of explosive perchloric ether; 1812-1909).

Boyle, Robert (nat. philos., chem., boiling point of liquids under pressure; 1627-1691).

Brahe, Tycho (astron., studied comets, stars, planetary motions and orbits; 1546-1601).

Broca, Pierre P. (Fr., surg. and anthropol., brain surg., located speech center; 1824-1880).

Cavendish, Henry (studied hydrogen, sp. grav. relative to water, electricity; 1731-1810).

Chittenden, Russell H. (phsiol. chem., biochem. of nutrition and digestion; 1856-1943).

Christofilos, Nicholas C. (nuclear phys., strong-focus prin., "magnetic bottle"; 1916-   ).

Compton, Arthur H. (phys., change in wave length of x-rays, work on cosmic rays; 1892-1962).

Copernicus, Nicholaus (founded mod. astron., math. of planetary orbits, dist. to sun; 1473-1543).

Curie, Marie S. (phys. chem., studied radio-active materials, died of leukemia; 1867-1934).

Dana, James D. (geol., studied earth's crust—mts., volcanoes, continents; 1813-1895).

Darwin, Charles G. (physics, x-ray diffraction, res. in atomic physics; 1887-1962).

Darwin, Charles R. (modern evolution. theory, *Voyage of Beagle, Origin of Species*; 1809-1882).

Davy, Humphrey (nitrous oxide as anesthetic, H ion in acid, safety lamp; 1778-1829).

Descartes, Rene (math., founded analyt. geom., sought mech. explan. of events; 1596-1650).

Durer, Albrecht (artist, scientific pict. rep., used magic sq. in art work; 1471-1528).

Eads, James B. (built bridges, river gunboats for Civil War, improved harbors; 1820-1887).

Eddington, Arthur S. (gen. theory of relativ., gravit. waves, space-time in geom.; 1882-1944).

Einstein, Albert (spec. and gen. theory of relativ., gravity and light; 1879-1955).

Erlanger, Joseph (physiol., res. on blood pressure, electric impulse of nerves; 1874-1965).

Fermi, Enrico (atomic sci., nuclear reactor and chain reaction, atom bomb; 1901-1954).

Ferrel, William (meteorologist, winds and ocean currents; 1817-1891).

Fischer, Emil (organic chem., work on synthesis of sugar, polypeptids, tannin; 1852-1919).

Fleming, Alexander (microbiologist, penicillin, work on immunology; 1881-1955).

Franck, James (phys., energy transfer, photochem. of chlorophyll; 1882-1964).

Franklin, Benjamin (work on elect., flow from + to —, statesman, philos.; 1706-1790).

Freud, Sigmund (psychol., psychoanalysis, sex and libido, Oedipus Complex; 1856-1939).

Friedmann, Herbert (zool., ornithol., brood parasitism in birds, an. symbol. in art; 1900-   ).

Galilei, Galileo (astron., math., dev. & used telescope, studied moon & Jupiter; 1564-1642).

Galton, Francis (eugenics, studied identical twins, inheritability of genius; 1822-1911).

Gay-Lussac, Joseph L. (laws of gases, volumetric analysis, bleaching chlorides; 1778-1850).

Geiger, J. Hans (gas ionization, geiger counter, radioactive period of radium; 1882-1945).

Geissler, Heinrich (glassblower, vacuum production over col. of mercury; 1814-1879).

Gray, Asa (plant geog. & taxon., thought species were preordained, author; 1810-1888).

Griscom, John (chem. teacher, med. prop. of cod-liver oil, iodine for goiter; 1774-1852).

Grissom, Virgil I. (astronaut, 2nd Am. in space, killed in fire on grounded missile; 1926-1967).

Haber, Fritz (synthesized ammonia from atmospheric nitrogen, gas warfare; 1868-1934).

Haeckel, Ernst H. (biogen. laws, intell. as evolving, org.-inorg. unity, God as energy; 1834-1919).

Haldane, John B.S. (genetics, meas. of gene linkage, gas mix & safe breathing; 1892-1964).

Hale, George E. (astron., sunspot movement, studied sun's mag. & geog. poles; 1868-1938).

Halley, Edmond (astron., comets, eclipses, aurora, cataloged stars of So. Hem.; 1656-1742).

Harshberger, John W. (botany, author, bot. ed. of Funk & Wagnall's Coll. Dict.; 1869-1929).

Harvey, William (phys. anat., role of capillaries, blood circ. per hr.; 1578-1657).

Heisenberg, Werner K. (quan. mech., atomic structure, pos. & veloc. of particles; 1901-   ).

Helmholtz, Hermann L. F. (physics, tone theory, color vision, Reiman's geom.; 1821-1894).

Hershel, John F. W. (astron., nebulae of No. & So. Hemis., wrote on diff. calculus; 1792-1871).

Herzberg, Gerhard (physics, atomic & molecular spectroscopy, planetary atmosphere; 1904-   ).

Hess, Victor F. (cosmic rays, radioactive indexes of mixed liquids; 1883-1964).

Hofmeister, Wilhelm F. B. (bot., ovum fert. & embryo dev., angio- & gymnosperms; 1824-1877).

Hooke, Robert (phys., math., modern algebra, topological groups; 1918-   ).

Hotchkiss, Rollins D. (molecular biol., gen. biol. of deoxyribonucleic acid; 1911-   ).

Humboldt, Friedrich, W. H. A. (nat. hist., geog. exploration in So. Am., meteorology; 1769-1859).

Huxley, Julian S. (biol., prag. ethical theory based on natural selection; 1887-   ).

Huxley, Thomas H. (zool., res. on tropical animals, helped popularize Darwin; 1825-1895).

Ingenhous, Jan (photosynthesis, studied heat conductivity; 1730-1799).

Kepler, Johannes (astron., planetary motion, studied eclipses, astrol. forecasts; 1571-1630).

Kihara, T. (physics, model to explain equation of gas states, structure of crystals; 1917-   ).

Kitasato, Shibasaburo (bacteriol., plague bacillus, diphtheria antitoxin; 1856-1931).

Koch, Robert (bacteriol., identified cholera bacillus, dev. bacteria cultures; 1843-1910).

Kornberg, Arthur (biochem., enzyme chem., discovered deoxyribonucleic acid; 1918-   ).

Lamarck, Jean B. P. A. (evolutionist, accepted inheritance of acquired traits; 1744-1829).

Langley, Samuel P. (astron. physics, extension of solar spectrum, aerodynamics; 1834-1906).

Lavoisier, Antione L. (oxygen in respiration, formation of acids & salts, gasometer; 1743-1794).

Leakey, Louis S. B. (anthropol., paleon., fossil discover. in Tanzania and Kenya; 1903-1970).

Lenard, Phillip E. A. (cathode rays, atom has structure and is mostly empty space; 1862-1947).

Lindemann, Frederick A. (chem., adviser to W. Churchill; 1886-1957).

Linnaeus, Carl (scientific naming of plants and animals, systematic botany; 1707-1778).

Malthus, Thomas R. (pop. grows geometrically, food supply arithmetically; 1766-1834).

Manton, Sidnie Milana (zool., res. on crustaceous embryology; 1902-   ).

Maxwell, James Clerk (kinetic theory of gases, electromagnetic theory of light; 1831-1879).

Mendel, Johann G. (geneticist, worked on peas, hybridization; 1822-1884).

Mendelejeff, Dmitry I. (chemist, periodic table of elements, studied petroleum; 1834-1907).

Mercator, Gerardus (geog., map projection, planisphere for use in navigation; 1512-1594).

Michelson, Albert A. (phys., speed of light, meas. diameter of stars; 1852-1931).

Millikan, Robert A. (phys., ionization chambers in experiments on electricity; 1868-1953).

Morley, Edward W. (chem., density and atomic wt. of oxygen and hydrogen; 1838-1923).

Moseley, Henry G. (atomic nos., x-ray wave length and atomic wt.; 1887-1915).

Muller, Hermann J. (genetics, mutations, influence of x-rays on genes; 1890-1967).

Murchison, Roderick I. (geol., res. on fossiliferous strata, geol. systems; 1792-1871).

Newell, Homer E. (phys., exploring upper atmosphere with rockets, space probes; 1915-).

Newton, Isaac (nat. philos., math., studied gravity and universal gravitation; 1642-1726).

Osborn, Henry F. (paleontologist, over 860 sci. & educa. papers; 1857-1935).

Oort, Jan Hendrick (astron., structure of galaxies, origin of comets; 1900-).

Oppenheimer, J. Robert (quantum theory, particle theory, atomic bomb; 1904-1967).

Pauli, Wolfgang (phys., beta particles, new subatomic particles; 1900-1958).

Pavlov, Ivan P. (physiologist, psychol., conditioned reflexes and brain areas; 1849-1936).

Piaget, Jean (Sw., psych., infant's concept of reality, dev. of logical ideas; 1896-).

Piccard, Auguste (explor. stratosphere & ocean depths, balloon & bathysphere work; 1884-1962).

Piyp, Boris I. (geol., specialist on volcanoes and hot springs; 1906-).

Pliny the Elder, (sci. encyclopedia, summarized ancient knowledge on science; 23-79 A.D.).

Prescott, Benjamin (biochem., immunology, Bright's Disease; 1907-).

Priestley, Joseph (chem. theologian, studied CO_2 produced in fermentation; 1733-1804).

Ptolemy, Claudius A. (astron., said sun, moon & stars revolved around earth; 2nd cent. A.D.).

Pythagoras of Samos (philos., math., py. theorem, kinship of all living things; c. 572-497 B.C.).

Raper, John R. (botanist., genetics of sexuality in higher fungi; 1911-).

Rhazes (Al-Razi) (Arab sci., Galen view of med., an. gut. sutures, plaster casts; 841-925).

Riemann, George F. B. (Riemann geom., foundation of Einstein's work; 1826-1866).

Romer, Ole C. (veloc. of light by eclipses re. Jupiter, const. transit inst.; 1644-1710).

Rontgen, William K. (x-rays, pressure & viscosity of fluids, prop. of quartz; 1845-1923).

Rush, Benjamin (cor. phys. & mental aspects of med., insanity as arterial disease; 1746-1813).

Russell, Bertrand A. W. (math., philos., logical founda. of math.; 1872-1970).

Rutherford, Ernest (nuclear theory of atom, atom is mostly empty space; 1871-1937).

Sears, Paul B. (ecol. postgalacial climatic seq. in No. Am., ecol. & culture; 1891-).

Shapley, Harlow (stellar photo., size & shape of Milky Way, pulsa. theory; 1885-1972).

Shaw, William N. (meteriol., air pressure & circ. of upper atmosphere; 1854-1945).

Sidgwick, Nevil V. (chem., electronic theory of valency; 1873-1952).

Simpson, George C. (meteriol., res. on thunderstorms & atmospheric electricity; 1878- ?).

Snell, Esmod E. (biochem., vitamins and amino acids in foodstuffs; 1914-).

Steinmetz, Chas. P. (elec. eng., lightning arresters on power lines, 100 patents; 1865-1923).

Stoddard, John T. (chem., physics, author; 1852-1919).

Straus, William L., Jr. (phys. anthropol., anat. of living and extinct primates; 1900-).

Thales of Miletus (nat. philos., isosceles triangle, est. size of sun & moon; c. 636-c. 546 B.C.).

Theophrastus (found. sci. botany, described over 500 plants, philos.; c. 372-c. 287 B.C.).

Tobias, Cornelius A. (biophys., radiation and medical phys.; 1918-).

Twort, Frederick W. (bacteriologist, disc. a virus that destroys bacteria; 1877-1950).

Tyndall, John (absorp. & radia. of heat by gases & vapors, blue sky & polariza.; 1820-1893).

Urey, Harold C. (chem., disc. heavy hydrogen, meas. of paleotemperatures; 1893-).

Van Allen, James A. (phys., high-alt. rocket res., Van Allen radiation belts; 1914-).

Vinci, Leonardo da (painter, anat., methematician, architect; 1452-1519).

Von Braun, Werner (space sci., dev. various space rockets and boosters; 1912-).

Vries, Hugo de (mutation theory re: new species, studied osmosis, plasmolysis; 1848-1935).

Wallace, Alfred R. (naturalist, zoo. of Malay Archipelago, mapped zoogeog. regions; 1823-1913).

Warburg, Otto H. (biochem., cancer cells grow without oxygen, damaged by radiation; 1883- ?).

Westheimer, Gerald (optom., eye focus, optical & photoelec. insts. to test vision; 1924-).

Whitehead, Alfred North (math., organic philos., examined nat.-sci. concepts; 1861-1947).

Wiener, Norbert (math., vector & differential spaces, founda. of cybernetics; 1894-1964).

Wilkins, John (math., co-founder of Royal Society, philos.; 1614-1672).

Williams, Carrol M. (biochem. of insects, endocrine control of metamorphosis; 1916-).

Williamson, William C. (paleobotanist, plant life forms in coal; 1816-1895).

Wolff, Kaspar F. (embryologist, blastoderm and intestine formation; 1733-1794).

Wren, Christopher (arch., math., designed St. Paul's Cathed. and Greenwich Observ.; 1632-1723).

Wyckoff, Ralph W. G. (crystallographer, biophys., electron microsc. in virus study; 1897-   ).

Yanofsky, Charles (biol., amino acid changes in protein re: mutation changes; 1925-   ).

Young, John W. (astronaut; 1930-   ).

Young, Thomas (theory of light, surf. tens. of liquids, Rosetta Stone work; 1773-1829).

Young, Wesley A. (vet. res. on pharm. prep. for domestic and zoo animals; 1898-   ).

Zeeman, Pieter (magneto-optics, light in vibrat. media—water, quartz, flint; 1865-1943).

Teachers and Educators

To a large extent the pattern of early education in America was determined by the religious turmoil of the Reformation period in Europe. With the control of education essentially in the hands of the church and clergy, educational content and procedures were geared to promote the doctrines and practices of the religious group which prevailed in the particular region.

Thus, most of the teachers and educators of early America were clergymen; or stated conversely, most of what formal education there was depended on the efforts of clergymen. This point can be noted in the characterizations of several persons listed for consideration under the present caption. The number of church affiliated schools and colleges in the nation's present educational structure offers one indication of current relationships between religion and education in the nation's social structure. The continuing legislative and court disputes about separating church and state in public education offers another indication.

However, the bulge in emphasis on narrow doctrinal aspects of Christianity, which so extensively entered into and dominated the intellectual and educational life of the Western world during the extensive Reformation turmoil and its aftermath, should be viewed in perspective relative to the outlook which preceded that period and the outlook which during several recent decades has been replacing it. Some of the persons listed herewith reflect the ends of the suggested continuum, in considerable perspective.

1. Concepts for Discussion

(a) The children of each generation in America have more to learn than their parents had, and the difference is becoming greater from one generation to the next.

(b) It is more important for young people to learn *how* to learn *effectively*, than it is for them to learn any specific body of subject matter.

(c) With a continuing increase in the amount which the individual adult has to know in order to participate significantly in the vocational and civic world, it is important that young Americans during their formal schooling develop appropriate attitudes toward continued learning during their adult years.

(d) If schools emphasize getting students to help one another to learn, the students may be developing certain attitudes and skills of cooperation which constructive American citizenship requires.

(e) By reading biographical material on some of the persons whose names are listed herewith, and by reflecting on what is read as well as on the substantial number of names listed, a student can get a fair idea of the long and gradual buildup that has led to the nation's present educational opportunities and expectations.

(f) The content and operation of the school program, at any particular time, should be such as to inform and to encourage those students who show promise of becoming good teachers for future generations.

2. Individuals to Consider

Abelard, Peter (teacher, theologian, scholastic philosopher; 1079-1142).
Alexander the Great (extended Greek culture eastward; 356-323 B.C.).
Alfred the Great (promoted education in early England; 849-899).

Bagley, William C. (teacher, author, editor; 1874-1946).
Bancroft, Cecil F. P. (educator, prin. of Phillips Academy; 1839-1901).
Barnard, Henry (college pres., public school reformer, *Am. Jour. of Educa.*; 1811-1900).
Bigelow, Melvin M. (educator, legal historian; 1846-1921).
Binet, Alred (Fr., developer of intelligence tests for the children; 1857-1911).
Bobbitt, Franklin (curriculum, school surveys, 1876-1956).
Bode, Boyd D. (teacher, author; 1873-1953).

Calvin, John (leader of Prot. Reformation in Switzerland; 1509-1564).
Cattell, James M. (psychologist, educator, author, founded Science Press; 1860-1944).
Channing, Edward Tyrrell (educator, writer; 1790-1856).
Charlemagne (king of the Franks, developer of educa.; 768-814).
Cheever, Ezekiel (Colonial schoolmaster, author; 1614-1708).
Cobb, Lyman (educator, spelling and arithmetic textbooks; 1800-1864).
Comenius, Johann A. (Moravian, educational reformer, bishop; 1592-1670).
Counts, George S. (educa. sociol., author, univ. prof., pres. Am. Fed. of Teachers; 1889-1974).

Demosthenes (Athenian, statesman and orator; 384?-322 B.C.).
Dewey, John (teacher, prog. educ., social analyst, philosopher, author; 1859-1952).

Edwards, Ninian W. (early promoter of education in Illinois; 1809-1889).
Eliot, Charles W. (educator, author, univ. pres.; 1834-1926).
Erasmus, Desiderius (Dutch, humanist, theologian, writer; 1466-1536).

Fairchild, George T. (teacher, agr. college pres.; 1838-1901).
Fichte, Johann G. (Ger., philosopher, teacher; 1762-1814).

Froebel, Friedrich (Ger., educa. reformer, founder of kindergarten; 1782-1852).

Goodspeed, Thomas W. (theologian, univ. developer; 1842-1927).

Harper, William R. (teacher of Hebrew, educator, univ. pres.; 1856-1906).
Harris, William T. (philosopher, educator, author; 1835-1909).
Hegel, George W. F. (Ger., philosopher; 1770-1831).
Herbart, Johann F. (Ger., philosopher and educator; 1776-1841).
Herodotus, (Greek, historian, inventor; 484?-425? B.C.).
Hopkins, Mark (teacher, moral philosopher, coll. pres.; 1802-1887).
Horace (Roman, poet, satirist; 65-8 B.C.).
Humbolt, Wilhelm von (Ger., philologist, diplomat; 1767-1835).

Inglis, Alexander J. (secondary education, school surveys; 1879-1924).

James, William (physchologist, educator; 1842-1910).
Jefferson, Thomas (defender of personal freedom, founder Univ. of Va.; 1743-1826).
Jesus (founder of Christianity; 4 B.C.?-29 A.D.?).
Judd, Charles H. (educator, author, administrator; 1873-1946).

Kandel, Isaac L. (educator, univ. prof., author; 1881-1965).
Kilpatrick, William H. (teacher, author, philosopher; 1871-1965).
King, Martin L. (Bapt. preacher, negro civil rights, bus boycott, 1964 Nobel Peace Pr.; 1929-1968).

Lathrop, John H. (teacher, univ. admn.; 1799-1866).
Locke, John (English, empirical philosopher; 1632-1704).
Loyola, Ignatius (Sp., soldier, ecclesiastic, founded Society of Jesus—Jesuit; 1491-1556).
Luther, Martin (Ger., theologian, leader of Prot. Reformation; 1483-1546).
Lyon, Mary (educator, founder of Mt. Holyoke seminary; 1797-1849).

McGuffey, William H. (author of *McGuffey's Reader*, univ. pres.; 1800-1873).
McMurry, Frank M. (educator, Am. exponent of Herbartian pedagogy; 1862-1936).
Mann, Horace (lawyer, education reformer in Mass.; 1796-1859).
Margolis, Max L. (teacher, Engl. translation of Hebrew Bible; 1866-1932).
Melanchthon, Phillip (Ger., Prot. reformer and educator; 1497-1560).
Mencius (Chinese, philosopher, teacher of Confucianism; 372?-289? B.C.).
Mohammed (Arab, prophet, founder of Islam; 570-632).
Morley, Margaret W. (teacher, early textbook writer for grade school; 1858-1923).

Parker, Francis W. (educational reformer and admn., Univ. of Chi.; 1837-1902).
Peabody, Elizabeth P. (promoter of kindergarten, publisher; 1804-1894).
Pestalozzi, Johann H. (Swiss, educational reformer; 1746-1827).
Plato (Greek, philosopher, teacher; author; 427-347 B.C.).
Plutarch (Greek, biographer and moralist; 46?-120?).
Porter, Samuel (educator, teacher of the deaf; 1810-1901).

Pythagoras (Greek, philosopher, math., religious reformer; c. 582-c. 500 B.C.).

Quintillian (Roman, rhetorician and critic; c. 35-95 A.D.).

Rogers, Harriet B. (teacher of the deaf, pioneer in using oral methods; 1834-1919).

Rousseau, Jean J. (Fr., educational reformer, *Emile*; 1712-1778).

Russ, John D. (physician, pioneer in teaching the blind; 1801-1881).

Russell, Bertrand (Eng., educator, math., philosopher, author; 1872-1970).

Sherwood, William H. (pianist, teacher, composer, founded music school; 1854-1911).

Socrates (Athenian, idealist philosopher, teacher of socratic method; 469?-399 B.C.).

Solomon (Jewish king, sage, temple builder; 10th cent. B.C.).

Soule, George (pioneer in business educa. in the South; 1834-1926).

Spencer, Herbert (English, philosopher; 1820-1903).

Stetson, William W. (educator, author, lecturer, school admn.; 1849-1910).

Stevens, Thaddeus (statesman, antislave leader, fought for free schools in Pa.; 1792-1868).

Stowe, Calvin Ellis (clergyman, educator, author; 1802-1886).

Suzzalo, Henry (educator, author, adviser to gov't.; 1875-1933).

Thorndike, Edward L. (psychol., educ., dev. Army intell. tests in W.W. I, author; 1874-1949).

Ticknor, George (educator, author, work in Spanish literature; 1791-1871).

Turner, Frederick Jackson (educator, history of Am. development; 1861-1932).

Veblen, Thornstein (economic and social control of education, author; 1857-1929).

Venable, William Henry (educator, author of fiction and nonfiction; 1836-1920).

Virgil (Roman, poet, author; 70-19 B.C.).

Waddel, Moses (educator, preacher, univ. developer; 1770-1840).

Wait, William Bell (educator of the blind, developed a variant of Braille; 1839-1916).

Washington, Booker T. (negro author, educator, work at Tuskegee, Ala.; 1856-1915).

Watson, John B. (behaviorist in psychology and educa.; 1878-1958).

Wharton, Francis (lawyer, clergyman, educator in Mass., author; 1820-1889).

Wiley, Calvin H. (promoter of public education and supt. of schools in No. Carolina; 1819-1887).

Willard, Emma Hart (educa. for women, female seminary—Troy, N.Y.; 1787-1870).

Wilson, Woodrow (educator, statesman, president, League of Nations; 1856-1924).

Wirt, William Albert (school admn., prog. educ., platoon system; 1874-1938).

Yale, Caroline Ardelar (educator, teaching the deaf, author; 1848-1933).

Young, Ella Flagg Ardelia (public school admn., first woman pres. of N.E.A.; 1845-1918).

Transportation and Communication

When anthropologists emphasize the importance of movement and contact among tribes in the development of civilization, and when psychologists emphasize the importance of language and other means of communication among individuals as basic in learning and in the development of thought, the role of transportation and communication in a complex culture should begin to loom up.

In writings on freedom and deomcracy, the point is often made that democratic relationships within and among nations demand the free movement of goods, ideas, and individuals. Since individuals produce both of the other items, individuals are the most important element in the trilogy. Yet it seems that there never has been a time, at least not within the past thousand years, when complete freedom of movement related to any one of the three items.

Most Americans know about tariffs, embargoes, and other obstructions to the free movement of goods. And efforts at various forms of censorship to prevent the free flow of ideas constitute an area of common knowledge. Moreover, we currently hear a great deal about restrictions placed by Russia, the Iron Curtain nations of Eastern Europe, Cuba, and other countries on the exit of persons who reside within their borders. Apparently some degree of restriction as to persons has been involved in most countries, at some time or other. Medieval cities often tried to prevent artisans from "leaving town" and thus from contributing their skills and imagination to some competing city. Nearing the close of World War II in Europe, there was substantial competition between Russia and the West to "capture" German scientists and technologists, so as to add the competence of these persons to the culture of captor nations and to prevent that competence from falling into the hands of competitor nations. The use of barbed wire, masonry walls, armed guards, police dogs, etc., to prevent the movement of people westward from the Iron Curtain nations of Europe constitutes the world's most conspicuous ongoing illustration of thwarted freedom of people to move. The barriers indicate where the people concerned prefer to live. The major restrictions established by the United States have related to persons who wanted to enter rather than to persons who wanted to leave. Our immigration restrictions which became pronounced following World War I have continued to be pronounced since that time, although there have been shifts in the sources from which the immigrants may come.

Evaluation of restrictions concerning the movement of goods, ideas, and people have to be made in terms of the conception of social or national well-being of the countries which set up the restrictions. A basic fact in this connection is that the people of any country vary substantially in their capacity and likelihood of "contributing to the country," whether one refers to the country which they would like to leave or the country in which they would like to live. Age, sex, education, vocational competence, economic status, attitudes and behavioral record, race, and religion have been among factors in restrictions. Previous comment noted restraints by medieval cities and Iron Curtain countries on the out-migration of skilled technicians and others. Apart from persons with delinquency and police records and persons who in an economic sense appear to belong permanently to a relief and dependency class, America's major restrictions on immigration have concerned points of national origin. While with respect to the migration of people reference is not usually made to a "most favored nation" status, as in regard to some aspects of trade, the results are similar. Thus, domestic considerations respecting such matters as influence on law and order, economic well-being, cultural adaptability, and ethnic background have been important in determining policy on the migration of people, as international political relationships have also been.

In a modern industrial society there is great range in the types of activities which are concerned with transportation and communication, in the sense noted in preceding statements. The list of persons noted in section two of this appendix indicates considerable range, although the list should be looked upon as only a sampling. However, several types of project interest might be developed through using selected persons as avenues of exploration. In such exploration, emphasis should be placed on the importance of smooth coordination of many varying elements, in the efforts of a widely diversified economy to operate in a democratic atmosphere of peace and prosperity. Where international considerations are involved, attention to alternative projections regarding possibilities seem especially important.

1. Concepts for Discussion

(a) The idea that no man is an island or can exist without contacts involving other persons is more true regarding the development of his mind and intellectual life than regarding most other aspects of life.

(b) Freedom for the movement of goods, ideas, and people both within and among nations must always be a matter of degree. Hence, anyone who is interested in expanding or in contracting that freedom should focus on the *criteria* used in determining appropriateness of the freedom that exists at a particular time.

(c) The only conception of freedom that is feasible in civilized society is a conception which is: (1) based on laws and other publicized regulations, and (2) in which all of the people have an opportunity for equal representation in determining what the laws and regulations shall be.

(d) With respect to personal freedom and cultural development, it is as important that educational institutions and news media be free from censorship, as it is that highway regulations be such as to foster maximum satisfactions for persons and corporations in using the highways.

(e) From the standpoint of personal freedom in a stable but developing society, it is as essential to have censorship or policing of education and the news, as it is to have policing of the highways.

(f) If there were complete freedom regarding the movement of goods, ideas, and people throughout the world, there would gradually develop a worldwide uniformity of ethnic, cultural and economic status. This would reduce any drive for improvement, since it would reduce the desire of any individual to excel or the desire of others to catch up.

2. *Individuals to Consider*

Abbey, Henry E. (theatrical mgr., Eur. talent in "road" tours of U.S.; 1846-1896).

Adams, Alvin (expressman, founded Adams Express Co.; 1804-1877).

Armstrong, George W. (expressman, trans. news & restaurant serv., N.E. rys.; 1836-1901).

Ayres, Leonard P. (statistician, pub. studies on schools and business; 1879-1946).

Babson, Roger W. (statistician, economist, bus. forecaster, Babson Inst.; 1875-1967).

Bailey, James A. (showman, Barnum & Bailey; 1847-1906).

Bancroft, Edgar A. (lawyer, diplomat, counsel to several rys.; 1857-1925).

Barnum, Phineas T. (showman, exposed the philos. of humbug; 1810-1891).

Barrymore, John (actor, international repute; 1882-1942).

Bellew, Frank H. T. (mag. illustrator and caricaturist; 1828-1888).

Bennett, Floyd (navy pilot, with Adm. Byrd in polar exploring; 1890-1928).

Bennett, James G. (editor, pub., *N.Y. Herald*, first marked use of teleg.; 1795-1872).

Blair, John I. (dev. of western rys., laid out sites for over 80 towns, philan.; 1802-1899).

Brady, Mathew B. (photographer, coverage of Civil War; 1823-1896).

Brentano, Lorenz (statesman, journalist, *Illi Staatszeitung*; 1813-1891).

Brown, Ethan A. ("father of Ohio canals," politician; 1766-1852).

Burnham, Daniel H. (Chi. architect, 1893 world's fair, city planning; 1846-1912).

Carbutt, John (photo. dry plates, contribs. to color photo; 1832-1905).

Castle, Vernon B. (dancer, flier, crashed while teaching cadets; 1887-1918).

Cather, Willa (author, novelist, Pulitzer Prize for 1922; 1873-1947).

Chanute, Octave (aerial nav., gliders, designed a biplane; 1832-1910).

Corning, Erastus (iron mfgr., first pres. N.Y.C. Ry., educator, politician; 1794-1872).

Crosby, Fanny (wrote about 6,000 hymns, taught at N.Y. Inst. for Blind; 1820-1915).

Curtiss, Glenn H. (aviator, built army dirigible, flying boat; 1878-1930).

Daly, John A. (playwright, prod., adapter, prop. of Daly's Theater, N.Y.; 1838-1899).

Dana, Charles A. (newspaper ed., N.Y. Trib., owner-editor of N.Y. Sun; 1819-1897).

Davenport, Homer C. (cartoonist, reform advocate, "Trust" figure symbol.; 1867-1912).

Delano, Frederick A. (ry. exec., gov't. official; 1863-1953).

Depew, Chauncey M. (lawyer, ry. counsel and president, politician; 1834-1928).

Douglas, Stepherd A. (important role in establ. of Ill. Cent. ry.; 1813-1861).
Douglass, Frederick (white-Indian-negro mix., abolitionist, journalist; 1817?-1895).
Dun, Robert G. (credit rating agency, R. G. Dun and Co.; 1826-1900).
Dunlap, William (playwright, theater manager, historian; 1766-1839).
Durant, Charles F. (first prof. Am. aeronaut, balloon flights; 1805-1873).

Eastman, Charles G. (journalist and pol. in Vt., poet; 1816-1860).
Erlanger, Abraham L. (helped org. Theatrical Syn., mgr. & producer; 1860-1930).
Evans, Oliver (inventor, first stationary high-pressure steam engine; 1755-1819).

Fessenden, Reginald A. (inventor, pioneer in radio communication; 1866-1932).
Fisher, Clara (actress, singer, stage artist; 1811-1898).
Fiske, Haley (insurance official—Metropolitan, public health and mortality rates; 1852-1929).
Forepaugh, Adam (showman, once rivaled Barnum's "Greatest Show on Earth"; 1831-1890).
Fox, George W. L. (actor, comedian, pantomimist—"Humpty Dumpty"; 1825-1877).

Garrett, John W. (rail exec. and org., Civil War trans. of troops; 1820-1884).
Gilbert, John G. (actor in stock cos., played "elderly roles"; 1810-1889).
Gould, Jay (financier, ry. directing and stock maneuvering; 1836-1892).
Graham, William F. (Billy) (evangelist, prominent in diff. countries; 1918-   ).
Graves, John Temple (jour., popular lecturer; 1856-1925).

Harrigan, Edward (playwright, actor, prod., wrote 39 plays; 1845-1911).
Harriman, Edward H. (ry. magnate and developer, banks, insurance; 1848-1909).
Hearst, William R. (pub.-owner-editor of newspapers and mags.; 1863-1951).
Hennessy, William J. (painter, illus. Tennyson, Longfellow, Whittier; 1839-1917).
Heywood, Ezra H. (abolitionist, pamphleteer, Civil War pacifist; 1829-1893).
Hill, James J. (rail. exec., financier, Gt. Northern, settlement of N.W. areas; 1838-1916).
Huntington, Collis P. (rail. magnate, some dubious practices; 1821-1900).
Huntington, Henry E. (rail. exec., nephew of Collis, book collector; 1850-1927).

Inness, George (top flight Am. landscape painter; 1825-1894).

Keith, Benjamin F. (vaudeville mgr., "contin. performance," org. Keith Circuit; 1846-1914).
Kennedy, Joseph C. G. (statistician, supt. of census, Internat. Stat. Cong.; 1813-1887).

La Mountain, John (aeronaut, early balloonists, bal. observer in Civil War; 1830-1870).

Langley, Samuel P. (scientist, aviation research pioneer, author; 1834-1906).
Lefferts, Marshall (engineer, early work with teleg. cos., pres. of one; 1821-1876).
Lindberg, Charles A. (aviator, first Atlantic solo flight, many awards; 1902-1975).
Litchfield, Electus B. (financier, ry. builder, also street rys.; 1813-1889).
Loew, Marcus (theater owner, motion-picture pioneer; 1870-1927).
Loveland, William A. H. (Colo. real estate and rys., Denver *Rocky Mt. News*; 1826-1894).
Lowe, Thaddeus S. C. (aeronaut, meteorologist, first photos from balloon; 1832-1913).

McVickers, James H. (theater mgr., stock cos., Yankee comedy; 1822-1896).
Majors, Alexander (freight operator, Pony Express, stagecoaches; 1814-1900).
Marconi, Guglielmo (inv. wireless teleg. 1900, Nobel Prize in physics; 1874-1937).
Markham, Charles H. (pres. Ill. Cent. Ry., modernized Chi. yards; 1861-1930).
Morley, Margaret W. (teacher, wrote pioneer textbooks on nature for children; 1858-1923).
Mulford, Prentice (jour., comic lecturer, "New Thought," pop. philos.; 1834-1891).
Mumford, Lewis (author, soc. philos., hist., city planner; 1895-   ).
Muybridge, Eadweard (pioneer in movie photo, *The Horse in Motion*; 1830-1904).

Neuendorff, Adolph H. A. (mus. cond., Am. prod. of Wagners Opera; 1843-1897).
Newell, Peter S. H. (cartoonist, illus. of periodicals and books; 1862-1924).

Odenbach, Frederick L. (meteorologist, estab. Jesuit seismolog. lab.; 1857-1933).
Ogden, William B. (real estate, rail. const. out from Chi. as a center; 1805-1877).
O'Neill, James (actor, played "Edmond Dantes" in *Monte Cristo* 6000 times; 1849-1920).
Osborn, William H. (rail. promoter and pres., philan.; 1820-1894).

Payne, John H. (actor, dramatist, editor, diplomat; 1791-1852).
Phillips, Wendell (abolitionist, reformer, lyceum speaker, author; 1811-1884).
Pidgin, Charles Felton (stat., inv. tools for mech. tabulation, novelist; 1844-1923).
Plant, Henry B. (express co. exec., rail. & steamship op., "Plant System"; 1819-1899).
Plowman, George T. (architect, etcher; 1869-1932).
Post, Wiley (solo flying record 1933, crashed in flight to Orient; 1899-1935).
Prentice, George D. (editor *Louisville Daily Jnl.*, strong Unionist; 1802-1870).
Pulitzer, Joseph (immigrant soldier, journ., Sch. of Journ. Col. U., Pulitzer Prizes; 1847-1911).

Randolph, John (orator, statesman, rigid adherence to his prins.; 1773-1833).
Rice, Dan (showman, famous Am. clown, crackerbox philos.; 1823-1900).

Ringling, Charles (circus prop., acquired Barnum & Bailey, Fla. land; 1863-1926).

Roberts, Benjamin S. (rail. eng., invented breach-loading rifle, mil. leader; 1810-1875).

Rogers, William Allen (cartoonist, illus. children's stories; 1854-1931).

Russell, William H. (stage coach operator, Pony Express; 1812-1872).

Santayana, George (poet, philosopher, novelist, critic; 1863-1952).

Savage, Henry W. (real-estate, theater prod., org. light-opera co.; 1859-1927).

Sellers, Isaiah (pilot on Miss. R., first to use pseudonym "Mark Twain"; 1802-1864).

Sewell, William J. (rail. exec., Pa. ry. lines in N.J., politician; 1835-1901).

Skinner, Otis (actor, played various roles, father of Cornelia Otis Skinner; 1858-1942).

Stanford, Leland (rail builder, transcont. ry., Leland Stan. U.; 1824-1893).

Strickland, William (made rail. surveys, eng., architect; 1787-1854).

Strong, William B. (rail. official, developed A.T. & S.F. Ry.; 1837-1914).

Upton, George P. (jour., music critic, wrote books, *Chi. Daily Trib.*; 1834-1919).

Vanderbilt, Cornelius (capitalist, railway industrialist, "Commodore"; 1794-1877).

Van Sweringen, Mantis J. (real est., rail. mgr. and speculator; 1881-1935).

Wacker, Charles H. (city planner, Chi. Plan Com., city beautification; 1856-1929).

West, Benjamin (almanac-maker, astronomer, univ. teacher, author; 1730-1813).

Wharton, Edith N. J. (author, novelist; 1862-1937).

Wheatley, Phyllis (negro slave bought by Mr. Wheatley, wrote poems, c. 1753-1784).

Wilson, Francis (actor, musical comedy, org. actor's strike; 1854-1935).

Wright, Wilbur (aviation pioneer with bro. Orville; 1867-1912).

Yates, Abraham (Anti-Federalist pamphleteer, N.Y. agrarian democrat; 1724-1796).

Ziegfeld, Florenz (theatrical prod., *The Follies, Sally, Show Boat*; 1869-1932).

Women

The purpose and content of this appendix item are quite different from those features of the other items. This item is concerned with women and lists only the names of women. A separate item on women is presented because some girls and young women think that their vocational and other participation in American culture is restricted because of sex.

No tabulation is necessary to support the observation that the participation of women is greater in some areas of the culture than in other areas. Thus, many women are teachers, social workers, novelists, and writers or journalists in nonfiction areas, but few are inventors, physicists, clergymen, or geographical and resource explorers.

This item attempts to present a broad swath of different types of significant activities in which women have gained a high level of recognition, rather than to differentiate particular areas in such a way that the listing approximates the relating frequency with which women engage in the particular areas. Young women who are contemplating or just embarking upon the vocational and related cultural aspects of their lives are typically interested in a comprehensive view of what has been done or might be done.

A few women are listed in the other appendix considerations, as for example in the listing on agriculture, science, etc. However, the number of women so listed is small because the number who have achieved in such fields is small as compared with the number of men who have thus achieved. Ordinarily the women whose names are included in the other appendix listings are not listed again in the present connection, although there may be some exceptions to this statement.

1. Concepts for Discussion

(a) There are economic, political, and psychological reasons why an industrial democracy should be interested in developing the potentialities of its female population. In a strictly economic sense, the productivity of women adds greatly to the gross national product and to the associated tax base. In a political sense, government which is expanding in services rendered and in responsibilities involved in defining and in meeting civic needs must rest on a population which has broad and continuously expanding civic education that is based not only on general reading and observation but also on direct participation. From the psychological standpoint, man's greatest intellectual and other freedoms reside in the opportunity to pursue interests along lines such that his achievements win the respect of others and reside in understanding why such recognition for any substantial percent of the population must rest on a stable but creative system of law and order. Persons who do not understand the foregoing and get the understanding worked into their habits and personality structures tend to lead stunted and frustrated lives which fluctuate between violence and neurotic disintegration. This consideration is important from both individual and social standpoints.

(b) Since biological development has evolved in such a way that reproduction among humans is on a bisexual basis, as it is among rats, cattle, elephants, etc., the lives and functions of members of the two sexes in the human world cannot be identical. This means that there is no mathematical or comparably scientific way to equate the rights and duties of the two sexes, and that the equating process must depend on some combination of ethical ideals and social pressures. The combination which has been looked upon as just or as constituting a balance has been a matter of dispute for several centuries—and will likely continue to be in future centuries. To refer to the situation as the "battle of the sexes" may be substantially irrelevant, except to note that any kind of social or ethical relationship which people develop must be such as to provide for nature's way of perpetuating the species—otherwise the species becomes extinct.

(c) Circumstances vary from time to time in any modern society concerning relative emphasis which the social group will place on begetting and rearing the next generation, as compared with other types of contribution to the culture. As a culture becomes more complex, more factors bear on the variations. Prospects for a simple relationship are slim.

(d) Since most street crime and associated violence involves the exercise of physical force against victims, it is a greater threat to women than to men. Hence, women have an especially large stake in maintaining peace and security, or law and order, in the streets and in places of public gatherings.

(e) Women should be in the uniformed police force of major cities and most other communities in about the same proportion as men are and should have the same types of authority, responsibility, and assignments as men have.

(f) The essential absence of women as prominent figures in the Watergate and in similar previous scandals has various implications, both positive and negative, respecting the status of women in American culture—particularly in those aspects of the culture which are most directly concerned with government, and with the role of law and moral integrity in our regulatory structure.

2. Individuals to Consider

Akers, Elizabeth Chase (poet, author, newspaper woman; 1832-1911).
Angela, Mother (Sisters of Holy Cross in U.S., founded St. Mary's Col. at N. Dame; 1824-1887).

Bacon, Alice Mabel (teacher, lecturer, writer; 1858-1918).
Bailey, Anna W. (Groton Heights, 1781, gave flannel petticoat for gun wadding; 1758-1851).
Barrymore, Ethel (actress, stage, movie, television; 1879-1959).
Bellamy, Elizabeth W. C. (teacher, author of romantic novels on life in South; 1837-1900).
Bickerdyke, Mary A. B. (nurse, "Mother Bickerdyke," aided Civil War wounded; 1817-1901).
Blackwell, Elizabeth (teacher, rec'd M.D. in 1849, helped org. C. War field nurses; 1821-1910).
Bleecker, Ann E. (poet, published in *Posthumous Works*; 1752-1783).
Blow, Susan E. (first Am. public kindergarten, St. Louis; 1843-1916).
Bocher, Maxine (mathematician, univ. teacher; 1867-1918).
Booth, Mary Louise (author, translator, editor; 1831-1889).
Bouvet, Marie M. (linguist, wrote books for young people; 1865-1915).
Brown, Charlotte E. (org. and first pres.—1890—Gen. Fed. of Women's Clubs; 1838-1895).

Cary, Annie L. (opera singer, acquired international reputation; 1841-1921).
Cary, Phoebe (poet with sister Alice, wrote hymn *One Sweetly Solemn Thought*; 1824-1871).
Catherwood, Mary Hartwell (novelist, story writer; 1847-1902).
Child, Lydia M. F. (abolitionist, novelist; 1802-1880)
Clarke, Mary F. (founded Cath. org. "Sister of Charity . . . ," Phila.; 1803-1887).

Colman, Lucy N. (antislave lecturer, abolitionist; 1817-1906).

Comstock, Elizabeth L. (Quaker minister, temp. & prison reform, philanthropist; 1815-1891).

Cooper, Sarah B.E. (founder of kindergartens, 1892 pres. Internat. Kgn. Union; 1835-1896).

Crandall, Prudence (educator, reformer, failed in effort to estab. negro sch. in Conn.; 1803-1890).

Darling, Flora A. (helped D.A.R. & other patriotic orgs.; 1840-1910).

Davis, Pauline K.W. (editor, worker for woman suffrage; 1813-1876).

Diaz, Abby M. (author, stories for children, social reformer; 1821-1904).

Dix, Dorothea L. (humanitarian, investigated jail & asylum conds.; 1802-1887).

Doyle, Sarah E. (educator, Brown Univ., founded R.I. Women's Club; 1830-1922).

Duncan, Isadora (made dancing a creative art; 1878-1927).

Dupuy, Eliza Ann (novelist; 1814-1881).

Eddy, Mary Baker (founded Christian Science Church; 1821-1910).

Estaugh, Elizabeth Haddon (Quaker founder of Haddonfield home for ministers; 1680-1762).

Farmer, Fannie M. (educator, editor, director of cooking school; 1857-1915).

Fleming, Willimina P.S. (astron., stellar photos, discovered stars and novae; 1857-1911).

French, Lucy V.S. (author, romantic novels and poems, lit. ed. of So. jours.; 1825-1881).

Fuller, Sarah M. (educator of the deaf, 1869 opened Boston Sch. for Deaf-Mutes; 1836-1927).

Gage, Matilda J. (woman's suffrage leader, co-authored book on woman suffrage; 1826-1898).

Gilbert, Anne J.H. (dancer, character actress, played in Western cos.; 1821-1904).

Gratz, Rebecca (*Ivanhoe's* Rebecca, founded Hebrew S. Sch. Soc., Phila. Orphan Soc.; 1781-1869).

Hanaford, Phoebe Ann C. (author, Universalist min., first woman ordained in N. Eng.; 1829-1921).

Hapgood, Isabel F. (translator, journalist, introd. Tolstoy, Gogol, etc., to Eng. sp. world; 1850-1928).

Hardey, Mother M.A. (Soc. of Sacred Heart, co-founder of a convent; 1809-1886).

Harrison, Elizabeth (kindergarten, author; 1849-1927).

Haskell, Ella L.K. (lawyer, politician, crusader for women's rights; 1860-1911).

Holley, Marietta (humorist, author, women's rights advocate; 1836-1926).

Howard, Ada Lydia (educator, first pres. of Wellesley College; 1829-1907).

Hyde, Helen (artist, color etching, woodblock prints; 1868-1919).

Irene, Sister (Sister of Charity—R.C., methods of foundling care; 1823-1896).

Isom, Mary Frances (librarian, work in W.W.I war camps and hospitals; 1865-1920).

Jacobi, Mary C.P. (physician, prof. at Woman's Med. Col. of N.Y.; 1842-1906).

Jewett, Sarah O. (author, early N. Eng. village life; 1849-1909).

Jones, Mary H. (labor organizer and orator, U.S. labor movement; 1830-1930).

Judson, Ann H. (Bapt. missionary to Burma, wrote acct. of the mission; 1789-1826).

Kennedy, Rose Fitzgerald (politics, social activities, philanthrophy; 1890-   ).

Klinglesmith, Margaret C. (lawyer, author, librarian; 1859-1931).

Ladd, Catherine (S. Car. schoolmistress, wrote fugitive verse; 1808-1899).

Lathrop, Julia C. (soc. work, Hull House, 1st woman on Ill. Bd. of Public Charities; 1858-1932).

Lee, Ann (founded Shakers of America; 1736-1784).

Lockwood, Belva Ann (teacher, lawyer, suffragist; 1830-1917).

Loeb, Sophie I.S. (soc. worker, journalist, secured welfare leg.; 1876-1929).

Low, Juliette M.K.G. (founder Girl Scouts of Am., 1912; 1860-1927).

Lozier, Cemence S.H. (physician and reformer, founded a woman's hospital; 1813-1888).

McCauley, Mary L.H. (Rev. War heroine, "Molly Pitcher"; 1754-1832).

MacDowell, Katherine S.B. (wrote short stories and novels; 1849-1883).

Magruder, Julia (novelist, short-story writer; 1854-1907).

Mayo, Mary A.B. (teacher, pioneer, Grange and Farmers' Institute worker; 1845-1912).

Mills, Susan L. T. (missionary, educator, pres. of Mills College; 1852-1912).

Mitchell, Maria (astronomer, educator, first prof. of astron. at Vassar; 1818-1889).

Mortimer, Mary (pioneer in higher ed. for women, Milwaukee Female College; 1816-1877).

Mosher, Eliza M. (physician, pioneer in phys. educ. for women; 1846-1928).

Murray, Louise S.W. (archaeologist, local historian; 1854-1931).

Nation, Carry A.M. (temp. reformer, saloon swasher, sold hatchet souvenirs; 1846-1911).

Ney, Elisabet (sculptor, statues and busts of Texas notables; 1833-1907).

Norris, Mary Harriott (educator, author, dean of women at Northwestern Univ.; 1848-1919).

Norsworthy, Naomi (psychologist, teacher, author; 1877-1916).

Nurse, Rebecca (victim of Salem witchcraft; 1621-1692).

Peabody, Elizabeth P. (educator, author, estab. 1st kgn. in America; 1804-1894).

Peale, Sarah M. (portrait painter, daughter of James Peale; 1800-1885).

Powell, Maud (violinist, toured in Eur., org. the Maud Powell Quartet; 1868-1920).

Prang, Mary A.D.H. (art teacher, author, edited art manuals; 1836-1927).

Reilly, Marion (educator, suffrage leader, dean of Bryn Mawr College; 1879-1928).

Richards, Ellen H.S. (teacher, chemist, home economist; 1842-1911).

Rogers, Clara K.B. (opera and concert sop., taught at N. Eng. Conserv. of Music; 1844-1931).

Russell, Lillian (comic opera singer, famous beauty; 1861-1922).

Salmon, Lucy M. (educator, college history teacher; 1853-1927).

Sangster, Margaret E.M. (author, ed. *Hearth & Home* and *Harper's Bazaar*; 1838-1912).

Seton, Elizabeth A.B. (founded Am. Sisters of Charity, two sons, est. girls' school; 1774-1821).

Severance, Caroline N.S. (founded women's clubs, Cleveland and elsewhere; 1820-1914).

Sewall, Mary Eliza W. (teacher, prin. of Girls' Classical School in Indianapolis; 1844-1920).

Shafer, Helen A. (educator, math. prof. and later pres. of Wellesley; 1839-1894).

Sharp, Katharine L. (author, 1897-1907 U. of Ill. librarian; 1865-1914).

Shaw, Anna H. (physician, Methodist minister, suffrage and temp. reformer; 1847-1919).

Sherwood, Katherine M. B. (journalist, reformer; 1841-1914).

Singleton, Esther (editor, music critic, author; 1865-1930).

Slocum, Frances (Indian captive, married a Delaware, would not return to white kin; 1773-1847).

Smith, Erminnie A.P. (geol., ethnologist on Iroquois Indians; 1836-1886).

Smith, Sophia (founded Smith College; 1796-1870).

Snow, Eliza Roxey (Mormon leader and hymn writer, wife of B. Young; 1804-1887).

Spalding, Catherine (found. Cath. "Sisters of Charity of Nazareth's" schools in Ky.; 1793-1858).

Stephens, Alice B. (illustrator, quiet scenes and incidents from classic fiction; 1858-1932).

Stephens, Ann S. (author, editor, Beadle "dime novels"; 1813-1886).

Stetson, Augusta E.S. (Christian Science leader—N.Y.C.; 1842-1928).

Stevenson, Matilda C.E. (ethnologist, author, study of Zuni Indians; 1850-1915).

Stone, Ellen M. (Congregational mission in Bulg., her capture got wide attn.; 1846-1927).

Stone, Lucy (abolitionist, woman suffrage leader; 1818-1893).

Strong, Harriett W.R. (hort., pioneer in Calif. walnut ind., irrigation; 1844-1926).

Terhune, Mary V.H. (author, writer, household mgmt.; 1830-1922).

Tubman, Harriet (fug. slave, abolitionist, leader in Underground Ry., wrote memories; c. 1821-1913).

Van Rensselaer, Martha (teacher, home econ., rural ext. work at Cornell Univ.; 1864-1932).

Walker, Mary Edwards (physician, suffrage worker, urged dress reform for women; 1832-1919).

Walker, Sarah Breedlove (pioneer negro businesswoman, beauty culture, philanthropist; 1867-1919).

Ward, Lydia Arms A.C. (author, Chicago civic leader; 1845-1924).

White, Ellen G.H. (Seventh-Day Adventist leader, helped found colleges in Mich., Calif.; 1827-1915).

Whitney, Anne (sculptor, poet, statue of Sam. Adams in Statuary Hall; 1821-1915).

Whittelsey, Abigail G. (editor, author, *Mother's Magazine*; 1788-1858).

Wiggin, Kate Douglas (author, pioneer kindergarten worker in Calif.; 1856-1923).

Willard, Mary Hatch (businesswoman, social worker, hospital supply service in W.W.I; 1856-1926).

Wister, Sarah (diarist, stories on life in Phila. under Brit. occupa.; 1761-1804).

Woodbury, Helen Laura S. (soc., econ., women in industry, child labor laws; 1876-1933).

Woodhull, Victoria C. (stock mkt. operator, women's rights, publisher; 1838-1927).

Wooley, Celia Parker (author, settlement worker, ordained Unitarian; 1848-1918).

Yale, Caroline Ardelia (educator, dev. oral methods for teaching the deaf; 1848-1933).

Zakrzewska, Marie Eliz. (physician, founder N. Eng. Hosp. for Women and Ch.; 1829-1902).

Miscellaneous

In efforts to classify any large number of divergent items, there is usually a substantial proportion that are easily placed in appropriate groups or classes, but several that do not seem to fit into any class, without setting up a separate class for each of the divergent items. Setting up a large number of classes as implied, with only one or a few items in many of the classes, distorts the whole idea of classification. One escape from the predicament is to provide a general class or catchall for the scattered and widely divergent items. Such terms as "other" or "miscellaneous" are used to label the catchall.

How large and divergent the miscellaneous class will be depends primarily on the number and range of all items to be classified and on the extent to which individual classes are actually established. In the present study only a few categories are separately designated, to suggest one way in which a project approach might be made to a general understanding of regulatory structure in organized society and of relationships between that structure and problems of law and order.

Accordingly, the persons listed in the present miscellaneous category reflect considerable variation in the type of interest shown. It is hoped that the list will further help students to sense the variation of interest and development that appears in American culture, and will suggest to students more conceivable avenues of interest with which it is possible for them personally to identify.

1. Concepts for Discussion

(a) Adults who have difficulty in classifying items without leaving a substantial miscellaneous residue have a problem similar to that of the young child who must learn to fit his own experiences into categories which society has established.

(b) In establishing laws and other regulations for a complex society, the scattered and unusual forms of behavior are the most difficult to provide for, much as the scattered and unusual items in an extensive list are the most difficult to classify. It is in situations of this kind that the judge, or other person who must decide what to do, needs the greatest leeway.

(c) In a complex society, an individual cannot operate effectively without classifying a large portion of his activities into categories which can be reduced to habit—so that he can devote major thought and energy to new kinds of experiences. In the social regulation of organized society, the same idea applies to the usual areas of social relationships in contrast with scattered areas of occasional or unusual relationships.

(d) In any growing or developing society, new discoveries or other new experiences usually occur in what may be called miscellaneous areas; that is, areas which could not previously have been regarded as categories because the material concerned did not previously exist. This idea applies to research on space or other areas of study, specialized school and educational programs, new developments in housing, new kinds of jobs in the employment world, changes in relationships with other peoples of the world associated with expanding international contacts, etc.

(e) For an idea, a law, or an individual to attain maximum significance, the item or individual must be integrated or associated into a functional relationship with other ideas, laws, individuals, etc. Hence, there is a need for continuing effort to move items out of the miscellaneous category into a category where the main theme or drift can be more meaningfully described.

(f) Creative individuals who make original contributions to some aspect of human well-being are likely to be considered unusual, miscellaneous, or "oddball" to some extent. It is important for other persons to be tolerant regarding such individuals because society depends on creativeness for whatever progress it makes. However, the creative persons should expect to accommodate themselves to curious outbursts from more typical persons. But the foregoing does not negate the continuing need for collective effort to weave particular miscellaneous items into some existing classification, or into some new one that is being developed.

2. Individuals to Consider

Abbey, Edwin A. (illustrator, mural painter, free-lancer; 1852-1911).
Alden, John (*Mayflower* Pilgrim, signer of *Mayflower* pact; c. 1599-1687).
Allen, Ethan (Rev. soldier, author; 1737/8-1789).
Anthony, Susan B. (temperance reformer, woman suffrage; 1820-1906).

Armour, Philip D. (Chi. meat packer, canned meats, refrig., philan.; 1832-1901).

Arnold, Benedict (Am. Rev. patriot and traitor; 1741-1801).

Austin, Stephen F. (founded Texas, diplomatic and military struggle; 1793-1836).

Bach, Johann Sebastian (Ger., organist and composer; 1685-1750).

Barton, Clara (organizer of Am. Red Cross, teacher; 1821-1912).

Beethoven, Ludwig (Ger., composer; 1770-1827).

Berger, Victor Louis (socialist, journalist, politician; 1860-1929).

Bienville, Jean B. LeMayne (explorer, founded Mobile and New Orleans; 1680-1767).

Bingham, Robert W. (newspaper proprietor, lawyer, diplomat; 1871-1937).

Bismarck, Otto E. P. ("Iron chancellor" of unified Ger., 1815-1898).

Bok, Edward Wm. (editor, author, social reformer, conservationist; 1863-1930).

Bolivar, Simon (leader of revolt in South America, liberator; 1783-1830).

Boone, Daniel (Quaker pioneer, Indian fighter; 1734-1820).

Booth, John Wilkes (actor, assass. Pres. Lincoln, thought slavery was God-given; 1838-1865).

Brahms, Johannes (Ger., composer; 1833-1897).

Breasted, James Henry (Egyptologist, archaeologist, textbook writer; 1865-1935).

Brisbane, Arthur (writer, editor, syndicated columnist, Hearst papers; 1864-1936).

Brown, John (abolitionist, raid on Harper's Ferry, treason; 1800-1859).

Bryan, William Jennings (political leader, Tenn. evol. trial of 1925; 1860-1925).

Bulfinch, Charles (architect, worked on U.S. Capitol Bldg.; 1763-1844).

Bull, Ole B. (Norw., violinist and composer; 1810-1880).

Byrnes, Thomas (police executive, reorganized N.Y. detective bureau; 1842-1910).

Canfield, Richard A. (art collector, protector of R.I. gambling houses; 1855-1914).

Carson, Christopher ("Kit") (trapper, guide, scout, Ind. agent, soldier; 1809-1868).

Caruso, Enrico (It. born opera tenor in Am.; 1873-1921).

Champlain, Samuel de (explorer, founded Canada, map and des. of St. Lawrence; 1567-1635).

Chaplin, Charles S. (American, movie actor and producer, born in England; 1889-1978).

Chiang Kai-shek (head of Chinese Nationalist govt. on Taiwan; 1886-).

Chopin, Frederic F. (Pol., pianist and composer in Fr.; 1810-1849).

Clark, George Rogers (soldier, explorer, surveyor—Ohio Valley and Ill.; 1752-1818).

Cody, William F. ("Buffalo Bill") (scout, meat for ry. builders, showman; 1846-1917).

Cooper, Peter (inventor, mfgr., philan., Cooper Union of N.Y.; 1791-1883).

Copley, John S. (painter of portraits, a pioneer Am. pastellist; 1738?-1815).

Coronado, Francisco V. (governor and explorer of Nueva Galicia—the Am. S.W.; 1510-1554).

Cortez, Hernando (Sp., explorer, conqueror of Mexico; 1485-1547).

Crevecoeur, Michel G. F. (Fr., writer on Am. frontier life—Pa., N.Y., N. Car.; 1735-1813).

Crockett, David (Tenn. hunter and politician, defender of Texas Alamo; 1786-1836).

Currier, Nathaniel (lithographic printer, publisher Currier & Ives prints; 1813-1888).

Curtis, Edwin Upton (lawyer, police com'r.; 1861-1922).

Damrosch, Leopold (violinist, conductor, composer; 1832-1885).

Darrow, Clarence S. (soc. reformer, criminal lawyer., Loeb-Leopold; 1857-1938).

Davenport, George (fur trader, helped found Davenport, Iowa; 1783-1845).

Decatur, Stephen (naval officer, Tripolitan War; 1779-1820).

Delano, Jane Arminda (nurse, teacher, Nat'l. Com. of Red Cross Nurses; 1862-1919).

Desoto, Hernando (Sp., explorer, 1541 discovered Miss. R.; 1500?-1542).

Dix, Dorothea L. (humanitarian, asylum reform., Supt. of Women Nurses; 1802-1887).

Douglas, Stephen A. (statesman, political leader, debated with Lincoln; 1813-1861).

Ericson, Lief (Norw., discoverer of Am. ?; fl. 1000 A.D.).

Farmer, Moses G. (teacher, pioneer Am. electrician; 1820-1893).

Fitch, John (paddle-wheel steamboat, screw propeller; 1743-1798).

Fremont, John C. (explorer, soldier, politician—Ore. Trail country; 1813-1890).

Gandhi, Mohandas K. (Indian, national leader and reformer, Hindi; 1869-1948).

Garrison, William L. (reformer, publisher, opponent of Negro slavery; 1805-1879).

Genghis Kahn (Mongol, conqueror of centeral Asia and E. Europe; 1162-1227).

Goethals, George Washington (engineer, soldier, builder of Panama Canal; 1858-1928).

Gompers, Samuel (labor leader, trade-unionism, labor-mgmt. negotiator; 1850-1924).

Grady, Henry W. (Ga. newspaper, *Atl. Const.*, reconstruction era; 1850-1889).

Hadley, Henry K, (music composer, conductor, promoted Am. composers; 1871-1937).

Hale, Nathan ("martyr spy" of the Rev. War.; 1755-1776).

Heifetz, Jascha (Rus. born violinist in Am.; 1901-   ).

Henry, Patrick (Revolutionary statesman, orator, politician; 1736-1799).

Hickok, James Butler ("Wild Bill") (stage driver, scout, U.S. marshall; 1837-1876).

Hitler, Adolph (Nazi, chancellor, dictator of Ger., suicide in Berlin; 1889-1945).

Homer, Winslow (painter, marine settings; 1836-1910).

Hudson, Henry (Eng., explorer, discovered Hudson river and bay; ?-1611).

Huntington, Daniel (painter of portraits, and of hist. and nature settings; 1816-1906).

Insull, Samuel (built utility empire which collapsed in 1932, fled to Europe; 1859-1938).

Jones, John Paul (merchant captain, naval officer and hero; 1747-1792).

Kagawa, Toyohiko (Jap., writer, social reformer, religious leader; 1888-1960).

Lesueur, Charles A. (Fr., artist, naturalist, explorer of Australian coasts; 1778-1846).

Lewis, Meriweather (explorer of Am. N.W., expedition to Oregon; 1774-1809).

MacDowell, Edward A. (musician, composer of various kinds of music materials; 1861-1908).

Madison, Dolly Payne (hostess for Pres. Jefferson who was a widower; 1768-1849).

Magellan, Ferdinand (Port., navigator, St. of Magellan; 1480?-1521).

Mao Tse-tung (Ch., communist leader, Chr. Peoples Republic; 1893-1976).

Markham, William (kin of Wm. Penn., helped locate Phila., *Frame of Gov't*; c. 1635-1704).

Mason, George (planter, statesman, political philosopher; 1725-1792).

Meeker, Nathan C. (jour., Union Colony agr. coop. in Colo., White Riv. Res.; 1817-1879).

Mendelssohn, Felix (Ger., composer and conductor; 1809-1847).

Michelangelo (It., painter, sculptor, architect, poet; 1475-1564).

Montessori, Maria (It., educator; 1870-1952).

Montezuma II (last Aztec emperor of Mex., conquered by Cortez; 1470?-1520).

Moran, Thomas (painter, panoramic Western landscapes, etcher; 1837-1926).

Muir, John (explorer Yellowstone and N.W., Alaska, conservationist; 1838-1914).

Newcomb, Simon (astronomer, published texts and astron. papers; 1835-1909).

Niemeyer, John Henry (artist, teacher of drawing; 1839-1932).

Osborn, Henry F. (paleontologist, evolutionist, princ. of "adaptive radiation"; 1857-1935).

Owen, Robert Dale (social reformer, New Harmony, Ind.; 1801-1877).

Paderewski, Ignace J. (Pol., pianist, composer, statesman; 1860-1941).

Penn, William (Quaker statesman, founder of Pa.; 1644-1718).

Pitt, William (prime minister of Brit. 1783-1801, Am. Rev.; 1759-1806).

Pizarro, Francisco (Sp., conqueror of Peru; 1470?-1541).

Pocahontas (daughter of Powhattan, saved ? John Smith, bond with Eng.; c. 1595-1617).

Polo, Marco (Venetian sailor, traveler in Asia; 1254?-1324).

Post, Wiley (aviator, set records alone and with Harold Gatty; 1899-1935).

Putnam, Israel (soldier, Revolutionary organizer; 1718-1790).

Sargent, Lucius M. (antiquarian, temperance leader, author; 1786-1867).

Savonarola, Girolamo (It., monk, reformer, martyr; 1452-1498).

Schoolcraft, Henry R. (ethnologist, explorer, author, Lake Superior Indian tribes; 1793-1864).

Sherwood, Robert E. (Am. playwright, dramatist; 1896-1955).

Sitting Bull (Sioux chief & med. man, Little Big Horn, Messiah agitator; 1834?-1890).

Sousa, John Phillip (bandmaster, composer, "Stars and Stripes Forever"; 1854-1932).

Stone, Warren S. (1903-25 head of Bro. of Locomotive Engineers; 1860-1925).

Sun Yatsen, (org. Chinese overthrow of Manchus, founded Kuomintang; 1867-1925).

Tecumseh (Shawnee Chief, Tippecanoe—1811, War of 1812, c. 1768-1813).

Thoreau, Henry D. (essayist, poet, transcendentalist, "Walden"; 1817-1862).

Thucydides (Athenian, historian; 460?-400? B.C.).

Tojo, Hideki (Jap., prime minister 1941-44, executed for war crimes; 1885-1948).

Trumbull, John (painter of the Am. Rev., 250-300 representations from Am. life; 1756-1843).

Whistler, James A. McNeill (painter, etcher, author; 1834-1903).

Wright, Frank Lloyd (Am., architect, "organic architecture," author; 1869-1959).

Wrigley, William (soap, chewing gum, baseball clubs & fields; 1861-1932).

Zimmerman, Eugene (cartoonist, "exaggerated distortions"; 1862-1935).

APPENDIX NO. 3

Pertinent Quotations

At various points in the present study quotations are presented. These indicate that for several centuries persons in socially responsible positions have been concerned about problems regarding the occurrence of lawlessness and corruption in public life and about possible ways to improve the situation at hand. Such persons have been engaged at different points from ourselves, along the continuum of struggle with regulating human associations.

It seems justifiable to philosophize that the aim has consistently been to regulate those associations in ways which seemed most constructive for the betterment of mankind in general, or at least most helpful from the standpoint of those in positions to reflect on the development and to exercise power within some type of group organization.

Attention to the thought and suggestions of our predecessors in the areas noted, along with our own, should be an asset to Americans in considering problems of the kinds examined in this study.

The great amount of quotable material available means that the selections presented herewith constitute only a small sample of the total that might seem usable. Quotations and original statements which appear in this appendix are grouped according to the five major divisions of the study. For convenient reference, the items presented are numbered consecutively within the respective divisions.

Division I

Cultural Development and the Regulatory System

1. There is no such thing as "natural law": this expression is nothing but old nonsense. Prior to laws, what is natural is only the strength of the lion, or the need of the creature suffering from hunger or cold; in short, need. (Stehdahl—1783-1842)

2. Necessity knows no law except to prevail. (Publilius Syrus—fl., 1 cent. B.C., maxim #553)

3. Now this is the law of the Jungle—as old and as true as the sky;
   And the Wolf that shall keep it may prosper, but the Wolf that
      shall break it must die. (Rudyard Kipling, 1895—1865-1936)

4. Nothing happens to anyone which he is not fitted by nature to bear. (Marcus Aurelius Antoninus—121-180 A.D.)

5. This is the law of the Yukon, that only the strong shall thrive;
   That surely the weak shall perish, and only the fit survive.
   Dissolute, damned and despairful, crippled and palsied and slain.
   This is the Will of the Yukon—Lo, how she makes it plain! (Robert S. Service—1874-1958).

6. Where there is no law there is no transgression. (Bible—Paul to Romans, IV:15)

7. I establish law and justice in the land. (Hammurabi—c. 2100 B.C.)

8. Fear cannot be banished, but it can be calm and without panic; and it can be mitigated by reason and evaluation. (Vannevar Bush, 1949—1890-1974).

9. Government—A sign of the divine grace. (Martin Luther—1483-1546)

10. Government—The biggest organized social effort for dealing with social problems. (Felix Frankfurter—1882-1965)

11. Nothing so weakens government as persistent inflation. (John Kenneth Galbraith,1965—1908-   )

12. The law is not concerned with trifles. (Anon., Latin legal maxim)

13. All government—indeed, every human benefit and enjoyment, every virtue and every prudent act—is founded on compromise and barter. (Edmund Burke, 1775—1729-1797)

14. Liberty exists in proportion to wholesome restraint. (Daniel Webster, 1847—1782-1852)

15. Reason in man is rather like God in the world. (Thomas Aquinas —1227-1274)

16. Prosperity doth best discover vice, but adversity doth best discover virtue. (Francis Bacon—1561-1626)

17. It is the greatest good to the greatest number which is the measure of of right and wrong. (Jeremy Bentham—1748-1832)

18. Government—A device for maintaining in perpetuity the rights of the people, with ultimate extinction of all privileged classes. (Calvin Coolidge—1872-1933)

19. Government—Just a device to protect man so that he may earn his bread in the sweat of his labor. (Hugh S. Johnson—1882-1942)

20. The law will never be strong or respected unless it has the sentiment of the people behind it. If the people of a state make bad laws, they will suffer from it. They will be the first to suffer. Suffering, and nothing else, will implant that sentiment of responsibility which is the first step to reform. (James Bryce, 1888—1838-1922)

21. The law of accumulation will be left free; the laws of distribution free. Individualism will continue, but the millionaire will be but a trustee for a season with a great part of the increased wealth of the community, but administering it for the community far better than it could or would have done for itself. (Andrew Carnegie, 1889—1835-1919)

22. Every man holds his property subject to the general right of the community to regulate its use to whatever degree the public welfare may require it. (Theodore Roosevelt, 1910—1858-1919)

23. Government—Mainly an expensive organization to regulate evildoers, and tax those that behave; government does little for fairly respectable people except annoy them. (Edgar W. Howe—1853-1937)

24. Power politics is the diplomatic name for the law of the jungle. (Ely Culbertson, 1946—1891-1955)

25. The people never give up their liberties but under some delusion. (Edmund Burke, 1784—1729-1797)

26. Government—A conspiracy against the superior man. (Henry L. Mencken—1880-1956)

27. For many centuries the sword and the cross were allies. Together they attacked the rights of man. They defended each other. (Robert G. Ingersoll, 1896—1833-1899)

28. Every tradition grows ever more venerable—the more remote is its origin, the more confused that origin is. This reverence due it increases from generation to generation. The tradition finally becomes holy and inspires awe. (Frederich Wm. Nietzsche, 1878—1844-1900)

29. Where it is a duty to worship the sun, it is pretty sure to be a crime to examine the laws of heat. (Voltaire, 1772—1694-1778)

30. Every king springs from a race of slaves, and every slave had kings among his ancestors. (Plato—427-347 B.C.)

31. The bitterest hatred is that of near relations. (Tacitus—1st and 2nd cents., A.D.) (This may apply also to nations—Punke)

32. (There is a) lunatic fringe in all reform movements. (Theodore Roosevelt, 1913—1858-1919)

33. The doctrine is that the universe was created by a being similar to man, but greater in every respect, in power, wisdom, and strength of passion, in fact by an idealized superman. (Sigmund Freud—1856-1939)

34. Civilization was thrust into the brain of Europe on the point of a Moorish lance. (Robert G. Ingersoll—1833-1899)

35. The law is the last result of human wisdom acting upon human experience for the benefit of the public. (Samuel Johnson—1709-1784)

36. The law: It has honored us; may we honor it. (Daniel Webster, 1847—1782-1852)

37. Love is the fulfilling of the law. (Bible—Romans XIII:10)

38. Whether one considers the law to come from superhuman power or to be distilled from human experience by one's peers, the practical results are much the same when one must satisfy a traffic ticket or face a charge of arson or of treason. (Punke)

Division II

The Courts and General Education on Lawlessness

1. Our government is the potent, the omnipresent teacher. For good or for ill, it teaches the whole people by its example. (Louis D. Brandeis, 1928—1856-1941)

2. The essence of free government consists in an effectual control of rivalries. (John Quincy Adams—1767-1848)

3. Crime—an act committed or omitted in violation of a public law either forbidding or commanding it. (William Blackstone—1723-1780)

4. Drunkenness is a kind of temporary death; the effect of a drug which temporarily dulls the senses and makes one unaware of his enveloping unhappiness. (Punke)

5. Reason is the life of the law; nay, the common law itself is nothing else but reason. . . . The law, which is perfection of reason. (Sir Edward Coke—1552-1634)

6. The life of the law has not been logic; it has been experience. (Oliver Wendell Holmes, Jr., 1881—1841-1935)

7. The law is good, if a man use it lawfully. (Bible—I Thessalonians V:21)

8. A good person once said that where mystery begins religion ends. Cannot I say, as truly at least, or human laws, that where mystery begins, justice ends. (Burke—1729-1797)

9. Where law ends, tyranny begins. (Pitt, 1770—1708-1778)

10. The law has no power to command obedience except that of habit, which can only be given by time, so that a readiness to change old to new laws enfeebles the power of the law. (Aristotle—384-322 B.C.)

11. The law must be stable, but it must not stand still. (Roscoe Pound, 1922—1870-1964)

12. The prophesies of what the courts will do in fact, and nothing more pretentious, are what I mean by the law. (Oliver Wendell Holmes, Jr., 1897—1841-1935)

13. Great cases like hard cases make bad law. (Oliver Wendell Holmes, Jr., 1904—1841-1935)

14. Ignorance of the law excuses no man; not that all men know the law, but because 'tis an excuse every man will plead, and no man can tell how to refute it. (John Selden—1584-1654)

15. There is no man so good, who, were he to submit all his thoughts and actions to the laws would not deserve hanging ten times in his life. (Montaigne—1533-1592)

16. Every great example of punishment has in it some injustice, but the suffering individual is compensated by the public good. (Tacitus—55-117 A.D.)

17. The people's good is the highest law. (Cicero—106-43 B.C.)

18. We must remember not to judge any public servant by any one act, and especially should we beware of attacking the men who are merely the occasions and not the causes of disaster. (Theodore Roosevelt, 1899—1858-1919)

19. Whenever monarchs err, the people are punished. (Horace—65-8 B.C.)

20. No higher duty, or more solemn responsibility, rests upon this Court than that of translating into living law and maintaining this constitutional shield deliberately planned and subscribed for the benefit of every

human being subject to our Constitution—of whatever race, creed or persuasion. (Hugo L. Black, 1938; Chambers v. Florida, 309 U.S. 227—1886-1971)

21. Facts are stubborn things; and whatever may be our wishes, our inclinations, or the dictates of our passions, they cannot alter the state of facts and evidence. (John Adams, 1770, re: Boston Massacre—1735-1826)

22. We are under the Constitution, but the Constitution is what the judges say it is, and the judiciary is the safeguard of our liberty and of our property under the Constitution. (Charles Evans Hughes, 1907—1862-1948)

23. I recognize without hesitation that judges do and must legislate, but they can do so only interstitially; they are confirmed from molar to molecular motions. (Oliver Wendell Holmes, Jr., 1917—1841-1935)

24. One precedent creates another. They soon accumulate and constitute law. What yesterday was fact, today is doctrine. (Junius—pseudonym)

25. We should never assume that which is incapable of proof. (G. H. Lewes—1817-1878)

26. Possession is eleven points in the law. (Colley Cibber—1671-1757)

27. Laws grind the poor, the rich men rule the law. (Goldsmith—1728-1774)

28. The verdict acquits the raven, but condemns the dove. (Juvenal—60?-140? A.D.)

29. Like every great democratic movement in American history, Jacksonian democracy eventually collided with the courts, running up sharply against their inclination to devise new guarantees for property and throw up new obstacles to popular control. (Arthur M. Schlesinger, Jr.—1917-)

30. What we call real estate—the solid ground to build a house on—is the broad foundation on which nearly all the guilt of this world rests. (Hawthorne—1804-1864)

31. Revenge is a kind of wild justice, which the more man's nature runs to, the more ought law to weed it out. (Francis Bacon—1561-1626)

32. Injustice is relatively easy to bear; what stings is justice. (Henry L. Mencken—1880-1956)

33. Do not pursue with the terrible scourge him who deserves a slight whip. (Horace—65-8 B.C.)

34. Judges are apt to be naive, simpleminded men, and they need something of Mephistopheles. We need education in the obvious—to learn to transcend our own convictions and to leave room for much that we hold dear to be done away with short of revolution by the orderly change of law. (Oliver Wendell Holmes, Jr., 1913—1841-1935)

35. There is no slavery but ignorance. Liberty is a child of intelligence. (Robert G. Ingersoll—1833-1899)

36. Freedom of speech may be meaningless without the opportunity and the will to become informed, and to develop and exercise the capacity to think. (Punke)

37. The attacks upon the Court are merely an extension of the unrest that seems to wonder vaguely whether law and order pay. When the ignorant

are taught to doubt, they do not know what they safely may believe. (Oliver Wendell Holmes, Jr., 1913—1841-1935)

38. We must not make a scarecrow of the law. (Shakespeare—1564-1616)

39. World history is the world's court. (Johann C. F. Von Schiller, 1786 —1759-1805)

40. Only our concept of time makes it possible for us to speak of the Day of Judgment by that name; in reality it is a summary court in perpetual session. (Franz Kafka—1884-1924)

41. When the judges shall be obliged to go armed, it shall be time for the courts to close. (S. J. Field—1816-1899)

Division III

The Police, Law-Enforcement and Correctional Agencies

1. The first requisite of a good citizen in this Republic of ours is that he shall be able and willing to pull his weight. (Theodore Roosevelt, 1902 —1858-1919)

2. I believe that every right implies a responsibility, an obligation; every opportunity, an obligation; every possession, a duty. (John Davison Rockefeller, Jr., 1941—1874-1960)

3. As citizens of this democracy, you are the rulers and the ruled, the lawgivers and the law abiding, the beginning and the end. (Adlai Stevenson, 1952—1900-1965)

4. The four pillars of government are . . . religion, justice, counsel, and treasure. (Francis Bacon—1561-1626)

5. It is not the function of Government to keep the citizens from falling into error; it is the function of the citizen to keep the Government from falling into error. (Robert H. Jackson, 1950—339 U.S. 382, 442—1892-1954)

6. Government—A trust, and the offices of the government are the trustees; and both the trust and trustees are created for the benefit of the people. (Henry Clay—1777-1852)

7. The art of government is not to let man grow stale. (Napoleon I—1769-1821)

8. No man is above the law and no man is below it; nor do we ask any man's permission when we require him to obey it. Obedience to the law is demanded as a right; not asked as a favor. (Theodore Roosevelt, 1903 —1858-1919)

9. The prince (president) is not above the laws, but the laws above the prince. (Pliny the Younger—62-113 A.D.)

10. Criminal—A name for the most obvious, extreme, and directly dangerous forms of . . . departure from the norm in manners and customs. (Havelock Ellis—1859-1939)

11. Criminal—An enemy of the human race. (Latin proverb)

12. Crime is not punished as an offense against God, but as prejudicial to society. (Froude—1818-1894)

13. Poverty is the mother of crime. (Magnus Auerlius Cassiodorus—490-575)

14. I have heard with admiring submission the experience of the lady who declared that the sense of being perfectly well-dressed gives a feeling of inward tranquility which religion is powerless to bestow. (Emerson—1803-1882)

15. There is no evil in the world without a remedy. (Sannazaro—1458-1530)

16. Punishment brings wisdom; it is the healing art of wickedness. (Plato —427-347 B.C.)

17. Justice is always violent to the party offending, for every man is innocent in his own eyes. (Daniel Defoe—1659-1731)

18. He that will not apply new remedies must expect new evils. (Francis Bacon—1561-1626)

19. Only the man who has enough good in him to feel the justice of the penalty can be punished; the others can only be hurt. (William E. Hocking —1873-1966).

20. It is better to prevent crimes than to punish them. (Cesare Bonesana di Baccaria—1738?-1794)

21. The object of punishment is prevention from evil; it never can be made impulsive to good. (Horace Mann—1796-1859)

22. The only medicine for suffering, crime, and all the other woes of mankind, is wisdom. (T. H. Huxley—1825-1895)

23. Nothing is more wretched than the mind of a man conscious of guilt. (Plautus—254?-184 B.C.)

24. Juvenile delinquents—Other people's children in trouble. (Jerry Dashkin)

25. The time that precedes punishment is the severest part of it. (Seneca —4 B.C.-65 A.D.)

26. Care should be taken that the punishment does not exceed the guilt; and also that some men do not suffer for offenses for which others are not even indicted. (Cicero 106-43 B.C.)

27. When men of talent are punished, authority is strengthened. (Tacitus —55-117 A.D.)

28. Whenever the offence inspires less horror than the punishment, the rigour of penal law is obliged to give way to the common feeling of mankind. (Edward Gibbon—1737-1794)

29. And folks are beginning to think it looks odd,
     To choke a poor scamp for the glory of God. (Lowell—1819-1891)

30. The offender never pardons. (George Herbert—1593-1633)

31. Let those who deserved their punishment, bear it patiently. (Ovid —43 B.C.-17? A.D.)

32. He that spareth the rod hateth his son. (Bible—Proverbs XIII:24)

33. It is true that liberty is precious—so precious that it must be rationed. (Lenin—1870-1924)

34. I begin by taking. I shall find scholars afterward to demonstrate my perfect right. (Frederick II, "The Great," King of Prussia—1712-1786)

35. Power, like a desolating pestilence, pollutes whate'er it touches. (Shelley—1792-1822)

36. In all ages, hypocrites, called priests, have put crowns upon the heads of thieves, called kings. (Robert G. Ingersoll—1833-1899)

37. Law stands mute in the midst of arms. (Cicero—106-43 B.C.)

38. It behooves a prudent person to make trial of everything before arms. (Terence—185-159 B.C.)

39. Freedom of opinion can only exist when the government thinks itself secure. (Bertrand A. Russell—1872-1970).

40. A little Rebellion . . . is the medicine necessary for the sound health of government. (Thomas Jefferson—1743-1826)

41. Men with the muckrake are often indispensable to the well-being of society, but only if they know when to stop raking the muck. (Theodore Roosevelt, 1906—1858-1919)

42. Social change affords new ways to promulgate old evils. (Punke)

43. I know of no method to secure the repeal of bad or obnoxious laws so effective as their stringent execution. (U.S. Grant, 1869—1822-1885)

44. Let well enough alone, lad, and ill(ness) too at times. (Kingsley—1819-1875)

45. That virtue which requires to be ever guarded is scare worth the sentinel. (Oliver Goldsmith, 1766—1728-1774)

46. A good remedy for some ills is to forget them, and devote effort to more promising things. (Punke)

47. Who can refute a sneer? (William Paley, 1785—1743-1805)

48. Let the meek inherit the earth—they have it coming to them. (James Thurber, 1960—1894-1961)

49. And do as adversaries do in law; strive mightily, but eat and drink as friends. (Shakespeare, *Taming of the Shrew*, 1593-1594—1564-1616)

Division IV

Educational Institutions and Activities

1. Life is an end in itself, and the only question as to whether it is worth living is whether you have enough of it. (Oliver Wendell Holmes, Jr., 1900 —1841-1935)

2. The earth belongs to the living, not to the dead. (Jefferson, 1813—1743-1826)

3. When we are planning for posterity, we ought to remember that virtue is not hereditary. (Thomas Paine, 1776—1737-1809)

4. Men fear thought as they fear nothing else on earth—more than ruin, more even than death. (Bertrand A. Russell—1872-1970)

5. It is advantageous that the gods should be believed to attend to the affairs of man; and the punishment of evil deeds, though sometimes late, is never fruitless. (Pliny the Elder—23-79 A.D.)

6. It is said that desire for knowledge lost us the Eden of the past; but whether that is true or not, it will certainly give us the Eden of the future. (Robert G. Ingersoll—1833-1899)

7. The ignorant man always adores what he cannot understand. (Cesare Lombroso—1836-1909)

8. The greatest dangers to liberty lurk in insidious encroachments by men of zeal, well-meaning but without understanding. (Louis D. Brandeis, 1928; Olmstead v. United States, 277 U.S. 438—1856-1941)

9. The value of a sentiment is the amount of sacrifice you are prepared to make for it. (John Galsworthy, 1922—1867-1933)

10. Men get opinions as boys learn to spell, by reiteration chiefly. (Elizabeth Barrett Browning—1806-1861)

11. Magnanimity in politics is not seldom the truest wisdom; and a great empire and little minds go ill together. (Edmund Burke, 1775—1729-1797)

12. The appearance of a single great genius is more than equivalent to the birth of a hundred mediocrities. (Cesare Lombroso—1836-1909)

13. More is experienced in one day in the life of a learned man than in the whole lifetime of an ignorant man. (Seneca—4 B.C.?-65 A.D.)

14. The boastful blockhead ignorantly read,
    with loads of learned lumber in his head.
(Alexander Pope—1688-1774)

15. One becomes a critic when one cannot be an artist, just as a man becomes a stool pigeon when he cannot become a soldier. (Gustave Flaubert, 1846 —1821-1880)

16. Beware the man of one book. (Thomas Aquinas—1227-1274)

17. Literature—the most seductive, the most deceiving, and the most dangerous of professions. (Burke, 1770—1729-1797)

18. I am always at a loss to know how much to believe of my own stories. (Washington Irving, 1824, *Tales of a Traveler*—1783-1859)

19. The great act of faith is when man decides that he is not God. (Oliver Wendell Holmes, Jr., 1907—1841-1935)

20. When is it an asset for an ignorant person to gain a general idea of how ignorant he really is? (Punke)

21. True science teaches, above all, to doubt, and to be ignorant. (Miguel de Unamuno—1864-1936)

22. Two things fill the mind with ever-increasing wonder and awe, the more often and the more intensely the mind of thought is drawn to them; the starry heavens above me and the moral law within me. (I. Kant, 1781 —1724-1804)

23. The contribution of psychoanalysis to science consists precisely in having extended research to the region of the mind. (Sigmund Freud— 1856-1939)

24. There are two cardinal sins from which all the others spring: impatience and laziness. (Franz Kafka—1884-1924)

25. The vagabond, when rich, is called a tourist. (Paul Richard—1874-)

26. There will never be a system invented which will do away with the necessity of work. (Henry Ford—1863-1947)

27. He that thinks with more extent than another will want words of larger meaning; he that thinks with more subtlety will seek for terms of more nice discrimination. . . . Yet vanity inclines us to find fault anywhere rather than in ourselves. He that reads and grows no wiser seldom suspects his own deficiences but complains of hard words and obscure sentences and asks why books are written which cannot be understood. (Samuel Johnson —1709-1784)

28. To the man who strives earnestly, God also lends a helping hand. (Aeschylus—525-456 B.C.)

29. God helps him who strives hard. (Euripides—5th cent. B.C.)

30. God helps those who help themselves. (Algernon Sidney—1622-1683).

31. Heaven's help is better than early rising. (Cervantes—1547-1616)

32. In certain trying circumstances, urgent circumstances, desperate circumstances, profanity furnishes a relief denied even to prayer. (Mark Twain —1835-1910)

33. Hell is full of good meanings and wishings. (George Herbert—1593-1633)

34. All the things I really like to do are either immoral, illegal or fattening. (Alexander Woolcott—1887-1943)

35. Make two grins grow where there was only a grouch before. (Elbert Hubbard—1856-1915)

36. There are many things of which a wise man might wish to be ignorant. (Emerson—1803-1882)

37. Your pettifoggers damn their souls,
    To share with knaves in cheating fools.
(Butler Hudibras—1612-1680)

38. Those who would administer (property) wisely must, indeed, be wise for one of the serious obstacles to the improvement of our race is indiscriminate charity. (Andrew Carnegie, 1889—1835-1919)

39. For as laws are necessary that good manners may be preserved, so there is need of good manners that the laws may be maintained. (Machiavelli —1469-1527)

40. The brave man inattentive to his duty, is worth little more to his country than the coward who deserts her in the hour of danger. (Andrew Jackson, at N. Orleans, 1/8/1815—1767-1845)

41. A straw vote only shows which way the hot air blows. (O. Henry— Wm. Sidney Porter—1862-1910

42. A fair-minded man, when reading history, is occupied almost entirely with refuting it. (Voltaire—1694-1778)

43. Meek young men grow up in libraries, believing it their duty to accept the views which Cicero, which Locke, which Bacon have given; forgetful that Cicero, Locke, and Bacon were young men in libraries when they wrote these books. (Emerson—1803-1882)

44. Meekness takes injuries like pills, not chewing, but swallowing them down. (Sir Thomas Browne—1605-1682)

45. A bright child's learning experiences should be enriched by the curriculum, not enveloped by it. (Punke)

Division V

General Implications of the Study

1. Beware of false prophets, which come to you in sheep's clothing, but inwardly they are ravening wolves. (Bible—Matthew, VII:14)

2. The sublime and the ridiculous are often so nearly related that it is

difficult to class them separately. One step above the sublime makes the ridiculous, and one step above the ridiculous makes the sublime again. (Thomas Paine—1737-1809)

3. All abuses of the world are engendered upon this, that we are taught to fear to make profession of our ignorance and are bound to accept and allow all that we cannot refute. (Montaigne—1533-1592)

4. Men reject their prophets and slay them, but they love their martyrs and honor those whom they have slain. (Dostoevski, 1879—1821-1881)

5. We make a ladder of our vices, if we trample those same vices underfoot. (St. Augustine—354-430)

6. We do not live to exterminate the miseries of the past nor to accept as incurable those of the present. (Fairfield Osborn—1887-1969)

7. There is a glory in a great mistake. (Nathalia Crane—1913-   )

8. If we would guide by the light of reason, we must let our minds be bold. (Louis D. Brandeis, 1932; New State Ice Co. v. Liebmann, 285 U.S. 311—1856-1941)

9. When a thought is too weak to be expressed simply, it is a proof that it should be rejected. (Vauvenargues—1715-1747)

10. Axiom: Hatred of the bourgeoisie is the beginning of wisdom. I call a bourgeoisie anyone whose thinking is vulgar. (Gustave Flaubert—1821-1880)

11. Two great European narcotics, alcohol and Christianity. (Nietzsche —1844-1900)

12. I find no hint throughout the universe,
    Of good or ill, of blessing or of curse;
    I find alone Necessity Supreme. (James Thomson—1834-1882)

13. It was a wise man who invented God. (Plato—427-347 B.C.)

14. A believer is a bird in a cage, a free thinker is an eagle parting the clouds with tireless wing. (Robert G. Ingersoll—1833-1899)

15. You cannot fly like an eagle with the wings of a wren. (William Henry Hudson, 1909—1841-1922)

16. I say to you in all sadness of conviction, that to think great thoughts you must be heroes as well as idealists. (Oliver Wendell Holmes, Jr., 1886 —1841-1935)

17. No pleasure is comparable to the standing upon the vantage-ground of truth. (Francis Bacon—1561-1626)

18. To the modern spirit nothing is, or can be rightly known, except relatively and under conditions. (Walter Potter—1839-1894)

19. Meaning is a relationship among persons, things, ideas, aspirations, etc. But the extensive experimenting and blundering that is often involved in arriving at a meaning, creates doubt on whether the full potential meaning of any relationship is every completely established. (Punke)

20. The good critic is he who relates the adventures of his soul among masterpieces. (Anatole France—1844-1924)

21. All ambitions are lawful except those which climb upward on the miseries or credulities of mankind. (Joseph Conrad, 1912—1857-1924)

22. Conscience is the perfect interpreter of life. (Karl Barth, 1857—1886-1968)

23. Some politicians and other public speakers become artists at treading on the brink of meaning. (Punke)

24. Familiar as an old mistake,
    and futile as regret.   Edwin Arlington Robison—1869-1935)

25. No man is justified in doing evil on the ground of expediency. (Theodore Roosevelt, 1900—1858-1919)

26. From fame to infamy is a beaten road. (Thomas Fuller—1654-1734)

27. The cook was a good cook, as cooks go; and as cooks go, she went. (Saki, 1904—1870-1916)

28. It is all one to me if a man comes from Sing Sing or Harvard. We hire a man, not his history. (Henry Ford—1863-1947)

29. We demand that big business give the people a square deal; in return we must insist that when anyone engaged in big business honestly endeavors to do right he shall himself be given a square deal. (Theodore Roosevelt, 1913—1858-1919)

30. Few rich men own their property. The property owns them. (Robert G. Ingersoll—1833-1899)

31. Civilized society is perpetually menaced with disintegration through primary hostility of men toward one another. (Sigmund Freud—1856-1939)

32. Men should stop fighting among themselves and start fighting insects. (Luther Burbank—1849-1926)

33.There is no grievance that is a fit object of redress by mob law. (Lincoln—1809-1865)

34. Disinterested intellectual curiosity is the lifeblood of real civilization. (George Macaulay Trevelyan, 1942—1876-1962)

35. The power and salvation of a people lie in its intelligentsia, in the intellectuals who think honestly, who feel, and can work. (Anton Chekhov —1860-1904)

36. Early in youth, as upon entering junior high school, a bright child should begin to realize that he will spend most of his life working with mediocrities and fools; and his development should become oriented accordingly. (Punke)

37. When you have eliminated the impossible, whatever remains, however improbable, must be the truth. (Arthur Conan Doyle—1859-1930)

38. In the history of the world, the man who is ahead has always been called a heretic. (Robert G. Ingersoll—1833-1899)

39. Public opinion is always in advance of the law. (John Galsworthy, 1922—1867-1933)

40. Every advance in civilization has been denounced while it was recent. (Bertrand A. Russell—1872-1970)

41. Sociability is as much a law of nature as mutual struggle . . . mutual aid is as much a law of animal life as mutual struggle. (Petr A. Kropotkin, 1902—1842-1921)

42. Psychoanalysis is Calvinism in Bermuda shorts. (Anon.)

43. There is no time like the old time, when you and I were young. (Oliver Wendell Holmes—1809-1894)

44. I only regret that I have but one life to lose for my country. (Nathan Hale, from the gallows, 9/22/1776—1755-1776)

45. The reformative effect of punishment is a belief that dies hard, chiefly I think because it is so satisfying to our sadistic impulses. (Bertrand A. Russell—1872-1970).

46. It is sad to rejoice alone. (Lessing—1729-1781)

47. Government—a necessary evil; the badge of lost innocence. (Thomas Paine—1737-1809)

48. The rule of joy and the law of duty seem to me all one. (Oliver Wendell Holmes, Jr., 1900—1841-1935)

49. All the ills of democracy can be cured by more democracy. (Alfred E. Smith—"Al,'' 1933—1873-1944)

INDEX